PAUL
the APOSTLE *of*
JESUS CHRIST

PAUL
the APOSTLE of
JESUS CHRIST

His Life and Works,
His Epistles and Teachings

TWO VOLUMES IN ONE

F. C. BAUR

Paul the Apostle of Jesus Christ: His Life and Works, His Epistles and
Teachings
By F. C. Baur

Hendrickson Publishers, Inc.
P. O. Box 3473
Peabody, Massachusetts 01961-3473

ISBN 1-56563-899-9

Reprinted in one volume from the original two-volume English edition:

Baur, Ferdinand Christian. *Paul, the Apostle of Jesus Christ: His Life
and Works, His Epistles and Teachings; A Contribution to a Critical
History of Primitive Christianity.* 2 vols. London: Williams & Norgate,
1873–1875.

Translated from the original German edition published in 1845.

Printed in the United States of America.

First Printing—November 2003

Library of Congress Cataloging-in-Publication Data

Baur, Ferdinand Christian, 1792–1860.
  Paul the Apostle of Jesus Christ : his life and works, his epistles
and teachings / F. C. Baur ; [translated from the original German].
    p. cm.
  Originally published: London : Williams and Norgate, 1873.
  Includes bibliographical references and index.
  ISBN 1-56563-899-9
  1. Paul, the Apostle, Saint. 2. Bible. N.T. Epistles of Paul—
Criticism, interpretation, etc. I. Title.

    BS2506.3.B38 2003
    225.9′2—dc22
[B]
                                               2003056761

TRANSLATOR'S PREFACE.

THE object of the Committee of the Theological Translation Fund is to place within the reach of English readers
who are not conversant with the languages of the Conti-
nent, the best results of recent Continental theological investigations. In accordance with this object, the Translator
of the present volume has endeavoured to give the meaning
of the Author clearly and concisely, and has avoided the
temptation of making smooth sentences and rounded periods.
The Translator is perfectly aware that the English is by no
means a model of diction or of style, but challenges criticism
as to the faithfulness of the translation—and as criticism, like
punishment, is useless unless remedial, hopes to profit ˙in the
second volume by the criticism on the first. If the book can
be readily understood by those for whom it is intended, its
aim will be attained.

A. P.

September 27th, 1873.

TABLE OF CONTENTS

VOLUME I.

FIRST PART.

VOLUME II.

APPENDICES

FIRST PART.

INTRODUCTION.

THE STANDPOINT OF THE INQUIRY—THE ACTS OF THE APOSTLES
AS THE SOURCE OF THE APOSTLE PAUL'S HISTORY—DIVISION
OF THE WHOLE SUBJECT.

To investigate critically the primitive history of Christianity, its origin and first development as they lie before us in the list of writings which form our New Testament Canon, is the great problem of our time; a problem which can only arise from the deepest centre of a universal interest and feeling. It may be justly said of the present age that its prevailing tendency is critical, and that its desire is not so much to shape a growing world, as to grasp one already grown and present, in the more important epochs of its development. The principal efforts of the age in the higher walks of science are critical and historical; of everything it is asked what is its influence on the present in its historical claims ? All data and facts are looked at on their own basis, above all it is sought to go back to the beginning, to the first elements in which everything is included, in order to arrive at a clear insight into the whole from the discovered relations of the individual parts. This independence of thought, attained after such great effort—after the painful toil of many centuries—naturally turns its gaze back into the Past, the spirit reposing in the self-certainty of its consciousness, is now first placed on a standpoint from which it can review the paths along which it has passed, driven by the force of circumstances, and it reviews them in order to illumine the unconscious Past with the consciousness of the inward necessities of the Present. If in so many walks of

1

human knowledge this critical task is the necessary mental process through which the consciousness of the Present becomes mingled with that of the Past, where can it be of greater importance than when the Present is linked with the Past by the strictest and closest ties, and when this union has its roots in the deepest interests of our spiritual being ? Christianity is on one hand the great spiritual power which determines all the belief and thought of the present age, the ultimate principle by which the self-consciousness of the spirit is produced and maintained, so that unless it were essentially Christian it would have no stability or firmness in itself. On the other hand, Christianity is in its very nature a purely historical problem, whose solution lies only in that Past in which Christianity itself had its origin ; a problem which can only be solved by that critical attitude of thought which applies to the Past the knowledge acquired in the Present. The great importance which this problem attained in our age as soon as the separate elements of its solution prepared long before-hand were collected in one point of view, and reduced to their definite expression, led to the critical Life of Jesus by Strauss. The keenness of this criticism which yet had the principal part of its force in the clearness with which it drew necessary deductions from long granted premisses, took the public by surprise, and made a painful impression by the negative character of its results, which it was thought could not be too quickly guarded against by hastily attempted refutations. What results followed, and what effects were generally produced on the consciousness of the age by this great critical agitation must not here be entered into, but the scientific claim of such a criticism must not have any doubt thrown on it by any thought of its possible result. It must be recognized as a decided need in the education of the age, and all that is said in so many quarters against the work of Strauss can only be of any value as laying down a challenge to us to go still deeper and more thoroughly into the critical process begun by him.

The criticism of the Gospel history, so far as it immediately concerns the life of the Founder of Christianity, with which so many weighty questions are allied, will long remain the most important object of the critical labours of our time. In view of the interests of the problem there next follows the historical and critical inquiry into the question how Christianity, so closely interwoven with Judaism, broke loose from it and entered on its sphere of world-wide historical importance. In regard to the life of Jesus, the conscious idea of Christianity and its principles, originated by him, and by him carried out through the devotion of his whole being, is what the Gospel history presents to us as the essence of the historical meaning of his life. But when we proceed from the Evangelical history to that of the time of the Apostles the practical realization of that idea becomes the proper object of historical research. This practical realization of the idea of Christianity was first dealt with when entering into the reality of its consciousness through the death and resurrection of Jesus, and becoming of itself a living power, the idea found in the bounds of the national Judaism, the chief obstacle to its universal historical realization.

How these bounds were broken through, how Christianity, instead of remaining a mere form of Judaism, although a progressive one, asserted itself as a separate, independent principle, broke loose from it, and took its stand as a new enfranchised form of religious thought and life, essentially differing from all the national peculiarities of Judaism is the ultimate, most important point of the primitive history of Christianity. Here also as in the Gospel history the individuality of a single life is the peculiar object of the historical and critical enquiry. That Christianity, in its universal historical acceptation, was the work of the Apostle Paul is undeniably an historical matter of fact, but in what manner he achieved this, in what light his relations with the elder Apostles must be viewed, whether it was in harmony with them or in contradiction and opposition to them, that he first authoritatively laid

1 *

down principles and opinions, this it is that deserves a most thorough and accurate inquiry. As in the Gospel history, historical criticism has here two statements before it, differing from each other, which must be weighed and compared, in order to get from them their pure historical value. These are the accounts contained in the Acts of the Apostles and the historical data comprehended in the Apostle's own Epistles. It is true that one would think that in all the cases where the accounts in the Acts do not altogether agree with the statements of the Apostle the latter would have such a decided claim to authentic truth that the contradictions in the Acts would scarcely be worth attention, but this rule, which would seem to spring from the nature of the case, has not up to this time been so much followed as it deserves. As far as the supposition of the thorough identity of the statements in the Acts of the Apostles and the personal declarations of the Apostle in his Epistles is maintained the existing discrepancies, even when they cannot be denied, are considered too slight and unimportant to have any further weight attached to them, and in some cases even opinions have ranged themselves on the side of the Acts of the Apostles, contrary to the clear assertions of the Apostle. Thus not only is historical truth set in a false light, but the justice and impartiality which are due to the Apostle in the investigation of his life and labours cannot be thoroughly employed. In order to show that in his relation to the other Apostles no serious differences existed, there is no hesitation in ascribing to him in many cases a course of action, which, if it really took place as is stated, throws a very equivocal light on his character. A statement of this part of the primitive history of Christianity, undertaken on the strict foundation of historical criticism, can therefore be nothing but an apology for the Apostle. Neander's History of the Apostolic Age is so little free from this one-sided manner of treatment, that it makes a point of bringing the whole historical material into apparent harmony, and in this way has aided in altering the point of view of the most important time of this period of the development of Christianity.

The Acts of the Apostles are presented then as the chief source of the history of the apostolic life and labours of the Apostle Paul. But the historian cannot take his stand on it without first making himself acquainted with the position it holds with regard to its historical object. Between the Acts of the Apostles and the Pauline Epistles, as far as the historical contents of the latter can be compared with the Acts of the Apostles, there will be found in general the same relation as between the Gospel of John and the Synoptical Gospels. The comparison of both these sources must lead to the conclusion that, considering the great difference between the two statements, historical truth can only belong to one of them. To which it does belong can only be decided by the undisputed historical rule that the statement which has the greatest claim to historical truth is that which appears most unprejudiced and nowhere betrays a desire to subordinate its historical material to any special subjective aim. For the history of the Apostolic Age the Pauline Epistles take precedence of all the other New Testament writings, as an authentic source. On this account the Acts must fill a secondary place; but there is also the further critical point that the same rule which defines the relation of the Synoptical Gospels to the Gospel of John, finds its application in the Acts of the Apostles; whilst in this place, and in order to indicate the standpoint of the following inquiry, I must express this opinion on the Acts of the Apostles, that I can find in it no purely objective statement, but only one which is arranged on subjective grounds; and I must also express a great wish to refer to a critical work which I venture to follow all the more, as it afforded me important results when I devoted myself to a quite different line of work some time ago.* Schnecken-burger designated the aim of the Acts of the Apostles as apolo-

* Schneckenburger " über den Zweck der Apostlelgeschichte," Berne, 1841. See my review of this essay in the Jahrbücher für wissenschaftliche Kritik, March, 1841. No. 46.

getic. According to the results of his inquiry, we have to consider this work as a defence of the Apostle Paul in his apostolic dignity and his personal and apostolic conduct, especially in Gentile matters in the face of all Jewish opposition and censure. The idea that runs through the whole, that of a parallel between the two Apostles Peter and Paul, lies at the root of each of the principal parts into which the Acts of the Apostles is divided* (Chapters i. to xii., and xiii. to the end). The unity of the work consists in this idea; its chief tendency is to represent the difference between Peter and Paul as unessential and trifling. To this end Paul is made in the second part to appear as much as possible like Peter, and Peter in the first part as much as possible like Paul. It is sought also to make both as nearly as possible of the same importance, so that one may sometimes be taken for the other, which, according to the undeniably Pauline author of the Acts of the Apostles, can only result in favour of Paul. But, as Schneckenburger points out, there is wanting in the second part any proof of Paul's righteousness according to the law, (such as zealous keeping of feasts, frequent journies to the Temple, personal asceticism, and circumcision ;) but on the other hand there is no trace of that side of Paul's piety which opposed itself to the law. The same Judaizing characteristics which meet us in the personal conduct of Paul, are evident in the account of his official labours. Paul observed the most fitting respect, not only towards the elder Apostles, who so completely agreed with him (Chapter xv.), but also towards the Jewish people—especially in this, that he, as is here brought intentionally to our notice, first proclaimed the Gospel to the Jews, and then, when they rejected him and his Gospel, turned to the Gentiles. Schneckenburger with much ingenuity further endeavours to prove that all the important omissions in the Pauline history are to be accounted for by this apologetic tendency of the Acts. They refer to persons or facts whose

---

* This idea and its influence on the views or the aim of the Acts of the Apostles I first commented on in my treatise über den Ursprung des Episcopats, Tübingen Zeitschrift für Theologie, 1838, pt. 3, p. 142.

mention or description would have given a completely different picture of Paul to that which is exhibited by the text as it stands, putting out of sight altogether as this does the Jewish prejudices and misrepresentations which we hear of in the Pauline Epistles. The most remarkable instance of this kind is the utter silence of the Acts of the Apostles with regard to the scene related in the Epistle to the Galatians between Peter and Paul at Antioch; and with this may be connected the omission of the name of Titus in the Acts. The first part of the Acts is constructed in accordance with the same apologetic aim. The Jewish opponents of the Apostle Paul, as we see especially in the Second Epistle to the Corinthians, would not allow that the visions which he claimed for himself were any proof of his apostolic mission. In this view the vision ascribed to Peter (Chapter x.) and its acknowledgment by the primitive Church is of importance as an indirect legitimation of the Pauline visions. But this vision has reference to the conversion of the first Gentile Cornelius. If therefore the Judaizers complained that the Apostle Paul devoted himself to the conversion of the Gentiles, whilst the Children of the Covenant still were for the most part unbelieving, the first part states that long before Paul, Gentiles had been baptized, and baptized actually by Peter, the head of the Judaizers. Thus the whole question of the admission of the Gentiles had been decided by a divine vision, by the recognition of the primitive Church, and by the most definite preaching and deeds of the Apostles. Paul therefore had only to tread in the footsteps of the older Apostle. Further, a comparison of the passages xv. 7, 14, shows an unmistakeable design to vindicate the earlier activity of Peter among the Gentiles, and through this precedent to impress on the activity of Paul, so blamed by some, the seal of legitimacy given by the assembled primitive Church. Above all, it is obvious how desirous the author of the Acts of the Apostles is to show how Peter began the conversion of the Gentiles. He did this by divine command after the indifference of the Jews in general had been proved.

Schneckenburger rightly finds another great proof of this apologetic tendency of the Acts of the Apostles in the fact that whilst the second part makes Paul believe and speak as much as possible in conformity with Judaizing claims, the same principles of equal participation by Jews and Gentiles in the Messianic salvation which Paul so circumstantially develops in the Epistle to the Romans, are laid down and pronounced to be real by the Jewish-Christian Apostle, in the first part. The universality of Christianity and the lawfulness of preaching to the Gentiles were so decidedly recognised by Peter that no doubt can be entertained that in the opinion of the narrator this doctrine has been already indicated in the words of Jesus, Acts i. 8.

Schneckenburger has incontestably proved that the Acts of the Apostles was composed from this apologetic point of view. If it is still further asked whether it was written exclusively in this apologetic interest, whether it does not also contain passages which cannot well be even reconciled with such a purpose, and in which the general aim seems to be to furnish a historical statement, we can even in this case find nothing of any importance which is in contradiction to the decidedly apologetic aim. The second part, which is occupied exclusively with the Apostle Paul, offers no difficulty in this respect, for we can perceive on reflection, that although the accounts of the travels of the Apostle contain more personal and special details than are required by the apologetic aim, still we can also undoubtedly see that the account itself throughout presents features in which the same aim of the author can be easily traced.

In the first part indeed the purely historical interest would seem to predominate over the apologetic one, if we did not take into consideration that the author in the parallel which he has in view must first have been certain of the necessary historical basis, and also that his apologetic aim must have been indirectly forwarded to a considerable extent by the care and accuracy which he brings to bear on his account of the circumstances and arrangements of the first Christian Church. He keeps back with the greatest care the especial Judaizing side of the primitive Church, hoping by this means to further all the more the chief aim of his work, the apology for the Apostle Paul, which thus takes the character of a simple historical narrative. In reality we ought not to set the apologetic in such direct opposition to the historical interest, that when the first is established the second will not unite with it, for the apologetic aim will even grow out of the established historical foundation. Another and much more important question here introduces itself, namely, how the supposition of the apologetic aim of the Acts of the Apostles to which we have referred, stands with regard to the historical trustworthiness of the work and the authorship of Luke ? Schneckenburger seeks to avoid as much as possible the awkward conclusion which might be deduced in this point of view from the result of his investigations. He refutes very carefully the opinions of those who differ from him, by saying they seem to throw a doubt on the historical trustworthiness of the Acts, and pronounces repeatedly and decidedly in favour of the theory that Luke was the author. But it is not possible for him to carry out his view of the aim of the Acts without sometimes granting more than seems to be compatible with the supposition of its being the work of an author standing in so close a connexion with the Apostle. Looked at in this light, how suspicious are such admissions as the following : Luke evidently did not intend to include in his plan a complete historical picture of Paul, but as pleasing an one as possible. He may not have incorporated in his work any unhistorical feature, yet there are wanting, in the interests of strict impartiality, the chief features of the Pauline character which meet us in his own writings (p. 58). The picture it presents of Paul and his labours is a partial one, not in conformity with the description he gives of himself in the Epistles, either in generalities or in special details, and is one that a Paulinist would not have represented without some subordinate apologetic aim (p. 92). There

may be really some difficulty in reconciling the later historical
facts of the Judaizing of Peter with the Pauline teachings and
labours which are attributed to Peter in the first part, and undoubtedly in the second part Paul seems to have altered more
to accommodate himself to the Jewish wishes and prejudices than
in fact was the case. At any rate, the characteristic Pauline
decisiveness nowhere appears either in teaching or action
(p. 210). That the author could not entirely get over the
Apostle's journey to Jerusalem and the facts so closely dependent on it, but for that very reason may have attributed quite
different motives to the journey (p. 113); that the objective
succession of events are internally improbable (p. 145); that he
has permitted himself to use an unhistorical hyperbole (p. 182),
&c. &c. All this Schneckenburger cannot deny; he accordingly passes over such points very lightly, and above all is most
careful to prevent any suspicion of historical fiction from attaching to the author of the Acts of the Apostles. But after
these admissions it is not possible that his historical trustworthiness should remain completely undisturbed.

Any writer who is purposely silent upon so many points, and
thereby places the facts of his narrative in a different light,
cannot certainly be considered as just and conscientious ;
especially when, as soon as he finds it his interest to do so, he
places himself in a wrong position with regard to true history.
If we go through the whole series of special instances, in which
the designed parallel between the two Apostles, made in the
Acts of the Apostles, is indicated by Schneckenburger, and
then carefully consider how analogous is the one to the other ;
who can believe that the author has taken all this only from the
history lying before him, with the simple intention of choosing
what was best for his purpose. This remarkable fact leads us
to the assumption of a special aim ; but what is gained by that
assumption, if the fact remains ? If matters really are as they are
here represented, we can only consider the author as useful for
mere reference, and it must be in the highest degree doubtful

whether he held the apologetic view he adopts, which he never once distinctly explains.

It is certainly apparent that a decided apologetic feeling lies at the root of his statement, and therefore it must be doubtful whether we can have a purely historical relation from him : and it can scarcely be denied that possibly, if not probably, he has in many cases altered the true history, not only negatively, by ignoring actions and circumstances which bear essentially on his subject matter, but also positively.

The most weighty reason for this opinion is, that the Paul of the Acts is manifestly quite a different person from the Paul of the Epistles. "Evidently," says Schneckenburger himself (p. 150), "we do not here get a full and entire account of Paul's relation to the law, but a one-sided one, and there is really nothing laid before us by which we can form an opinion of the other side of this relation." When the author, who in the historical narrative of Paul, describes him so exactly, and who represents the accusation of his unfaithfulness to the law as a slander, by making him perform an act of legal conformity (Acts xxi. 20, &c.), in regard to which Paul can only clear himself by the exercise of the subtlest casuistry, (Romans iii. 31. νόμον οὐ καταργοῦμεν διὰ τῆς πίστεως, ἀλλὰ νόμον ἱστῶμεν), the conjecture is surely allowable that a special purpose is to be served in presenting Paul to the readers of the Acts in this particular light.

The two views which together make one Paul are, in fact, so divergent and heterogeneous that, although the author may be valuable as an historically faithful referee, the connection that is necessary to harmonize them is by no means self-evident, and must after all be sought for in the Apostle himself, that is to say, the historical character of the author can only be maintained at the cost of the moral character of the Apostle. When the whole bearing of the case, as set forth in accordance with Schneckenburger's investigation, is considered, it is impossible for us to remain within the limits which he sets to himself,

where they appear to be only arbitrary ; the results of his inquiries draw us on from the mere supposition of an apologetic
aim to a much further point, which places the question as to
the aim of the Acts of the Apostles and its author in a different
position. If the idea of an undeniably existing apologetic interest
be maintained then follows the unanswerable question—What
can have decided the author to sacrifice historical truth to this
bias? That this can only have been done on very weighty grounds
is certainly a natural supposition, but these grounds do not concern the person of the Apostle, or any matters which touch him
very nearly. Why then, if the Apostle needed an apology,
could not the best apology have been found in an open historical
detail of his apostolic life and labours ? in the entire results of
his whole conduct in his apostolic calling ? The reasons for
the mode of treatment really pursued can only be sought for in
circumstances which, in the interest of the community, made
such concession necessary on the part of a disciple of Paul.
These circumstances took place at a time when, in consequence
of all those efforts which we see from the Epistles of the Apostle
himself were made in the most strenuous manner by his Jewish-
Christian opponents, the Pauline doctrine was so severely
repressed that it could only maintain itself through a concession,
which modified the hardness and bluffness of its opposition to
the law and Judaism, and by this means put itself into a position
as far as possible harmonizing the antagonistic views of the
powerful Jewish-Christian party opposed to him. As far as we
can follow the course of these circumstances we find it undeniable that they did exist, that they extended far into the second
century, and that they were powerful enough during that
period when a newly-established Church was rising out of the
conflict of heterogeneous elements, to produce other literary
results of a similar tendency. If we keep clearly in view these
circumstances in their connection and in the meaning they took
in their gradual development, we shall be carried on by them to
a point when we can no longer maintain the authorship of Luke,

as far as regards the Acts of the Apostles, in the form in which we possess them. Still it may not be impossible that preparations, collections, narratives, chronicles, especially those concerning the last journey of the Apostle, from the hand of Luke may be the foundation of the Acts. That the name of Luke has been prefixed to it presupposes only that as its whole purpose is preeminently devoted to the life and labours of the Apostle Paul, the work is evidently written in his interest, and can only have proceeded from the immediate circle of the Apostle. Was not this in the mind of the author, when in one place he allows himself, by the expression " We," to be brought forward as in existing and intimate relations with the person under consideration? Who is it that speaks of himself in this form? He calls himself by no name—the name of Luke nowhere occurs in the Acts of the Apostles—but as Luke (Colossians iv. 14) is represented as standing in such close relations with Paul, why should not the author have put himself by the use of " We " in the place of Luke, and identified himself with him? Perhaps an existing account of the journey from the hand of Luke was the cause of this. In such passages the author is very willing to be considered as one person with Luke ; but he does not dare as the writer of the Acts of the Apostles, to come forward openly in the character of Luke, for he was well aware of the difference in dates, and could not so completely forego his own identity. The apologetic interest of his statement does not depend on its historical character, but limits and modifies it. Unhistorical as it appears in many points, on which we can bring to bear proofs from the Apostle's own declarations, it is on the other hand in agreement in many instances with other passages in the received history of that time. The Acts of the Apostles therefore, although it must be judged of in quite a different manner from that generally employed, with regard to its author, its aim, and the time of its production, remains a highly-important source of the History of the Apostolic Age. It is, however, a source which needs strict historical criticism before it can win a place as a trustworthy historical picture of the persons and circumstances of which it treats. The foregoing remarks may be useful as indicating a general standpoint from which to conduct the historical examination of the life and labours of the Apostle Paul. The fixing of the historical value and character of the Acts of the Apostles depends chiefly on the answer to the question—How does it stand related to the historical contents of the Pauline Epistles ? and the sentence pronounced must in the first place be founded on the strictest inquiry into the most important moments in the history of the life of the Apostle. This inquiry into the life and labours of the Apostle, resting on the criticism of the Acts of the Apostles, is the most important object of a statement comprehending the whole historical meaning. The results of this inquiry can only be judged of in the first place by the historical position of the Pauline Epistles, and by the question—To what extent the Epistles, ascribed to the Apostle, are to be held as genuine ; and from this it follows that a true explanation of the Pauline teachings can only be given on the foundation of those Apostolic teachings which are accepted as genuine. The whole subject then divides itself into three closely-connected parts. 1. The life and work of the Apostle. 2. The historical position and meaning of his Epistles. 3. The subjects and relations of his teaching.

THE LIFE AND WORK OF THE
APOSTLE PAUL.

CHAPTER I.

THE CHURCH AT JERUSALEM BEFORE THE APOSTLE'S CONVERSION.

THE conversion of the Apostle Paul to Christianity is so important an event in the history of the recently established Church, that it can only be properly conceived by taking into consideration the position which the Church had occupied during the short time of its existence. But the only thing of which we have any certainty during this earliest period, is that which is so closely connected with the name of the Apostle Paul, and to which he himself bears witness (Galatians i. 18, 23, 1 Corinthians iv. 9), namely, that he became a Christian and an Apostle from being a persecutor of the Christian Church. Even in the earliest times persecutions had fallen on the Church at Jerusalem. Persecutions are spoken of in the Acts of the Apostles, but in such a manner that historical criticism must bring its right of doubt and denial to bear on the statement.

When in the well-known manner, into which we will not here further inquire, the Christian Church, so weak in the beginning, had organized itself, first inwardly by the power of the Spirit imparted to it as the principle of a new animating consciousness,* and then outwardly after the rapid increase of its numbers, by the first regulations of its social life, a series of measures was taken against the Apostles by the Jewish rulers, induced by a miracle of healing wrought on a man lame from his birth

* Compare, with respect to the occurrences at the Pentecost, my treatise in the Theol. Studien und Kritiken 1838 p. 618, for the newest researches on the γλώσσαις λαλεῖν in the first Christian Church.

by the Apostles Peter and John on their way to the Temple. The description of this first persecution of the Apostles is characterized by the same idealizing tendency which is especially seen in the delineation of the primitive Church. In the statement as a whole, as well as in its individual features, a design is evident which it is impossible to consider as the natural historical result of the facts. In short, the Apostles must appear in their full glory. From the beginning, this glorification is the aim of the narration of the chief occurrences as well as that of the individual minor circumstances attending them. The greatness and superiority of the Apostles, whose glorification is the object in view, are put in a still clearer light, and are brought all the more prominently forward, as such a treatment tends also to exhibit the shame and humiliation of the opposite party. This is the more palpable as it is very evident that events are related in the most exciting manner possible by all the means at command, and with the greatest parade. Everything is calculated to advance this end. As soon as the Apostles were seized in consequence of the miracle and of the discourse delivered after its performance, preparation was made to treat the affair with all gravity and the greatest formality. Early on the next morning (for there was no time left for such a proceeding on the evening of the preceding day) chapter iv. 3, the members of the Sanhedrim, the Elders and Scribes, Annas and Caiaphas, the High Priests, of whom we hear at the condemnation of Jesus, and all those who belonged to their party assembled together. No one whose name was of any importance must be wanting. Even all those members of the Sanhedrim who from various circumstances were not present in Jerusalem were obliged to return in all haste to the capital* in order to take part in the proceedings. And what resulted from all this? Nothing more than that the whole assembled Sanhedrim allowed

* So must these words be taken, iv. 5: συναχθῆναι—εἰς Ἱερουσαλήμ, where εἰς does not mean so much as ἐν, and must not be taken as stating that the dwellers in Jerusalem had assembled in Jerusalem.

itself to be told by the two Apostles under examination that the cause of this judicial inquiry against them was a good deed wrought on a suffering man, and that the worker of this miracle was Jesus Christ of Nazareth, by them crucified and slain, and to whose saving name this healing wrought on a suffering man gave undeniable testimony.*

In order to strengthen still further the impression which cannot fail to have been made on the Sanhedrim, we are carefully shown how much it had been mistaken in its estimate of the Apostles. It had taken them for uneducated persons of low rank, who at the condemnation of Jesus had given so many proofs of their weakness and timidity, but now it greatly wondered at them for the boldness and magnanimity with which they behaved, iv. 13. This change in the Apostles is mentioned as now perceived for the first time by the members of the Sanhedrim with much astonishment, although they must have seen with what kind of men they had to deal by those occurrences in the Temple, which had so roused their attention. This incomprehensible want of perception in the Sanhedrim is made use of in the interests of the Apostles under examination. Even this is not enough: the greatest difficulty brought forward, which the Sanhedrim must have had to meet and struggle with, was the presence of the lame man who had been healed, which testified in the highest degree to the truth of the claims of the Apostles. If it is asked how it came to pass that the lame man who had been healed was present at this transaction, the account says only, iv. 14: τον δὲ ἄνθρωπον βλέποντες σὺν αὐτοῖς ἑστῶτα τὸν τεθεραπευμένον οὐδὲν εἶχον ἀντειπεῖν, and the interpreters cannot say anything in explanation of this certainly remarkable occurrence. Had he, as at first would appear, been himself summoned to the assembly of the Sanhedrim, or had he (as has been already remarked by the author, iii. 11) never left the Apostles' side since the time of the cure wrought on him, but

---

* The words iv. 13: ἐπεγίνωσκόν τε αὐτοὺς ὅτι σὺν τῷ Ἰησοῦ ἦσαν, take their new meaning for the first time when used in this assembly.

2

had followed them to prison and from prison to the judgment hall? Whether we assume the one or the other to have been the case, the members of the Sanhedrim evidently so lost self-command at the presence of this man (which they could have hardly admitted) that they could not meet the defendants in the least thing touching the chief points of the inquiry, although they must have known that they would have to do so; thus showing a want of forethought unexampled in such a court. In fact the members of the Sanhedrim did not know what they wanted; the points which they ought to have well considered and settled beforehand, they first thought of when assembled— what had been plainly seen by all Jerusalem then first flashed on their blinded eyes. If this miracle was such a public one (iv. 16), they could not have been in ignorance of it—they must before that time have been in a situation to come to some conclusion in what manner best to meet the assertions of the Apostles. That the matter had no further result before such blind and weak-minded judges as these members of the Sanhedrim appear throughout the whole narrative to have been, is the only thing about which no wonder can be felt, although a certain amount of surprise must be excited as to how the writer could have thought that he had accounted for the failure of the whole proceeding (really owing to the confusion of the Sanhedrim), by the remark that nothing could be done for fear of the people, iv. 21. If the people had been so much to be feared, the rulers would never have dared to seize and imprison the Apostles (iv. 3) in the midst of their discourse to the assembled crowd astonished by the miracle. All this can only be disregarded by taking a standpoint from which the Apostles are thought to be the more glorified the more the ill deeds of their enemies are brought forward to their humiliation and confusion.

This is however but the first part of this transaction, which, if not altogether dramatic in its development, at least tends in that direction. A second part follows, which is but a mere

repetition of the first with this important difference, that everything in it is on a larger scale. It now appears that not merely
one, but a great many miracles had been worked, not only on
one suffering man, but on sick and suffering of all kinds ; and
the vigilance of their enemies was again directed to the Apostles,
not because a great crowd of people came to them from Jerusalem only, but also from all the neighbouring cities. As in
the first instance it was the two Apostles Peter and John who
were seized and thrown into prison, and then brought before
the Sanhedrim, now it is the whole number of the Apostles who
are so treated.* The first time their enemies had at least so
far got possession of the two Apostles that they kept them in
prison through the night and were, able to produce them the
next morning before the Sanhedrim. But now the Apostles
who were in prison were freed in the night by an angel of the
Lord, who led them out of the prison and commanded them to
teach as before in the Temple, and when the next morning the
assembled Sanhedrim in full solemn conclave caused the
Apostles to be summoned before them by their servants, they
were astonished by the news that the gates of the prison had
been found most carefully closed and the guard standing before
the door, but on opening the prison no one was therein. In
the perplexity in which the members of the Sanhedrim were
now plunged, they accidentally received tidings that the men
who had been put in prison were in the Temple holding discourse before the people. The Apostles allowed themselves to
be entreated with gentle words to present themselves again
before the Sanhedrim. Force would not have availed, as the
people the day before the imprisonment of the Apostles would
have stoned the Temple keeper and his servants. But when
the Apostles repeated their former declaration that they ought

---

* They are now throughout spoken of simply as, οἱ ἀπόστολοι, v. 18, 29, 49; as
also the signs and wonders which gave cause to the expression: διὰ τῶν χειρῶν τῶν
ἀποστόλων ἐγένετο, v. 12; when immediately before the question is of ἅπαντες,
i.e. ἀπόστολοι.

2 *

to obey God rather than man, and that God the Father had raised the Crucified Jesus from the dead, the same scene was renewed. Great was the exasperation, and the turn which the affair seemed to be taking was so important at this point, that the actual consequences afford a striking contrast to the intentions and arrangements of the opposing party, and the slight punishment which, in addition to the insignificant prohibition, was laid on the Apostles only served to intensify their conviction : ὅτι ὑπὲρ τοῦ ὀνόματος αὐτοῦ κατηξιώθησαν ἀτιμασθῆναι, v. 41.

In all this who can see anything else than an enhanced and exaggerated repetition of the narrative of the scene already related, having for its foundation the idea of setting forth the Apostles in their full greatness and worth, in the glorified light of the higher power, under whose protection and guidance they stood ? If we can see no natural connexion and result from the circumstances as they were first related, how great does the improbability become when the same occurrences are represented as happening for the second time with exaggerated details ? The simple putting together of the separate points through which the whole of the events related move, cannot possibly make any other impression on an unprejudiced mind. It is self-evident that if a well-digested judgment on the probability or improbability of the whole is to be pronounced, all the facts of the narrative ought to be taken together and considered in their relation to each other. The affair however appears in a totally different light in the statement given by Neander, as follows : " Meanwhile the great work which the Apostles had performed before the eyes of the people (the healing of the lame man), the power of the word of Peter, the fruitless trial of force, resulted in increasing the number of the disciples to two thousand."*

When the Apostles, without troubling themselves about the command of the Sanhedrim, had (as they declared openly they

---

* The conversion of the two thousand is however reported before the trial of miraculous power.

would do) worked more and more with word and deed to spread the Gospel, it could not be otherwise than that they should again be brought before the Sanhedrim as refractory. When the President of the Sanhedrim reproved them for their disobedience ; Peter renewed his first protestation (v. 29). The words of Peter had already excited the rage of the Sadducees and fanatics, and the voices of many were raised for the death of the Apostles, but among the crowd of angry men one voice of moderating wisdom made itself heard, we see clearly that the words of Gamaliel protected the Apostles from suffering the usual punishment of scourging in consequence of their disobedience to the commands of the Sanhedrim, and subsequently caused the former prohibition to be renewed.*

Represented in this light the whole affair takes a different position, but is this representation a correct one ? By what right does it ignore the miraculous release of the Apostles from prison, which is of such great moment in this part of the narrative, when the release itself is told as a miracle, and not merely as an incidental minor occurrence ? If the silence about this event had its foundation in the fact that the narrative without it would seem to be simpler, more natural, and more probable, it would also seem to give room for a doubt which would change the whole aspect of the affair, and on this account it must not be passed over in silence, but be very carefully considered. With the same justice which throws a doubt on this part of the narrative, we may also doubt about another portion, and thus arises the inevitable question what especially in the whole section is historical and unhistorical ? But to omit everything which does not suit the theory entertained, and to use the rest of the materials with the modifications which such omissions render necessary—to interpolate as auxiliary aids,† now this

---

* Geschichte der Pflanzung und Leitung der Christl. Kirche durch die Apostel. Ed. 1841. vol. i. p. 62.

† Neander allows himself to make use of such an aid, page 62, in reference to iv. 1-22, when he conjectures thus : " Perhaps also the secret (if not absolutely declared) friends which the cause of Christ possessed from the first among the members of the

event and now that, in order to make the whole hang well together and appear probable, and then to present the results of
the omissions and additions in a narrative thus treated, as an
undoubtedly veracious historical relation,[1] is nothing else than
the acknowledged rationalistic method, which makes its own arbitrary history. And even if this method does not strictly carry out
its rationalistic principles, but takes miracle (which it here sets
on one side) under its protection, and considers it as a substantial element of a continuous narrative of the objective side of
the events, then it is easy to see where such a method of treatment must lead, and how necessary the alternative becomes
either to confine ourselves to a simple, literally correct narrative of the facts, or to allow historical criticism (if we cannot
altogether ignore its existence) full scope to exercise its rights.

If in the narrative as a whole we recognize this tendency in
the development of the chief events, we see it no less in the
minor occurrences, but in some respects more clearly and unmistakeably. The Apostles are throughout represented as
exalted, superhuman beings, who affect all around them by
their indwelling, supernatural, miraculous power, who, with
imposing mien, exert an influence over assembled crowds, and
draw to themselves with irresistible power all who listen to
their preaching. How clearly is this expressed when we are
told that great fear fell upon the whole Church, and upon all
who heard these things in consequence of the miracles which
were performed : v. 11. How vividly the impression that their
greatness made is delineated when we hear, that when they, *i.e.*

Sanhedrim operated in favour of the accused." Secret friends of the cause of
Christ among the members of the Sanhedrim ! How far this idea is removed from
anything that is related in the Acts ! From what can such a completely arbitrary
and improbable hypothesis arise ? Apparently from the fact that all the relations
of the affair have not been understood. But this hypothesis granted—is the problem
even then solved ? So little is this the case that another difficulty is even raised,
which is artistically concealed, and as much as possible ignored. There is nothing
more blameable than a method of treating history, which instead of looking freely
openly, and impartially at events from their own foundation, sets its own arbitrary
ideas in the place of historical truth.

the Apostles, were all together in the Porch of Solomon, where the largest assemblies usually gathered, they composed a single isolated group, which no man dared to approach, and the universally high estimation in which they were held is expressed by the fact that the people kept at a certain distance * from those whom they held to be superior, superhuman, perhaps magic beings, whom no man ought to approach. The idealized picture of the Apostles, which is visible throughout the whole account, is here clearly and decidedly expressed.

The bright light which is shed over the assembled Apostles centres itself in its richest glory on the person of the Apostle Peter, who stands at the head of the twelve. In the first division of the account, iii. v. the Apostle John shares this pre-eminence with the Apostle Peter—but in the rest of the narrative it is only the Apostle Peter who is raised above his fellow Apostles in the same proportion in which they are raised above other men. Whilst the Apostles collectively perform signs and wonders in great numbers, the Apostle Peter's very shadow brings about these miraculous results, and when at the first trial John is at least mentioned as being with Peter, iv. 19, at the second Peter alone is spoken of, and represented as being the spokesman of the rest. But the chief point of the apostolic activity of Peter is the miracle which was worked on Ananias and Sapphira. It may be taken as a fact that these two persons were on historical grounds considered accursed in the history of the first Christian Church. They may have exhibited a course of thought and action directly opposed to the example of self-sacrifice and unselfishness given by Barnabas, who is placed in direct contrast with them; this may have caused their names to be so hated and despised that in their death, which immediately

* ἄπαντες, v. 12, is commonly taken as referring not merely to the Apostles but to Christians generally. Zeller also " Apostelgesch." page 125, brings this forward in favour of the theory that a community existed, ii. 42, 44, 48. But v. 12, has to do with the μεγαλύνειν of the Apostles, on account of what proceeded from them, and as through this a φόβος seized the πᾶσα ἐκκλησία, they reverentially avoided setting entirely aside such beings (κολλᾶσθαι).

followed, men could only see divine punishment—but all this is so intimately connected with the view here taken of the πνεῦμα ἅγιον which is represented as the divine actuating principle of the Apostles, that it cannot be divided from it, and indeed, can only be explained by it. As the πνεῦμα ἅγιον, animating all Christians, is a divine principle, imparting to them an elevated and peculiar character, so it is bestowed in a special manner on the Apostles. Their human individuality stands in so secondary a place to this animating divine principle that they seem to be only the instruments and organs of it, and all that they do bears in itself an unmistakeably divine character. In this sense must be taken the words of Peter, when as the first Apostle in whom the πνεῦμα ἅγιον resided in its full strength and importance, he said to Ananias, v. 4, οὐκ ἐψεύσω ἀνθρώποις, ἀλλὰ τῷ Θεῷ. But if a striking representation were needed of the activity of this principle dwelling in the Apostles and of the divine character imparted to them by it—how could this be better made than by narrating a case in which a doubt is cast on it, thereby putting the Holy Spirit itself to the proof. This happened with regard to Ananias and his wife Sapphira, inasmuch as they had agreed together on a course of conduct the results of which could only take place on the supposition that the divine principle animating the Apostles did not bestow on them divine omniscience, which one would have thought the most essential attribute of the πνεῦμα ἅγιον. What other result could follow from such a course of conduct than the divinely decreed punishment of both by sudden death? For they had sinned not against man, but against the organs of the Divine Spirit, against God himself.

There would be no necessity to speak of the endeavours to put a natural interpretation on this event, which have been made by Heinrichs and other interpreters, if this mode of explanation had not received fresh support and authority from Neander. For it is nothing else but an endeavour of this kind which Neander makes, when he says, page 38 : " If we reflect what

Peter was in the eyes of Ananias : how the hypocritical, super-stitious man must have been dismayed and astonished at seeing his lie brought to light—how the reproving holy earnestness of a man, speaking with such divine insight into his conscience, must have worked on his alarmed mind, and the fear of punish-ment from a holy God must have seized him : then we do not find it so inconceivably difficult to believe that the words of the Apostle brought about this great event, and that the divine and the natural are here brought together in the closest con-nection."

According to this, we have to look at the death of Ananias as a natural event, that it may be taken as such psychologically. But, even if such an event as sudden death, as the direct psychological consequence of a violent mental shock is not im-possible, the case before us cannot be considered from this standpoint. The rarer and more uncommon such a death is, the more unlikely is it to have happened twice consecutively in the space of three hours. For the death of Sapphira must be treated in the same manner, and Neander does not hesitate to give it the same psychological explanation: "When Sapphira, without being at all aware of what had happened, after a lapse of three hours entered the assembly, Peter first of all endeavoured by questioning her, to work on her con-science. But when, without being induced to reflect, or persuaded to repent, she persisted in her dissimulation, Peter accused her of agreeing with her husband to try the Spirit of God, whether or not it could be deceived by their hypocrisy. He then proceeded to threaten her with the divine punishment which had just overtaken her husband. The words of Peter strengthened in their effect by the impression made on the conscience of the deceiving woman by the dreadful occurrence, operated in the same manner as in the case of her husband just before." If such an event (granting that it really occurred) is in the highest degree uncommon, its immediate recurrence de-prives it of all probability. But if we set it aside for this reason, the narrative of the author leaves us no other alternative than the supposition of an evident miracle. The sentence of Peter on Ananias is spoken in so threatening a tone, that the death of Ananias immediately succeeding it can only appear as the completion of the threatened punishment. This is seen even more distinctly in the speech addressed to Sapphira : " ἰδοὺ οἱ πόδες τῶν θαψάντων τὸν ἄνδρα σου, ἐπὶ τῇ θύρᾳ καὶ ἐξοίσουσί σε," v. 9. A death which follows immediately on such a decided declaration cannot be looked on as accidental, but as an intentional, miraculously-performed act. If it be considered as a merely accidental, natural event not happening according to the expressed intention of the Apostle, a new doubt arises, namely, whether it would not have been the duty of the Apostle, when so shortly before he had seen so unexpected and fatal a result of his words, rather to endeavour to moderate than to enhance the impression which could not fail be made on Sapphira ? Without the adoption of the miraculous theory, no satisfactory meaning can be attached to this narrative. But if the natural explanation, as Neander gives it, is not meant to be taken in its entirety, it may be looked on as a gentle way of uniting the anti-miraculous and miraculous theories—a way by which, when he had learnt to look at the supernaturalism of the miracle as something natural, he was enabled again to merge the natural into the supernatural.

There is nothing in this connection said by Neander about a divine punishment, which here would be an important matter, in order to secure the first operations of the Holy Spirit from the admixture of the most dangerous poison, and to secure a proper respect for the apostolic authority ; but it must be expressly remarked that the Divine and the Natural appear here to be in the closest connection. In what light we ought to view this connection between the Divine and the Natural, Olshausen tells us rather more clearly, by reminding us that "the absolute distinction between the natural and supernatural is not indispensable— there is nothing to prevent us from giving a purely natural explanation of the death of Ananias; but by the adoption of this theory the miraculous character of the event is not set aside. The natural itself becomes miraculous through its adaptation to the circumstances and surroundings, and such is the case with this death, which, taken in connection with the sentence of the Apostle spoken in the power of the Spirit, and penetrating Ananias like a sword, self-convicting him of sin, was in reality a miracle ordered by a higher power." But what end do these half measures in investigation serve? The absolute distinction between the natural and supernatural is indispensable, for the idea of miracle demands such a distinction; as a miracle, if it is not something essentially or absolutely different from the natural, is not a miracle at all. But the illogical blending of two essentially different ideas—the neutralizing of the natural and supernatural into an indifferent third, which on the one hand shall be as much natural as supernatural, but on the other hand neither supernatural nor natural, is exactly nothing at all. Two views only can be taken of this event. The death of Ananias and Sapphira was either natural—the natural result of terror and the consequence of an apoplectic fit, and for that very reason no miracle, and not the result of the will or words of the Apostle—or it was a miracle, and then not the mere result of fear and apoplexy, for even if fear and apoplexy were the immediate cause of the death, they did not operate in a natural manner, or the death would have been no miracle; but they had this result, owing to the will of the Apostle and the divine miraculous power accompanying his words. It is therefore clear, that if so great an importance is attached to the naturalistic theory of Neander and Olshausen, which states that a strictly natural construction may be put on the death of Ananias and Sapphira, the true point of sight is totally displaced. Attendant minor causes are made into principal ones in an illogical manner; and a third set of incidental causes brought into view, of which the narrative says nothing, because the narrator is very far from supposing that what he relates as miracle would ever be taken for an accidental natural event. If we decide on adopting the strictly miraculous theory, the miracle remains in its severity, and the less this severity is in unison with the rest of the New Testament miracles, or vindicates itself on satisfactory grounds, the more justly will this miracle be brought under criticism which must throw a doubt on the historical character of the whole passage to which it belongs.

We will here glance at the whole series of circumstances which are related concerning this miracle. The glorification of the Apostles is the aim to which everything tends, together with the exhibition of them as high, super-human unapproachable beings, in direct contrast to their enemies. This is worked out generally by completely ignoring any satisfactory connexion of ideas, thus betraying that one dominant intention underlies the whole account; and a miracle, such as the one under notice, can have no claim to be judged from any other point of view. In its entirety it serves only as an introduction to, or as the cause of the following events, and bears all the tokens of such an aim. The desire of enhancing the glory of the Apostles requires the enemies of the cause of Jesus to be represented as taking fresh steps, necessarily involving their own shame and humiliation. But, above all, the attention of their opponents had to be directed anew to the Apostles. On this account something had to take place, to which indifference would be no longer possible. The cause of Jesus must win the sympathy of the people, the preaching of the Apostles must cause a very considerable increase in the number of believers. But the preaching of the Apostles had not of itself produced such great results, therefore a great point must be made, the interest of the people must be aroused by some event of a palpable and striking nature. How could this be better effected, than by a miracle worked by the Apostles? But it was not every miracle that would have served this purpose. It could only be one which would not have a merely transitory importance, but one which, by its very nature, could excite and arrest public attention. No miracle could better fulfil these conditions than the healing of the man lame from his birth, who had never walked before, but who immediately used the power given to him in such a manner, that all eyes were instantly drawn towards the miracle that had been wrought. The narrative itself represents the miracle from this point of view. As soon as it is performed the lame man springs up, walks about, accompanies the Apostles to the Temple, walking and leaping and praising God, and publishing what had happened to him, so that all the people saw him, and were filled with wonder and astonishment at the change, iii. 8-10. He even remained an inseparable companion of the two Apostles, in order that, by the side of the worker of the miracle, he might bear witness to the miracle worked, iii. 11; and appear with the Apostles at the judicial meeting of the Sanhedrim, without anyone knowing how he obtained admittance. Then again, the narrative relates carefully how publicly known the miracle had become throughout Jerusalem, and how it had been the more recognized as a highly-extraordinary event, because the lame man was known as a beggar, of more than forty years old, who sat daily at the gate of the Temple, iii. 2, 4, 14, 16, 21, 22. As soon as the dominant idea of the whole is rightly understood, how clearly shown is the relation in which each separate feature stands to the whole—how necessary one seems to the other! And if the historical character of the chief occurrences must be doubted, how little can we hold as historical facts, the individual minor circumstances, which furnish us with the motive and are the groundwork of what follows. Every individual trait shows plainly the internal intentional connexion which binds the whole together, in order that the end at which it aims may be advanced.

This peculiar idealizing tendency of the whole account does not affect the Apostles exclusively, the glorifying ray of its light shines also on the whole Church of the Believers. The glory which falls to the share of the Apostles concerns especially the Holy Spirit which dwelt in and animated them; but it is the same Spirit with which all the believers are filled. In them also this Spirit is a divine principle, which raises them above the general modes of action, and makes them shine in a higher light. In this light they are represented in both the short accounts, ii. 42-47; iv. 32-37; in which the peculiar aim of the author is to give a universal characteristic to the first Christian Church of that time. That which is reported of the Apostles, namely, that they shared the wonder, honour and love of the whole population of Jerusalem, is also the distinguishing praise won by the first Christian Church. Ἐγένετο δὲ πάσῃ ψυχῇ φόβος, ii. 43 ; ἔχοντες χάριν πρὸς ὅλον τὸν λαόν, ii. 47 ; χάρις τε μεγάλη ἦν ἐπὶ πάντας αὐτούς, iv. 33. It is self-evident how little the persecution of the Christians, which broke out so soon afterwards, confirms this account. Such a representation of the relations of the first Christian Church to the whole people, can only be the result of a desire to embellish—and every feature in the narrative testifies to this. The favourable impression, which arouses good-will and trust made by the Church on the people, must in accordance with the rest of the narrative, have been mainly owing to the spirit of unity and harmony which animated all the members of this body, bound them together, and showed itself especially in their social arrangements with regard to the general community of goods established among them by the division of property. We should expect to have here a correct historical representation of the social relations of the primitive Church ; but that this is by no means the case must be granted by those even who have the highest opinion of the historical credibility of the Acts of the Apostles. "In the narrative of the Acts [itself," remarks Neander, p. 34, "there is a great deal which contradicts the assertion of such a community of goods. Peter expressly says to Ananias that it lay with himself whether to keep the piece of ground or to sell it ; and that even after it was sold he was at liberty to do what he would with the proceeds, v. 4. In the sixth chapter of the Acts of the

Apostles there is an account of a proportionate division of alms to widows, but no word is said of a common purse for the use of the whole church. We find, xii. 12, that Mary possessed a house of her own at Jerusalem, but not that she had bought it at the expense of the common purse. These instances show clearly that we must not think that we have arrived at a solution of the question of the relations of property in the first Church." But nothing else is said on the subject in direct terms by the writer. The contradiction which his picture presents to the facts he relates, forces itself upon us—that picture which, as Neander says, " must not be taken literally "—so that we must acknowledge as a fact, that other interests besides historical ones underlie the description. It is also incontestable that there is a desire manifested to represent this primitive Church in the beautiful light of a complete unity, from which all that is disturbing and dividing in the social relations of humanity has been banished, by abolishing from its midst all distinction between rich and poor. But this fact has no place in reality; and from the very nature of the case can have no such place—for how can we imagine that in a Church, which at that time, according to the declaration of the writer, iv. 4, consisted of 5000 members; all those who possessed houses and landed property " sold them," iv. 34; and that not one individual in the whole Church possessed a private dwelling. And if (as it must be concluded from the text) it was an established rule that every member should sell all that he possessed, and put the proceeds as a contribution in money into the common purse—why is it told, as a remarkable fact, that Joses Barnabas, iv. 36, should sell his land, and bring the price and lay it at the Apostles' feet? We must again conclude that what the writer represents as a universal arrangement of the first Christian community cannot have been true in its widest acceptation. May we not, however, take as the historical truth, that " a common purse was established, out of which the needs of the greater part of the poorer members of the Church were relieved ; out of which, perhaps, the special expenses which the Church as a whole incurred (such as the preparations of the feasts), were defrayed, and that in order to do this the more easily, some of the property was sold? There may also have been established a similar state of things in the earlier union of men and women ' joined together in Christ,' and in the subsequently arranged general collection for the poor in the Apostolic Church," (Neander, p. 36).

The representation of our author is in no way borne out by all this—and if no other data were at our disposal, we should not be at liberty to assign to it historical truth. A narrative to which historical credibility must be denied as a whole, leaves us in uncertainty as to how much truth may lie at its foundation. We must deny to this narrative such historical foundation, and consider it as an unhistorical representation, which, for the most part at least, affects to proceed on an historical basis. But in order to obtain the exact historical facts of which neither of the extracts in question say anything, we must add to the particulars we possess what, according to Epiphanius (Haer. 30), the Ebionites said of themselves. This was, that the epithet " poor," which they gave themselves, and considered as an honourable distinction, they took on account of their having sold their possessions in the time of the Apostles, and laid the price at their feet. Thereby they underwent poverty and shame, and therefore, as they say, they were everywhere called " poor." Our researches have already shown that this is in very near accordance with both the passages from the Acts of the Apostles, which must not be taken in any other light, for the Acts can have no authority whatever in anything relating to the Ebionites, owing to the well known hatred of this sect to the Apostle Paul. We have here also a historical datum which tell us of a similar τιθέναι παρὰ τοὺς πόδας τῶν ᾿Αποστόλων as a characteristic feature of the apostolic time. But we must not suppose the poverty of the Ebionites originated at that time, or that they then sold all their possessions. The supposition

is much more natural that they were poor from the beginning,
that they considered their poverty as something honourable
and distinctive, and that they wished it to be viewed as something self-chosen, as the result of their own free choice. To
this end they contributed by really at first selling whatever property they possessed, and laying the money realized by such
sales at the Apostles' feet. What we ought to look at as
the historical truth is not so much the action, as the intention and manner of treating worldly goods, lying at the root
of the action—and as the intention must be accepted as real,
the event must be taken as the natural outcome of the intention. What the Acts of the Apostles states respecting the
social relations and arrangements of the first Christian Church
is not to be understood as referring to its real, total, and general
social condition, but only to the universal, individual willingness
shown in many instances like that of Barnabas, where worldly
riches and possessions were given up for the sake of the cause
of Jesus, the proceeds brought as an offering to the common
fund, and in this sense laid at the Apostles' feet. But the general
community of goods and actual renunciation of worldly possessions mentioned in the Acts of the Apostles only shows us in a
remarkable manner the peculiar essence of mythic tradition.
This generally prefers the concrete, living, and perceptible, and
therefore mere intention seems too bald and empty. Intention
must be realized in action, if it has to have life and meaning,
and take its place as a fit subject for tradition. This may also
explain the following discrepancy—that while the Ebionites
affirmed that they became poor through the τιθέναι παρὰ τοὺς
πόδας τῶν Ἀποστόλων, the Acts of the Apostles declares that by
the same process all poverty and need were banished from the
Church. Even though this may be taken relatively, it is yet
distinctly expressed in the words οὐδὲ γὰρ ἐνδεής τις ὑπῆρχεν ἐν
αὐτοῖς, &c. If we look only at the intention which prompted
the renunciation of these worldly goods and possessions we
must hold fast the idea of poverty, but if we think that

3

the property was actually realized for the good of the community, the idea of its needy condition must be entirely set aside.

If it is asked how much special historical value can be found in the whole section, Acts iii.—v. the actual results are very small; and the consideration of the circumstances related in it gives us reason to suppose that this first period of the early Christian Church was very bare of important events. The fact that bears the most decided impress of historical reality, namely the advice given by Gamaliel, seems to imply that the enemies of Jesus troubled themselves very little about his disciples during the time immediately following his death. And even when, doubtless in consequence of the supposition that instead of diminishing they were increasing and flourishing, they took more notice of them, it was not worth while to take any very strict measures against them. Even the hostile attitude of the two sects of the Pharisees and Sadducees, as it is represented in the statement of Gamaliel and the members of the Sanhedrim, with reference to the disciples of Jesus, can scarcely be taken as historical. It has been remarked with justice,* "Although the Sadducees had allied themselves for the same object with Caiaphas the High Priest, who had condemned Jesus, and afterwards endeavoured with special zeal to ruin the Apostles, we find no historical trace that Caiaphas himself was a Sadducee, the Sadducees first appeared with true party spirit against the Apostles in the matter of the resurrection of Jesus."

It is exactly this which must make us suspicious about the part which the Sadducees first played in the matter ; for it is very evident that because the doctrinal discourses of the disciples could contain nothing of more consequence than the testimony to the resurrection of Jesus, they could have no more decided, no bitterer opponents than the Sadducees—the declared enemies of the doctrine of the resurrection. The repeated inten-

* Comp. Meyer Apg. v. 17.

tional declarations that the Sadducees had given the greatest impulse to the hostile measures against the disciples, iv. 1, v. 17, and
had especially shown great vexation that the resurrection of Jesus
from the dead was preached as a fact (διὰ τὸ καταγγέλλειν ἐν τῷ
Ἰησοῦ τὴν ἀνάστασιν τὴν ἐκ νεκρῶν, iv. 2) have quite the appearance of such an a priori combination. But if the Sadducees had
the greatest interest in urging on the suppression of the disciples of Jesus although all the plans and measures taken were
fruitless, what could have caused this failure but the influence
of the opposite party, that of the Pharisees? It must have
been a very weighty authority which could exert so much influence over the Sadducees and still their rage, who else could
have done this but the most prominent Pharisaic leader of that
time, the renowned Gamaliel? And yet Gamaliel does not
seem quite fitted for the part assigned to him, or for the
moderate and peaceful nature of the advice ascribed to him,
when we call to mind that the most zealous persecutor of the
Christian Church of that time, Saul, had been educated in his
school and on his own principles. Therefore, we must also let
alone the person of Gamaliel and reduce his celebrated advice
to the mere opinion prevailing among the Jewish rulers at that
time, that it might be the best way to leave the cause of
Jesus to its fate, in the full assurance that its little importance would soon be made obvious.* During this period,

* That Gamaliel could not really have spoken the words as they are put into
his mouth by the author of the Acts, v. 35, is shown by the striking chronological
error in the appeal to the example of Theudas, who, according to Josephus (Antiq.
xx. 8) first appeared as a false prophet and agitator about ten years later, under the
Procurator Cuspius Fadus. As Cuspius Fadus became Procurator of Judea about
the year 44 of the Christian Era, the revolt of Theudas could not have occurred before that time. How little does the view expressed in the words of Gamaliel, Acts
v. 38, agree with the statement of facts as related in the whole section comprising
Chapters iii.—v. If all these miracles were really performed, as is here said, and so
publicly that the Sanhedrim itself could not ignore them, nor bring forward anything against them—if the man lame from his birth was healed by the word of the
Apostle, and if the Apostles themselves without any human intervention, were freed
from prison by an Angel from Heaven—how could Gamaliel as an unbiassed
thoughtful man, resting his judgment on experience, express himself so problemati-

3 *

in which the disciples of Jesus were not disturbed by their
enemies, they had time to gain fresh confidence in their
belief in the resurrection, and to strengthen themselves by
winning new adherents to their cause ; and the best opportunity
for doing this offered itself in Jerusalem. It cannot but be
considered as a momentous period in the cause of Jesus when
the disciples resolved to remain in Jerusalem. Here only could
they assist one another by uniting all who believed in Him who
had risen ; here only did a field of action open before them, rich
in probable results. Not without reason does the Acts of the
Apostles date back this resolve of the disciples to the command
given by Jesus shortly before his departure, namely, that they

cally as he does here, and leave it to the Future to decide whether there was anything divine in these things ? If the miracles here related were really performed,
so much as this must have been quite evident—that they were publicly recognized,
authentically witnessed matters of fact, on which no one could throw any doubt.
For what could Gamaliel be waiting in order to give a decided opinion on the
matter ? For fresh miracles which would not prove anything more than those
already performed ? Or for still greater additions to the number of adherents to
the disciples from among the people? But even in this view everything had
already occurred which could be expected to occur. Every discourse of the Apostles had been followed by the conversion of thousands—the whole people hung with
awe and wonder on the preaching of the new faith, so that even the rulers did not
dare to employ force for fear of being stoned. What mighty testimony to the
popularity of the new doctrines, and to the danger to which the Sanhedrim was exposed, is given by the fact that the universal inclination of the people could no
longer be withstood. If on the other hand we suppose that Gamaliel could not
deny the miracles that had been performed, but did not consider them as divine,
even then we cannot understand why he should express himself so weakly and undecidedly, and vote for the cessation of any measures of interference. If the miracles were looked at as having been performed, but not as being divine, how could
there be any doubt that a still worse deceit was being carried on, the investigation
and punishment of which ought to have been a highly important duty of the Court ?
If we conclude that the events took place, as the narrative says they did, but as we
can scarcely think they did—the wise advice of Gamaliel fails of effect, as too
much had already happened to allow such a matter to remain undisturbed. Either
the testimony of truth must have been recognized, or active steps taken against
such a palpable deceit. But the two statements which here lie before us—on one
side the nominal facts, on the other the wise measures counselled by Gamaliel do
not agree. Either that may really have occurred, which is said to have done so—and
Gamaliel did not give such advice, or if he did give it, it did not hold the same relation to what is said to have taken place as is represented.

should not leave Jerusalem, but remain there till the promise of
the Holy Spirit should be fulfilled, through whose power they
were to be his witnesses in Jerusalem, in all Judea, in Samaria,
even unto the ends of the earth, Acts i. 4. We must understand
by this gift of the Spirit the confidence and boldness with which
the disciples proclaimed the Gospel and endeavoured to work in
its interest;* and the actual results show us the internal connexion, founded on the nature of the case, which these two
points bear to each other, the stay in Jerusalem, and the imparting of the Holy Spirit which was connected with it. The
same phenomenon which the history of the first development of
Christianity presents to us, namely, that the larger cities, such
as Antioch, Rome, Corinth, and Ephesus, became the first sites
of Christianity, and the starting points of its growing activity,
meets us also in the fact, that the first Christian Church was
established in Jerusalem. But here we must work on a decidedly lower scale than that employed in the Acts of the
Apostles, when it speaks of the conversion at one time of many
thousands—indeed, we can scarcely accept the same number of
hundreds. We have a remarkable instance of how little these
numbers are to be relied on in Acts i. 15. We are there told
that after the ascension of Jesus the disciples altogether num-
bered a hundred and twenty. But on the other hand, the
Apostle Paul, whose testimony has an earlier and a greater
claim to credibility, speaks of five hundred brethren to whom
Jesus appeared at once after his resurrection. If the small
number be manifestly incorrect, the subsequent statement of
much larger numbers (Acts ii. 41, iv. 4) is no more worthy of
credit, and we must come to the conclusion that the lesser
number precedes the greater, in order to give a more vivid impression of the speedy and important growth of the Church.
Even if we consider the persecution of Stephen, we cannot
think of the Church at Jerusalem as so important and as con-

---

* Compare especially the passages, iv. 31: ἐπλήσθησαν ἅπαντες πνεύματος
ἁγίου, καὶ ἐλάλουν τὸν λόγον τοῦ θεοῦ μετὰ παρρησίας; also vi. 5, 10.

sisting of such a number of believers, as we must suppose it to have done if we accept all the increase to it mentioned in these passages of the Acts of the Apostles, ii. 41, iv. 4, v. 14, vi. 1, 7. From all this there is strongly impressed upon us the conviction that if we wish to make a proper statement of the affairs of this earliest period, we must not place much weight on isolated events and on the conclusions dependent upon them. This remark applies equally to the speeches contained in this part of the Acts of the Apostles which were delivered. on various occasions by the Apostle Peter, and to the Christian Hymn, iv. 24. They may be taken as fragmentary pictures of the circle of action and ideas in which this first Christian Church moved, and as spoken evidence how the first disciples of Jesus sought to bring about, both in themselves and in others, Faith in Him, the Risen and Ascended One, and to place such faith in conformity with the Jewish stand-point on which they stood, by associating with it those passages in the Old Testament which might be taken as bearing reference to the Messianic appearance of Jesus. But however suitably these passages may fit in with the historical narrative, they cannot make the historical agreement more apparent, and we must consider the relation in which they are placed to the facts narrated as a very accidental and capricious one. The inquiry we have hitherto pursued gives rise to the question, whether the author of the Acts of the Apostles has followed his own free composition or a tradition independent of it, in writing the unhistorical contents of this portion of his work. Doubtless both elements exist here in very close connexion.

Taking into consideration the theatre on which the events of the narrative are carried on, which is the sacred circle of the first Christian Church, we are disposed to assign no mean share to tradition ; but a writer like the author of the Acts of the Apostles, cannot deny himself the right to use even traditional materials in a free and independent manner.

So little do we here stand on firm historical ground, that

not being able to place any confidence in the statement with regard to the persecution of the Apostles and of the first Christian Church, we cannot attach any feeling of historical reality to the ideally related scenes, which, according to the Acts of the Apostles, necessarily followed—namely, the martyr death of Stephen and the persecution of the Christians involved in it.

On the same day on which Stephen the first martyr fell as a victim to his energetic activity in spreading the new doctrine, there broke out a great persecution of the Church at Jerusalem. The Christians all left Jerusalem and scattered themselves in Judea and Samaria; only the Apostles, as is expressly stated, remained behind in Jerusalem, viii. 1. This may justly surprise us. We should suppose that they had been selected from the rest for the very reason, that their dignity would not allow them to fly before danger and leave the appointed scene of their labours; although the Apostle Peter, when placed in a similar position, does not seem to have been of this opinion, xii. 17. However, it cannot be doubted that they remained behind in Jerusalem, where we immediately afterwards find them, viii. 11. But if they remained we cannot believe that they were the only ones who did so, but rather that the persecution first directed against the Hellenist Stephen was in fact carried on against the Hellenistic part of the Church, which, with Stephen, had placed itself in direct opposition to the existing Temple worship. But the Hebraistic part, which, with the Apostles, more closely adhered to it (Luke xxiv. 53, Acts iii. 1, 11, iv. 1, v. 25), were not so much persecuted as enemies. Had all the Christians in Jerusalem left the city with the sole exception of the Apostles, something more would certainly have been said of the return of the fugitives to the Church, which still continued to exist in Jerusalem. But the only mention of the Church is that it still spread wider, and founded new churches in other places. One of the fugitives, Philip, remained in Cæsarea (viii. 40, xxi. 8), after he had proclaimed the Gospel in Samaria; although, as he

is named with Stephen as one of the seven deacons, we should
almost have expected that he would have returned to Jerusalem
as soon as circumstances permitted. We must therefore suppose that this first persecution of the Christians brought on
important results to the Church in Jerusalem. The two elements
composing it, the Hellenistic and Hebraistic, closely allied, but
allied apparently through a certain difference, now became outwardly separated from each other. 'At that time the Church
at Jerusalem was purely Hebraistic; as such it adhered closely
to its strictly Judaizing character, and a strenuous opposition to
the liberal Hellenistic Christianity was consequently developed.
It would seem that the Church at Jerusalem was desirous at that
time, in order to further its Jewish interests, to bring the Christian churches which were at a distance from Jerusalem into
closer relations of dependence on itself, that the free development of Hellenistic principles might be hindered. Another aim
is indicated by the sending the Apostles Peter and John into
Samaria in order to impart the Holy Spirit, by laying on of
hands, to the Samaritans, already nominally converted and baptized by Philip. This scarcely gives a clear representation of
the affair, as it involves the supposition that there was an outward gift of the Spirit accompanied by miraculous signs, bestowed by the Apostle as the immediate organ of the Holy
Spirit. In the same manner as Peter and John were sent into
Samaria, Peter travelled into Judea, Samaria, and Galilee, and
visited the churches established there (iv. 31, xi. 1, &c.), and
was received in the name of the Church at Jerusalem, and in
the interests of its Judaistic principles; but there is nothing
said of imparting the Holy Spirit to the newly-converted by the
hands of the Apostles. We might suppose that Barnabas also,
when it was known in Jerusalem that the Christian faith was
accepted in Antioch, made a similar journey of visitation to
that city. But this is very doubtful. Neander himself says
(p. 139.) : "Astonishment and mistrust seem to have
been awakened in Jerusalem by the news that in Antioch

had arisen among the Gentile Christians a self-established church, which did not hold the ceremonial law in observance." But if this were the case Barnabas the Hellenist would scarcely have been selected for the visit to Antioch, as his liberal principles, so nearly allied to the Pauline standpoint (as was proved by the sequel), could not have been unknown at that time to the Christian Church. There is every indication that he did not undertake the journey to Antioch as an errand from the Church, for there is no trace of his being in any way dependent on the Church at Jerusalem. It even seems doubtful if he had been in Jerusalem before he went to Antioch, where his name (ix. 27), is associated with events which we will show can scarcely have happened in the manner related. Perhaps therefore, after the persecution which followed the death of Stephen, he had left Jerusalem, and at last found with Paul in Antioch the sphere of action which promised greater freedom to his individuality. The actual division between the two elements of the Church formerly allied together, became wider and wider, but did not now originate. The persecution itself shows that there was a previous antagonistic relation between the Hebraistic and Hellenistic Jews in Jerusalem ; but we must apparently seek for the first germ of the continued dissension between the two divisions of the Church in Jerusalem, in the facts related, Acts vi. 14. We have here an account of the neglect of the Hellenist widows in the apportioning of the daily gifts and the openly declared dissatisfaction of the Hebrews. That γογγυσμὸς of the Hellenists against the Hebrews brings us down at once from the ideal harmonious relations of the primitive Church to the sphere of the common affairs of life, and must have had deeper grounds in the dislike between the two parties, from which such disputes as these derived importance. So much was made of the grievance, as well as of the means that were taken to soothe it, that we are apparently justified in concluding that the Church had strengthened itself in an overwhelming manner from among the Hellenists, even without reckoning the selection of the first deacons from that party. This of course enabled the liberal turn of thought which was exhibited by the Hellenists in their separation from the Hebrews, to become more developed. If this selection was really made as is related, we may take it as a token of the spirit in which it was made, and in which the attendant circumstances had their foundation, that one of the deacons chosen in consequence of this separation was Stephen, with whom we are now to become more intimately acquainted.

CHAPTER II.

According to the Acts of the Apostles the first disciples of Jesus adhered as nearly as possible to the Jewish religion and to the national worship. The only thing that divided them from the rest of the Jews was the conviction at which they had arrived, that the promised Messiah had appeared in Jesus of Nazareth. They saw nothing antagonistic to their national consciousness in this belief in Jesus as the Messiah. And yet this simple undeveloped belief contained, on the Jewish side of its consciousness, an element of discord which necessarily widened the division between Judaism and Christianity. That this antagonism of Christianity to Judaism was first expressed by Stephen in a manner which showed he had attained a clearer consciousness, is perfectly evident by the fact of the persecution to which he fell a sacrifice; but there is more doubt attendant on the statement made in the Acts of the Apostles as to the form in which he first gave his decided expression of this antagonism. He must have had disputes with the different Hellenistic communities in Jerusalem, to whom he had doubtless turned with especial confidence that they, as Hellenists, would have understood the views and principles which he considered as the essence of his Christian faith. The accusation against him was made only by false witnesses, according to whom he had expressed himself in an irreligious manner against the Jewish Temple worship and the Mosaic law, and had proclaimed the impending destruction of the Mosaic religion through the teachings of Jesus of Nazareth. What was true and what false in this accusation the Acts of the Apostles does not say; whether founded or unfounded is left to be deduced from Stephen's speech in his own defence. If this speech be the work of Stephen himself, it is incontestably one of the most important documents of that period, and we must accordingly refer to it as such; but a strict inquiry is first necessary, and to this end the contents of the speech itself must be examined, as the latest interpreters, instead of penetrating into its argument and internal arrangement, find in it a disconnected variety of meanings. The greatest obstacle to our acceptance of this speech . arises from the fact that Stephen takes so little notice of the special accusation against which he is defending himself; he only takes up the affair as regards his own person from a general point of view, and from this point he and his affairs are throughout considered. The contents of the speech divide themselves into two parts running parallel to one another; on one side are enumerated the favours which from the earliest times God bestowed on His people, whilst on the other the behaviour of the people towards God is set forth. Hence arises the prevailing idea of the speech.

As the favours which God from the beginning bestowed on the people were great and extraordinary, so also from the beginning the attitude of the people towards the Divine will was unthankful and contradictory; so that where a thoroughly harmonious relation ought to have subsisted, the greatest antagonism prevailed, and in the same proportion in which God on the one hand had done everything to draw the people to Him and raise them to Himself, the people had turned away from God. Whilst the speaker takes up the relation of the people to God from this general point of view, it becomes clear how his own affairs are involved in it; but the relation itself appears as the special and particular point of the speech. Stephen was accused of having spoken irreverently, not only against the Mosaic law, but also against the Temple. In evident reference to this accusation, the Temple is a main subject of the course taken by the speech. The

Temple is the ultimate goal to which the promises tend, the most concrete point of their fulfilment. And in the Temple also, on account of the contrast in which God and the people are placed in this speech, the spirit which from the beginning had been peculiar to the people, would necessarily manifest itself. As the speaker takes refuge in the general relation of the people to God, from the accusation brought against him, or rather from the feeling which the people testified by this accusation against him and the Divine cause which he advocated, the historical tone of the speech seems necessary by the nature of the case. The speaker goes back to the earliest times in order to enrol the position in which he himself was placed among the great series of wonderful occurrences which comprise the contents of the history of the Jewish people. These epochs, which are scattered through the Jewish history, form the most important features of the speech.

The first part of the speech treats of the period of Abraham, up to the time when the people had formed themselves into a nation in Egypt, and when Moses had led them out into freedom. During this first period, the goodness of God to the people manifested itself in its highest form, inasmuch as the promises given by God to his chosen Abraham were not confined to him alone, but extended to his descendants, and the people who should proceed from them. And for the people's sake he was obliged to leave his home and kindred, and wander in the land where his people once dwelt, but where he himself should not possess land enough on which to set his foot. The land was promised to the people; and, although Abraham at that time had no child, it was all assigned to his descendants, vii. 5.

The destiny of the people was then foretold, and it was announced as the highest point of the promises that they should serve God in the place where now the Temple stood. A token was given, that all the promises to Abraham should be fulfilled for his descendants. This token was Circumcision, and by it all the descendants of Abraham, directly after their birth, were to assert their full claim to the promises given to him. Next, after all had been arranged with regard to posterity (οὗτος, viii. 8), this was treated in detail, beginning with Isaac. How little share the patriarchs themselves had in the land of promise, according to the spirit of the divine promises, can be seen in the history of Joseph, who was sold into Egypt, and then in that of the rest of the patriarchs who followed him there, after suffering the most extreme want in the land of promise. Little as they had enjoyed the promised land during their lifetime, after their death it became evident how sparingly the promise had been fulfilled towards them. After their death in Egypt, their bones were indeed brought back to Palestine, and buried in the burial place of Abraham ; but even then Abraham had been obliged to get this burial place into his possession by paying a certain sum of money ; and after all it did not lie even in the actual promised land, but only in Sichem, in the country of the Samaritans so hated by the Jews. Thus, even in death, they were not allowed to rest in peace in the land of promise.

The second part of the speech includes the period extending from the residence of the people in Egypt and the Exodus of Moses, to the times of David and Solomon. During the time treated of in the first part of the speech, the people did not exist as a nation ; therefore the subject-matter relates to what God resolved to do for the nation about to be formed. Of course there could be then no question of the relation of the nation to God ; but so much the more is this relation insisted on in the second part of the speech. For in the beginning of the second period, which the second part of the speech omits, the descendants of the patriarchs had formed themselves into a great nation; and as soon as this was done, God let nothing be wanting to bring about the fulfilment of the long promised blessing. But now how did the people behave ? First of all, they showed themselves incapable of understanding the great deed performed by Moses—who had been so wonderfully preserved for his great work, and so carefully educated for it, vii. 25. Next in one special instance they broke out into open opposition against him, vii. 27. For these reasons Moses was obliged to flee from his brethren in Egypt. Notwithstanding this, God, through him, afterwards carried out the appointed work of leading the people out of Egypt, by sending Moses, who had been rejected by his brethren, as their leader and deliverer to Egypt, from whence he led them out with signs and wonders. But against this Moses, from whom the people received the promise of a prophet like unto himself—this Moses who, in the solemn assembly at Sinai, was the mediator between the people and God (or the angel who spoke with him in the place of God), and who received there the law as " lively oracles,"—against this man the people committed an act of disobedience by which they turned again to Egypt in an idolatrous sense, and even forced Aaron to make for them a golden calf, as a symbol of the ancient, honoured gods of Egypt; and not content even with this one worship, they fell into all kinds of idolatry. Yet God did not on this account delay the fulfilment of what he had once promised. The ancient words of promise: λατρεύσουσί μοι ἐν τῷ τόπῳ τούτῳ, 7, had not been fulfilled. The σκηνὴ τοῦ μαρτυρίου (whose idolatrous antitype was the σκηνὴ of Moloch, vii. 43, the typical idea being carried out by the speaker in the commencement of vii. 44), which accompanied the Israelites in a tabernacle through the wilderness, and was brought by them into the promised land—remained in the same form until the time of David. To realize the word of promise in this respect was reserved for the third period.

This third period, to which the third part of the speech refers, comprehends the age of David and Solomon. Instead of the moveable tabernacle carried from place to place, David and Solomon established the Temple at Jerusalem, as an established site with which the worship of God should be permanently connected. But now the godless and carnal temper of the people manifested itself more openly, for they changed the general aspect of their religion with the change of the place where they worshipped. Now that they possessed a regular Temple, their religion took the form of a Levitical worship connected with the Temple, and consisting of a formalism composed of outward rites and ceremonies. What did the Prophets who appeared after this time contend for, if not for a spiritual worship of God ? What else was the cause of the suffering and persecutions which they underwent—of the martyr deaths which so many of them died, as forerunners of the coming Messiah, except this constant struggle against the merely external worship of the people, which was altogether opposed to the adoration of God in spirit and in truth ?

This last portion of the speech is undoubtedly conceived according to this view, and in it the speaker depicts the images that pass before his mind in a few striking words, and it is clearly evident how this conclusion of the speech is in agreement with its design as a whole, as well as with the apologetic aim of the speaker. This point appears to me to need a more exact inquiry.

If we look at the conclusion of the speech in the usual manner, the question may arise whether the speaker meant that the exclusive tendency of the people towards the outward and ceremonial, developed in the existing Temple worship, was to be considered as a fresh token of their perversity, or whether he did not intend to point out that the building of the Temple itself was to be looked at from this point of view. The question is by no means answered by the fact that it is said of David, after he had craved permission from God to build a " dwelling for the God of Jacob "—that " he found favour before God." These words only mean that David laid this entreaty before God in the full confidence of possessing the grace of God which had been vouchsafed to him ; but that the entreaty itself was the subject of divine favour there is no record whatever. Neither

must we omit to mention that it said of David, his wish was
εὑρεῖν σκήνωμα τῷ θεῷ ᾽Ιακὼβ, but the building of a special
οἶκος is ascribed to Solomon of whom nothing is predicated.
Is not a disapproving sentence passed on the building of the
Temple itself—in so far as it confined to a settled, narrow spot
the worship of that God, whose sphere is the great free Universe—the natural Temple of God? This sentence being
implied by the direct contrast presented to the statement
Σολομῶν δὲ ᾠκοδόμησεν αὐτῷ οἶκον, immediately after the words,
" Albeit the Most High dwelleth not in temples made with
hands—as saith the Prophet, Heaven is my throne, and earth is
my footstool, what house will ye build me? saith the Lord, or
where is the place of my rest? Hath not my hand made all
these things ?" The external, sensuous, ceremonial worship
of the Jews may not have been the necessary consequence of
the building of the Temple, yet the speaker considers it from
this point of view—and that he really does so consider it is
clear from the contrast which he draws, not only in the two
passages, vii. 46 and 47—but also in what he says of the "tabernacle of witness," vii. 44. For why should it have been
here said that the "tabernacle of witness" was possessed
by the fathers in the wilderness in the form in which Moses
had been ordered to make it, " after the fashion he had
seen," by the Being who spoke with him—God, or the
angel standing in the place of God, if it had not been
mentioned with the view of calling attention to the great
difference between the Ideal and the Real, and at the same time
to the difference between a spiritual and sensuous worship of
God? According to the opinion of the speaker as here indicated, the "tabernacle of witness," free, moveable, wandering
from place to place, bound to no particular spot, and therefore
keeping the worship connected with it in constant motion,
fulfilled much better the aim of a spiritual service of God, than
the massive, stationary Temple, with its stern fixed worship—in
which the real, external, material phenomena were so much the

more predominant, because they were no longer kept down and penetrated by the invisible Ideal—the Heavenly "Form" which Moses had seen. David also keeps nearer and more faithfully to this Ideal in the σκηνὴ τοῦ μαρτυρίου, inasmuch as with him the question is of a σκήνωμα that he wishes to put in the place of the σκηνὴ, and it was Solomon, whose reign was marked by so different a tendency, who really " built a house" for God. If this (as cannot be doubted) is the real and exact sense, which the speaker intended to express in the last part of his speech, we must not understand the former words of promise λατρεύσουσί μοι ἐν τῷ τοπῷ τούτῳ as referring immediately and exclusively to the Temple. The meaning which the speaker intended to give these words in the conclusion of his speech can only be this, " If we are by this place, to understand the Temple only, it must be in accordance with that external and sensuous turn of thought which lying at the root of the Temple worship, gives rise to the perversity of the prevailing form of worship, and maintains that God can be worshipped in no other place than in a temple raised to Him by the hands of men." In this way the speech answers sufficiently the apologetic aim of the speaker—although it partakes so little of the outward form of a defence. If, as had been alleged, the speaker had reviled the holy place, he had of course protested against the outward ceremonial worship to which at that time the true essence of religion was perverted ; and his protestation proceeded from the same interest in the true spiritual worship of God which had animated the prophets. This, then, was what the speaker had to urge in his own defence ; but he cannot have concealed from himself that it was such a defence as must force him to resign all expectations of inducing his judges to acknowledge the justice of his cause. The futility of such a defence is manifest from the beginning. Whilst the speaker addresses himself to the task of contrasting the goodness and grace of God towards the people, with the behaviour of the people towards God, he shows by the same means through which he places the greatness of the Divine goodness and grace in the fairest light, that the perversity of the people is throughout exhibited in its depth, considering the promises which even before the actual establishment of the nation, could belong to no other people. He shows how ingratitude and disobedience, with that overwhelming bias towards materialism which the people had always manifested, must really have been their truest and most characteristic nature, because from the beginning—from the first moment in which they began to be a nation—they showed no other inclination. But what is so deeply rooted in the inmost being of an individual or of a nation, must be looked on as an innate and natural passion, and must at some time or other, and in some manner, show itself outwardly; is an invincible tendency against which it is useless trouble to struggle. This recurring idea of the speaker is the reason, that from the beginning of his sketch, a parallel is visible between the earlier and later times, and Moses is represented as a type of what afterwards was fulfilled by Christ. Moses appears as a deliverer (λυτρωτὴς, vii. 35), the people also receive from him the words of life (λόγια ζῶντα, vii. 38) out of his mouth comes the promise ; (προφήτην ὑμῖν ἀναστήσει κύριος ὁ θεὸς ἐκ τῶν ἀδελφῶν ὑμῶν, ὥς ἐμέ, vii. 37). How then can we wonder that this prophet like unto Moses, had to endure what Moses endured, only in a greater degree, owing to the more confirmed perversity and opposition to the Divine Will that characterized his time ? How can we wonder that if the prophets—the foretellers of the Coming One—were persecuted and slain, that the Righteous One when He came, also found betrayers and murderers ? How wonder that the same fate overtook all those who sought to labour in the same spirit ? With such accusers and judges the speaker could not expect any better result from his defence. The people must have been false to their inmost nature if they had not sacrificed him to their own want of comprehension of a spiritual worship of God, and the hatred of it proceeding from the want. Therefore the suppressed feeling of the

4 *

speaker, hitherto restrained by the facts of history to an indirect statement of the chief idea of the speech, breaks out at
at its close without further moderation or forbearance in the
words; σκληροτράχηλοι καὶ ἀπερίτμητοι τῇ καρδίᾳ καὶ τοῖς ὠσὶν
ὑμεῖς ἀεὶ τῷ πνεύματι τῷ ἁγίῳ ἀντιπίπτετε, ὡς οἱ πατέρες ὑμῶν
καὶ ὑμεῖς. Τίνα τῶν προφητῶν, &c. Οἵτινες ἐλάβετε τὸν νόμον εἰς
διαταγὰς ἀγγέλων καὶ οὐκ ἐφυλάξατε, vii. 51. This it was, therefore, that the speaker had at heart from the beginning, and
now first uttered freely and openly. The accusation brought
against him of irreligion in regard to the τόπος ἅγιος and νόμος,
and the sentence of condemnation pronounced thereby on the
Christian faith, fell back on his accusers and judges, but his
own fate was at the same time decided. The question which
some interpreters have raised as to the conclusion of the
speech, and which is commonly answered in the affirmative,
bears with it its own answer. The question is, whether
Stephen was interrupted by his hearers or not; whether,
therefore, his speech was or was not really finished? Of
course it was interrupted, inasmuch as his passionate words
must have provoked his hearers to a point, at which there
could be no further question of giving any longer hearing to a
continuation of the speech, but it was not interrupted in one
sense—as he had in reality said all that he had to say. What
could he have added that would have furthered the whole plan
and development of his speech? He had laid bare to their
deepest root the impure motives that lay at the foundation of
the accusation raised against him—he had kept back nothing
that could have been said directly or indirectly about the characteristics of his enemies—he had carried on his speech to a
point from which the chief reproach which had been made
against him about the τόπος ἅγιος had received an exhaustive
examination, and of what use could any further continuation
of his speech have been?

That he did not intend to say anything more about the time
of the prophets, is shown by the comprehensive summary in
which (vii. 49 and 52,) he includes this period in a grand whole;

he had already gone over this period, and could not well refer
to it again. It may be thought that he had something further
to say with regard to the reproach made against him with
reference to the Mosaic law. But that is scarcely likely. The
high respect with which he spoke of Moses would defend him
from this part of the accusation, as would also the manner in
which he treats of the giving of the Law from Mount Sinai—
of the law itself, as " lively oracles "—as well as his recognition
of the Divine origin and spiritual contents of the Mosaic law,
and the manner in which with regard to the reproach of the
τόπος ἅγιος he gives a turn to the matter which throws the
accusation back on his enemies. This he does also with the
other reproach concerning the νόμος, as is shown in the concluding words : ἐλάβετε τὸν νόμον εἰς διαταγὰς ἀγγέλων, καὶ οὐκ
ἐφυλάξατε. But could he not have pursued this οὐ φύλαττειν
still further ? But this οὐ φύλαττειν τὸν νόμον is sufficiently
explained by what he had already said in the former part of
the speech regarding the disobedience of the people towards
Moses, and their constant tendency towards idolatry. From
whatever side we look at this matter, we find that the aim of
the speaker was attained, and the carrying out of the main
idea of the speech fulfilled. And even if the natural end of
the speech had not been reached at the point where we find
it ended, we must remember how flat and superfluous anything that the speaker might have had to urge in his own
defence would necessarily have appeared, after so emphatic and
energetic an apostrophe.

The more remarkable in contents and form this speech undeniably appears according to the foregoing analysis, the more it
seems to be the work of a man possessing such a mind as that
of Stephen, whose superiority in mind and wisdom had already
been expressly stated by the author, vi. 10. If, on the contrary, we conclude that a speech so thorough-going, so com-
pactly arranged in design and execution, cannot be supposed
to have been unpremeditated, as this necessarily must have
been, we may still say that by a speaker who had long had

these ideas in his mind, and had brought them into this close connection by close familiarity with them, no great difficulty in delivering the speech would be felt, and less still because the historical form which the speech takes would make an unpremeditated one very easy. We must also remember how exactly the speech replies to the charge brought against Stephen. How telling and striking is all that is said in answer to the charge, how deeply the speaker goes into the matter he handles, in order to reach the deepest root of those motives of his enemies which prompted the accusation.

On the other hand there is so very much to be said for the contrary view, that it is impossible to suppose that we have here the speech of Stephen himself in its original form. This speech, which so well answered its purpose of refuting the charge of the opposite party in the most complete and humiliating manner, and tracing it back to the furthest point of its futility, is, for this very reason so constructed, that the speaker could hope to effect nothing in the interests of his own personal defence. It may never have entered into his mind for a moment that his sentence could not fail to be in accordance with such a decided provocation on his part; for Stephen did not belong to that class of men who think more of their own personal interests than of the universal cause of truth. Further reflection will show us the improbability, that his enemies, angry and irritated as they were, still manifested so much forbearance and patience as to listen to a defence of such length, and deferred the outbreak of their passion until the speaker had completely attained the aim which he had proposed to himself. Does it not seem probable that it was the interest of the author to find what he thought a fitting place for a speech containing such matters as this, when we see it represented that in the outbreak which followed directly the speaker had concluded the idea of his speech, the hearers first appear to exhibit an angry suspicion, that they had been listening so long in deceived expectation of something else, and listening also to views exactly contradictory to their own? This was also the case with the Apostle Paul's speech at Athens. But the circumstances under which Stephen delivered this speech must be taken into consideration on this head. His affair must have been placed under the notice of the Sanhedrim, and if the stoning immediately followed the speech, it must be looked upon as a sentence of death carried out at the command of the Sanhedrim, or at least with its connivance. Now, it is well known that the Sanhedrim could not pass a capital sentence without the sanction of the Roman Governor. But there is nothing said of the concurrence of the Roman Governor in this capital sentence, and there is no fact stated which necessarily would lead us to suppose that the carrying out of the sentence followed so immediately on the occurrences that took place before the Sanhedrim that nothing could have happened in the interval. It is generally maintained in view of this deviation from the legally established rule, that the stoning of Stephen could not have taken place before the year 36, as in that year Pilate, under whom it is thought that the Sanhedrim would not have been permitted to carry out such an independent proceeding, was recalled from the Procuratorship of Judea. It is therefore supposed by some that the most correct date for the sentence on Stephen is in the interval before the successor of Pilate, the new Procurator Marcellus, arrived, and when L. Vitellius the Proconsul of Syria, who came to Jerusalem in the year 37, was very favourable to the heads of the Jewish nation.* Others, as Neander, Olshausen, and Meyer, think that they can settle the difficulty which exists with reference to the relation of the Sanhedrim to the Roman Governor by the remark, that the whole of the proceedings against Stephen were of a very " tumultuous " character. " Perhaps," says Olshausen, " the Sanhedrim, obliged to avoid a collision with the Roman magistrates, passed no formal sentence of condemnation; but connived at its execution, which was carried out by some fanatics." But in this case also the whole blame of the responsibility must be laid on the Sanhe-

---

* Jos, "Antiq." xviii. 6, 7.

drim. And what idea can we form of this supreme spiritual tribunal, when, notwithstanding that it had not much to fear from the Romans with regard to the legal form, it allowed such an outburst of fury to take place under the eyes of the Sanhedrim itself, even through the actual co-operation of some of its members (vi. 15. vii. 54, 57 :) before it was possible that a legal sentence could have been passed; and that such a sentence was never passed we must assume as certain. What natural connexion is there between the following facts : that Stephen was dragged before the Sanhedrim from a street riot, then dragged away again in a riotous manner to be stoned to death outside the city—and that these enraged enemies of his showed so much gentleness and forbearance that they could listen to a speech of such length and of such purport between these two outbursts of fury ? That Stephen was seized and stoned in a tumultuous insurrection is indisputably the best-established fact with which we have to deal. Does it not seem, taking into consideration the difficulties that we have above stated, that the more riotous the whole proceeding against Stephen must have been, the more improbable is it that in this case there was any transaction at all before the Sanhedrim ? If we dismiss all idea of the scene before the Sanhedrim, how natural and simple do all the occurrences appear! Stephen then fell a sacrifice to a suddenly aroused popular tumult caused by his energetic public teachings; and although the speech which he is said to have delivered may have so well suited his individual character, and have been so correctly stamped with his declared religious views; although it so well fulfilled the conditions needed by the author of the Acts of the Apostles in order to complete his statement; still what is there to prevent the supposition that it is nevertheless the work of the historian himself? That he does not consider himself as overstepping the bounds of his license as a historian by putting speeches into the mouths of persons treated of in his history is shown by many other similar instances in the Acts of the Apostles. If he considered this as part of his historical task, why should be not in this place have represented a man who appeared so prominently in the history of that period, who drew so much attention to himself by the religious opinions which he defended, and by the fate which he underwent, as allowed to speak for himself? How could this aim have been better advanced, than by a speech publicly delivered before a court, in which the affair ought properly to have, been arranged? How such a proceeding would have been received by the Sanhedrim, considering the circumstances immediately preceding it, is very little taken into consideration by an author who looked at relations and occurrences from a distance. This opinion forces itself on us if we endeavour to form a purely historical idea of the progress of the affair and we are not then surprised to find that the author brings the matter before the Sanhedrim. But, as it seems to me, this leads us on to another point of view. It is clear that in the dying Stephen is reflected the image of the dying Saviour. As Jesus died with the prayer, that the sins of his enemies might be forgiven, so the last words of the dying Stephen are : κύριε μὴ στήσῃς αὐτοῖς τὴν ἁμαρτίαν ταύτην. And as Jesus yielded up his spirit to the Father, so did Stephen to the Lord Jesus.*

To this constantly recurring parallel drawn by the author between the first martyr and the dying Saviour must be ascribed the fact that the scene in reference to Stephen is laid before the Sanhedrim. As the Saviour raised himself to the glory of the Father through a similar death, so the radiant, divine light streaming on him from the throne of God, must also shine on the first of the martyrs who followed him. Therefore, not only in that solemn moment which glorified him in his imitation of

---

* It is worthy of remark that both these expressions of Jesus adopted by Stephen, are only found in the Gospel of Luke, xxiii. 24, 36. The three other Evangelists certainly do not give them. It is natural that the author of the Acts of the Apostles should adhere closely to the Gospel of Luke, but is it as natural that Stephen should have so exactly confined himself to these expressions of Jesus, which are found in Luke's Gospel?

Jesus, when he saw the " heavens opened and the Son of Man standing at the right hand of God," ready to receive him,* but even before the scene in the Court of the Sanhedrim, his judges saw " his face shine as though it had been the face of an angel." What can be more reasonable than to think that this parallel with Jesus, which is here so evidently intentional, was intended also to be visible in the statement of what occurred previous to the stoning. This is rendered still more clearly evident by another fact implied by it, namely, that the charge against Stephen was only a repetition of that already made against Jesus, that he had said : δύναμαι καταλῦσαι τὸν ναὸν τοῦ θεοῦ, Matthew xxvi. 61, Mark xiv. 58, with the addition τοῦτον τὸν χειροποίητον· That Stephen's attack on the existing temple worship was the cause of the outbreak of fury against him to which he fell a victim cannot be doubted. And as false witnesses were brought against Jesus with the same charge (Matthew xxvi. 60, &c.) false witnesses must not be wanting in this case (although there is very little said with reference to the falsity of their testimony), and as the condemnation of Jesus took place before the Sanhedrim, so the same conditions must

* A modern critic only could here add the question, "How Stephen could have seen the Heavens opened in the room in which doubtless the sitting of the Sanhedrim was held ?" Meyer answers the question as follows : " The Heavens may have been visible to him through the windows of the session chamber." Neander and Olshausen in regard to this difficulty, adopt without hesitation the theory (which is also advanced by Meyer) of an ecstasy, a prophetic spiritual gift of seeing, possessed by Stephen, and taking the form of a symbolical vision, so that by only looking at the Heavens they seemed to open before his eyes. How paltry and arbitrary do interpretations become when they try to account for things which (in themselves really unimportant) ought to be carefully sifted if a purely historical statement is in question ! We may dismiss Meyer's looking from the window, and also the mere hypothesis of the ecstasy, and take for granted that what the author represents as having been seen, really had existence only in his own eyes at the moment of writing. We may take the perfectly analogous example, vi. 15, ἀτενίσαντες εἰς αὐτὸν πάντες οἱ καθεζόμενοι ἐν τῷ συνεδρίῳ εἶδον τὸ πρόσωπον αὐτοῦ ὡσεὶ πρόσωπον ἀγγέλου. It is said that Stephen was so glorified that men thought they saw an angel in him. This view of Stephen can certainly only have been taken by his friends and adherents—it is perfectly clear that there is here only related the subjective Christian side of an objective phenomenon, which involuntarily attracted the notice of the opposite party.

be fulfilled in this case.   In short, everything in the whole matter must be exactly similar.   People, priests, scribes, elders,
and the whole Sanhedrim must be set in motion.   Acts vi. 12,
vii. 1, and Matthew xxvi. 57—59.

Notwithstanding all this it cannot be doubted that the attack of Stephen on the Jewish national worship, was the cause
of the outbreak of violent anger to which he fell a victim.
Even if the author of the Acts of the Apostles means to indicate
that the accusation brought against Stephen was the result of
false testimony, the parallel charge brought against Jesus cannot be held as completely false.   What was false in the testimony of the false witnesses may only have referred to the form
in which they brought forward the real accusation—perhaps in
the special mention of the Temple, whose destined destruction
(particularly as it really followed) was the pregnant and concrete
expression of all that opposed the existing national worship, and
could only be supposed to proceed from an inimical Gentile
feeling.   Judging by the accusation, which was the same
already made against Jesus, the Jews had undoubtedly conceived a real dread of the great change which their religion
would undergo through Christianity.   That the essence of true
religion did not consist in outward ceremonials, connected with
a temple service confined to an appointed spot, was the one
great idea, through which, at that time, Judaism saw itself
superseded by Christianity.   This inevitable rending asunder
of Christianity from Judaism, whereby Judaism would be rendered negative as an absolute religion, and by which its final
extinction was threatened, had been realized by Stephen; the
high, liberal standpoint which he assumed, fostered in him the
energetic zeal with which he laboured in the cause of Jesus—and
in proportion to this was the opposition more earnest, which he
drew down on himself.

This spirit of Christianity, asserting itself all at once in its
full power and importance in Stephen, is an astonishing
phenomenon, as we are accustomed to see him take a very

subordinate standpoint with regard to the Apostles. But in this affair there is no mention made of the Apostles—it is Stephen alone who wages this fresh battle against the enemy—and whilst he considers the temple worship with all its outward forms as something already antiquated and dying out of itself—the Apostles always remain immoveably true to their old adherence to the Temple. Although this relation of Stephen to his immediate surroundings places him in so high a position, we must consider also the more extended spiritual connection in which he stands. The establishment of a Hellenistic Church in Judea, and the bordering countries, viii. 1—4, ix. 31, xv. 3, is due to that persecution whose cause and victim he was; but Hellenists scattered in many other distant places, becoming more and more independent of the cramping connection with the Mother Church at Jerusalem, took the important step of preaching the Gospel not exclusively to the Jews, but to the Gentiles also. Even in these places, the first impulse may have been received from the same Hellenistic circle of ideas in which Stephen worked; for as soon as men felt, what had been so clear to Stephen, that they were no longer bound to the old cramping forms of Judaism, they also saw that the dividing boundaries between Jew and Gentile could no longer be considered as absolutely necessary. Stephen and Paul, whom we are accustomed to place in the most complete opposition to each other on account of the martyr death of the former, here stand forth in close resemblance. The most violent persecutor of Stephen, and of the Hellenists who shared his opinions, soon after entered on the new path of Christianity, first trodden by Stephen, and certainly the powerful impression which the idea of Christian consciousness first excited by Stephen made on Saul, who so suddenly became Paul, must explain the fact that from the first moment of the change that took place in him, both these things appear in such close connection—his conversion to Christianity, and his appointment to the apostolic office among the heathen, Gal. i. 15, 16. Because in Stephen, whom he had persecuted, he had seen what was meant by that change so unbearable to a Jew, a change which set aside the Jewish monopoly of religion, and substituted for it a universal system, in which Jew and Gentile stood equal side by side, he could now in this transition state of his consciousness without any further mediation, adopt the exact opposite of all that he had hitherto clung to in the true Jewish interests. If we take the ideas contained in the speech of Stephen as indisputably his own, we may easily perceive a still closer connection between Paul and Stephen. If we are not quite entitled to do this, we cannot but think that in the direction taken by the speech the historical basis was laid, from which the original ideas of Pauline Christianity began to be developed by Stephen, who, in this case, was the forerunner of the Apostle Paul. The Jews, who had become believers, could have had nothing more bitter to experience than the knowledge that the Messiah had been rejected by the nation for whom he had been especially destined. This could be explained only by the analogous fate of the prophets, and by the feeling and character of the people, which was shown to be the same now as it had been in all the past ages of their history. If we infer that the motive of the Messianic salvation for the Gentiles is to be sought in the rejection of the Messiah by the Jewish people, after such repeated instances of their disobedience, xiii. 17; such a result of the religious history of the Jews, affording so striking a contrast to the lofty ideas of the Jews as to the distinctive favour of God towards their nation, induces a deeper reflection as to the cause of this not lying merely in the character of the people, but also in the peculiar nature of the aspect of the Old Testament religion, in the essence of the law, in the subjective if not in the objective impossibility of attaining salvation by the law. If, as we may after all assume, there had already taken place in Stephen a breach between his religious consciousness and the Mosaic Law, there was undoubtedly also awakened in him a desire to bring about a relation between the Law and the Gospel—at least in so far that he made the progress of the history of the Old Testament religion the subject of the intention that lies at the root of the speech ascribed to him. We are accordingly justified, as far as regards the historical position he fills, and in view of the inner process by which the development of his Christian consciousness was carried on, in recognizing him as the most direct forerunner of the Apostle Paul.*

* Schneckenburger, "Ueber den Zweck der Apg.," p. 184, says that this speech of Stephen's has for its main idea a preparation for the one with which Luke makes Paul conclude the Acts of the Apostles, xxviii. 25. The state of the case could not have been put more emphatically than was done by Stephen, that the Jews in general, and in their entire peculiar individuality, were not capable of receiving the Messianic salvation. This concluding thought of the speech is the real point aimed at, to which all the other ideas lead up. There is patent in the speech of Stephen a general sentence on the Jews on account of their acknowledged bearing towards the Gospel as it is described in the Acts of the Apostles ; and we may say that in this general sense the sentence can only have been so decidedly pronounced as the result of the facts of a later time. We may here also see a further proof of the unhistorical character of the speech. The historical importance which Stephen must have possessed cannot on the other hand be understood except by placing this thought at the foundation of the collision between him and the Jews. Stephen's historical importance lies in his being the predecessor of Paul. How is it then explained, that in the writings of Paul himself there is not the slightest mention of such a predecessor ? The answer can only be found in the breach with Judaism, which was his conversion, in the originality of his religious ideas—the directness of his manifestation of his belief, Galatians i. 16. These of themselves exclude the idea of any preparatory means for his adoption of Christianity.

CHAPTER III.

ON the road to Damascus, whither Saul, breathing out threatenings and slaughter, was pursuing the Hellenists who had been scattered abroad by the fierce persecution raging in Jerusalem, occurred that great change which so completely transformed him. We possess three accounts of this occurrence which made such an important epoch in the life of the Apostle; the principal one in Acts ix. 1—25, and two others, Acts xxii. 1—12, and xxvi. 9—20. It is a disputed point whether we are to believe the account given by the author in the first of these passages, or the narrative of the Apostle himself in the two others. We are not justified in ascribing a strictly authentic character to the statement in the Acts of the Apostles; it is only from the author that we get this account, and an author too, who, as we have seen by his report of the speech of Stephen, knows well how to use his literary license. But if we grant, as Neander does, that the difference in the three accounts may be founded on a want of accuracy and detail in the speeches of Paul, we may reject the Pauline authenticity of these speeches on the same ground for we cannot tell how far this want of accuracy goes, nor whether this or that detail is to be omitted. The comparison of the three accounts shows several discrepancies. The most worthy of remark is that in ix. 7. The companions of Paul are made to hear the voice that spoke to him, but in xxii. 9, they do not hear it. It is generally thought that this difference is very easily accounted for by the supposition that the companions really did hear a sound—that of the thunder which accompanied the phenomenon, but not the articulate words which were spoken to Paul. But how unsatisfactory this is, when there is nothing said of any other φωνὴ except the φωνὴ τοῦ λαλοῦντος, whilst it is expressly stated on the one hand that the voice that spoke to Paul was heard likewise by his companions, and on the other hand that it was not.*

That in the first account, ix. 7, the companions "saw no man," but in the two others, xxii. 9, xxvi. 16, they saw as Paul did a "shining light" is of course (as the appearance of the light is mentioned in the first passage as an objective ·matter of fact) just as slight a contradiction, as the statement which is made in the last passage that the voice spoke in the Hebrew tongue. More striking than these instances is it, that according to the first account the companions of Paul remained standing, but according to the third they fell down with Paul, whilst the second has only the vague expression ἔμφοβοι ἐγένοντο. It is also remarkable that the information given by Christ in both the two first accounts to Ananias about the calling of the Apostle, in the third is given by Christ to Paul himself, and this is a difference not to be easily passed over, at least by those who wish to believe in the authenticity of the Apostle's own relation of this event. If we resolve with Olshausen, to set all these differences aside once for all, we must accept the account simply as it is given us, and if we find variations in the narrative, consider that we often find such in the Gospels, but that they only concern unimportant minor points which alter the credibility of the event as a whole so little that they in reality tend to establish it. But certainly the account given by Paul himself ought to have the precedence over that of Luke, who relates the occurrence very shortly, and may easily have overlooked some minor occurrences of which he was not an eye-witness. But all this is in the highest degree arbitrary, and we must not impute such a want of precision to an author

---

* τὴν φωνὴν οὐκ ἤκουσαν τοῦ λαλοῦντός μοι, is said xxii. 9, and on the contrary ix. 7, has ἀκούοντες τῆς φωνῆς. And this φωνὴ is certainly the φωνὴ λεγοῦσα αὐτῷ.

whose authority in general stands so high, that we give unquestioning belief to his accounts of miracles, for little as contradictions and want of precision are looked on as tokens of the trustworthiness of an author, they cannot, in this instance, be taken as attaching a character of credibility to the narrative but rather as tending to cast a doubt on other circumstances related in it. In reality these differences which are appealed to as examples of varying narration easily reconcileable would be considerable enough to indicate a difference in the tradition, if it were not that they are found in the accounts of the same author, and if this author had not already given many proofs of the free manner in which he handles historical materials.

Instead therefore of taking refuge in the usual manner in a forced and arbitrary reconciliation between what has been shown to be contradictory, such as the hearing and the not hearing, the standing upright and the falling down, we must confine ourselves to the question, What does the author intend by relating the event now in one way and now in another? As far as concerns the question with regard to the discrepancy between the expressions ἀκούειν and οὐκ ἀκούειν τὴν φωνὴν τοῦ λαλοῦντος, it can easily be seen that the author in the passage, ix. 7, decides on the plan of ascribing the ἀκούειν τῆς φωνῆς to the companions of the Apostle also, because by so doing, he can prove in the best possible manner the objectivity of the occurrence, which must be more credible if the same voice which the Apostle describes as having addressed itself specially to him was also heard by others. But in both the other passages, especially in the second in which it is expressly said that the companions did not hear the voice, the contradiction may arise from its having occurred to the author that as the Apostle himself is speaking, it might be favourable to the interests of the Apostle to represent this voice as one addressed to him alone, belonging especially to him, and not heard by his companions. In furtherance of the aim which is apparent in these two speeches, it is essential that no doubt be felt as to the Apostle being the sole and especial object of this strange phenomenon. But its objectivity, on which no less stress must be laid, can only be sufficiently proved by the special statement that the companions of the Apostle suddenly saw a light streaming down from Heaven in the clear noon day, which is stated here, as in xxvi. 13, as a confirmation of the fact. That the discrepancies of which we are treating are to be explained chiefly by such a bias on the part of the author, seems also to be confirmed by a particular remark made in the third passage, that the voice which talked with Paul spoke in the Hebrew tongue. If we look back to the first speech delivered before the Jewish people (xxii.) we shall find that it contains no special reason to justify the particular remark (xxi. 40) that it was spoken in the Hebrew language; but as we must suppose that the third speech which was delivered before the Roman Procurator Festus and the Jewish King Agrippa, was spoken in Greek, the remark as applied to this speech would not have seemed superfluous, for the attempt to make the hearers suppose the unlikely fact that Jesus spoke to Paul in the very Greek words he repeated to them might have cast an improbable light upon the whole affair.

It is also easily seen why in one of these two speeches of the Apostle the addition is made to the words addressed to him by Jesus, σκληρόν σοι πρὸς κέντρα λακτίζειν, xxvi. 14, as this kind of proverbial speaking is peculiarly adapted to heighten the effect of the principal idea on the hearers, which throughout it is the great desire of the speaker to do, and this idea is that he was unavoidably constrained to take the step so distasteful to the Jews, by the power of an objective impression made upon him. The narrative of the author himself does not however need such a strengthening of the chief idea of the matter; the discrepancy between the standing and falling of the companions is, like their hearing and not hearing, a contradiction which can only be reconciled from the standpoint of the author. The most striking proof of the powerful impression made by the phenomenon was of course the throwing down of the Apostle and those who accompanied him, but if the author described the impression in the first place by the strong expression ἐννεοὶ, this is a sufficient compensation for the falling down; that they should have remained standing suits better the word ἐννεοὶ than that they should have fallen, and they must be represented as standing because it is necessary to show that they saw no one from whom the voice could have proceeded. In short, as far as concerns the difference in the words spoken by Jesus in calling the Apostle, it is perfectly evident that separate events in the first passage are summarized and placed together in the third; and this is of no importance, as the words addressed to Ananias by Jesus are evidently only a continuation of his conversation with Paul, but the free treatment of the author is especially shown in these details of the minor circumstances attending the chief event.

If, however, we succeed in reconciling the three above-named passages in the Acts of the Apostles, we see by the very means employed to reconcile them that every detail of the narrative must not be taken as of the same value, those that are essential must be carefully separated from those of less importance. The chief point is stated by the Apostle Paul in his Epistles. It was the most decided conviction of the Apostle, that as Jesus had appeared to the Apostles and the other believers, so at last he had visibly manifested himself to him, 1 Cor. xv. 8, iv. 1. But the Apostle does not give any explanation as to the way and manner in which this manifestation took place, as in his Epistles he is very reticent about these facts, and scarcely mentions or hints at them. That they were facts, we must conclude from the two speeches which we find in the Acts of the Apostles, and if the parallel between the appearance manifested to him, and the former appearances of the risen Jesus is satisfactory to us, and makes us willing to accept the idea of an

5 *

outward objective fact, the expression of the Apostle, Gal.
i. 15, εὐδόκησεν ὁ Θεὸς ἀποκαλύψαι τὸν υἱὸν αὐτοῦ ἐν ἐμοὶ,
shows us the deeper meaning of the matter in such a way as to
prevent our laying too much stress on the outward appearance.
We are on this account more justified in trying to find out
what is to be accepted in the narrative of the Acts of the
Apostles, and what is not. The chief point lies unquestionably
in the inquiry, whether the appearance of Jesus is to be considered as an external or internal fact? The whole statement
in the Acts of the Apostles leans to the supposition of a material
appearance; the most important point against this supposition
is the express assertion of the author that the companions of the
Apostle who saw a bright flash of light, saw no person. The
decided expression, ix. 7, εἰστήκεισαν μηδένα θεωροῦντες, is here
of the more importance, as, in matter of fact, there is nothing in
the three narratives in the Acts of the Apostles to lead to the
idea of a material, visible, objective appearance of the person of
Jesus. Neander also (p. 119) assumes this to have been a
spiritual fact in the mind of Paul, a spiritual manifestation of
Christ to his deeper self-consciousness, and by assuming this we
lose nothing of the real, divine part of the matter, as the external manifestation is only an adjunct, and the material perception can have no greater certainty and reality than a fact
present to a higher self-consciousness. But Neander (p. 122)
feels obliged to return again to the idea of a real visible appearance, since the Apostle, 1 Cor. xv. 8, places the appearance of
Christ vouchsafed to himself, on an equal footing with all the
other appearances of the risen Christ, and this opinion must
have all the greater weight, because (2 Cor. xii. 1) it is shown
that the Apostle knew perfectly well how to distinguish between a state of ecstasy and a state of ordinary consciousness.

As to what concerns the latter point, it follows from the very
reasonable grounds adduced by Neander himself (p. 121), that
the appearance of Jesus which is here spoken of cannot have
been intended to be taken as an ecstatic vision, like that re-

ferred to in 2 Cor. xii. 1, but does it therefore follow that as a spiritual fact it had nothing in common with an ecstatic vision, if not in his normal yet in his higher self-consciousness? This cannot be maintained, and although the Apostle makes a parallel between this appearance of Jesus and the other appearances of the risen Christ, it does not follow in the first place that this appearance must have been an external one (for even with an internal appearance, the fact of the ἑωρακέναι and ὀφθῆναι would seem certain); and secondly, if the parallel were actually to imply an external appearance, the rule which Neander himself lays down (p. 97) in reference to Cornelius would apply here; and Paul, being the only witness for the objective reality of the appearance, can only be accepted as a sure witness of what he believed he really saw. We cannot, however, here avail ourselves of this subjectivity, as, according to the express declaration of the author, not one of the companions of the Apostle saw the form of Jesus, so there is no room for the supposition of an objective material appearance. However much the Apostle may have certainly believed that he actually saw the form of Jesus, he only really bears testimony to what he believed he saw. Here we have arrived at a point from which, without any difficulty, the connexion of the rest of the narrative may be perceived. To the question whether the appearance of Jesus was really an outward and visible one, there is allied the further inquiry whether the words which Paul believed he heard from the Jesus who appeared to him, were really audible. Had we only the testimony of the first passage on this point, the question would be answered immediately in the affirmative; but as the author is directly in contradiction to himself on the subject, we can only answer by what we can gather from the analogy of the whole, and not from isolated statements. As far as concerns the analogy it can be shown certainly, that just as little as the appearance of Jesus was a real and outward one, so little could the words which Paul thought he heard, have been outwardly audible. Just as easily as he might have believed that he saw

Jesus without an outward visible objective form of Jesus, so he might have believed that he heard words, which to him only, not to others, and not in general were outwardly and object-ively audible. This connection between seeing and hearing can be explained also psychologically. If the Apostle was once convinced that Jesus appeared to him, he must also have supposed that there was some decided reason for this appear-ance, and for what reason should Jesus appear to him ; except to present himself to him, the persecutor, as the object of the persecution ? And even if the belief in such an appearance of Jesus had not already existed in the Apostle, even if he were not already filled with belief in the supreme worth of Jesus, instead of with his former unbelief, when the faith in the appearance came to him, there must have come also in the closest and most direct connexion with it, the resolve to become a preacher instead of a persecutor of the Christian cause.

So considered, what are the words which the Apostle thought that he heard from the form of Jesus, and, which, if the Appear-ance itself was only a spiritual fact, he may have heard from some spiritual voice, what are they but the necessary expla-nation of the fact itself, and of the idea immediately connected with it? Just as little as it is possible to divide words and ideas, just as necessarily as the idea expresses and clothes itself in words, just so close and immediate is here the connexion of one with the other, of the Seen and the Imagined, with the Spoken and the Heard. Hitherto we have remained entirely within the sphere of the Apostle's consciousness, but now we must step over the boundary which divides the inner from the outer, the subjective from the objective, in reference to what the companions of the Apostle may at least have seen, even if they heard nothing. If they did not see the person of the being who manifested himself, they may have seen the stream of heavenly light by which they and the Apostle were surrounded. The well-known modern hypothesis, so often repeated, that this light was a flash of lightning which suddenly struck the Apostle and laid him and his companions senseless on the ground, is really mere hypothesis, and as it not only has no foundation in the text, but is rather opposed to the acknowledged tone of the author, we shall make here no further mention of it, but to say that the question is the more forced upon us, whether or not this stream of light must not be taken, after all, as an objective reality. The narrative clearly means it to be so taken, but it is another question whether or not so celebrated a fact as the conversion of the Apostle Paul is a point on which mythic tradition may be made available. It must be borne in mind in order that the supposition of the mythical may not be held as completely arbitrary, that the essence of a myth consists in the outward objective expression of an inner subjective idea. The more indispensable and direct this passage from the subjective to the objective, from the inner to the outward, the less practical seems here the idea of the mythical, although this is the point at which the natural province of the myth begins. In this sense the necessary transformation already discussed of a direct, inexplicable sudden impression into a decided idea, and of the idea into words, belongs to the province of the myth, it is also here an inward process which becomes an outward one, a transition from the subjective to the objective, the idea becomes expressed, it clothes itself in words and outward signs, and takes material shape and form. But in this case it is a necessary mental process, that the mythical, whilst appearing in its direct, inner connexion with the logical, shall become especially mythical as soon as its passage from the subjective to the objective, from the inner to the outward has no longer any inner logical necessity, but relies more on a subjective need, and appears only as the accidental and more or less unbiassed statement of an abstract thought, or as a matter lying beyond the province of the senses, although in a palpable and material form. From this point of view the phenomenon, as far as regards the companions of the Apostle, must be considered. Although the fact be firmly established that the ascended, glorified Jesus appeared to the Apostle Paul on the way to Damascus, tradition cannot be contented with the abstract thought of a fact presenting itself only to the inner, deep self-consciousness of the Apostle. The inner phenomenon must in some way become an outward one, if it is to have its full traditional importance and concrete truth. But that the inner perception present only in the mind of the Apostle did not become an outward perception to those who accompanied him, in the visible form of Jesus appearing in the heavenly light, is to be explained by the fact, that even original tradition in its strictest form has its fixed boundaries which it does not arbitrarily overstep. The original maintains its veracity as a spiritual matter of fact, by asserting that Jesus appeared in a visible manner to the Apostle only, and this tradition must also acknowledge. But if he had been actually visible, and only to the Apostle, how can tradition have assumed that the heavenly light without which no Divine appearance can be imagined, spread over all the surroundings of the Apostle. Jesus could not really have appeared without some outward token of his nearness and presence. The strange brightness surpassing that of the sun at mid-day, that suddenly shone round the Apostle and his companions, is accordingly nothing but the symbolic and mythical expression of the certainty of the real and immediate presence of the glorified Jesus, elevated to heavenly dignity. As soon as the appearance of Jesus is thought of in this manner, we see that it must have brought about in all who witnessed it, the effects which always result from heavenly phenomena of this kind; its overpowering influence threw them all on the ground, or at least riveted them to the earth in rigid astonishment.

The occurrences in Damascus form the second part of the miraculous narrative in the Acts of the Apostles. The adherents of the so-called natural mode of explanation have experienced as much difficulty about these as about the principal event itself.* Although the latter is thought to have been very

* Neander gives no further explanation of the occurrences at Damascus.

easily met by the lucky hypothesis of a flash of heaven-sent lightning, the complicated events in Damascus cannot be accounted for in so simple and easy a manner. This is especially the weak place in the natural mode of explanation, and the cold hands of the aged Ananias, the vivid delight of Paul at his appearance, the sudden stepping forth from the dark chamber to the light, and the three days' fasting, are only weak unskilful means of releasing the Apostle from the darkness of the cataract produced on him by the lightning flash. But how difficult it is to bring Ananias and Paul in a natural manner into such mutual relations as must have existed, according to the narrative in the Acts of the Apostles. It may on the other hand be justly asked, Who can believe that these two visions, so exactly fitting into each other, Paul learning through one, that Ananias was coming to him to restore his sight, and Ananias receiving through the other the command to go to Paul and help him, can have been received by some lucky chance? Just as little can these visions be taken as miracles in the ordinary sense. With our author, visions are precisely the means employed to bring persons widely separated and unknown to each other into correspondence. As in the history of the conversion of Cornelius, he and Peter are drawn together by two visions, so here this also is the case with Ananias and Paul, only the visions of the two latter are more strictly and unmistakeably connected. As Paul in his vision saw Ananias coming to him, so Ananias in the vision which he had, is apprized of the nature of Paul's vision. As we may readily suppose, it must have been very difficult for Paul, after his arrival at Damascus, to find an introduction to, or to win confidence from the Christians residing there, so we must suppose that he could not have succeeded in doing this without some great extraordinary preparation, and such a preparation must appear the more necessary as Paul in the state of blindness in which he had been ever since the appearance of the light from Heaven on the way to Damascus, had been so dependent on help from strangers. Who would dare to venture near a man, whom until now they had known as the bitterest enemy and persecutor of the Christian name? and how could he himself, a man so blinded and prostrate, place any confidence in his neighbours who might be willing to take care of him?

Here then the Deity must himself step in and complete the work already begun. Ananias accordingly receives, in a divine vision, the command to go to Paul, and to afford him the help he needed, and to Paul himself Ananias is shown in a vision as the man destined to assist him. The charge which Ananias received lies in so close a connection with the miracle he wrought on Paul, that from the miracle itself we first come to a right understanding of the chief subject matter of the vision. According to the narrative in the Acts of the Apostles, Paul had been blinded by the mighty light of the appearance of the Lord. He came blind to Damascus, and was there alone for some days in that condition until he was released from it by Ananias. But was this blindness an actual one? And was his release from it by Ananias an actual miracle? This question is suggested to us by the narrative itself, in which the close connection between the cure of the blindness and the laying on of hands, and the aim of the latter operation, namely, the gift of the Holy Ghost, deserves the most special attention. Ananias indeed received in his vision the command to go to Paul and lay his hands on him that he might receive his sight, and as soon as he had come to Paul and had laid his hands on him, Paul received his sight and was filled with the Holy Ghost, and there fell from his eyes as it had been scales, and he " forthwith saw." Is not then the πλησθῆναι πνεύματος ἁγίου that ought to be the immediate consequence of the laying on of hands, in itself, a healing of blindness, an ἀναβλέπειν in a spiritual sense— and does not the expression, ix. 18—εὐθέως ἀπέπεσον ἀπὸ τῶν ὀφθαλμῶν αὐτοῦ ὡσεὶ λεπίδες indicate that they were no real scales, that there was no real blindness and no real cure?

If we remember the condition to which the Apostle must have
been reduced by the appearance of the Lord, how can we think
of him in any other manner than with a downcast, introspective
look, absorbed in his own situation, in deep earnest meditation
on the sins that weighed so heavily upon him and which weight he
had incurred during his recent course of action? Christian baptism first shone upon this dark night of his spiritual life with the
bright light of the consciousness of sin forgiven, and caused him
again to see clearly! The narrative itself points to such a state
of mind, brooding on itself, closed to all outward impressions,
entirely occupied with itself and struggling from darkness into
light, by showing us Paul after some days residence in Damascus, as not only seeing nothing, but eating and drinking
nothing, and only after receiving baptism as taking food and
resuming his full powers of life, ix. 9-18. But even if we look
at the condition of the Apostle, not only immediately after the
phenomenon, but before its occurrence, whilst he was still the
strenuous Pharisaic zealot, jealous for the law, and the persecutor of all who turned away from it, what is the great contrast which this first state presents to the second in which we
find him? Is he not also in the first place a blind man, who
has to be cured of his blindness? Grotius has remarked on
the words, ix. 8, ἀνεῳγμένων δὲ τῶν ὀφθαλμῶν αὐτοῦ, οὐδένα
ἔβλεπε, " ea fuit imago Pauli, qualis antehac fuerat, speciem
habens hominis eruditi in lege, quum plane animo cœcus
esset." And on ix. 18, ὡσεὶ λεπίδες, "adumbrantes velum illud,
de quo agit Paulus," 2 Cor. iii. 14. Grotius maintains further,
that this expression, although figurative, is of fitting and
marked significance, as showing the spiritual condition of the
Apostle. The author himself represents the Apostle as acting
in accordance with this figurative expression, when he makes
him repeat in his speech the words of the Lord, which called
him to his appointed office, xxvi. 18, he is to be sent to the Gentiles. ἀνοῖξαι ὀφθαλμοὺς αὐτῶν καὶ ἐπιστρέψαι ἀπὸ σκότους εἰς
φῶς, καὶ τῆς ἐξουσίας τοῦ σατανᾶ ἐπὶ τὸν θεὸν, τοῦ λαβεῖν αὐτοὺς

ἄφεσιν ἁμαρτιῶν, καὶ κλῆρον ἐν τοῖς ἡγιασμένοις, πίστει τῇ εἰς ἐμὲ. May not the conversion of the Apostle itself be described in the same manner, as a passage from a state of darkness and blindness to a state of light, and vision with clear and open eyes. Taking all these points into consideration, does it not seem reasonable to consider as tradition all that is related in the Acts of the Apostles of the blinding of the Apostle, and the wonderful cure of his blindness by Ananias. The Apostle himself does not in any single instance mention these occurrences in his life in any of his Epistles. The tradition doubtless arose from the expressions which, in their figurative and material shape, indicate the great change in the inner, spiritual life of the Apostle, having been taken as literal and not figurative. This result may have been brought about by the great contrast afforded by the Apostle's earlier and later mental tendencies and religious modes of thought; and this result always follows the progress of mythical tradition. Spiritual blindness thus becomes bodily blindness : the looking up in a spiritual sense becomes the falling off of scales which had covered the eyes. There must also be a certain fixed time, in which one thing shall result from another. No better opportunity for the blinding could be found, than the moment when the Apostle had seen the dazzling appearance of light in which the Lord appeared. If, in order to substantiate the outward appearance, tradition represents an extraordinary heavenly light as spreading around, at the moment when the Apostle saw the Lord, this could not happen according to the usual conditions of such heavenly phenomena, without leaving behind on the person chiefly interested a token in the shape of blindness. And if also, the condition in which the Apostle was after that appearance, and the consequent change in himself must be taken really as a condition of perfect unconsciousness of the outward world, then everything concurs to place that blindness which affected the Apostle before he had attained to the clear light of the Christian life, in the period between the appearance of the Lord to him, and the act of his reception into the Christian community. What had begun miraculously was obliged to be miraculously carried on, and was brought to its culminating point when, after the crisis of the struggle into light was fully past, the Apostle became a new man by his actual reception into the Christian community. But the greater the change in the outward condition of the Apostle, the more fitting it seems that this should have been effected by special divine preparation, and (as is the case also with the conversion of Cornelius) two corresponding visions are represented, as the means most likely to advance the end. A special divine communication, such as the Apostle could only have received in a vision, must in this case appear to be all the more necessary, as without it the special outward act of imparting the Holy Spirit to the Apostle, by the laying on of hands by Ananias, could not have been considered as valid, as Ananias was not an Apostle. All these details in the tradition agree so well together, so close is the connection throughout between all the subsequent details, that we feel we have arrived at a point from which we can discover the genesis of this tradition. We cannot but assume that the blindness of the Apostle was no real physical blindness; then the miracle of healing is no longer needed; and if Ananias was not sent to Paul for this purpose (for it was to this end he was chiefly desired to go, according to Acts ix. 17, ὁ κύριος ἀπέσταλκέ με, ὅπως ἀναβλέψῃς), the statement also falls to the ground that Ananias received this charge in a divinely sent vision; and the whole tenor of the matter takes a completely different complexion from that given to it in the Acts of the Apostles. It therefore remains doubtful whether Ananias really came into such close relations with the Apostle Paul during this critical period of his life—whether his name did not get mixed up in the account of the conversion in an accidental manner. In the speech of the Apostle delivered before the Jewish people, the following is predicated of Ananias : ἀνὴρ εὐσεβὴς κατὰ τὸν νόμον, μαρτυρούμενος ὑπὸ πάντων, τῶν κατοικούντων Ἰουδαίων, xxii. 12. How easy it is to imagine that there was a particular interest at work in thus representing the Apostle Paul as from the beginning in close connection with a man who stood in such good repute with the Judaising party which was always so suspicious of the Apostle.

Although the historical and critical treatment of the narrative of the conversion of Paul, as given in the Acts of the Apostles, does not allow us to consider it as simply miraculous, yet if we look at it from a psychological point of view, the supposition of a miracle, if not necessary, may yet be allowable. Who can venture to say that such a change in the religious and spiritual life of the Apostle may not have been developed in his inmost being in a simply natural manner ? or who can dare to make the assertion that even the most sudden transition from one extreme to another lies outside the pale of psychological possibility ? or that such a phenomenon must be held as contrary to nature ? as if being contrary to nature made a miracle possible ! If the adoption of a miracle is so objectionable in itself, it is so certainly on psychological grounds, and especially in cases in which the miracle is to be considered only as an important disturbance of the natural development of the inward spiritual life of an individual. Neander, although in his statement and examination of this important question he for this reason adheres to the miraculous theory, still in no way allows a magic influence to have been in operation on Paul, whereby he was carried away and changed against his will. It is rather set forth as a point of his inmost being, without which the most essential, the inner revelation of Christ, to his highest self-consciousness would not have been possible, without which, no outward impression would have had any availing power, without which any outward impression, however strong, would have been merely transitory. But if once the theory of an inward connecting point is advanced, is it anything else but a setting forth of the principle, by which the whole change is referred to natural causes ? It becomes therefore the task of historical criticism to investigate, if what in itself is possible, did actually occur in accordance with the statements before us, without the interposition of a special miracle. So clear and

simple does that seem that we can only wonder how the
modern interpreters of the Acts of the Apostles embrace these
highly exaggerated miraculous theories. In a manner not
quite suited to the case Olshausen indicates as a reason for the
words, xxvi. 14, σκληρόν σοι πρὸς κέντρα λακτίζειν* (to which a
wrong meaning is given,) the Augustinian doctrine of "gratia
irresistibilis," only with this difference, that, by the assertion
that in *this* appearance of our Lord, Grace was manifested in an
overpowering strength, it is by no means sought to deny that
there may have been moments in the subsequent life of Paul
when by unfaithfulness he may have forfeited the grace vouchsafed to him. This is exactly the worst modification of this
doctrine of irresistible grace, as by it two completely different
standpoints become confused with each other, the ordinary
theory of free-will, and its opposite, that of absolute dependence. The consequence, or rather the cause, of this illogical
blending of heterogeneous theories is a theory of miracle which
thoroughly destroys the continuity of the spiritual life, the arbitrary assertion that there are circumstances in the life of man in
which (as Neander well puts it) " the individual is carried away
and transformed by magic influence against his own will." In
this view of the conversion of the Apostle Paul miracle is of
course assigned its full right, but this is the only advantage, and
what is believed to be gained by it on one hand, in favour of

* According to Olshausen, the meaning of these words can be only as follows:—
" Thy striving against the overpowering strength of grace helps thee not. Thou
must therefore submit." This meaning can only be forced from the words by an
interpreter biassed in favour of the Augustinian dogmatism. It appears certain
that these words ought to be taken as referring not to the subjective, but to the
objective, uselessness of striving. Their meaning therefore would be: " Thou
persecutest me in the belief that I am not the true Messiah, but as thou must be
now convinced that I am the true Messiah, how can thy undertaking be anything
but vain, and redounding to thy own destruction ? " This reading receives a
completely favorable corroboration from the parallel in the speech of Gamaliel, v.
39. οὐ δύνασθε καταλῦσαι αὐτὸ, μήποτε καὶ θεομάχοι εὑρεθῆτε. " You will not
effect anything by your reaction; the end will show on the contrary that you will
draw on yourselves the worst consequences, for only the worst is to be expected
when a direct opposition to God is in question."

the glorification of divine grace, is lost on the other by the sacrifice of the moral dignity of the Apostle.

The facts of the conversion and calling of the Apostle must have been of the greatest importance to the author of the Acts of the Apostles in furthering his apologetic aim. They are therefore not only related at length in chapter ix. but are also stated with the same detail and accuracy in the two speeches which are put into the mouth of the Apostle Paul himself, chapters xxii. and xxvi. We see from the epistles of the Apostle how his enemies always reproached him with not having been, as the other Apostles, a disciple of Jesus, and for not having been called to be an Apostle by Jesus himself during his earthly life. Against such a reproof and such an attack on the apostolic authority of Paul, a fact must have weighed strongly, by which he was connected with Jesus by a relation not less direct than that which bound the rest of the Apostles to him. The Apostle himself maintains with the most decided emphasis that he also had seen Christ the Lord, 1 Cor. ix. 1, that Jesus had manifested himself to him as well as to the other Apostles—even if after the others—still really and truly. 1 Cor. xv. 8. And not only once did this happen, but by repeated ὀπτασίας καὶ ἀποκαλύψεις τοῦ κυρίου, he claims for himself direct communion with the Lord : 2 Cor. xii. 1. But there still remains the great and essential difference between his calling and that of the other Apostles, namely, that the reality of the former depended on a momentary appearance which he maintains to have taken place—on a vision—an ὅραμα, whose truth only existed in the sphere of his own subjective consciousness, and therefore lies open to the possibility of being the result of self-deception. And as together with his calling to the office of an Apostle he received also a peculiar, decided commission to proclaim the Gospel to the Gentiles, so the whole question as to the participation of the Gentiles in the Messianic Salvation, which was so bitter a cause of dispute between the Apostle and the Jewish Christians, rests also on the truth and reality of the visionary appearance by which the Apostle believed himself to have been called. The more problematical the apostolic authority so delivered must be, the more earnestly must a writer who has so decided an apostolic tendency as the author of the Acts of the Apostles, endeavour to procure every possible guarantee for his Apostle. The authority of Paul, according to the nature of the circumstances under which the Acts of the Apostles was composed, can be legitimatized in no better manner than by the authority of Peter. If we can look to a precedent that Peter also saw a really divine vision in which he received an important charge, a charge which concerned a no less weighty matter than the adoption of the Gentiles into the Messianic kingdom, what objection can be taken to the vision which was the cause of Paul's being called to the office of an Apostle among the Gentiles? According to the whole plan and economy of the Acts of the Apostles it can not surprise us that we really do find in it such a legitimation of the Apostle. It is contained in the account of the conversion of Cornelius, which the author of the Acts of the Apostles, chapters x. and xi. apparently places purposely between the conversion of the Apostle, chapter ix. and the actual commencement of his apostolic office among the Gentiles, xi. 25. The detailed and circumstantial manner in which this is related, shows us in the clearest way how much importance the author attaches to it. If everything had taken place as it is here related, and as it is commonly believed to have done, there would be no need of saying anything about an especial apologetic aim of the author. But how is it possible to take such a series of miraculous occurrences all depending on one another as having actually happened? If we remember that this is not a question of miraculous events, merely occurring in the external world, but of operations from the higher world in an individual circle of religious thought and feeling, operations depending on one another and re-acting on one another, and having as consequences, resolutions and

6

opinions which were not likely to have been the result of religious and spiritual development ordinarily produced, we cannot then accept such a direct influence of a higher causality on the spiritual nature. The persons concerned must have been passive organs for the proclamation of ideas which, according to the divine plan, were to be introduced to the world as a purely supernatural revelation. We must notice how little the persons here treated of betray any clear consciousness, or even any suspicion of the consequences depending on their actions. Cornelius indeed received instructions to summon Peter to come to him, but he did not know what end was to be answered by his coming, x. 33. Peter involuntarily followed the summons sent him, x. 20. The opinions which he had hitherto held regarding the relation of the Jews to the Gentiles would rather have held him back from the command contained in the vision he had received, (28) but he understood so little of its real meaning and aim, that the light flashed upon him for the first time through the surprising discovery of the exact correspondence of the two visions with each other. It was not of his own free conviction and decision that he determined on his course of action, but through the overpowering impression of new miraculous events, which had immediate effect, and by which the destined result was completely carried out. Obviously Peter serves here as a mere organ, and we see, without doubt, in what outward relation the religious ideas and convictions here introduced stand to his religious consciousness and the steps of his religious development.

The entire series of these events is wanting in historic connexion, neither has it a natural point of contact. It has no result at all commensurate with the extraordinary preparation made for it. The Church at Jerusalem indeed allowed its doubts to be hushed by the assurances of Peter ; but how little influence these really had, the narrative in chapter xv. shows, and Peter himself always recurs to the cause of these events as to something of the highest antiquity, xv. 7, (ἀφ' ἡμερῶν ἀρχαίων,

&c.), about which nothing had been thought in the interval, and which now for the first time had attention drawn to it. With what aim did all this happen, if at that time it suited so little the stage of development then attained by Peter? could it have been in order to furnish him later on with a resting point for his religious consciousness, at a time in which he could not any longer need one? Or must we think it all took place for the sake of Cornelius? How passive he himself is, however, in all the events that befall him! and how little his personality seems concerned in reference to them! No satisfactory aim seems to be furthered by such a miracle, and how does so studied and complicated a series of miraculous occurrences agree with the character of the Gospel history? Such a narrative of such an important character, cannot be held as a mythical tradition. All through it we see that the details are connected with each other, that they are bound together by a single, exhaustive and studied combination of deliberate meaning into a complete whole, one vision corresponding to the other, and the consequences of each only happening at a certain moment and in a certain manner, and thus only are they enabled to fit into the whole. For this reason also the remark with which Neander prefaces his statement, "that we are not justified in assuming that Cornelius was able to separate clearly the objective and actual from the subjective side of his own comprehension of that which was placed before him as a subject for his investigation and examination," is completely aimless and useless; as it must not be supposed that anything else was included in the series of details than what is related, as that would betray somewhat of a subjective deceit.

If one of these details is put out of its place, or considered in a different relation, the whole becomes disarranged and confused and loses coherence and connexion. Such combination and coherence as are here presented are foreign to a myth. Such a narrative cannot be looked upon as the casual product of mythical tradition, but as a free composition, originating in a certain

6 *

design. From this point of view, the two visions which are so essential in the matter must be held to be the spontaneous, visible form in which the ideas presented are clothed, as in the accounts of the earliest Christian times visions are not uncommonly presented, merely as visible and poetical media. The chief idea with which they have to do appears so decidedly as the preponderating one, that we can scarcely avoid seeing that the persons and events which are placed before us are only destined to carry out the idea of the whole, and bring it into notice. As soon, therefore, as the means of furthering this end are so far advanced that the aim of the statement is attained, the idea is abruptly withdrawn from the material husk which enveloped it; and now the full consciousness has dawned upon Peter of what the author makes him utter as the ruling idea of the whole, x. 34, that "there is no respect of persons with God; but in every nation he that feareth him and worketh righteousness is accepted with him." These words, as modern interpreters rightly remark, can only be so taken in the whole connexion in which they stand in opposition to the Jewish exclusiveness : God receives into the Messianic kingdom those who believe in Jesus, not with any regard to whether or not they are descended from a special theocratic nation ; but looking only to the moral worth and sensibility of each separate individual. The speech of Peter immediately following seeks to remove any idea of exclusiveness from the labours of Jesus. The idea here brought forward could not be more directly and emphatically confirmed than by the outpouring of the Holy Spirit which anticipated baptism, x. 44. How evidently was it thus shown that the Gentiles were not to be excluded from the reception of the Holy Spirit as the principle of Christian consciousness, how clearly is the conclusion drawn that the outward form of adoption is not to be refused, when the inward desire of and inclination for the Holy Spirit is present, this being the chief condition, and all else merely superfluous. Peter accordingly repeatedly takes as the chief idea, resulting from the whole (x. 47, xi. 16, 17), this especial thought, that as the Gentiles as well as the born Jews, had at one time received the gift of the Holy Spirit, and attested its reception and operation by the same outward manifestations as those at the feast of Pentecost, and the λαλεῖν γλώσσαις and the μεγαλύλειν τὸν θεὸν, there could be no distinction between Jew and Gentile with regard to the Messianic kingdom. From this it must necessarily follow that with respect to the adoption of the Gentiles into the community of the followers of Jesus as the Messiah, nothing was demanded (as would have been the case with enforced circumcision) which involved as a condition that they must become Jews in order to become Christians. As the whole matter is embodied in visions—for the figurative and symbolical always favour visions—this thought is also presented in a symbolic form. The distinction between clean and unclean in the relation between Jews and Gentiles, is founded specially on the Mosaic laws with respect to eating, by which the Jews were forbidden to taste the flesh of certain animals which were held to be unclean. The Gentiles, to whom this eating of flesh was not forbidden, became for that very reason unclean to the Jews, who had to be on their guard against defilement in their intercourse with the Gentiles when this involved eating and drinking together. The idea that the difference hitherto subsisting between Jews and Gentiles with regard to clean and unclean things, was no longer of any importance, is very strikingly exhibited by the figure of a vessel in which clean and unclean things were contained, and commanded to be used as food without any distinction. The extreme hunger which Peter had experienced just before the vision, is also connected very closely with the aim and purpose of the vision; as he must have felt the prohibition against eating certain beasts which were destined for the food of and use of man, as an unnatural restriction. The removal of the distinction between the idea clean and unclean was expressed also by the symbolical vessel, as in it there was no difference made between clean and unclean beasts, and also by its imme-

diate descent with all its contents from heaven. As the difference between clean and unclean with regard to the animal world,
rested on a certain dualistic view, on the idea of a clean and
unclean creation, so also with regard to the relations of Jew
and Gentile, the existing wall of partition between the old
customs and the prevailing views could be removed in no better
way than by the introduction of the thought that God was the
God of the Gentiles as well as of the Jews. As from the
Divine standpoint there can be no unclean creation—no man
is to be considered " common or unclean," (compare x. 28, and
15), so Jesus, as the Messiah, is the common Lord of all in the
peace of his Gospel, πάντων κύριος, (36), and ordained of God to
be the Judge of quick and dead. (x. 42.) All this combines
to set forth concisely and distinctly a certain decided idea, but,
although after what has been said no further remark is needed
to show that this idea was intended to be brought home especially to the recognition and consciousness of Peter, yet it is
necessary for us to notice that the circumstances attending its
presentation betray a great desire on the part of the author to
show that the Church at Jerusalem also acknowledged the idea
brought forward by Peter. He expressly mentions the opposition which Peter's act of imparting the Gospel to the uncircumcised and unclean, received from the Church at Jerusalem,
and makes Peter relate circumstantially the whole course of the
affair in his own vindication. The author would not have
allowed himself this repetition if he had not attached great
weight at this period of his narrative to the impression which
the affair made on the Church at Jerusalem. Accordingly
after hearing this vindication, the Church at Jerusalem held its
peace and glorified God in that he had extended his salvation
to the Gentiles, (xi. 1-18). The behaviour that the members
of the Church exhibited in the sequence of this affair shows
undoubtedly how strange all this must have appeared to them
at that time. Can we not understand how Peter so easily
succeeded in his vindication of a step calculated to excite such

great opposition, when we see that he appeals to the fact that before he had ended his introductory speech : ἐπέπεσε τὸ πνεῦμα τὸ ἅγιον ἐπ' αὐτοὺς ὥσπερ καὶ ἐφ' ἡμᾶς ἐν ἀρχῇ. xi. 15. This fact is thus included with the feast of Pentecost and the miraculous γλώσσαις λαλεῖν. So actual and public a miracle could of course further no better end than silencing the doubts of the Church. But if the miracle of the λαλεῖν γλώσσαις was taken by Cornelius and those baptized with him as having been performed for no other reason than that they (as Neander states, page 105) should feel themselves impelled to express their feelings in inspired praises of God who in so miraculous a manner had led them to salvation, would the Church at Jerusalem have been content with such a vindication ? Must we also in favour of this vindication retract what we have already allowed to be a well-founded result of the enquiry into the λαλεῖν γλώσσαις ? Certainly not, but it therefore follows that this vindication before the Church at Jerusalem, (especially as regards the consequences it seems to have had), cannot be held to have occurred as the letter of the narrative would have us believe.

However little such a narrative can lay claim to historic credibility, it suits the apologetic tendency with which the Acts of the Apostles is written. However we may decide on the traditional element which lies at the root of the history of the conversion of Cornelius, its adoption into the narrative, and the place assigned to it can can only be accounted for by the apologetic interest of the author of the Acts of the Apostles. Paul must be represented as entering on his apostolic work among the Gentiles under the shield of the Apostle Peter, who himself converted the first Gentile, and the heavenly appearance on which alone Paul grounds the proof of his apostolic calling, becomes legitimized in the most authentic manner, by a similar vision to that sent to the Apostle Peter. We can well imagine what great weight this must have had in the apologetic interest of the author of the Acts of the Apostles, if we consider to what attacks the Apostle Paul was exposed, both at the commencement of his career and long afterwards from the Jewish-Christian party, on account of the peculiar nature of his call. In the Pseudo-Clementine Homilies the principle is enunciated, with peculiar reference to the Apostle Paul, that those revelations only should be considered true and trustworthy which are attested by outward communications and testimony, and not merely by appearances and visions. This is one of the chief subjects of controversy between the persons who are represented as conversing in these Homilies; and the arguments adduced on each side are only of use in making us see clearly the importance this matter must have had to the Apostle and his party. "Thou hast boasted, objected Simon Magus to the Apostle Peter, (Homily xvii. 13.) that thou hast entirely understood thy Teacher, (the true prophet Christ) because thou hast personally seen him present, and hast listened to him, and that it would be impossible for any other man to have the like certainty by means of any appearance or vision. (ὁράματι ἡ ὀπτασίᾳ.)— Now, that this is untrue, I will show thee. He who clearly hears what another says is not fully convinced by what is said. For he must think in his mind, ' Does not a man who is merely an appearance, lie ? ' But a vision certifies the truth, for when it is seen, the conviction comes to him who sees it, that it is something divine." To this Peter replies, " Thou maintainest that more can be learnt through a vision than through a real operating presence (ἡ παρὰ τῆς ἐνεργείας.) On this account thou thinkest that thou art better informed about Jesus than I am. The prophet alone deserves all belief, as we know before hand that he surely is, and he gives, as the learner wishes, an answer to questions asked him. But he who believes a vision, a form, or a dream, has no security and knows not whom he believes ; for he may indeed be deceived by an evil demon, or a deceitful spirit, which really is nothing, and if he asks who it is that appears*—it can answer what it

* As Paul asks, Acts ix. 5, τίς εἶ κύριε.

will. It stays as long as it pleases, and vanishes like a sudden flash of light, without giving the desired information to the inquirer. In a dream no one can ask what he desires to know, since the mind of the sleeper is not in his own power. For this very reason we ask, out of curiosity, many things in a dream, and learn without asking what is of no interest to us, and when we awake we are discontented because we have neither asked nor heard what we wanted to know." The Magus rejoins that even if belief is not to be conceded to all visions, still those visions and dreams sent by God cannot be false; that only the righteous can see a true vision, not the wicked; and Peter answers that he cannot agree to this, and pursuing his argument he says, "I know that many Idolaters, carnal-minded men given over to all sorts of sins, see visions and true dreams, and some also have seen demoniacal appearances. I maintain that mortal eye cannot see the incorporeal form of the Father or of the Son, because they shine in purest light. It is therefore not out of jealousy, that God does not allow himself to be seen by men who are fettered by their fleshly nature. For who can see the incorporeal form even of an angel, much more of the Son? But if any one sees a vision (ὀπτασία) he must remember that it may proceed from an evil demon: and that ungodly persons see visions and true dreams is certain, and I can prove this from the Scriptures." Then are adduced the instances of Abimelech, Genesis xx.—of Pharaoh, xli.—of Nebuchadnezzar, Daniel iii. 5. "All these were ungodly persons and yet saw sights and visions and true dreams. It results from this that a man who sees visions, dreams and appearances, need not be concluded to be necessarily a pious man. For the truth springs out of an indwelling pure feeling in the pious man, which does not seek the truth in dreams, but is bestowed on good men with consciousness and judgment. Thus the Son was revealed to me from the Father—I therefore know how important the revelation is (τίς δύναμις ἀποκαλύψεως, *i. e.* how essential it is) from my own experience. For as soon as the Lord questioned me, (Matthew xvi. 14.) something rose in my heart and I myself knew not what had happened to me. Then I said, ' Thou art the Son of the living God.' He who on this occasion called me blessed first told me that it was the Father who had revealed this to me. Therefore I perceived that this which was revealed to me without outward manifestation, without visions and dreams, was something spiritual. And thus it is that in the truth which God implanteth in us is contained the seed of all truth. This is either concealed from, or revealed to us by the hand of God, for God acts towards every man according to his deserts. To manifest itself by dreams and visions is not a characteristic of revelation, but a token of divine wrath— for it is written in the Law that God being wroth with Moses and Aaron said (Numbers xii. 6.) ' If there be a prophet among you, I, the Lord, will make myself known unto him in a vision and will speak unto him in a dream. My servant Moses is not so, for with him will I speak apparently (directly, ἐν εἴδει) as a man speaketh to a friend.' Thou seest how laws and dreams are tokens of anger. But what a man wishes to impart to a friend goes from mouth to mouth direct, and not through figures and dreams and sights, which he uses in communicating with an enemy : So although our Jesus may also have appeared to thee, manifested himself to thee, and spoken to thee, he had done so in wrath, as to an adversary, and for that reason he has employed appearances, and dreams, and other outward revelations. But can a man be instructed and ordained for the office of Teacher by means of a vision ? If thou sayest this is quite possible, then I say, Why did the Teacher avoid communication for a whole year with those who watched continually for him, and how can these believe that he revealed himself to thee? How can he have appeared to thee, who art not even in agreement with his doctrine ? If thou really didst become an Apostle by communion and instruction, if only for a time, then expound his sayings, explain what he said and did, love his Apostles, and dispute not with me who was with him; for thou hast striven against me as an adversary, against me, the strong rock, the corner pillar of the Church. If thou hadst not been an adversary, thou wouldest not have so vilified and abused me and my preaching, that men would not believe what I myself heard from the Lord when I was with him, as though I were worthy of condemnation when I was really worthy of praise. Yea, verily, when thou callest me accursed, Gal. ii. 11, thou accusest God who revealed Christ to me, thou attackest Him who has blessed me through this revelation. If thou wishest in deed and truth to become a fellow-worker in the cause of truth, then learn from us as we have learnt from Him, and when thou hast become a disciple of truth, then become a fellow-worker with us."

Such was the opinion prevailing on the Jewish-Christian side at the time the Pseudo-Clementine Homilies were composed, with regard to the apostolic calling of Paul : and that we are not here exhibiting a mere extreme heretical opinion of a later date is testified by the Epistles of the Apostle himself, in which it is represented in exactly the same light. This opinion then was the general one of the opposing Jewish-Christian party. Even if this opinion had been held at the time of the authors of these Homilies, in a modified form by a part only of the Jewish-Christians ; if Paul had even been considered in his apostolic relation to Peter, as filling a position in which he by no means held any advantage over Peter, and in which he must share with him the glory of being the Apostle to the Gentiles—we should still see here the result of the efforts by which the Pauline party generally, and the author of the Acts of the Apostles especially, had so far provided for the Apostle Paul the acknowledgment of his apostolic dignity. This could not have been brought about without concessions and modifications of various kinds on the side of the Pauline party. The Petrine party, above all, must have conceded it in view of the superiority which it implied on the part of its Apostle, and the principles

on which this rested. The author of the Acts of the Apostles
must have consented to include in his statement this criterion
of the apostolic calling, which the Homilies present as the only
one. On the election of the Apostle Matthias in the place of the
traitor, Peter enunciates the principle, i. 21, 22, δεῖ οὖν τῶν
συνελθόντων ἡμῖν ἐν παντὶ χρόνῳ, ἐν ᾧ εἰσῆλθεν καὶ εξῆλθεν εφ᾽
ἡμᾶς, ὁ κύριος Ἰησοῦς, ἀρξάμενος ἀπὸ τοῦ βαπτίσματος Ἰωάννου
ἕως τῆς ἡμέρας ἧς ἀνελήφθη ἀφ᾽ ἡμῶν, μάρτυρα τῆς ἀναστάσεως
αὐτοῦ γενέσθαι σὺν ημῖν ἕνα τούτων. In the same sense Peter
says in his speech, with regard to the conversion of Cornelius,
x. 41, that they, the Apostles, are the μάρτυρες προκεχειροτον-
εμένοι ὑπὸ τοῦ θεοῦ οἵτινες συνεφάγομεν καὶ συνεπίομεν αὐτῷ (the
following words, μετὰ τὸ ἀναστῆναι αυτὸν ἐκ νεκρῶν, are, as De
Wette also says, obviously not in agreement with the words
directly preceding, but should be taken with ἐμφανῆ γενέσθαι,
40). It cannot be denied that a certain design which bespeaks
a special·reason is evident in the express enunciation and enforcement of the principle, that the witnesses of the risen Jesus
should be those only who through living communion with him,
through the constant coming and going with him, the eating
and drinking with him, were specially destined by him for this
purpose. This indeed seems to be recognized by the author of
the Acts of the Apostles himself as a criterion of the apostolic
calling, which might be made use of against his Apostle. But
the more that he places this to the credit of the Jewish-Christian
party, the more does he expect from that side a willingness to
make its Apostle yield to his ; and, provided only that the exclusive primacy were assured to the Apostle Peter, he desires to
win from the Jewish-Christians the concession that there might
exist another mode of receiving the apostolic mission, namely,
through apparitions and visions, especially as these also by
extraordinary divine ordination fell to the share of the Apostle
Peter himself, in furtherance of the important aim of the conversion of the Gentiles.

CHAPTER IV.

BETWEEN the conversion of the Apostle and his actual entrance into the sphere of his apostolic work, there intervenes a time of which we will speak later, as the account of it in the Acts of the Apostles varies considerably from the Apostle's own statement. In general this interval has been considered as the period in his life in which he matured the powerful impression which he had received from his sudden conversion, into a thorough religious conviction, which served as the strong groundwork of his apostolic labours. As there is nothing known of his outward actions during this interval, which he himself says (Gal. i. 18) lasted several years, it is more likely that he lived an inner life in his own introspective, deep thoughts, in his newly-won Christian consciousness. When we consider his individuality generally, as well as the kind and manner of his conversion, which was so sudden and thorough a transformation of his inward man, we cannot but think that he did not first go through any various preliminary steps; but as soon as he was once settled and fixed in his own mind, he became at once what we see him to have been afterwards.

So soon, as he himself says (Gal. i. 16), as God had been pleased to reveal his Son to him, that he might preach his Gospel among the heathen, a new world entered on his consciousness, and his own independence preserved him in the purity of his individuality from troublesome dependence on others. This much is certain, that as he grounded his whole apostolic works and actions entirely on the directness of his apostolic call, and as all that he was, he only wished to be through Christ who had appeared to him, he would not have neglected to institute inquiries into the history of the life of Christ. He who could speak so decidedly and in such detail about matters of fact in the Gospel history as the Apostle does, 1 Cor. xi. 23, &c., xv. 8, could not have been unacquainted with the rest of its chief incidents.

The Apostle of the Gentiles first entered on his widely-extended and momentous life, in Antioch, where before his coming a new metropolis of the Christian world had begun to arise, in consequence of the important events already mentioned in the history of the development of Christianity.* From thence, with his greatest friend Barnabas, he undertook his first missionary journey, which was first directed to Cyprus, and the countries of Asia Minor, Pamphylia, Pisidia, Lycaonia and their cities, Perga, Antioch, Iconium, Lystra and Derbe. The discourses of the two Apostles which were accompanied by miracles secured a ready acceptance of the Gospel among the Gentiles, but for that very reason called down on them the hostile opposition of the Jewish party. In the whole account the apologetic tendency and the literary freedom of the author of the Acts of the

---

* As an indication of the important position which Antioch had assumed in the affairs of Christendom, we may take the remark in xi. 26, that the disciples were called Christians first in Antioch. This name must have been commonly current among the people at the time when the Acts was written; which is the only meaning of χρηματίζειν. The name χριστιανοί only occurs in two passages in the New Testament, Acts xxvi. 28, 1 Peter iv. 16, and was used by opponents as a distinctive appellation, as it was afterwards also used by the writers of the second century; but the opponents who gave the name must have been Gentiles, as Jews would not have so used the name χριστός, which was sacred among them. The Gentile origin of the name causes the author to connect it with the city of Antioch, which was the first Gentile site of Christianity. But whether it originated in Antioch is very doubtful, on account of the Latin form of the name. The name Christiani is first mentioned by Roman writers, and as one in use among the people; it is used by Tacitus and Suetonius on the occasion of the incendiarism of Nero and the cruelties then practised against the Christians. "Nero," says Tacitus, Ann. 15, 44, "subdidit reos, et quæsitissimis pœnis affecit, quos per flagitia invisos vulgus Christianos appellabat. Auctor nominis ejus Christus." Compare Suetonius, Nero, 16. Already, in Nero's time, the people had called the hated sect, "Christians." The author may have assigned the origin of this name to Antioch because he thought that as a Gentile name, it must have originated in the first Gentile city in which Christians existed.

Apostles are shown in a manner which places its historical contents in a very questionable aspect.

The miracles which the Apostle may have performed in this first missionary journey in the company of Barnabas bear most undoubted tokens of the apologetic parallel with Peter. One of Peter's most celebrated apostolic actions was his victory over Simon Magus. According to the Acts of the Apostles, Peter met the sorcerer in Samaria, when the Apostle himself for the first time visited the region beyond Judea on his apostolic errand. Parallel with this is the meeting of the Apostle Paul with Elymas the sorcerer in Cyprus, on his first missionary journey. The first important act of Paul's apostolic life in foreign lands is the conviction and punishment of the sorcerer. In both cases the apostolic acuteness shows itself in the instantaneous unveiling of the deep obstinacy which usually lay at the root of sorcery when it came into contact with Christianity. Although the sorcerer Elymas is placed in a different relation to Christianity to that occupied by Simon Magus, the main idea of the speech against the former is the same as in the speech of Peter, viii. The speech, xiii. 10, &c., evidently refers to viii. 21, &c. The main idea in viii. 21, ἡ γὰρ καρδία σοῦ οὐκ ἔστιν εὐθεῖα ἐνώπιον θεοῦ, is again pursued in xiii. 8, &c., wherein the sorcerer is described as ζητῶν διαστρέψαι ἀπὸ τῆς πίστεως, πλήρης παντὸς δόλου καὶ πάσης ῥᾳδιουργίας διαστρέφων τὰς ὁδοὺς κυρίου τὰς εὐθείας. This is an example of how imitation generally supplies a want of originality by exaggeration. It seems by this that the sorcerer Elymas did not endeavour to introduce himself into the Christian community by secret means like Simon Magus, but set himself in direct opposition to Christianity, for which reason the speech against him contains still stronger expressions than that against Simon (especially in xiii. 10, υἱὲ διαβόλου). But the exaggerated copy is most evidently apparent in the fact, that whilst there is no punishment pronounced against Simon, although he is commanded to pray to God for forgiveness of his sins, a miracle of punishment takes place with regard

to Elymas. This punishment itself is nothing else than a
figurative representation of the main idea by which the sorcerer,
or rather sorcery itself, is characterized. As sorcery in contrast
to the true religion is untrue, perverted, erroneous, and therefore gropes about in the dim light, shelters in the darkness,
blind, seeing nothing, so this is symbolized in the punishment
destined for the sorcerer, παραχρῆμα δὲ ἐπέπεσεν ἐπ᾽ αὐτὸν ἀχλὺς
καὶ σκότος, καὶ περιάγων ἐζήτει χειραγωγούς, ii. How clearly
the hand of the copyist has been at work here! for all these
traits are only the carrying out of the οὐκ εὐθεῖα καρδία, viii. 21.
This first important apostolic act of Paul is also remarkable,
because from this time the Acts of the Apostles gives him his
own especial apostolic name, Paul, instead of Saul, the name he
had hitherto borne. Henceforth, he is named not after but before Barnabas. It cannot be doubted that this change of name
here has some reference to the Roman Pro-Consul Sergius
Paulus, converted by the Apostle Paul. This is not contradicted
by the explanation of Jerome : "Apostolus a primo ecclesiæ
spolio, Proconsule Sergio Paulo, victoriæ suæ trophæa retulit
erexitque vexillum ut Paulus ex Saulo vocaretur,"—only the
erection of these trophies is not ascribed to the Apostle himself,
but merely to the report which joined the change of name
already adopted by the Apostle to an important act of his apostolic life. How could the arrival of the Apostle of the Gentiles
at his full glory be better shown than by the conversion of a
Roman Pro-Consul ? The Roman form of the name hints also
at the conversion of a Roman.

The conversion of a Roman Pro-Consul must also have been
the important fact by which the Apostle verified the meaning
of the name which he bore as the Apostle to the Gentiles in a
manner worthy of notice. The Gentile name Paul is the proper
name by which to denote an Apostle to the Gentiles. In considering the account of this bestowal of a name from this point
of view, we have a parallel to the genuinely apostolic act of the
Apostle Peter, Matt. xvi. 16. As Peter then, through his per-

suasion, steadfast as a rock, that Jesus was the Christ and the Son of God, bore witness to the true meaning of his name, and was no longer to be called Simon, but Peter, so Paul adopted, as a memorial, the name of the Roman Paul, whom he had converted, thus giving public evidence that, as an Apostle to the Gentiles, he had a right to bear that name.

Even the conversion of so distinguished a Roman was not a sufficiently prominent fact to fix special attention to this period in the life of the Apostle; it had to be rendered more important and rich in results, by the victorious opposition to and struggle of the true divine faith with false, magical and demoniacal beliefs. For this reason, the moment at which the name of Paul receives its meaning, is the moment of the address which overpowers the sorcerer, xiii. 9. Σαῦλος δὲ, ὁ καὶ Παῦλος, πλησθεὶς πνεύματος ἁγίου, καὶ ἀτενίσας εἰς αὐτὸν εἶπεν, &c. So two different moments in the life of Peter are joined in one act, that Paul may enter on the scene as an Apostle to the Gentiles in his first important apostolic action.

Such narratives as those of the two sorcerers in Acts viii. and xiii. are no doubt commonly considered worthy of historic credence, because sorcerers and enchanters were very general phenomena of that time, and received ready acceptance from men of the first standing. Of course this cannot be denied, and we see an example of the kind in Josephus (Antiq. xx. 7), where he mentions the sorcerer, Simon of Cyprus, who was much thought of by Felix, the Roman Procurator of Judea; and the more common certain phenomena of the age are, the more natural it is that tradition and poetry should borrow their materials from them. It is for this reason, that if we wish to prove the truth of the narratives in the Acts of the Apostles, we must not appeal to Alexander of Abonoteichos, described by Lucian, whose prophecies were eagerly sought after by the most important men in Rome, and whose most zealous adherent was the Roman statesman Rutilianus.* It is clear that in this

* Neander, Gesch. der Pfl. p. 148.

7

impostor, Lucian does not intend to sketch any historical personage, but only to give a picture of the customs of his time. That the Acts of the Apostles gives to the sorcerer the name of Bar-Jesus, and says of him that he was a Jewish false prophet, also testifies nothing to the truth of the narrative, as a Jew he would be all the more fit to be brought forward in this manner as an adversary of the Apostle Paul. But the conversion of the Roman Pro-Consul has a very slight degree of probability. The Acts of the Apostles does not give us any further particulars on the subject, it merely says without mentioning baptism that he " believed," and that, in consequence of the miracle wrought on the sorcerer, he was further impressed with the reality of the doctrine. And how can we think that a conversion took place in that class to which a Roman Pro-Consul belonged, and in the manner which is here related, when all internal evidence is wanting as well as any outward testimony, to prove that the impression received was anything else than a momentary effect. If such minor circumstances do not in any way strengthen the truth of the narrative generally, they must be looked upon from the general point of view from which such narratives must be considered, with reference to the entire nature of the historic statement of which they form the ingredients.

The Apostle Paul is said to have wrought a second miracle during the same missionary journey at Lystra in Lycaonia, on a man lame from his birth, xiv. 8, &c. This miracle also presents a duplicate to the one wrought by Peter, and described iii. 1, 4. Here, as there, it is a χωλὸς ἐκ κοιλίας μητρὸς αὐτοῦ, iii. 2. xiv. 8. The relation in which the worker of the miracle is placed to the lame man, is indicated in both places by the word ἀτενίζειν (ἀτενίσας αὐτῷ—εἶπε [Παῦλος] xiv. 9 ἀτενίσας δὲ Πέτρος εἰς αὐτὸν—εἶπε, iii. 4—and the miracle following is in both cases described by the same words, ἥλλετο καὶ περιεπάτει, xiv. 10, ἐξαλλόμενος ἔστη καὶ περιεπάτει, iii. 8. Only the first narrative where the lame man is described as a beggar presents several additional corroborative features ; and the second merely says

of the lame man, Πίστις τοῦ σωθῆναι.   As the two miracles are
exactly alike we might indeed hold the similarity of the two
narratives, as very natural, if there were not visible in both
cases a special design, rendering necessary such a miracle, so
exactly fitted to awaken great attention, and to point out the
Apostle unmistakeably as a worker of miracles.   This end could
be best carried out by a miracle wrought on a lame man who
had never been seen to walk, but who now sprang at once to
his feet, and went about in the sight of all the people, walking
and leaping and praising God for what had happened to him.
As this incident (iii. 8.) is related with a purpose, so in xiv. 10,
the healed man in the same way mixes with the crowd of people, (ἥλλετο καὶ περιεπάτει οἳ δὲ ὄχλοι ἰδόντες, &c.)*   The leading

---

* Neander thinks himself obliged to add to his merely referential and translated
text the following remark : " To believe this (that the lame man rose and walked
at the mere word of the Apostle) is really incumbent only on him who recognizes
the new divine power which was bestowed on mankind through Christ.   But even
to him who is fettered by no mechanical views of nature, who recognizes the might
of spirit over nature, and a hidden dynamic agreement between soul and body,
there is at least nothing so incredible in the direct influence of divine strength
working on the whole inner being of man, bringing about effects of quite a different
kind from those attainable by the general remedies in the power of nature."   In a
historical critical investigation of the narratives in the Acts of the Apostles, I hold
it quite superfluous to go into the general dogmatic question as to whether miracles
are possible, for in such an investigation it is not needed to enquire into the possibility
of miracle, but only into their credibility, and in this idea are comprised all the
questions with which criticism has to do.   But when others, in evasion of the
critical questions which as historians they should have investigated, give unqualified assent to every miracle which is related in any one of the New Testament
writings, and think themselves obliged to call to their assistance a theory of
miracles, without being able to adduce in its vindication any better argument than
the accusation that those who do not embrace this view of miracle are wanting in
true insight into Christianity and nature,—such persons must put up with this
accusation being thrown back on themselves.   As positive grounds are taken it is
easy to see how weak they are.   The accusation that he who does not believe a
miracle in the Acts of the Apostles like the one in question, does not acknowledge
the divine strength of life bestowed on man through Christ, gives a very dishonouring
idea of Christianity, as it must necessarily follow that miracle belongs so essentially
to Christianity, that everywhere, where Christianity is not accompanied by miracle it
does not manifest its divine life-giving power.   As it is acknowledged that no miracle
now takes place, at least none of the same kind as those now in question, if we do
not take the legends of the middle ages and of the modern missionary accounts as

7 *

thought of the writer of the history, is, that Paul had wrought as great and astonishing a miracle as Peter had done, and by the whole affair had made such an impression on the Gentiles that none more powerful or more striking could be made. In this thought also the narrative is in strict accordance with the preceding one. In consequence of the miracle, Paul and Bar-

miracles, and if those who do not share this belief must refuse to recognize the divine life principle of Christianity, Christianity must long have been extinct. It is therefore only just to make it understood, that a man may fully acknowledge the divine life-principle of Christianity, even if he does not consider every one of the miracles related in the New Testament as a real actual miracle, because the letter of the narrative so describes it. As far as concerns the reproof of taking a mechanical view of nature, we may say that a mechanical view of nature is one which, instead of accepting a living natural organism, supposes a purely external relation between cause and effect, and considers nature as a machine, set in motion from time to time by a force applied from without. This is however the precise view of nature which lies at the root of the theory of miracles, for every miracle may be considered as an interruption of the natural order, not to be explained by any natural cause, and dependent on a connection between cause and effect, regulated by an inherent law, the result of an external causality working irregularly, provided we do not in this theory of miracles admit the arbitrary idea, which is necessitated by the mechanical natural theory. It is not evident what the power of spirit over nature has to do with the connection of soul and body as a vindication of the theory of miracle. What Schleiermacher, in the well-known proposition in his doctrine of faith, has said in regard to the divine omnipotence, " that we cannot be decided as to whether the divine omnipotence shows itself most in the interruption of the order of nature, or in the sustaining it in the usual course," refers in the same way to the power of spirit over nature. Spirit shows its power over nature, not in interruption and disturbance of the arrangements of nature, but, as its essence is legality, through the fact that it is the law itself. However, judging by the argument in the above extract, the power of the spirit over nature and the hidden dynamic connection between soul and body seems to be remembered with a view to the partial naturalizing of miracle. A miracle such as the one in question, viz., the healing of a man lame from his birth by a mere word, is supposed to become more credible, if we think of it, first, as the action of divine power on the whole inner being of the man, and then of the healing itself as the result of the direct influence of this action, so that the healing is the consequence of the hidden but natural connection between soul and body. Miracle must also be explained psychologically, it follows certainly from the dynamic connection between soul and body, that the active healing power works through the mediation of the soul operating on the body according to its own laws. But how does the divine power itself affect the soul ? In a natural or spiritual manner ? If in a natural manner, then there is no further question of miracle. And it must then be explained how the healing which resulted from it is nevertheless represented as a miracle. If it affects the body in a supernatural manner, the miracle remains, and it is not evident what nabas were held by the astonished people to be gods, who had come down from heaven to earth in the likeness of men. They called Paul Hermes, and Barnabas Zeus, and in this delusion preparations were made by the priests of Zeus in Lystra, for a solemn sacrifice to the two above-mentioned gods, when the two Apostles, who from ignorance of the language did not mark what was going on, interfered just in time to prevent, with great difficulty, the completion of the hateful act which was already so far advanced. The whole affair considered in all its bearings has certainly a very strange and romantic aspect, and we cannot avoid asking why, among all the miracles which the Apostle wrought, this should have had so remarkable a result? why this idolatrous scene at Lystra should have taken place? why the people should so suddenly have gone from one extreme to the other, that on account of the insinuations of some Jews from Antioch, they chased with stones out of the city and left for dead, the same Apostles to whom just before they had been willing to offer sacrifice as gods? All that we can say on this subject is comprised in what Olshausen remarks, " The Gentiles took Paul and Barnabas for Hermes and Zeus,

---

is gained by the argument, which goes to prove that it can be explained naturally. Where a miracle is accepted, (unless we are playing with idle words,) there must also be accepted an interruption and disturbance of the order of nature; but in accepting miracle, it is perfectly the same whether it is accepted from one point of view or another, and perfectly useless to try to conceal this interruption of the order of nature by speaking of the hidden dynamic connection between soul and body, thereby awakening suspicion that the interruption of the order of nature is not so easily disposed of, as is really the case. If we do not hesitate to heap miracle upon miracle, then we must not hesitate to confess without affectation or equivocation that we are always ready to tear away every thread of the order of nature on any available occasion. Perhaps we may convince ourselves that the belief in miracles at least might be grounded on better reasons than are here used, and that it may not be so superfluous in some isolated cases to inquire whether, in consequence of the entire nature of a narrative of a miracle, we are, I will not say obliged, but entitled, to accept the real actual miracle theory. But as such things are generally treated, it can be no great task to defend any such legendary miracle with such striking words as " New divine life power," " Mechanical view of nature," " Power of spirit over nature," " Hidden dynamic agreement between soul and body," &c.

because these gods did once visit Philemon and Baucis the ancient inhabitants of this place. These occurrences are specially interesting in so far as they show that the belief in the ancient doctrines of the gods still had deep root in the life of the people, for we must remember that this event took place in a small remote town where the philosophical enlightenment of the Augustan age had not yet penetrated." But if we appeal to the tradition of Philemon and Baucis, what right have we to assume, that not only had the Greek and Roman poets who relate the tradition, transplanted its scene into Phrygia and the neighbouring countries, (this locality being a favourite theatre for primitive mythical occurrences of this kind), but that the inhabitants of these places themselves entertained it as a native tradition and really preserved it as a foundation of their religious belief. There is also unquestionably a very great difference between a fact such as is described here, and what is spoken of by Homer, and pathetically described by Neander as " a belief spread widely among the heathen from the most ancient times, springing from the depth of the human breast, from the undeniable feeling of the connection of the human race with God, a belief that the Gods descend in human form in order to dispense benefits among men." Still less can we understand, how, according to Neander's assertion, this belief was furthered by the religious ferment at that time existing. Religious ferment rather promotes doubt and unbelief, and although that age with its unbelief was still at the same time much addicted to a faith in a direct union with the higher supernatural world, still it was by no means the child-like faith of the Homeric world, which was still at that time cherished, or to which men had recurred; but it was rather a belief in Sorcery, uniting the natural and supernatural worlds, supported on a belief in the power of Demons. For this reason we should have thought it much more natural if the people in their astonishment at the workers of the miracle had taken them for sorcerers and magicians, instead of seeing in them an Homer, *i. e.* Homeric incarnation of the Gods. This may be elucidated by an example lying near at hand. The same locality which is assigned to the tradition of the pious couple Philemon and Baucis, also belongs to the well known soothsayer and miracle worker, Apollonius of Tyana.* According to his biographer, Philostratus, he was supposed by the inhabitants of the country in which he was born to be a son of Zeus, but even this must be taken on the authority of the exaggerated statement of Philostratus, and the truth is that originally he held no higher place in the estimation of the people than that of a sorcerer.

The historic trustworthiness of this narrative is not such as to confirm the opinion that this belief in the appearance of the Gods of the Homeric and Pre-Homeric age, was existing at the time we were speaking of. We are undoubtedly reminded by it of the old traditions of the appearance of the gods, especially of the tradition of Philemon and Baucis, but criticism, instead of taking such tradition as a confirmation of the historic truth of the facts here related, has to turn back and ask, whether the pretended fact itself is to be looked at as anything but an imitation of the ancient mythical occurrence. The apologetic parallelism between the two Apostles, gives here also the simple key to the explanation of the pretended fact, which fact is all the more incredible, that the miracle on whose reality it relies, is no less incredible. It is especially stated in the narrative in the Acts of the Apostles, with respect to the elder Apostles and to Peter, that they were honoured by the people with a true religious veneration as superhuman beings. The Apostles collectively are thus depicted, v. 11, &c.

---

* Ovid says, Metamorphoses, 8, 719, after he had described the transformation of the aged couple into two trees entwining together,

" Ostendit adhuc Tyaneïus illic
Incola de gemina vicinos arbore truncos."

The author of the Acts of the Apostles describes Peter in a very especial manner as being looked upon in the light of a lofty superhuman being, by a Gentile, when Cornelius at the entrance of Peter into his house fell with religious reverence at the Apostle's feet (πεσὼν ἐπὶ τοὺς πόδας προσεκύνησεν, x. 25,) and Peter taking him up said: ἀνάστηθι, κἀγὼ αὐτὸς ἄνθρωπός εἰμι. Just in the same sense the two Apostles say to the Gentiles at Lystra, who were worshipping them as gods, ἄνδρες, τὶ ταῦτα ποιεῖτε, καὶ ἡμεῖς ὁμοιοπαθεῖς ἐσμεν ὑμῖν ἄνθρωποι, (xiv. 15.) If the author of the Acts of the Apostles wished to make his Apostle Paul participate in this reverence and glorification, resulting from a deep impression of his superhuman dignity, what better opportunity could be afforded, than among the inhabitants of a country in which the traditions of the faith of bygone ages still subsisted, meaning that the gods appeared in the likeness of men, and until they were recognized and worshipped as gods by those who were awe-struck at the miracles wrought by them.*

But will the speeches and doctrinal discourses which the Apostle delivered during his first missionary journey give us a truer picture of his apostolic activity ? We might justly expect this to be the case. The more independently the Apostle entered on his path the more ought we to gather his very self from his works, the fresher he came to the work laid upon him, the more clearly he ought to display the Pauline spirit in his speeches. But with regard to this also we are deceived in our expectations. How little does the lengthy address with which

---

* That just the same two gods who are said to have appeared to Philemon and Baucis, viz., Hermes and Zeus, (Jupiter huc specie mortali cumque parente venit Atlantiades positis caducifer alis,)—Ov. Met. 8, 626, here enter on the scene—seems to indicate that the author was thinking of this very tradition, or at least of one very similar. The appearance of these gods was also at that time accompanied by miracles exciting astonishment, The author of the Acts of the Apostles shows here how he usually fills the part of a literary, descriptive, and learned writer, and knows how to utilize this peculiarity in his statement, as a connoisseur in mythology. Compare what he says, xix. 24, about the Ephesian Artemis, and, xvii, about the description of Athens.

the Apostle makes his first appearance in the synagogue at
Antioch, bear a Pauline character ?   How striking on the contrary is the dependent relation in which it stands to the speeches
delivered in the preceding part of the Acts of the Apostles.
The speech takes in its first part a purely historical character.
It begins with a narrative of the favours which God had shown
from the earliest times to the Israelites, in that he chose their
fathers, exalted their descendants in Egypt to be a peculiar
people, led them out of Egypt by His miraculous power,
accompanied them through the wilderness, and bestowed on
them the Land of Canaan as their own possession, and especially in that He had given them David, the man after His own
heart, for a King.   Such a review of the favours and guidance
of God, since the days of the patriarchs, is given in the speech
of Stephen, (vii.) only this speech starts from a different point
of view, and is carried on into further details which are here
abridged.   Both speeches take for their leading idea the time of
the patriarchs, the period in which the people were in Egypt
and that of King David. (Compare especially xiii. 17. τὸν λαὸν
ὕψωσεν with vii. 17. ηὔξησεν ὁ λαὸς καὶ ἐπληθύνθη ἐν Αἰγύπτῳ.)
The next chief division of the speech, v. 23-31, harmonizes most
with the two speeches of the Apostle Peter, v. 37-41. (John the
Baptist is not here in any way brought forward) and iii. 13-17.
Compare especially οἱ ἄρχοντες αὐτῶν τοῦτον ἀγνοήσαντες, &c.
&c. xiii. 27. and κατὰ ἄγνοιαν ἐπράξατε ὥσπερ καὶ οἱ ἄρχοντες
ὑμῶν, iii. 17.   Ὁ δὲ Θεὸς ἤγειρεν αὐτὸν ἐκ νεκρῶν. οἵτινες
εἰσι μαρτύρες αὐτοῦ πρὸς τὸν λαὸν, xiii. 30, and ὃν ὁ Θεὸς
ἤγειρεν ἐν νεκρῶν, οὗ ἡμεῖς μάρτυρες ἔσμεν, iii. 15. The succeeding
clause, v. 32-37, is in connection with Peter's speech, where the
same argument is drawn from the same passage of the Psalms
which is here also the principal passage.   For the conclusion
which follows : διὰ τούτου ὑμῖν ἄφεσις ἁμαρτιῶν καταγγέλλεται,
καὶ ἀπὸ παντῶν, ὧν οὐκ ἠδυνήθητε ἐν τῷ νόμῳ Μωσέως
δικαιωθῆναι, ἐν τούτῳ πᾶς ὁ πιστεύων δικαιοῦται, xiii. 38, 39 ;
there can be of course no parallel with the preceding, but

must not these concluding words give us the impression that
the author may himself have felt, after he had made the Apostle
Paul speak long enough in the manner of Peter that he ought
now to make him say something specially Pauline. If the
most general thought in the Pauline doctrine of justification
as it is represented in the epistles of the Apostle were to be
abstracted and set forth separately, it could not be done in a
more complete manner than this. But consequently, how
foreign is the relation in which this doctrine stands to the text
of the speech, how purposeless it is to introduce it here for
the first time at the end of the discourse! This part of the
speech seems to have made a like impression on Olshausen, for
he remarks on xiii. 37, "It is a striking thing in the Christian
consciousness of the later Church that the Apostle Paul here
lays all the stress on the resurrection, and not on the death of
the Lord, as does Peter also in the speeches in the first part of
the Acts. Yes: Paul here joins as it seems the ἄφεσις ἁμαρτιῶν
to the resurrection, as in his epistles he presents the death
of Christ as the source of the forgiveness of sins. In this
view the Apostle's manner of teaching may be thoroughly
understood, if we reflect that in the missionary speeches by
which men were to be convinced that Christ was the Messiah,
he could not develop more closely the contents of the Gospel,
but felt it of the most importance to lay the foundation of the
belief in the Messiahship of Jesus. But the death of Christ
was an occasion of offence and had therefore to be kept in the
back ground, on the other hand, the resurrection contained
a special strength of argument, and therefore it is made a predominant subject of the speech." If the striking feature of
this speech be explained by the occasion of offence which the
death of Jesus was to the Jews, we must remember that this
offence could never be avoided, that no speech of this kind
could have been delivered without speaking of the death of
Jesus, neither was the death of Jesus left in the back ground
(in this speech it is by no means so left, xiii. 27-29.) but on

the contrary, it is placed in such a relation to the Gospel doctrine of salvation, that it appears as an essential portion of it.
Two ways of treating the subject are open, either that the
death of Jesus should be so spoken of, as to add greater weight
to the resurrection, or so treated as to be considered the cause
of the forgiveness of sins of course still taking the resurrection for granted. The first manner is the tendency of the
speech of Peter, the other, the peculiar Pauline way of treatment. But if, in considering the peculiarities of this speech,
it is asserted that there is not so much said about the death as
about the resurrection, still nothing is explained, as we cannot
perceive why there is nothing said about the forgiveness of
sins through the death of Jesus, nor why the latter does not
serve as a ground for the belief in the Messiahship of Jesus,
the explanation seems to be evaded by saying that the speech
does not so much bear the stamp of Paul as that of Peter. It
does not, however, bear this stamp in the above extract from
Olshausen, but in the preceding one, and if the peculiar
Pauline idea of the insufficiency of the law for justification is
again enunciated, xiii. 38-39, it by no means follows as Olshausen thinks, that the authenticity of the speech is thus confirmed
in the strongest manner, for the way in which this is done
serves as we have already seen only to make it more doubtful.

It results from all this, that we cannot place ourselves on the
standpoint of the author, and only from that standpoint could
it be possible to give a recapitulation of the earlier speeches of
the Acts of the Apostles, as is here done; and to make the
Apostle Paul deliver a speech so thoroughly characteristic of
Peter that its Pauline conclusion seems to be purposely arranged in order to remind the reader, of what he might have
otherwise forgotten, namely, that it really was not Peter but
Paul who was speaking. The threat contained in the concluding words is evidently connected with what is afterwards
related with regard to the consequences of the speech, namely
that the Gospel was rejected in the most decided manner and

with the greatest hatred against the Apostle, by the Jews at Antioch, xiii. 45. That which really afterwards happened is foreseen by the speaker, little as such a change in affairs could be expected after xiii. 42. A speech which indicates so clearly the links by which its individual elements are joined can have no great claim to Pauline originality. What then remains certain to us concerning this first missionary journey of the Apostle, during which Christian churches in so many places were founded and organized? The history gives no further information about the churches in the places it names, and it will be shown in the sequel, how much uncertainty prevails as to which of the Apostles the Acts of the Apostles intends to set forth as having been the first to preach the Gospel to the Gentiles, after it had been rejected by the Jews, according to what had been predicted of them.

CHAPTER V.

WE now for the first time arrive at a point from which we
may gain some positive result, as we can take the historical
testimony of the Apostle himself, together with the statement
in the Acts of the Apostles, which latter is for the most part of
negative value in historical criticism. But this result can only
be attained by a criticism which works on different principles
from the usual ones.

The two first chapters of the Epistle to the Galatians form a
historical document of the greatest importance in our investigations into the true standpoint of the Apostle and his relations to the elder Apostles. But if these chapters are to be
of any value in the interest of the truth of the history, we
must first of all free ourselves from the common arbitrary suppositions which generally attend this enquiry, by which the
most complete harmony is established between the author of
the Acts of the Apostles and the Apostle Paul, and one narrative is used as a confirmation of the other. It is self-evident
that as the Apostle appears as an eye-witness and individual
actor in his own affairs, his statement alone ought to be held as
authentic. Then again an unfavourable light is thus shed on
the Acts of the Apostles, the statements in which can only be
looked at as intentional deviations from historical truth in the
interest of the special tendency which they possess. But if we
entirely ignore the fact that such a position of the Acts of the
Apostles with regard to history cannot be surprising considering the results of the foregoing enquiry, we then have to deal
simply with the discrepancies that really lie before us. All

attempts at the reconciliation of the two accounts as they are generally presented by interpreters and critics are but useless trouble, and they not only result in a heterogeneous mixture of the meaning of the Apostle's words, but also in the conceal- ment of the truth of the historical facts, or at least in placing them in a false light, and in ascribing to the character of the Apostle what can only redound to his disadvantage.

In order to make as much use as possible in the interest of historical truth of so authentic an account as that which the Apostle himself gives to the elder Apostles of the course of his Christian development, and his whole apostolic position, we must not overlook what he testifies as to the events most closely depending on his conversion. Here we meet at once with discrepancies between this account and that of the Acts of the Apostles, which show very seriously the want of historical truth in the latter. According to Acts ix. 22, the Apostle re- mained for some time in Damascus after he had been baptized by Ananias and received into the Christian community, and during this time was zealously occupied in accordance with his newly-gained convictions in seeking to persuade the Jews in Damascus of the truth that Jesus was the Messiah. But as he was waylaid by the Jews and his life endangered, his leaving the city of Damascus became necessary, and he went to Jerusalem, ix. 26. Now in the Epistle to the Galatians, i. 16, the Apostle himself says that immediately after his conversion he went not to Damascus but into Arabia, and from there again back to Damascus, and then three years afterwards travelled to Jeru- salem. The cause of his leaving Damascus was undoubtedly the danger with which he was threatened by the Ethnarch of King Aretas in Damascus, and although this cause is not spoken of in the Epistle to the Galatians, it is mentioned by the Apostle himself (2 Corinthians, xi. 32), and it cannot be placed in any other period than is there assigned to it. In this part of the circumstance indeed the two accounts agree; in the rest the difference is great enough: not only does the Acts of the

Apostles pass over in complete silence the journey of the
Apostle into Arabia, but speaks of his sojourn in Damascus as
merely of some days' duration, whilst the Apostle himself says
that years elapsed between his conversion and his journey to
Jerusalem. Even if we put a wide construction on ἡμέρας ἱκανὰς,
ix. 23, and justly place the journey to Arabia in this time, as is
done in Galatians, i. 17, we do not get the length of the sojourn
in Arabia. We must then certainly confess that the expression
ἡμέραι ἱκαναὶ has no fitting reference to a time extending over
full three years. But if we are inclined to set aside the expression, this would be only possible in the case of the connexion of
this passage, making it probable that ἡμέραι ἱκαναὶ really is to
be understood as a space of time comprising several years. This
is not the case : indeed, the facts are exactly contrary ; what is
said (ix. 26), about the return of the Apostle to Jerusalem,
that he παραγενόμενος εἰς Ἱερουσαλὴμ ἐπειρᾶτο κολλᾶσθαι τοῖς
μαθηταῖς καὶ πάντες ἐφοβοῦντο αὐτὸν, μὴ πιστεύοντες, ὅτι ἐστὶ
μαθητής, places us manifestly in a time which could not have
been very distant from the conversion of the Apostle, still
preserving the fresh impression of so unexpected an occurrence
and one so incredible, and which is therefore described by
the author of the Acts of the Apostles as having been reckoned
not by years but by days. The Apostle endeavoured when he
came to Jerusalem to ally himself with the disciples as one who
belonged to them and was as one of them (we may compare on
this idea, κολλᾶσθαι, v. 13) ; but they all timidly avoided him,
they would not come near their old enemy and persecutor, because they did not believe that he was a disciple. How could
this have been possible, if at that time a period of more than
three years had elapsed since the conversion of the Apostle ?
and if, during that time, he had not merely laboured in the cause
of the Gospel in distant Arabia, where his sojourn perhaps did
not last long ; but in Damascus, which was not far distant from
Jerusalem ? Could he not have arranged that a more accurate
knowledge should have been imparted of that remarkable oc-

currence, especially as the aim of the Apostle's journey to
Damascus corroborates the supposition of intercourse between
the two cities, and this same aim must also be taken as the
subject of the Apostle's labours at this time Acts ix. 20.
Besides, had not many real proofs been for a long time given
of the change that had taken place in him ?

In both the speeches in which the author of the Acts of the
Apostles makes the Apostle himself tell the story of his conversion, his journey to Jerusalem is mentioned in direct connexion with it, and without any indication of a long interval
having elapsed between the two occurrences (xxii. 16, 17,
xxvi. 20). It is true that in both these passages the narrative
is so condensed that the second really proves nothing, but
simply serves to confirm the first. But between these and the
narrative in the Epistle to the Galatians there is a contradiction
which cannot be got over, and which shows how completely
untenable is the supposition that the author was placed in a
position which allows him to be quoted as an authority. But
as this conspicuous discrepancy is not only most important in
itself, but enhances deeply and fatally the difference between
the two narratives, how futile it is to contend about minor
points. The Apostle, in the Epistle to the Galatians, asserts in
the most decided and solemn manner that he had not received
his Gospel from man, but immediately through the fact that
God had revealed His Son in him. Immediately after he had
received from God the charge to declare the Gospel to the
Gentiles, he " conferred not with flesh and blood," neither with
men in general, nor especially with the Apostles who were connected with him by common national ties (expressed also by
σὰρξ καὶ ʼαῖμα), neither did he go to Jerusalem to the elder
Apostles, but into Arabia, and from thence to Damascus, and
then at the expiration of three years first went to Jerusalem.

It is clear that here the Apostle does all in his power (ἃ δὲ
γράφω ὑμῖν, ἰδοὺ ἐνώπιον τοῦ θεοῦ ὅτι οὐ ψεύδομαι, i. 20), to
meet the assertion that now for the first time since his conver-

sion he was in such a relation to the elder Apostles that his apostolic mission could be looked upon as an emanation from their apostolic authority. He wishes to enter on his apostolic mission under the influence of a revelation vouchsafed to him alone, in a perfectly free and independent manner, unbiassed by any human interposition. In this view it certainly appears most probable that he spent the first period after his conversion in Arabia and Damascus, not in Jerusalem nor in any place where he could enter into any nearer relations with the elder Apostles. Even when he returned to Jerusalem at the expiration of three years, after a time had elapsed in which he must have decided on what his apostolic character should be, his aim seems in no way to have been to get his call authorized by the elder Apostles, but only to make the acquaintance of Peter, who during their fifteen days intercourse sufficiently showed that he had nothing to allege against Paul's apostolic call. If the Apostle had been in companionship with the rest of the assembled Apostles, or even with some of them, this intercourse would have appeared in his being legitimately received by them as an Apostle. For this reason he lays peculiar stress on the circumstance that during that time he saw no Apostle but Peter, for Peter could not have authorized him to assume the apostolic office without the express consent of the rest of the Apostles, although by his own behaviour towards Paul he gave the most valuable testimony to his entire acquiescence in the apostolic mission of the latter. Every idea of the authorization of the apostolic office of Paul by the other Apostles during the period immediately succeeding, is done away with by the fact that Paul was in Syria and Cilicia, and did not come into contact with the Church in Judea. The chief point towards which these remarks tend, is undoubtedly that which is expressed by the Apostle in a tone of the deepest and most assured confidence, namely, that during the whole period treated of in chap. i. nothing took place between him and the other Apostles which could be taken as a sign of subordination or dependence

on his part. He would not be disposed to give up any of his
independence, because the more dependent on the rest of the
Apostles he appeared the more the independence of his call
might be called in question. But if we take into consideration
·that the opponents of the Apostle, as we see in his Epistles,
made use of the authority of the other Apostles to his disadvantage in the churches, and placed his doctrine in opposition
to that of the other Apostles, what necessity was there for his so
insisting on the independence of his position ? If he had ever
acknowledged the relation of dependence on the rest of the
Apostles ; if he had not emphatically persisted in declaring that
not only by their permission, but because he was as much an
Apostle as they were, he had thrown off their authority with
regard to any difference in doctrine existing between himself
and them, he would have failed in establishing and maintaining
a principle which it was his office to uphold against the other
Apostles as the most essential one of Christianity. The whole
significance of his apostolic labours depended on the fact that
he was a specially called Apostle, and independent of all the
other Apostles. In this way only could he, with regard to the
mode of his adoption into Christianity, claim the right which
each of the other Apostles asserted he possessed ; and it is perfectly clear of what great moment this was to Paul, of what
great importance it must have been for his interest to insist on
his well-grounded right with every sign of determination, by the
simple statement of the actual historical truth. But how does
the statement in the Acts of the Apostles agree with this ?
What does the author say, when we compare his account with
the direct assertion of the Apostle himself? Exactly the opposite of what the Apostle has asserted in the most decided and
most solemn manner. In Acts ix. 27, the Apostle is represented as actually having passed some time with the Apostles
assembled in Jerusalem, and this soon after his conversion.
Should we wish to pass over this discrepancy on which we
have before remarked, and assume that Acts ix. 27, speaks of

the same residence of the Apostle in Jerusalem, which he him-self mentions, Gal. i. 17, it is very clear that the impression, which the Apostle was most careful in endeavouring to guard against, namely that of any appearance of his having received an authorization of his apostolic office from the rest of the Apostles, here obtains the highest confirmation. We cannot avoid seeing this, if (as is stated, ix. 27) he really were intro-duced by Barnabas into the circle of the Apostles (for so must these words be taken in any case, ἤγαγε πρὸς τοὺς ἀποστόλους, even if one or other of the Apostles may have been absent) and then laid before them an account of the occurrences on the road to Damascus for their decision and recognition. If this account be held as authentic it would really make the Apostle a liar, and it is simply incredible that he should have given the assurance ἃ δὲ γράφω ὑμῖν, ἰδοὺ ἐνώπιον τοῦ θεοῦ ὅτι οὐ ψεύδομαι. On the other hand his statement cannot but appear strange beside that of the author of the Acts of the Apostles, as the difference between him and the Apostle seems greater the more closely we consider it. What a striking contradiction lies in this, that the Acts of the Apostles represents the Gospel as being preached by the Apos-tle at that time in Jerusalem, as well as in Judea, whilst he himself, Galatians i. 22, says he was not personally known to the Christian churches in Judea, that they had only heard that their former persecutor was now preaching the faith which he formerly sought to destroy, and praised God on that account.

How does this agree with the παῤῥησιάζεσθαι ἐν τῷ ὀνόματι τοῦ κυρίου Ἰησοῦ (ἐν Ἰερουσαλὴμ) and with the assertion put into the mouth of the Apostle himself, xxvi. 20 : τοῖς ἐν Δαμασκῷ πρῶτον καὶ Ἰεροσολύμοις εἰς πᾶσάν τε τὴν χώραν τῆς Ἰουδαίας καὶ τοῖς ἔθνεσιν ἀπαγγέλλων μετανοεῖν. At what period then can this have taken place, if not during that in which, according to the Apostle's own assurance it did not occur ? for he never went afterwards with such an object to Jerusalem. If he had for a long while laboured with all boldness in proclaiming the Gospel in Jerusalem he could not have been so unknown in the churches of Judea. The Acts of the Apostles gives a character of publicity to the residence of the Apostle in Jerusalem at that time, to which it could never pretend according to the description given of it by the Apostle himself. How can we think that in the short space of time in which he was occupied by his self-imposed errand, that of conferring with the Apostle Peter, he could have acted in such a manner as is described in the Acts of the Apostles. In connection with the whole of this anomalous statement, the Acts of the Apostles gives another cause for his departure from Jerusalem. In his zeal for the Gospel he came into collision with the Hellenists, and, because they sought to put him to death, the brethren brought him for safety to Cæsarea. Not mere Jews, but Hellenists are here named, apparently under the supposition that they must have been in antagonism with him as a converted Hellenist, because this had been already the case with Stephen, Acts vi. 8, and because afterwards the Hellenists showed themselves especially hostile to Paul. The Apostle himself says nothing at all of this. We see at once that in his journey to Jerusalem he did not intend to remain long there, and to open there for himself a field of labour for the preaching of the Gospel. As he was destined from the beginning to be an Apostle to the Gentiles, he wished to enter on his appointed field of labour in Syria and Cilicia; but he took Jerusalem on his way thither, in order, as was very natural, to inaugurate his relations with the elder Apostles, now that so much was developed in him, and he was decided as to the standpoint he should maintain.

Fourteen years after, it may have been after that journey which is spoken of Galatians i. 18, after his conversion, or at any rate after a greater number of years had elapsed, the Apostle again went to Jerusalem. If we had not the Acts of the Apostles to refer to, which describes the apostolic activity which had been in operation during this time, we should be obliged to assume that he had fulfilled the purpose with which he had left Jerusalem and gone into Gentile countries. The

Apostle was now labouring as an apostle to the Gentiles; he had converted many Gentiles and founded many Christian churches; but the greater the strides were which the Gospel made among the Gentiles, the greater was the importance which the Gentile Christians assumed over the Jewish Christians, and the more doubtful men were in Jerusalem, as to whether the Gentiles could directly participate in the Messianic salvation without the intervention of Judaism. That question which had made but little apparent difference on the occasion of the Apostle's first journey to Jerusalem, because the matter to which it referred then lay in the far distance, now was of the greatest practical importance. This question was whether such a Gentile Christianity as the Pauline Christianity had now become, ought to be recognized and tolerated from a Jewish standpoint. It could not be denied that in Jerusalem and Judea a very important part, if not indeed the whole of the Jewish Christians, was against this recognition. According to Acts xv. 1, as soon as the zeal of the Apostle began to bring forth greatly increasing fruits in Gentile countries, steps began to be taken in Jerusalem in order to put hindrances in his way. Therefore from the very nature of the case, it might be expected that the Apostle after a long interval, should resolve on a fresh journey to Jerusalem in the interest of his apostolic office among the Gentiles. That this resolution to go to Jerusalem was inspired by an ἀπο- κάλυψις, a special divine command summoning him thither (Galatians ii. 2), does not in any way set aside the cause above assigned to the journey, but rather shows all the more certainly that this matter was then occupying his mind in a very vivid and important manner, and the reason of this must be sought in the posture of affairs at that time. He accordingly resolved to journey to Jerusalem and to take counsel with the members of the Church there, and with all the Apostles who might be in the city, upon the principles which he followed in the promulgation of the Gospel, and in virtue of which he considered himself the Apostle of the Gentiles. He also resolved to lay his Gospel before them in order to see how it stood with regard to them, and that by a public statement of his views and principles it might be put to the proof whether or not he could maintain them, although he himself was not in the slightest degree doubtful or uncertain on the point. Therefore he made a fresh journey to Jerusalem, but how this journey (Galatians ii. 1), stands related to the journeys to Jerusalem narrated in the Acts of the Apostles has been endlessly treated of in modern times, as if it were an absolute impossibility to come to a certain result on the subject. The Acts of the Apostles makes the Apostle, after the journey, ix. 26 (which must apparently at least be assumed to be the journey in Galatians i. 18,) travel twice from Antioch to Jerusalem in company with Barnabas, xi. 30, xv. 2. As the Apostle, Gal. ii. 1, seems to speak of a second journey after the first, i. 18, (although $\pi \acute{a} \lambda \iota \nu$ is not so strong as $\delta \epsilon \acute{\nu} \tau \epsilon \rho o \nu$), so also does it seem that we may assume it to be the journey in Acts vi. 30. But in Acts xi. 30, not the slightest hint is given of such an aim of the journey, whilst that spoken of in xv. 2, at least touches in a general manner on the matter in question. If we should be inclined to take the journey in Acts xv. 2, as being referred to in Gal. ii. 1, rather than the journey in xi. 30, on the other hand the possibility of going beyond Acts xi. 30, becomes cut off by the following argument : the Apostle could not certainly have given up his object between the journeys spoken of in Acts xi. and xv. His object required that no communication with the Apostles should be mentioned as occurring between Gal. i. 18, and ii. 1 ; else the proof of his teachings being independent of the tuition of the rest of the Apostles would be wanting ; he would have been concealing something which would have worked disadvantageously in the cause of the independence he was asserting, and he would not have given a faithful account of the circumstances of his life as far as they regarded this independence. If the object of the Apostle (Gal.

i. and ii.) was confined to a mere intention of showing that he had learnt his doctrine from no man, not even from the Apostles, we might justly rejoin that it therefore much more depended on the Apostle to assert the independence and freedom of his apostolic authority by spoken arguments. For this reason it could not have been his intention to give a complete narrative of his journeys to Jerusalem; he only wished to render those events conspicuous which would be of the most value as decided proofs of the independence of his apostolic authority. The first period of his apostolic labours was the only one that could have been affected by the assurance that he stood towards the elder Apostles in no such relation as would have any influence on his doctrine. If he had once taught and worked as an Apostle, independently of the other Apostles, it would not have mattered whether he had been with them in Jerusalem or not, he might have received his doctrine even directly from them, but the way and manner in which the rest of the Apostles acknowledged his principles would be of the greatest importance. It seems then clear that he does not call attention to his journey to Jerusalem (Gal. ii. 1), as following another journey before spoken of, but only on account of the particular transactions which took place in consequence of it. But there still remains something behind all this which is not so easily disposed of. If we fairly consider the words we must conclude (especially if we think of the meaning of the preposition διὰ used in Gal. ii. 1), the most probable view to be, that the Apostle never went at all to Jerusalem during that interval. In Galatians i. 19, he makes a certain exception which he would not have been able to do if in the interval he had been to Jerusalem. The question then presents itself, whether it is of any special consequence to bring the journeys of which the Apostle here speaks so entirely into harmony with those mentioned in the Acts of the Apostles? What specially would be gained by taking as identical the journey, Gal. ii. 1, and that in Acts xi. 30, or xv. 2? If we take it as identical with xi. 30, we then indeed have this advantage, that the journey, Gal. ii. 1, follows chronologically on the first, i. 18, just as the journey, Acts xi. 30, follows the first, ix. 26 ; but this is all, and it does not in any way result from this external resemblance that the journey, Acts xi. 30, is really and truly identical with that in Gal. ii. 1. Not only is there no further point of resemblance in regard to the cause and object of the journey, to which a completely different aim is assigned in Acts xi. 30 ; but the question may be raised whether the journey, Acts xi. 30, is not an erroneous statement, a mere fiction, which is not so very unlikely a supposition in such a narrative as the Acts of the Apostles. If we suppose that the Apostle (Gal. ii. 1), only mentioned his second journey, we do not really know whether that is the one, Acts xi. 30. But granting this, we find that in regard to Acts xi. 30, everything is so uncertain and undefined, that the identity with this journey fails, and is more likely to exist with that in Acts xv. 2. But if we grant this, thinking it more probable from the external chronological facts, and the internal relations of the affair, what do we then gain ? It is clear that the same reason which militates against the identity of Gal. ii. 1 and Acts xi. 30, may also be alleged against that of Gal. ii. 1 and Acts xv. 2, for it may justly be argued in defence of the identity of Gal. ii. 1 and Acts xi. 30, that the whole circumstances of the affair in Gal. ii. 1 are not so completely in harmony with the transactions in Acts xv. 2, that we are really justified in upholding the identity of the two journeys. And if the advantage of maintaining the authenticity of these two journeys can only be maintained by giving up Acts xi. 30, of what use is the supposition that what the Apostle says (Gal. ii. 1), regarding his journey to Jerusalem should exactly coincide with the account in Acts xv. 2, &c. ?

Reasoning from what we have hitherto observed, we have every cause to be distrustful of a statement like that of the Acts of the Apostles, which agrees so little with the Apostle's own account, and the only result possible for us, is to ignore the idea of an identity which does not exist, and—without any further regard to whether the discrepancies are greater or lesser—entirely to separate the two statements. Only if we endeavour from this point of view to get at the true historical facts by a comparison of the two statements, the following important items of difference show that no doubt can exist as to which side we ought to take.

We find, according to the Acts of the Apostles, an account of a formal public meeting of such a description that the consultations and resolutions resulting from it have from the earliest times caused it to be taken, not without reason, as forming the first Christian Council; not only were the Apostles and Elders of the Church at Jerusalem gathered together at it, xv. 6, but the members of the Church generally took part in the meeting, xv. 12, 22. There was a dispute about the question before the assembly; speakers rose, who introduced and explained the different points of view, the whole was under the guidance of the Elders of the Church at Jerusalem, who as we may well suppose did not in this capacity forego their precedence in the assembly, and who gave the last and finishing stroke to the discussion by passing a formal resolution, the contents of which, together with some points more intimately concerning themselves, were sent in a letter from their own hands, as a command from the Holy Spirit, by especially chosen men to the Churches in Antioch, Syria and Cilicia. Of all this the Apostle knows nothing at all : he only says, as if he wished to contradict such a statement of the affair, ἀνεθέμην αὐτοῖς τὸ εὐαγγέλιον, ὃ κηρύσσω ἐν τοῖς ἔθνεσι, κατ᾽ ἰδίαν δὲ τοῖς δοκοῦσι. Neander has not left quite unnoticed an important circumstance on this affair which is often overlooked. He remarks, "As Paul in the Epistle to the Galatians speaks only of his private transactions (κατ᾽ ἰδίαν) with the three chiefest Apostles, this would at first sight seem to contradict completely the narrative in the Acts of the Apostles ; and this contradiction would seem to indicate that the same facts are not spoken of in both the narratives." Neander indeed is also of opinion that "if we assume that before there was any public council in Jerusalem, there may have been many private consultations, we may aid in establishing a perfect harmony between the two accounts; as it is self-evident that before the affair was spoken of in a large assembly, Paul had come to an understanding with the Apostles with regard to the principles established by it." Still we should of course have expected that there would have been some mention in the Epistle to the Galatians of such a large assembly. But nothing is said of it, and this is only a new proof of the arbitrary and uncritical nature of such an attempt to harmonize the two accounts. How can we suppose that the Apostle would speak of minor circumstances, and leave quite without mention the chief matter, the special transaction which alone could decide the whole affair. It is quite impossible to take up this position. If we understand the words, ἀνεθέμην αὐτοῖς τὸ εὐαγγέλιον, as referring to the chief transaction, it would be a thoroughly vague and inappropriate reference, in which it would be impossible to find what, according to the Acts of the Apostles we ought to find, and the chief difficulty would still remain, that in this manner the principal occurrences by which the Apostles must have been influenced, are removed to an earlier date, and these private transactions become at once the most important. But looking at the matter in the right light we can not find any such meaning in these words. They do not describe any especial transaction, but they are only a vague expression followed immediately by the more decided κατ᾽ ἰδίαν δὲ τοῖς δοκοῦσι. We must take the passage to mean as follows: "I travelled to Jerusalem in order to present my Gospel to the members of the churches there, and truly I specially applied myself not (as Neander says) to introduce the matter by means of private transactions, but to set it at once in its true light, and to present it to those most worthy of preference in the most exact and direct manner." For this very reason the Apostles are here

throughout called οἱ δοκοῦστες, because they were of the highest
authority in the eyes of the Church at Jerusalem, (the Apostle
gives us purposely to understand that they took this high position only in a subjective, not in an objective manner, so that he
was at full liberty to reject their authority) and must therefore
be considered here as chief personages, whose attention to any
matter rendered further interference superfluous.   In the whole
passage there is no question of any other transactions than with
the δοκοῦντες, *i. e.* with James the president of the Church at
Jerusalem, and the two Apostles, Peter and John.   De Wette,
who assumes that Galatians ii. 2, contains two different communications, can show no ground for his supposition.   Had
there been two different assemblies, we might say that the Acts
of the Apostles is silent on the secret conference, in accordance
with the peculiar characteristics of its manner of narration,
which would make it wish to deal with the affair as a public
one.   But as the Apostle himself, if the public assembly had
really taken place as the Acts of the Apostles relates, would
not have been silent on it as an important event, it follows from
his silence that the Acts of the Apostles first gave a publicity to
the affair which it never would have received from the authentic
report of the Apostle.   It is only in the narrative in the Acts
of the Apostles, and in the interest to which it is devoted, that
these transactions take the character of a Synod which reminds
us of a form of later times.

But the most important point is, that the Acts of the Apostles represents the elder Apostles as agreeing with the Apostle
Paul with regard to his views and principles in such a manner
as never could have taken place according to the Epistle to the
Galatians. We learn from the Acts of the Apostles, that it was
specially some members of the Church of Jerusalem, who had
been converted to the Christian faith from the sect of the
Pharisees, who were not willing to receive Gentiles into the
Christian community, except under the condition of their submitting to the Mosaic circumcision, xv. 5.   But the Apostles

themselves were very far from sharing in this view, and supported the proposal made by the Apostle Paul in the most obliging and appreciative manner. The Apostle Peter referred to the conversion of Cornelius, and declared that it was tempting God to lay a yoke on the necks of the disciples, (not only on those of the Gentiles, but of the Christians generally,) which neither they nor their fathers were able to bear, because they believed that the grace of Christ was sufficient for salvation. This then is the conviction expressed, that the Mosaic law was no longer binding on Christians, whether Jew or Gentile. The author of the Acts of the Apostles seems purposely to represent the views of the Apostle Peter as the freest and most advanced in order to make those of James, the chief leader in these transactions, more clear to those who saw the matter in a more modified form. For James immediately agrees with the opinion of the Apostle Peter in all essential points, and with this aim recals the utterances of the Prophets, according to which the entrance of the Gentiles into the service of the true God depended on the building again of the fallen theocracy of David, he consequently withdrew his proposal, as far as regarded the Gentiles who might be converted, and recommended that the observance of the Mosaic law should be the only obligatory yoke laid upon them. For the rest, the Law is considered in the true Pauline spirit as a yoke, (comp. Gal. v. 1,) and, if in reference to the Gentiles, it were once recognized as too great a burden, no further step would be necessary to make it appear in itself an unbearable yoke. From this point of view it is considered by the Apostle Peter.*

---

* We may take as genuine or not, according as we look at the argument in favour of the prophetic passage from which they are extracted, the last words $\dot{\epsilon}\sigma\tau\iota$—$\alpha\dot{\upsilon}\tau o\tilde{\upsilon}$ in the quotation, xv. 10, $\gamma\nu\omega\sigma\tau\acute{\alpha}\ \dot{\alpha}\pi'\ \dot{\alpha}\iota\tilde{\omega}\nu o\varsigma\ \dot{\epsilon}\sigma\tau\iota\ \tau\tilde{\omega}\ \theta\epsilon\tilde{\omega}\ \pi\acute{\alpha}\nu\tau\alpha\ \tau\grave{\alpha}\ \ddot{\epsilon}\rho\gamma\alpha\ \alpha\dot{\upsilon}\tau o\tilde{\upsilon}$. In any case these words contain a clear explanation. James affirms what Amos prophesied, namely, that the worship of the true God, which is to be one day universal among mankind, can never really be general unless the Gentiles are freed under the Mosaic law. As the divine prophecy is infallible, so it must be the will of God that the Gentile should be free under the law. About the sense of these words there cannot well be any doubt, but we are not quite so sure about the meaning

If we compare with this statement the narrative which the Apostle himself gives of the whole bearing of the case, everything appears altered. The question was by no means first agitated by mere individual, pharisaic-minded members of the Church at Jerusalem, we here see a conflict between the Pauline and Jewish Christianity. The elder Apostles stood so little in connection with this conflict that they are rather placed on a standpoint from which they had never before looked on Judaism. There is nothing clearer than that there was no question of anything but circumcision, with regard to which the Jewish-Christian party maintained that the Gentiles could not take part in the Messianic salvation, except on the condition that they would submit to circumcision. But circumcision included all Judaism in itself—it was the hardest condition which could be laid on the Gentiles; by it they would be forced to abjure their heathenism and become Jews, and lay themselves under an obligation to observe all Jewish rites. The

of 21. Neander takes the passage as do many interpreters with Schneckenburger, " Über den Zweck der Apostgesch." p. 23. As far as regarded the Jewish believers, as Jews, no special precept was needed ; of these there was now no question ; they knew what as Jews they ought to observe, for in every city where Jews dwelt, the Mosaic law was read every Sabbath in the synagogue. " These words," remarks Neander, " cannot possibly be understood as being intended to apply to the laws given to the Gentiles. In this assembly there needed no motive to lay so much on the Gentile Christians, much less to impose any more on them, and these words supply in no way whatever any further motive." These motives do not lie so far from the sense of the words as Neander thinks: if we take them in this way, Moses, *i.e.* the Mosaic law has already been long preached in the cities—has been read in the synagogue every Sabbath, but nevertheless there are very few who trouble themselves about accepting the law. But now, as the worship of the true God without the fetters of any law is preached, many turn to him, and it is incontestable that the ceremonial law is the only hindrance to the universal spread of the true religion. This explanation is given by Giesler. But it is doubtless the most simple plan to understand 21 as supplying a motive for sending a letter to the Gentile Christians, and requiring such an ἀπεχέσθαι from them. For such a claim James says so ancient a worship as the Mosaic is specially fitted. The more generally and regularly the Mosaic law became known, the more clearly would its incontestable authority be manifested.

question was also whether the Gentiles could become Christians directly as Gentiles, or only through the mediation of Judaism by first becoming Jews. The Apostle, in order to show the energy with which he opposed this question, says that " even Titus had not been compelled to submit to circumcision," *i.e.* that he was not really obliged to be circumcised, but that this compulsion was sought to be put upon him when the Apostle took him to Jerusalem, and that this compulsion was met and combated with all earnestness. This is easily seen by the whole context, and we cannot say with De Wette (inasmuch as it would assume that the Apostle had so desired it) that this would amount to contradicting the apologetic aim of this account : and the spirit of the transactions and resolutions (Acts xv, Gal. ii.) is clearly not to be explained by Acts xv.; and as far as regards the apologetic aim of the account, we see by the great earnestness with which the Apostle here defends the cause of his Gospel, that he had not to do merely with the παρείσακτοι ψευδάδελφοι but with the Apostles themselves. Why did he wish to go to Jerusalem himself? why did he so especially wish to treat of the matter with the Apostles, if he had not had good grounds for supposing that the Apostles in Jerusalem were by no means strange to the impression created by the παρείσακτοι ψευδάδελφοι ? The course of the transactions shows how the Apostles behaved with regard to the principles of these false brethren. They are the opponents against whose principles the Apostle contends. That in regard to the circumcision of Titus having been enforced, the Apostle does not once speak with certainty, but assumes that it may really have been sought to impose such a compulsion on him, and the reason for this can only have been that he, an uncircumcised Gentile, was the companion of the Apostle himself. It must have seemed at first to the Apostle, and to him who was the immediate object of the demand, and who was placed in the midst of those who advocated circumcision, that any resistance against such influence could scarcely be carried out. But just for this reason the Apostle seems to have taken Titus with him to Jerusalem, that he might take up the affair at its strongest point, and give an immediately practical direction to the strife of principles, or else that he might impart to the Gentile Titus some portion of his own zealous opposition to the Jewish-Christians. There is no trace in the Epistle to the Galatians of any compliance on the part of the Apostle with what, according to the Acts of the Apostles, was achieved with the most willing agreement of the elder Apostles; but, according to the assurances of the Apostle himself, was the result of the most powerful opposition, the most energetic repulsion of the most decided pressure. Not for a moment even, says the Apostle, did I give place to them by the subjection required of me, in order that the truth of the Gospel, the principles of true Christianity freed from Judaism, might be upheld and carried on in the churches founded by me.* The Apostles themselves have

---

* Nothing can be more absurd than the explanation given, not merely by a Tertullian, c. Marc. 5, 3, but even by interpreters of the most modern times, of the passage Galatians ii. 1; according to which περιετμήθη must be added to διὰ δὲ—ψευδαδέλφους—and Titus therefore must have been circumcised, if not by compulsion, still out of tender regard to the false brethren. If Titus were circumcised for the sake of the false brethren, how can the Apostle say without the greatest contradiction that he "did not give place by subjection, no, not for an hour." The affairs of the Gentile-Christians could not be divided from those of the Jewish-Christians—it would have surrendered its principles by the circumcision of Titus. That it would have been directly against its principles is testified by the emphatic οὐδὲ, ii. 5. How can such passages as these be misunderstood? and how can the historical enquiry into Primitive Christianity be founded on such misapprehension? Highly inconvenient truly is the interrupted mode of speech employed by the Apostle, verse 4; but as far as we can gather the sense, it is this:—the matter about circumcision would have been a cause of dispute with the false brethren if I had not felt myself obliged to take this decisive step towards the maintenance of my Gospel principles. The παρείσακτοι ψευδάδελφοι are those τίνες κατελθόντες ἀπὸ τῆς Ἰουδαιὸς, of whom the Acts speaks, xvi. They were thus called by the Apostle because they came to Antioch as members of the Church at Jerusalem, Gal. ii. 4, in order that they might be able to investigate on the spot the report which had reached Jerusalem, that in Antioch the Mosaic law was completely shaken off—and then that they might immediately bring to bear their own stringent Jewish principles. The Apostle is evidently aware of the persevering nature of these people, as he designates them as παριεσάκτοι ψευδαδ. and παρεισῆλθον,

not wrought any change in my views and principles, at least
they have only influenced me as the δοκοῦντες εἶναί τι, as such
they appeared to me worthy of all submission. "Therefore,"
says the Apostle, with a truly rational consciousness of his
evangelical freedom, "whatever a man's outward position or
personal authority may be, even if he were an Apostle and
chief of the Church at Jerusalem, it maketh no matter to me!
A merely outward condition of this kind can be of no importance to me. God looketh not at the outward and personal.
Only from this it may chance that the reason may be shown
of the charge against me, yet even in this view I cannot see
that I am obliged to abjure the principles on which I have
hitherto acted. For they have brought nothing against me
concerning which I have given them any right, or which I can
appropriate as an ameliorating addition to my views. So little
is this the case, that they were obliged on the contrary to
acknowledge how well grounded and well arranged my views
and modes of action were. Instead therefore of the Jewish-
Christian party thinking that my Gospel of Gentile Christian-

because they came as Jewish Christians into a Gentile Christian Church like
that of Antioch, in order to introduce into that Church certain principles, which
until then were unknown in it, and which seemed to be in opposition to Gospel
truth. The whole point of view would be altered if, as is generally done by
interpreters, we take the Apostle as having considered these παρεἰς. ψευδάδ.—
as enemies of Christian freedom, not merely in reference to the Church at
Antioch, but to the Christian Church generally. The Christian freedom which
they opposed only existed in Antioch ; nothing was known' of it in Jerusalem,
where, on the contrary, the Mosaic law was enforced with peculiar severity on
the Christians. Therefore it is not to be overlooked that these were interfering
and false brethren only in their relation to the Church at Antioch, but not
to that at Jerusalem, to this latter they belonged, and in it their zeal for the law
would only be reckoned as honourable to them. Here first in the history a decided
contest presents itself between Jewish and Gentile Christianity: what was looked
upon in Antioch as a servitude in direct opposition to the idea of Christian freedom,
was considered in Jerusalem as true and genuine Christianity. We also see
undoubtedly that this question was first touched upon in Jerusalem at this time.
Therefore it is an unnecessary remark of De Wette's, that " the Jewish-Christians
who came to Antioch went later on to Jerusalem itself."—Whence could they have
come to Antioch if not from Jerusalem ? and where else could the principles which
they maintained have been the ruling ones but at Jerusalem ?

ity, as opposed to Jewish Christianity, appeared ungrounded
and untenable, its independence was fully acknowledged." But
this acknowledgment by no means appeared in the beginning:
the Apostle obtained it by means of argument : the chief results
of which he shortly points out, Gal. ii. 7, &c. His enemies
must be convinced that the Gospel of uncircumcision was con-
fided to him, as that of circumcision had been to Peter, or in
other words that there existed not only a Jewish Christianity
but also a Gentile Christianity independent of Judaism.
They must also acknowledge that the Gentiles might have a
direct share in the Messianic salvation, without first becoming
Jews. In the complete self-consciousness of his standpoint, the
Apostle places himself in opposition to Peter, so that we have
before us man against man, teacher against teacher, one
Gospel against another, one apostolic office against another,
and the argument on which the Apostle relies is the decided
matter of fact success to which he is enabled to refer. The
Apostle says, (ii. 8, in the words ὁ γὰρ ἐνεργήσας Πέτρῳ εἰς
ἀποστολὴν τῆς περιτομῆς ἐνήργησε καὶ ἐμοὶ εἰς τὰ ἔθνη), that as
an Apostle he could not have accomplished so great a success
among the Gentiles, if God to whom this success must be
referred, had not willed to establish it as a fact that there
might truly be an εὐαγγέλιον τῆς ἀκροβυστίας. The reality of
the animating principle may be generally concluded from the
reality of the consequences. This is the meaning of the
Apostle's words : " I am in fact the Apostle of the Gentiles, and
as the Gentiles would never have been converted to the Gospel
if I had not grounded my Gospel on the foundation of freedom
from the law, who will maintain against me that this form of
the Gospel has not an equal right of existence ? indeed it could
not have had any existence at all if it had not been the will of God
that it should exist." In this manner the Apostle also appeals
to the results of his efforts in the cause of Christianity as a
proof that he was a true and genuine Apostle of Christ. In
the same sense he speaks in direct terms of the grace given

9

him, understanding by it the Divine principle lying at the
root of his apostolic activity, without which supposition the
existence of such consequences could not be thought of. The
Jewish Apostles could not but acknowledge this, they could
not deny the facts, and neither could they see in them the
operation of an ungodly, unchristian principle. They gave to
him and Barnabas the right-hand of fellowship, recognized
them as accredited companions in the work of the Gospel, and
promised at the same time to put no hindrance in their way,
even if they continued as hitherto to spread the Gospel to the
Gentiles, without imposing the law on them. So far all is in
agreement, but we cannot believe that a full reconciliation took
place at this time between these widely sundered views and
principles. The κοινωνία was always a division, it could only
be brought into agreement by one party going εἰς τὰ ἔθνη, the
other εἰς τὴν περιτομὴν, *i.e.* as the Jewish Apostles could really
allege nothing against the principles on which Paul founded
his evangelical labours, they were obliged to recognize them
in a certain manner, but this recognition was a mere outward
one, they left it to him to work on these principles still further
in the cause of the Gospel among the Gentiles; but for themselves, they did not desire to know anything more about them.
The apostolic sphere of operation therefore became divided into
two parts; there was an εὐαγγέλιον τῆς περιτομῆς, and an εὐαγγέλιον τῆς ἀκροβυστίας; and an ποστολὴ εἰς ἀτὴν περιτομὴν, and an
ἀποστολὴ εἰς τὰ ἔθνη: in one the Mosaic law prevailed, in the
other it did not, but each depended inextricably on the other.*

---

* If we place before us the real issue of the affair, how striking is the conversion
of Cornelius, with which Peter opens his discourse at Jerusalem! (Acts xv. 7.)
Peter is made to say, " Men and brethren, ye know how that a good while ago God
made choice among us that the Gentiles by my mouth should hear the word of the
Gospel and believe. And God who knoweth the hearts bare them witness, giving
them the Holy Ghost, even as he did unto us, and put no difference between us
and them, purifying their hearts by faith." Who can help detecting here a
consistent adherence to a plan on the part of the author—but who can help finding
it necessary to use that same consistent adherence as an argument against the statements in the Acts of the Apostles. Just as little as Peter could have spoken at
Jerusalem in so Pauline a manner as the author of the Acts of the Apostles

The standpoint from which the elder Apostles looked at Paul cannot be sufficiently kept before us. It is as clear as possible that at this time at least, fourteen years after the conversion of the Apostle Paul, their circle of vision did not extend beyond Judaism. They knew nothing at all of a direct Gentile Christianity, existing without any co-operation from their side ; they were therefore first brought to recognize it by Paul, and their recognition appeared entirely as a concession which they were forced to make. They could do no otherwise, for they were not in a condition to resist the strength of circumstances and the overpowering personal influence of the Apostle. But they only consented not to oppose the Pauline Christianity, which with regard to their principles they were bound to oppose, and stipulated that they should be allowed to hold themselves passive towards it, or in one word to ignore it. So that as the

---

represents him to have done, could he have appealed to the transactions with Cornelius. The one cannot be separated from the other. But if he cannot have appealed to what took place with Cornelius, what security have we that he was so intimately connected with the conversion of Cornelius as the Acts of the Apostles relates. It is not clear that the author of the Acts of the Apostles would have made the Apostle Peter appeal to such an event in the same interest which influenced him when he gave a place to the narrative of Cornelius in his history. He who represents Peter as saying what he could not under the circumstances have said, prejudices himself, and gives rise to the suspicion that the statement is not very strictly historical. Peter would not have acknowledged that liberal view of the Mosaic law and the principles dependent on it for the first time when the pressure of circumstances and the imposing presence of the Apostle Paul left him but little choice. He would have done this long before, and in a manner which would have showed that he did so, not under the authority of any other man, but through the immediate impulse of the divine Spirit. The apostolic independence of Peter was not strengthened by this representation, but it tended to establish more firmly those more liberal views on which the Pauline preaching of the Gospel was based, even before the Apostle Paul himself entered with the divine sanction on the sphere of his labours. How much it is the intention of the author of the Acts of the Apostles to refer to the conversion of Cornelius, and then to make the chief idea of the Pauline Christianity appear in it, is shown also in the thought contained in Acts xv. 9, " And put no difference between us and them, purifying our hearts by faith." That things held to be unclean might not be unclean, is set forth in the conversion of Cornelius and the vision accompanying it, and as already, x. 43, the participation in the forgiveness of sins is made to depend upon faith in Jesus; so, xv. 9, the Pauline πίστις is brought forward as the true principle of a state which is well pleasing to God.

9 *

matter stood only two alternatives presented themselves. Either
the Jewish Apostles agreed with the Apostle Paul in the principles of his εὐαγγέλιον τῆς ἀκροβυστίας, or not. If they agreed
with him, they ought to consider it a duty to work with him
for the conversion of the Gentiles, else they would not be carrying out their apostolic office to its full extent, as they knew it
ought to be carried out ; they would have recognized theoretically as true and right what by their practical behaviour they declared objectionable. If they did not agree with him they ought
not to have yielded as much as they really did ; they could not
consider it as an indifferent matter, that with regard to the Gentiles the principle was adduced that salvation could be obtained
without Judaism, without the observance of the Mosaic law.
They could not recognize this principle without also recognizing
the obligation to work not merely for the εὐαγγέλιον τῆς περιτομῆς,
but also for the εὐαγγέλιον τῆς ἀκροβυστίας. Although they
did not do this, still it must be concluded from the sincerity
of the confession made to the Apostle Paul, that they were in
an unsettled state regarding these views and opinions, which
necessarily involved them in contradictions and inconsequences.
They could bring nothing forward in refutation of the principles
and facts which the Apostle Paul made use of against them,
and still they could not free themselves from the limited standpoint of Judaism on which they had hitherto stood. As they
had now made a concession by giving the right hand of fellowship, nothing else remained than to assume as indifferent a
position as possible towards Pauline Christianity. We have
here presented to us the exact origin of those two sections of
Jewish Christianity with which we become more nearly acquainted in the history of the succeeding period. There grew
up within Jewish Christianity itself a strict and a liberal party.
The stricter one wished to impose the general principles
of all Jewish Christians on Gentile Christians also, and
this in their full significance, so that without Judaism no man
could obtain salvation. This class of Jewish Christians could

not be indifferent to the Pauline Christianity, it was forced to
fight against it—and thus when the Gentiles would have claimed
a participation in the salvation of the Messianic kingdom,
(against which claim when once it had been allowed nothing
could be alleged) this could only be granted on the condition
that they should not be pronounced free from the observance
of the law. They saw perfectly well that if the necessity of the
law was not recognized in the case of the Gentile Christians,
its absolute importance to Judaism was at an end.   They were
therefore the declared opponents of the Apostle Paul, and introduced themselves into all the churches founded by him, that
after he had accomplished their conversion to the Gospel they
might follow with the condition without which it never should
have taken place, and without which it would be a perfectly
fruitless work, namely, the imposition of the law.   The more
liberal party was in principle in harmony with the stricter one,
only after the concessions made by the Jewish Apostles to the
Apostle Paul, they could not practically act against him in the
same manner ; they renounced the consequent carrying out · of
their principles, and limited their operations to Judaism.   We
cannot but think that the Jewish Apostles were at the head of
this party ; but the other, which owing to its strictness felt itself in no way hampered as to its practical activity by any
vagueness of opinion, must from the very nature of the case have
been of the most historical importance.   In the period immediately succeeding these transactions at Jerusalem, it is shown
how the two parties behaved with regard to each other, and how
each sought to get the upper hand.

In the closest connection with these circumstances stands
that scene between Paul and Peter at Antioch, which from the
earliest times bore such evil notoriety, and was so important
with regard to the standpoint of both parties. If the elder
Apostles had been really and truly convinced of the merely
relative value of the law and its worthlessness in regard to the
grace of the Gospel, would Peter have been guilty of such

double dealing towards the Gentile Christians in Antioch out
of timid regard to the Jerusalem Jewish Christians, whose visit
to Antioch had already shown that this resolution at Jerusalem
could not be taken as the Acts of the Apostles represents it to
have been, with the general consent of the whole community
of Jewish Christians? Would that same Peter have so acted
whom the Acts of the Apostles shortly before had shown as
speaking in so decidedly Pauline a manner, and this indeed
in Jerusalem itself before the whole Church, a few members
of which would have been sufficient to excite anxious timidity
in the mind of the Apostle? How striking and abrupt is here
the contrast between Paul and Peter! How open and un-
sparing is Paul's censure! How harsh and vehement his
speech! How keenly he exposes the contradiction in which
Peter found himself involved through his irresolution! The
Acts of the Apostles indeed says nothing of all this. In a representation deviating so much from the truth as this account of
the transactions at Jerusalem, there could indeed be no place
for a scene like this; and for this reason not only does this
discrepancy between the Acts of the Apostles and the Epistle
to the Galatians become more apparent, but it also becomes
indubitable that the silence of the Acts of the Apostles with
regard to so public an occurrence, is an intentional one. Where
we expect to find the dispute between Peter and Paul mentioned, the Acts of the Apostles only speaks of a παροξυσμὸς
between Paul and Barnabas, and even this quarrel is assigned
to another cause to that given to it Gal. ii. 13. Why is it
silent as to the chief cause of the quarrel from which certainly
even this παροξυσμὸς arose, if it were not from the advisability
of keeping silence as to all disputes at that period? On the
same grounds it did not dare to mention the name of Titus,
who was obnoxious on account of these very events, in the list
of the friends and companions of the Apostle.* We see clearly

---

* Instead of the uncircumcised Titus, the name of the circumcised Timothy is
everywhere brought forward. That the same Paul who in Jerusalem refused with

that it wishes to throw a concealing veil over all these occurrences in Jerusalem and Antioch, and by the mention of the less important quarrel between Paul and Barnabas, to divert attention from the chief fact and chief subject of the dispute. Nothing could be more abhorrent to its apologetic and conciliatory tendency than the renewal of a subject which made the Apostle Paul appear in so unfavourable a light in the eyes of the Jewish Christians; an event of which the offensive impression (as we gather from many things) operated for so long a period after its occurrence, that even at that time every effort was made to soften it as much as possible, and to cause the whole affair to be forgotten.* We may at least learn enough from this, to

all his might that Titus should be circumcised, and this out of regard to the Jews and Jewish-Christians, should soon after himself have caused Timothy to be circumcised out of the same regard to prejudice, Acts xvi. 3, belongs undoubtedly to the simply incredible side of the Acts of the Apostles. This act would have been a complete denial of principle on the part of Paul. That Timothy had up to this time never been circumcised, although his mother was a Jewess, would seem to indicate that he was reckoned as a Gentile, like his father. If he were now circumcised as a Gentile, and by the wish and connivance of the Apostle, in order that he might not be any longer looked on as a Gentile, as his father was, Acts xvi. 3, what could either Jews or Gentiles think on the subject, but that it was a proof that circumcision was not so indifferent a thing as the Apostle once considered it? This deed performed on Timothy stands in the most evident contradiction, not only to Gal. ii. 3, but to Gal. iii. 28 and v. 11. Even if the submission to circumcision on the part of Timothy was a completely voluntary act, as Olshausen especially maintains, the Apostle would never have allowed Timothy to become his companion, as by so doing he would have exposed himself to the merited reproach of want of principle, and inconsequence of reasoning. As we are forced to consider the circumcision of Timothy in this light, the λαβὼν περιέτεμεν αὐτὸν, Acts xvi. 3, cannot be ascribed to the Apostle.

* How Paul is reproached in the Pseudo-Clementine Homilies, 17, 18, for having said of Peter, Gal. ii. 11, that he was κατεγνωσμένος! Εἰ κατεγνωσμένον με λέγεις, θεοῦ τοῦ ἀποκαλύψαντός μοι τὸν Χριστὸν κατηγορεῖς καὶ τοῦ ἐπὶ ἀποκαλύψει μακαρίσαντός με καταφέρεις. Peter says this to the Magus Simon,—but that the Apostle Paul is meant, there is no doubt. In the preceding part of the Homily, it is said by Peter to James: Τινὲς ἀπὸ τῶν ἐθνῶν τὸ δι᾽ ἐμοῦ νόμιμον ἀπεδοκίμασαν κήρυγμα, τοῦ ἐχθροῦ ἀνθρώπου ἄνομόν τινα καὶ φλυαρώδη προσηκάμενοι διδασκαλίαν. Καὶ ταῦτα ἔτι μου περιόντος ἐπεχείρησάν τινες ποικίλίας τισὶν ἑρμηνείαις τοὺς ἐμοὺς λόγους μετασχηματίζειν εἰς τὴν τοῦ νόμου κατάλυσιν. ὡς καὶ ἐμοῦ οὕτω μὲν φρονοῦντος μὴ ἐκ παρρησίας δὲ κηρύσσοντος, ὅπερ ἀπείη. This is also referred to Gal. ii. 12, only the affair is reversed. Against the assertion of Paul, that Peter really agreed with his (Paul's) view of the Mosaic law, and

justify us in excusing the harsh attitude of the Apostle towards
Judaism, but this fails in the first period after his conversion,
in regard to which Tertullian says, c. Marc. I. 20, "Paulus adhuc
in gratia rudis—ferventer, ut neophytus, adversus judaismum
aliquid in conversatione reprehendum existimavit." On the
same grounds the modern interpreters, in their chronological
discussions on the journey of the Apostle, Gal. ii. 1, place this
at an earlier date, and take Acts xi. 30 as the second journey.
They also appeal to the fact that the behaviour of the Apostle
towards Judaism, was afterwards much milder and more
yielding. But what proof have we of this, if we do not get it
from the Acts of the Apostles, whose contradiction of the
Epistle to the Galatians is sufficiently evident? What the
Apostle, 1 Corinthians iv. 12, says, "that unto the Jews he
became a Jew that he might gain the Jews," can certainly not
be taken in a sense which would involve his denying essential
principles. He can only have been a Jew unto the Jews in the
same manner in which he was a Gentile to the Gentiles. The
most certain proof that the Apostle afterwards thought so himself, and considered his relation to the elder Apostles from the
same point of view, is given by the Epistle to the Galatians itself,
for how else could he express what he thought of the consequences of the occurrences at Antioch in such a manner, in a
letter written so short a time afterwards? Is then anything
omitted which could be alleged in mitigation of the impression
which must have been made by such a long existing dispute
between the two Apostles?

What the Acts of the Apostles represents as the result of the
apostolic transactions in Jerusalem is also at complete variance
with the Apostle's own accounts. According to the proposal
of James it was resolved, as is related in the Acts of the

---

that it had been a mere ὑπόκρισις in Peter to deny his true opinions out of fear of
the Jewish Christians, Peter here protests, and says that the assertion that in the
matter of the abolition of the law, he surrendered his real opinion for want of
παῤῥησία, is an arbitrary interpretation of his speech.

Apostles, that the Gentiles should "abstain from eating flesh offered to idols, from blood, from things strangled, and from fornication." James, as has already been remarked, stood in a certain sense between the two chief parties, between the Pharisaic-minded zealots of the law on one side, and Barnabas, Paul and Peter on the other, in order that the Gentile Chris-tians might neither be entirely freed from any respect to the Mosaic law, nor yet be subject to that which to those among them who were willing to accept Judaism, always appeared as the heaviest burden of the law, and therefore must have been the chief obstacle, the greatest hindrance to the Gospel among the Gentiles, namely, circumcision. This resolution formally entered into by the whole assembly, was sent to the churches in Antioch, Syria and Cilicia in the shape of letters, by delegates chosen from the midst of the Church at Jerusalem, accompanied to Antioch by Paul and Barnabas, in the name of the Apos-tles, Presbyters, and brethren of the Church at Jerusalem. The author of the Acts of the Apostles intentionally renders the importance of this resolution very prominent. It was passed, say the letters, with a view of quieting minds, and chasing away the anxious fears which were spread abroad by some who clung to circumcision and the strict observance of the Mosaic law. On this account it will be expressly remarked what lively joy was awakened in Antioch by the resolutions conveyed thither, and the agreement between the Church at Jerusalem and this at Antioch, as it was testified by the delegates from Jerusalem. The author of the Acts of the Apostles remarks again with evident intention on the momentous character of this decree. When not long afterwards Paul and Silas entered on a second missionary journey and visited the churches founded during the first—they "delivered unto them," Acts xvi. 4," the decrees ordained by the Apostles and Elders at Jerusalem," that they might thereby rule themselves (παρεδίδουν αὐτοῖς φυλάσσειν τὰ δόγματα τὰ κεκριμένα ὑπὸ τῶν ἀπ.), and the consequence of this was that the "churches were established in the faith,

and increased in number daily." Beneficially as this decree
operated in the cause of the Gospel, so also on it essentially depended its further spread among the Gentiles.   As the
affair is here represented, the transactions at Jerusalem and the
decree made there at that time, betoken a very important
epoch in the most ancient history of Christianity : the critical
question, at that time most prominent, whether Christianity
should be subordinate to Judaism or not, was decided in favour
of Christianity.   Should we not expect that the Apostle Paul
would not have left so weighty a decree wholly unmentioned in
an Epistle to the Galatians, whilst he speaks of the very same
transactions, and with reference to the question how far this
decision had been arrived at ?   The condition of the κοινωνία
was, ἵνα ἡμεῖς μὲν εἰς τὰ ἔθνη, αὐτοὶ δὲ εἰς τὴν περιτομὴν—would
not this have been an opportunity of paying regard to the common and reconciling relations that existed between the ἀποστολὴ
περιτομῆς and the ἀπόστολη εἰς τὰ ἔθνη, instead of placing them
in such harsh opposition as is done by the words above quoted ?
But we find in the Apostle's writings not the slightest indication that at that time any such important a decree had been
made, but rather the most decided assurances to the contrary.
The Apostle says expressly, ii. 10, Μόνον τῶν πτωχῶν ἵνα
μνημονεύωμεν.   The only condition which was attached to the
independence of the Apostle in the sphere of his apostolic
labours, was then the μνημονεύειν τῶν πτωχῶν, which it is impossible to understand otherwise than as a conciliatory promise
which the Apostle gave from love of peace, that he would
engage to support the poor church at Jerusalem by contributions which he would collect in the churches of the Gentile
Christians, and this, says the Apostle, he was " also forward to
do," as we indeed find he was from his epistles.   But does not
this μόνον include something besides this stipulation ?   And how
comes the Apostle to place this promise of contributing to the
poor, which after all was a minor part only of the transaction, as
its sole aim, when far more important ends were involved in the

object of the transaction itself, namely the sufficiency of the
Mosaic Law ? It is not here said that there is any question of a
κοινωνία concluded between Paul and Barnabas on one side, and
James, Peter and John on the other, as between all these,
according to the Acts of the Apostles, no difference existed,
and there is no cause for mentioning this result, but notwithstanding this it is implied by the Apostle : it has been already
shown that one of the chief differences in the two accounts is
that the parties who are described as engaged in the dispute
are not the same. There can be no longer any idea of a reconciliation between the two accounts, but the difference already
shown rather grows wider. We find a private transaction instead of a public assembly, and a dispute between the Apostles
themselves, instead of between the Apostles and the Pharisaic
minded members of the Church at Jerusalem ; and we cannot
find any definition of the decree which, according to the Acts of
the Apostles, was ordained, and this for the natural reason that
according to the Epistle of the Galatians such a decree never
existed. That it is not accidentally omitted, with all that
depends on it, is incontestably shown in the Epistle to the
Galatians, as also in the rest of the Apostle's Epistles. In the
Epistle to the Galatians the Apostle contends with the Judaising
opponents, who were desirous of imposing circumcision on the
Galatian Church as a necessary condition of salvation, Gal. v. 1.
In order to do this the Apostle explains his entire relation to
the ἀποστολὴ τῆς περιτομῆς. What would forward this more
than an appeal to the decree ? How could these opponents
be better repulsed than by a decree made in Jerusalem itself,
through which circumcision had been declared to be a burden
as unbearable as it was unnecessary ? We may even go so far
as to say that if he referred to this transaction at all it was incumbent on the Apostle, not to leave such a decree entirely
unnoticed in a case on which it so especially bore. He
could not have been silent on it without prejudicing the truth of
the affair, as his statement would be chargeable with keeping

back one of the chief events which would have been useful against his opponents. What importance then could such a decree, which must have had such great weight with the Gentile Christians, have had in its results, if no use at all were made of it in a case like this, in which it was so eminently fitted to maintain the ground already won ? Just the same reasoning may be applied to the other arrangements of this pretended decree.

The Apostle is also silent in a perfectly inexplicable manner, in many instances where we might expect not only a mention, but an express application. It is known how often in his Epistles he speaks of many reasons for eating flesh offered to idols. He is indifferent to the matter in itself, but lays particular stress on the obligation of paying regard to the weaker Christian brethren. So the Apostle declares especially in 1 Cor. viii. concerning the εἰδωλόθυτα, about which we can perceive he has been questioned by that part of the Corinthian Church to which his epistle is addressed. This inquiry would not have been put, if, as the Acts of the Apostles sets forth, this decree had been ordained to be laid before almost every church of the Gentile Christians, and its observance had been made a necessary condition of the existing Christian communion between the Gentile and Jewish Christians. But the Apostle himself, although he might be indifferent to the question as to the eating of meat offered to idols on its own merits, and as regarded himself, could not have declared his indifference to the relations the question held at that time, because the observance of a positive command given for such a purpose could never have been looked on with indifference. It cannot be doubted that the Acts of the Apostles intends to convey the idea that all these commands were to be observed in all the Gentile Christian churches for the future. According to xv. 20. (compared with 22 and with 28, 29,) ἐπιστεῖλαι αὐτοῖς (ἔθνεσι) τοῦ ἀπέχεσθαι ἀπὸ τῶν ἀλιστ., it was resolved that it was indispensable that these arrangements should be submitted to. Neither can we say that they were made merely in reference to the churches

in Antioch, Syria, and Cilicia, because they were troubled by
these Judaising zealots, for it is evident by the express remark
of the author, xvi. 4, that they were delivered for observance
to the churches in Derbe and Lystra by Paul himself on his
arrival at those places; and also that they were observed in all
the new churches in the same manner—Paul going to Corinth
immediately afterwards and founding the church there.
Neander also finds it worthy of remark that the Apostle in
regard to the disputes in the Christian church at Corinth,
about the eating of meat offered to idols, did not appeal
to the decree of the apostolic assembly at Jerusalem, in
order to establish the rules for the Gentile Christians with regard to this sacrificial meat. But with reference to this subject
as well as to the question of why the Jewish Christians, who
wished to enforce circumcision on the Gentiles, did not oppose
the observance of this decree, Neander explains, that it belongs to the characteristic manner of Paul not to appeal to a
positive outward command, to a νόμος, but to the inner law in
the conscience of the believer, defining what the spirit of the
Gospel demanded. Neander must himself have felt how unsatisfactory this explanation is, for he remarks further, "It
seems, although the observance of this decree was firmly established by the Apostle in Palestine, that beyond Palestine it
had but very little influence. As this decree depended on a
mutual agreement, it must follow that as one of the parties, the
Jewish Christians, did not fulfil the conditions whilst they refused to acknowledge the uncircumcised as brethren, the obligatory force of the agreement failed on the other side also, that is
on that of the Gentile Christians, who, through the observance
of this decree, would have been brought into nearer communion with the Jewish Christians." Neander here grants so
much that from what he concedes we may get an idea of the
opinion he has arrived at. How did it happen then that these
decrees were of so little value out of Palestine, where alone it
was of importance that the Jewish Christians did not fulfil the

conditions, and indeed never had fulfilled them from the beginning ? For if those τινὲς ἀπὸ ʼΙακώβου could so openly and decidedly appear in opposition to the decrees so soon after the council at Jerusalem, and that too at Antioch, in the very church for which the decrees were ordained, we can only conclude that up to that time the decrees had had very little heed paid to them. And if these depended on a mutual agreement, how comes it that there was never any remonstrance raised by the Gentile Christians against this violation of the agreement on the part of the stricter and more prejudiced party ? If we conclude it to have been in favour of the Gentile Christians that the obligation to observe these decrees was removed, we cannot see what interest could have been served by concluding such an agreement. The original state of the case was that each side looked at the law as it liked. But if the Jewish Christians wished to enforce circumcision on the Gentile Christians this mediating agreement must have been concluded for the greater tranquillity of the Gentile Christians, because they could only be freed from the observance of this burdensome part of the law with the consent of the Jewish Christians. If however the Jewish Christians did not hold to their agreement, if they insisted afresh on circumcision, the tranquillity which the agreement had bestowed on the Gentile Christians would be disturbed, and they would find themselves plunged again into the restless state of uncertainty as to whether they could be saved without circumcision. But if now, so shortly after the agreement had been made, they could so entirely disregard it, it might be fairly argued that they might have been tranquillized before and without any such agreement, and we cannot avoid coming to the conclusion that laws which not only were never kept, but whose existence was not called for by any special need, really could never have been made. It is true that Neander appeals to Acts xxi. 25 as a proof that the Apostles always held fast to the observance of these decrees in Palestine, but this passage only bears testimony to the interest which the author of the Acts of the Apostles had in calling to remembrance the decrees mentioned by him in a former place. There is wanting throughout the Acts of the Apostles an independent proof of the observance of these decrees, and this is the only proof to which any value could be attached. It is not by any means likely that the Apostles even held fast to the authority of these decrees in Palestine. For why should they have done so? Only to compel the Jewish Christians to recognize the decrees as far as they regarded the Gentile Christians. But if so little resulted from this compulsion as the history shows, how powerless must the authority of the Apostles have been with the Jewish Christians!—is it not more likely that the recognition of these decrees was not enforced, or that the decrees never existed at all!

However small the probability that these decrees were observed or even that they existed at that time, later on this improbability becomes certainty. Even Neander remarks, " It was later that these decrees received a stronger legal authority through the predominance of another tendency in the Church." This word " later" shows us from what point of view, according to the Acts of the Apostles, we are expected to consider the stipulation under consideration, as existing at that time, but the history says nothing of the validity which these arrangements subsequently took, being a consequence of the earlier legal ordinance. From the earliest date the Gentile and Jewish Christians had stood in opposition to each other with regard to circumcision; whilst the latter firmly adhered to it, the · former in no way recognized any obligation as to its adoption, but considered baptism as an outward and perfectly sufficient substitute. The situation of affairs at that time is precisely indicated by what the Apostle Paul says in opposition to those zealots for the law who, as members of the Church of Palestine, or at least under its influence, maintained the necessity of circumcision in the churches founded by the Apostle out of Palestine. Galatians v. 2, compared with iii. 27 : Ἴδε ἐγὼ Παῦλος λέγω ὑμῖν, ὅτι ἐὰν περιτέμνησθε, Χριστὸς ὑμᾶς οὐδὲν ὠφελήσει—ὅσοι γὰρ εἰς Χριστὸν ἐβαπτίσθητε, Χριστὸν ἐνεδύσασθε, οὐκ ἔνι Ἰουδαῖος οὐδὲ Ἕλλην. The next step that was taken was the leaving off of circumcision by the Jewish Christians, not indeed in Palestine, where the Ebionites and Nazarenes still continued strong adherents to the Mosaic law, but amongst the foreign Jewish Christians, the Hellenists, who accordingly show the great importance which they bore in the most ancient history of the Christian Church, as a reconciling medium between Jews and Gentiles, and through this mediation paving their own way to Christianity. How this took place is not distinctly evident as there exists a lack of information, still some hints are afforded which are worthy of consideration. It is striking to find with what contempt circumcision is treated in the Epistle of Barnabas, which if we do not take as having been written by the Barnabas known to us, still must be taken as a Hellenistic work, as having the name Barnabas attached to it. "Now first," says the author, chap. ix. in a series of allegorical interpretations by which he endeavours to elucidate the meaning of the Old Testament, "are our ears circumcised for the right understanding of the Divine words? The circumcision on which they place their trust is now recognised as null and void. For God intended no carnal circumcision, they were wrongly advised, being deceived by an evil angel."

Here we have circumcision as it was observed by the Jews as a Mosaic law, even ascribed to demoniacal influence. In the Epistles of Ignatius there is a difference made in the same way between an outer and an inner circumcision, and a true and false Judaism.* Another remarkable sign of the change in the views and customs of the Hellenists with regard to circumcision is given us by the Clementine Homilies. There is no other

---

* Epistle to the Philadelphians, c. 6. He who proclaims the one God of the Law and the Prophets, and denies that Christ is the Son of God, is a liar, καὶ ἔστιν ὁ τοιοῦτος τῆς κάτω περιτομῆς ψευδοιουδαῖος.

memorial which so clearly testifies as does this document to the influence which Judaism extended over Christianity down to the second half of the second century. Although Judaism is so very prominent in it, there is not the least question of circumcision, but so much the more the importance of baptism and the new birth is held up as a means for the abolition of heathenism, (the ἀφελληνισθῆναι, Hom. iii. 9,) and the command of James to the elders of the Church at Jerusalem not to yield up the discourses of Peter sent by him, to any one but a circumcised believer is the only trace of a reference to the ancient value attached to circumcision. Without doubt this rejection of circumcision had its ground in the conviction that the Gentiles could never be won over by any other means. How much the supplanting of Judaism and the spread of the only true religion signified to the Hellenistic Jewish Christians, is seen also in these Homilies by their making their Apostle Peter entirely an Apostle to the Gentiles. The Acts of the Apostles also considers the subject from this point of view, when it makes the increase that the Christian Church received from the Gentiles entirely owing to it. But the more that Judaism yielded to heathenism with regard to circumcision, with the greater justice could the observance and consideration of the Mosaic law be urged to the full extent on the Gentiles. This point, which the Acts of the Apostles joins to the release from the obligation of circumcision we find, as far as we can learn, to be the existing normal state of Christian opinion in the apostolic time.

When the Apostle Paul wrote his first Epistle to the Corinthians there was still a weakness in regard to the εἰδωλόθυτα. The Apostle still advises their rejection, not only on account of the regard which ought to be paid to weaker Christians, but also because the enjoyment of them would be μετέχειν τραπέζης δαιμονίων, 1 Corinthians x. 21. This became afterwards the prevailing view. In this sense the Clementine Homilies, viii. 4, enjoin the ἀπέχεσθαι τραπέζης δαιμόνων, and it was especially

10

urged against the Gnostics, as they were generally looked upon as Gentiles, that they declared εἰδωλόθυτα ἐσθίειν, as something indifferent and not defiling. In the period in which the Church was first established as a whole out of heterogeneous elements, it held fast to the ἀπέχεσθαι τοῦ πνικτοῦ καὶ τοῦ αἵματος (from the flesh of beasts which were killed by strangling, which were strangled in their blood, and from blood generally*). All this agrees with the views which prevailed in the first Christian Churches about heathenism, founded on the Jewish representations of demons as being the idols of the heathen world, and indeed the originators of all that was heathen.† The most remarkable in the series of the apostolic ordinances is nevertheless the ἄπεχεσθαι τῆς πορνείας. Interpreters rightly find it very striking, that, as Neander expresses it (page 166,) the disciplinary ordinances, which although appointed for a certain time and certain conditions were valid for all time, arose from a somewhat objective moral prohibition of immorality. Meanwhile Neander is of opinion that the connection in which this prohibition stands, gives the best explanation of the cause and relations of this special statement. The πορνεία is here only mentioned in the same relation as the foregoing points, on account of the close connection in which they seemed to the Jews to stand with the worship of idols; men were already accustomed from the writings of the Old Testament to associate idolatry with immorality; excesses of this sort are really bound up with many branches of idolatry, and in general a

---

* In the writings of the Gallic Churches of Paris and Vienna, in Eusebius, H. E. vi, it is said, in reference to the well-known reproof made against the Christians, πῶς ἄν παιδία φαγοίεν οἱ τοιοῦτοι, οἷς μηδὲ ἀλόγων ζώων αἷμα φαγεῖν ἐξόν.

† In this connexion we find in Origen contra Celsum, vii. 30, τὸ μὲν γὰρ εἰδωλόθυτον θύεται δαιμονίοις καὶ οὐ χρὴ τὸν τοῦ θεοῦ ἄνθρωπον. κοινωνὸν τραπέζης δαιμονίων γίνεσθαι, τὰ δὲ πνικτά, τοῦ αἵματος μὴ ἐκκριθέντος ὅπερ φασὶν εἶναι τροφὴν δαιμόνων, τρεφομένων ταῖς ἀπ' αὐτοῦ ἀναθυμιάσεσιν ἀπαγορεύει ὁ λόγος ἵνα μὴ τραφῶμεν τροφῇ δαιμόνων, τάχα τινῶν τοιούτων πνευμάτων συντραφησομένων ἡμῖν ἐὰν μεταλαμβάνωμεν τῶν πνίκτῶν· ἐκ δὲ τῶν εἰρημένων περὶ τῶν πνικτῶν σαφὲς εἶναι δύναται τὸ περὶ τῆς ἀποχῆς τοῦ αἵματος.

strict idea of chastity is very far removed from the standpoint
of natural religions.   There is no question here of any special
moral precept of Christianity; had there been, the command
would have been given not so much as a secondary, but as a
positive one, and would be much more enforced from the whole
connection of the Christian Faith and Life than is done in the
Epistles of the Apostle.   All that comes before us here is the
ancient Jewish opposition to anything which might appear to
have any connection with idolatry, and this opposition became
transferred to the new Christian Churches."   This explanation
I cannot consider satisfactory.   For how could a special prohibition against participation in the immorality bound up with
the Gentile idolatry have seemed necessary to Christians if they
did not in general need the inculcation of the prohibition.
Only he who generally manifested indifference to immorality,
could hold it as something allowed by Gentile idolatry.   But a
self-accusing prohibition against the immorality of the Gentile
idolatry must have been the less necessary for Christians, as with
the prohibition of participation in the εἰδωλόθυτα there fell away
every inducement to the immorality bound up with it.   If we
take the πορνεία in the sense Neander does, we do not perceive
why here the ἀπέχεσθαι πορνείας should find a special place
close to the ἀπέχεσθαι εἰδωλοθύτων—as it is included in it—
and such a useless addition is not to be expected in legal definitions of this kind, we therefore see ourselves again reduced
to the necessity of taking the πορνεία in a general sense, and
the ἀπέχεσθαι πορνείας as a general moral precept: and this, as
has been acknowledged, is highly unlikely.   What Olshausen
gives as the only true explanation is equally untenable, namely,
" that we must bear in mind the much greater freedom in sexual
relations among the Greeks and Romans, which was an abomi-
nation to the more serious Jews, and seemed to them even as
refined fornication."   By means of this expression, comprising
not merely gross, but refined errors of this kind, greater
care and circumspection in their intercourse with the female

10 *

sex were recommended to the Gentile Christians, in order
that no cause of offence might be given to the Jewish Christians." But who can believe that all this is expressed in
the word πορνεία ? How vague and arbitrary would be the
whole idea of this πορνεία, for such legal definitions ought
to have had a precise meaning and be applied to a precise object. As the rest of the ordinances related to
especial individual cases, so this also must be assumed to hold
good with the πορνεία. In this view the explanation of Von
Gieseler (in the Abhandlung über die Naz. u. Eb. in Staüdl. u.
Tzsch. Arch. f. K. G. p. 312) deserves precedence, and we cannot but wonder how Neander and Olshausen have left it
entirely disregarded. Von Gieseler supposes that πορνεία here
may mean incest, which deserved special mention, as among
Gentile nations unions among blood relations were held admissible. This meaning the word πορνεία has also, 1 Corinthians
v. 1.

If we assume that in this period of the Christian Church,
of which we have the most ancient post-apostolic memorials, the
institution of second marriages was looked on as fornication
and adultery, and so designated by the oldest Christian
authors, we can the less have any doubt that through the
word πορνεία those marriage unions were indicated, which
according to the views prevailing at that time among Christians, were considered unlawful, and as tokens of an unchaste
and carnal mind. This explanation suits very well with the
context. For as partaking in the Gentile sacrifices and the
eating of things strangled, and of blood, were looked on as
a Gentile corruption, because through them men were brought
into communion with demons, the gods of the Gentiles, so
also those marriage unions, and especially the contracting of
second marriages, appeared inadmissible, as leading away
from the true God, and as an opposition to Monotheism. He
who contracted so unchaste a union gave, by his deed, a
token that he, as the Clementine Homilies express it, had no

monarchical soul, *i.e.* no soul capable of appreciating the highest unity. He must here remember the Old Testament representation of the chosen people, owing, as it were, marriage fidelity to God, and the New Testament idea of the union of Christ with the Church as his Bride, then, just as Christian marriage is spoken of in the Epistle to the Ephesians, vi. 22, and as there is seen in this union between man and wife an image of that holy indissoluble relation, therefore, in the demands specially made on the chiefs of a Christian Church, 1 Tim. iii. 2, one of the peculiarities required of the ἐπίσκοπος was that he should be μιᾶς γυναικὸς ἀνήρ. From this point of view, everything which was not suitable in regard to the married life in the Christian sense could be designated as an idolatrous, Gentile πορνεία.

All these definitions, which must have been given in Jerusalem, bear unmistakeably the impress of a time in which there was no sympathy bestowed by the Gentile-Christians on the Jewish-Christians of Palestine, who would neither abate anything of the strictness of the Mosaic law, nor allow of any milder definition of it. Their sympathy was rather given to the liberal-minded foreign Hellenists. Whilst there is not the least hint in the Pauline Epistles as to the agreement which, according to the Acts of the Apostles, was formally arranged in Jerusalem, (for in 1 Corinthians vi. we find no such hint, even granting the matter treated of relates to this subject,) in all the post-apostolic writers on the other hand all these points are represented as the existing normal conditions of the Christian life. How is it likely therefore that the author of the Acts of the Apostles himself belonged to this later time, that in the apostolic council in Jerusalem, he referred to the earlier apostolic period, and to a decree of the Apostle himself, that which had of itself become a praxis, characterizing the Christian life in the relations which Jewish and Gentile-Christians held to each other? The Pseudo-Clementine Homilies place us in just the same sphere of the relations of life. When the Apostle

Peter, in the character of the Apostle to the Gentiles, organized the Gentile Churches founded by him in Tyre and Sidon, he gave them the following precepts, Hom. vii. 4, 8 :—Ἔστι δὲ τὰ ἀρέσκοντα τῷ θεῷ—τραπέζης δαιμόνων ἀπέχεσθαι, νεκρᾶς μὴ γεύεσθαι σακρὸς, μὴ ψαύειν αἵματος, ἐκ παντὸς ἀπολύεσθαι (or according to Cotelier's emendation, ἀπολούεσθαι), λύματος, τὰ δὲ λοιπὰ ἑνὶ λόγῳ, ὅσα θεὸν σεβόντες ἤκουσαν Ἰουδαῖοι, καὶ ὑμεῖς ἀκούσατε ἅπαντες, ἐν πολλοῖς σώμασιν μίαν γνώμην ἀναλάβοντες. The Apostle left this precept behind him at Tyre, and when he went from thence to Sidon, he there gave a similar one. Ἡ δὲ ὑπ' αὐτοῦ (God) ὁρισθεῖσα θρησκειά ἐστιν· τὸ μόνον αὐτὸν σέβειν, καὶ τῷ τῆς ἀληθείας μόνῳ πιστεύειν προφήτῃ, καὶ εἰς ἄφεσιν ἁμαρτιῶν βαπτισθῆναι, καὶ οὕτῳ διὰ ἀγνοτάτης βαφῆς ἀναγεννηθῆναι θεῷ διὰ τοῦ σώζοντος ὕδατος· τραπέζης δαιμόνων μὴ μεταλαμβάνειν, λέγω δὲ εἰδωλοθύτων, νεκρῶν, πνικτῶν θηριαλώτων, αἵματος, μὴ ἀκαθάρτως βιοῦν, ἀπὸ κοίτης γυναίκος λούεσθαι, αὐτὰς μὲν καὶ ἄφεδρον φυλάττειν, πάντας δὲ σωφρονεῖν, εὐποιεῖν, μὴ ἀδικεῖν, &c. If we deduct from this what belongs especially to the Clementine view of Christianity, and if we take into consideration that baptism is here put in the place of the circumcision which had been abandoned, we have the four points presented to us in the Acts of the Apostles. For there can be no doubt that the μὴ ἀκαθάρτως βιοῦν, or the παντὸς ἀπολούεσθαι λύματος, corresponds to the ἀπέχεσθαι πορνείας, and includes in itself what is apparently to be understood by the πορνεία. Any express prohibition of second marriages is not indeed to be found in the Clementine Homilies ; but as the πορνεία, or μοιχεία, is considered next to idolatry to be the greatest sin, and as the greatest stress is laid on the fact that everything in human life has a strict monarchical form and direction, it is rightly assumed that second marriages would therefore scarcely need an express prohibition, for it would be thought self-evident that they were included under πορνεία, or μοιχεία.

In the passage first quoted it is clearly stated that the Jewish

Christians considered the observance of the decrees in question as the essential condition by which alone they could enter into perfect communion with the Gentile Christians. In this modified form the two heterogeneous elements first approached to a unity. But how far both sides still stand apart in that time in which we first become really aware of the existing difference!

CHAPTER VI.

IT was one of the grandest moments in the life of the Apostle when, after these transactions at Jerusalem, he defended the great cause of his Gospel and apostolic mission before the assembly of the elder Apostles and the whole Church of Jerusalem, penetrated as he was with a deep consciousness of its truth, as he expresses it in his Epistles. One of the ideas developed by his first journey to Jerusalem was now a matter-of-fact reality, evident to all eyes. The Apostle had given utterance to a real, undeniable truth when he characterized the cause of his Gospel as the cause of God. If this, on the part of the Apostle, was the most powerful evidence of its truth, on the other hand the great practical importance which the matter now took made the opposition of its enemies more decided and energetic. As Barnabas soon after the transactions at Jerusalem showed signs of lukewarmness, it was in fact the Apostle alone who had to wage the whole battle with the power of Judaism, which up to that time had been so closely interwoven with Christianity. After he had spent some time in Antioch, he undertook a new missionary journey, prompted by the deep self-consciousness evolved by the events at Jerusalem and Antioch, and by the conviction which these had freshly established, that the cause of his Gospel could never be crushed by merely human power, but that it contained in itself the whole future of the history of the development of Christianity. In this journey he not only revisited the countries in Asia Minor where he had before been, but took the more important step of carrying over the doctrine of the Gospel from Troas to Macedonia, and from thence spreading it further in the countries of Europe. It is quite according to the usual method of classic antiquity (a method which is by no means strange to the author of the Acts of the Apostles) that so important an era, including so much of the future history of the cause of the Gospel, should be inaugurated by a vision of the night. In this vision a man from Macedonia appeared to the Apostle with a prayer that he would go over to Macedonia and help them (xvi. 9). As the author of the Acts of the Apostles is desirous to show the inherent desire of the Gentile world for the salvation of the Gospel by every sign and token in his power, so here, by this man of Macedonia, he symbolizes the desire for salvation with which not only the people of Macedonia, but those of Europe humanity generally, appealed to the Apostle as the ambassador of the newly revealed salvation. Although by such an embellishment of history the literary individuality of the author of the Acts of the Apostles may be gratified, its acceptance would only involve us in a series of narratives in which we should again see the rest of the events in the life of the Apostle by the magic light of miracle, and their historical truth covered by a thick veil.

The occurrences which are assumed to have taken place during the Apostle's visit to Philippi, in Macedonia, belong to the most miraculous order of those which the Acts of the Apostles relates of him. Interpreters and critics (not excepting Neander) indeed pass over these suspicious passages with their accustomed facility, but it cannot be denied that there is very much in them to which we may make valid objection. The chief difficulty is in the narrative beginning chap. xvi. 20, but the one preceding it where its immediate cause is presented, is strange enough. Whilst Paul and Silas, as is related, lingered some days in Philippi they were followed, as soon as they were outside the city on the way to the Jewish Proseuche, by a damsel possessed with a spirit of divination, with the loud cry, "These men are the servants of the Most High God, who show us the way of salvation." After the damsel had done this for many days, Paul at last turned angrily to her, and in the name of Jesus Christ commanded the spirit to come out of her. But as those persons whose slave she was, lost the important gains which they were wont to obtain from her prophetic powers, they excited a popular tumult against Paul and Silas, on the charge of political intrigue, and accomplished the arrest of the Apostle and his companion. The attempts of modern interpreters to explain this matter more clearly only place its improbability in a stronger light. The πνεῦμα πύθωνος is treated in a very peculiar manner. Modern interpreters reject the theory of ventriloquism, which the expression πμεῦμα πύθωνος would imply, and of which we get a hint in certain earlier occurrences ; but Olshausen and Neander are positive that they find the solution they desire of this phenomenon in the phenomena of somnambulism. " In the recognition of the spiritual characteristics of the Apostle by the damsel," says Olshausen, " there may be perceived the same *clairvoyance,* of which such numerous examples are found in those Gospel histories which relate the healing of those possessed by demons." In the same sense Neander (page 242) speaks of the " phenomena of the somnambulistic state taking the form of convulsions,* in which the impression of what the damsel had before heard of Paul reacted on, and became mingled with, her own heathen ideas." According to this explanation there is impressed on us, to say the least, a doubt as to how the Apostle could have treated the damsel as one possessed by an evil spirit, if she had merely been in a state of somnambulism. Olshausen gives no explanation of this, but Neander says (page 244), " There is no ground for assuming that an error could not possibly exist in the light of the Apostle's Christian conscious-

---

* We may observe by the way that there is not the least hint in the text of convulsions, or of a condition of ecstasy. I must likewise declare, as wholly foreign to the question, the assertion that persons who imparted oracles in an ecstatic condition, under the influence of powerful convulsions, could never return to that condition after their conversion to Christianity, as there is not a single word said in the text on the chief point on which the assertion is based, the conversion of the slave.

ness on such a subject as this, which does not affect belief in truth, but belongs to a perfectly different and lower province, namely, the question whether this must be taken as a phenomenon explicable from the nature of the human soul, from its natural powers, its connection with the corporeal organism, or as the consequence of possession by a personal evil spirit." It is very evident what dangerous consequences lie in this explanation for a standpoint like that of Neander. As Neander expressly says, that in a case like the foregoing, the possibility of error on the part of the Apostle may be assumed. Why may not this assumption be permitted in other like cases? Olshausen has already brought the demoniacs of the Gospel under the point of view of somnambulistic phenomena. May we, following the lead of Neander's assertion, suppose the possibility of error in the religious consciousness of Jesus himself? For the demoniacs of the Gospel are never described as being in a condition of somnambulism, but as being possessed by evil spirits.

With what right can it be further maintained, that a question of this sort does not properly belong to the sphere of belief in truth? As long as the doctrine of demons holds its peculiar place in the series of truths of the Christian faith, the question of the influence of demons, and its extent, must undoubtedly have a real religious importance, and it cannot be concluded without inconsequence that an Apostle enlightened by the divine Spirit may have been in error on the question whether in a certain case a demoniac influence existed or a natural phenomenon. If, however, we let such questions rest as they are, the supposition of a condition similar to the phenomena of somnambulism is in any case refuted in these passages. If the damsel was not really possessed by an evil spirit, how could the Apostle command the spirit with which she was afflicted to come out of her? What must we think of the preceding change in the damsel, if the Apostle was so much at fault respecting the cause of the malady with which she was visited?

Must we accept it as an operation of his miraculous power, in a case in which he did not even know on what object to direct it ? And how must we explain the displeasure which the outcries of the damsel excited in the Apostle, and the reproving earnestness which he brought to bear on them, if no evil spirit here asserted its existence ? Neander seems to have this question seriously before him, as he remarks (page 243), " The Apostle commanded the spirit which held her heart and reason imprisoned to come out of her. If this was not a personal evil spirit, it was yet under the control of an ungodly spirit. That which is free in man—which rules over all natural impulses and powers—was made subservient to such a spirit as this. And through the divine might of him who restored peace and harmony to the distracted soul of the demoniacally-afflicted damsel, she found herself in a changed condition, freed from the power of the ungodly spirit, and never again liable to become subject to such a condition." According to this, we are to suppose, an ungodly spirit, which is no personal evil spirit, a state of bondage to natural impulses and powers from which no one can free himself, and yet, at the same time, a state into which one can enter by choice and free-will. But what is gained by such half measures in reasoning ? To what purpose is such a rationalizing of miracles, when in other places there is no hesitation in heaping miracle on miracle ? We openly confess therefore, as the letter of the text requires, that an evil spirit is here spoken of, and that from our present standpoint we can distinguish the actual fact from the Apostle's conception of it, as little as from the account of the author. The displeasure of the Apostle and the miraculous act performed by him can therefore have no other reason than that, although the evil spirit unwillingly bore witness to the truth, the Apostle did not wish to see the acknowledgment of the truth promoted by demoniacal help. But the demon who here asserted his existence is called πνεῦμα πύθωνος. If we grant that the expression does not exactly necessitate the idea of such a spirit as the Pythian Apollo, yet it must be looked on in any case as something characteristic that it is here stated that the demon was " a spirit of divination." There existed also a special class of spirits of divination, who whilst they possessed, in common with the demons of the general Jewish-Christian idea, the superior knowledge that pertained to their race, had also the power of prophesying. But does not this lead us still further back into the heathen ·statement, which Plutarch (De def. Orac. 9.) indicates as something highly foolish and childish. "τὸν θεὸν αὐτὸν ὥσπερ τοὺς ἐγγαστριμύθους Εὐρυκλέας πάλαι, νυνὶ Πύθωνας προσαγορευομένους, ἐνδυόμενον εἰς τὰ σώματα τῶν προφητῶν ὑποφθέγγεσθαι, τοῖς ἐκείνων στόμασι καὶ φωναῖς χρώμενον ὀργάνοις." But if it is insisted that the demon as such was a spirit of divination, how can we think, how reconcile it with sound psychological ideas, that a demon as a superior being taking possession of men, was at the same time so completely in the service of the men it possessed, that the latter could make what use they pleased of the divining power of the demon, and could drive what bargain they pleased? This in fact surpasses even all that is said in the Gospels concerning the relations of demons with those possessed by them, and shows clearly that those interpreters who throw no doubt on the reality of demoniac possession feel that in this case they must take another course ; affording a fresh proof that a coherent narrative cannot be made out of the occurrences related.

The chief difficulties, however, as we have said, concentrate in some of the facts, to which those already spoken of form only the introduction. The contents of the narrative are shortly these : The masters of the slave, deprived of the gains which they made by her, owing to the expulsion of the spirit of divination, excited the people to an uproar by a charge of political innovation brought against Paul and Silas ; the result of which was that the Duumviri of the city of Philippi caused the two Apostles to be scourged with rods, thrown into the

deepest prison, and held in the strictest confinement. But at
midnight Paul and Silas raised a loud hymn, heard by all the
prisoners, which was followed immediately by a severe earthquake, causing the doors of the prison to be thrown open
and the fetters of the prisoners to be loosed. At the sight of
the open doors the keeper of the prison, thinking that the
prisoners had escaped, was about to throw himself on his
sword, when Paul called out to him with a loud voice that they
were all there, and he, falling at the feet of Paul and Silas,
asked, " What must I do to be saved ?" The answer was,
" Believe on the Lord Jesus Christ." The word of God was
then declared to him and to all his household, and they received
Christian baptism, whereupon this keeper of the prison, as an
expression of his joy, that same night arranged a festive meal.

Scarcely had the day broke when the Duumviri sent the
command to release Paul and Silas. But Paul declared that
they had suffered the indignity as Roman citizens, and it was
not fitting that they should be put out privily; that the
Duumviri should come in person and take them out of prison.
These magistrates, learning for the first time that they had
allowed these proceedings to be taken against Roman citizens,
actually came in person, led the Apostles out of prison, and
prayed them with friendly words to leave the city.

This simple summary of the chief points in the narrative
shows clearly enough how signally the whole course of the
matter fails in natural connexion. This objection by no means
applies merely to the miracle included in the account, the
reality of which is insisted on. The interpretation which
takes the earthquake, as a merely natural circumstance,
is in direct contradiction to the words and meaning of the
author. Neander gives this turn to the passage (page
245): " At midnight Paul and Silas joined in praising God in
prayer because an earthquake shook the foundations of the
prison." I can only see in this interpretation a transposition
which the text does not justify, as the author certainly does

not intend to represent the earthquake as the cause of the prayer, but as the consequence and operation of it. How can we believe that not only were the doors of the prison opened by the earthquake, but that it even loosened the fetters of the prisoners? Let us leave the miracle as we find it, as it is the only one in this part of the narrative which contains a certain kind of connexion; and let us take the circumstances which followed into consideration.

Whilst the two Apostles were singing and praying so loudly that all their fellow-prisoners heard them, the keeper of the prison alone lay in a deep sleep. When at last (as we must suppose, as soon as he was alarmed by the earthquake) he awoke and saw the doors of the prison opened, the first thing he did was to draw his sword in order to kill himself, without seeing whether the prisoners were really fled as he feared or not, before he resolved on this desperate deed. He also apparently never thought that the earthquake which awakened him might possibly have been the cause of the doors standing open, in which case no blame would have fallen on him; and when Paul called to him with a loud voice that they were all there, he threw himself at the feet of Paul and Silas without any visible cause. How did he know that the convulsion of the earth which he also took as miraculous had happened expressly for the sake of the Apostles? and assuming (although the author does not say so) that Paul and Silas had informed him of this, what could have decided him to place such implicit confidence in them on so short an acquaintance, and how could the Apostles themselves have given the assurance they did so confidently (28) in the darkness (29), which any of their fellow-prisoners might easily have made available for the purpose of flight? Is it likely further, that the keeper of the prison who just before would have killed himself on the spur of the moment, because he feared he had betrayed his trust without knowing how, now so completely forgot this fear and its cause—the Duumviri—that he carried off the two prisoners with him to his house and entertained them at a festival, as if he now at once were freed from all responsibility, although he could have no ground for the assumption that the Duumviri had changed their views with regard to the prisoners, and would leave him unpunished, with the trust of his office violated, and the express commands he had received contravened ? With the dawn of day the Duumviri, they who had the day before taken such harsh measures, and seemed about to take some still harsher, did indeed send the further command to let the two prisoners go ; but there is no connection to be seen here.* If we say they may have acted so strictly on the preceding day, merely on account of the people, this does not seem a very probable course of proceeding for Roman magistrates, and (xvi. 35) would rather give us to understand that although they were not over well pleased with the affair, yet the narrative undoubtedly tacitly implies that they had received a warning to act thus from the earthquake of which they must have been aware.

The improbabilities are not even yet sufficient. The Duumviri now first perceive that they have made a mistake in thus treating Roman citizens, and in order to spare themselves further disagreeable consequences, they go in person to the prison to ask forgiveness of the prisoners, and to promise they would not carry the affair any further. Can we imagine that Roman magistrates would conduct themselves in such a manner, and in a case where their official dignity was at stake, commit so striking an error which they could not retrieve ? Either it was a common practice to ask those who were liable to punishment first of all whether or not they were Roman citizens, or else it was concluded that those who were to be punished would pro-

---

* That this warrant of discharge was received by them in consequence of the impression they made on the gaoler, as Neander supposes, is the less likely, as so important a circumstance would not possibly have been overlooked by a faithful author. The narrative evidently will not warrant any outward motive of that kind.

claim their citizenship, and avail themselves of its privileges, as we find in a like case, Acts xxii. 25. If the first had been the case here, the enquiry would not have been omitted, but if the latter, if Paul and Silas had claimed the benefit of their Roman citizenship, the Duumviri would have been without justification. But in any case, we cannot conceive how it was they did not resolve in the first place to ward off the injustice about to be committed, as it was their duty to do, and as Paul did Acts xxii. 25, before he was beaten with rods, when he said to the centurion (εἰ ἄνθρωπον Ῥωμαῖον καὶ ἀκατάκριτον ἔξεστιν ὑμῖν μαστίζειν;) In this case the Apostles first said they were Roman citizens after they had received their punishment. Were they not themselves to blame for this? or could they reckon beforehand, that in a matter where the means by which they could have sufficiently secured themselves lay in their own hands, God had resolved to effect their complete release, and this by so striking a vindication? This is really the idea that lies at the foundation of this miraculous narrative. From the first the most illegal measures were taken against the two Apostles, and in the harshest manner. They were not merely beaten with rods, but thrust into the darkest dungeon, and watched with the greatest care, without any one seeming to know exactly what great crime they had committed. No enquiry was instituted, no legal forms were observed, nothing was done which was customary in Roman tribunals, and all this evidently with a view that God should have the more opportunity to give a complete vindication. It is a kind of triumphal cry to which Paul gives utterance, when he says to the despairing keeper of the prison (xvi. 28), "Do thyself no harm, for we are all here!" as though he would say, "It is by no means the case that we have made use of this miracle which has taken place on our account in order to set ourselves free. Ye must however now perceive whom ye have seized, and of how much ye are guilty against our honour." It is not enough that the keeper of the prison be converted in one moment, he must also directly prepare a festive meal, in order to show all honour to his distinguished prisoners. And all this—the conversion of the keeper of the prison and his whole household, their first instruction in Christianity, the baptism of the converted, the entertainment—happened in the same night, in the course of the few hours between midnight and morning. So powerful and enthralling was the impression made by the miracle, and in so august a light do the two Apostles appear! The Roman magistrates are now obliged to condescend so far as to repair to the prison in person in order to offer the fullest compensation to the two Apostles for the injustice they had endured. The question here may well be raised, whether such a trenchant claim for satisfaction, gratified by such a trifling outward formality, was thoroughly suitable to the character of the Apostles and worthy of them. Wetstein is the only one of the older interpreters who takes into consideration this question which so naturally presents itself. " Hoc Paulus debebat sibi ipsi, si enim clam abiisset, paullo post rumor fuisset sparsus, effracto carcere ipsum aufugisse, quæ res famæ et auctoritati apostolicæ apud Philippenses et alios multum nocuisset." But there is in fact no question of a secret dismissal comprised in the command sent by the Duumviri, and although the Duumviri may have set the Apostles free by an official command, and did not exactly lead them out of prison personally, we do not see how in any reasonable manner it can be inferred that Paul and Silas fled secretly. Everything was publicly conducted, and if the Apostles found it necessary to demand a special public recognition of their innocence, why did they ask for a vindication of their honour, which so easily gives rise to the idea that they were exhibiting egotistical feeling and carrying it to excess ?

Wetstein says still further, " Porro etiam jure civili et naturali tenebatur immunitem suam et civitatem Romanum asserare ; quid enim sunt immunitatem et jura, si quis ea negligat, et sibi eripi patiatur ? si alii omnes idem facerent, et qui nunc vivunt, et posteri ipsorum perpetuæ addicentur servituti et mancipiorum loco habebuntur. Boni autem civis est, facere ne˙ sua negligentia alii, quibuscum vivit, cives, et præcipue liberi nepotesque deterioris fiant conditiones quam fuissent absque eo." All this is quite true ; but we must all the more wonder why the Apostles, as it was their clear duty to do, did not at first make use of their Roman citizenship, and protest against so unjust and insulting a transaction. Even if they had wished not to claim the privilege till afterwards, we cannot see any reason why it must have been done exactly in this form.* In one word, the result of the judicial enquiry instituted against the Apostles is that they come out of it with increased glory, that they appear as lofty, unapproachable beings protected by Divine power.

This entire series of improbabilities brought together with such evident design, must cast the gravest suspicion on the historical character of the narrative. Even if it does not bear a mythical stamp, there is a shadow of the mythical over it. This is also a decided copy of what had before occurred at Philippi.

---

* Neander, p. 246, takes another direction, in order to vindicate the conduct of the Apostle. "If anything fanatical had been mixed up with the holy enthusiasm with which Paul bore all shame and suffering in the cause of the Lord, he certainly would have done nothing to escape from the shame which he might have avoided without prejudice, and with advantage to his office, and this in order to receive as an apology to his dignity what he might have received on account of his citizenship. This is not far from what in later times the morality of the monkish spirit called humility." Of such humility we indeed see no trace, but the question is not now of this, but rather of the contrary, he who stands not far from one extreme, is for that very reason not free from the suspicion of standing too near the other. Olshausen thinks that he can remove all difficulty by the remark that the Apostle may have acted towards mankind, generally, according to the jus talionis, whose legality they alone were in a condition to estimate. But is this the morality of Christian principle ? Whither must such a moral evasion lead in the judgment of others, and in what direct contradiction does this jus talionis stand to the command of Jesus, Matthew v. 38, 39. Again, it must be taken into consideration, with regard to Silas, that all token of Roman citizenship in his case is wanting —nothing at all is said of it—but on the other hand we cannot blame Grotius when he says that Paul here speaks "communicative"—he ascribes only " per synecdochen," the Roman citizenship to his companion Silas, but then it must be granted that the Romans would scarcely have been willing to allow such a synecdoche, since the nature of their legal relations would scarcely allow such an application.

11 *

The whole tenor of the narrative tends to exhibit the disgrace
of the opponents who are themselves made to aid in this design,
whilst they are interfering in so remarkable a manner with the
two preachers of the Gospel. Nothing less is done to them
than to beat them with rods, to put them in chains, and to
thrust them into the darkest dungeons. But if a fitting satisfaction for this were demanded, something would be necessary
on their side to enable them to act in the best and most legal
manner. To this end nothing could more naturally offer itself
than the well-known fact that the Apostle Paul was in possession of Roman citizenship. But if he were to make use of
this right with any result, nothing must be alleged against it
by Roman magistrates. Romans must acknowledge Roman
citizenship. Roman magistrates would therefore be obliged to
relinquish all proceedings of any kind whatever against the two
Apostles, as illegal. But Roman magistrates could only be
supposed to be in a Roman municipal city, and such a city was
Philippi as a Roman colony. Also at the first mention of the
city of Philippi it was remarked that it was a Roman colony,
and everything that is related of the residence of the two
Apostles in Philippi seems only to be told, as an introduction to
what afterwards took place between them and the Roman
magistrates. They were obliged to pass many days at the
house of Lydia, because the affair with the possessed damsel is
represented as extending over many days,* and this occurrence
was the cause of the more important events which followed.
Everything is here introduced with this ulterior motive, to
enhance the effect of the chief scene, the glorification of the
Apostle and his companion. And what is the foundation of
all this? The apologetic parallel between the Apostle Peter

---

* Not without reason does it seem specially indicated (xvi. 18) that the damsel
acted in this manner during several days (17.). This is evidently the cause of
the Apostle's " grief " (the διαπονεῖσθαι, iv. 2). This " grief " is given as the most
immediate cause of the expulsion of the demon. The more cause the Apostle had
for " grief " in the behaviour of the damsel, the more unjust appears what afterwards
occurred.

and the Apostle Paul. Twice was Peter in a miraculous manner released from prison. The first time when he had been thrown into a dungeon with the rest of the Apostles at the command of the Sanhedrim, v. 19 ; the second time when, after the execution of the elder James, king Herod destined the same fate for him, xii. 3. The Apostle Paul must therefore not be back-ward in giving a similar token of the divine miraculous power which animated him. If according to the analogy of the charac-ters in the Acts of the Apostles the Pauline miracle is only to be looked at as a reflex of the Petrine, then the question as to the actual reality of such miraculous narratives must be raised upon the first event, of which the latter is but a copy. The copy can only be understood from the original. It will therefore not be out of place in the interest of the enquiry before us if we look a little closer into the nature of this Petrine miracle which is here reflected in Paul.

The narrative of the hostile measures which king Herod Agrippa took against the Christian Church at Jerusalem, (Acts xii.) stands altogether alone. There is nothing said about the cause which led the king to act in so extremely harsh a manner all at once towards the Apostles who had remained unmolested in Jerusalem during the first persecution, nor why the elder James, who is otherwise not specially mentioned, had drawn particular attention upon himself. Neither is there any question of what took place in the sequel in Jerusalem against the Apostles there, and the whole proceeding is so much the more astonishing, as Josephus is not only completely silent on these events, but espe-cially praises the mild, beneficent mind of the king, who was in no way inclined to cruelty.* There is only one indication of a point of contact between the Acts of the Apostles and the narrative of Josephus. According to Acts xii. 3, the king seems to have

* Antiq. 19, 7, 3: Ἐπεφύκει δὲ ὁ βασιλεὺς οὗτος—ἡδόμενος τῷ χαρίζεσθαι καὶ τῷ βιοῦν ἐν εὐφημία χαιρῶν, κατ' οὐδὲν Ἡρώδῃ τῷ πρὸ ἑαυτοῦ βασιλεῖ τὸν τρόπον συμφερόμενος ἐκείνῳ γὰρ πονηρὸν ἦν ἦθος ἐπὶ τιμωρίαν ἀπότομον—πραὺς δὲ ὁ τρόπος Ἀγρίππα καὶ πρὸς πάντας τὸ εὐεργετικὸν ὅμοιον.

been actuated when he took these persecuting measures by his desire to render himself pleasing to the people. Josephus especially brings forward this desire for popularity and indeed connects it with a strong adherence to the national worship.* In this respect, what is stated in the Acts of the Apostles seems to be confirmed. The zeal of the king for the established national worship would have made him hate a sect which however closely it might adhere to Judaism, still because it acknowledged the name of Jesus who had been condemned by the Jewish authorities, had excited against itself a suspicion of religious innovation. On the other hand we find no trace of the harsh measures against the Christian Church at Jerusalem being calculated to gain popularity ; —indeed Josephus relates a case in which judging by analogy the contrary seems to be indicated. I mean the well known narrative in which he relates the death of James the Just in accordance with the text of the tradition. He says, Antiq. xx. 9: Ὁ δὲ νεώτερος Ἄνανος ὃν τὴν ἀρχιερωσύνην ἔφαμεν παρειληφέναι, θρασὺς ἦν τὸν τρόπον καὶ τολμητὴς διαφερόντως· αἵρεσιν δὲ μετῄει τὴν Σαδδου-καίων, ὅπερ εἰσὶ περὶ τὰς κρίσεις ὠμοὶ παρὰ πάντας τοὺς Ἰουδαίους καθὼς ἤδη δεδηλώκαμεν· ἅτε δὴ οὖν τοιοῦτος ὢν ὁ Ἄνανος, νομίσας ἔχειν καιρὸν ἐπιτήδειον, διὰ τὸ τεθνάναι μὲν Φῆστον, Ἀλβῖνον δὲ ἔτι κατὰ τὴν ὁδὸν ὑπάρχειν, καθίζει συνέδριον κριτῶν· καὶ παρα-γαγὼν εἰς αὐτὸ (τὸν ἀδελφὸν Ἰησοῦ τοῦ λεγομένου Χριστοῦ Ἰάκωβος ὄνομα αὐτῷ, καὶ) τινὰς (ἑτέρους) ὡς παρανομησάντων κατηγορίαν ποιησάμενος παρέδωκε λευσθησομένους. Ὅσοι δὲ ἐδόκουν ἐπιεικέστατοι τῶν κατὰ τὴν πόλιν εἶναι καὶ τὰ περὶ τοὺς νόμους ἀκριβεῖς, βαρέως ἤνεγκαν ἐπὶ τούτῳ, καὶ πέμπουσι πρὸς τὸν βασιλέα (the King Agrippa of Acts xxv. 13, the son of Herod Agrippa, Acts xii. 1), κρύφα παρακαλοῦντες αὐτὸν ἐπισ-τεῖλαι τῷ Ἀνάνῳ μηκέτι τοιαῦτα πράσσειν· μηδὲ γὰρ τὸ πρῶτον ὀρθῶς αὐτὸν πεποιηκέναι. Τινὲς δὲ αὐτῶν καὶ τὸν Ἀλβῖνον

---

* Antiq. 10, 7, 8: Ἤδεια γοῦν αὐτῷ δίαιτα καὶ συνεχὴς ἐν τοῖς Ἱεροσολύμοις ἦν, καὶ τὰ πάτρια καθαρῶς ἐτήρει διὰ πάσης γοῦν αὐτὸν ἦγεν ἀγνείας, οὐδὲ ἡμέρα τις παρώδευεν αὐτῷ, τῆς νομίμης χηρεύουσα θυσίας.

ὑπαντιάζουσιν ἀπὸ τῆς Ἀλεξανδρείας ὁδοιπορο*ῦντα* καὶ διδάσκουσιν ὡς οὐκ ἐξὸν ἦν Ἀνάνῳ χωρὶς τῆς ἐκείνου γνώμης καθίσαι
συνέδριον. Ἀλβῖνος δὲ πεισθεὶς τοῖς λεγομένοις γράφει μετ᾽
ὀργῆς τῷ Ἀνάνῳ, λήψεσθαι παρ᾽ αὐτοῦ δίκας ἀπειλῶν, καὶ ὁ βασιλεὺς Ἀγρίππας διὰ τοῦτο τὴν ἀρχιερωσύνην ἀφελόμενος αὐτὸν
ἄρξαντα μῆνας τρεῖς Ἰησοῦν τὸν τοῦ Δαμναίου κατέστησεν.

It is confessedly very doubtful whether Josephus really
speaks especially of James in this place; the passage is in all
probability to be read without the concluding words, which
seem to be only a Christian gloss. But at the same time
scarcely anything else except Christians can be understood by
that παρανομήσαντες. And indeed, if the apocryphal sounding
narrative of Hegesippus (Euseb. H. E. ii. 23) contains any
truth regarding the death of James the Just he must at that
time have perished by some violent means or other. According
to Hegesippus James the Just was stoned, and not at the
instigation of the populace, but at that of the chiefs of the
sect (τινὲς τῶν ἑπτὰ αἱρέσεων τῶν ἐν τῷ λαῷ (Eus. ib.) by
which we understand the Pharisees to be meant, because at
the same time mention is made of their doctrine of the denial
of the resurrection, (αἱ δὲ αἱρεσεῖς αἱ προειρημέναι οὐκ ἐπίστευον
οὔτε ἀνάστασιν, οὔτε ἐρχόμενον ἀποδοῦναι ἑκάστῳ κατὰ τὰ ἔργα
αὐτοῦ).

If we now compare the case related by Josephus with that
mentioned in the Acts of the Apostles we easily perceive that,
as at that time of which Josephus speaks, a deed of violence
had been committed against a member of the Church at
Jerusalem, and perhaps even against its chief, such an one
may have already happened earlier under King Herod Agrippa.
Apparently at that time a high priest belonging to the sect of
the Sadducees aided in the matter. At any rate, according to
Josephus, Antiq. xix. 6, 4, the King stood in a very close connection with the then High Priest. That in any case an act of
cruelty was committed against the Church by Herod Agrippa,
and as the Acts of the Apostles relates, the elder James

died a violent death, receives still further confirmation from the
original Christian legends concerning the death of this king,
which—according to the kind of death described by Josephus—would not have been represented in the manner related,
(Acts vii. 19)* if there had not existed a reason for such a narrative being given with immediate reference to the Christian
Church. But the above quotation from Josephus shows quite
clearly how unpopular such persecuting measures were, and
the conclusion is very obvious, that the act of violence subsequently committed by the High Priest Ananus excited general
displeasure among all the right-thinking orderly inhabitants
of Jerusalem, and occasioned the measures spoken of by

---

* If we compare the narrative of the death of the king (Acts xii. 19), with that
in Josephus, Antiq. xix. 8, 2, we see a remarkable similarity running through all
the differences which exist in the accounts. Josephus also places the sickness and
death of the king in direct connection with the festivities of the day, and with the
indecorous honour which was shown to the king by the sycophantic people. The
historical fact which lies at the root of both narratives, namely the sudden death of
the king, occurring shortly after the festival days, allows of no doubt; and Josephus
also seems to have considered it as a divinely sent punishment, or else he would not
have placed it in such direct relation to the superhuman honours of which he speaks.
Josephus indeed does not say anything of an angel of death, but speaks of an owl
as the ominous prophet of death. Still less does Josephus say anything of the
king's living body being devoured by worms; according to his narrative, the sickness was only a very severe pain in the bowels; but even this account of the sickness shows evidently a point of connection with the Christian legend. The piercing,
gnawing, inwardly devouring pains—what are they when mythically presented but
worms devouring the living body? But what inducement could there be to paint
the disease from which the king died in such glaring colours as to attribute it to the
gnawing worms which torment the damned in hell? (Mark ix. 44, compare Jos.
66, 44). We may answer this question if we call to mind that King Antiochus
Epiphanes is reported to have died in the same manner, that king so hated by the
Jews, the cruel persecutor of all true worshippers of God, the enemy of true
religion, who with presumptuous audacity assumed a hostile attitude towards the
Most High. Compare Macc. iv. 5. This deadly enemy of the Jewish name, the
tyrannical Antiochus Epiphanes, seems to exist again in the person of King Herod
Agrippa, who persecuted the believing disciples, put to death the Apostle James,
and intended the same fate for the Apostle Peter; the overbearing, ungodly adversary, who at last even usurped divine honours. How clearly we see here a legend
expressed in the Christian interest; and when we compare a Christian legend so
purposely prepared with the narrative of Josephus, what light is thrown on the
historical events out of which it arose !

Josephus, so that the Roman Procurator Albinus thought himself obliged to interfere, and King Agrippa, on just the same ground, deprived the High Priest Ananus of his office. These steps were not received with greater favour by the people than similar ones had been when taken by Herod Agrippa ; and those individuals who exercised most influence over the King, were of a different opinion in the matter. On this account we need not hesitate in laying to the credit of his acknowledged bias, what the author of the Acts of the Apostles says regarding the satisfaction of the people at the proceedings of the King. This bias is the more evident as the remark, xvi. 3, that it " pleased the people," stands in the closest connection with the preceding narrative of the miracle and the chief occurrence in it, namely the saving of Peter, ἐκ πάσης τῆς προσδοκίας τοῦ λαοῦ τῶν Ἰουδαίων. xii. 11. From this well-grounded historical statement we get a certainly not improbable connexion with that which the Acts of the Apostles relates in the same manner concerning the Apostle Peter. The same fate threatened the Apostle Peter, and he would have been publicly executed, had it not been that the celebration of the feast of the Passover, which occurred at the time, caused a delay. The intentions of the King however would not thus have been delayed, but the Apostle Peter would have been released in a perfectly unexpected manner. According to the narrative in the Acts of the Apostles, this occurred by a miracle, but in pursuance of the views above stated, how natural it is to suppose that the King himself desisted from his purpose, and of course unexpectedly released the Apostle Peter, because in the interval he had ascertained how unpopular his proceedings were, and how little the execution of the Apostle James had found that favour with the people which he had anticipated. If we look at the release of the Apostle from prison with as little doubt as we do on his imprisonment, how can we explain it otherwise than by some such sudden a turn in affairs as seems to be indicated by the circumstances spoken of by the author of the Acts of the

Apostles and in part by Josephus? According to Acts xii. 19, King Herod left Jerusalem directly after the release of the Apostle Peter and went to Cæsarea. Josephus agrees with this, and says at the same time the third year of his reign was over.* As the beginning of his reign was coincident with the reign of the Emperor Claudius, *i.e.* the end of January of the year 41 A.D., we are justified, according to Josephus, in placing the departure of the King to Cæsarea at the time in which it is placed by the Acts of the Apostles, directly after Easter, A.D. 44. This departure of the King, who, as Josephus says, would not else have left Jerusalem for some time, must have been caused by some special reason which determined him to take this step. We must now take into consideration that Josephus directly after says in explanation of this, that the King had deprived the High Priest Matthias of his office, Antiq. xiv. 4. This dismissal must have taken place on some special grounds, as Matthias had been elected High Priest by King Herod himself, under conditions which certainly implied friendly relations. (Antiq. xix. 64.) After the execution of which Josephus speaks in the former place, and which perhaps is that of James the Less, the High Priest Ananus, as the instigator of the proceedings which had been so much disliked, was deprived of his office. In the case of which we are now speaking, may not the dismissal of the High Priest Matthias have been owing to the same cause?

The Apostle Peter also is truly released from prison in a manner perfectly unexpected, after what had occurred to James the elder; but the miraculous way in which this was brought about by an angel of the Lord is only a Christian legend or poem, which explains in its own manner the darkness which at that time enveloped the whole matter, and ascribes the happy issue of the whole affair to the direct operation of a higher causality. If the Apostle were unexpectedly set free, as soon as the release

---

* Antiq. xix. 82: τρίτον δὲ ἔτος βασιλεύοντι τῆς ὅλης Ἰουδαίας πεπλήρωται καὶ παρῆν εἰς πόλιν Καισάρειαν.

becomes represented as a miracle, we are forced, as the most immediate consequence, to perceive that the intentions of the enemy are frustrated in the most surprising manner. On this account not only is the wondering expectation with which all the people waited for the promised show of a public execution brought prominently forward, v. 11 ; but it is also remarked as a remarkable circumstance that the Apostle was released in the night which preceded his destined execution. Can we wonder that on the next morning when the affair was discovered the greatest commotion ensued, and that the deceived King vented his anger on the soldiers to whose charge the prisoner had been consigned, and that he caused the death destined for the Apostle to be inflicted on his keepers. In such a case as this, if once the legend takes this direction, everything is turned to account which can heighten the dramatic effect. And we have accordingly here a circumstantial relation of measures taken in the most careful manner for watching the prisoner. Four quaternions of soldiers had been detached to keep watch at night alternately, so that two soldiers to whom the prisoner in the middle was bound by two chains were inside the prison, and two others stood outside the door, xii. 4, 6. It must be seen also that this truly Roman proceeding was nothing extraordinary on the part of a King accustomed to Roman manners and customs, but at the same time heedful of national customs ; but then why are all these details of this strict watch given here, and not in chapter xvi., where one should expect to find them, as being customary in a Roman colony ? Evidently because they would not have accorded with the scene with the keeper of the prison in chapter xvi., whereas in chapter xii. they are quite in the right place, in order to show incontestably how important this matter was considered, and how much we must confess was done in order to make the release of the Apostle from prison impossible. But was there any reason for such great fear and apprehension ? No one could have expected a miracle—the Christians themselves did not think of one,* and if such an expectation had existed, the measures taken would have been thought perfectly useless. But again we find something in this very peculiar; as though the enemy had a presentiment of what did really afterwards happen, and took every precaution which seemed to them possible against it; and yet in order to make sure could only presuppose the affair as certain, in order to provide the better against its not taking place. This is evidently a mode of proceeding which bears with it an irony in the contrast of the intention with the result—but an irony which can only be appreciated from a Christian standpoint. But if the affair really took place as is here represented, how unlikely it appears. How badly the four soldiers placed with such care on guard must have fulfilled their duty, if so shortly before daybreak they allowed themselves to be so completely overcome with sleep, that the Apostle could have escaped unhindered from the midst of his keepers lying around in slumber. This must have been shortly before daybreak, because if it had been earlier, the escape would not have been first discovered in the morning (xii. 15); but at least when the third τετράδιον was released, between the third and fourth night watches. This profound sleep of the keepers must therefore have been brought about in a miraculous manner, and in reality the miracle is here evidently brought to view in a series of events which have every resemblance to magical operations. The Apostle likewise lying in a deep sleep was awakened by a blow on the side, suddenly freed from the chains which fell from his hands, stood up, dressed himself and went out without any hindrance through gates and guards. And even after he had successfully passed through the gates and guards of the prison, the iron gates leading into the city are made to spring open before him, as though not to neglect a theatrical idea,

---

* The Acts cannot picture strongly enough the great astonishment of the disciples at the Apostle's miraculous release from prison, xii. 23-16. And yet we cannot avoid asking, Why were they so much astonished? would they not rather have expected such a miracle, as one had already happened in a perfectly similar case, Acts v. 19.

which is here made of special effect. The effect which a series of miracles so completely out of the sphere of reality must have is indeed indicated by the author himself, when he remarks that the Apostle thought he had seen a vision, and that only after he had again come to his full consciousness was he able to decide exactly between reality and vision—truth and fancy. But we cannot ignore the question how the Apostle, who alone is of any worth here as a witness, could have been so certain that all this had been performed by an angel, if he had not been more clearly conscious of what had happened. The miraculous narrative thus bears with it its own refutation.

If the historic fact to which the two miraculous narratives, Acts xii. and xvi. (as well as the earlier one Acts v. 19, &c.) have been made to refer, possesses any probability, a further conclusion may be drawn as to the relations existing at that time in the Christian Church at Jerusalem. As the members of this Church still strictly adhered to the Jewish religion, observed its laws and customs, and only separated themselves from the rest of the Jews because they believed in Jesus as the Messiah which had appeared, it cannot be supposed that the Jews in Jerusalem placed any great obstacle in their way. They were willingly tolerated as long as they did not come to any such openly pronounced breach with the Jewish laws, as had been the case with Stephen and the Hellenists allied with him. But it was far otherwise with the chiefs of the Jewish nation. The establishment of a sect whose Founder they had removed out of the way by a public sentence of condemnation, must have been peculiarly disliked by them. It is therefore not improbable that the persecution of the Christians had really been of an earlier date, and as, according to Josephus, those who were appointed to the highest offices of state were chiefly Sadducees, we may believe the author of the Acts of the Apostles, when he says that such oppressive measures were generally taken by the Sadducees. This party would undoubtedly have taken further steps of this kind if they had had full liberty of action, and had not been restrained partly by regard to the Roman Procurator, and partly by the disposition of the people. But anything besides which is represented as proceeding from the general position of the affair is very uncertain. All the rest may be concluded to be a miraculous narrative, which can be placed to the account of tradition, or to the peculiar mode of statement employed by the author of the Acts of the Apostles ; in any case we must look upon it as a peculiar feature in the Acts of the Apostles, that such important miracles as those we have been considering, are always represented in it as twofold. Nothing extraordinary can happen to Peter which is not repeated with regard to Paul : and again, nothing can be shown about Paul, at all affecting him in a peculiar manner, without the exact counterpart being shadowed forth as affecting Peter. This original peculiarity of the mode of statement adopted by the author of the Acts of the Apostles is clearly presented to us in the miracle related in Acts xvi.

CHAPTER VII.

FROM Philippi the Apostle took his way with his two companions, Timotheus and Silas, to Thessalonica, and from thence
to Athens. After a short stay there, he went on further to
Corinth, in order to remain a longer time in a place better
adapted for his work. During the year and a half of his stay
there, he founded, under great difficulties, the first important
Church in Greece. After he had made from thence a journey
to Jerusalem and Antioch, the city of Ephesus became the
chief seat of his labours; the results of which, according to
the Acts of the Apostles, were of such importance in resisting
the demoniacal and magic power of the old religion and its
idolatrous worship as to give rise to a public contest between
the old and the new faiths. He travelled once more from
Macedonia into Greece, and then after a residence of three
months took that important journey to Jerusalem, which had
already filled him with the most gloomy forebodings when he
summoned the Ephesian elders to him at Miletus, and expressed to them his presentiments. According to the statement of the Acts of the Apostles, the most determined hatred
was shown towards the Apostle by the Jews in every place
where he dwelt, either for a long or a short space of time.
With regard to the persons named as Aquila, Priscilla and
Apollos, there are several special points of agreement with the
Epistles of the Apostle. He met Aquila, a Jew of Pontus, and
his wife Priscilla in Corinth, when he went there for the first
time. Apollos, a Jew of Alexandria, with whom Aquila and
Priscilla became acquainted at Ephesus, was there at the time

when the Apostle took his way through Galatia and Phrygia to Ephesus, and from thence to Corinth, where his activity was exerted in rather a peculiar manner in the development of the relations at that time existing in the Corinthian Church. In this part of the Acts of the Apostles, the chief part of the life and work of the Apostle is presented to us, partly by his speeches, partly by miracles, in both of which critical survey can only recognize, through the veil of much foreign matter, a very obscure reflection of historical truth.

The celebrated speech which the Apostle delivered at Athens is introduced by a narrative to which historical criticism must take as much exception as it does to the speech itself. The chief reason for this critical doubt is the evident design which pervades the whole. Everything belonging to the acknow-ledged characteristic traits of the Athenian character is pur-posely sought for, and arranged in order, so that the contrast which in this brilliant seat of Grecian culture, must have been presented between Christianity and polytheistic heathenism, and between the Christian and the popular character, may be brought forward as prominently as possible. How completely the historian carries on his narrative from this point of view is shown from its very commencement. This reigning idea to which all that follows bears reference, namely the striking contrast between Christianity and heathenism, as the latter appeared in its most brilliant aspect in Athens, is ascribed to the Apostle himself, when the author represents him as moved by the most intense emotion at the first view of the city so "wholly given to idolatry." The Apostle is described here as acting differ-ently from his usual custom. Instead of waiting for the way to be opened for the preaching of the Gospel to the Gentiles through the Jews and proselytes in the synagogue, and seeking an opportunity for religious conversation among those whom he met in the public places, the Apostle is shown as disputing with the Epicurean and Stoic philosophers, adherents of the same philosophic sects which afterwards raised the greatest opposition against Christianity, and in all his connection with the Athenians, they are represented as repeating the behaviour they had already shown on other similar occasions. How clear it is that there was present in the mind of the author, when he put these words into the mouths of the Athenians, ξένων δαιμονίων δοκεῖ καταγγελεὺς εἶναι, that which had been charged against Socrates when he was accused. Xenophon. Memor. 1. 1, οὒς μὲν ἡ πόλις νομίζει θεοὺς, οὐ νομίζων, ἕτερα δὲ καινὰ δαιμόνια εἰσφέρων, and what does the mocking speech of the Athenians mean, τί ἂν θέλοι ὁ σπερμολόγος οὗτος λέγειν: except the same light, trivial, sophistical banter, that serves Aristophanes in the " Clouds " as a veil beneath which he can make the seriousness of the Socratic philosophy, whose founder was also in the eyes of the people only a σπερμολόγος, the subject of his wit and mockery. How strikingly the author paints the well-known ironical popular wit, in the characteristics which he ascribes to the Athenians, when he represents them, according to the polytheistic mythological manner, as including in a divine pair Jesus and the ἀνάστασις.*

If the historian had wished, according to his evident intention, to give a general view of the characteristics of the Athenians, he ought just as little to have omitted their very characteristic irony, as their equally peculiar curiosity, which he goes on to describe in almost the same words in which it is painted by the old authors themselves. It therefore could only have been curiosity which awakened in the Athenians a certain interest in the Gospel preached by Paul, and which caused them to grant a hearing to a discourse of the Apostle delivered in the Areopagus. But even this appearance of the Apostle

---

* So must the words, xvii. 18: τὸν Ἰησοῦν καὶ τὴν ἀνάστασιν, undoubtedly be taken. Among the modern interpreters of the Acts, Meyer in especial finds it very strange that the philosophers thought the Ἀνάστασις to be a goddess revealed by Paul. If Luke had aimed at this in his explanatory note, he would have indicated it more decidedly; and would the Athenian philosophers have been so ignorant? Of course it could not have been ignorance on the part of the author, but irony : and then does not the author sufficiently show this sense of the expression when he twice puts the article before the word.

in the Areopagus throws a new and very doubtful light on the
whole affair, and is exactly the point from which we can most
clearly see the connexion of this narrative.   We must ask
accordingly, why was it precisely in the Areopagus that the
Apostle delivered his discourse ?   The most likely answer
undoubtedly is that to the Areopagetic court of justice was
committed the care of matters of religion.   The Apostle would
be brought for his legal defence to the Areopagus, on account
of the ξένα δαιμόνια which he was accused of introducing, as
Chrysostom among the elder commentators supposes, ἦγον αὐτὸν
εἰς τὸν ἄρειον πάγον οὐχ ὥστε μαθεῖν ἀλλ᾿ ὥστε κολάζειν ἔνθα
αἱ φονικαὶ δίκαι.   But there is not the least hint of this ; the
whole affair as treated by the Apostle and shown by the sequel,
makes it perfectly clear that curiosity was the only motive
which prompted the Athenians to lead the Apostle to the
Areopagus, for they saw in him only a harmless enthusiast,
but not a dangerous heretic ; here it is not unimportant to remember that we must not think of the locality of the court of
justice strictly so called, but of the open space which was on
the hill.   In this case also we may suppose that the same
irony is shown in the choice of a locality, which is displayed in
the whole treatment of the Apostle.   The narrative very decidedly represents the Athenians as taking up the affair with
an ironical temper, (δυνάμεθα γνῶναι, τίς ἡ καινὴ αὕτη ἡ ὑπό
σου λαλουμένη διδαχή ; ξενίζοντα γάρ τινα εἰσφέρεις εἰς τὰς
ἀκοὰς ἡμῶν. βουλόμεθα οὖν γνῶναι τί ἄν θέλοι ταῦτα εἶναι.
19-20.) and so little is there any thing serious mixed with it that
the scene is laid in the Areopagus, for the express purpose of
contrasting the importance of the place with the confessed insignificance of the affair.   But just as little as there seems to
be any doubt as to why the Apostle was led to Areopagus, so
much the more striking is it that the Dionysius converted by
the Apostle should be called the Areopagite.   This surname
would seem to indicate that Dionysius, as a member of the
Court of Justice, had become acquainted with Christianity, and

had been converted to the Christian faith at the time when the
Apostle delivered his speech before the assembled court. Why
should the name be here expressly brought forward, if not to
indicate the occasion of his conversion? Or can it be held as
an accidental circumstance that when the Apostle was led to
the Areopagus, one, among the few converted by him, was an
Areopagite? But if he had been converted as an Areopagite,
we must assume that the Apostle appeared before the whole
assembled Court of Justice. How shall we explain this am-
biguity with regard to the cause of the speech of the Apostle in
the Areopagus? The explanation as I believe is as follows:—
Ecclesiastical tradition speaks of a Dionysius with the surname
of Areopagite who was the first Bishop of Athens. According
to Eusebius (H. E. iv. 23.) Bishop Dionysius of Corinth wrote
an epistle to Athens, as he had done to other churches, in
which he admonished the members of the Athenian Church to
faith and to a Gospel manner of living, as since their Bishop
Biblius had died as a martyr in the persecutions of these times,
they had become indifferent, and had almost fallen away from
the Christian faith, until Quadratus the successor of the martyr
Publius re-animated their faith by his zeal. Eusebius remarks
that in the same epistle Dionysius mentions Dionysius the
Areopagite as the first Bishop of Athens, who was converted
by the Apostle Paul. The interpreter of this passage in Eusebius rightly observes that if Publius who died as a martyr
under Marcus Aurelius had been the immediate successor of
Dionysius the Areopagite, the latter must have been Bishop of
Athens for more than 70 years. There must have been other
Bishops between Dionysius and Publius, but the tradition says
nothing of them, it speaks only of the first Bishop, Dionysius
the Areopagite. Must we look upon our passage in the Acts
of the Apostles as the source of this tradition? We should of
course be obliged to assume this, if we had no other reason
for doubting the historical trustworthiness of the narrative
contained in it. But as we have already seen, other reasons

12 *

do exist, and thus we are justified in reversing the matter and assuming that Dionysius the Areopagite was imported into our passage in the Acts of the Apostles from ecclesiastical tradition, and only on this supposition can the whole scene in the Areopagus be satisfactorily explained. An old ecclesiastical legend mentions one Dionysius an Areopagite, as among the first who accepted the Christian faith in Athens; but does not say whether he was really an Areopagite, or had only received that surname because it was thought to show the goodwill towards Christianity of a member of that honourable senate. But in order still further to show the reason of his conversion, the legend says, in mentioning the surname, that he was converted in the Areopagus itself, and on what occasion can we imagine this conversion to have been more likely to occur than at the time when the Apostle came to Athens on his journey from Macedonia to Corinth. There cannot therefore be any doubt that the Apostle entered the Areopagus itself. Doubtless the legend gave no further account of the occasion on which this happened, as the author of the Acts of the Apostles found. So much the more was he therefore at liberty to carry out the idea which he had proposed to himself, by means of the Areopagite Dionysius mentioned in the legend. The whole nature of the passage leads to no other supposition than that the author intended to describe, by the reception which the Apostle received in Athens, how Christianity was considered and judged in the time when the author lived, as well by the educated people generally, to whom the Athenians were the highest ideal of the finest spiritual culture, as by the principal philosophic sects, the Epicureans and the Stoics, whose chief seat was also at Athens. Judging from what he says, there was floating before his mind a time in which Christianity had indeed drawn on itself the observation of the educated and the philosophers, but a time also when it was considered by them with marked contempt as a fanciful folly. The irony, which at a later date took so cutting and bitter a tone in Lucian and

Celsus, spoke also at that time, only in a milder and more gentle form. It is a fact worthy of special remark, that the author makes the doctrine of the resurrection the chief point on which the whole transaction between the Apostle and the Athenians turns. From the very beginning this doctrine is maintained against the Gentile opponents as the most characteristic of Christianity. Against it was especially directed the mocking scorn with which the Apostle was met, and as soon as it was introduced into his speech, it was enough to cause the audience to declare that they would no longer listen to him, or to anything he had to say further. In this is shown the same offence which the Gentiles took with regard to accepting this doctrine as soon as they became more familiar with Christianity, and the first persecutions gave occasion for a more decided expression of the Christian hope of a resurrection, as a compensation for the suffering martyrs. To such a time as this we must take this passage as referring. The author of the Acts of the Apostles wished to depict the marked supercilious scorn on the part of the Gentiles towards the Christianity with which they were scarcely yet acquainted. Such a scene as this in Athens was especially suited to such an aim. The ironical inquisitive Athenians, treating all things, even the holiest, in a light and frivolous manner, were the worthiest representatives of this side of the Gentile character. The occurrence in the Areopagus, which seems to pre-suppose the traditionally given name of the Areopagite Dionysius, may therefore not have been intended to be taken seriously, as the author's principal point of view was a completely different one. Many things which are not taken literally in poetry and legend, must be looked upon quite differently when the affair is considered as a reality, so the author had no scruple on this occasion in representing this solemn venerated spot as having been thrown open to the public, who had gathered together to satisfy their curiosity and indulge their love of ridicule.

The most striking point in the speech, after its carefully designed introduction, is the sudden change with which it passes to the doctrine of the resurrection as soon as its principal object is attained, namely, the exhortation to the acceptance of Christianity. We see that as soon as it is in any way possible, this doctrine is designedly introduced, and brought forward as the chief doctrine of Christianity, although the Apostle must have known from experience that it was precisely the point adapted to give the most offence to the Athenians. To what purpose then did the speech so studiously include the resurrection, when the subject might so easily have been avoided, or at least longer postponed? This speech is commonly brought forward as an example of apologetic teaching, and as greatly redounding to the praise of the Apostle's wisdom in instruction. But has it been also considered that it contributes above all to the advantage of the chief idea in which the speaker was interested? Is it then so remarkable a token of a discourse being to the purpose, that the hearers, before the speaker had arrived at the explanation of his principal thought, should take so great offence at the contents of his speech as to go away? It rather would seem to follow that the Apostle, if he were not acting in opposition to the wisdom in teaching, which characterized him in so high a degree, could not have delivered this speech as we possess it. It is only the author who wishes to bring plainly before us the obstacle which this doctrine of the resurrection presented to educated Gentiles like the Athenians, in conformity with the main idea which he is carrying out in this passage. Even that part of the speech in which interpreters think they perceive most clearly the Apostle's renowned wisdom in teaching, presents a totally different aspect if we consider the doctrine of the resurrection, mentioned at the conclusion, as the chief topic of the speech itself. It cannot be disputed that the speaker, much to the credit of his speech, conformed as nearly as possible to the religious opinions of his audience, placed himself as much as possible on the same standpoint with them, in order by these means more easily to win them over to his own

views. Although the contents of this speech are so strictly
monotheistic, it contains many propositions whose chief ideas
are found in almost the same words in Greek and Roman
authors. The speaker, in one of the principal ideas of the
speech, quotes the exact words of a Greek poet, thus giving
undoubted evidence that by such a quotation he wished to
place himself on a common footing of agreement and sympathy
with his hearers. It was in conformity with his chief aim to
represent the age of polytheism as a time of ignorance, which
God had been willing to overlook, provided that the Gentiles
would now change their opinions, and turn to Him. The
necessity of such a conversion is shown by an idea which lay
within the religious consideration of the Gentiles, the idea of
future retribution. But when, notwithstanding that the speech
had been so cleverly carried on up to this point, the result
aimed at, and almost attained, was suddenly frustrated by words
involuntarily uttered by the speaker, and it seemed as if he
would never be permitted to complete the argument he had
begun. We can only accept this failure as the natural historical issue of the matter, as we must also do if we accept as a
fact that the Apostle was guilty of so striking an offence
against apostolic wisdom in teaching, as to broach designedly
the characteristic Christian doctrine of the resurrection, which
at that time was the most prominent obstacle to the acceptance
of Christianity by the Gentiles. But as both these suppositions
are equally improbable, we can only see in this speech an arbitrarily introduced effect of the author. In proportion as the
points of resemblance which the author makes the Apostle
point out between the religious consciousness of the Gentiles
and his own monotheistic standpoint were true and manifold,
so the impression which the Christian doctrine of the resurrection made on the educated Gentiles was harshly offensive.
The resurrection of Jesus, the fact which to Christians was
the greatest confirmation of their Christian faith, made the
whole of Christianity the most incredible affair to the Gentiles,

and a folly most worthy of ridicule. To give a graphic picture of this side of the Gentile conception of Christianity is the chief design of the author of the Acts of the Apostles in this passage. Everything else is throughout made subservient to it, and the speech put into the mouth of the Apostle is especially intended to further the design.

Among the individual features which show us the unhistorical character of this speech, as well as that of the whole passage, I think we must specify in particular " the Unknown God " of the Athenians. The fruitless trouble which interpreters have given themselves with regard to the historical authentication of this " Unknown God " is well known. All that can be historically proved is that in Athens, as well as in other places in Greece, there were altars which were dedicated to unknown Gods—that is, to Gods whom men did not know how to name. As it admits of no denial that unknown Gods, in the plural, would not have fulfilled the aim of the Apostle's argument, some of the modern interpreters have made the existence of an " Unknown God " in Athens a direct historic postulate. It is maintained that the ἀγνώστῳ Θεῷ must be literally correct, or it would compromise Paul as a σπερμολόγος. We cannot imagine that the Apostle would, at the climax of his noble speech, have brought an absolutely false statement before the Athenians.* Neander also has argued on this side : " Although we investigate exactly all the records of antiquity, and compare the whole religious scope of the polytheistic religion of Nature, we find throughout no real foundation for any denial of the existence of altars actually bearing the inscription to which Paul refers. Altars may indeed have been raised on many occasions dedicated to an " unknown God," when it was not known which God had been provoked, and therefore was to be appeased " (page 262). Of course this is in itself not impossible, but criticism must

---

* Compare Meyer on this passage.

not be content with mere possibility, but must endeavour to find out the probable. But as far as regards the historical credibility of our passage, what right have we to assume as indubitable the very point which is in question? What right have we to pay so little heed to the testimony of the ancients who only speak of the ἄγνωστοι θεοὶ, and not of a ἄγνωστος θεὸς, as to bring forward as a historical fact the worship of an ἄγνωστος θεὸς, in spite of their silence on the subject? Is not this supposition the more arbitrary, as it may well be imagined that the ἄγνωστος θεὸς of the Acts of the Apostles may have originated in the ἄγνωστοι θεοὶ of the ancients? In reality no other theory can be accepted if we consider the matter carefully. Neander endeavours to prove that the Apostle gives a faithful quotation, by asserting that the altar he refers to may have been dedicated not to the unknown God, but to an unknown God, but the theory rather goes to prove the contrary. Granting the unhistorical character of the whole passage, we must of course grant that the altar with the inscription ἀγνώστῳ θεῷ was not simply dedicated to " the unknown God," but to one whose name was accidentally not known : and how can we overlook the fact that the Apostle must have been guilty of open violation of the truth if he explained this very God to have been the One whom he preached, as being the true God, the Creator of heaven and earth. If this were only "an unknown God," he would not be distinguished from the rest of the known Gods by any peculiar idea, but only by the accidental circumstance that his name was not known, or that no decided name had been given him ; he would be exactly in the same class with the rest of the deities of the polytheistic faith, from whom the true God of monotheism is different in every essential point, and it is evident that there may quite as well be several unknown Gods of this sort, as one. If we look at the matter in this light we can see why, in the passages quoted from the ancients, the question is always of altars to " unknown Gods," and never of an altar to an " un-

known God." The polytheistic faith in itself implies so
completely that there is no question of one God only, but on
the same grounds that it allows there may be one unknown God,
it also allows that there may be several. In this worship of
the nameless and unknown there is betrayed in a very remarkable manner, the unsatisfying nature of polytheism, that innate
misgiving that there does exist something of which the conscious knowledge and name are still wanting ; in other words,
that negative nature of its principles which makes polytheism
a necessary step in the transition to monotheism. This thought,
which is the true one for the Apostle's line of argument, and
leaves it indifferent whether he starts from ἄγνωστοι θεοὶ in the
plural, or from one ἄγνωστος θεὸς only, cannot however be
deduced from the account in the Acts of the Apostles, where
undoubtedly we see that the chief point in the Apostle's argument lies in the unity of the ἄγνωστος θεὸς.* Such a confusion between the historically proved ἄγνωστοι θεοὶ and the
ἄγνωστος θεὸς, which is so unhistorical and foreign to the nature
of polytheism, could only have been adopted by an author
standing at a distance from the events related, so that he has
nothing to fear from contradiction as to place and circumstance,
which would have been the case with the Apostle Paul. It is
easy to see that there stands in very close connection with this
the tendency in the speech to represent the Apostle as bringing
forward as much as possible those points on which the religious
consciousness of the Athenians most nearly approached to
Christianity. To this end the author made use of the fact of

---

* When Neander (p. 263) says, " Paul used this inscription, which included a
deeper meaning, as an additional point in order to indicate the higher unknown
longing which lies at the root of polytheism," it must be remarked on the other
hand that in any case—even assuming the theory of a deeper meaning which the
Athenians were scarcely in a condition to originate, there remains a striking incor-
rectness in identifying this " unknown God," with the God of the New Testament
—and that such an identification could have any probability only if it were in exact
accordance with the inscription. As soon as we are obliged to draw conclusions
about the unknown from the unknown, we see traces of design rather than of
depth of reasoning.

which he was aware, that in Athens, unknown gods were worshipped. But at the same time he imagined he could fix and express the true thought that was floating in his mind by substituting ἄγνωστος for ἄγνωστοὶ, and as soon as the plural had given place to the singular, it was easy enough to make this ἄγνωστος θεὸς into the true God of the Jewish-Christian faith, although it was a mere play upon the words.

The second speech which we have now to consider, that farewell speech which the Apostle delivered to the Elders of the Ephesian Church whom he had summoned to Miletus before his last journey to Jerusalem, undoubtedly bears the impress of a later time. How could the idea have originated with the Apostle to deliver such a farewell speech and to summon the Ephesian Elders to Miletus for the express purpose? Could he already then have foreseen with the decided certainty expressed in the speech, that he stood at the summit of his apostolic course, that his work was ended, and that by all those amongst whom he had hitherto preached the kingdom of God his face should be no more seen? Is this same feeling, this same view of his course as being already closed, exhibited later on by the Apostle? When he sees himself at Jerusalem in danger of falling into the hands of the Jews and of being offered up as a sacrifice to their hatred, would he have appealed unto Cæsar for any other reason, except with a view of escaping the danger threatening him in Jerusalem, and of securing the continuation of his apostolic work with the preservation of his life by a just decision of his cause in Rome? Does not the Acts of the Apostles itself (xxiii. 11) represent the Apostle, although in prison, as nourishing the joyful confidence that he should yet bear witness in Rome as well as in Jerusalem to the cause of the Gospel? What could authorize this confidence if, according to the express assertion in this speech, he had seen the end of his apostolic work in the imprisonment he was enduring at Jerusalem? And what completely different views as to his position and to the future the Apostle must have

entertained not long before, when in writing the Epistle to the
Romans he speaks in the most cheerful manner of the journey
which he intended making to Jerusalem, and at the same time
passes lightly over the probable dangers without however seeking to ignore them: (παρακαλῶ δὲ ὑμᾶς, ἀδελφοὶ—συναγωνίσασθαί
μοι ἐν ταῖς προσευχαῖς ὑπὲρ ἐμοῦ πρὸς τὸν θεὸν ἵνα ῥυσθῶ ἀπὸ
τῶν ἀπειθούντων ἐν τῇ 'Ιουδαίᾳ). Romans xv. 30, 31. He also
connects the fortunate completion of this journey, which he confidently hopes for, with the plan of a further journey into Spain
and the West. Romans xv. 22, 32. There is no trace whatever
here of that utterly sorrowful picture of the future which floated
before the mind of the Apostle in the farewell speech at Miletus : it is rather a clear, joyful, hopeful view, which he takes of
the future; he hopes to return from Jerusalem, and visit the
Roman Christians, ἐν πληρώματι εὐλογίας τοῦ Χριστοῦ (29) ἐν
χαρᾷ, evidently with quite a different χαρά with which (Acts xx.
24) he is ready to τελειῶσαι τὸν δρόμον—καὶ τὴν διακονίαν διαμαρ-
τύρασθαι τὸ εὐαγγέλιον.* Can we imagine that the Apostle's
position and frame of mind could have so completely changed
in so short a space of time ? It cannot be said that the words
uttered by the Apostle in this farewell speech, with regard to
the future that lay before him, were merely vague forebodings,
the results of the temporarily depressed state of his feelings,
and on that account that they need not be required to be in
exact accordance with what actually followed. This cannot be
maintained; for the speech, as a leave-taking, which it certainly
was, did not only fulfil the purpose of a final farewell, but
everything it indicates regarding the impending fate of the
Apostle agrees so exactly with what actually occurred that it is
impossible to look on the words as the expression of a vague,
accidental presentiment. The Apostle already in spirit sees
himself bound and on his way to Jerusalem. Every city

---

* I abstain here from uttering my doubts as to the authenticity of this part of
the Epistle to Romans, as in any case κατ' ἄνθρωπον must be used in this manner
in the argument.

through which his way led him brought Jerusalem before him,
and awakened in him the thoughts of bonds and imprisonment.
Although the several circumstances which led to his imprisonment at Jerusalem were of course in the far distance, yet the
chief fact itself stood clearly before his mind exactly as it
really afterwards occurred—the fact, that with his arrival at
Jerusalem a time of captivity would begin, which would ever
after set a limit to his free apostolic work. How could he at that
time have foreseen this so decidedly, or have been able so exactly
to predict what was first resolved on four years afterwards, and
then in a manner apparently totally unexpected by the Apostle ?
Must not this incline us to the theory that the speech was not
really so delivered by the Apostle, but only put into his mouth
by the author *post eventum* ? This theory is supported also by
some very trustworthy criticisms of a later literary period.
The πρεσβύτεροι τῆς ἐκκλησίας (17), the ἐπίσκοποι, who τὸ
πνεῦμα τὸ ἅγιον ἔθετο ποιμαίνειν τὴν ἐκκλησίαν τοῦ κυρίου, ἣν
περιεποιήσατο διὰ τοῦ αἵματος τοῦ ἰδίου (28), are here brought forward with an emphasis of which there is no trace in the genuine
Epistles of the Apostle Paul. · The more weight must be laid
on this as it is connected with another subject, which as it in
reality was closely allied with it, is here mentioned at the same
time. The exhortations to watchfulness, and true care for the
church, which the departing Apostle here gives, were addressed
especially to the πρεσβύτεροι, or ἐπίσκοποι, because as the author
represents him as saying to them, xx. 29, ἐλεύσονται μετὰ τὴν
ἄφιξίν μου λύκοι βαρεῖς εἰς ὑμᾶς, μὴ φειδόμενοι τοῦ ποιμνίου, καὶ
ἐξ ὑμῶν αὐτῶν ἀναστήσονται ἄνδρες λαλοῦντες διεστραμμένα, τοῦ
ἀποσπᾶν τοὺς μαθητὰς ὀπίσω αὐτῶν. That by these dangerous
wolves so destructive to the flock, are meant False Teachers there
can be no doubt—but we cannot overlook the fact that these
are the false teachers who arose in the midst of the Christian
Church itself, and drew disciples after them by dissent from
the true doctrines. How distinctly the existence of sects of
Heretics is here indicated, as they existed possibly at the close

of the first century, but which probably had their origin at the beginning of the second, and this is also spoken of as a spreading evil of that time in the Christian Church. But of all this we find no trace in the genuine Epistles of the Apostle, which only speak of other kinds of false teachers and opponents of the Apostle. In the so-called pastoral letter of the Apostle only is there somewhat of a parallel to this passage, but the less doubt that there is of its being spurious, and of its date as being far removed from the apostolic period, the more decidedly does it show by its agreement with the Acts of the Apostles on this point, that the speech bears the stamp of a later period, and we must naturally conclude that the author himself could not entirely ignore the fact of the difference of date, as he makes these dangerous heretics first appear just after the departure of the Apostle, (μετὰ τὴν ἄφιξίν μου (29.) The conclusion is obvious, that throughout this speech, that which is represented as a prophetic seeing of the Future on the part of the Apostle, was really placed in his mouth as a *vaticinium post eventum*.

It is therefore clear that the author of the Acts of the Apostles made use of the time in which the Apostle Paul, on his last journey to Jerusalem, came into the neighbourhood of the church in whose midst he had so long laboured, in order to make him deliver a formal and solemn farewell speech, and in it, before these witnesses, to give an account of his apostolic mission up to that time. This was a moment full of importance, a critical turning point in the life of the Apostle : he was leaving the chief theatre of his apostolic activity to which he was bound by so many solemn ties of the Past and thoughts of the Future. His departure from this sphere of labour was at the same time his departure from his apostolic path ; he was now for the last time the free uncontrolled working Apostle, and immediately afterwards there would begin for him a period of imprisonment from which, last as long as it might, he would never again be free. In this solemn sense the author of the

Acts of the Apostles spoke, when from his own standpoint he considered the course of events which had developed itself in such close connection from one important point ; and he believed that it was his duty as a thoughtful author, following the development of events with all attention, to give this particular one its full weight. But the affair could only be thus considered from the standpoint of a later time. However much the principles enunciated may be worthy of the Apostle—however much the feelings and thoughts he is made to express, and the whole scene presented to us may be beautiful, elevating, tender, and moving, it is to the author, not to the Apostle that all must be referred, and we must even hold as extremely doubtful whether in reality anything corresponding to this scene ever occurred. The fact that only the Elders and Bishops of the Church they represented, were summoned by the Apostle, shows the spirit of a later time. If the speech was not really so delivered, the occurrences which followed at its conclusion, (36-38,) cannot be divided from it, and we here see truly how well the author of the Acts of the Apostles understood how to paint in living colours a situation so full of emotion, and at the same time to what extent he thought himself justified in availing himself of his literary freedom.

The parallel with the Apostle Peter, up to this point kept in view, is not directly brought forward in the two speeches now under consideration ; still they must be reckoned as apologetic. Such a picture, comprehending so wide a circle of activity more or less rich in results, such a fidelity to his office, so unreservedly and self-sacrificingly proved,* can only tend to the renown of the Apostle, and to the dispersion of the prejudices nourished against him. But we again decidedly meet

---

* A special passing reference to Peter may, however, be contained in the words, xx. 20. οὐδεν ὑπεστειλάμην τῶν συμφερόντων, τοῦ μὴ ἀναγγεῖλαι ὑμῖν καὶ διδάξαι ὑμᾶς δημοσίᾳ καὶ κατ᾿ οἴκους. Compare 27. It seems that the rectitude in the office of teacher, free from all taint of hypocrisy, which the Jewish Christians claimed for their Peter in order to protect him from the reproach of the ὑποστέλλειν, Gal. ii. 12, is here also employed in vindication of the Apostle Paul.

the apologetic parallel between the two Apostles, when in the same section of the Acts of the Apostles we turn from the speech to the miracles, and to other tokens of the apostolic activity.

The first narrative relating to these, Acts xix. 1, is one of the most obscure and difficult parts of the Acts of the Apostles, and can only be rightly understood from the point of view of this parallel. The question is about the disciples of John, who had only been baptized with the baptism of John, but received the baptism of the Lord Jesus from the Apostle Paul. To this class belongs also the Alexandrine Apollos, mentioned xviii. 25, for it is also said of him that he had only known the baptism of John. On one side these men were described as Christians, they were even called disciples, $\mu a \theta \eta \tau a i$ (which expression cannot possibly be taken in any other sense than the general one, and must be understood as referring only to the disciples of Jesus (xx. 1) and also believers $\pi \iota \sigma \tau \epsilon \acute{v} \sigma a \nu \tau \epsilon \varsigma$ (xx. 2) ; and it is said of Apollos, xviii. 25, that not only was he instructed in the doctrine of the Lord, but he taught the things of the Lord, and pursued them with all the fervour of his spirit. On the other hand, these men are again described as not being precisely Christians. They were therefore baptized in the name of the Lord Jesus, because John, whose baptism alone they knew, had only baptized them into the faith of one who was to come after him. That this One who was to follow John had really now come seems still to have been unknown to these disciples of John. Although Apollos appears to have been acquainted not only with the doctrine, but with the person of the Lord ($\tau \grave{a} \pi \epsilon \rho \grave{i} \tau o \tilde{v} \kappa v \rho \acute{i} o v$, xviii. 15), yet his knowledge must have been very incomplete and imperfect, as Aquila and Priscilla undertook to instruct him more exactly in the divine doctrine. How can we believe both these statements and unite them in a coherent account? We might, indeed, say with Olshausen that these disciples of John formed a third party, occupying a place between those of

his school, who, like the Apostles, had decidedly joined the
Church, and those who openly opposed Christianity, making
the Baptist the Messiah, and who were the Zabians of a later
time. This third party, who indeed had been led by the
Baptist to Jesus as the Messiah, and who were illumined by
his light, knew nothing further of him. This was probably
owing to their connection with Palestine having been early
interrupted, partly through the journies which these disciples
of John made to pour out the Holy Spirit into Gentile lands.
But this is neither very probable in itself, nor very applicable
to Apollos, of whom it is expressly stated that he ἐλάλει καὶ
ἐδίδασκεν ἀκριβῶς τὰ περὶ τοῦ κυρίου. How can this be said of
him, if he knew nothing further of Jesus than what John
the Baptist had taught about him, and when once the opportunity was afforded him of learning to know τὴν ὁδὸν τοῦ
κυρίου, how could he have left the most important thing of all
unlearnt? Just as vague is the relation of these disciples of
John to the Holy Spirit. According to Olshausen the meaning
of their words is that they considered God to be an inflexible,
self-contained, incommunicable Unity, without recognizing the
qualities of Father, Son, and Spirit, dependant on the existence of the Spirit, without which God could not be thought of
as living, and as communicating and revealing himself. But
already, as Jews, they must have known the Holy Spirit as the
Principle of Divine Revelation, notwithstanding they say,
xix. 2, simply ἀλλ' οὐδὲ, εἰ πνεῦμα ἅγιόν ἐστιν ἠκούσαμεν.
Undoubtedly these words can only be understood as referring
to the imparting of the Holy Spirit as the peculiar Christian
principle; but there is no clear connected idea in this explanation, unless by the imparting of the Holy Ghost we mean
those outward signs which the Acts of the Apostles considers
as the most essential and characteristic, namely, the λαλεῖν
γλώσσαις and the προφητεύειν. Of these the disciples of
John knew nothing, and these were the points that distinguished them from the Christian μαθηταί in the strictest sense

13

of the word. The best explanation is given in the passage
xi. 25, where Peter says that as soon as he began to speak in
the house of Cornelius, the Holy Ghost fell on Cornelius and
those Gentiles who were with him, in the same manner as it
had done in the beginning; and he remembered the saying of
the Lord, Ἰωάννης μὲν ἐβάπτισεν ὕδατι, ὑμεῖς δὲ βαπτισθήεσθε ἐν
πνεύματι ἁγίῳ. Here also we undoubtedly see what we ought
to understand in the Acts of the Apostles, by the βάπτισμα
Ἰωάννου, and the βάπτισμα εἰς τὸ ὄνομα κυρίου Ἰησοῦ. As the
Holy Spirit, as soon as it descended on Cornelius and those
baptized with him, immediately gave outward signs by the
λαλεῖν γλώσσαις and the προφητεύειν, so also with regard to
the disciples of John; he who has experienced in himself these
operations of the Spirit, even if he knew the doctrines of the Lord
and believed in him, was yet on the level of the Baptism of
John, and could only become a Christian in the fullest sense
when he was baptized with the Holy Spirit. We cannot however remain at this point; but must endeavour to come still
closer on the traces of these disciples of John. As the λαλεῖν
γλώσσαις and προφητεύειν, in the sense in which the author of
the Acts of the Apostles chap. ii. undeniably uses them, can
only be held as a mythical picture of the operation of the Holy
Spirit, we fail in finding in them a characteristic mark of
distinction with regard to the disciples of John, as soon as we
substitute fact for the veil of myth. In what light must we
consider these disciples, if they really were Christians, and yet
stood on so humble a level that the Christian inspiration did
not assert itself in them in so lively a manner as in the rest of
the Christians? This disadvantage may have had its root in
the imperfection of their Christian knowledge, and of their
Christian life generally, but how could it have formed a decided
token whereby they were distinguished from other Christians;
because at that time, as always, Christians were divided into the
perfect and the imperfect; into those who were actuated in a
deeper and more living sense by the Christian principle, and

into those who felt this in a lesser degree. All this subject is connected with the λαλεῖν γλώσσαις and προφητεύειν in the sense in which these are taken in the Acts of the Apostles, and only so far as we hold these mythical features as exact realities, can the disciples of John be granted to have been a peculiar class of Christians. This is shown undeniably by Apollos being associated with the disciples of John. In the description of him, xviii. 26, the definition ἐπιστάμενος μόνον τὸ βάπτισμα Ἰωάννου (which is evidently intended to make the transition easy from Apollos to the disciples of John, who are immediately after mentioned, and to assign him a place in the same class with them) may be altogether omitted, and then does not what is related of Apollos for the first time stand in a clear light? We must, from the very nature of the case, look upon this Apollos as one who as an Alexandrian did not adhere to the strict Judaism of the Jerusalem party, but who yet had not become familiar with the Pauline Christianity, nearly as he approached it, and easily as he could have accommodated himself to it. This form of Christianity he first learnt more thoroughly from Aquila and Priscilla, the trusted friends of the Apostle, and thus he came forth from the isolated position which he had hitherto occupied between the Jewish apostles and the Gentile apostle as a colleague of a peculiar kind, in order that he might ally himself with the Apostle Paul, as we find he did in the Epistle to the Corinthians. If anything stands in the way of this clear and satisfactory explanation, does not the βάπτισμα Ἰωάννου present a still greater obstacle to such an explanation? Must we not rather think that the peculiar phenomenon which is presented in Apollos as a historical fact, may have been the cause which called these disciples of John into being, these disciples who cannot have existed in the form in which they are presented. In opposition to the βάπτισμα Ἰωάννου, which is the only one spoken of in connection with Apollos, is the βάπτισμα εἰς τὸ ὄνομα τοῦ κυρίου Ἰησοῦ, now first manifesting itself in a peculiar class of persons by the λαλεῖν γλώσσαις and the προφητεύειν.

13 *

There is a special design, as may easily be seen, in these repeated "gift of tongues," and the disciples of John are brought forward in the interest of this design. Why should the author of the Acts of the Apostles make such a point of once more mentioning this λαλεῖν γλώσσαις, except for the evident purpose of adding to the glory of the Apostle Paul, whose laying on of hands was immediately followed by this miraculous result. It is only for this reason that in the case of Apollos, whose βάπτισμα Ἰωάννου needed the completion of the βάπτισμα εἰς τὸ ὄνομα τοῦ κυρίου Ἰησοῦ, there is no mention made either of baptism and laying on of hands, or of a λαλεῖν γλώσσαις and προφητεύειν, as Aquila and Priscilla could not in these matters represent the Apostle. As long as it is the laying on of hands by the Apostle only which operates in such a manner, he can appeal to it as a testimony of his genuine apostolic character. This it certainly is the desire of the author of the Acts of the Apostles to represent, and for no other reason than that the Apostle Paul shall not be found wanting in any advantage which characterized the Apostle Peter. As, according to the statement in the Acts of the Apostles, Peter, by the conversion of the first Gentile Cornelius, took precedence of Paul the special Apostle to the Gentiles, and as the Acts of the Apostles represents the λαλεῖν γλώσσαις as being only bestowed where the Holy Spirit revealed its operations in a new class of converts to Christianity, so at the time of the conversion of Cornelius by Peter a λαλεῖν γλώσσαις must be represented as occurring among the events on that occasion.

The conversion of Cornelius, as represented in the Acts of the Apostles, forms one of the most brilliant moments in the apostolic life of Peter, and so evident a manifestation of the Holy Spirit on the occasion must contribute to his glorification. But although Paul is placed after Peter as an Apostle to the Gentiles, he is as much as possible put on the same footing with him; the λαλεῖν γλώσσαις is made to accompany him as a direct effect of his apostolic mission, and to give proofs of the presence of the Holy Spirit. But to what class of men must this fresh λαλεῖν γλώσσαις be represented as being imparted? The first time it had been ' bestowed was at the first Pentecost, to those converted from Judaism, as the organ of the Holy Spirit given by the risen Jesus, and the second time it had fallen on the first-fruits of the Gentiles at the conversion of Cornelius. Now, if the λαλεῖν γλώσσαις was to be considered in the same light as heretofore, it should be imparted to a class of men, composed of neither Jews nor Gentiles. For this purpose the disciples of John are brought forward, as they formed a peculiar class of half-believers, standing between the unbelieving Jews and unbelieving Gentiles. They were neither Gentiles (for they were born Jews), nor Jews like other Jews (for they believed in Jesus); and yet they were not Christians, for the Holy Spirit had not yet been manifested to them as to the rest of the Christians: they were a third class—half Christians, who now were for the first time made Christians in the full sense by the λαλεῖν γλώσσαις. So simple is the solution of the enigma of the strange appearance of these disciples of John, if we refer the matter to the desire entertained by the author of the Acts of the Apostles to make good the parallel between the Apostles Peter and Paul, through this new and striking proof of the apostolic authority and activity of the latter!

The Acts of the Apostles represents Corinth and Ephesus as the chief seats of the apostolic labours next to Antioch, which was the starting-point of the Apostle, and where he returned from time to time, as he also did to Jerusalem. (xviii. 22.) In both these cities the Apostle spent a long period, unbroken by any interval of travel. But according to the Acts of the Apostles the city of Ephesus especially was the theatre of the Apostle's most brilliant and most successful labours. Here, after he had left Corinth, the Apostle fixed his residence—here he spent two whole years—here (as his farewell speech at Miletus testifies) he found his most appropriate sphere of

action. Here, however, the author does not speak of any
λαλεῖν γλώσσαις as accompanying the Apostle's preaching—he
only mentions a series of miracles and signs as setting forth its
results in the most beautiful light, and contributing as much
to the glorification of Paul, as the miraculous deeds related v.
14, did to that of Peter. During the two years' residence of
the Apostle Paul at Ephesus, says the Acts of the Apostles, xix.
10, all the dwellers in Asia, Jews and Gentiles, heard the word
of the Lord, and by the hand of Paul, God worked miracles of
so uncommon a nature that even handkerchiefs and other linen
that had come into direct contact with the body of Paul were
carried to sick persons, and their sickness departed from them,
and the evil spirits went out of them. This brilliant sketch
of the apostolic labours has a striking antitype in that passage respecting the Apostle Peter, v. 14, and even the purely
mythical trait is analogous ; that whereas in one case it was
the shadow of Peter falling on the sick which cured them, in
the other, handkerchiefs and aprons which had touched the
Apostle manifested an inherent miraculous power, just as
relics did in after times. Such copying as this shows also
a peculiar desire to enhance the importance of the whole
matter, and this is done in so truly apocryphal a manner, that
it is extremely difficult to get hold of anything historical.
Among the miraculous deeds of the Apostle Peter is the driv-
ing out of unclean spirits, v. 16. But the demons themselves
are here represented as working in the promotion of the faith
of Christ, whilst they punish the misuse of the name of
Jesus which the Jewish exorcists allowed themselves.* The

---

* Although already in the Gospels demons were cast out in the name of Jesus
(compare for example, Mark xvi. 17) so here, Acts xix. 3, a conquering power of
some kind over demons is ascribed to the ὄνομα τοῦ κυρίου Ἰησοῦ, which we first find
in the post-apostolic time. Compare here Justin's dialogue with the Jew Tryphon.
Ch. 85. Christ, it is here said, is the κύριος τῶν δυνάμεων. ὡς καὶ νῦν ἐκ
τῶν ὑπ' ὄψιν γενομένων ῥᾷον ὑμᾶς πεισθῆναι, ἐὰν θέλητε. Κατὰ γὰρ τοῦ,
ὀνόματος αὐτοῦ τούτου, τοῦ υἱοῦ τοῦ θεοῦ, καὶ πρωτοτόκου πάσης κτίσεως καὶ
διὰ παρθένου γεννηθέντος καὶ παθητοῦ γενομένου ἀνθρώπου, καὶ σταυρωθέντος

demoniac, whose evil spirits seven Jewish exorcists had endeavoured to cast out in the name of Jesus, filled with wrath at
the impure motives from which they acted (for demons possess
a higher intelligence), fell upon the exorcists, treating them
with such violence that they fled naked and wounded, and as
this was known to all the Jews and Gentiles dwelling in Ephesus, general fear prevailed, and the name of the Lord Jesus
became " greatly magnified." Many indeed who already believed, but who at the same time practised sorcery, now burnt
all the books that contained their magic formulas in one enormous pile. Οὕτω κατὰ κράτος, says the Acts of the Apostles at
the conclusion of this narrative, ὁ λόγος τοῦ κυρίου ηὔξανε καὶ
ἴσκυεν. This is accordingly the point of view from which the
whole narrative is to be considered. It gives us a truly striking picture of the all-conquering power with which Paul
worked in the spreading of the faith in Jesus; but it betrays
too distinctly the stamp of a later post-apostolic period. Let
it be granted that the circumstance which caused these
operations really occurred, as related (and this can only be
granted on the unhistorical supposition of the reality of these
demoniacal possessions), and even then we cannot suppose
that the Apostle, who should be judged by the result of his

ἐπὶ Ποντίου Πιλάτου ὑπὸ τοῦ λαοῦ ὑμῶν, καὶ ἀποθανόντος καὶ ἀναστάντος ἐκ
νεκρῶν, καὶ ἀναβάντος εἰς τὸν οὐρανὸν πᾶν δαιμόνιον ἐξορκιζόμενον νικᾶται καὶ
ὑποτάσσεται. Origen, c. Cels., 1. 25, whilst he speaks of the secret importance
of the name, adds : τῆς ὁμοίας ἔχεται περὶ ὀνομάτων φιλοσοφίας καὶ ὁ ἡμέτερος
Ἰησοῦς οὗ τὸ ὄνομα μυρίους ἤδη ἐναργῶς ἑώραται δαίμονας ἐξελάσαν ψυχῶν καὶ
σωμάτων, ἐνεργῆσαν εἰς ἐκείνους. ἀφ᾽ ὧν ἀπηλάθησαν. Is not this statement in
agreement with the passage in the Acts now under consideration? By the υἱοί
Σκευᾶ Ἰουδαίου ἀρχιερέως ἑπτὰ is generally understood, seven real sons of a Jewish
High-Priest (Olshausen makes the ἀρχιερεὺς, a chief Rabbi, who, perhaps, was the
head of the Ephesian Jewish community), but without doubt the expression υἱος
ought to be taken in the sense in which, according to the Jewish mode of writing,
the scholars of a master were called his " sons." The High Priest Sceva may therefore have been held by these and other Jewish exorcists as a celebrated master in
the art of sorcery. That they were seven, has merely reference to the idea that
demons sometimes took seven-fold possession of a man. Such a union of spirits
mus require a similar union of strength to operate against it.

power, in the inner working of the spirit, would have set any value on a propagation of the faith of Christ carried on by such means as the demoniac, or rather the demon itself, repudiated.

If the believers in Ephesus had given up the sorcery which was still mixed with Christianity, only because they deduced from such practices the doctrine that they might come to an evil end if they trifled with demons in so equivocal and insincere a manner, what would such a Christianity have been but the exchange of one form of superstition for another? And yet the author of the Acts of the Apostles gives utterance here to this verdict on the whole affair, οὕτω κατὰ κράτος ὁ λόγος τοῦ κυρίου ηὔξανε καὶ ἴσχυεν. Such a view is in itself so unworthy of the characteristics of an Apostle, and is so completely in conformity with those of a later period that we cannot but be doubtful about its origin. At the same time we cannot ignore the fact that the narrative, 13-20, as well as that which follows, 21-40, seem to have originated only in an *a priori* abstraction. The intention of the author, as we have already said, was to give as brilliant a picture as possible of the labours of the Apostle at Ephesus. To this end the Paganism opposed to Christianity, and requiring to be overcome by it, must be clearly presented.

Now Ephesus was doubly celebrated for its magic and its worship of Artemis. Accordingly with respect to both these facts, the mighty progress which the cause of the Gospel made through the labours of the Apostle is brought prominently before us. That Ephesus was a celebrated seat of magic is testified by the universally known Ἐφέσια γράμματα. By the very nature of the case the worship of demons was bound up with magic. If a man denied magic he must also deny demon worship. The demons themselves co-operated to this end, for· as intelligent spirits penetrating into inward things they hated a syncretism in which Christianity was so unlawfully allied partly with Judaism and partly with Heathenism. From such data is the narrative in xiii. 20 computed. But as it was the

author's design to represent here the victory which through
Paul, the Gospel had won over Heathenism in the form in
which it at that time existed in Ephesus, the celebrated
temple worship of the Ephesian Artemis could not be passed
over in silence. Could there have been given a greater proof of
how the Gospel was spreading in an ever-widening circle, than
that the great Artemis of the Ephesians was losing her worshippers? that the world-renowned silver shrines no longer could
find purchasers? and that the whole guild of silversmiths employed in making them lost their occupation, and very naturally
broke out into open violence against the man who was the
original instigator of this great change in the aspect of affairs?
The connexion in which the narrative of the tumult of Deme-
trius appears in the Acts of the Apostles is taken from a point
of view from which the successful labours of the disciples can
only be considered as an ideal picture, without at the same time
offering any real security as to the truth of the individual
statements, for of these in many instances no clear account is
preserved.   We must therefore conclude that the historical result of the whole passage, xix. 10-40—of the simple report
of the Apostle himself, 1 Cor. xvi. 9, of his residence in
Ephesus, θύρα γάρ μοι ἀνέῳγε μεγάλη καὶ ἐνεργὴς καὶ ἀντικείμενοι
πολλοὶ (compare xv. 31.) is not carried out.   And it is even
more evident as the comparison of the two passages, v. 14, &c.
and xix. 11, &c. shows, that the more the author here kept
Peter before him as a model, the more must the picture of the
Apostle Paul's operations testify to the parallel between the two
men.

I might consider from the same point of view the narrative of the youth who at the evening discourse of the Apostle
at Troas, fell down from an open window on the third floor,
and was brought to life again by the Apostle, Acts xx. 7, &c.
There is of course every probability that the young man was
not really dead, and the whole occurrence can very naturally be
explained without the intervention of any miracle.   On the

other hand the account of the historian supposes a miracle to
have been worked. That the Apostle hastened to the youth
and " laid himself on him," proves nothing against the miracle
theory, as sometimes accessory means of this kind were
employed in miraculous acts, although they were not indispensable to the miracle. The words γὰρ ψυχὴ αὐτοῦ ἐν αὐτῷ ἐστιν
may indeed signify " his life is still in him ;" but how does
this prove that Calvin's commentary, " non negat fuisse
mortuum quia miraculi gloriam hoc modo extingueret—sed
sensus est, vitam illi redditam esse Dei gratiâ," as Meyer among
the modern interpreters expresses it, is only a strange evasion ?
How, as is here specially pressed on our attention, could the
author say distinctly, xx. 9, ἤρθη νεκρὸς, if he did not really
mean the reader to understand that the youth was dead ?
Although the whole occurrence may have happened in a perfectly natural manner, the writer must have considered it to
have been a miracle, and must have designed to represent it as
such. What could have decided him to take this course, if it
were not that he thought that as a raising from the dead had
been among the miracles wrought by the other Apostles, and
especially by the Apostle Peter, the Apostle Paul ought to be
represented as not behind them in this respect.* This accidental

---

* In the narrative of the miracles which the Apostle Peter performed in Lydda
and Joppa, Acts ix. 23, &c. the accounts in the Evangelists of the different miracles of Jesus are collected together succinctly, and ascribed to the Apostle Peter.
In this way is treated the cure of the paralytic, ix. 33-55 (compare especially Mark
ii. 1, f.)) and a raising from the dead, ix. 36-43. As the raising of the young man
at Nain, Luke vii. 12, has for an especial motive that the youth was the only son
of his mother, and that she was a widow—so here there is a similar motive, only it
is in a connection which it would very naturally take, as there is so much said about
almsgiving and good works. A life that had been spent in so many good works is
most pathetically brought into notice by the widows who stood around weeping, displaying the clothes and garments which the dead woman had made for them, such a
life should not be snatched from the world or should again be given back to it. On
this account, this restoration to life is brought forward as a supreme event in the
Gospel of Luke as here in the Acts. As it is expressed in Luke, καὶ ἔδωκεν αὐτὸν
τῇ μητρὶ αὐτοῦ. So here 41, φωνήσας δὲ τοὺς ἁγίους καὶ τὰς χήρας παρέστησεν
αὐτὴν ζῶσαν. For the rest the narrative rests on the three Evangelists, Matthew
ix. 18, &c. xxiii. 26 ; Mark v. 22, &c ; Luke viii. 41, especially on the account in

and natural occurrence could be easily utilised for the purpose of this parallel. In the same manner may also be treated the narrative, xxviii. 8-10, in which the Apostle appears as a miracle-worker, but which in reality contains no miracle at all.

Mark. We may compare Mark v. 40, ἐκβαλὼν ἅπαντας καὶ κρατήσας τῆς χειρὸς τοῦ παιδίου λέγει αὐτῇ ταλιθὰ κοῦμι—καὶ εὐθέως ἀνέστη τὸ κοράσιον—with Acts ix. 40. ἐκβαλὼν δὲ ἔξω πάντας ὁ Πέτρος. εἶπε· Ταβιθὰ ἀνάστηθι: ἡ δὲ—ἀνεκάθισε. (Com_pare Luke vii. 14.) εἶπε ·νεανίσκε, σοὶ λέγω ἐγέρθητι· καὶ ἀνεκάθισεν ὁ νεανίας δοὺς δὲ αὐτῇ χεῖρα ἀνέστησεν αὐτήν. The supposition, however, is very patent that the name of the woman Ταβιθὰ is only borrowed from the Ταλιθὰ κοῦμι of Mark. The name Ταβιθὰ, Roe-deer or Gazelle in Hebrew and Syriac, means the same as Ταλιθὰ, with which it is interchangeable, by Paranomasia, and signifies maiden generally, and as Mark v. 41, adds, ὅ ἐστι μεθερμηνευόμενον τὸ κοράσιον, the author of the Acts follows with ἣ διερμηνευομένη λέγεται δορκάς.

CHAPTER VIII.

THE sad and gloomy forebodings with which, according to the Acts of the Apostles, the Apostle Panl set out on his journey to Jerusalem, and which he expressed in his farewell speech at Miletus, were too well grounded, although their complete fulfilment did not immediately take place. Scarcely had the Apostle arrived in Jerusalem when there happened a series of events, whose result was to place him in the hands of the Roman tribunal at Jerusalem, and then after a two years' arrest at Cæsarea he was led to Rome as a Roman prisoner, in order to receive the ultimate decision of his fate from the Emperor, to whose sentence he had appealed as a Roman citizen. Here, if anywhere, in the most public part of the Apostle's life, we might be entitled to expect from the Acts of the Apostles a statement which would admit of no doubt as to its historical truth. But we are deceived in this expectation. The false position with regard to Judaism which as we have seen is given to the Apostle by the Acts of the Apostles very naturally brought on the catastrophe which followed in Jerusalem. It cannot be doubted that it was caused by the hatred which the Jews had long cherished against the Apostle, as being an apostate from and an enemy to their religion. All through the Acts of the Apostles we find this brought forward as the reason for representing the Jews as being the most bitter enemies of the Apostle, not only as opposing his preaching of the Gospel with all their power, but also as trying every means to sacrifice him to their hatred. But if we ask what was the special cause of this deadly hatred on the part of the Jews towards the Apostle, we find no satisfactory answer to the question in the

Acts of the Apostles : as it is in accordance with the apologetic interest to conceal as much as possible the true relation of the Apostle Paul to the Jews as well as that to the Jewish Christians. The only explanation which can be given is as follows : That the Acts of the Apostles represent the occurrences at Jerusalem and Antioch in quite a different light from that in which we see them placed in the Epistles of the Apostle himself—that it makes him accommodate himself to Judaism in a manner to which he could not possibly have committed himself without falsifying all the logical consequences of his principles. In this view we have already said how little belief ought to be given to the assertion of the Acts of the Apostles that Timothy allowed himself to be circumcised on the persuasion of the Apostle. In the same light we ought to consider those actions ascribed by the Acts of the Apostles to the Apostle, which testify at the same time to a clinging to the customs and institutions of Judaism on his part, which, if it does not itself stand in direct contradiction to his well-known principles, at least places his mode of action in an highly equivocal light. Twice does the Acts of the Apostles purposely state that the Apostle did not neglect the usual visits to Jerusalem at the times of the festivals. The Acts represents him as saying, xxviii. 21, Δεῖ με πάντως τὴν ἑορτὴν τὴν ἐρχομένην ποιῆσαι εἰς Ἱερόσολυμα. Even this journey he made under the influence a vow which was connected with the undoubtedly Jewish custom of shaving the head.* He did not wish to be detained on his last journey, because, as we are told Acts xx. 16, he hasted εἰ δυνατὸν ἦν αὐτῷ, τὴν ἡμέραν τῆς πεντηκοστῆς γενέσθαι εἰς Ἱεροσόλυμα. The Apostle himself says very simply, Romans xxiii. 35, in speaking of this journey, that he now goes to Jerusalem, διακονῶν τοῖς ἁγίοις, in order to convey thither the contributions collected in Macedonia and Achaia. In any case this

---

* Most commentators take the κειράμενος, Acts viii. 18, as relating to the Apostle. Perhaps also his inclination to the acceptance of the Nazarite sacrifice, xvi. 26, may be thought remarkable.

must have been the chief aim of the journey, as in 2 Corinth. viii. 9, where the same contributions are spoken of as being a very important part of the Apostle's affairs. But whilst the Acts of the Apostles says nothing directly on this subject, on the other hand it brings into great prominence the visit to the feast, about which the Apostle is perfectly silent, and this is evidently done with a view of making the Apostle appear as a faithful adherent of the Jewish national worship. But if the Apostle had throughout shown such an adherence to the ancient religion of his fathers, would he so far have depreciated it as to deny the necessity of circumcision? And how shall we explain the great collision into which the Apostle came with his brethren in the faith, and the irreconcilable hate with which he was persecuted by them? The faith in Jesus as the Messiah cannot have been the origin of this hatred, or it would have been shown in the same manner against the Jewish Christians who lived together with the Jews in Jerusalem. It can only be explained by his teaching of the law, and naturally it could not be otherwise than that the Jews should consider him a deadly enemy to their religion, if, on the one hand, he was desirous of making the Gentiles Jews, in order that he might make the Gentiles partakers of the Messianic salvation exclusively ordained for the Jews, and on the other hand of relieving them from the necessity of circumcision, by which alone the Gentiles could partake of the blessings of Judaism. As soon as circumcision was no longer of value as the specific characteristic of Judaism, the essential difference between Jew and Gentile was removed, and with it the absolute importance of Judaism. Therefore in the doctrine which the Apostle held as essential, namely that circumcision was no longer necessary, there was seen only the most direct contradiction of the principle of Judaism. But explicable as is the enmity of the Jews to the Apostle, the statement in the Acts of the Apostles is just as inexplicable—for why should the hatred of the Jews be directed exclusively towards him, and not equally towards the elder Apostles, who were completely in accord with him on the subject of circumcision? But if, as we may assume from the epistle to the Galatians, the elder Apostles did not agree with him on this point, if they, like the Jewish Christians generally, rather adhered more closely to the necessity of circumcision, then we must naturally suppose that the Apostle was held as an enemy on account of his doctrine of freedom from the law, not only by the Jews, but by the Jewish Christians also. How can it be otherwise than that a narrative which presents the whole position of the matter in quite a different light to that which really existed, should also make the events springing from it appear in another form? And if at the same time it cannot pass over in complete silence the real state of the matter, it can only by mentioning it, involve a self-contradiction. From this point of view the account in the Acts of the Apostles of the arrest of the Apostle in Jerusalem is constructed, and from this point of view we must consider it with its accompanying events. In it we meet with difficulties and contradictions, in which we see nothing but the natural collision which must ensue in the wider sphere which affairs take in their actual operation, between a historian who from the beginning had taken up such a false position with regard to historical truth, and the real matters of fact.

This view likewise is very striking in regard to the first point with which the Acts of the Apostles begins the relation of these last occurrences in Jerusalem. The Apostle went, on his arrival in Jerusalem, to James the head of the Church at Jerusalem. In an assembly of the collected Elders, he gave utterance to a detailed account of the results of his apostolic labours among the Gentiles up to that time; all that he had to say on this subject was received with the most sympathetic recognition. But at the same time he was made aware that in Jerusalem it had been said that his teaching had been opposed to circumcision. Then in order to meet the opposition which his appearance in Jerusalem would excite, he was advised to join himself to four men, doubtless members of the Jerusalem

Christian Church, who were already under a Nazarite vow and as a necessary obligation to share the charges of carrying out their vow. For thus he would testify to all that those things whereof they were informed concerning him were nothing, and that he also exactly kept the law. This advice the Apostle followed. But even if it is not self-evident that he could ·not have resolved on such a course of action, which, unless he were unfaithful to his principles, could only serve to refute a report circulated against him, and thus mitigate the hatred of his enemies, we cannot overlook the design of the narration of this act, and what end it is destined to serve. The Apostle was accused of having incited all the Jews present to forsake Moses, by maintaining that they ought not to circumcise their children nor observe the law. Acts xxi. 21. This accusation was not untrue—it was matter of fact that the Apostle preached a doctrine among Jews and Gentiles which as a necessary consequence removed the obligation of circumcision, because the reason for this custom, which had hitherto been considered of all importance, now appeared utterly aimless. But if the Apostle now entered on a course of action apparently designed to impress his opponents with the idea that he still adhered strictly to the law (στοιχεῖς καὶ αὐτὸς τὸν νόμον φυλάσσων as well as others) what was said of him would have been false (ὧν κατήχηνται περὶ σοῦ οὐδὲν ἐστι)—false also that he was an opponent of circumcision. How could James the brother of the Lord commend such an act, from the point of view of the motive which the Apostle had when he resolved on it? What opinion can we have of the character of these men if we can conceive them capable of such a mode of action? The author of the Acts of the Apostles himself felt this—for he limits the διδάσκειν ἀποστασίαν ἀπὸ Μωυσέως very decidedly to the Jews which were among the Gentiles, xxi. 21, (compare 25) and the accusation itself implies in the strongest sense a direct opposition to circumcision and to the Mosaic law. (λέγων μὴ περιτέμνειν αὐτοὺς τὰ τέκνα μηδὲ τοῖς ἔθεον περιπατεῖν, xxi. 21) verse 25,

also bears reference to this. It means that nothing must interfere with the freedom of the Gentile Christians, but it is far
from being asserted that for them alone the φυλάσσεσθαι τό τε
εἰδωλόθυτον &c. is of value and not circumcision. How could
the Apostle maintain the necessity of circumcision for the Jews,
if he ignored it for the Gentiles? The reference of these
transactions in Acts xv. to an occurrence which cannot have
taken place as related, shows the interest the author has in
representing the affair in a light of which there is not the least
hint throughout the whole preaching of the Apostle concerning
the law of Judaism. Commentators on the Acts of the Apostles
therefore hold it as unlikely that the Apostle Paul should have
inculcated direct opposition to the observance of the law, and
think that he only decidedly attacks as un-Christian the dependence of salvation on such observance.* But nevertheless he
worked in the most decided manner against the opinions held
by the Jewish Christians concerning the observance of the law,
and could in no way turn away from himself the reproach that
his whole doctrine tended to the up-rooting of the law.
Can these interpreters then find it very intelligible that the
example of the Apostle, and the entire spirit of his teachings
caused many Jewish Christians to renounce conscientiously
the observance of the Mosaic law altogether? How weak and
unworthy of an Apostle is the evasion to which he must have
had recourse in order to have any foundation for the assertion,
ὧν κατήχηνται περὶ σοῦ οὐδέν ἐστιν ἀλλὰ στοιχεῖς καὶ αὐτὸς τὸν
νόμον φυλάσσων ? It was certainly very far from the Apostle's

---

* Thus Olshausen, on Acts xxi. 17-26—and also Neander, p. 425, say, "Paul
always attacks the outward observance of Judaism only in so far as the justification
and salvation of man were made dependent on it." What Neander says against me
does not in the least alter the case. The Apostle himself, 1 Cor. vii. 18-20, expresses
the principle that the Jews should remain Jews after their conversion—that Christianity does not pretend to change any of those outward things—which may remain
as ever merely outward; but even in this way the whole former view of them is
changed, and any one may see that if circumcision is no longer made necessary to
salvation, its merely outward retention can have no value, and sooner or later must
end, even for the Jews themselves.

14

intention to give a colour to such an observance of the law. In
his own Epistles he states in the frankest manner that he is an
opponent of circumcision, and says that adherence to it is in
opposition to the principles of his teaching. Here again we
find that it is the Epistle to the Galatians which throughout
consistently maintains its irreconcileable contradiction to the
Acts of the Apostles. " See—I, Paul say unto you," declares
the Apostle unreservedly, Gal. v. 2, 3, 6, 11, 13, "that if ye
be circumcised Christ shall profit you nothing. For I testify
again to every man that is circumcised that he is a debtor to
do the whole law." " For in Christ Jesus neither circumcision
availeth anything nor uncircumcision, but faith which worketh
by love." " And I, brethren, if I yet preach circumcision, why
do I yet suffer persecution ? then is the offence of the cross
ceased." " Ye have been called unto liberty." It is not said
that the Apostle speaks in this manner only against the Galatian Gentile Christians. When he declares in the same Epistle,
" Ye are all sons of God through faith in Christ Jesus, for so
many of you as are baptized in Christ have put on Christ, and
are therefore neither Jew nor Greek." He expressly establishes
the principle that no difference can be acknowledged between
Jew and Gentile. With what appearance of truth could he
come before the Jews with the statement, " All that you have
heard of me is not in the least true. I am, as much as you, an
adherent to and an observer of the law !" Would this have
been a less objectionable ὑπόκρισις than that with which the
Apostle himself so unreservedly charged Peter. It is impossible that the Apostle should have resolved on such a course of
action on the grounds given by the author of the Acts of the
Apostles ; and if the grounds be wanting on which a certain
course of action depends, how doubtful the action itself becomes ! How can we imagine any reasonable grounds for
recommending such a course of action to the Apostle ? The
immediate result showed unmistakably how vain and purposeless were the advice and its consequences. It is therefore only

the author of the Acts of the Apostles who wishes to represent the Apostle as a faithful adherent to and observer of the Mosaic law, and also here and everywhere (especially in xxviii. 17) to place completely in the background, or rather entirely to ignore, the real difference between him and the Jewish Christian party, and, in one word, who is desirous to represent the Apostle to the Gentiles at any cost as an Apostle to the Jews, which he certainly neither was, nor, according to his own express declaration, ever would be.

The advice thus given to the Apostle must have had for its motive the fact that there were so many thousands of believing Jews in Jerusalem who were all strict zealots for the law (xxi. 20). But here also springs up an insoluble difficulty. We must ask, how did all these thousands of believing Jews come into a church, which, according to all accounts, could not have been very important? The Jewish inhabitants of Jerusalem in general might perhaps be correctly spoken of as consisting of "many thousands," and the supposition seems very clear that the words τῶν πεπιστευκότων, added on to ᾽Ιουδαίων, are spurious. It cannot be alleged against this supposition, which I have before brought forward, that if Paul had been told that there were in Jerusalem many thousand Jews who were all zealous observers of the law, it would have been a self-evident proposition. This would not have been told to Paul as something with which he was before unacquainted, but merely in order to recommend to him the course which it would be best for him to pursue. A statement, to which the grounds of critical objection lie so deep, cannot be established by such patching up of weak places. If, according to Neander's idea,* "that this number need not be taken as an exact one," we pass over the "many thousands," there still remain the "believing Jews" about whom the Apostle was warned, and also the

---

* A writer who at first makes thousands upon thousands converted at every preaching of the Apostles may truly not make much difficulty at last in speaking about myriads!

14 *

Jewish Christians of that Church, in which the Apostle, as had been immediately before said, had found so friendly a recep-- tion from the brethren. Even these were now described to him as zealots for the law, from whom he had to fear the most extreme measures, on account of the accusation brought against him of preaching apostacy from the Mosaic law. How can we entertain both these ideas? Supposing that we assume that all the members of the Church at Jerusalem might not have been equally suspicious of the Apostle, and adverse towards him, yet how the few brethren who formed the exception would have sunk into insignificance in comparison with the great mass of the Jewish Christians in that Church which saw in the Apostle nothing but the worst enemy of the law.* For it is not likely that we have here described in the disposition of these zealots for the law, that same hatred against the Apostle which soon after broke out in so threatening a manner in spite of advice, which although well meant, was not to all appearance likely to end favourably.†

* Kuinöl remarks quite unreservedly in his just appreciation of this difficulty on ἀδελφοὶ (17). "Apostoli et presbyteri nam coetus non favebat Paulo," but is harshly treated by Meyer, who finds this remark "very strange," as it (20) speaks of an increased enmity of the zealots, carried on even to a refusal of a friendly reception. But is not this really the undeniable meaning of what follows? The suspicion against the Apostle was so great that men saw in him no brother in the faith, but only an apostate. We can by this explain how it was that such an opposition existed between these Ἰουδαῖοι πεπιστευκότες and the ἀδελφοὶ, in a church which had been established under the immediate direction of the Apostle. Neander is completely silent on this point. If also, as by Zeller Apostgesch. (page 280) the words (21) must be taken as meaning to express suspicion, the affair is not much altered. Simple suspicion may have sufficiently excited such fanatic jealousy.

† The author however himself indicates that this opinion of the Jewish Christians was connected with the appearance subsequently mentioned, v. 22. But if the words: πάντως δεῖ πλῆθος συνελθεῖν are not to be directly understood to refer to a tumult, but only of a collection of the curious, what is thereby gained? The most favourable views are not to be imputed to a multitude which has flocked together out of curiosity, because an apostate and a preacher of apostacy, has ventured to let himself be seen in Jerusalem, and indeed in such a case only a chance incident would be needed to give a practical bearing to such hatred. But this συνελθεῖν is nothing less than a συνδρομὴ τοῦ λαοῦ, as in v. 30. It is also

And why should we not suppose such a disposition against the
Apostle among the Jewish Christian inhabitants of Jerusalem,
as well as among the Jewish inhabitants, as all those who are
referred to by James, are described by him as declared foes and
opponents ? Does not everything which is here said about the
great apprehension for the Apostle awakened at that time by
the zeal for the law among the inhabitants of Jerusalem, coincide completely with the feeling which was afterwards entertained against the Apostle Paul by the Ebionites, who were so
nearly allied to the Jewish Christians. We can only wonder
how a writer who hitherto has taken the greatest pains to
conceal, as much as possible, the true relation in which the
Apostle stood to the Jewish Christians, should have here come
forward for once with the bare naked truth, and this too in a
connection in which the matter in hand had a practical importance, and must have caused, by its results, the Jewish Christians to appear in a very equivocal light. But the clear literal
meaning of his words can leave us in no doubt on the matter,
and even if, as the πόσαι μυριάδες seems to indicate, the Jewish
Christians of Jerusalem had unwillingly perhaps joined with the
Jewish inhabitants of the city (for really there cannot have been
so great a division between the Jews and Jewish Christians
of Jerusalem),* what he has once said cannot be unsaid,
and his testimony is of all the more value, as it must be
looked on as wrung from him against his will by the might of
historical truth. We must then conclude, according to the
statement of the author of the Acts of the Apostles himself,
that the Jewish Christians in Jerusalem saw in the Apostle
Paul an apostate from the law, and a preacher of this apostacy
among both Jews and Gentiles. As they held this opinion of

evident that v. 28, οὗτός ἐστιν—πάντας πανταχοῦ διδάσκων, refers to v. 21,
ἀποστασίαν διδάσκεις, &c.

* Ἰουδαῖοι οἱ πεπιστευχότες are therefore in general true adherents of the law—
orthodox Jews, whether or not they are believing or unbelieving Jews in reference
to Christianity. The expression is evidently used by the author in this sense as
concerning Judaism merely.

him, no one can be astonished at the supposition that they
could not be so indifferent and uninterested as is generally
supposed, in the events with which the scenes immediately succeeding were the undeniable results of these views and opinions.
  Without doubt the actual course of the subsequent narrative,
and in fact the only one which can with any certainty be
deduced from it, is, that the appearance of the Apostle in
Jerusalem caused a tumultuous scene, in which he was saved
from the hands of the Jews by the Roman military power, but
on the other hand suffered imprisonment at the hands of the
Romans. The motives of these circumstances are mixed up in
the closest manner with the apologetic tendency which reigns
over the whole, and in accordance with which the Acts of the
Apostles represents the pretended advice to the Apostle as
being followed. The more free, accordingly, that he became
from the charge brought against him, the more apparent
become the groundlessness and unreasonableness of the hatred
which burst out against him as an apostate. This thread runs
through the whole series of transactions following the imprisonment of the Apostle. It is an artistically constructed compli-
cation which is by no means calculated to present a clear
natural statement of the matter. If we turn to the chief scene
of this narrative, to the trial of the Apostle before the Sanhedrim, xxiii. 1-10, which is developed with a certain dramatic
interest, how unlikely and unintelligible, even how unworthy
of the Apostle, does everything appear. At best the artifice is
astonishing which the Apostle must have employed in order to
bring the two parties composing the Sanhedrim, namely the
Sadducees and the Pharisees, into a quarrel, and by this quarrel
not only to avert the attention and passion of the Sanhedrim
from himself, but to gain for himself the goodwill of one
of the parties. After the violent outburst of passion from
both sides, which interrupted the discourse of the Apostle, as
soon as it was begun, he commenced with the bold declaration,
whilst thinking of the opposition between the two parties

of the Sadducees and Pharisees, " I am a Pharisee, the son
of a Pharisee; of the hope and resurrection of the dead
I am called in question." This one question is represented as
having had the immediate result not only of placing the Sadducees and Pharisees in the most violent opposition, but of
bringing over the Pharisees to the side of the Apostle, and
making them declare openly that they found no fault in him.
Here especially arises the question whether it was exactly in
accordance with the truth, that the Apostle should take up the
subject of the quarrel with his enemies in this manner ? If
the Apostle agreed with the Pharisees about the faith in a
resurrection, of course he could hardly have said with truth
that he stood there for judgment because he had preached
Jesus as the One through whom the hope of the people of
Israel of resurrection from the dead must be fulfilled. For as
soon as the sense of the words of the Apostle, περὶ ἐλπίδος καὶ
ἀναστάσεως νεκρῶν ἐγὼ κρίνομαι, is taken as Neander takes it, it
is then clear that between him and his opponents, the question
of a faith in a resurrection from the dead was not raised, but
only the inquiry, whether or not Jesus had risen from the
dead. But this fact could be denied without prejudice to the
doctrine of a resurrection. Although the Apostle indeed agreed
in this last instance with the Pharisees, he at once separated
from them with regard to a fact without which the doctrine of
a resurrection could have no meaning nor value for him. It
was here at least completely useless for him to cling to this
point of agreement, which only included the mere possibility
of the resurrection of Jesus, but proclaimed aloud the great
chasm between possibility and reality, and accordingly it was
most evident that, as a Pharisee, he stood for judgment on
account of the common belief of the Pharisees. The Apostle
claimed expressly to be judged as a Pharisee. Even if there
does not here appear an incoherent and equivocal evasion of the
truth of the peculiar matter in dispute, we must express an
opinion that the statement which traces the whole difference

between the Apostle and his opponents to the doctrine of the resurrection must be considered in this light. The Apostle must have known perfectly well that there was no question here of the doctrine of the resurrection, in regard to which he was in accordance with those who believed in the resurrection of Jesus, and with those Jewish-Christians of Jerusalem who no longer contested this belief, but that the real cause of offence was that which distinguished him from all these, namely, his preaching of the law. There is in this view also an evasion of the real cause of dispute, which does not seem to be in accordance with the Apostle's frank love of truth; and the remark of Grotius on v. 6: "non deerat Paulo humana etiam prudentia, qua in bonum evangelii utens columbæ serpentem utiliter miscebat et inimicorum dissidiis fruebatur," still less suffices for the vindication of the Apostle, as it sets in a yet more striking light the very point in question. But, setting aside all these moral considerations, we can scarcely imagine that a single expression undesignedly let fall by the Apostle regarding the resurrection could have kindled so fierce a fire. Parties, which differed from each other on such essential points, and yet in so many ways were in practical agreement, and who were also united in one and the same school in the Sanhedrim, must long before have so far relaxed their points of difference, that it would have been impossible for these to have again been the objects of so violent a dispute on this occasion, unless now, as in a former case, there was a question of a mere stratagem for the defence of the accused. But we have both parties disputing with a fury and a passion which blinded them to their own interests, as it had done in the first instance, when they quarrelled about these opposing doctrines. The intention of the author of the Acts of the Apostles in this narrative appears all the more clearly from the absence in it of any historical probability. The Acts of the Apostles throughout makes the Apostle Paul stand in as close a relation as possible to Judaism; his real, essential opposition to it is passed over in silence and placed completely out of sight. In furtherance of this view, a common point of agreement is established between Judaism and the teachings of the Apostle. It is evidently the intention of the author, partly to adopt the prejudices which may have existed on the part of the Jewish-Christians against the Apostle as an opponent of the law, and partly to represent the hatred of the Jews towards the Apostle in a still more disadvantageous light. As the Apostle here stood before the Sanhedrim in opposition to both Sadducees and Pharisees, and was yet partly allied to the Pharisees by the belief in a resurrection, an opportunity was afforded to the author of so representing the matter, as to show that the Pharisees were not so much the peculiar enemies of the Apostle as the Sadducees were. The Apostle was a victim only to the partial hatred of a single sect. In the connection of ideas in which the author introduces the matter, he allows us also to penetrate into the difference of doctrine between the Pharisees and Sadducees by the remark made xxiii. 8. After there had been so much question up to this time of the Pharisees and Sadducees, and even of their disagreements, what makes the author now state so precisely the differences in their doctrine ? If he were only treating of a matter of fact in a simple and historically true manner, he would certainly not have specially brought forward an idea which is represented as an established fact throughout the Gospels, unless with the intention of setting the opposition of the Apostle to the Sadducees and Pharisees in such a light as to present a decided picture of the difference of doctrine existing between these two parties. From his knowledge of this difference in doctrine he seems to have constructed his account of the behaviour of the Apostle before the Sanhedrim. He allows himself to be so far misled by the efforts he makes to unite as far as possible the party of the Apostle with the Pharisaic party, as almost to make the Pharisees into Christians. It is not enough that he finds a common ground of resemblance in the doctrine of the resurrection—the other points of difference, the belief in angels and spirits, must be utilized to the same end, whilst the Pharisees, acknowledging the Apostle's side as their own, declare openly that they can find no fault with this man, and even say in addition (v. 9) εἰ δὲ πνεῦμα ἐλάλησεν αὐτῷ, ἢ ἄγγελος. This bears out what the Apostle, in his speech to the people, xxii. 6-18, said of the appearance of the risen Jesus, and the Pharisees seem prepared accordingly to yield to the Apostle, as far as regards the reality of this appearance ; but, in the very moment in which they are about to acknowledge this openly, the author makes them suddenly interrupt their declaration, as though they themselves were astonished at such a concession. We may say with Neander (page 432) that "the concluding words of the interrupted speech, μὴ θεομαχῶμεν, are certainly a gloss, and a gloss disturbing the sense, because this was assuredly more than the Pharisees from their standpoint could have meant." The matter in hand in no way depends on the question whether the interrupted words which must have been completed in some way, were in fact completed in this manner or otherwise ; and it is clear that the preceding words contain much more than could have come into the minds of the Pharisees from their standpoint. Those who were inclined to grant so much could never again object to the Christian faith. Besides, how can we think that the Pharisees, while they were in the Sanhedrim as judges of the Apostle, and as champions of their own doctrines would, on account of the mere appearance of the identity of his faith with their own, consider as not worth any further attention all those points which, as Pharisees, they must have felt as most obnoxious in the Apostle, and points too which comprised the special charge against him, namely, indifference to the profanation of the Temple, and uprooting of the authority of the Law ? All this is in the highest degree unlikely, and shows very clearly that the whole of this transaction before the Sanhedrim, in the form in which we have it, is purposely introduced by the author of the Acts of the Apostles, and that he does not pay due regard to maintaining the dignity of the Apostle's character. It must, therefore, be here said openly that this public statement of a tumultuous scene between the Apostle and the High Priest is something so unworthy of the Apostle that thanks are owing to any criticism which, on sufficient reasons, would free the Apostle from this blot on his character. The author of the Acts of the Apostles has here in his mind something that tells against rather than in favour of the historical character of his statement —the trial of Jesus before the Sanhedrim ; but how unlike the Apostle seems to the image of him who " lived in him." " Ubi est illa patientia Salvatoris qui quasi agnus ductus ad victimam non aperuit os suum, sed clementer loquitur verberanti ; si male locutus, argue de malo, si autem bene, quid me caedis ?" Thus does Jerome decide on this passage (contra Pelag. iii. init.), and the impression left by these words is not effaced when he adds : " Non Apostolo detrahimus, sed gloriam Domini prædicamus, qui in carne passus carnis injuriam superat et fragilitatem." Olshausen also decidedly states that it appears unlikely that the Apostle should have used an abusive word, he would by such a behaviour have violated the decorum due to so high a court of justice, and confounding the person with the office would have given vent to his feelings with regard to the man where only the office was concerned.* Neander indeed is of opinion that these passionate words contain the truth, and that the Apostle, when made aware that it was the High Priest whom he had thus vilified, retracted his words at once, by saying that he had not thought that it was the High Priest to

---

* It is really incomprehensible how Olshausen from his standpoint could have committed himself to such an opinion on the behaviour of the Apostle. If the literal reading is worth so much, it cannot be doubted that the Apostle really behaved as is represented, and further it is certain that the Apostle as the most direct organ of the Holy Spirit, must here be an infallible authority, and we must therefore not judge the behaviour of the Apostle according to our human standard of morality, but rather arrange our standard of morality according to the behaviour of the Apostle!

whom he was speaking, and to whom, of course, according to the law, reverence was due. But how little is it remembered in this theory that the simple words οὐκ ᾔδειν cannot mean "non reputabam." They can only mean "I did not know;" but the Apostle could not in earnest say that he had not recognized him, and therefore could only have said, "I did not know that he was High Priest" in an ironical sense. But if those words are to be taken in an ironical sense the irony shows that he ranged himself on the side of the Pharisees, and with them made common cause against the Sadducees. This was also shown by the stratagem by which he immediately afterwards placed his special enemies the Sadducees, at whose head was the High Priest Ananias, in the greatest embarrassment, and it is thus clear that he had little intention of retracting.

The same tone and character reign from beginning to end in the behaviour of the Apostle. I disagree with the opinion pronounced by Neander on this passage, as follows (page 421) : "The art which the Apostle has here employed makes us acknowledge in him the man who, with Christian circumspection knew how to command the violence of his feelings, and with Christian prudence to turn circumstances to account without any prejudice to truth." I can neither see here any " Christian repression of passion" or any Christian "turning circumstances to account without prejudice to truth ;" and I consider it unjust that the picture of the Apostle's character which we gain from his Epistles should be distorted by the warped delineation of an author who lived at some distance of time from the apostolic period, and who wrote in the interests of a party.

If the two extracts, xxi. 17-26, xxiii. 1-10, are related in the manner above shown, it must be granted how little we are justified in considering the rest of the passage with the narrative connected with it from an historical point of view, even if it is not possible for historical criticism with the evidence at its disposal to attach the general suspicion which it must cherish, to every individual statement. According to the result of our inquiry on the passage xxiii. 1, &c., it must be held as extremely doubtful whether or not any such transaction as this before the Sanhedrim took place. If this is doubtful, what security have we that the two speeches said to be delivered by the Apostle —one in chap. xxii. before the Jewish people, the other chap. xxvi. before King Agrippa—really were so delivered as stated by the author. The first at any rate must have been delivered under circumstances which were scarcely calculated for such a discourse. Is it likely that the Roman tribune, who had arrested the Apostle in a highly tumultuous scene, should have given permission to a prisoner, whom he held to be a rebel of a most dangerous kind, to deliver a public speech, and about whom he knew nothing except what he heard from himself, —that he was a Jew of Tarsus in Cilicia, and this too directly after he was brought into the castle—especially when it could not be foretold how this speech would operate on people already in a state of suspicious excitement? Is it likely that the people in this state of passionate excitement would have listened so long and so patiently to the hated speaker, whom they had just condemned as worthy of death? At any rate we must again pronounce the fact as very remarkable, that this speech like that of Stephen, and the one delivered by the Apostle in the Areopagus, is so systematically arranged that the speaker is interrupted at a certain point, and in this case at a point when he begins to speak of his mission to the Gentiles, xxii. 21, reminding the people of the most peculiar and immediate reason for their hatred against him. This point occurs too just at that moment when he had completed all he could under such circumstances say in furtherance of his main idea. Both speeches have a thoroughly apologetic tendency. The chief idea which the Apostle carries out is as follows : the duty to which he had hitherto devoted himself among the Gentiles was by no means either arbitrarily chosen, or the accidental result of a free subjective resolution, but it was rather the consequence of a higher call vouchsafed to him, brought to a resolve by an objective fact, the operation of whose

overpowering influence he had been unable to withstand. Of
course such an apology seems not inappropriate to the aim
which the Apostle had in view in delivering both speeches, but
it also suits in a remarkable manner the apologetic tendency to
which the author of the Acts of the Apostles generally sets
himself to further. And the question rather arises from it
whether the Apostle, if he thought himself obliged to speak
apologetically against his opponents, was obliged also to refer
in the manner he did to the matter of fact on which his whole
apology is founded. But this is not the case, and in none of
the epistles of the Apostle, in which he has to vindicate himself
against opponents of different kinds, is there any decided indication of this kind respecting the outward matter of fact which
the Apostle here, twice in succession, makes the chief subject of
his detailed discourses. But such an apology strictly considered
is not at all suited to the situation in which the Apostle found
himself in chap. xxii. We must not here forget that the peculiar cause of the hatred of the Jews against the Apostle was
not so much his faith in Christ, as his attack upon the law. As
long as he did not vindicate himself on this last subject, any
apologetic attempt must have been in vain; but in the whole
of the speech there is no vindication, and we cannot suppose
the reason to have been that he was interrupted, and would
have spoken on the subject if he had continued the speech. In
the second speech also in which the Apostle was at full liberty to
express himself fully and in detail, nothing is said on this point,
although it is in general designedly brought forward in the
Acts of the Apostles, as if in this case it did not affect the
Apostle Paul more than the other Apostles. In the position of
the Apostle at that time such an apology would have been of
no great value, but the affair must take a different aspect from
the standpoint of an author who has to vindicate the Apostle,
not merely in his relation to the Mosaic law, but generally
with reference to his apostolic authority. What could be
better adapted for this aim than the repeated circumstantial

mention of the extraordinary fact by which, against his own will and intention, he had been placed in the path of action in which he had hitherto worked as an Apostle.

If these two speeches, especially the first, can scarcely be considered as having been really delivered, the point of view is strongly urged upon us, that the arrest of the Apostle in this narrative portion of the Acts of the Apostles, seems to have been intended as a testimony to his innocence, and this arrest is separated from the undoubtedly more simple issue of the affair by a series of transactions in which the same scene, always resting on the same views, is constantly repeated, partly by the Apostle himself, partly by others, whose opinion seems to have been of importance. The Apostle's speech before the people has this aim, but it was not possible for the Apostle to bear witness of his innocence before the people, therefore the objective point of view was necessarily presented, on which the cause of the Apostle was to be generally decided. The transactions before the Sanhedrim were brought about by the Roman tribune, to whom the true cause of the tumultuous popular riot against the Apostle was unknown, with the intention γνῶναι τὸ ἀσφαλὲς, τὸ τί κατηγορεῖται παρὰ τῶν Ἰουδαίων (xxii. 30.) As the Apostle succeeded in drawing the party of the Pharisees over to his interest, and received from them the declaration: οὐδὲν κακὸν εὑρίσκομεν ἐν τῷ ἀνθρώπῳ τούτῳ (xxiii. 9) a public recognition of his innocence and the justness of his cause was achieved. The mild, benevolent, careful behaviour which the Roman tribune manifested towards the Apostle, must be chiefly explained, according to the Acts of the Apostles, by the favourable result of the transactions before the Sanhedrim. The fresh steps which were taken by the Roman Procurator Felix, in the form of a Roman prosecution of the Apostle, gave the latter a fresh opportunity of proving not only the injustice of the accusation brought against him, but also of exhibiting his Jewish orthodoxy in a way which makes the various religious points which divide him from his opponents appear as a highly indifferent matter. But here also we cannot imagine how the Apostle could say with a clear conscience, ὁμολογῶ δὲ τοῦτό σοι, ὅτι κατὰ τὴν ὁδὸν ἣν λέγουσιν αἵρεσιν, οὕτω λατρεύω τῷ πατρῴῳ Θεῷ πιστεύων πᾶσι τοῖς κατὰ τὸν νόμον καὶ τοῖς ἐν τοῖς προφήταις γεγραμμένοις—(also according to the first commandment, Genesis xvii. 14) ἐλπίδα ἔχων εἰς τὸν Θεὸν, ἣν καὶ αὐτοὶ οὗτοι προσδέχονται ἀνάστασιν μέλλειν ἔσεσθαι νεκρῶν δικαίων τε καὶ ἀδίκων—ἢ αὐτοὶ οὗτοι εἰπάτωσαν τὶ εὗρον ἐν ἐμοὶ ἀδίκημα, στάντος μοῦ ἐπὶ τοῦ συνεδρίου, ἢ περὶ μιᾶς ταύτης φωνῆς ἧς ἔκραξα ἑστὼς ἐν αὐτοῖς ὅτι περὶ ἀναστάσεως νεκρῶν ἐγὼ κρίνομαι σήμερον ὑφ᾽ ὑμῶν (xxiv. 41, &c.). The cause of the Apostle is here again placed in a very equivocal light, but he reaps the advantage by the Procurator Felix not deciding against him, but treating him with attention and forbearance. A new and very solemn transaction occurred in the presence of the Jewish King Agrippa and his sister Berenice under the successor of Felix—the new Procurator Porcius Festus—who, although convinced of the innocence of the Apostle, xxv. 18, by his compliant attitude towards the Jews necessitated an appeal on the part of the Apostle to the Emperor. This appearance of Paul before the King first happened at the special request of the latter (xxv. 22), and then again (verse 26) owing to the desire of the Procurator to have the opinion of the King as a Jew, in order that he might be in a situation to have something to report to Rome on the affair, although this opinion of the King could only be founded on the one-sided representation of the Apostle himself. The Apostle accordingly relates afresh before this solemn assembly the history of his conversion, together with the repeated assurance of his Jewish orthodoxy, evading at the same time the special points of the accusation against him. The result of this scene is the unanimous decision of the whole assembly : ὅτι οὐδὲν θανάτου ἀξίον ἢ δεσμῶν πράσσει ὁ ἄνθρωπος οὗτος, toge-gether with the especial declaration of Agrippa against Festus, ἀπολελύσθαι ἐδύνατο ὁ ἄνθρωπος οὗτος, εἰ μὴ ἐπεκέκλητο Καίσαρα (xxxvi. 31, 32). The author of the Acts of the Apostles has to treat of this result, he does not however desist from making it very evident of how much value such a decision was in the mouth of a man who had to exert a knowledge of all Jewish customs and religious questions, and who also knew something of the history of Jesus, (xxvi. 3). The question especially put to the King by the Apostle (verse 27) πιστεύεις βασιλεῦ Ἀγρίππα, τοῖς προφήταις, with the answer purposely given by the Apostle himself, οἶδα, ὅτι πιστεύεις, to what do they lead, except to a strengthening of the importance which the decision of the King received by this assurance of his orthodoxy? But it can scarcely be imagined that the decision of a King who was not very worthy of respect in a moral point of view could have been so pleasing to the Apostle; nor that he would have prized so much the opportunity of pleading his cause before the King, as the author of the Acts of the Apostles represents him to have done in the outset of his speech, xxvi. 2.

15

CHAPTER IX.

In consequence of the appeal made to the Emperor, the
Apostle with some other prisoners was brought from Cæsarea
to Rome at the command of the Roman Procurator Festus, by a
Roman centurion whose humane conduct is much lauded in
the Acts of the Apostles. The detailed relation of this journey,
apparently taken from an account of it by Luke, although here
and there betraying another hand, is for the most part authentic;
and what the Acts of the Apostles gives with regard to the
life of the Apostle is of very little importance in the history of
his apostolic labours. As soon as the Apostle arrives in Rome
we see him again placed in antagonistic relations to the Jews,
and these in their results require a more lengthy discussion.
The thing most worthy of remark contained in the Acts of
the Apostles regarding the life of the Apostle is the notice
given at the conclusion, that the Apostle remained two whole
years in Rome, and held free intercourse with all that came to
him, working unhindered for the kingdom of God by the
preaching of the Gospel of Christ. What makes this concluding remark which has been so much discussed, so enigmatical, is that it assigns a period of two years, at the expiration of
which a change may be supposed as taking place in the circumstances of the Apostle, and something definite as succeeding.
But what could this have been? If after so long a delay the
appeal of the Apostle to the Emperor was then decided and the
Apostle consequently set at liberty, it does not seem conceivable
that the author of the Acts of the Apostles should pass over
in utter silence an event which would have been the result of

all that had gone before, and which would so exactly have been in accordance with the apostolic tendency of the work.*

The general idea is, that the Apostle at the expiration of these two years, being free either through the decision of the Emperor or for some other reasons, immediately took another journey and went into Spain, but afterwards suffered a second imprisonment at Rome, and at last died as a martyr in Rome at the same time as the Apostle Peter. A second Roman imprisonment is first spoken of by Eusebius, but the reasons for this supposition which it seems was traditional, even in the time of Eusebius, are only the so-called Epistles of the Apostle, which without it were thought not to be intelligible.† The decision to which we come on this pretended fact, as well as on the others which overstep the boundary line set by the Acts of the Apostles, must depend chiefly on the question, what trust can be given to the historical connection with which the history of the further destiny of the Apostle is entwined. We cannot even here separate Paul from Peter, both must even at the end share the same fate. This is full of significance. We cannot fail to see in it the mythical traditional continuation of the parallel which the author of the Acts of the Apostles has all along instituted between the two Apostles. The legend arising from a definite idea attains its resting point in a belief spreading over the universal consciousness of the period, that Peter and Paul, as the two most glorious Apostles, together founded the Roman Church, and after this common work died the same

---

* In order to explain this conclusion of the Acts of the Apostles, Schneckenburger remarks, page 126—"He came to Rome and there preached unmolested. '*μετὰ πάσης παρρησίας ἀκωλύτως.*' Is not this a fitting conclusion? Is it not quite in harmony with the bias running through the whole history of Paul?" Certainly, but if the author of the Acts of the Apostles had had no more positive end to carry out, Paul would not really have been found innocent and released.

† H. E. ii. 22. Τότε μὲν οὖν ἀπολογησάμενον αὖθις ἐπὶ τὴν τοῦ κηρύγματος διακονίαν λόγος ἔχει στείλασθαι τὸν ἀπόστολον· δεύτερον δ' ἐπιβάντα τῇ αὐτῇ πόλει τῷ κατ' αὐτὸν (Νέρωνα) τελειωθῆναι μαρτυρίῳ ἐν ᾧ δεσμοῖς ἐχόμενος τόν πρὸς Τιμόθεον δευτέραν συντάττει ἐπιστολὴν ὁμοῦ σημαίνων τήν τε προτέραν αὐτῷ γενομένην ἀπολογίαν καὶ τὴν παραπόδας τελείωσιν.

15 *

death as martyrs in the same city. Here the legend attains its
aim, but its real point of action only consists in what belongs to
the life history of the Apostle Paul. Paul did actually come to
Rome—the office in which he had hitherto laboured among the
people, as the Apostle to the Gentiles, had led him thither—and
it can also be looked on as an historical fact that he died there
as a martyr. But all that we find in reference to Peter is from
the first very doubtful and legendary. It cannot be disputed
that he laboured for the Gospel beyond the bounds of Judea.
At least the Acts of the Apostles represents him as not only
going into Samaria, but also as travelling into the Phœnician
cities, and according to Gal. ii. 11, he also went to Antioch.
But on this point further information is wanting, and the passage, 1 Cor. ix. 5, establishes no correct conclusion. The Apostle
Paul indeed here says of himself, μὴ οὐκ ἔχομεν ἐξουσίαν, ἀδελφὴν
γυναῖκα περιάγειν, ὡς καὶ οἱ λοιποὶ ἀπόστολοι, καὶ οἱ ἀδελφοὶ τοῦ
κυρίου καὶ Κηφᾶς, but this περιάγειν can only be meant of the
Apostle himself, and the sense of the words can only be thus—
whether he had not the right to take with him on his missionary
journeys an ἀδελφὴ γυνὴ as the rest of the Apostles had an ἀδελφὴ
γυνὴ. In any case it may well be assumed that the foreign missionary activity of the Apostle Peter, was directed exclusively to
the Jews, according to the arrangements made Gal. ii. 9. Of
course there is some mention of the martyrdom of the Apostle
Peter in the New Testament, but it is only in the apocryphal
sounding addition to the Gospel of John, xxi. 18, 19, and here
as well as in the fourth epistle of Clement of Rome, chap. 5, no
place is ever specified. The legend of his residence in Rome is
without doubt to be referred to the passage, 1 Peter v. 13, as the
interpretation of Babylon by Rome agrees best with the whole
nature of the Epistle. Perhaps we may see a slight allusion to
this legend in the two passages, Acts xix. 21, and xxiii. 11.
At the time, when the Apostle Paul first took the resolve to
travel from Ephesus, by Macedonia and Achaia to Jerusalem, he
very emphatically declared ὅτι μετὰ τὸ γενέσθαι με ἐκεῖ, δεῖ με

καὶ Ῥώμην ἰδεῖν, and when he had successfully undergone the trial before the Sanhedrim, and the stormy scene with which it ended, the Lord must be represented as appearing to him on the following night, and encouraging him with the words, θάρσει ὡς γὰρ διεμαρτύρω τὰ περὶ ἐμοῦ εἰς Ἱερουσαλὴμ, οὕτω σε δεῖ καὶ εἰς Ῥώμην μαστυρῆσαι. In both these passages the idea is so expressly conveyed that the highest aim of his efforts, the fairest point of view of his completed apostolic course is the εἰς Ῥώμην μαρτυρῆσαι, that it cannot have taken place without some special intention. It may not be too bold to suppose that the idea of the Apostle Peter (who is represented by the legend as being already at Rome) may have floated in the mind of an author who throughout shows so decidedly apologetic a tendency. Whether this is so or not, the Apostle Paul had the actual truth on his side, but in order as clearly as possible to vindicate his claims, the author of the Acts of the Apostles makes him express beforehand his knowledge of his destination.

In proceeding from the commencement of this legend to its further development, we find it divided into two different branches, one of which takes an Anti-Pauline, the other a Petrino-Pauline direction. The first of these forms is connected with Simon Magus, on whose account Peter came to Rome. The Acts of the Apostles represents them as meeting in Samaria. When the Apostle perceived the perverse condition of the Magus by his endeavour to partake of the Holy Spirit by unlawful means, he recognized the danger of corruption which threatened Christianity through the Magus. Although this may really have been connected with the historical person of the Magus, it is easy to see in the Acts of the Apostles that he is the mythical representation of a Samaritan popular deity. As the Samaritan religion was considered as heathen, so he was the representative as well of the heretical Christianity mixed with heathen elements as of heathenism itself;*

* Die Chr. Gnosis, p. 306. Christenthum der drei ersten Jahrh. p. 1, 8, etc. treats exhaustively and accurately of Simon Magus.

and the Apostle Peter travelled from place to place, from
land to land, from east to west, only to follow the Magus
going before him, to combat him in every form, and to refute
the godless doctrines promulgated by him. In this form the
legend plays the chief part in the pseudo-Clementine Homilies,
and in the writings connected with it. In the same form Eusebius recognizes it. As soon as the Magus had fled before the
Apostle from the east to the west, and had so far carried his
magic arts in Rome itself that he was there honoured as a God
and had a statue erected to him—Peter also appeared there.
Παραπόδας γοῦν ἐπὶ τῆς αὐτῆς Κλαυδίου βασιλείας ἡ πανάγαθος
καὶ φιλανθρωποτάτη τῶν ὅλων πρόνοια τὸν καρτερὸν καὶ μέγαν τῶν
Ἀποστόλων, τὸν ἀρετῆς ἕνεκα τῶν λοιπῶν ἀπάντων προήγορον,
Πέτρον, ἐπὶ τὴν Ῥώμην ὡς ἐπι τηλικοῦτον λυμεῶνα βίου χειρα-
γωγεῖ ὅς ὅιατις γενναῖος τοῦ θεοῦ στρατηγὸς τοῖς θείος ὅπλοις
φραξάμενος, τὴν πολυτίμητον ἐμπορείαν τοῦ νοητοῦ φωτὸς ἐξ
ἀνατολῶν τοῖς κατὰ δύσιν ἐκόμιζεν φῶς αὐτὸ καὶ λόγον ψυχῶν
σωτήριον, τὸ κήρυγμα τῆς τῶν οὐρανῶν βασιλείας εὐαγγελιζόμενος.
What is said here as well as by Justin Martyr in the "apology,"
regarding a statue erected to this Simon in Rome, in an island
on the Tiber with this inscription, " Simoni deo Sancta," is an
evident mistake, a confusion of Simon Magus with the Sabine
Roman god Semo Sancus, (which also may have been originally
allied with the ancient Eastern Sem-Semo), but the important
legend of the Magus and the Apostle Peter cannot have been
derived from this. For this cause then the Apostle came at so
early a period to Rome. Eusebius at the close of his narrative (ii. 15) appeals for the truth of this tradition to Clement
of Alexandria, who has related the history in the sixth book
of his Institutes, and to the corresponding testimony of
Bishop Papias of Hieropolis. It is here truly doubtful whether
Clement and Papias are of any value as witnesses for the whole
of the foregoing striking narrative of Simon Magus and
Peter, or only for that part of it which refers to the Gospel
of Mark.

About the reason which Mark may have had for composing his Gospel in Rome, Eusebius says : "the great impression which Peter had made on the Romish Christians by his brilliant victory over Simon Magus, had produced the lively wish in them to possess a written memorial of the Christian doctrine he had delivered to them. So on their pressing entreaty, Mark the companion of Peter, became the author of the Gospel handed down under his name." As we see in Eusebius vi. 14, Clement really speaks of Peter's activity in teaching in Rome, but whether this is also to be gathered from the elder Papias is doubtful, as Eusebius can scarcely have meant this by the passage (iii. 39) quoted by him from the works of Papias, in which it is only said that the Gospel of Mark arose from the doctrinal teachings of the Apostle Peter. In the meanwhile the Romish origin of the Gospel of Mark seems to have been an ancient tradition, which nevertheless may have been well known to Papias, and if it were well known to him why should he not have been acquainted with all the rest which stood in close connection with it? Mark indeed came to Rome only as the companion of Peter, but for what cause could Peter at so early a period have come to Rome, if the presence of Simon Magus there had not afforded one? It is very possible that the legend in this form had a certain antithetical relation to the Apostle Paul. If Simon Magus be heathenism personified, then the Apostle Peter, who travelled everywhere after him, combating him and converting the people from his false doctrines, would with justice be specially described as the Gentile Apostle, which he really was not, but ought to have been, in order not to leave Paul alone to enjoy this renown. The pseudo-Clementine Homilies expressly ascribe this title to the Apostle Peter, as he himself says, iii. 39. "ὁρμᾷν εἰς τὰ ἔθνη τὰ πολλοὺς θεοὺς λέγοντα, κηρύξαι καὶ διδάξαι, ὅτι εἷς ἐστιν ὁ θεὸς ὃς οὐρανὸν ἔκτισε καὶ γῆν καὶ τὰ ἐν αὐτοῖς πάντα ὅπως ἀγαπήσαντες αὐτὸν σωθῆναι δυνηθῶσιν." This sphere, which we are accustomed to see occupied exclusively by Paul, as the Apostle to the Gentiles, is here described as being equally filled by Peter, and in this same homily the matter takes a truly surprising aspect—it exhibits in Simon Magus, conquered by the Apostle Peter, no less a person than the Apostle Paul himself. It has been already shown what unequivocal attacks upon the Apostle Paul these Homilies contain, how especially they seek to represent him, according to their theory of revelation, as an Apostle forced on a wrong track, and as one who dispensed with all true authority. This attack runs through all the contents of these Homilies. What is so strongly advanced by Peter against Simon Magus, namely that he had called him a κατεγνωσμένος (Hom. xvii. 19) is stated with reference to the Apostle Paul (Gal. ii. 11). There is the same reference when Peter, in the letter to James which precedes the Homilies, chap. ii., speaks of a difference of doctrine which he not only knew of as a prophet, but because he could already see the beginning of evils. " For some among the Gentiles," he says, " have rejected the lawful doctrine which they received from me, and have adopted the lawless and unworthy doctrines of a man opposed to me. And already in my lifetime some have undertaken through artful interpretation of my teachings to transform them into exhortations to the abolition of the law, as if I myself did not think and teach freely and candidly the very opposite. This conduct of theirs is nothing but opposition to the laws of God, which were given by Moses, and testified to our Lord when he said with regard to his own everlasting duration, ' Heaven and earth shall pass away before one jot or one tittle of the law shall fail.' Thus spoke He of whom are all things. But those persons who, I know not how, seem to know my meaning, and to understand that of the teachings which I deliver, better than I do myself, say of those teachings, that their doctrine and intention are such as I never intended them to be. If such persons in my lifetime dare to utter such lies, how much more will they dare to lie after my death !"

It cannot well admit of doubt that by this ἄνθρωπως ἐχθρὸς, whose ἄνομος καὶ φλυαρώδης διδασκαλία the Gentiles accepted, was understood the Apostle Paul. He is also that πλάνος of whom Peter, Homil. ii. 17., says, that before him Simon Magus had gone to the Gentiles—he after him. ἐπελθὼν ὡς σκότῳ φῶς, ὡς ἀγνοία γνῶσις, ὡς νόσω ἴασις. οὕτως δὴ ὡς ἀληθὴς ἡμῶν προφήτης εἴρηκεν, πρῶτον ψευδὲς δεῖ ἐλθεῖν εὐαγγέλιον ὑπὸ πλάνου τινὸς καὶ εἶθ' οὕτως μετὰ καθαίρεσιν τοῦ ἁγίου τόπου εὐαγγέλιον ἀληθὲς κρύφα διαπεμφθῆναι, εἰς ἐπανόρθωσιν τῶν ἐσομένων αἱρέσεων. The false Gospel of this heretical teacher following on the true one, is Pauline as to the abolition of the law, and the words μετὰ καθαίρεσιν τοῦ ἁγίου τόπου are not merely a chronological definition, but also an allusion to Acts xxi. 28, according to which passage the Jews fell upon Paul with the cry, οὑτός ἐστιν ὁ ἄνθρωπος, ὁ κατὰ τοῦ λαοῦ, καὶ τοῦ νόμου καὶ τοῦ τόπου τούτου πάντας πανταχοῦ διδάσκων, ἔτι δὲ καὶ Ἕλληνας εἰσήγαγεν εἰς τὸ ἱερὸν καὶ κεκοίνωκε τὸν ἅγιον τόπον τοῦτον. With regard to the occurrence here related, the attitude of the Apostle Paul, so inimical to any forced abolition of the Mosaic law, and the other institutions of Judaism, are designated as a καθαίρεσις τοῦ ἁγίου τόπου, in order to represent this wild, characteristically heathen disturbance about the law, as at the same time a prelude to the destruction by the Romans of Jerusalem and the Temple—the τόπος ἅγιος.

All these accusations bespeak the genuine Ebionitish spirit and character of these Homilies. The Ebionites saw in the Apostle Paul only an apostate from the law, a false teacher, whose collected Epistles they cast away.* And Epiphanius could have mentioned, if he had chosen, many other things concerning their abuse of the Apostle Paul. As men would rather consider those who have become hated heretics, and innovators in religious matters, as never having been members of the religion against which they so sorely offended,

---

* Irenæus contra haer. 1, 26. Eusebius, H. E. 3, 27.

so the Ebionites maintained that Paul was no Jew by birth, but a Greek or Gentile, springing from Gentile ancestors, and who only at a later time had become a proselyte to Judaism. To account for his inimical attitude towards Judaism there is a tale which reminds us of many other charges originating in the same spirit. The Ebionites asserted that when Paul came at a later period to Jerusalem and remained there for some time, he courted a daughter of the high-priest. With this view he became a proselyte, and allowed himself to be circumcised. But as he did not succeed in obtaining the fulfilment of his wishes, he wrote in wrath and vexation against circumcision and the Sabbath, and the law generally.* If on the other hand we assert that the Ebionites took so inimical a position against the Apostle Paul on account of their extreme heretical tendencies, still we must not forget that Ebionitism from the beginning comprised the same elements which at last constituted it a heresy, and the Jewish-Christian opponents already combated by the Apostle Paul in his Epistles, give the most undoubted testimony as to what feeling prevailed against the Apostle Paul, in that most ancient period of the first existing opposition between Ebionitism and Paulinism. These views and feelings against the Apostle Paul are brought forward throughout, in a greater or less degree, as the decided Ebionite element is of a more or less defined character. As Papias and Hegesippus belonged to the Jewish-Christian or Ebionite party, it cannot be surprising to find even in the few fragments of their writings which have been handed down, traces which make us certain of their anti-Pauline tendency. Papias is very desirous (as he testifies of himself in Eusebius (H. E. iii. 39) to collect together and keep in remembrance all which he thought worth mention, of the actual and enduring sayings of the immediate disciples of the Lord, which he held to be of more importance than their writings. To this end he made enquiries specially

---

* Περὶ τοῦ ἁγίου Παύλου ὡς βλασφημοῦντες αὐτὸν λέγουσι, πόσα ἔχω λέγειν; Haer. 30, 25.　　　　　　　† Epiphanius, Ch. 16.

of those who had stood in the most immediate connection with the original disciples of Jesus. "Οὐ γὰρ," he says, "τοῖς τὰ πολλὰ λέγουσιν ἔχαιρον ὥσπερ οἱ πολλοὶ, ἀλλὰ τοῖς τάληθῆ διδάσκουσιν, οὐδὲ τοῖς τὰς ἀλλοτρίας ἐντολὰς μνημονεύουσιν, ἀλλὰ τοῖς τὰς παρὰ τοῦ κυρίου τῇ πίστει δεδομένας καὶ ἀπ' αὐτῆς παραγινομένας τῆς ἀληθείας." Therefore he carefully asked for what Andrew, Peter, Philip, Thomas, Matthew, or any other of the disciples of the Lord had said. There is no mention made here of the Apostle Paul, but it is not improbable that a man who laid so much weight on tradition which went back directly to the doctrine and person of Christ, should have had in view the Apostle Paul and his adherents, in speaking of those who τὰς ἀλλοτρίας ἐντολὰς μνημονεύουσι, in opposition to those who had been the recipients of the utterances of truth from the Lord himself.* Photius has preserved a remarkable fragment on Hegesippus, in his epitome of a work of the Monophysite Stephen Gobarus. The writings of Stephen Gobarus consist of a series of articles in which he has collected together the contradictory declarations of the teachers of the Church. On this point he says, ὅτι τὰ ἡτοιμασμένα τοῖς δικαίοις ἀγαθὰ οὔτε ὀφθαλμὸς εἶδεν ὄντε οὓς ἤκουσεν, οὔτε ἐπὶ καρδίαν ἀνθρώπου ἀνέβη, and continues in contrast to this : Ἡγήσιππος μέντοι, ἀρχαῖός τε ἀνὴρ καὶ ἀποστολικὸς ἐν τῷ πέμπτῳ τῶν ὑπομνημάτων, οὐκ οἶδ' ὅτι καὶ παθὼν μάτην μὲν εἰρῆσθαι ταῦτα λέγει καὶ καταψεύδεσθαι τοὺς ταῦτα φαμένους τῶν τε θειῶν γραφῶν καὶ τοῦ κυρίου λέγοντος· μακάριοι οἱ ὀφθαλμοὶ ὑμῶν οἱ βλέποντες καὶ τὰ ὦτα ὑμῶν τὰ ἀκούοντα. The first extract is taken from 1 Cor. ii. 9, and the charge of false doctrine seems therefore to point to the Apostle Paul. The charge of falseness is based on these words and in opposition to them the declaration of the Lord, Matthew xiii. 16, is stated. In this passage Jesus esteems his disciples blessed because they see and hear what many prophets and righteous men desired to see, and to hear, and had not

---

* Bibl. Cod. 232.

seen and heard. The reason of their blessedness is the direct presence of the person of Jesus which was granted to the Apostles in their special relation to him. This utterance of the Lord seems to Hegesippus to be completely in contradiction to what the Apostle Paul says : 1 Cor. ii. 9. " ἀλλὰ, καθὼς γέγραπται ἃ ὀφθαλμὸς οὐκ εἶδε, καὶ οὖς οὐκ ἤκουσε, καὶ ἐπὶ καρδίαν ἀνθρώπου οὐκ ἀνέβη ἃ ἡτοίμασεν ὁ θεὸς τοῖς ἀγαπῶσιν αὐτὸν ἡμῖν δὲ ἀπεκάλυψεν ὁ θεὸς διὰ τοῦ πνεύματος αὐτοῦ," and as Hegesippus undoubtedly understands these words to refer to the way and manner in which Paul was asserted to have been called to the apostolic office by a special revelation, we have here the same opposition as is set up in the pseudo-Clementine Homilies, when these deny the true characteristics of apostleship to the Apostle Paul, because he had become an Apostle only by a visionary revelation, and not, as the other Apostles, by immediate intercourse with Jesus. Because this sanction of the apostolic office was wanting to him, Hegesippus declares him to be according to the Ebionite view a liar, and his assertion that a man may become an Apostle without any outward hearing or seeing, to be a groundless one (μάτην εἰρῆσθαι ταῦτα). There is no reason whatever why we should take the words of Hegesippus in any other sense than that which they themselves precisely express, as all that we know of Hegesippus leaves us in no doubt of his Ebionitism. It is highly unsatisfactory to suppose with Neander that he may have said this, not out of opposition to Paul, but in eager zeal against the opponents of the material millenium which the Pauline passages already quoted and many others tend to oppose, in order to do away with the sensuous ideas of future happiness.* Such zeal for the material millenium would indeed point him out as a genuine Ebionite, from whom we must therefore expect the usual Ebionite views of the Apostle Paul.† It is only the strongest expression of these

---

* Gesch. der. Chr. Kal. u. Kirche, 2' A., p. 1160.

† It can only be alleged against this reading of the quotation from Hegesippus referring to the Apostle Paul, that according to another fragment of the same

views when it was said directly of the Apostle Paul that he was no Jew but a Gentile—a Samaritan—that Simon Magus who was conquered by the Apostle Peter, and it may be that this form of the legend, according to which Peter in the dispute with the Magus followed him to Rome, originated in the anti-Pauline tendency of Ebonitism.

The other form of the legend represents the two Apostles as in fraternal agreement instead of being at enmity. They work together in their vocation, share the same martyr-death, and the scene of their common and glorious martyrdom is Rome, the Eternal City of the world. The comparison of the different witnesses on this legend shows clearly how it keeps decidedly in view this common object in Rome. Clement of Rome, the oldest witness on this point, merely speaks of the martyrdom with which the two Apostles ended the great work of their life. In his first Epistle to the Corinthians (chap. iii.), he reminds this church, which was again divided into parties, of the great mischief which is excited by envy and malevolence, and exhorts it to order and unity. After quoting some Old Testament examples as proofs of this truth, he continues (chap. v.) : Ἀλλ'ἵνα τῶν ἀρχαίων ὑποδειγμάτων παυσώμεθα, ἔλθωμεν ἐπὶ τοὺς ἔγγιστα γενομένους ἀθλητάς· λάβωμεν τῆς γενεᾶς ἡμῶν τὰ γενναῖα ὑποδείγματα. Διὰ ζῆλον καὶ φθόνον οἱ μέγιστοι καὶ δικαιότατοι

work of Hegesippus (Eusebius, H. E. iii. 32) the church up to the time of the first Gnostics had remained a pure untainted virgin, and only after the holy company of the Apostles was broken up, the ἄθεος πλάνη had their beginning. But it must not be forgotten that the Church at that time remained only ἐν ἀδήλῳ που σκότει φωλευόντων εἰσέτι τότε τῶν, εἰ καὶ τινες ὑπῆρχον παραφθείρειν ἐπιχειρούντων τὸν ὑγιῆ κανόνα τοῦ σωτηρίου κηρύγματος. At that time also ὑπῆρχόν τινες. As Peter speaks of such τινες in the Homilies, and also in the epistle to James, chapter ii., ἔτι μου περιόντος ἐπεχείρησάν τινες, &c. Although Hegesippus attaches no further importance to this τινες, because the immediate presence of the Apostle seemed to him so overpowering that a heretical element, even did it exist, could not flourish. The expressions αὐτὴ ἡ ἀλήθεια, ἡ ἔνθεος σοφία, in reference to the Person of Christ, which point out the truth to the Prophet in the Homilies, are very convincing as to the Ebionite character of Papias and Hegesippus. The living voice of this truth Papias thought he perceived in the traditions which he collected.

στύλοι ἐδιώχθησαν καὶ ἕως θανάτου ἦλθον. Λάβωμεν πρὸ
ὀφθαλμῶν ἡμῶν τοὺς ἀγαθοὺς ᾿Αποστόλους. ῾Ο Πέτρος διὰ
ζῆλον ἄδικον οὐχ ἕνα, οὐδὲ δύο, ἀλλὰ πλείονας ὑπήνεγκεν πόνους
καὶ οὕτω μαρτυρήσας ἐπορεύθη εἰς τὸν ὀφειλόμενον τόπον τῆς
δόξης. Διὰ ζῆλον ὁ Παῦλος ὑπομονῆς βραβεῖον ὑπέσχεν ἑπτάκις
δεσμὰ φορέσας ῥαβδευθεὶς λιθασθεὶς, κῆρυξ γενόμενος ἔν τε τῇ
ἀνατολῇ καὶ ἐν τῇ δύσει, τὸ γενναῖον τῆς πίστεως αὐτοῦ κλέος
ἔλαβεν, δικαιοσύνην διδάξας ὅλον τὸν κόσμον, καὶ ἐπὶ τὸ τέρμα
τῆς δύσεως ἐλθὼν, καὶ μαρτυρήσας ἐπὶ τῶν ἡγουμένων, οὕτως
ἀπηλλάγη τοῦ κόσμου, καὶ εἰς τὸν ἅγιον τόπον ἐπορεύθη
ὑπομονῆς γενόμενος μέγιστος ὑπόγραμμος. It may be reasonably doubted here whether the μαρτυρεῖν of Peter is to
be understood as referring specially to his martyrdom, or
merely in a wider sense to his witness to the truth through
his apostolic labours. But in this case there is so little advantage conceded to Peter over Paul that the former is really
shown to hold a secondary place. Not only are the long enduring labours of Paul described with precise details, but it is
expressly shown that he was a herald of the faith in the west as
well as in the east, and arrived at the end of his career as the
Teacher of the whole world. But there is not a word said
tending to show that the two Apostles suffered martyrdom together; we must therefore rather conclude on the contrary, that
it was said only of Paul and not also of Peter that he worked in
the west as well as in the east. Both Apostles truly became
martyrs in the wider sense, but even here the difference must
be pointed out, that Paul as ἐλθὼν ἐπὶ τὸ τέρμα τῆς δύσεως καὶ
μαρτυρήσας ἐπὶ τῶν ἡγουμένων is called the great example of
steadfast endurance. At a later period when the martyrdom
of Peter was an established fact, there was at any rate some
contradiction on the point whether both the Apostles suffered
martyrdom at the same time. We find in the transactions of
a Roman Synod, held under Bishop Gelasius I., the following
sentence in reference to Peter, " Cui data est etiam societas
S. Pauli, qui non diverso sicut hæretici garriunt, sed uno

tempore eodemque die, gloriosa morte cum Petro in urbe
Roma cum Nerone agonizans coronatus est."* It is true that
here the question is only of a difference in the point of time,
but as soon as we find it said that they did not share the same
martyrdom in the same place, at the same time, the whole
aspect of the affair is changed, and from the *garrire* charged to
the heretics, we may conclude that there was a further difference, resting on an older tradition. But the same interest,
in which the Apostles are placed in relation to each other and
in which we really see them in the passage quoted from Clement of Rome, although they are here again more separated,
shows more and more in the further development of the legend
that they as much as possible had everything in common.
They not only suffered a common martyrdom at the same time,
and in the same place, that is to say in Rome, but it is no accidental connection that unites them, they had entered on the
journey to Rome from the same point of their common labours,
in view of the same martyrdom. This fact is especially
brought forward in the testimony of the Corinthian Bishop
Dionysius, who lived soon after the middle of the second
century. Eusebius quotes him as a witness of the common
Roman martyrdom of both the Apostles in the words (ii. 25),
ὡς δὲ κατὰ τὸν αὐτὸν ἄμφω καιρὸν ἐμαρτύρησαν, Κορινθίων
ἐπίσκοπος Διονύσιος ἐγγράφως Ῥωμαίοις ὁμιλῶν ὡδέ πως παρίσ-
τησιν· ταῦτα καὶ ὑμεῖς διὰ τῆς τοσαύτης νουθεσίας τὴν ἀπὸ Πέτρου
καὶ Παύλου φυτείαν γενεθεῖσαν Ῥωμαίων τε καὶ Κορινθίων συνεκεράσατε. Καὶ γὰρ ἄμφω καὶ εἰς τὴν ἡμετέραν Κόρινθον φυτεύσαντες
ἡμᾶς ὁμοίως δὲ καὶ εἰς τὴν Ἰταλίαν ὁμόσε διδάξαντες ἐμαρτύρησαν
κατὰ τὸν αὐτὸν καιρόν. The two Apostles not merely suffered
the same martyrdom in Rome—they were also the common
founders of the Corinthian as well as of the Romish Church—
as Irenæus says in the well-known passage: "maxima et
antiquissima et omnibus cognita, a gloriossimus duobus Apos-

---

* Contra hær. iii. 3.

tolis Petro et Paulo—Romæ fundata et constituta ecclesia."
The two Apostles stand side by side like brothers united together in death as in life, both share the same renown. But
this equilibrium is soon lost in the preponderance of one over
the other. It is not only the simple historical truth which
places them so fraternally together, the legend represents a rival
interest springing up between them ; and Paul who in the first
form of the legend took such an adverse part, is now everywhere made to give place to Peter who has gained the upper
hand of him. If both Apostles, as Tertullian says,* "Felix
ecclesia totam doctrinam cum sanguine suo profuderunt," it is
then only Peter who "passioni dominicæ adæquatur," whilst
Paul "Johannis" (the Baptist) "exitu coronatur," which is
further strengthened by the statement of Origen,† that Peter
after the preaching of the Gospel in Pontus, Galatia, Bithynia,
Cappadocia, and Asia, had at last come to Rome also. ἐν Ῥώμῃ
γενόμενος ἀνεσκολοπίσθη κατὰ κεφαλῆς, οὕτως αὐτὸς ἀξιώσας
παθεῖν, wherein Ruffinus in his translation of the Ecclesiastical
History of Eusebius gives the following commentary : "Cruci-
fixus est deorsum, capite demerso, quod ipse ita fieri deprecatus
est ne exæquari Domino videretur," although Tertullian takes
no objection to the adæquari passioni dominicæ. Their graves
even are not in the same place. The Presbyter Caius, living
under the Roman Bishop Zephyrinus, first speaks as Eusebius
maintains of the martyr graves of the two Apostles. In his
work against the Montanist Proclus he may have mentioned
the place, "ἔνθα τῶν εἰρημένων ἀποστόλων τὰ ἱερὰ σκηνώματα
κατατέθειται," in the words "Ἐγὼ δὲ τὰ τρόπαια τῶν Ἀποστόλων ἔχω δεῖξαι· Ἐὰν γὰρ θελήσῃς ἀπελθεῖν ἐπὶ τὸν βατίκανὸν,
ἢ ἐπὶ τὴν ὁδὸν τὴν Ὠστίαν, εὑρήσεις τὰ τρόπαια τῶν ταύτην
ἱδρυσαμένων τὴν ἐκκλησίαν," and Eusebius maintains, in proof of
the trustworthiness of the traditions concerning Peter and

---

† De praeser. haer. c, 36. Compare adv. Mark iv. 5. Petrus passioni dominicæ
adæquatur.
† In the passage in Eusebius, H. E. iii. 1. Compare Dem. Ev. 37. H. E. 2. 25.

Paul that the places where the two Apostles were buried were generally known up to this time and were called by this name.* Caius does not indeed particularly describe the τρόπαια of the Apostle, but there can be no doubt that already at this time the legend had assigned to the Apostle Peter the more distinguished place in the Vatican, and to Paul on the contrary that outside the city on the way leading to Ostia. Still more striking is the subordination of Paul to Peter in the narrative of Lactantius: "quumque jam Nero imperaret, Petrus Romam advenit, et editis quibusdam miraculis, quæ virtute ipsius Dei, data sibi ab eo potestate faciebat, convertit multos ad justitiam, Deoque templum fidele ac stabile collocavit. Qua re ad Neronem delata, quum animadverteret, non modo Romæ, sed ubique quotidie magnam multitudinem deficere a cultu idolorum et ad religionem novam, damnata vetustate, transire, ut erat execrabilis ac nocens tyrannus—Petrum cruci affixit et Paulum interfecit." † Here Paul is only casually mentioned, the legend confines itself to Peter only, he alone is the first and special founder of the Roman Church. As without doubt Simon Magus again plays a part in so general a review of his miraculous deeds, this narrative presents that form of legend which receives its thoroughly complete legendary shape in the apocryphal Acta SS. Apostolorum Pauli et Petri. According to these Acta, when Paul came to Rome Peter was already there with Simon Magus. The greatest part of the people were converted by the preaching of the two Apostles.

Peter indeed converted Nero's wife Livia, and Agrippina the wife of the Prefect Agrippa; Paul converted many soldiers and dependants of the Court; but the Magus working against them out of envy still obtained followers by his magic arts, although Peter strove against his sorcery by the miracles which he worked, by healing the sick, expelling demons, and raising

---

* Πιστοῦται τὴν ἱστορίαν ἡ Πέτρου καὶ Παύλου εἰς δεῦρο κρατήσασα ἐπὶ τῶν αὐτόθι κοιμητηρίων πρόσρησις. H. E. 2-25.

† De Mort. persecut. C. 2.

the dead. The contest of the two Apostles with the Magus carried on before the Emperor Nero ended indeed by the Magus being struck dead to the earth by the prayer of the Apostles, as he was about to ascend flying to heaven, and after his death, being divided into four parts and changed into a stone consisting of four flints; while the two Apostles were put to death as martyrs by Nero's command. Paul was beheaded outside the city, Peter was crucified, and by his own desire, on a reversed cross; for as the Lord who had come down to earth from heaven had been raised on a cross standing upright, so he who was summoned from earth to heaven, ought to turn his head to the earth and his feet to heaven. It may be seen by the explanation which Peter himself gives on this subject to Nero,* that the relation of Paul to Peter is worthy of being remarked. " Everything that Paul has said is true ; for a long time I have received many letters from our Bishops all over the world, about what Paul said and did. When he was a persecutor of the law† the voice of Christ called to him from heaven and taught him the truth, because he was not an enemy of our faith through malevolence but through ignorance. For there were before us false Christs such as Simon, and false Apostles and Prophets, who attacked the sacred writings and sought to abolish the truth. Against these there could only be opposed a man who from childhood had devoted himself to nothing else than the investigation of the secrets of the Divine Law, and the defence of truth and the persecution of falsehood. But as his persecution did not arise from malevolence but only from a defence of the law, the truth appeared to him out of Heaven, and said

---

* Philo, part ii. p. 11.

† Διώκτου γὰρ αὐτοῦ ὄντος τοῦ νόμου, φωνὴ αὐτὸν Χριστοῦ ἐκ τοῦ οὐρανοῦ ἐκάλεσε. If Paul was converted as a persecutor of the law, then his conversion to Christianity is represented as a conversion from his enmity to the law. Law and truth, or Christianity, are here identical. From this standpoint, the original Ebionitish one—the Apostle's persecution of Christianity was confounded with his Christian Antinomianism. He was to be converted from his Antinomianism if he were to be of any value as an Apostle.

' I am Jesus whom thou persecutest, cease from persecuting me, for thou shalt be seen to fight against the foes of truth.' " In this form has mythical tradition as completely as possible perpetuated its conciliatory tendency. Not only are all the elements of the legend adopted, but the two Apostles are brought as closely together as is possible whilst granting the superiority of Peter. Peter is in Rome with the Magus, but the scene 'is now laid in the reign of Nero, in order that the Apostle Paul may take part in it. There is now still a slight trace to be found of his Ebionite identification with the Magus, for his conversion by Christ is necessary for the purpose of the contest with the Magus. In proportion as he is recognized by Peter, as an Apostle and a brother, must he be subordinate to him. Only through him is he legitimatized. When the two Apostles prepare for the last and crowning act, the conquering of the Magus, the Acta make Paul himself say to Peter : " It becomes me to pray to God on my knees—but it becomes thee to bring to nothing what thou seest the Magus do, because thou wert first chosen by the Lord." Peter was the special miracle-worker and conqueror of the Magus.*

If we look through the legend in its various forms and modifications we cannot ignore the interest which it takes throughout in the cause of Peter. Considering the actual facts which lie at the root of the matter, Paul has indisputably the nearest and most unequivocal claim to having founded the Roman Church, and yet it is Peter who eventually gathers all the conclusions drawn from these facts to himself, and leaves Paul scarcely any share

---

* The form in which these Acta have come down to us cannot be very ancient; but the traditional elements which they contain are much older. Origen scarcely says anything of the crucifixion, κατὰ κεφαλῆς, neither of the appearance of Christ related also in these Acta, as having been vouchsafed to Peter before his martyrdom, when Christ told him he should be crucified again. Wherefore Origen refers to πράξεις Παύλου. In Joh. 1, xx. c. 12. Compare De princ. 1, 2. Fortasse hæc Acta, remarks Thilo, Part ii. p. 24, fuerunt Petri et Pauli sicut probabile est, Prædicationes Petri et Pauli fuisse unum idemque scriptum quod modo sub alterutrius modo sub utrius que nomine allegatur.

in the matter. This evident bias not only necessarily casts suspicion on the legend, but it opposes the real historical facts in a manner which can only be explained by the same bias. The Acts of the Apostles which bears a documentary character, most particularly, in its account of the travels of the Apostle to Rome, says nothing of a meeting between Peter and Paul in Rome, and thus so far confirms the supposition which is generally advanced, that the companionship of the two Apostles began after the time when the Acts of the Apostles concludes. If the two Apostles really (as the Corinthian Bishop Dionysius seems to assert) travelled from Corinth to Italy and Rome in company, this must have been a different journey from that described in the last chapter of the Acts of the Apostles, since not the least trace is found either in the Acts of the Apostles, or in the Epistles reputed to have been written during Paul's imprisonment at Rome, that he had been in company with the Apostle Peter during his journey (which besides did not touch at Corinth) or during his stay at that time in Rome. If this were the case he must have been liberated from his imprisonment, and then immediately afterwards have undergone a second with Peter. On what can we found the probability of such a supposition? As the testimony of Eusebius (as has been already remarked) rests only on references drawn from the second Epistle to Timothy, so this Epistle can alone afford a proof of this supposition. The genuineness of the pastoral Epistle however has for so long a time been called in question, and the right of doubt so fully acknowledged that nothing certain can be established on such insecure data. We may therefore lay so much greater weight on the passages from the Clement of Rome above quoted. Neander decidedly maintains that the τέρμα τῆς δύσεως, the borders of the West to which Paul went, do not mean Rome, but must naturally refer to Spain. We must conclude by this account of Clement that Paul carried out his resolve to travel into Spain, or that at least he left Italy, and we are therefore obliged to assume that he had been liberated from his Roman imprisonment.* This is however a very ungrounded conclusion, and in spite of all Neander's protestations I must maintain that the well-known expression τέρμα τῆς δύσεως must be taken differently. The question, as Schenkel also rightly acknowledges, is whether Clement speaks of a τέρμα τῆς δύσεως in an objective sense, which was the τέρμα for all the world, or in a subjective sense, which would make it a τέρμα for Paul only. For all the world it would indeed have been the τέρμα τῆς δύσεως of the extreme west; for Paul it must have been the place that set the last western limit to his further progress. If this limit to his apostolic labours were set in Rome, why should Rome not have been called τέρμα in reference to the Apostle, as it lay in the western land in a place most nearly answering to the description τέρμα τῆς δύσεως? † He came εἰς τὸ τέρμα τῆς δύσεως must, as I have before stated, mean simply, he came to his appointed goal in the west, which as it lay in the *Occident,* was the natural goal of his *Occidiri,* and this meaning can very naturally be extracted from the words. If any further objections are advanced to this explanation I refer to my former remarks.‡

If these two points of support are withdrawn from the supposition of a second imprisonment, it falls to pieces, and positive grounds may be taken against it, that is, the improbability that the Apostle under the circumstances as they then existed, should have been released from one imprisonment only to undergo another. If in accordance with the most probable reckoning we place the arrival of the Apostle Paul in Rome in the spring of the year 62, and take the two years' duration of his imprisonment, of which the Acts of the Apostles speaks,

---

* Gesch. der Pflanzg. 3rd Ed. p. 455.

† Schenkel. Theol. Stud. u. Krit. 1841, page 71. Die zweite Gefangenschaft des Apostel Paulus.

‡ Compare Tüb. Zeitschrift für Theol. 1831, p. 4. Die Christus-Partei, &c., p. 149, and the so-called Pastoral Briefe, p. 63. Tüb. Zeitschrift f. Theol. 1838. 3. Ueber den Ursprung des Episc. page 46.

what can be more natural than to suppose that the Apostle became a victim in the year 64, of the Christian persecution under Nero, which is described by Tacitus (Annal. 15. 44)? How unlikely is the assumption that he was freed at so fatal a period for the Christians after an imprisonment of two years' duration! and how can we imagine that the scene was repeated so short a time afterwards under circumstances so nearly similar! We may all the more take a stand on this reading of the catastrophe in the life of the Apostle,* as the combinations are so arbitrary in which we see it involved, as soon as it is attempted to bring it into the necessary agreement with the data involving a second imprisonment.†

For the same reason, the more improbable that a second imprisonment of the Apostle Paul appears, the more problematical becomes the martyrdom at Rome of the Apostle Peter. It is rendered·impossible by its connection with the history. The two Apostles may have been together in Rome, and died there —but they could not have done so unless we submit their common residence in Rome to the limits assigned in the Acts of the Apostles. The accounts of the Apostle Paul do not authorize us in overstepping these limits ; but what probability has the martyrdom of the Apostle Peter at Rome, if we consider it according to the historical value of the testimony in its favour. The oldest and most authentic testimony which we possess in the Epistles written by Clement of Rome in Rome itself, says nothing of a martyrdom of the Apostle, and Dionysius of Corinth only, speaks decidedly on the point. But what a mean idea we must form of the historical trustworthiness of these testimonies if we only hold to the one, which, in direct opposition to the Apostle's Epistles to the Corinthians, represents not Paul alone as the

---

* We may compare for example the combinations (which else are not the worst of their kind) made by the author of the treatise in the Theol. Quartalschr. Ueber den Auferthalt des Apostels Petrus in Rom. 1820. Page 628. 1830. P. 636.

† Neander, page 454, does not himself understand the expression of Paul, μαρτυρεῖν ἐπὶ τῶν ἡγουμένων, to mean a martyr death.

founder of that church, but associates Peter with him. We must conclude that Peter went to Corinth as little as that he was the founder of the Corinthian Church. It must have been the Petrine party in Corinth who, desirous of usurping the merit of having founded the Corinthian Church, caused the assertion to be made that Peter had been in Corinth. We may lay especial weight on the testimony of Dionysius of Corinth, in opposition to that of Caius of Rome, not only because he lived half a century earlier, but also because of the interest which Caius may perhaps have had in enhancing the glory of the Roman Church by such a fact. Dionysius openly testifies that the two great Apostles died in Rome, and not in Corinth. Dionysius, indeed, lived half a century before Caius, but the former even was separated by an interval of more than a century from the circumstance to which he bears witness. He therefore can only testify to the legend handed down to his time of the common journey of the two Apostles from Corinth to Rome, and their martyrdom, which ensued. And we have no means of knowing whether this legend is merely a legend or the account of a real historical fact. The bias which Caius of Rome had to his own Church, is of course not to be found in Dionysius ; but the question is not whether the one or the other is the originator and author of the legend in a special interest, but only whether an unhistorical legend even in their day traditionally handed down, was believed and related by them as historically true. This possibility certainly cannot be disputed, and if the readiness with which such legends are believed, would seem to presuppose a certain interest in them, how easily can we imagine such an interest as existing in the case of Dionysius of Corinth ! Legends tending to the glorification of the Apostles were in general readily believed. And indeed most willingly in cases where at the same time the glorification of the church to which the believers belonged was enhanced. Was not this also the case here ? Was it not then highly honourable to the Corinthian Church that the two great Apostles should be represented as having been at Corinth together, at the most glorious moment of their lives, that they had been directed thither either by common agreement or by a higher call, in order to set out thence on the journey to their martyrdom in the capital of the world—to that death which was to glorify their whole lives ? And does not this interest in placing the city of Corinth on the same footing as the city of Rome, and in making the light shed by the two Apostles glorify both cities, show itself in the writings of the Corinthian Bishop ? "Thus have ye also," (he writes to the Roman Christians) "by your admonitions (the epistle of the Roman Bishop Soter to the Corinthians, which Dionysius was answering) brought into union what Peter and Paul founded." (τὴν ἀπὸ Πέτρου καὶ Παύλου φυτείαν γενηθεῖσαν 'Ρωμαίων τε καὶ Κόρινθίον συνεκεράσατε, *i.e.* ye have renewed the union in which both the Churches founded by the same Apostles—the Corinthian and the Roman, are joined together.) " For after both Apostles had planted our Corinth for us " (εἰς τὴν ἡμετέραν Κόρινθον φυτεύσαντες ἡμᾶς, founded our Corinthian Church) " they went together teaching in the same manner into Italy, and died the same martyr death at the same time." Does not a special interest betray itself in these transformed facts of history, where, contrary to all historical facts, Peter is represented as the founder of the Corinthian Church as well as Paul ?

In the case of the third in our list of witnesses, Caius of Rome, we may well grant the possibility of a special interest ; but the more that it is considered that he wrote in Rome itself, that he gives the precise localities of the Vatican and of the road to Ostia, the more unlikely it is that there should be any error in this statement, because thousands would directly have contradicted his mistakes. Caius indeed speaks of the τρόπαια of the two Apostles in Rome with exact reference to the locality, but of what value can the testimony of an author be who is separated by the interval of nearly half a century from the fact of the death to which the graves bear witness? His testimony is only of value as showing that what he states about the two Apostles was told and believed in Rome at the time when he wrote. Of course it is incredible that there is any error in this statement, and thousands would have immediately contradicted him, if he had stated as the current Roman tradition, that of which no one in Rome knew anything. People do not confound fact with legend. There can be as little doubt that it was really a legend, as that it had no historical foundation.

But the contents of a legend do not enhance its historical trustworthiness. Neander himself acknowledges that the later tradition of the crucifixion of Peter, which in his humility he thought it too much honour to endure in the same manner as the Holy One had done, and therefore prayed to be crucified with his head downwards, bears the stamp of a later and more sickly piety, than that of simple apostolic humility.* How dearly bought is the theory of the Apostle Peter's presence in Rome, which is a purely historical question for Protestants and not of the slightest consequence to him, if it is only to be gained at the price of sacrificing the genuine apostolic character to a mere empty show of humility! But if we only take our stand on Tertullian's "adæquari passioni dominicæ," what probability can even this have had in the circumstances under which the Apostles must have died.† If the two Apostles had formed one sacrifice to a Roman persecution of the Christians, there would have been no difference made between them in respect to the way and manner of their execution, least of all such a difference as would so exactly have carried out the legend of the remarkable rival interests between them. The localities of the two graves even betray the existence of the

---

* Page 473.

† If we believe with Tertullian in his "Petrus passioni dominicæ adæquator," we must for the same reason believe with him in the truth of the martyrdom at Rome by oil of the Apostle John, which is attested in the same passage.

same rival interest, since Paul, the more foreign preacher of Christ, was allotted a grave on the road to Ostia, whilst Peter was glorified by obtaining the highest honour of a martyr's grave in the widely renowned theatre of the persecution in the garden of Nero. That which in the Epistle of Clement of Rome is vaguely represented as a martyrdom, grows with the growth of the legend into a firmly established and widely localized tradition.*

It has been so far necessary to enter into the connexion of the legend affecting the two Apostles in order to be able more exactly to determine what facts lie at their foundation. It appears from our foregoing investigation, that the life history of Paul is the historical foundation and point of connection from which the web of tradition has spun itself in different directions. Everything which is represented as having actually occurred is true of Paul and not of Peter. What is related of Peter is only the traditional reflex of the historical reality belonging to the life of Paul. But the legend resulting from this implies that Paul must first have renounced all that was of importance in the results of his life, in order that it might be transferred to that of Peter, and only retained any peculiar worth to which his right was incontestable in a manner which showed that any honour he possessed was but the reflected splendour of the higher glory streaming from Peter. Thus the legend has freely handled in its own interest the three historical facts which have been under our consideration—namely the

* Nero's amphitheatre was at the foot of the Vatican. Tacitus, annal. xiv. 14; in the same place were the gardens of Nero. Peter is represented as having been buried there, where a Church was afterwards built to him. Compare Roma antica di F. Nardini, Ed. iv. di A. Nibby, T. iv. Rom. 1819, page 358, where the Italian antiquarian asks, forse Nerone immanissimo in far strage di Christiani usò poi pietà in distruggere il suo circo per concedervi loro la sepoltura? In the description of the City of Rome V. E. Plattner. C. Bunsen, &c. ii. 1, 1832, page 52, it is remarked on the words of Caius quoted above, 'Εγὼ δὲ τὰ τρόπαια, precisely considered this can only be a testimony that the Apostle here suffered in this persecution, the city of the martyr death may be the token of the victory of the Christians, even if it were not his burial place. But Eusebius evidently understands the words of Caius as referring to the graves of the Apostles.

apostolic mission to the Gentiles, the residence in Rome, and the martyrdom there. There are accordingly three special explanations of the different forms of the legend. In order to displace Paul from the sphere in which he first moved in his apostolic work among the Gentiles, Peter is represented in opposition to him as the true Gentile Apostle, and he himself as having adopted the part of a false Apostle preaching Gentile doctrines. Scarcely had historical truth been in so far brought to bear on the subject as to allow Paul to maintain his historical existence, and to place the two Apostles on an equal footing in dignity, than Paul is made to yield the first place to Peter in everything which men either could or would not recognize as his peculiar right, such as the establishment of the more important churches, the Roman and the Corinthian, the honour of martyrdom suffered in Rome, and the burial there. It is impossible not to see in all this the reflex of the different forms of the relations in which the chief parties in the apostolic and post-apostolic ages, stood with regard to each other. It cannot be doubted that the Jewish Christians saw in the Apostle Paul only the opponent and enemy of the law, and of the continuance of the Jewish Christianity which rested upon the law, and that they ought to oppose him by all the means at their disposal, in all the Gentile Christian Churches. But the greater the progress was which Christianity made among the Gentiles through the efforts of the Apostle Paul and his followers, the less could it fail in establishing what, in spite of the influence of the Jewish Christians, must have been taken as the principles of Pauline Christianity. Thus there arose a contradiction which could not continue to exist in its rude aspect if the Christian Church was to preserve its unity. That it did so preserve it, is a historical fact; but it is a false statement to say that it was Pauline Christianity alone which won the victory over the Jewish Christianity which opposed it. The two parties, by concessions on each side, became so mingled that in many instances we find Judaism still bearing the upper hand, and writings such as the Acts of the Apostles, and many of the post-apostolic Epistles of the Canon testify to what concessions the Pauline party submitted, either voluntarily or forced by the power of circumstances. Thus in the legend concerning the fate of the two Apostles, we have not placed before us a picture describing the end of their life and of their characteristics, but only of that of the parties depending on their persons and histories. So considered, and treated in their true character, these legends, notwithstanding their unhistorical contents possess a true historical value, as living pictures of the age, with its actuating motives and its efforts, displaying also how essentially different history becomes if we not only accept as history what is mere legend, but also if we continue to add to an already unhistorical series of facts, in order to complete the connection of legends which do not exactly fit into each other. An example of this we have in the theory of the second imprisonment of the Apostle Paul, and we must once for all free ourselves from this groundless view, in order that we may not render still more aimless and incorrect our free enquiry into the relations of the first Church in that most ancient time.

SECOND PART.

EPISTLES OF THE APOSTLE PAUL.

SECOND PART.

THE EPISTLES OF THE APOSTLE PAUL.

INTRODUCTION.

THE foregoing inquiry shows what a false picture of the individual character of the Apostle Paul we should obtain if we had no other source than the Acts of the Apostles from which to derive our knowledge of it. The Epistles of the Apostle are then the only authentic documents for the history of his apostolic labours, and of the whole the relation in which he stood to his age, and in proportion as the spirit that breathes through them is great and original, so do they present the truest and most faithful mirror of the time. The more we study the Epistles the more we perceive that a rich and peculiar life is summed up in them, as the most direct testimony to it. Only in the Epistles is that shadow, whose false image the Acts of the Apostles brings forward in the place of the real Apostle, placed in direct contrast with him. That all these thirteen Pauline Epistles, which Christian antiquity unanimously recognized, and handed down as the Epistles of the Apostles, can not make equal claim to authenticity, and that many of them have against them an overwhelming suspicion of unauthenticity, is a result of later criticism, which is still gaining more general acceptance. If we consider the present state of the criticism of the Pauline Epistles it may now be the place to form our judgment in accordance with the foregoing inquiry, on the same classification, on which Eusebius, in his classic passage on the canon, proceeded, when he delivered his judgment on the writings composing the canon of the New Testament, drawn from the historical testimony lying before him.   The Pauline Epistles divide themselves into Homologoumena, and Antilegomena.

In the Homologoumena there can only be reckoned the four Epistles which must on all accounts be considered the chief Epistles of the Apostle, namely the Epistle to the Galatians, the two Epistles to the Corinthians, and the Epistle to the Romans.   There has never been the slightest suspicion of unauthenticity cast on these four Epistles, on the contrary, they bear in themselves so incontestably the character of Pauline originality, that it is not possible for critical doubt to be exercised upon them with any show of reason.   All the rest of the Epistles, which are commonly ascribed to the Apostle, belong to the class of Antilegomena ; but even according to the idea attached by Eusebius to the word, this does not by any means imply a positive assertion of actual unauthenticity, but only indicates the opposition to which their authenticity has been partly already exposed, and that to which it may still further be exposed, since among all these lesser Pauline Epistles, there is not a single one against which, from the standpoint of the four chief Epistles, some objection or other cannot be raised.   In their entire nature they are so essentially different from the four first Epistles, that even if they are considered as Pauline, they must form a second class of Epistles of the Apostle, as they must have been composed for the most part at a later period of his apostolic course.   But as Eusebius himself makes another division of his Antilegomena, and establishes another class which he designates as spurious, in reference to which opposition no longer remains a mere inward doubt, but brings to light the overwhelming probability of real unauthenticity, so in these deutero-Pauline Epistles there is nothing wanting to make the critical sentence incline more and more to this view as regards them.   According to my views, and those of other critics, the so-called Pastoral Epistles must be placed in this subdivision of the Pauline Antilegomena.

It follows then that there are three classes of Pauline Epistles, a classification which rests also on an ancient authority. The Marcionite canon, whose 'Απόστολος is the most ancient collection of Pauline Epistles known to us, does not contain the generally received thirteen Epistles of the Apostle; but only ten, excluding the three Pastoral Epistles. In any case the Pastoral Epistles in their relation to the Canon of Marcion make a separate class, and on that account perhaps are not comprehended in it. If they are wanting because they were not in existence at the time, they of course would not be afterwards included as spurious in a collection which only professed to contain genuine Pauline Epistles. If they were in existence at the time, but unknown to Marcion (and this is scarcely credible if they had been long existing as genuine Pauline Epistles), their relation to this Canon remains the same, they were not included because they were not Pauline writings. Thus if, being already recognized writings, they were excluded from the Marcionite Canon, they were excluded as being writings which were held by the compiler of this Canon not to be Pauline : and by this exclusion they must be condemned as not Pauline, and must be also considered as writings which, if not dating from a notoriously later period, still at least are wanting in the genuine Pauline character. From the standpoint of the Marcionite Canon, these Epistles must be in any case considered as composing the last class of the Epistles generally ascribed to the Apostle Paul. If we proceed from the Epistles which are wanting in the Canon to those which it really contains, we find two classes which agree with the above classification, namely a series of Pauline Epistles of the first class, and another of the second class. According to Epiphanius, (Hær. 42. 9.) the Pauline Epistles in the Canon of Marcion were arranged as follows : —Galatians, 1 and 2 Corinthians, Romans, 1 and 2 Thessalonians, Ephesians (but to which Marcion has affixed the inscription, "To the Laodiceans") Colossians, Philemon, and

17

Philippians. In this arrangement of the Pauline Epistles we must bear in mind the prominence given to the Epistle to the Galatians, and the reason of this may be found in the importance which this Epistle must have held in the teachings of so decided an anti-judaistic follower of Paul as Marcion. The rest of the Epistles must also have been arranged from the point of view of their greater or less importance with regard to the teachings of Marcion, but we cannot understand why the two Epistles to the Corinthians should precede that to the Romans, and still less why the rest should follow precisely in the order they do. If we assume that this arrangement is in accordance with the order of time in which they were written, the two Epistles to the Thessalonians stand in the way, as in this case they ought not to come just after the Epistle to the Romans, but ought to precede the whole, as they were the first written. And yet we must recognize a certain reference to the order of time in the fact that the Epistles to the Thessalonians follow immediately the four principal Epistles. If we consider all these facts, we can only explain the Marcionite Canon by the supposition that it consists of two separate collections. The first collection is composed of four Epistles. Galatians, 1 and 2 Corinthians, and Romans, which could only be so placed by following a chronological order. The second collection must also have been arranged chronologically—although we cannot rightly understand why it was commenced with 1 and 2 Thessalonians, and why the Epistle to the Philippians follows immediately that to Philemon. However we may decide on the question of there being two collections, a very remarkable phenomenon of this Canon remains certain, namely, that we find in it, in a second series, all those lesser Pauline Epistles which in many respects are so different from the chief Epistles that they afford more or less occasion for critical doubt, and the supposition very naturally presents itself, that unless weighty reasons are brought forward against their unauthenticity, the secondary position of these collected Epistles can only be owing to their having been first brought forward as deutero-Pauline, after the collection of genuine Pauline Epistles had been concluded. As they professed to be Pauline Epistles they would in that case have been united with the original genuine Epistles of the Apostles, but the way and manner in which they are connected with them betrays their later origin, and it is just as natural that they should be separated from the others, being later Epistles although held as Pauline, as it is natural that the Pastoral Epistles opposed to the Marcionite teaching, should be entirely excluded from that Canon. In this way this Canon has become allied to the name of a man who made an epoch in the history of Pauline Christianity, which to him seemed the only pure, real Christianity, and in this respect is of the greater importance, as there is generally ascribed to the heretic a critical datum, which is not without importance in the interests of modern criticism on the Pauline Epistles.*

* As the importance of the reasons which are added against the origin and character of the lesser Epistles cannot, according to all probability, be diminished by further unrestrained critical inquiry, but, on the contrary, rather strengthened, it is really the simplest and most natural way of proceeding to divide the Epistles standing in the Canon under the name of the Apostle, into authentic and unauthentic, Pauline and pseudo-Pauline, and to arrange the later ones according to their probable chronological order.

THE FIRST CLASS OF THE PAULINE EPISTLES.

THE GENUINE EPISTLES OF THE APOSTLE.

CHAPTER I.

THE EPISTLE TO THE GALATIANS.

ACCORDING to general opinion, the Galatian churches (αἱ ἐκκλησίαι τῆς Γαλατίας, Gal. i. 2) were founded by Paul himself. The passages i. 8, iv. 13, 19, in which the Apostle speaks of his preaching the Gospel among the Galatians, would seem to leave little doubt on this point, but the Acts of the Apostles gives us no certain information about the time and occasion when it took place. It is true that the founding of these churches, according to the account in the Acts of the Apostles, can only be placed during the time of the second journey of the Apostle (xvi. 6, &c.) as he went at that time into Galatia, and on the third journey when he again went into Galatia, he only "strengthened" the disciples who were already in existence there, Acts xviii. 23. Yet it is remarkable that the author of the Acts of the Apostles, xvi. 6, without saying anything of the founding of a Christian church, represents the Apostle as travelling through Phrygia and Galatia, and, as we must see, represents also this journey as being so hurried that we can hardly suppose that his residence in those countries was a lengthy one. And to this conclusion we are necessarily led by the Acts of the Apostles. With regard to the members of this church, the general opinion is that they consisted partly of Jewish and partly of Gentile Christians. That there were Jewish Christians among them is all the more probable as many Jews lived in Asia Minor generally, and therefore also in Galatia (compare 1 Peter i. 1.) ; and we may also suppose that the Apostle would not have spoken of the Law and of the Old Testament as he does in Galatians iii. 2, 13, iv. 3, 31, if there had not been Jews among the readers of his Epistle. This last observation however does not carry much weight, as a knowledge of the Old Testament is supposed to have been possessed also by those Gentiles who were inclined either to Judaism or Christianity. It may therefore remain doubtful whether there were any Jewish Christians in the Galatian Church, and although this is not in itself entirely improbable, yet it cannot be taken as certain, for the Epistle itself in many places (compare iv. 8, v. 2, vi. 12) undeniably bears witness that the Apostle was speaking to Gentile Christians.

What the Apostle designed in writing this Epistle to the Galatian Church is seen very decidedly in the Epistle itself. The Galatian Christians were very near falling away from the Gospel as it had been preached to them by the Apostle, i. 6, iii. 1, 3, iv. 9, &c., 21, v. 2, &c., 7. This was the result of the influence of strange teachers, who had entered into these churches after the Apostle, and made the Galatian Christians go astray in Christianity through the fear that they could not be saved by a doctrine like that of the Apostle Paul. These teachers represented to them that before all things they must submit to circumcision, v. 2, 11. Here we first meet with those Judaising opponents with whom the Apostle had to maintain so severe a struggle in the churches which he founded, and they indeed here completely show that rugged Judaistic stamp which marks them as opponents of the Pauline Christianity. Their opposition to the apostolic work of the Apostle Paul did not indeed go so far as to deny to the Gentiles participation in the Messianic salvation ; in this respect they allowed the limits of Judaism to be broken through, but they were on this account all the more zealously desirous to hold fast the principle that even in

this wider sphere, salvation could only be obtained in the form
of Judaism. To Judaism there must always belong an absolute
right over the Gentiles. It was therefore simply impossible
that a man should be saved by Christianity unless he acknowledged Judaism, and submitted to everything which Judaism
prescribed as the necessary conditions of salvation. Whilst
they placed this principle in the highest place of all, they set
before them the especial task of repairing the injury which the
Apostle Paul had done in preaching his Gospel of freedom
from the law, by using all energy in enforcing the necessity of
observance of the law, that the Gentiles might not be so much
converted to Christianity as to Judaism. Where, according to
their views, the Apostle Paul stood forth as an innovator and as
revolutionary, they were desirous of interposing with their
conservative principles to repair the evil, and to make the
new ideas and doctrines, in which the salvation of mankind was
comprised, depend entirely on the positive foundation of
Judaism. It lies in the very nature of the case that they
should exhibit themselves as the opponents of the Apostle
Paul, and that wherever they come in contact with him, they
should manifest the most decided and obstinate opposition to
him; but this opposition does not justify us in seeing in them
nothing but heretics, impostors, and corrupters,—nothing but
persons who from bad motives made it their business to interfere with the beneficent work of the Apostle, hindering and
disturbing it. Of course the Apostle Paul himself thus represents them, but we must not forget that party is here opposed to
party, and each side takes up the affair in question and judges
of it from its own particular standpoint. We have no reason
for assuming that these opponents of the Apostle were not
thoroughly in earnest in the views and principles which they
defended, or that they did not act up to them in perfect good
faith as far as we can see; and indeed the whole impression
which they make on us is that of men so entirely rooted in the
opinions and principles for which they contended, that they

could not separate themselves from them or raise themselves above them. In one word, they were Jews or Jewish Christians of the genuine old stamp, who could so little find a place in the more liberal atmosphere of Pauline Christianity that they thought the very ground of their existence would be cut from under them, if Judaism was no longer to have its absolute power and importance. But it is by no means here sought to deny that they permitted themselves to employ the most unjust accusations and most malicious calumnies against the Apostle Paul, since these are never wanting in every strife of parties, but we must not displace the point of view of the whole matter in question ; and therefore it behoves us to place to the credit of the Apostle's opponents, the narrowing influence of their Jewish standpoint, which naturally increased their inability to raise themselves from their low state of religious consciousness to a higher and a freer one.

These considerations tend to establish the point of view from which this Epistle of the Apostle is as a whole to be considered. It places us in the midst of the great excitement of the critical struggle which had begun between Judaism and Christianity, in the decision of the momentous question whether there should be a Christianity free from Judaism and essentially different from it, or whether Christianity should only exist as a form of Judaism, that is to say, as nothing else than a modified and extended Judaism. But as everything which Christianity possessed or was likely to attain in respect to its essential distinction from Judaism had been first brought to an historical reality by the Apostle Paul, and still entirely depended on his personal influence, the peculiar theme of the Epistle is the vindication of Pauline Christianity, which at the same time must necessarily be also the personal vindication of the Apostle. In this conflict with Judaism and its champions he assigned to himself the task of explaining more clearly the grounds of his apostolic standpoint, which he only could do from his own immediate Apostolic consciousness. Therefore, the first thing

with which he begins is a reference to the directness of his
apostolic calling, or his peculiar standpoint, showing that he
had not arrived at this standpoint by means of any human
influence, but entirely through the direct action of his own
self-consciousness, by which he became aware of his inward
divine call, i. 6—16. This independence of the principle on
which his apostolic call rested he maintained in opposition to
the elder Apostles—first, negatively, inasmuch as he became
an Apostle of Christ in a manner perfectly independent of
them, and what he was as an Apostle he already was in the
fullest sense before he came into any outward communication
whatever with them, i. 17, 18 ; and secondly, positively, inasmuch as in this communication with them he not only surrendered nothing of this principle in order to hold his own
against them, but was enabled to win for it the most unequivocal and triumphant recognition. This took place at three
different times, which stand in regular order in their relation
to each other, a gradation by which he makes good his own
claim in a convincing, practical and authentic manner. For
in the first place, at the time of his journey to Jerusalem, no
one could in any way lay claim to his peculiar standpoint,
i. 18, 19 ; in the second place, when matters came to an open
quarrel, he severed himself so completely from the elder
Apostles, that they were obliged to recognise the equal claim
of his apostolic mission, ii. 1, 10 ; and in the third place, when
Peter in Antioch disputed the principles which had before
been acknowledged, the error was so manifestly on his side
that he was forced to consider himself as thoroughly in the
wrong, ii. 11, &c. The personal vindication here passes over
naturally to the dogmatic, to the root of the main subject, that
the principle of justification, which alone secures salvation to
man, lies only in faith in Christ and not in the works of the
law. This proposition is brought forward in the first place,
iii. 1, 5, as the direct result of the Christian consciousness ;
secondly, as a fact proved to be true from the Old Testament,

inasmuch as the real contents of the Old Testament are the
promises given to Abraham, in which the law was but
accidentally included, iii. 6, 18. Thereupon follows wider
discussion on the nature of the law, in which the inferior relation of the law to the promise is further insisted on, together
with the merely relative importance which the law possesses in
its position between the promise and faith in a mediating sense,
although this is in no way an unimportant one. The explanation
of the Apostle is still further continued, and treats of the difference between the preparation and the fulfilment, between the
carnal and spiritual minds—the servitude of the " heir as long
as he is a child," and his freedom when he becomes of age. Christianity is the absolute religion, the religion of the spirit and
of freedom, with regard to which Judaism must be looked at
from an inferior standpoint, from which it must be classed with
Heathenism, as ἀσθενῆ καὶ πτωχὰ στοιχεῖα τοῦ κόσμου. The
reason for this, is first objectively given in the inner nature of
Christianity in its comparison with the nature of Judaism, then
subjectively, in the life of spirit and freedom experienced by
Christians themselves, iv. 1, 11 (what next follows, iv. 12, 30, is
an expression of the Apostle's sorrow and pain at the falling
away of the Galatians).—Secondly, the reason is deduced from
the Old Testament, through an allegorical interpretation of the
two sons of Abraham, Isaac and Ishmael, who hold to each
other the relation of bondage and freedom. The hortatory and
practical part of the Epistle contains, first, an exhortation to per-
severance in the freedom of the spirit, by means of real faith,
and a warning against a relapse into Judaism, v. 1—12 ;
secondly, a challenge to that moral activity by which true
freedom and the spiritual life are proved, and a warning against
the misuse of freedom. This moral activity is considered
generally, v. 13—15, and in particular with reference to the
circumstances of the Galatians, v. 26, vi. 10. Finally, in vi.
11—18, we have the conclusion of the Epistle, consisting of a
brief emphatic summary of what had been said before, together

with a blessing.   The Epistle may accordingly be divided into three chief parts, one personal and apologetic, one dogmatic, and one practical.   All three are intimately connected with each other.   The dogmatic part of the Epistle consists partly of the evidence of the apostolic authority of the Apostle, and partly it naturally passes over to the practical side, inasmuch as the νόμος is one of the chief ideas of the dogmatic part.   It was necessary to show that freedom from the law does not by any means necessitate the abolition of moral obligation.

The composition of this Epistle is placed by many at a very early, and by others at a much later date.   The general opinion is that it was written soon after the Apostle's second journey, Acts xviii. 2, 3, and Rückert, Credner, and others have sought to establish this opinion more decidedly by combinations of a very subjective kind.   If to this Epistle be assigned a decided place in the series of Pauline Epistles chronologically arranged, its relation to the two Epistles to the Corinthians and to the Epistle to the Romans comes under consideration.   In this respect we have in it a highly important statement with reference to the opponents with whom the Apostle had to contend among the Galatians as well as among the Corinthians.   There can scarcely be any doubt with regard to these Judaising opponents, that from the way in which the Apostle opposed them, the conflict was now for the first time being carried on. We see that this is the first time this subject has been handled ; the Apostle perceives that he is absolutely obliged to give an account of how he was summoned to his apostolic office, and he speaks of it in such a manner as he could not have done, if he had ever before come in contact with these opponents in the same way.   He puts himself thoroughly in opposition to them ; as thoroughly as can only be done when for the first time the full importance of a principle dawns upon a man, and when the maintenance of this principle against a vexatious opposition constitutes the task of his whole life.   This same idea of a perfectly new party contest, in which an individual aim is set forth is shown also in the opposition of the opponents. Circumcision is treated of as the most necessary recognition of the value of the Mosaic law. It is certainly remarkable that in the Epistles to the Corinthians there is no longer any mention of this subject. Although indisputably the same Judaising opponents are in question, the party feeling which in the Epistle to the Galatians we see in its most direct, and so to speak in its rudest form, is in these Epistles modified, and the contest is removed to another arena. On all these accounts the Epistle to the Galatians can only have the first place assigned to it, in comparison with the three other Epistles, and this place it also holds in the Marcionite Canon. In the same way as the mention of the opponents with whom the Apostle had to contend, places it in a near relation with the two Epistles to the Corinthians, so its dogmatic contents bring it into close connection with the Epistle to the Romans. But here also the relation is a perfectly analogous one. What in the Epistle to the Romans is the complete, and in every sense thoroughly developed Pauline doctrine, we see drawn in outline, and yet quite distinctly in the Epistle to the Galatians. We may therefore, beginning with this Epistle, pursue the development of the idea of the Pauline doctrine through various critical stages throughout the four chief Epistles of the Apostle. It has already been shown in our former inquiry, of which the chief foundation was the Epistle to the Galatians, what weight as an historical document this Epistle possesses. It enables us to arrive at a more correct idea of the original and true position of the Apostle Paul towards the other Apostles ; and at the same time it shows the process of development by which the essential principle of Christianity first attained a decided place in its struggle with Judaism.

CHAPTER II.

These two Epistles stand in chronological order between the Epistles to the Galatians on the one hand, and the Epistle to the Romans on the other, and they form the centre of the important sphere of action in which the Apostle moved as the founder of Gentile Christian churches. That which is presented in its simplest elements in the Epistle to the Galatians, and which in the Epistle to the Romans passes over to the abstract sphere of dogmatic antithesis, widens out in the Epistles to the Corinthians into the full reality of concrete life, with all the complicated relations which must have existed in a Christian church of the earliest period. The Corinthian Church was the peculiar creation of the Apostle, it had been, as he himself says (1 Cor. iv. 15), a child begotten by him and nourished in all love ; but such a child also as needed his fatherly correction and instructing care in every way. With no other church did he stand in so close and confidential a relation, to none did he address so many and such important Epistles, in none had he undergone so many experiences of different kinds, above all in none had he such a difficult and important problem to solve. All this was in consequence of the Corinthian Church being the first Christian one which existed in the classic ground of ancient Greece. How could the Greek spirit disown its original nature, when it underwent its new birth into Christianity ? There is nothing more natural than that Christianity should at first break out into phenomena of a peculiar kind, among a people like the Greeks, whose spiritual activity and versatility, whose political party spirit had a new theatre opened before them, in the newly acquired sphere of action, and this especially in a city like Corinth, where Greek culture and Greek sensuality stood in such close connection. But hence also arose a fact which was of peculiar importance in the personal relation of the Apostle to the Corinthian Church, and which gave him such manifold opportunities of placing before us the underlying, purely human phase of his many-sided individuality, and this fact was that the same Judaising opponents, with whom we are already acquainted, introduced a new and deeply penetrating element into the life of this Greek Christian Church, yet in the first stage of its development. But it must have been evident to their opponents themselves, if they had any tact at all, that they must take quite a different attitude in this thoroughly Greek Church, than in the one in Asia Minor, and that it was incumbent on them to appear in a more polished, more refined, and less strictly Jewish form, especially as they must meanwhile have given up much in their religious consciousness to which they had at first jealously adhered. Their opposition to the Pauline Christianity no longer proceeded from the purely Jewish standpoint, which laid the greatest stress on circumcision alone, it now took peculiarly Christian ground, and above all other subjects concerned itself with the true Christian idea of the apostolic authority, but in proportion as it was intense and thorough, it was all the more personally dangerous to the Apostle himself.

In the first Epistle the Apostle treats of a series of circumstances which at that early period had a special interest for a church still in its infancy. The chief matter with which he concerned himself was the party spirit which existed in the Corinthian Church through the influence of the Judaising opponents. It had split into several parties, which were called by names denoting their several opinions, i. 12. The names Paul, Apollos, Cephas and Christ betoken as it seems so many different parties. Very naturally the party of Paul is first placed before us. The Corinthians had not deserted the Apostle, they had only divided themselves into parties, and

those members of the Church who had remained most faithful
to the Apostle, as we see from the contents of both the Epistles,
still continued to form an overwhelming majority. When
different parties were formed in Corinth it cannot be wondered
at that one of these should be called by the name of Apollos.
Apollos was, according to the Apostle, undoubtedly his fellow-
worker in the cause of the Gospel at Corinth, and if, as is
related of him, Acts of the Apostles xviii. 24, he had attained
such eminence through Alexandrine education and literary
acquirements, it may easily be understood how there might
be many persons in Corinth, who owing to the peculiarly Greek
spirit of his discourses became so prepossessed in his favour
that they gave him a certain precedence over the Apostle Paul.
But why did not the favourable reception which other like-
minded teachers met with from a portion of the Church, appear
to the Apostle as indicating such a dangerous party spirit, and
one so earnestly to be opposed ? Some other circumstances
must have occurred therefore before the expressed predilection
for Apollos could have been considered by the Apostle as a
token of a doubtful tendency in the Church. We must seek
for the peculiar cause of division and schism in the names of
the two other parties. With the name of Peter, an opposition
to Paul is naturally connected. As far as we know, Peter himself was never at Corinth, but under the authority of his name
a Jewish Christian element had, without doubt, been introduced
into a Church consisting almost entirely of Gentile Christians.
In this sense only can the Apostle mean to affix the name of
Cephas or Peter to one of these parties. We should have
expected that the Apostle would have taken as the subject of
his objection, the principles propagated by the Judaising opponents, but the contents of his Epistle do not carry out this
expectation. The Jewish doctrines of the absolute value of the
Mosaic law, and the necessity of its observance for salvation,
are no where combated as they are in the Epistles to the
Galatians and the Romans, and there is no mention made of

the law, and all that depends upon it. It is vain throughout the whole of both the Epistles to the Corinthians, to look for any trace which may help to bring us into a closer knowledge of the real existence of these parties, only the last chapter of the second Epistle leaves us in no doubt whatever that this opposition had by no means ceased. At the conclusion of the Epistle (xi. 22), the Apostle so openly unveils the Judaism of his opponents, and describes them as false with such sharp words, with all the authority of a born Jew who had become a teacher of Christianity, that we are easily enabled to understand the reason of his polemic against them; but we are no nearer to the desired explanation of their principles. The Judaism of his opponents appears here in a new form, and we may ask whether by means of these party relations we cannot see deeper into the fourth of these parties described by the Apostle—the so-called party of Christ. Here we come also to a most difficult question, which we must endeavour as far as possible to answer if we wish to arrive at a clear understanding of the circumstances of the Corinthian Church, and the position of the Apostle in it.

Who were these οἱ τοῦ Χριστοῦ?* Amongst the interpreters and critics who in modern times have directed their attention to this question, Storr and Eichhorn have advanced theories which exhibit a natural opposition to each other, inasmuch as whilst the one adheres too closely to something special, the other on the contrary loses himself in generalities, but both have a common ground of agreement in neither relying on a decided point of support in the contents of the Epistle, nor in even giving a clear idea of the subject. According to Storr†

---

* I first investigated these questions in a treatise in the Tübinger Zeitschr. für Theologie, 1831, pt. 4, p. 6: Die Christus-partei in der korinthischen Gemeinde, der Gegensatz des petrinischen und paulinischen Christenthums, der Apostel Petrus in Rom.

† Notitiæ historicæ epistolarum Pauli ad Corinthios, interpretationi servientes. Tub. 1758, p. 14. Opusc. acad. Vol. ii. p. 246. The same opinion supported by Flatt. Vorlesungen über die beiden Briefe Pauli an die Cor. by Bertholdt, Hist.

οἱ τοῦ Χριστοῦ were those members of the Corinthian Church who had made the Apostle James the chief of their party as being the ἀδελφὸς κυρίου, in order that through this material relationship of the head of their sect to Jesus, they might claim for it a precedence which would exalt it over the Petrine party. The Apostle indeed might have had good reasons for hinting at this carnal idea of relationship to Christ, 2 Cor. v. 13, in the expression Χριστὸν κατὰ σάρκα γινώσκειν; but if Storr cannot bring forward anything else in support of his theory than that the Apostle 1 Cor. ix. 5, speaks of the " brethren of the Lord," and xv. 7, speaks of James especially with Peter, of what value is such an hypothesis ? According to Eichhorn,* οἱ τοῦ Χριστοῦ may have been the neutrals who stood apart from the strife of parties ; they did not depend on Paul, nor Apollos, nor Peter ; but only on Christ. In order to give some sort of colouring to the idea of these neutrals, Pott endeavours to establish Eichhorn's theory, by a comparison of the passage 1 Cor. iii. 22, where Paul, after enumerating the schisms in the Corinthian Church which he had before denounced, brings forward as the main point of his argument the words πάντα ὑμῶν ἐστιν, εἴτε Παῦλος, εἴτε Ἀπολλὼς, εἴτε Κηφᾶς, πάντα ὑμῶν ἐστιν, ὑμεῖς δὲ Χριστοῦ, and does this in such a manner that we must look upon the views and doctrines of the Χριστοῦ ὄντες as those approved of by the Apostle himself. These same οἱ τοῦ Χριστοῦ are meant in i. 12, whilst in iii. 22 the Apostle asserts that the Corinthians themselves τοῦ Χριστοῦ εἶναι, and he wishes to point out to the followers of the sects, the doctrines of the true Teacher, to which οἱ Χριστοῦ already had given their adherence. The sources from which they derived their Christian doctrine were equally the teachings of Paul, Apollos, and Peter ; but in order to avoid any appearance of sectarianism they did not dis-

---

Krit. Einl., p. 339, by Hug. Einleitung in die Schriften des N. T. 3rd Ed., p. 360; and by Heidenreich, Comment. in 1 Corinthians, Vol. i., 1825, p. 31.

  * Einleitung in das N. T. Vol. iii. p. 107.

  † Epist. Pauli ad Cor. Partic. 1, 1826. Proleg. p. 31.

tinguish themselves by the name of the teacher who first instructed them in the principles τοῦ εἶναι Χριστοῦ, but simply called themselves τοῦ Χριστοῦ. In both the passages quoted above, there a Χριστοῦ εἶναι is indeed spoken of, but, as a more correct comparison will easily show us, in a very different sense. In the passage, i. 12, the words ἐγὼ δὲ Χριστοῦ are merely the indications of a sect, just as the three sentences immediately preceding them point out as many other sects. These words cannot however be taken as referring to the adherents of a so-called Party of Christ, were the Apostle to be understood as wishing to indicate it, as alone possessing a divine unity bestowed by Christ, in opposition to those sects and the other sectarian divisions and distinctions lying outside them. Therefore if οἱ Χριστοῦ were the neutrals, the neutrals themselves were nothing else than a sect, as Neander also supposes them to have been. " They may indeed have maintained that they were Christians in a false sense ; very probably the conceit of the Corinthians caused some to come forward, in these disputes as to whether the teachings of Paul or Peter or Apollos were the only true and perfect ones, who thought and asserted that they were better acquainted with Christianity than Paul, Peter or Apollos—some who out of verbal or written tradition, interpreted to suit their own foregone theories and opinions, made a Christ and a Christianity for themselves, and who now in their arrogant zeal for freedom wished to make themselves independent of the authority of the selected and enlightened witnesses of the Gospel, professing to have as perfect a system of doctrine as they had, and who in their presumption called themselves disciples of Christ as a distinction from all others." This view again can only be received as a modification of that of Eichhorn. What, after all this, are we to think of the peculiar characteristics of this so-called Party of Christ ? If they wished to set up a Christ and a Christianity of their own in opposition to the chiefs of the other sects, to whose authority the adherents of those sects submitted, their relation to Christ must have been brought about in some way similar to that which had been the case with the other sects, and we cannot see if they claimed to have a more perfect doctrine than others and to know Christianity better than Paul, Apollos and Peter, how they could have made good their claim to this precedence with any better success than any other of the sects. Therefore either οἱ Χριστοῦ were no sect to be classed with the other sects mentioned with them, or they indeed formed a sect, but a sect of which we must at the same time perceive we have at this day no data by which to form a clear conception of its tendencies and peculiarities.

In order to arrive at a clearer understanding as to the probability of the last mentioned point, it seems to me that the theory which J. E. Chr. Schmidt has given, in a treatise on 1 Cor. i. 12, is not without importance; namely, that there were really but two parties, one that of Paul and Apollos, and the other, as Schmidt expresses it, that of Peter and of Christ. Taking into consideration the acknowledged relation in which Paul and Peter, one as the Apostle to the Gentiles, the other to the Jews, really stood towards each other, or at least the relation in which they were thought to stand towards each other by the chief parties of the oldest Christian Church, there can be no doubt that the chief difference lay between the two sects which called themselves after Paul and Cephas. It follows that the two other parties, that of Apollos and that of Christ, differed less from each other, than from the former, of Paul and Apollos, and the relation also of the parties of Paul and Apollos must be viewed in the same light. We see from many passages that Paul placed Apollos completely on his own side and considered him as an authorized fellow-worker with himself in the preaching of the Gospel, and we find nothing in the contents of either of these Epistles of the Apostle, which would lead us to suppose that there was any important difference between them. Still I will not deny, what is generally believed, that the Apostle, in the passage in which he speaks of the distinction between the σοφία κόσμου and the σοφία θεοῦ, had the party of

Apollos especially in view, but on the other hand it must be granted, that the mental tendency here pointed out must have been more or less the ruling one in the Corinthian Church as a whole. The Apostle represents it as still fettered in this σοφία τοῦ κόσμου, and the yet deeper and more thorough sense of the real Christian life in the inward man, he represents as a feeling which in the present state of their spiritual life, the Corinthians had yet to attain. Although therefore the predominance of this mental tendency, especially in so far as it consisted in an over-estimate of the outward forms of teaching, as opposed to its quality and the nature of the doctrine itself, divided the party of Apollos from that of Paul, and although the adherents of these parties set the teachers who were at their head, in a relation to each other which the teachers themselves in no way recognized, the difference cannot have been so essentially and dogmatically fixed that the two parties of the adherents of Peter, could not be reckoned as one sect ; and if we look at the matter from this side, we can very well imagine that the relation between the party of Cephas and that of Christ may have been a similar one. Even if both sects must be considered as one and the same in the chief point, this does not at all affect the relation which must have subsisted between the parties of Paul and Apollos. The Apostle, 1 Cor. i. 12, may also have intended to multiply the names, in order to depict the overbearing party-spirit in the Corinthian Church, which expressed itself in the multiplication of sectarian names, which indeed indicated different colours and shades of party opinion, although not exactly different parties. Let us, therefore, first investigate the question wherein the chief opposition consisted between the parties of Peter and Paul.

In the above named treatise, Schmidt finds the chief cause of the difference between the two parties in the presumption, which led the Jewish Christians to consider themselves true Christians, and which would scarcely allow them to reckon the Gentile Christians as real Christians. Among the first Christians there was a party which arrogated Christ to

18 *

itself in a special manner—this was the Jewish Christian party. Christ, the Messiah, came in the first place for the sake of the Jews, to whom alone he had been promised ; the Gentiles might thank the Jews that Christ had come into the world. Among such proud men as these Jewish Christians, would not the presumption arise that Christ, the Messiah, belonged to them alone ? Exactly in this manner the presumption did arise, as we see from 2 Cor. x. 7. They called themselves τοὺς τοῦ Χριστοῦ —disciples of Christ—disciples of the Messiah,—or, changing slightly the name, χριστιανούς. If these Christians were Jewish Christians no doubt can arise that they formed one party with the sect of Peter. But if we agree with this, something else must have lain at the root of such a presumption on the part of the Jewish Christians, because it is quite incredible that they as Jewish Christians with such a presumption, which excluded the Gentile Christians from a participation in the Messianic salvation, should have gained an entrance into a Church consisting for the greater part of Gentile Christians. Therefore, however rightly Schmidt may see the ground of this opposition between the parties of Peter and of Paul, in the claim that the Petrine party made to be οἱ τοῦ Χριστοῦ, we may still enquire how this may be more exactly and certainly determined than has hitherto been done.

In order to answer this question, we shall certainly not be proceeding on an arbitrary assumption, in supposing that the chief accusation which the opposite party brought to bear against Paul, would have been recognised in some way in these Epistles of the Apostle. But the vindication of the apostolic authority constitutes a chief portion of the contents of these Epistles—this authority not being willingly yielded in its full sense to the Apostle Paul by his opponents. They would not recognize him as a real and genuine Apostle, on the ground of his not being in the same sense as Peter and the rest of the Apostles, τοῦ Χριστοῦ, and not like these having been in the same direct connection with Jesus during his life on earth ? Peter himself had no share in the party which went by his name in Corinth, as it must be concluded, from what we have already seen, that Peter was never in Corinth at all ; but it may well be supposed that the false Apostles who went about calling themselves by the name of Peter, eventually extended their travels to Corinth.

In the second Epistle, in which especially Paul speaks openly against these opponents, and directly contends with them, he calls them plainly, xi. 13, ψευδαπόστολοι, ψευδάδελφοι, ἐργάται δόλιοι, μετασχηματιζόμενοι εἰς ἀποστόλους Χριστοῦ. They also wished to be the true ἀπόστολοι Χριστοῦ, or to be in the closest connection with them, and in this sense to be Χριστοῦ ὄντες. The special zeal of the Jewish Christians for the Mosaic law, may also in this last respect be essentially the actuating motive, but since in a Church of Gentile Christians, such as was the Corinthian, they could not expect a favourable reception, if they had immediately brought forward their principles, they fell back on the special ground of their Judaistic opposition, they attacked the apostolic authority of the Apostle, and endeavoured in this way to work against him. According to this supposition, the relation of the party of Peter to that of Christ seems very simple and natural. Just as those of Paul and of Apollos did not esentially differ; so these two were not different parties, but only one and the same party under two different names, so that each name only denoted the claim which that party made for itself. They called themselves τοὺς Κηφᾶ, because Peter held the primacy among the Jewish Apostles, but τοὺς Χριστοῦ, because they relied on the direct connection with Christ as the chief token of genuine apostolic authority; and on this very account would not recognize Paul, who had been called to be an Apostle in a perfectly unusual and peculiar manner, as a genuine Apostle, enjoying the same privileges as the others, and thought they ought to place him at least far down in the ranks of Apostles.

On this account also their designation, evidently intentionally chosen, was τοῦ Χριστοῦ not τοῦ Ἰησοῦ or τοῦ κυρίου. The idea of the Messiah must be brought forward as the complete actuating organ of the Messianic happiness and blessing of the higher life, whose principle is Christ, in order to indicate all that those who belonged to this name had received from the most direct tradition, from an outward and actually experienced connection with the person of Jesus as the Messiah.

We must now endeavour as much as possible to establish the view here brought forward, by extracts from some principal passages of the two Epistles. Perhaps indeed the first apologetic section, in which the Apostle gives a vindication of his apostolic authority and work, (chap. i. 4), contains some indications that he may have had in his mind those adherents of the party of Peter who claimed to be considered as τοὺς τοῦ Χριστοῦ. When the Apostle, ii. 26, maintains with all his energy, ἡμεῖς δὲ νοῦν Χριστοῦ ἔχομεν (so far as the divine πνεῦμα is the principle of his Christian consciousness)—when, iv. 1, he desires his readers to remember that they have to look on him as ὑπηρέτης Χριστοῦ—when, iv. 10, he asserts that he as the least of the Apostles is willing to consider himself as a μωρὸς διὰ Χριστοῦ, in so far as on good grounds they hold themselves as φρόνιμοι ἐν Χριστῷ; when, verse 15, he reminds them that although they might have μυρίους παιδαγωγοὺς ἔχειν ἐν Χριστῷ, they could not have πολλοὺς πατέρας; in all passages such as these it is tolerably clear that he referred to the sects which he had just before mentioned; those parties who in the Apostle's opinion wished to make themselves known in an obnoxious manner, and in a perfectly peculiar sense as οἱ τοῦ Χριστοῦ ὄντες, and these special references lie behind the general apologetic tendency of all this section of the Epistle. In any case, an important passage of this section is to be found ix. 1, &c. The Apostle with a sudden transition here speaks in his own person, while still very closely connecting the portion of his Epistle, beginning ix. 1, with the contents of the chapter immediately preceding, and

he skilfully avails himself of the opportunity thus offered for
an apologetic discourse. In the foregoing eighth chapter then,
the Apostle had discussed the cause of the question which had
been laid before him, about the use of meat offered to idols at
the participation in the Gentile sacrificial feasts, and had given
his opinion that cases might arise when it would be necessary
to give up, out of consideration for others, what according to
a man's own views he would be perfectly justified in maintaining.
He puts this idea in such a manner as to give himself an opportunity of considering many things alleged to his disadvantage by his opponents in a light which with regard to his apostolic call can only appear as a voluntary renunciation. As an
Apostle he had also certain rights of which he as well as the
other Apostles might avail himself of; but that he had never
done so because a higher consideration had bidden him make
no use of them, Οὐκ εἰμὶ ἐλεύθερος; οὐκ εἰμὶ ἀπόστολος; οὐχὶ
Ἰησοῦν Χριστὸν τὸν κύριον ἡμῶν ἑώρακα; am I not free? am I
not an Apostle? and truly an Apostle as well as any other
Apostle? have I not seen the Lord Jesus Christ? Wherefore
the appeal to the ἑωρακέναι Ἰησοῦν Χριστὸν, τὸν κύριον ἡμῶν,
as a vindication of the ἀπόστολος εἶναι, if his opponents did
not deny him the real apostolic character, because he had not
seen the Lord as they, or rather the Apostle at the head of
their party had done, and had not lived in direct communion
with him? This also must be the genuine token of the Χριστοῦ
εἶναι. But that these opponents of the Apostle belonged also
to one class with the adherents of the party of Peter is clear
from the following words, verse 5, μὴ οὐκ ἔχομεν ἐξουσίαν
ἀδελφὴν γυναῖκα περιάγειν, ὡς καὶ οἱ λοιποὶ ἀπόστολοι καὶ οἱ
ἀδελφοι τοῦ κυρίου, καὶ Κηφᾶς. The Χριστοῦ εἶναι held good
in all these cases in the sense already discussed; it held good
for the Apostles in general who had enjoyed communion with
Jesus, it availed in a narrower sense for the ἀδελφοὶ Κυρίου,
inasmuch as they stood in a still nearer connection to the
Lord as his relatives; and it held good in the narrowest sense

for Peter, inasmuch as Jesus himself had assigned him a certain
precedence over the other Apostles, and he represented the
whole relation between Jesus and the others in the most complete manner in his own person. But Paul thought that he
himself, in the full consciousness of his apostolic dignity, and
the rights and claims connected with it, ought not to take a
secondary place, even to Peter. In token that he possessed
the same rights as the other Apostles, and especially the right
to live at the expense of the churches to whom ho preached
the Gospel, the Apostle appeals first, to what holds good in
law and custom in common life, (verses 7, 8.) ; secondly, to a
precept of the Mosaic Law, which indeed primarily referred to
animals needed for the use of man, but which might equally be
applied to the greatest things as to the least, (9-12) ; and thirdly,
to the customs prevailing in the Mosaic sacrificial worship, (13.)
But however well grounded his claim to be an Apostle might
be on these accounts, still he had never made any use of them,
because such a practice did not seem to him to be consistent
with the plan of the Gospel, and would place himself in a
mercenary light. Accordingly, living constantly in the consciousness of the chief aim to which he had devoted himself, he
subjugated his whole personality to the interests of others and
the regard to be paid to them, and his carnal nature he held in
such subjection that it was forced to yield to the power of his
spirit, (15-17). This whole section contains indeed a most
ample refutation of the supposition that the opponents of the
Apostle had ascribed the humility and unselfishness with which
he preached the Gospel in the churches, to the self-evident
consciousness of the Apostle, which did not allow him to dare
to place himself in a situation to assume the same rights as
the other Apostles. On account of this demeanour indicating
only weakness and want of self-confidence, they thought they
themselves had the less cause to be obliged to keep back the
selfish and self-seeking πλεονεξία (2 Cor. xii. 14.) of which the
Apostle elsewhere accuses them. But the more these charges

were connected with the chief attack on his apostolic dignity the more it must have seemed to the Apostle to be for his interest to vindicate himself from them, and to place his behaviour in its true light. As here the Apostle's apology refers in its main point to the ἑωρακέναι ᾽Ιησοῦν Χριστὸν, τὸν κύριον ἡμῶν ; without explaining more clearly the peculiar nature of this ἑωρακέναι he expresses his desire of holding fast in general to all that placed him on a level with the other Apostles. And he says also that as in any case a peculiar material revelation of the Lord could be predicated of himself, he accordingly (xv. 8.) declares in the same connection, that the Lord had appeared to him also as to the other Apostles. Just as the important exposition of the doctrine of the resurrection which follows seems to demand an equally authentic attestation of the chief points on which it relies, namely, that Jesus rose from the dead, and was really seen as so risen, so the theory cannot be excluded, that with regard to the chief points in which his opponents wished to involve the question of his apostolic authority, the Apostle evidently made use of the opportunity which here naturally offered itself, of placing himself in the same position with the disciples who were associated with Jesus during his life, and of vindicating his apostolic call by the criterion of a direct material appearance of the Lord.

The polemical references which the Apostle so freely uses in both Epistles are as openly and directly prominent in the second as in the first; still it is at the end of the Epistle that the Apostle confronts his opponents boldly without seeking any further compromise, and regards them steadfastly and keenly.

In the earlier part of the Epistle it is especially the passage v. 1-16, which contains a fresh interest full of meaning by its reference to his opponents. The Apostle assures the Corinthians at the outset in different terms of the love which should arouse their confidence, and seeks to convince them of the purity of his views and endeavours. In answer to the reproaches of his opponents he sets forth the results which had attended

his teachings through the strength given him by God, by
means of the διακονία τῆς καινῆς διαθήκης. The greater the
superiority of the καινὴ διαθήκη, the greater also is the superiority of the διακονία. But in striking contrast to this the
Apostle, iv. 7, continues " are the sufferings of all kinds with
which I as a weak fallible man have to struggle—sufferings
which threaten every moment to overwhelm my strength—still
I am preserved through them all by the might which conquers
death through life, by which Jesus was raised from the dead.
Therefore I do not allow my sufferings to hinder me in the
duties of my office." Sufferings only serve to educate the inward man, the true real man, for future glory ; this idea makes
the Apostle in chapter v., speak of the moment at which the
earthly body in whose bonds we now groan, will be changed
into a glorified heavenly body, v. 1-4. This confident expectation of a condition essentially belonging to our Christian
consciousness, in which when we are absent from the body we
are present with the Lord, or at least are in the most intimate
connection with him, now requires in all our acts and efforts
the most conscientious reference to Christ, by whom the judgment exactly corresponding to our moral conduct will be pronounced (5—14.) " This consciousness accompanies me in
my apostolic labours, and you yourselves must bear me this
witness ; you ought to be comforted by that which in this
respect testifies to my utmost consciousness, and holds good
against my opponents, and maintains my honour against them,
namely, that throughout I have not consulted my own person,
my own interests. I labour in the spirit of the love by
which Christ so offered himself up for us that we can only live
in him ; and all our former ties and relationships have ceased
to exercise any decided influence on us, wherefore we see ourselves placed in a perfectly new sphere of consciousness and
life. The principal actuating cause by which we are raised to
this completely new order of things, is the reconciliation which
God has effected through the death of Christ between himself
and man. Whilst this reconciliation is precisely the peculiar

burden of my apostolic preaching, the object of my labour; it is really only Christ in whose name I work—only God, whose voice is allowed to be heard through me. What then is there about my person which can justify my opponents in accusing me of a vain self-praise and of self-seeking views ?" In this connexion the expression used by the Apostle, Χριστὸν κατὰ σάρκα γινώσκειν, is especially worthy of remark. The Χριστὸς κατὰ σάρκα can only be the Christ or Messiah of Judaism, and accordingly the Apostle says in a sense which is as grammatically natural as satisfactory : " if it were the case that formerly I knew no other Messiah than the Messiah of Judaism—such an one as all the peculiar prejudices and material inclinations of my nation presented to me; and if I were not prepared to raise myself to the new stage of spiritual life on which I now stand —where I live in Christ who died for me, as for all, yet now I do not any longer acknowledge this conception of the Messiah as the true one. I have freed myself from all prejudices, from all the material ideas and expectations which had naturally taken hold of me from my nationality—which had devolved upon me as a born Jew." If this is the sense of the passage, it can scarcely be thought otherwise than that the Apostle in the expression Χριστὸν κατὰ σάρκα γινώσκειν wished to glance at his opponents who prided themselves especially as being τοὺς τοῦ Χριστοῦ ὄντας. Was it not exactly a κατὰ σάρκα Χριστὸν γινώσκειν, on which they took their ground when from the standpoint of Judaism and the conception of the Jewish Messiah they thought themselves obliged to deny to the Apostle the genuine apostolic character, and this because he had not been in that direct outward material communion with Jesus during his life on earth, of which those Apostles could boast who were originally called to the apostolic office by Jesus himself. The peculiar circumstance from which the εἶναι ἐν Χριστῳ must have been derived the Apostle says, on the contrary, was not so much the earthly and national appearance of Jesus, in which however the σάρξ in the above sense still had its share, but rather the death of Jesus, in so far as the old life died with his death, and the new life which was to be awakened in us took its beginning. That which essentially distinguishes the national Jewish Messiah from the Christ of the true Christian consciousness, is the sufferings and death of Christ—the great significance of the death on the cross which the Apostle represents as above all the culminating point of the Christian doctrine, and which he not without reason brings forward with all his energy against his opponents in these two Epistles. Therefore if the earthly life of Jesus as the Messiah and the visible communion with him during his life on earth be taken to a certain extent as something existing for itself, and his whole appearance on earth be not rather looked at by the light of his death on the cross, thus stripping it of the earthly, this is still a Χριστὸν κατὰ σάρκα γινώσκειν, we still fall back on that which is directly presented to us, conditioned by its natural relations, to which we must first die : but, on the contrary, if we look at his death as the great turning point, in which the καινὴ κτίσις is brought to light,—in which the old things vanish away and all things become new —then everything falls to the ground, which seemed to give the opponents, or rather the Apostles, on whose authority the opponents relied, their peculiar lofty precedence, owing to their direct communion with Jesus during his earthly life; but which really had its foundation in relations in which the Apostles, as born Jews, were involved. Therefore also he, the Apostle called so late, is enabled to place himself in the same rank with the witnesses of the resurrection of the Lord. He also has recognized in Jesus the One who, as the One who had died and was raised again to life, caused the full meaning of the Christian consciousness and life to appear to us, and established in us the true Χριστοῦ εἶναι.

Another passage, x. 7, is very nearly allied to those we have above examined. In chap. x. the Apostle enters on the consideration of the reproach made against him by his opponents that he was wanting in personal energy. He declares that he will show, on the contrary, that he knows how to act with all energy and earnestness, with the greatest confidence as to results whenever a matter of importance is involved. At the same time he refutes the reproach made against him, that in him the genuine token is wanting of a Χριστοῦ ὢν. Unless we look arbitrarily on the outward appearance only, in what is the Χριστοῦ εἶναι better than the ἐξουσία εἰς οἰκοδομὴν—the strength and energy with which a man labours at the furtherance of the cause of Christianity? He does not say τὰ κατὰ πρόσωπον βλέπετε, so much of the opponents themselves as of certain members of the Corinthian Church who had already given heed to them, and were in danger of allowing themselves to be still further led astray. " If in respect to my person you maintain what I must be κατὰ πρόσωπον—this is a proof that you chiefly look at the outward appearance, and judge according to the outward appearance only," (πρόσωπόν, as v. 12). These words are generally considered as referring to the so-called party of Christ, and Storr and Flatt understand them according to their view, with regard to their external relations to each other. As the Apostle is speaking of the Χριστοῦ εἶναι, the reference is to those who considered themselves in a special manner as τοὺς τοῦ Χριστοῦ—certainly very naturally—only I can find nothing at all in this passage, which would justify the conclusion that οἱ τοῦ Χριστοῦ were a party at all! The Apostle is rather concerned with his opponents, inasmuch as in contradistinction to him they boasted of a closer outward communion with Jesus or with the immediate disciples of Jesus—and especially with Peter the first of the Apostles—and in this wished to place the real criterion of the Χριστοῦ εἶναι.

But that these Χριστοῦ ὄντες belonged to one and the same class as the party of Peter, and the whole Judaising party of opposition, is clearly shown by the connection with what follows, where the Apostle speaks of the ὑπερλίαν ἀπόστολοι. What he advances against his opponents in reference to the Χριστοῦ

εἶναι, 7, appears to me to have been this : "If anyone maintains so confidently of himself that he is a genuine disciple of
Christ, and stands in real relations with him, according to
his subjective opinion, because he believes that he once did so
perceive the matter, (this secondary idea lies as much in the
word ἑαυτῷ as in πρόσωπον, which contains in itself the idea
of the subjective dependence on personal motives), he considers
also the outward connection with Christ as the peculiar token
of the true union with Christ, then such a man must on the
other hand concede to me the right of deciding on the true
union with Christ and this according to another token which I
hold to be true.   In this view I can, in any case, assert of myself, with the same right as do my opponents on their part, that
Χριστοῦ εἶναι.   What tokens of Χριστοῦ εἶναι the Apostle means
to indicate in reference to himself is seen by what follows.
" This right, that of considering myself as Χριστοῦ ὄντα, from
my own standpoint can so little be denied me, that in fact it
ought rather to be acknowledged even if I were to advance
still further pretensions.   Even were I to claim a still greater
authority than I really do, my claims would still be true and
well-founded ; I should have no fear of being brought to shame
because I employ my privilege of working as an Apostle, only
εἰς οἰκοδομὴν, and not εἰς καθαίρεσιν ὑμῶν, because I only endeavour to work in furtherance of the true welfare of the
Church.   With such good right do I believe that I am justified
in maintaining that I am Χριστοῦ."   What the Apostle wishes to
make available as a peculiar token of the Χριστοῦ εἶναι in opposition to the κατὰ πρόσωπον βλέπειν, is the aim of the οἰκοδομὴ,
the genuine Christian, beneficent, edifying form of his apostolic
activity, as he further says in verse 13 : "Of course I am very
far from placing myself in the same class with those who ascribe
to themselves, with conceited selfishness, an arbitrary self-made
measure of praise, and seek to enhance their own glory at the
cost of the advantage of others.   My glory lies in those things
which I have been actually enabled to effect in my apostolic

calling, within the bounds which God has appointed to my circle
of action, in favour of the cause of Christianity; insomuch as I was
the first who brought Christianity to Corinth, and hope to have
so planted it there, that its operations may open for me a yet
wider circle of action. So little is it necessary for me to seek
my glory in a foreign sphere, and so little can anything else
than real worth be of any value in the cause of Christianity."
The contrast of which the Apostle here speaks, allows us with
reason to suppose that the opponents not only worked against
his authority, but also called in question his merit of being the
special founder of the Corinthian Church. They indeed came
to Corinth after the Apostle, but as they did not acknowledge
Paul as a true Apostle, as Χριστοῦ ὄντα, they assumed to themselves the glory properly belonging to him, at least in so
far as they pretended to have been the first to plant true
Christianity.

With chapter x. 7, begins the section in which the Apostle
turns completely against his opponents, and exhibits himself
clearly in the freest outpouring of feeling with regard to his
whole relation with them. The tone in which he expresses
himself against them becomes, in chap. xi., stronger and more
vivid—there is a cutting irony mingled with his words, and the
picture which he holds up to us of his opponents stands forth
in more decided and ever more repulsive features. " Ye hear
indeed," he says, xi. 1. to his readers, " patiently enough the
sayings of the fools (my opponents who would exalt themselves
with vain presumption), ye should give me a moment's hearing
when I as a fool speak to you in the same language. (For my
vindication and my praise can only appear as folly from the
high standpoint from which my opponents look down upon
me). I am jealous over you with a godly jealousy (I am seized
as by a holy jealousy) when I think that the love, to which
I as the founder of the Christian Church in Corinth have the
justest right, may be handed over to others who have only
opposed all my aims. I have espoused you to one husband, to

present you as a chaste virgin to Christ. But I fear, as the serpent beguiled Eve through deceit, that your thoughts also may be turned away from the unfettered truth, against Christ. Indeed if one were to come who would preach another Christ whom I have not preached, or if ye were to receive another spirit from the One ye have received, or another gospel than the one ye have accepted (*i.e.* were it possible that there might be another Christianity, which must be taken as the real and true one now first preached to you by such another teacher, if I then had either not imparted the truth to you, or had done so only very incompletely and improperly) then indeed "ye might well bear with him.") (It is this then which brings the Apostle into the most decided antagonism with his opponents—the question between the two parties consisted of nothing less than that of a true or a false Christianity. The opponents of the Apostle truly preached another Jesus and another Christianity, whilst they accused the Apostle of not preaching the true ones.) "But even this is a perfectly unlikely supposition. That Christianity which I have preached to you is the only true one, and deserves all belief. For I suppose that I stand in nothing behind the 'very chiefest Apostles.'" The ὑπερλίαν ἀπόστολοι may have been the opponents of the Apostle themselves, those who are afterwards called ψευδαπόστολοι. But as these ψευδαπόστολοι, who in Corinth relied especially on the authority of the Apostle Peter, came to Corinth from Palestine—and without doubt stood in some connexion with the Jewish Apostles of Palestine—the ὑπερλίαν ἀπόστολοι may well have been the Apostles themselves whose disciples and delegates the ψευδαπόστολοι claimed to be. The expression ὑπερλιαν ἀπόστολοι may therefore signify the over-estimation which was sought to be ascribed to the authority of the Apostles in prejudice to that of Paul. This is also indicated by the expression οἱ δοκοῦντες στύλοι εἶναι used Gal. ii. 9, in reference to James, Peter, and John, which is only a way of saying why they were considered as forming a certain party desirous of commanding public opinion. "However great," says the Apostle accordingly, "may be the success of the pretensions advanced by the other Apostles in my disfavour, nothing can assail the truth of the Christianity which I teach." In what follows, the Apostle declares that he thinks he has every right to claim recognition for his apostolic calling, inasmuch as by his whole behaviour towards the Corinthian Church he had publicly afforded an insight into the essence of the Christian doctrines as well as borne testimony by his whole life to the purity of his zeal for the cause of Christianity. "For," he declares firstly, "I have in the most disinterested manner never once made any claim upon you for my support, while my opponents in whom you trust (οἱ τοιοῦτοι ψευδαπόστολοι ἐργάται δόλιοι, μετασχηματιζόμενοι εἰς ἀποστόλους χριστοῦ, as he calls these false teachers who gave themselves out by name as the Apostles of Christ, verse 13), only endeavour with every art of guile and deceit to make some gain out of you, and use you as the instruments of their interested designs.—Verses 7-20." Secondly, he says, "My whole life has been a series of hardships, sacrifices, and dangers, which I have undertaken for the cause of Christianity," 20-23. This passage alone sets it beyond doubt that these opponents were born Jews, of genuine Israelite descent. They therefore must have undoubtedly belonged to the party of Peter, and upheld the authority of the Apostle Peter. The Apostle, continuing in a tone of irony, allows the opprobrious insinuation ἀφροσύνη of his opponents, in order that under this mask he may place himself on the same footing with his presumptuous, vain, self-asserting opponents, and in order to be enabled in his own vindication to speak in a manner which indeed appears to be only foolish, vain self-praise, but which would be rather preferred by the Corinthians, accustomed as they were to the speeches of his overbearing opponents (compare 19, 20, 21). He then asks the question (22), Ἐβραῖοί εἰσι; κἀγώ· Ἰσραηλῖται εἰσι; κἀγώ· σπέρμα Ἀβραάμ εἰσι; κἀγώ. He also says, if there is any idea of such a

19

καυχᾶσθαι κατὰ τὴν σάρκα (18) of a καυχᾶσθαι depending only
on natural accidental advantages, it can apply to me equally
with my opponents. But they do not only claim to be genuine
Israelites, but also as such, διάκονοι Χριστοῦ. If it appears to
them merely folly on my part that I venture to claim equality
with them with respect to the above-mentioned advantages,
they will in all probability consider it as complete madness
(παραφρονεῖν here plainly means much more than the expression before used ἀφροσύνη), when they find that I shall even
have to claim the advantage over them, inasmuch as I can
appeal to something more real than to these advantages of
theirs, as the actual proof of my apostolic ministry. These
same persons who have so high an opinion of themselves as
born Jews, also maintain that they are the true διάκονοι
Χριστοῦ. In the following chapters, also, the Apostle
carries on the vindication of his apostolic authority, and
indeed adds a third reason in proof of the right he has to
make known his Apostolic office to the two he has already
mentioned in chap. xi. This third reason consists in the
extraordinary revelations which had fallen to his lot, especially
an extacy into which he had been thrown during the first
period of his apostolic career. Still he did not appeal to these
revelations as a cause of boasting. Rather he bore about in
his body a certain suffering which ever kept alive in him the
feeling of his human weakness as a corrective of any exalted
opinion of himself, and which caused him to put his whole
trust in divine help. Above all, he had only been induced to
say all that he had done in his own praise, because the
Corinthians had said nothing in his vindication against his
opponents, which they should properly have said. How far
he was from being behind the other Apostles they themselves
had the best right of judging, as he had borne witness among
them in every way of his genuine apostolic manner of action
and ministry; and nothing had been wanting in their Church
of all that had fallen to the share of any other Church in Chris-

tendom. There cannot be any reasonable doubt that the mention of the ὀπτασίαι and ἀποκαλύψεις to which the Apostle here
appeals, has a very close connection with his apologetic aim and
the character of his opponents with which he occupies himself. If, as Judaising teachers of Christianity, they took their
stand on the views which must have been those peculiarly of
the parties of Peter or of Christ, namely, the material relation
to Jesus and intercourse with him, which had been shared by
Peter and by disciples who had been called by Christ and
educated by him for their office; if they appealed to these
things as the true criterion of the Χριστοῦ εἶναι and the
apostolic call, then the Apostle Paul, when he referred to the
last and highest point of his appeal in favour of his apostolic
office, could only set an inward spiritual experience against the
outward material experiences of the rest of the Apostles. This
inward experience then consisted in those extraordinary
phenomena which, as the inward proofs and revelations of the
Divine, as matters of fact present to his direct consciousness,
had awakened in him belief in Christ—that ἑωρακέναι Ἰησοῦν
Χριστὸν τὸν κύριον ἡμῶν, to which he had already appealed
(1 Cor. ix. 1), and which at the same time belonged to one
class with the ὀπτασίαι and ἀποκαλύψεις κυρίου which he here
speaks of, even if it is altogether probable that the extacy
described in verse 2, &c., is precisely the same with the
phenomenon related in the Acts of the Apostles (chap. ix.), and
which brought about the conversion of the Apostle. Such
ὀπτασίαι καὶ ἀποκαλύψεις might appear to the opponents of the
Apostle as imaginary visions which could make no claim to
objective truth, in comparison with the outward matter of fact
relations in which the other Apostles had lived with Jesus, and
according to the principles which Peter (Acts of the Apostles
i. 21) had laid down on the occasion of the election of the
Apostle Matthias. But for the Apostle himself the phenomena
which had been interwoven with his inner life were nothing
less than firm incontestable facts; and just as he had volun-

19 *

tarily evaded speaking of them in order to avoid any appearance of vain self-exaltation, so in this place where it behoves him to be silent on nothing which might serve in the vindication and establishment of his apostolic authority, he cannot omit appealing to them. But the more that he cannot conceal from himself, that this testimony to his apostolic call belongs to the sphere of his own immediate consciousness, the more solicitously in the whole contents of these two Epistles does he seek to make good those active proofs to which the character of objective reality could be least denied—namely, the great trials through which he had borne testimony to his apostolic ministry and the great success with which he had been attended in his efforts to further the cause of Christianity. Compare 1 Cor. iii. 8-15 ; ix. 15, &c.; xv. 10 ($\pi\epsilon\rho\iota\sigma\sigma\acute{o}\tau\epsilon\rho\sigma\nu$ $a\dot{v}\tau\tilde{\omega}\nu$ $\pi\acute{a}\nu\tau\omega\nu$ $\dot{\epsilon}\kappa o\pi\acute{\iota}a\sigma a$) 2 Cor. x. 12, &c.

The passage (2 Cor. iii. 1, &c.) gives, in a manner well worthy of attention, an explanation of the entire matter in dispute between the Apostle and his opponents, when it treats of a question of principle which from the beginning essentially divided the Apostle from the elder Apostles. Its subject matter is of $\dot{\epsilon}\pi\iota\sigma\tau o\lambda a\grave{\iota}$ $\sigma\nu\sigma\tau a\tau\iota\kappa a\grave{\iota}$, of letters of " commendation " which certain persons ($\tau\iota\nu\grave{\epsilon}\varsigma$ as the $\tau\iota\nu\grave{\epsilon}\varsigma$ $\dot{a}\pi o$ $\dot{}I a\kappa\acute{\omega}\beta o\nu$—Gal. ii. 12, opponents of the Apostle) had brought with them to Corinth. It can only have been sought to testify by these letters that the bearers were to be considered as real credible preachers of the Christian doctrine certificated by recognized authority. Under what other names then, can these letters have been brought forward, except those of the elder Apostles, and in what else can the cause of the facts that such commendatory and certificated letters were thought necessary, consist, except in the opposition of parties which were so widely severed from each other that any one who wished to appear as a teacher was obliged, in order not to be taken for a false teacher, to give open proof to which party he adhered, and to whose principles and teachings he gave credence. The more important the authority on which such messengers relied, and the more universally acknowledged it was, the more undoubtedly could they reckon on their reception and influence, and from what other place could they bring with them so satisfactory a legitimation as from Jerusalem.* The ἐπιστολαὶ συστατικαὶ, indicates besides that there is a higher authority standing in the back-ground, behind the opponents with whom he is contending, and which the Apostle perceived as being antagonistic to his own—he therefore in these Epistles takes occasion to explain fully the principle of his apostolic authority. This he does in chapter iii. If no one were admitted to be a real, authenticated teacher of Christianity except he were recommended from Jerusalem and brought with him a "letter of commendation," this could only be because no others were to be recognized as Apostles except the elder ones. This the Apostle could not concede, and yet with regard to his apostolic office and apostolic authority he only appealed to that εὐδόκησεν ὁ θεὸς ἀποκαλύψαι τὸν υἱὸν αὐτοῦ ἐν ἐμοὶ, Gal. i. 15, and consequently to a mere fact of his own consciousness. And starting from these ἐπιστολαὶ συστατικαὶ he maintains, in order to produce some objective fact, that he also like his opponents has an Epistle of commendation, but indeed a very different one! His letters of commendation are the Corinthians them-selves, and written indeed in his own heart. What they are as Christians, concerns him so nearly, that it becomes an essential

---

* That such a legitimation belonged to the principles of the Judaizers, and was customary among them, is clear from passages from the pseudo-Clementine writings, which serve also as an explanation of the ἐπιστολαὶ συστατικαὶ. In the 4th Book of the Recognitions, C. 34, the Apostle Peter says the devil sends abroad into the world, false Prophets, and false Apostles, and false Teachers who indeed speak in the name of Christ, but do the will of the devil; he exhorts them therefore to use caution, "et nulli doctorum credatis nisi qui Jacobi fratris Domini ex Hierusalem, detulerit testimonium vel ejus quicunque post ipsum fuerit. Nisi enim quis illuc ascenderit, et ibi fuerit probatus quod sit doctor idoneus et fidelis ad praedicandum Christi verbum, nisi inquam inde detulerit testimonium, recependus non est sed neque propheta, neque apostolus in hoc tempore speretur a vobis aliquis alius præter nos." Compare Homily, II. 35.

part of his own self-consciousness. And because it shall not only be said what they are to him, but also what they are objectively with regard to his acceptation by others—he adds that these letters written in his inmost heart are also lying open before the eyes of the world, manifest to every man, laid before the general consciousness of the world, composed under the commission of Christ, written not with ink but with the Spirit of the living God, not in tables of stone, but on the fleshly tables of the heart; i.e. the legitimation of his apostolic authority, is the fact of the success of his preaching of the Gospel, the fact that through him the Corinthians had been constituted into a Christian Church. He who founds Christian Churches may with justice be considered as an Apostle of Christ, because there can be no question but that Christ is working in and through him. It is the result of the operation of the cause, of the principle, which must be pre-supposed before the idea of a decided operation can be formed, in the same manner as in 1 Cor. ix. 2, the Apostle says to the Corinthians in arguing against those who were not willing to allow his claim to be an Apostle: εἰ ἄλλοις οὐκ εἰμὶ ἀπόστολος, ἀλλά γε ὑμῖν εἰμὶ, ἡ γὰρ σφραγὶς τῆς ἐμῆς ἀποστολῆς ὑμεῖς ἐστε ἐν κυρίῳ, ἡ ἐμὴ ἀπολογία τοῖς ἐμὲ ἀνακρίνουσιν αὕτη ἐστί. In the same way in Gal. ii. 7, he grounds his εὐαγγέλιον τῆς ἀκροβυστίας on the fact that the same things which led Peter to εἰς ἀποστολὴν τῆς. περιτομῆς, operated powerfully in himself to bring forward εἰς τὰ ἔθνη—i.e. so that the operation of this ἐνέργιεν is the existence of the Gentile Christian Church. But the greater and more evident the success of his ministry, the more certain it is that he only derived its express apostolic authentication from God and Christ, whose servant he is—and he derives it from Christ as the founder of a new διαθήκη whose principle is the πνεῦμα. The more perfectly this principle is realized in him, the more able he is to bring forward a result corresponding to this principle. The question therefore can only be as to what it comprises and how he can prove its possession.

The whole stage of the development on which the religious consciousness of the Old Testament relies is the subject in opposition to which the Apostle develops the idea of the πνεῦμα as the Christian principle, iii. 11-18. He fixes as the essential difference between the two διαθῆκαι, in their two chief ideas γράμμα and πνεῦμα, the ἀποκτείνειν on one side, and the ζωοποιεῖν on the other, and accordingly makes this objective difference appear in its subjective character from the point of view of the question how the religious consciousness, which lies at the foundation of the Old Testament narrative of the shining light on the face of Moses, stands in relation to each of the two διαθῆκαι. This shining light is a symbol of the character of the old διαθήκη, as well with regard to its advantages as to its defects. Its advantages consisted in having a shining light in which the majesty of God reflected itself in such a manner, and from which it might be concluded that if the old had such a glory, the new would have one still more radiant and supreme. But the defects of the old διαθήκη consisted in the transitory nature of that shining light in the face of Moses; and even still more in the fact that the Israelites on account of the veil which covered the face of Moses in order to shade their eyes from the shining light, did not perceive its actual extinction, and therefore believed that it still continued after it had already become extinct. This veil, the symbol of Mosaism, still continues to lie on the consciousness of the Jews, this is the barrier in their religious consciousness which prevents their realizing the finite nature of the old διαθήκη. In contrast to this concealment and narrowness which belongs to the character of Judaism is the πνεῦμα as the Christian principle, unfolding the complete knowledge of the truth, exalted above all merely outward considerations, into the oneness with Christ, into the identical, absolute, self-certainty of Christian consciousness. If where the Spirit is, the Lord is also, then the Lord himself is the Spirit, iii. 16—so also he who has the Spirit in the sense meant by the Apostle is in the διακονία

τοῦ πνεύματος iii. 8—and is also a διάκονος Χριστοῦ (xi.
23.) The opponents with whom the Apostle was engaged at
Corinth, considered themselves as διάκονοι Χριστοῦ. As they
were not Apostles themselves, but were forced to support
themselves on some apostolic authority, they must have considered those to whose authority they appealed as especially
ἀποστόλους Χριστοῦ, but only in the same sense in which they
themselves claimed to be διάκονοι Χριστοῖ. They were not
Apostles, but if, as the Apostle says, they were μετασχηματιζόμενοι
εἰς ἀποστόλους Χριστοῦ, then by ἀπόστολοι Χριστοῦ we must
understand that they called the Apostles on whose authority they
relied and whose representatives they desired to be, Apostles
of Christ in the same emphatic sense in which they themselves
wished to be διάκονοι Χριστοῦ, and the Apostle himself, x. 7.
speaks of the Χριστοῦ εἶναι. In what else could the distinguishing criterion of their Χριστοῦ εἶναι consist, as distinguishing
them from the Apostle Paul, except that the elder Apostles
on account of the direct companionship in which they stood
with Jesus during his earthly life might claim to be the only
authenticated preachers and ministers of the Messianic salvation? And on what other standpoint could the Apostle himself
rest in maintaining the apostolic authority than the very one
which we see him assume in these two Epistles, obliged as he
was to set the inward and spiritual in opposition to that which
his opponents made so much of in a material sense, and to
recognize the principle of true companionship and the genuine
apostolic ministry only in the Spirit which is the Lord himself?
Therefore it is self-evident how he could not justify himself to
his nearest opponents in Corinth without referring to the
Apostles whose representatives they claimed to be. That he
was in no whit behind them, that he could claim for himself
the same rights as they did, and bore in himself the same
apostolic consciousness, is the view from which he proceeds to
the highest point of his conflict with them, xi. 5; and to which
he adheres throughout his whole discourse, as is shown by the

repetition of this chief idea, xii. 11. Whilst far removed from approaching them in regard to the acknowledgment of their apostolic dignity, yet he cannot put up with its exclusive assertion on the part of his oponents. That he did not wish to dispute with them as to what they were in themselves, but only as to what they assumed to be in their own too high estimation, he gives us to understand by the strikingly selected expression οἱ ὑπερλίαν ἀπόστολοι. The Apostles were placed in opposition to him, as if he were nothing in comparison with them (οὐδέν εἰμι he says, xii. 11, in a true sense for him, but still in allusion to this) and as if he were of no value as an Apostle of Christ. If in maintaining his apostolic authority, he had only said that he was in no respect behind such opponents as he characterizes in chap. xi. as those ψευδαπόστολοι, ἐργάται δόλιοι μετασχηματιζόμενοι εἰς ἀποστόλους Χριστοῦ, what a mean opinion he must have entertained of himself and of his apostolic dignity? He could only have intended to measure himself with the veritable Apostles themselves, and σημεῖα τοῦ ἀποστόλου of which he speaks, xii. 12, can be understood as on no other comparison.

If, according to the meaning of the chief passage which we have already granted, all the matters in dispute between the Apostle and his opponents must be referred to the idea of the Χριστοῦ εἶναι, as far as this can be taken as the chief criterion of the apostolic authority (although in a very different sense), it was very probable that those who especially wished to be considered as οἱ τοῦ Χριστοῦ, assumed also to be that Χριστοῦ εἶναι against whom the Apostle Paul was obliged to set up and hold fast with all possible determination his principle of apostolic authority.

We may then assume that the question respecting the party of Christ is here answered in as nearly correct a manner as is possible from the available data, but against the view here taken certain objections were raised, as soon as it was brought forward, and these objections must here be shortly considered.*

It is granted that what is predicated of οἱ τοῦ Χριστοῦ is corroborated by many antithetical references in both Epistles, and may even appear as the only correct solution of the difficulty; but it is thought that by this theory the difficulty is not overcome, that the party of Christ is distinguished only by name from the party of Peter, whilst the relation of the parties stands in direct contradiction to the foregoing party names; or which is the same thing, that the identity of the party of Peter with that of Christ is nowhere indicated. If this is not indicated, we fail to find in 1 Cor. x. 7, any dispute with the party of Christ, but only the statement which the Apostle brings against his opponents of Peter's party, namely, that he was of Christ as well as they. Could we indeed find a passage in which it was said clearly and decidedly that the party of Peter was one and the same with that of Christ, the matter would be very easily decided. But as such a one is not to be found, we are led to a process of combination by which on comparing together what seem to be data having a certain connection, and by paying strict attention to the peculiar ten-

---

* Compare Neander, Gesch. der Pflanzung u. Leitung der christlichen kirche durch die Apostol. 1832, 1. Thl. p. 298. Billroth. Commentar. zu den Briefen des Paulus an die Korinthier. Leipzig. Einl. p. xix. Rückert, Der erste Brief Pauli an die Korinthier. Leipzig, 1836. Schenkel. De Ecclesia Corinthia primæva factionibus turbata. Disquisitio critico-historia ad antiquissimum ecclesiæ Christianæ statum illustrandum pertinens, Basil. 1838. Goldhorn Die Christuspartei zu Korinth. im Zeitalter der Apostel. im Illgen's Zeitschr. für hist. Theol. 1840. Dähne Die Christuspartei in d. Apost. kirche zu Korinth. Halle, 1841. There may also be compared with these what I have on the other hand remarked in the Tübinger Zeitschr. für Theol. 1836, und in den Jahrb. für wissensch. Kritik. 1839. In the commentaries of Olshausen, Meyer, De Wette, Osiander, &c., the views of their predecessors are repeated, and combined now in one way, now in another, which only tends to convince one more of the necessity of bringing to a clear and firm point these strangely confused representations, which are so often contradictory, and this can only be done by a general historical view of the matter.

dencies of the author, we are enabled to arrive at a greater or less probable result. In what other light can the passage quoted be placed, when seen from this standpoint, if we remember that it is indisputable that in the passages which refer to the personal relations of the Apostle to his opponents, the criterion of apostolic authority (to maintain which against his opponents is the Apostle's task) is not treated of in a general Christian sense, but in an apostolic one. If accordingly we approach the reality of the matter by a process of combination, it is self-evident that the theory here adduced can only be considered from the points of view of relative probability, and then we must ask, what other theory than the one here adduced can be put forward with as great a claim to probability ?

According to Neander, the adherents of the party of Christ must have been those who kept to Christ only, to the exclusion of the Apostle ; those who recognised Christ only as Teacher, and who were desirous of receiving what he taught, as truth direct from himself without any mediation. This was such an arbitrary and subjective tendency, such an assumption of appropriation of the revelation vouchsafed by God, and at the same time such a breaking loose from the divinely arranged plan of development, that it could only result in an arbitrary proceeding manifesting itself in the forms in which the Christian doctrines themselves were received. It may easily have happened, that where one party desired to attach itself especially to Paul, another to Apollos, and a third to Peter, another might finally start up, which would not be called by any of these party names, but which constituted for itself in its own manner a different Christianity independent of apostolic preaching. The subjective form of thought which this party assumed may have been either more mystical or more rationalistic. Neander himself thinks that the rationalistic was the most prevailing tone, as according to his account the party of Christ must have been a philosophical sect, which made of Christ only a second,

perhaps a more exalted Socrates.* This is the principal view
in opposition to my own, and it is divided from it, inasmuch
as it endeavours, instead of identifying the parties of Christ
and of Peter, to find as far as possible a specific difference
between them. But what led to this idea, and how much it is
wanting in even probable grounds, is shown by the modification
which it has received from Rückert. He maintains that the
party of Christ was not, as Neander says, composed of persons
of philosophical culture who had made for themselves their own
philosophical view of Christ; but he places us in this dilemma,
that either the party of Christ took its stand as a party among
the other parties, or set itself up as the only true Church over
the rest of the sects. The first idea cannot be entertained,
as Christ could not have been looked upon as a mere teacher
such as Paul, Apollos, or Cephas, therefore the second must
be accepted. The party of Christ placed itself at the head
of the others, would neither be considered as of Paul nor of
Apollos nor of Cephas, but acknowledged Christ alone as its
Lord and Master; but it did not do this in the sense in which
Paul desired once that all men should be χριστοῦ. In what
sense then did it do this? The party of Christ must naturally
have been a separate party, or it would not have been reckoned
by the Apostle amongst the rest; further, it must have recognized Christ as Lord and Master, or it would not have designated
itself by his name, but it could not have acknowledged him in
a fitting manner, or else Paul would not have described it as
merely a party. But what is all this but a series of purely
abstract definitions, out of which we can get no concrete idea

---

* Neander thus indicates in the first edition, the opinion that the party of Christ
must have held of him. In the following edition this very striking indication of
Neander's views is suppressed, on what ground is not stated. But of course this
parallel shows in the most decided manner that these disciples of Christ who placed
him on the same footing as Socrates would not have been allowed to continue
within the pale of Christendom. The name itself οἱ τοῦ Χριστοῦ, contradicts the
theory of Neander. Whilst the name betokened them to be a sect, and bespoke
real Christianity for this sect in a special sense, this opinion held by it of Christ
would make of it a completely unchristian sect.

of what specially constituted this party. If we cannot even say what it was negatively, nor even what made it positively a party, we cannot think of it as a party at all. It cannot have been a philosophic sect, as Rückert expressly calls it; but can it have been, according to Neander's distinction, a mystical one? Schenkel, Goldhorn, and Dähne at least consider the adherents of the party of Christ to have been visionaries, in a sense which involves a yet further antagonism between their theories and my own. Whilst I see the chief importance of the Christ to the party of Christ, consists in his bodily connection with his disciples through the intercourse of outward material life, according to the opinion of these critics he must have been a spiritual Christ revealing himself in visions from heaven. The disciples of Christ boasted of a special inward union with Christ, by means of which they declared themselves independent of all the unlimited distinctive authority of the Apostles, but this their glory they did not rest on a special outward relation with Christ, but only on an inward one, revealed from heaven in visions, to which they appealed instead of to the apostolic doctrinal traditions. To this Schenkel refers what is said by the Apostle, 2 Cor. xii. 1, of his ὀπτασίαι and ἀποκαλύψεις, as the Apostle in this place only and nowhere else (and, as he himself says here, only forced to do so by his opponents) speaks of his ὀπτασίαι and ἀποκαλύψεις. His opponents must have been boasting of their special visions and revelations of Christ, and because they gloried in such, they had thrown off all apostolic authority. This therefore clearly shows that the party of Christ had called themselves by the name of Christ and not by that of an Apostle, because they held all Apostles as of no value. The reason of this must have lain in the occurrences at the feast of Pentecost. From the thoroughly direct manner in which the Divine Spirit descended from heaven upon them, it must have been concluded that nothing was to be obtained from apostolic instruction, and this conviction must have been strengthened by the sudden conversion of the Apostle Paul in consequence of a heavenly vision. We cannot accordingly wonder that since that time there arose men who were only willing to rely on the Spiritual Christ. But what are we to think of this Spiritual Christ? With the precarious suppositions on which the hypothesis rests, he floats before us so completely in the air that in neither Epistle does he stand on the firm ground of a real existence. How can we assume that the Apostle shared those visions and revelations of which he speaks with those very opponents with whom he was contending? We may indeed see, in this party of Christ, now indicated in one way, now in another, those neutrals independent of all apostolic authority, those adherents of a philosophical or Spiritual Christ (a wider modification of one and the same idea) and we may also see the specific division between the party of Christ and that of Peter which the words of the Apostle seem to require. But we cannot get at any clear and definite idea of the party in question ; neither is it likely, that if it was so characteristically different from all others, this difference must have been palpable in the way and manner in which the Apostle spoke of these parties. Where then does he speak of a party so peculiarly and so essentially different from all others? or how can it be supposed that he indeed did battle with all the others, but passed over in complete silence that very one which stood in the rudest antagonism not only to Pauline but to apostolic Christianity, and which threatened to destroy its foundations. If we agree with Neander, that what the Apostle in the first chapter of the first Epistle says of the disagreements between the Corinthian parties applies equally to the party of Christ, we can indeed appeal in confirmation of this to the declaration of the Apostle himself, iv. 6, where he speaks of a μετασχηματίζειν in reference to himself and Apollos, and this can only be understood as implying that what was before said in immediate reference to the parties of Paul and Apollos may now be applied also to both the others. But the same difficulty presents itself here also. If what is said of one applies also to the others, it must be possible to bring them altogether under the same idea. But how can this be possible if the party of Christ was so far divided from the three other parties in refusing to recognize an apostolic authority? This distinction is not made by the Apostle, and the recognition of an apostolic authority is very naturally not treated of generally in the chief passages of the two Epistles, but only in those special ones in which the Apostle feels himself compelled to make good his claim in opposition to that of the other Apostles.

But if all these modifications of the chief opposition to the views taken by me will not suffice to give a clear and distinct definition of the party of Christ, and cannot be founded on data contained in the two Epistles, we find ourselves again face to face with the question, whether it is so impossible, on the supposition of the identity of the parties of Christ and of Cephas, that the Apostle should have been justified in speaking of them as of two separate parties? This is in truth the only argument which can be advanced against my theory, and I can see no difficulty in it which does not vanish as soon as we go closer into the relations of the parties in the Corinthian Church. The chief opposition undoubtedly concerned the Apostle Paul. The authority of the Apostle Peter was set up against his. But this relation of opposition may have had a double aspect. The party called itself after Paul, the other after Peter; there was here nothing so far disparaging to or excluding the Apostle Paul: party stood opposed to party; each one held to its own Apostle as its head; but as soon as we penetrate a little further, and wish to arrive at the reason why Peter was followed and not Paul? why the preference must be given to one rather than to the other? and when this reason can only be found on looking at the matter from the Jewish standpoint on which the chief opponents of the Apostle in Corinth stood, and found only in the fact that Peter, not Paul, had been a personal disciple of Christ, then this state of opposition becomes an exclusive one; a principle is established involving as a necessary consequence that Paul was not to be considered as a true Apostle, because the most essential requirements of true apostolic authority were wanting in him. In the extreme ranks of the opposition against the Apostle stood those persons who were designated under the name of the party of Christ, and the nature of the matter requires that the party of Christ in this sense must be represented as those from whom proceeded this opposition against the Apostle Paul, founded on distinct grounds, those Judaising false teachers who had come to Corinth with their letters of recommendation (2 Cor. ii. 1). For the whole party the name was brought forward of the Apostle Peter, to be used in direct opposition to the name of the Apostle Paul, and concealing the ground of the opposition. This view of the relation between the parties of Peter and of Christ is not only very easily put in agreement with the passage 1 Cor. i. 12, but is even confirmed by it. For as the Apostle here first speaks of himself, then of Apollos, then of Cephas, and last of Christ, it is clear that here a relation is intended to be understood in which Apollos stood nearer to him than Cephas, and the party of Christ was still further from him than that of Cephas. Therefore, also, the Apostle immediately and characteristically grasps the whole question in its most extreme point which is here treated of, the name of the party of Christ ; beginning his reply boldly with the words μεμέρισται ὁ Χριστός : is this name (Χριστοῦ, as a party name) not the most undoubted proof that Christ is torn in pieces by your party spirit ? Each party must as a Christian party have desired to claim a share in Christ ; then, if there was a peculiar " party of Christ," how was the one Christ divided in whom all things were to be united and all differences were to vanish ? This the Apostle says just as if the party of Christ were the peculiar seat of the opposition against him, and the centre of the prevailing party spirit in Corinth.

If one is thoroughly satisfied on this point I do not in fact see what can further be alleged against the view in question.

The whole contents of both Epistles stand in the most fitting relation to it. Let it be granted that no further reference to the name of the party of Christ can be perceived, the matter itself on which it alone depends agrees in the most complete manner with all that this view implies. Both names indicate the same party, so that what is said against the party of Peter, holds good with regard to the party of Christ. Indeed if both parties had together formed the opposition to the Apostle Paul in the Corinthian Church we can fully comprehend and enter into the earnest and trenchant polemics against an anti-Pauline Judaising Christianity which runs through both Epistles. But the name does not so completely vanish from the Epistles that this theory does not also receive the necessary confirmation from this point also. As Billroth remarks, not without reason, " Although among the passages treating of the party of Christ, the passage 2 Cor. x. 7 only serves decidedly as a proof of my theory, yet this passage renders any doubt superfluous, and the want of more passages containing special mention of the party of Christ is very simply explained by the name of the party itself." It is true, if once the matter is firmly established, that in many passages we cannot mistake the allusions to the name of the party of Christ, but such passages cannot be used as direct proofs, because the name Χριστὸς has a peculiar meaning in every case. But the name of the party of Christ appears all the more remarkable in the passage above quoted. We see plainly that in the Χριστοῦ εἶναι there is here a question of something which the opponents and false teachers, whom the Apostle fought against, employed in order to make good their own side against the Apostle (εἴ τις πέποιθεν ἑαυτῷ Χριστοῦ, εἶναι, τοῦτο λογιζέσθω πάλιν ἀφ᾽ ἑαυτοῦ ὅτι καθὼς αὐτὸς Χριστοῦ οὕτω καὶ ἡμεῖς Χριστοῦ). How fitting is the allusion which the Apostle, in pursuance of his former plan, here makes to the name of those who maintained that they were especially and exclusively οἱ τοῦ Χριστοῦ. In this name was concentered in its most extreme form all the opposition against the Apostle,

20

and in this name also was there founded a reason for all that was brought against him, against which, from this standpoint, any vindication would seem to be in vain. With great reason therefore the Apostle calls this name to his own mind and that of his readers, whilst he proposes to himself, partly to establish that fact which he considers as the most direct and undeniable token of his apostolic authority, and partly to stand forth against his enemies without any further consideration or evasion, in the most open and decided manner, and to represent them in their complete nakedness, as ψευδαπόστολοι, ἐργάται δόλιοι, μετασχηματιζόμενοι εἰς ἀποστόλους Χριστοῦ. This polemic of the Apostle contained in the foregoing passages, as well against the party of Peter as the party of Christ, attains its natural conclusion in the assertion that the opponents were what they claimed to be only in appearance, in a false deceitful sense, and that they were not true but only false ἀπόστολοι Χριστοῦ.

But we must now direct our attention to the point how according to this theory of the relations of the Corinthian parties, the whole polemic of the Apostle, and the whole arrangement of composition of both these Epistles conditional on it, agree together in the most harmonious unity. Each of the parties named in 1 Cor. i. 12, has its just right given it in the polemic of the Apostle, each has its appointed place assigned it in the list given in this passage, and each has exactly the fitting thing said for it in its turn. The first important section of this polemic, 1 Cor. i. 12, iv. 21, is first of all directed against the party of Paul and that of Apollos, and on this account does not even hint at the peculiar antagonism between Pauline and anti-Pauline Christianity. The Apostle combats both these parties as is his usual manner and custom, and especially places himself throughout this discussion in as wide and general a sphere of vision as possible, although this attitude prompted by a deep impression of the true spirit of Christianity is so often wanting in the fundamental conception of partizanship. That he here also had already in view both the other parties, he himself indicates iv. 6, ταῦτα μετεσχημάτισα, &c. This is commonly taken as referring to iii. 4, &c. But the Apostle, in iii. 22, speaks of Cephas and Apollos with himself, and why could he not have mentioned Cephas also in iii. 4, 5? I would rather refer this μετασχηματίζειν to the whole section, i. 12. All that the Apostle says in this section, the relation of the σοφία τοῦ θεοῦ to the σοφία τοῦ κόσμου, testifies in the most natural way to the existing difference between the parties of Paul and Apollos. Whilst the Apostle ascribes the love of the Corinthians for the σοφία κόσμου, to their sensuality, or that they were σαρκικοὶ and not πνευματικοὶ, iii. 1, and points out as the source of their divisions and party strife, the carnal mind that still dwelt in them, and kept them on so low a level of Christian life, in whose consciousness they then ought to examine themselves, and see how little they were fitted to set themselves up as judges of their teachers; all these exhortations naturally applied also to the party of Peter. The sectarian spirit showed itself also in that party in the same carnal tendency devoted to egotistical interests; and the over self appreciation taking pleasure in haughty empty speeches with which the Apostle reproachfully credits party spirit in general, must apply especially to the party of Peter. But besides it must not be overlooked how the Apostle in 1 Cor. iii. 5, as well as in 2 Cor. xi. 13, speaks of διάκονοι Χριστοῦ. Without doubt the party of Peter arrogated to itself the name διάκονοι Χριστοῦ, and with regard to this it must not be considered as accidental that the Apostle, 1 Cor. iii. 5, had already spoken of the disputes of the Corinthian parties about the idea of the διάκονοι, the true ministers of the Lord. We may see also from the section 1 Cor. i. 12, iv. 24, how from the beginning the Apostle never lost sight of this opposition, but at first evades it with a certain forbearance and reticence, and then gradually proceeds from the indirect to the direct combat with his opponents.

20 *

This transition he makes 1 Cor. ix. 1, for here his polemic, after treating hitherto of the parties of Paul and Apollos, turns to that of Cephas. Accordingly he neither avoids indicating this party by its name, nor coming forward with the assertion that he had the same rights with the rest of the Apostles, with the brethren of the Lord and with Cephas, whom he mentions by name, ix. 5.

The indirect polemic passes into the direct, 1 Cor. ix. 1, &c. but attains its extreme height only in the second part of the second Epistle, x. 13. Still here the Apostle speaks of various different matters before finally approaching his opponents : we see that it costs him a certain inward struggle to take this last but absolutely necessary step. He first says everything else that he has to bring against the Corinthians, but still always has his eye on his opponents. Then when everything else is said and everything is ready, he comes forward against his opponents in the way we have already seen—in a discourse in which the more the subject is pursued to its climax, the more the peculiarities of the party of Christ are treated of and justice done to it, as far as it can be divided from the party of Peter, according to the passage already pointed out, 1 Cor. i. 12.

Besides the existence of parties, which is the chief point of which the Apostle never loses sight throughout the two Epistles, there were in the Corinthian Church many more special circumstances, more or less disturbing to the regulation of the Christian life. With respect to these phenomena the Apostle explains himself for the most part in a very explicit manner, partly on account of the questions which had arisen about them in a letter from the Corinthians to him, before his Epistle. The chief circumstances of this kind were the following—an unchaste relation causing great scandal, in which some one in the Corinthian Church had lived with his step-mother (chap. v.), to which category also belong the other immoralities prevailing among the Corinthian Christians, which are repeatedly

and earnestly reproved by the Apostle, v. 9, &c. xvi. 12, &c.
2 Cor. xii. 21 : the custom of bringing law disputes before
Gentile judges, and even of judging Christians by their law,
vi. 2 ; the question as to the advantage of married or celibate
life, chap. vii. as well as that of participation in Gentile sacrificial feasts and the use of meat offered to idols, chap. viii.—the
liberty which the Corinthian Christians permitted themselves
of covering the head in the Christian assemblies, chap. xi. 1,
&c. An abuse of the solemn institution of the Lord's supper,
xi. 17 ; the difference of opinion as to the value of the so-called
λαλεῖν γλώσσαις, especially in its relation to the προφητεύειν,
chap. xii. 14 ; and finally the question as to the resurrection
from the dead, which was denied by some of the members of
the Corinthian Church. All these occurrences, and the questions agitated in consequence of them, give us a very clear
and vivid picture of the condition of the Corinthian Church ;
yet it would be most interesting, to know more decidedly how
the various parties were concerned in these various occurrences,
and what share the Corinthian party spirit had in them. We
can however be sure only of this, that the Gentile Christian
element was throughout overwhelmingly preponderant. And
yet that the Judaising opponents of the Apostle, who had
even here thrust themselves on him and established themselves
firmly, were enabled to form this energetic opposition against
him which he so earnestly resisted.

The relation of the second Epistle to the first deserves to be
somewhat more closely examined. It has been already remarked that the polemic of the Apostle against those opponents, whom he attacks in the first Epistle, is pursued in the
second, and that precisely the strongest declarations with
which the Apostle most directly meets his opponents with all
decision and energy, are found in the last chapter of the
second Epistle. But all the more strong is the contrast between the sharp and vehement tone of this last chapter, and
the temper shown in the first part of the Epistle, in which the

Apostle betrays the greatest uneasiness and apprehension both with regard to the reception of his former letter, and his entire relation to the Corinthians, and takes great pains in the most pressing manner and with the most anxious care to secure for himself, by repeated assurances of his love and sympathy, the confidence of the Corinthians, which he feared was cooling towards him. Different theories have been advanced in the endeavour to explain this striking change of tone in the second Epistle—however the chief question is, what reason the Apostle could have had to have been in such great uneasiness and anxiety as to the impression made by his first letter. The contents of our first Epistle do not seem to furnish a sufficient motive for this anxiety. On this account, as well as because in both Epistles not only a mission of Timothy is mentioned, but also of Titus, (and in this the two Epistles do not seem to be in harmony) we are irresistibly drawn to the conclusion that our second Epistle does not stand in that close connection with the first which is commonly supposed. Our second Epistle, it is maintained,* does not refer to the occurrences which are brought before us in the first, but to the reception of a letter carried by Titus which we no longer possess. In fact there do occur in our second Epistle several passages, such as ii. 3, 4. vii. 12, which although they generally refer directly to the circumstances treated of, 1 Cor., still on closer inspection present great difficulties with regard to this theory, and their evidence is calculated to give us occasion to suppose that something intervened between our two Epistles with regard to the relation of the Apostle to the Corinthians, besides the news brought to the Apostle by Titus about the operation of the first Epistle. The whole tone and character of the reproof in 1 Cor. is not conceived and carried out in the manner we should expect from Paul according to his usual custom. It is therefore highly probable that in the Epistles mentioned in 2 Cor. ii. 3, those things especially which are there

---

* Compare Bleek, Erörterungen über die Cor. Briefe Theol. Stud. u. Krit, 1830.

spoken of, had been made far more prominent and of far higher importance, in accord with the whole subject of the Epistles, than those passages in 1 Cor. respecting the person accused of incest. If therefore the τοῦτο αὐτὸ, 2 Cor. ii. 3, really referred to something which the Apostle had written with respect to this relation, which of course is highly probable, we are led to conclude that it was not intended to apply to the first Epistle, but to a subsequent one, wherein Paul had written about this subject in a yet more vehement manner. Meanwhile it is indeed also possible that this did not refer at all to that incestuous person and the Apostle's remarks on him, but to some other special person of whom Paul had heard through Timothy, and whom he had accordingly spoken of in his Epistle sharply and sternly. The verse next following, 2 Cor. iii. 5, does not necessarily oblige us to think of this incestuous man, but if we give up the idea of this reference we must also resign the possibility of ascertaining exactly what the special matter was, and can only surmise in general that some one of the immediate precepts of the Apostle had been disregarded in a peculiarly striking manner. I cannot consider this opinion to be well grounded, and it seems to me to be much more probable, considering the characteristics of the Apostle, that the generally accepted relation between the two Epistles that we possess, should not be disturbed. We need only remember with what vehemence and indignation he speaks of the occurrence mentioned in 1 Cor. v. 5, and how this occurrence, as soon as the Apostle has said what he had to say on the chief subject of his letter, is the first special circumstance to which he addresses himself. The Apostle takes up this matter seriously enough, and at the same time treats it so notoriously as a decidedly exceptional thing, that it is against all probability that the peculiar occurrence which is spoken of in the same decided manner 2 Cor. ii. 5,* should have been any other than the one referred to 1 Cor. v. If we take farther into consideration,

---

* As ὁ τοιοῦτος, he is designated, 2 Cor. ii., as well as in 1 Cor. v. 5.

what the Apostle writes to the Corinthians with regard to this individual, in the most solemn manner, with all the emphasis of his apostolic authority, and which he also sets forth as his absolute command, we can well understand what anxiety and care this affair must soon after have occasioned him. To speak plainly he had written a letter which he himself must have regarded as a rash and overhasty one, and in which, by neglecting its evident consequences, he had laid himself open to his opponents. Indeed, he afterwards retracted the grounds on which he had proceeded, for he expresses himself pleased with something which was the exact opposite of that which according to his first decided declaration had taken place. The most natural sense of the passage in question, 1 Cor. v. 3, I find to be that given by the most modern commentators, namely, that the Apostle, by virtue of the strength of Christ that dwelt in him, credited himself with the authority to give over the criminal to the power of Satan, and this indeed through some disease which should fall upon him at that moment in which he should be cast out from Christian fellowship in the most solemn manner by the assembled Church, where the Apostle himself was only present in his miraculously operating spirit. How the expression παραδοῦναι τῷ σατανᾷ is to be taken, is here indicated by the Apostle in a sentence twice repeated in this case, of a miraculous punishment of bodily sickness (for nothing else than this can be understood by ὄλεθρος τῆς σαρκὸς), and the excommunication recorded in verses 2 and 13, to arrange which the Church was to be assembled. But neither of these, as we see from the second Epistle, had happened.

The miraculous punishment did not proceed from the Apostle, nor the exclusion of the criminal from the Church, from the Corinthians.* I agree also with Rückert's explanation of the

---

* The passage, 1 Cor. v. 4, contains no unimportant criterion by which to judge of the nominal miracles of the Apostles. The consciousness of miraculous power, the δύναμις τοῦ κυρίου, was of course felt by the Apostles, and in this consciousness they may have looked upon the special results of their ministry as operations of a

meaning of the second passage belonging to this matter, 2 Cor. ii. 6; the Apostle certainly says openly, v. 6, he is willing to be contented with the punishment decreed by the Corinthians, and does not require any of a more severe kind, which he could not have said if he had really demanded any such. From v. 10, it is clearly enough to be seen that the χαρίζεσθαι did not now first proceed from him, but had been originated before without any question of him, so that he now could only acquiesce in what had taken place in order not to put himself in open disagreement with them by persistence in his former commands. The Corinthians accordingly had confined themselves to a mere reproof, and even what had been done in reproving this man had not been the work of the Church as a whole but only of a part of the community. But if the matter stood thus, as Rückert very justly remarks, Paul must have found himself in no inconsiderable dilemma. His commands had not been followed; only a part of the community, although it might have been the largest part, had taken the matter to heart, the remainder, as might have been expected by the feeling of the Church towards him, had not even done this—his authority was greatly set at nought. What was he to do now?' Insist on his former orders? He might be sure that he should find no truer obedience, and the scandal would be all the greater. He could not enforce obedience, and the affair would only make a bad impression on all sides. There was here nothing else to be done but what in similar cases had been dictated by prudence— to give another turn to the matter—by which an open breach might be avoided, and the evil not indeed cured, but concealed until in better times the proper attitude might be again assumed. This turn was to approve of what had been done, even although it had been done without his consent, to represent it as his wish, and to bring the whole matter under a Christian point of

powerful energy, as σημεῖα, τέρατα, and δυνάμεις. Compare 1 Cor. x. 21. 10-28, 2 Cor. xii. 12. But in a case like that in 1 Cor. v. 4, this is so decidedly expressed, and there is so little question of a real miracle, that elsewhere the same state of things may also be suspected.

view. This was now publicly done, partly through the concession
that the punishment which the man had undergone may have been
sufficient, partly through the admonition to forgive him.   The
whole tone in which the Apostle wrote our Epistles to the Corinthians, the restlessness and anxiety, are very naturally explained by this position which he with great justice assumed.
He had taken a step whose consequences now first were clearly
evident to him.* It must now especially have appeared very
doubtful to him with regard to his opponents, for as we see
from the Apostle's Epistles themselves his opponents did not
forbear from making use of this overthrow of his authority.
When he is absent, said they, he can indeed make severe
speeches and is full enough of boastful vain-glory, but when
it comes to real action, he does not trust himself to be personally present, (x. 10-11. Compare iii. 1, v. 12.)   Without
doubt this was the reason which caused the Apostle to vindicate himself so solicitously as he does in the beginning of
his Epistle, with regard to his long contemplated journey to
Corinth, which had not yet been carried out.   An Epistle
written under such circumstances must of course contain a
predominant apologetic tendency, but the apology is by no
means a merely personal one, it passes immediately into a
general one, into an apologetic examination of his apostolic
office, which he represents in both its phases, bringing salvation to some, and working ruin to others; representing it
also in its difference from the ministry of the Old Covenant, and in its ennobling consciousness experienced by
himself; and as soon as he has satisfactorily fulfilled this
apologetic aim, and inspired the Corinthians with new confidence, he encounters his opponents with fresh courage, and a

---

* Rückert has no hesitation in saying with regard to 1 Cor. v. 5, " This is a
matter which we cannot divest of the stamp of passion which never can turn to be
of any use. And that he dictatorially issued commands to a Church by which his
authority was much lowered, and which he had no means of enforcing, does not
redound to his credit.'' Who will blame the unprejudiced critic that he says this
openly ?

still severer polemic, in order to put himself completely in opposition to them. In no other of the Apostle's Epistles are we allowed to look deeper into the pure humanity of his individuality, and into the special proofs of his relation to the Churches than in this second Epistle to the Corinthians, no other shows his characteristics more clearly, as soon as we do not seek out of a false interest to conceal that which is truly human in him. If it be granted that the second Epistle stands in this relation to the first, there can be no reason, except those assigned in considering 1 Cor. v. 9, for supposing the existence of a lost Epistle to the Corinthians. The Apostle had written to the Corinthians before the two Epistles which we possess, as he himself says 1 Cor. v. 9, but we do not know anything further of this lost Epistle, than what we may gather from the above-named passage. This Epistle cannot have had equal weight with our two Epistles—as the way and manner in which the Apostle speaks of the circumstances which make up the chief subject of our first Epistle does not allow of the supposition that there had been much previous communication between him and the Corinthians. The composition of our two Epistles is commonly placed in the years 57-59, in the period in which the Apostle after leaving Corinth, Acts xviii. 18, took up his residence for some time at Ephesus, Acts xix. 1, xx. 1. There seems no doubt that in his journey to Greece, Acts xx. 2, he came again to Corinth, and during his residence there wrote the Epistle to the Romans; but whether this visit was the second or third is not so easily decided, as in the passages in the Epistles where the Apostle speaks of a journey to Corinth, the special difficulty is that we do not know whether the third time of which he speaks is to be understood as meaning the actual journey, or the mere intention of performing it.

According to my idea the latter is the more probable, if we consider the connection in which the passages involving this question stand to one another. When he says, 2 Cor. xii. 14, ἰδοὺ τρίτον τοῦτο ἑτοίμως ἔχω ἐλθεῖν πρὸς ὑμᾶς—τρίτον τοῦτο, can quite as well apply to ἐλθεῖν as to ἑτοίμως ἔχω, and therefore we do not know whether the Apostle now resolved for the third time to go to Corinth—or whether he had already taken the third journey. In order to get at the real state of the case we must go back to the beginning of the Epistle, where he also speaks of a visit to the Corinthians. 'Εβουλόμην, says he, i. 15, πρὸς ὑμᾶς ἐλθεῖν πρότερον ἵνα δευτέραν χάριν ἔχητε, &c. Πρότερον, he could only have been desirous of going if he had already formed a decided plan of travel, and consequently wished to carry out such a plan before this one, and if the Corinthians were to have a δευτέρα χάρις—there must have been one already—with reference to which this first one would be the second, and on which in this case they would be justified in relying as designed for a δευτέρα χάρις. As the Apostle could only speak of a δευτέρα χάρις if he journeyed direct from Ephesus to Corinth, and from thence to Macedonia; but not if he first went to Macedonia, and from Macedonia to Corinth; inasmuch as his plan of travel at that time only included the three points—Ephesus, Corinth, and Macedonia; we must therefore grant that the πρότερον ἐλθεῖν could only have been the δι' ὑμῶν διελθεῖν εἰς Μακεδονίας. It was a δευτέρα χάρις, only in the same way as was the after-mentioned ἐλθεῖν ἀπὸ Μακεδονίας (if not as πάλιν ἀπὸ Μακεδονίας, still as ἐλθεῖν ἀπὸ Μακεδονίας), according to the intention of the Apostle, and in entire agreement with 1 Cor. xvi. 5. He still adheres to the original plan of a journey from Macedonia to Corinth, only he intends, without giving it up, to travel rather in the direct way, from Ephesus to Corinth and from thence to Macedonia. He had already twice resolved to go to Corinth, and had indeed formed the plan of two visits (a δευτέρα χάρις) without either of these plans and intentions having been carried out at the time of his writing to the Corinthians, and this is the very reason which induces him to speak of it, that he may refute the supposition that it was owing to his fickleness and want of purpose that he had not performed what he had undertaken, and his opponents on this account may have been justified in accusing him, (as they doubtless did) of a want of sincerity and of interested motives, which must have weakened in a great degree, all confidence in his apostolic authority. He protests against all the obviously unfavourable views which might be taken of his non-appearance; but as we do not here learn from him how often he had been in Corinth, and of which time he is here speaking, we must conclude that there is no mention made of an actual journey, but only of an intended one, and of plans of travel. All the more may we expect to find precise information about the number of his journies when he gives the positive reasons for his not going to Corinth. Ἔκρινα δὲ ἐμαυτῷ τοῦτο, says the Apostle, 2 Cor. ii. 1. τὸ μὴ πάλιν ἐν λύπῃ πρὸς ὑμᾶς ἐλθεῖν, and nothing seems more simple than to conclude that as the Apostle had already once been to Corinth, ἐν λύπῃ, and that this was not on the occasion of his first visit, it must have been that when he wrote our second Epistle he had already been twice at Corinth. But where can we find an appropriate time to which we may assign this second journey? If it were before our first Epistle that the occasion arose for his having gone to Corinth for the second time, and that he could only have gone ἐν λύπῃ, we must have in our first Epistle an indication of one kind or other to this effect, as the despatch of an Epistle earlier than our first could not have been passed over in it. It is especially worth consideration that the general question whether the Apostle went two or three times in all to Corinth is scarcely at all treated of, but attention is directed to the special character of the second journey which represents him as having been in Corinth between his first journey and the writing of our first Epistle, but only ἐν λύπῃ, that is under circumstances which laid him under a strong obligation, indeed which left nothing else possible, than to depart with the threat of taking still harsher measures against the Corinthians if they did not improve. But this theory makes the whole contents of

our first Epistle to the Corinthians, and the tone in which the
Apostle speaks of the whole condition of the Church and of its
various failings, simply impossible. Of what nature can those
irregularities have been, which already had existed and had
disturbed the good understanding between the Apostle and
the Church? We have no alternative but to suppose that they
were irregularities of the same kind as those which he reproved in so many ways in our first Epistle. The more specially,
and urgently that he here speaks of the different failings and
crimes of the Church, the less is it to be supposed that at a still
earlier period he has had any other reason for displeasure. He
speaks of everything which is treated of in our first Epistle as
of something with which he had become acquainted, and of
which he had been obliged to speak only shortly before, as he
himself expresses it. It is a question of fresh circumstances
and relations now first entered into, about which, as we see
clearly, he for the first time speaks to the Corinthians. Of
the parties into which the Church was divided, he had
first heard through the household of Chloe, (1 Cor. i. 11.)
He had also only heard generally of the prevailing immorality,
and the particular case which seemed to require a special step
on his part, v. 1. The misunderstanding which he has to
correct, v. 9, in regard to the μὴ συναναμίγνυσθαι πόρνοις,
which he had mentioned to the Corinthians in a letter previous
to our first Epistle, could scarcely have existed, if the affair had
been before verbally treated of. The questions relating to married life, which he explains in detail in chap. vii. had been first
raised in a letter to the Corinthians, vii. 7. And as we may
clearly see from the whole explanation of the Apostle that there
has been no question of all these things between him and the Corinthians, so this is likewise obvious with regard to all the other
subjects on which, in the rest of his Epistle, he partly expresses
his anger and disapprobation, and partly gives advice and precepts. No where do we meet with the slightest indication that
the Apostle had had previous cause to find fault with the Cor-

inthians on these or similar subjects ; that any differences had
arisen between him and them ; that he had given any advice
which had not been followed, or uttered any threats which had
not been heeded. Still less can we take as probable a journey
of this kind as occurring between our two Epistles. If our
first Epistle will not leave us room to suppose any such important break in time, which must be accounted for by the
theory of a further journey taken by the Apostle, it may be
concluded from the second Epistle as expressly as from the
first, that nothing could have previously taken place which it
would be necessary for us to possess as an explanation, without
our being able to perceive that such was the case. But it must
be asked, is it so essential to make the words, 2 Cor. ii. 1,
ἐν λύπη and πάλιν refer so directly to each other, that a second
ἐν λύπη must follow at once on a journey ἐν λύπη ? How would
it then be if the Apostle had changed the place of the participle
ἐλθών, which he would correctly have connected with πάλιν,
and if he had taken it with the following ἐλθεῖν, as would be
generally done in an epistolary style, especially when we must
suppose the affair to have been already known.

According to the foregoing remarks what forcible reason can
remain for taking the τρίτον τοῦτο, 2 Cor. xii. 14, in any other
sense than the following—" twice already I have proposed to
myself to come to you without it being possible to me to fulfil
my intention, but now that my thrice repeated design is about to
be realized, I will declare to you what attitude I shall assume towards you." On a casual glance the passage xiii. 1, which begins
with the words τρίτον τοῦτο ἔρχομαι πρὸς ὑμᾶς, would seem to
silence all doubts on the subject of a third journey, but on a
stricter examination it gives a still more complete solution of
the question respecting this journey. What then is there to
prevent these words being taken grammatically and made to
express the idea that the Apostle only says he has now for
the third time formed an intention of visiting them? And if,
instead of here finding an indication of a second journey already

previously taken,—as when he speaks of a journey he may really mean only an intended one, and the Epistle as a whole may be designed as a vindication of a journey intended indeed, but not yet carried out,—is it not self-evident in this connection what "the word of two or three witnesses" must signify? Can we not easily comprehend what he intends to say, when the passage quoted is taken in its peculiar sense? there is nothing more natural than to suppose that he means to say in an emphatic manner, "if according to the principles of the Mosaic Law what is attested by two or three witnesses is to be considered as true and legal, then this thrice intended journey of mine is to be taken in its full meaning; it is certain that it will receive immediate fulfilment." If we are convinced not only of the possibility but the probability of the above explanation, we shall be prepared to assume as the authentic result of our investigation that this passage sets forth as the last, special declaration of the Apostle, that he had only been once in Corinth and was now going there for the second time. Considered grammatically the words ὡς παρὼν τὸ δεύτερον do not refer so much to an actual as to a proposed occurrence. (Compare 1 Cor. v. 3.) In the vivid desire of the Apostle to give now at least no more room for doubt with regard to his immediate visit to Corinth, and to hold up his plighted word as about to be certainly realized, absence becomes presence to him, he considers himself already for the second time in Corinth, and thus being present, although absent, he tells them what must infallibly happen.

Let us give up the fiction of a journey for which we can find no reasonable grounds; and without which everything connected with the subject becomes far clearer, simpler, more natural and historically probable.

CHAPTER III.

The Epistle to the Romans is not only chronologically connected with the two Epistles to the Corinthians; there is an inward link between them, and it is from the standpoint of the Epistle to the Romans that we first get an insight into the rich result of the Spiritual Life which the Apostle exhibited in his own person, as well as into the strict logical sequence with which he developed and carried out his Christian principles, and into the grandeur of the circumstances in which he moved. We have already remarked the relation in which the Epistle to the Galatians and that to the Romans stand to each other, in the interest of a bold and deep-laid system founded on essential principles, and how their whole contents are to be explained by this system which is pursued and developed throughout. This systematic character of the Epistle to the Romans, comprehending a grand harmony of ideas, distinguishes it completely from the two Epistles to the Corinthians, which are rather characterized by the variety of their contents, and the abundance of profound spiritual ideas allied to and explained by the different relations of life. This aspect of the Epistle is also manifest in the attitude assumed by the Apostle with regard to the opposition, which it was the continued aim of his apostolic efforts to combat and overcome. He had not fulfilled his mission as the Apostle to the Gentiles, whilst the absolute importance which Judaism, and the Jewish Christianity identified with it, claimed for themselves as well in their principles as in their ultimate consequences, was not separated from them, and reckoned according to its merely relative value.

21

Just as in the Epistle to the Galatians he had emancipated Christianity from Judaism, by freeing it from circumcision, the outward sign of subjection which Judaism wished to impose on it as the necessary condition of salvation, so in the two Epistles to the Corinthians, he had established the principle that the call to, and participation in the Messianic salvation ought by no means to depend exclusively on the authority of the Apostles directly appointed by Jesus, but that he, the Apostle to the Gentiles, was an Apostle possessing equal rights with them. Now in the Epistle to the Romans he proceeds to do away with the last remaining portion of the Jewish exclusiveness, by taking up and representing it as the mere introduction to the Christian Universalism which extended to all nations. Although hitherto Jewish Christianity, in maintaining the absolute importance of Judaism, had not hindered him from establishing a special independent sphere of action in Gentile Christianity, free and independent of Judaism, yet the thought seemed to prevail, prompted by the religious consciousness of the Jewish Christians, that Jewish and Gentile Christianity could not merely exist side by side, but that the latter would gain a complete over-mastering power over the former; and that this was to be looked for as the final result of the apostolic ministry among the Gentiles. And as Messianic salvation seemed to fall to the share of the Gentiles in proportion as the Christian Universalism, embracing all nations without any distinction, became a reality, then the opposition between the Jews persisting in their unbelief, and the Gentiles continually more and more converted to the Faith, could only result in the rejection of the Jews and the acceptance of the Gentiles. This is the standpoint taken by the Apostle in the Epistle to the Romans and its theme, which can only be maintained by a statement of aims and intentions differing completely from the views hitherto presented.

In general, the origin and aim of the Epistle is considered from a purely dogmatic point of view, without inquiring exactly

into the historical cause of the Epistle and the relations it bore
to the Roman Church, and therefore attention is especially
directed to it, as though the Apostle only intended to
give a comprehensive and connected representation of the
whole of his doctrinal ideas, so to speak, a compendium of
Pauline dogma in the form of an apostolic letter. Since more
earnest efforts have been made to get at the explanation of the
Epistle, it has been thought, indeed, that there is no sufficient
reason for adopting this idea, for even if the Apostle endeavoured in his Epistle to reconcile the local disputes which,
according to the theories of Eichhorn* and Hug,† must have
existed between the Gentile and Jewish Christians in the
Roman Church, the whole design of the dogmatic writing
indicates decidedly a general aim, instead of one grounded
on special circumstances occurring in the Roman Church,
and this general aim has for its purpose to set forth the
importance of the Christian doctrine, and to show how it alone
is adapted to the requirements of Human Nature, for whose
needs neither Heathenism nor Judaism are adequate.‡ In
agreement with Tholuck, both De Wette and Olshausen explain
the Epistle in this sense. De Wette thinks that the Apostle
wished, at least by letter, to influence a Church which was so
important to him, and in connection with the chief doctrines of
his Gospel to show that salvation was to be attained through
faith, and not through the works of the law : he wished at the
same time, in sight of the capital of the world, to represent the
Christian Faith as the only means of salvation for all the world
—Jew and Gentile, and the Christian revelation as the revelation for the whole world. The Epistle to the Romans

---

* Einleitung ins. N. Testament. 3. page 214.

† Einl. ins. N. Testament, 2. vol. 2, page 361.

‡ Compare Tholuck in the first four editions of his Exposition of Paul's Epistle
to the Romans. This exposition, which first appeared in 1824, together with
lengthy extracts from the exegetical writings of the Fathers of the Church and the
Reformation, is of value as marking an epoch in the history of the explanation
of this Epistle.

21 *

is the only one of the Epistles of the Apostle, wherein he designedly sets forth his doctrine in detailed connection, for in the other Epistles he only treats of special needs, doubts, errors, and questions, and thus continually pre-supposes the whole of his doctrine. The Apostle does not, as in the Epistle to the Galatians, set up this doctrine of salvation by faith alone, in opposition to Jewish Christian errors, but merely in opposition to Judaism. He had little opposition to expect from the Gentiles, but he took much to heart the pretensions of Judaism, which, in accordance with the prevailing tendency at that time, was even disposed to unite with Gentiles in opposing Christianity.* Olshausen finds still more decidedly in the Epistle to the Romans, a purely objective representation of that aspect of the Gospel which was grounded only on the general opposition between Jews and Gentiles—but not on the special distinction between Jewish and Gentile Christians which was only found in the Church itself. The whole statement presents a purely objective aspect, and every subject except the truth of the Gospel is treated of in a secondary manner. But naturally it is part of the truth itself that it takes its stand against error of all kinds, and in this way it appears also in the Epistle to the Romans. The doctrinal wisdom of the Apostle prompted him to represent the doctrine of the Gospel in such a manner that the warning against the errors which the Christians were necessarily obliged to con-front lay in the very statement of them.† But there is no-where to be discovered in the Epistle to the Romans any decided aim, except the effort to lay the Gospel before the Roman Christians in its natural relation to the law, and in its results on life, and this without any contest with the Jewish Christians, and without having any regard to quarrels with

* Kurze Erklärung des Briefs an die Römer, 3rd Edition, Einl. page 2.

† This is the most extreme point of the purely dogmatic view. De Wette at least concedes the opposition to Judaism, but every direct antithetical reference is here excluded.

them, unlike the mode pursued in the Epistle to the Galatians, where such contests and disputes are undoubtedly discussed.* Large as is the number of Commentaries on the Epistle to the Romans in modern times, they all contain the same exclusive idea of its aim as having regard to special relations, and they express this idea in studied-variety, now in this way, now in that; as for example, when the chief purport of the Epistle is made to consist in strengthening the Roman Christians in their new faith, by representations of the necessity and grandeur of the salvation proclaimed by the Gospel, of its divine value and harmony with the former revelation, as well as of the sad results of Gentile superstition, and of the law of sin as distinguished from the ideal spiritual life of the true Christian, and also in inciting and encouraging the Roman Christians to the proper realization of the Christian ideal. Even when persons are obliged to make certain concessions on my account, or at least to notice the anomalous views advanced by me, so little do they relinquish the purely dogmatic point of view, that they show a more decided antagonistic interest by levelling and straightening all the rough places and difficulties which they think must attend the concrete circumstances of the origin of an Epistle, thereby providing that the dogmatic aspect shall in no way be diminished by the historical, and that in an Epistle like that of the Romans, the attempt shall not be made to deviate from the strictest normal bounds of Luther's theory of justification by faith.† Now whether this view is probable

---

* Der Brief des Ap. Paulus an die Römer, Königsberg, 1855, pages 50-54.

† In this sense Philippi, the chief representative of the strict, orthodox, dogmatic view of the Epistle, says in his Commentary, 2nd Edition, page 14 : " There is scarcely any other opposition to be imagined against the Pauline universalism than that which was received by all Jewish Christian false teachers and sects. The Apostle, accordingly, in the Epistle to the Romans is only contending as one of these—he only combats the Judaistic justification by works, but not the intended exclusion of the Gentile world generally, and indeed he combats the justification by works of Judaism, but not that of the Jewish Christian part of the Roman Church. Had the Roman Jewish Christians taken this direction, he would have seized upon the fact, and would have met them as well as the Galatian false teachers

in itself, whether the Epistle to the Romans itself, little as it seems to give a decided reason for its historical origin, does not still contain data sufficient to place the latter among its other subjects, is the question which we must in the next place endeavour to answer.

The analogy with those Epistles which alone can be compared with the Epistle to the Romans does not in general serve favourably for the view commonly taken. The Epistle to the Galatians and the two Epistles to the Corinthians, which can alone be properly considered as belonging to the genuine type of Pauline Epistles, give a completely different representation of the origin of the Epistles of the Apostle. There were special circumstances and requirements which caused the Apostle to compose these Epistles, but here we are not only brought face to face with these circumstances (chiefly employed by him in elucidating the developments of the doctrine already advanced) but we see also the operation of the overwhelming pressure of the circumstances which claimed and necessitated his writing, if he did not wish to see his work frustrated. In the Epistle to the Romans alone analogous circumstances are set forth, and in this view we can only wonder at the prejudice, with which the interpreters of the Epistle to the Romans have hitherto taken up the relations of the two chief elements in the Epistle, chapter 1-8, chapter 9-11. If we act on the supposition that the main tendency of the Epistle, and the special aim of the Apostle are contained in the dogmatic portion with which the Apostle opens the Epistle, and that the train of thought which he takes in the spiritual conception of his Epistle must have been the same as he lays down in its outward form, then of course we must from the beginning place before us a purely dogmatic standpoint from which to consider the Epistle

and the Galatian Church, and no consideration of any kind whatever would have induced the Apostle to the Gentiles to treat in a mild manner this tendency, which uproots the very foundation of the Gospel. The same position must besides be maintained, if the Roman Church had not exhibited the accustomed Galatian exclusiveness, but the Jewish exclusiveness by which I characterize it."

to the Romans. The dogmatic contents of the Epistle, as the Apostle presents them in the first eight chapters, form the chief grounds on which he proceeds, the original foundation on which he places the whole fabric of his Epistle; but all else that it contains—and especially that which is found in the following chapters, ix.-xi.—stands in a subordinate secondary relation to that chief portion of the Epistle, to which (after the Apostle has set forth its special theme) it is joined as a necessary result and practical application; so that without it, the Epistle following its main idea would still have been a complete whole, and the aim for which the Apostle destined it would still have been attained. This part therefore of the Epistle, by some interpreters (for instance, by Tholuck, p. 341, and De Wette, p. 4) is especially designated as a historical corollary, or supplement, in which the Apostle is desirous of declaring himself on the results which must necessarily follow the doctrine he had hitherto preached—namely, the exclusion of the unbelieving Jews from the Christian salvation; as if the necessity of doing this had now first forced itself upon him, when, at the end of his undertaking, he reconsidered it as a whole. If this is the common view taken of the two chief sections of the Epistle, it may with justice be met with the question, whether the matter may not be looked on from the reverse direction; and whether, if we take this standpoint, a more favourable view may not present itself of the aim and tendency of the Epistle, as well as of the historical circumstances in which it originated? The centre and pith of the whole, to which everything else is only an addition, would then be comprised in that part of the Epistle which is contained in the three above-named chapters : here we must take our stand, place ourselves in harmony with the original conception of the Apostle, from which is developed the whole organism of the Epistle as it is presented to us, especially in the first eight chapters. In furtherance of this view, we must first of all consider more closely the contents of the three chapters (ix. x. xi.) themselves.

In these chapters the Apostle answers the question, how it is to be explained, that so great a portion of the Jewish people, who for ages had been the chosen people of God and the recipients of all kinds of Divine promises, had really no participation in the salvation bestowed by Christ; whilst, on the contrary, the Gentiles adopted the position left vacant by the people of God? The answer which the Apostle gives to this question consists chiefly in the following points :—First, it does not depend on natural descent, but only on spiritual son-ship to God, and election by His free grace. As therefore all born Jews do not belong to the true people of God—God chose his people from among the Heathen also (ix. 24), because the imparting of salvation is only a free gift of divine grace ; and, accordingly, the way to attain salvation in Christ is not the νόμος δικαιοσύνης, pursued by the Jews, but the δικαιοσύνη ἐκ πίστεως, which stands open to Gentiles as well as to Jews, chapter ix. ; secondly, although, according to the νόμος δικαιοσύνης appointed by God, which is the δικαιοσύνη ἐκ πίστεως, the born Jews have no legal claim to Divine salvation, it is only their own fault if they have no share in it. For salvation can only spring from belief in the preaching of the Gospel, with regard to which there is no difference between Jew and Gentile (x. 12), but all Jews have not given ear and belief to the Gospel, chapter x. ; thirdly, notwithstanding this, the promises given by God to the Jewish people, are not absolutely unfulfilled towards them, and God has not absolutely rejected his people. For not only at this present time also there is a remnant according to the election of grace (λεῖμμα κατ' ἐκλογὴν χάριτος, xi. 5) among those who truly believe, but also the obduracy and the blindness which still characterize so many Israelites with regard to the Gospel may be looked at as something merely temporary ; so that as God never repents of his promise, Israel may one day be saved. The rejection of a part of the Israelites, or their present unbelief of the Gospel, only serves as a glorification of Divine grace.

Meanwhile the believing Gentiles have stepped into the place of the unbelieving Jews, their παράπτωμα is ἡ σωτηρία τοῖς ἔθνεσιν, their παράπτωμα is πλοῦτος κόσμου, their ἥττημα πλοῦτος ἐθνῶν (xi. 11-12). Divine grace is glorified in its relation to the whole matter, for it is evident that it belongs to the plan of God to permit the Gentiles to participate in His grace (πώρωσις ἀπὸ μέρους τῷ 'Ισραὴλ γέγονεν ἄχρις οὗ τὸ πλήρωμα τῶν ἐθνῶν ἔλθη, 25). What is loss on one side is gain on the other; but this also gives occasion for hope that those who have for a time turned away from God may one day be saved. For if the Jews are jealous of the grace of God, in which the Gentiles participate, they ought through this jealousy to stir themselves up that they also may come into possession of this grace (xi. 11-14).

If we consider more closely this whole section, and the chief subjects involved in it, we see that it treats throughout of the relations of Judaism and Heathenism, as well as of the relation of both to Christianity; and if, at the same time, we consider with what earnestness and interest the Apostle handles this subject, how especially he brings it forward in the words expressing such deep and vivid feelings with which he makes the transition to it (ix.-1) (— λύπη μοι ἐστὶ μεγάλη, καὶ ἀδιάλειπτος ὀδύνη τῇ καρδία μου ηὐχόμην γὰρ αὐτὸς ἐγὼ ἀνάθεμα εἶναι ἀπὸ τοῦ Χριστοῦ ὑπὲρ τῶν ἀδελφῶν μου τῶν συγγενῶν μου κατὰ σάρκα)—it does not certainly appear probable that he would have devoted so important a part of his letter to answering this question, if he had not had close at hand some special material reason for doing so, and this was afforded him by the circumstances of the Roman Church. And such a reason can only be found in the direct opposition to the idea pursued by the Apostle throughout this section, and in the objection also which might still have been raised against the participation of the Gentiles in the grace of the Gospel, or against the Pauline universalism, namely the religious opinion so deeply rooted in the consciousness of Jews and

Jewish Christians, that as long as Israel did not participate in this grace as a nation, as a people chosen by God, the participation in it by the Gentiles appeared as an encroachment on the Jews, as an injustice against them, as a contradiction of the promises given by God to the Jews as the people of God. The main idea which lies at the root of the whole discourse, the object which is treated of from both sides, is the theocratic supremacy of the Jewish nation, the absolute precedence which it claimed to possess over all other nations, and of which it now saw itself about to be irretrievably deprived, by the Pauline universalism. In order to comprehend the crisis at which this subject of dispute had arrived in its full importance, we must obtain a clear idea of the point to which Paulinism had at that time attained in its anti-Judaistic development, and also of the completely different standpoint which was taken by the Apostle in the composition of the Epistle to the Romans, from the one he occupied at the time of his Epistles to the Galatians and Corinthians. There is no longer any question of that rude conflict, when Judaism brought forward the most material side of its opposition by absolutely commanding circumcision in that most repulsive manner, which we find recorded in the Epistle to the Galatians, and just as little is a personal interest treated of, such as we see in the Epistles to the Corinthians, in which the Apostle had to ward off the attacks on his apostolic authority.

The Epistle to the Romans leaves all these subjects behind it, as of vanished importance : the whole conception of the question is a different one, just as the whole tone of the Apostle is different; for in this Epistle he has no longer to deal with opponents whose antagonistic attitude excited him to such vehement, bitter retorts; he turns with confidence to his readers ; expresses with all sympathy his lively interest in their salvation, which he also sets before them as the subject of the most earnest anxiety ; he is persuaded that in them he sees a church with which he can more easily come into harmony than with any other. If everything subordinate, special, personal, were abstracted, the question which even then would remain would be the most important which could possibly exist for Judaism, namely, whether the difference between Gentiles and Jews, was completely abolished by the universalism of Pauline Christianity. The complexion taken by the circumstances of the period must have been the subject of the most earnest consideration among the most thoughtful section of the Judaizers. The Epistle to the Romans is the last of the apostolic letters, written at a time when the Apostle was contemplating a step so full of importance in regard to the matter in hand, as a journey to Jerusalem. Time pressed for a decision. As he had resolved to bring to a crisis the great cause of dispute between Judaism and Paulinism, and to venture on the bold attempt of uniting and reconciling them by his personal presence at Jerusalem, the chief seat of Judaism, he felt compelled at the same time and acting on the same interest, to come to an understanding with that Church, which besides being the most important one in the West, was the one on whose receptive inclination and kind feeling he thought he could most depend in issuing an address which the exigences of the then state of things seemed to require. Whilst, through the labours of the Apostle pursued for many years, so many Gentiles had already accepted the Christian faith, and whilst the number of converted Jews was still a very small one in comparison to the number of the whole nation, the fact seemed still unfulfilled, on which the Jewish Christians rested their Messianic faith, namely that in Jesus, He had appeared who was the subject of the old national promises. How could He be the Messiah of the nation when the nation steadfastly refused to believe on him, and seemed to persist more and more in its unbelief? when looking at the mutual relations of the Jewish and Gentile Christians it would seem that everything which was expected of the Messiah was more applicable to the Gentiles than to the Jews? It was not forgotten that although

the Jewish Christians might not wish to exclude the Gentiles
from the Messianic community, still as Jewish Christians they
would not renounce the precedence which as Jews they claimed
over Gentiles.   Besides, they must either represent the apparent
contradictory incongruity between the existent state of things,
and the ancient promises, as being the fault of their Messianic
belief itself, or there must have existed among them most
earnest religious scruples with regard to the way and manner
in which the Gentiles had been called to the Christian faith ; for
what else would have augmented to such a degree the number
of the converted Gentiles, that the superiority in the Messianic
Churches seemed to be passing from the Jewish to the Gentile
ones, and the former to be more and more taking a secondary
place ; and what else would have brought about the facility with
which the Gentiles had entered into the Messianic community
since the Apostle's programme of the abolition of the law ?   If
they had been even released from the obligation of circumcision
they would not have been permitted so complete a dispensation
from all the requirements of the law, as the teaching of the
Apostle with regard to faith necessarily involved.   In this manner
would such Jewish Christians decide who thought more fairly,
and who did not adhere with the same tenacity as others to all the
prejudices of Judaism ; but who still could not quite relinquish
those deep-seated religious scruples produced by the dispropor-
tion that existed between the aspect of the Christian world at
that time, and that which it would have presented if it had been
regulated according to the ancient national promises.   And
the less this class of Jewish Christians assumed a harsh
and repelling attitude towards the Apostle, as was indeed the
case, there must naturally have arisen a more weighty solicitude
in his own mind to overcome these scruples, and in proportion
as they entered more deeply into the whole of the relations
between Judaism and Christianity, and became more closely interwoven into their nature, to endeavour to establish a more
thorough system of overcoming them.

There is in the Acts of the Apostles a remarkable confirmation of the theory, that the chief point of the antagonism between Judaism and Paulinism lay essentially in the claim for precedence, with which the Jewish Christians as born Jews set themselves up against the Gentiles and Gentile Christians, and that this was the unpardonable offence to which even the best intentioned among the Jews could not reconcile themselves, even when they desire to favour Paulinism, and this confirmation stands in the closest connection with the peculiar tendency of the Acts of the Apostles to favour the Apostle Paul. How is it, that the portion which especially relates to the apostolic labours of the Apostle Paul, always designedly states that the Apostle everywhere preached the Gospel first of all to the Jews, and only when the Jews, as everywhere happened, rejected him and his Gospel, turned to the Gentiles ? It is in reality highly remarkable how consistently the Acts of the Apostles repudiates this priority of the Jews, and makes the Apostle act according to the words which it puts into his mouth. (Acts of the Apostles, xiii. 46.) ὑμῖν, says he to the Jews, ἦν ἀναγκαῖον πρῶτον λαληθῆναι τὸν λόγον τοῦ θεοῦ ἐπειδὴ δὲ ἀπωθεῖσθε αὐτὸν καὶ οὐκ ἀξίους κρίνετε ἑαυτοὺς τῆς αἰωνίου ζωῆς ἰδοὺ στρεφόμεθα εἰς τὰ ἔθνη.) Immediately after his conversion the Apostle had risen up in the synagogue in Damascus, and had sought with all his might to persuade the Jews dwelling in Damascus, that Jesus was the Messiah; but the consequence was that he was obliged to flee from Damascus, because the Jews were lying in wait for him. (Acts of the Apostles, ix. 20, &c.) However this passage may be reconciled with the account of the Apostle himself (2 Cor. xi. 32,) that he was obliged to flee on account of the persecution of the Ethnarch of King Aretas, it can scarcely be held as accidental on the part of the author of the Acts of the Apostles that he should name the Jews as the instigators of the danger that threatened the Apostle. That the Apostle should have made his first visit to Jerusalem after his conversion.serve the purpose of an attempt at conversion, is not only contrary

to the expressed declaration of the Apostle himself that a completely different reason drew him to Jerusalem, but is also not
reconcilable with the fact of the short duration of his residence
there (Gal. i. 18). But the Acts of the Apostles represents
him as preaching the Gospel there with all boldness, and especially as carrying on controversies with the Hellenists. The
lying-in-wait with which he was threatened by the Jews was
the cause why he went to Tarsus (Acts of the Apostles, ix.
28). According to another passage in the Acts of the Apostles
(xxii. 18) after the speech which the Apostle delivered to the
Jews in Jerusalem, immediately before his capture, he received
from Jesus himself in an extatic vision seen in the Temple
the command to leave Jerusalesm speedily, because the Jews
there would not accept from him, the former persecutor of the
disciples of Jesus, any testimony in favour of Jésus. For this
reason Jesus tells him he is to be sent far away to the Gentiles.
But still, the Acts of the Apostles continues, the Apostle did
not consider himself as exclusively an Apostle to the Gentiles.
When, some time after, he undertook the first Missionary
journey, they were especially Jewish synagogues which he first
sought out (xiii. 5-14, xiv. 1) ; and even if he at the same time
brought Gentile proselytes into them, still his discourses were
always directed to the Jews alone (xiii. 15-41) ; and there
must have been a special motive to determine the Apostle on
addressing himself to the Gentiles. This restricting motive
is shown with regard to the Jews in the most striking
manner by the Apostles (xiii. 42-52). Paul and Barnabas
had preached the Gospel with successful results among the
Jews and proselytes in the synagogue at Antioch in Pisidia.
When the Jews saw the universal inclination of the people
towards the Apostles they opposed them, but the Apostles with
all boldness declared that it was indeed necessary that the
Word of God should be first preached to the Jews, but as they
rejected it, and judged that they were not worthy of eternal
life, they (the Apostles) now turned to the Gentiles. It is then

remarked that when the Gentiles heard this they rejoiced, and glorified the Word of the Lord, and those who were "ordained to eternal life believed." We must conclude, therefore, that if the Jews had not assumed this hostile attitude, the Gentiles, desirous as they might have been to receive the Gospel (48), would really have received scarcely anything of it, and Paul would have remained an Apostle of the Jews ; for the fact that Gentile proselytes existed in the Jewish synagogue would not have constituted him an Apostle to the Gentiles, as is shown by the opposition of ἔθνη to προσήλυτοι. Compare 46, 47, with 43. But who can believe that the Apostle's ἀποστολὴ εἰς τὰ ἔθνη depended on so accidental a circumstance, which here appears still more accidental, as this fact of many Gentiles being desirous of accepting the Gospel ? And yet this scene is re-peated again and again, and even in quick succession. In Lystra, in Lycaonia, the Gospel was preached to the Gentiles, but only after it had been expelled from Iconium by the unbelieving Jews (chapter xiv). This is still more brought under our notice (chapter xviii. 1), where the founding of the Corinthian Church is related. The Apostle first allies himself with the Jew Aquila, who just at that time had come to Corinth from Italy with his wife Priscilla, and he discoursed every Sabbath in the synagogue, thereby converting Jews and Greeks. But when the companions of the Apostle, Silas and Timotheus, who had remained in Macedonia, arrived, he first urged on the Jews with great emphasis the testimony that Jesus was the Messiah. And when the Jews withstood and reviled him, he shook off the dust from his garments (compare xiii. 51) and said to them, "Your blood be upon your own heads ; I am clear : from henceforth I will go unto the Gen-tiles." And with these words he departed into another quarter, and went to the house of a certain man named Justus, who worshipped God, and lived near the synagogue. Here it is manifestly the opposition of the Jews which gives the signal for the decided resolve to preach the Gospel to the Gentiles.

For if up to that time Gentiles as well as Jews had been converted (4), this had taken place in the synagogue, and the
Jewish synagogue still remained as the means of gaining Gentiles to go on the way to the Gospel. But as if an outward
legitimation was needed in order to remove this restriction,
the vehement energy with which Paul devoted himself to the
preaching of the Gospel after the arrival of Silas and Timotheus
at Corinth, would seem to have been absolutely intended to
call forth an opposition which would authorize him to lay the
Gospel immediately before the Gentiles, without any further
regard to the Jews.

But what fitting reason can we think of for this mode of
action ? Besides, it would not be of any effect on the unbelieving Jews, but among the believing Jews it might very
easily have had the result of making them fall off from the
Gospel, as they might have taken offence at the Gospel being
preached to the Gentiles also. But if this was not to be feared,
to what purpose was it to wait for a cause to be first given by the
unbelieving Jews ? We must even say that here an unworthy
reason is given by the Apostle for his ἀποστολὴ εἰς τὰ ἔθνη.
Either he was convinced, that it was decidedly the will of God
that the Gospel should be preached to the Gentiles, or not. If he
really had this conviction, he could not have possibly allowed the
actual success of his Gentile apostleship to depend upon whether
certain Jews bore themselves in a hostile and inimical manner
towards him : even if these feelings had not caused any public
manifestation of this kind, a great disinclination towards the
Gospel must have been presupposed to exist on the part of the
greatest portion of the Jews ; if he did not possess this conviction he could not have gained it by so accidental an occurrence as the one under consideration. And what can we think
of the stability of the Apostle's principles, and the searching
decision of his mode of action, if he had been able to content
himself with such incompleteness in the most important matter
of his apostolic office ? But the author of the Acts of the

Apostles must have considered such an occurrence as this as not unimportant with regard to his special design, for he again has recourse to it. In Ephesus also, whither the Apostle went from Corinth in order to take up his residence there for a longer period, the occurrence is again repeated which had taken place at Corinth, xix. 8, &c. He went into the syna- gogue, and discoursed boldly in order to make converts to the kingdom of God. But when some (or as τινὲς perhaps ought more properly to be taken, certain, special Jews—according to the custom now generally recognized of not giving the exact names) hardened themselves, and would not allow themselves to be instructed, but openly reviled the doctrine—he departed from them, separated the disciples, and held his daily discourses in the school of a certain Tyrannos, for the space of two years, with such success that all the dwellers in Asia, Jew and Gen- tile, heard the word of the Lord. Here also a σκληρύνεσθαι καὶ ἀπειθεῖν, a κακολογεῖν τὴν ὁδὸν, and indeed ἐνώπιον τοῦ πλήθους, must be brought before the notice of the people, as a public testimony, and at the same time in order to establish an undeniable case against the Jews, before the Apostle could enter on his full apostolic career, and begin his labours as an Apostle to the Gentiles. At the close of the Acts of the Apostles this scene is again referred to by the Apostle, who ascribes great importance to it, and this indeed in Rome which is especially worthy of remark from our point of view. As soon as the Apostle arrived in Rome (xxviii. 17), his first pro- ceeding was to call together the chief of the Jews, in order to lay before them the reason of his imprisonment, and to state that it was not on account of having transgressed against his nation and the customs of his fathers that he had been de- livered prisoner from Jerusalem into the hands of the Romans. The cause of his imprisonment was the Hope of Israel (the belief in the Messiah, which he shared in common with all his countrymen.) The Jews declared that they had not heard anything disadvantageous to him from Judæa, and

22

spoke of their desire to hear from him, what he held concerning that sect (Christianity), which as they knew, was everywhere so specially spoken against. On an appointed day they
repaired to the Apostle, and in a discourse, which lasted from
the morning to the evening, he endeavoured to persuade them
concerning Jesus, " out of the law of Moses and out of the
prophets :" and some believed his words, and others not. But
when they did not agree among themselves and departed, the
Apostle gave them a parting word to this effect : " Well spake
the Holy Ghost by Esaias the prophet unto our fathers, saying,
Go unto this people and say, hearing, ye shall hear, and not
understand, and seeing, ye shall see, and not perceive ; for the
heart of this people is waxed gross, and their ears are dull of
hearing, and their eyes have they closed, lest they should see
with their eyes, and hear with their ears, and understand with
their hearts, and should be converted, and I should heal them.
Be it known therefore unto you," says the Apostle in conclusion,
" that the salvation of God is sent unto the Gentiles, and that
they will hear it." We see immediately that the concluding
declaration is the practical result of the entire transactions
with the Roman Jews. The step which the Apostle now intended to take, of preaching the gospel to the Gentiles must
be justified by the antagonism of the Jews. But what a want
of sufficient motive is here ! how evidently the opposition of
the Jews, not amounting to obstinate unbelief, but only to a
rejection of the arguments advanced, is seized upon as giving
a reasonable colour to the determination, which without
such a pretext, would seem to be almost without justification !
And how does such a representation of the matter agree with
the circumstances of the Roman Church, as we are made
acquainted with them in the Epistle to the Romans itself ?

   The most admirable of Olshausen's Commentaries on the
Epistle to the Romans draws attention to the great difficulty
which exists in this passage of the Acts of the Apostles with
regard to its relation to the Epistle to the Romans, which rela-

tion he justly says, is not sufficiently considered in the investigations into the object of the Epistle to the Romans.   " If," writes
Olshausen,* " we think of the circumstances of the church of
Rome at the time when the Epistle to the Romans was composed, in the light in which they are generally considered, the
history of Paul in this capital is perfectly inconceivable.   The
Roman Church was divided into two parties, the Gentile and
the Jewish Christians.   The strict Jewish Christians observed
all the outward law of Moses, with circumcision, Sabbath
worship, &c.   On the other hand, the Gentile Christians were
free from all this.   Must we not necessarily assume from this
state of things that the Roman Jewish Christians adhered
to the synagogue in Rome?   As in Jerusalem the Jewish
Christians remained in the temple, and were not released from
the Jewish observances, so also the Roman Jewish Christians
would not separate themselves from the synagogue.   But now
let us read the narrative in the Acts of the Apostles, xxviii. 17,
according to which the Christians were utterly unknown to the
heads of the Roman synagogue, and ask whether, on its own
showing, this idea has any claim whatever to probability?
There is no ground for assuming that there was a designed
concealment ; but if this supposition is inadmissible, there
remains no choice but to say that the heads of the synagogue
knew really nothing of the Christians in Rome.   The speech
of Paul (xxviii. 17-20) is undoubtedly in an abbreviated form,
he would have spoken in it of his faith in Christ, as is indicated
by the mention of the ἐλπὶς τοῦ Ἰσραὴλ.   Thereupon the Jews
said : περὶ τῆς αἱρέσεως ταύτης γνωστόν ἐστιν ἡμῖν, ὅτι πανταχοῦ
ἀντιλέγεται.   Would any persons have spoken in this manner
of a sect which was present before them and whose disputes
and struggles were well known ? · This would be very difficult
to show as at all probable !   And following on this we have
the transaction with Paul (xxviii. 23) who, in order to prove

---

* In the work already cited.—Introduction, p. 45, &c

22 *

the Messiahship of Jesus, expounded the Scriptures to them during the whole of one day. This excited disputes among the Jews themselves, which, according to the common view, must have been a mere juggling trick, as the Jews must have long known about Jesus and decided against him. Only in cities where no churches existed do we find Jews so un-prejudiced as these in Rome appear to have been, but where through the establishment of a church they had acquired some knowledge of the Gospel, they allowed no Christian to preach doctrinal discourses. But as there must have been a church in Rome, the question arises how this anomalous attitude on the part of the Jews can be explained?"

The more pressing is the question here treated of, the more desirous we are to get at its solution. The only possible explanation of the phenomenon in question is this. " We must suppose that owing to the Jewish persecution under Claudius, the Christians in Rome were induced to make their differences with the Jews appear in the strongest and clearest light, probably in consequence of the influence which the Pauline disciples of that time had exercised on the Roman community. Four or five years after this persecution of the Jews at the beginning of the reign of Nero, Paul wrote the Epistle to the Romans. That many Jews at that time may have ventured to return to Rome, may have some probability, but those who went back must have kept themselves in concealment there, and it would have been very natural for the Roman Christian Church in its own interest to keep them as much as possible at a distance. Even three years later, when Paul went in person to Rome, Judaism there cannot have been very important, perhaps none of the old members of the Jewish community who had lived there before the persecution under Claudius had again returned, and the new members may have been unaware of the former existence of a Christian Church. Thus it may have happened, that in a period comprising eight or ten years the Christian Church in Rome may have become

completely separated from the Jews there, and in such a
state of separation do we find it according to this concluding
account in the Acts of the Apostles." But if this is the
only solution possible of the enigma, how is it possible to
overlook so striking a contradiction as that which it meets
in the Epistle to the Romans itself? A Church, which for
such a length of time had attracted to itself in so great a
degree the notice of the Apostle Paul (i. 13, xv. 22,) that
he himself wished to go to Rome, a Church whose circumstances appeared important enough to him to require so detailed
and comprehensive an Epistle, a Church of which he himself
says, that its faith was known throughout the whole world,
(εὐχαριστῶ τῷ θεῷ μου—ὅτι ἡ πίστις ὑμῶν καταγγέλλεται ἐν ὅλῳ
τῷ κόσμῳ, Romans i. 8. Compare xvi. 19, ἡ γὰρ ὑμῶν ὑπακοὴ
εἰς πάντας ἀφίκετο.) Could such a Church have been so unknown to the Roman Jews, who must have had the greatest
interest in becoming acquainted with a Christian Church consisting for the most part of their own countrymen, and which
they found established in one and the same city as themselves,
that they, as is represented in the Acts of the Apostles, could
speak of Christianity as a matter strange to them, with which
until now they had never come into contact, and which was
only known to them by hearsay? May we not also meet this
assertion with the same question which Olshausen asks with
regard to the commonly accepted view : " Would any person
have spoken in this manner of a sect which was present before
them, whose disputes and struggles were well known ? This
would be very difficult to show as being probable !" Just as
difficult would it be to make it appear possible that only the
Jews in Rome had not seen or perceived what every man in his
sound senses must have seen and perceived, for it lay open
to all the world, and must have been thoroughly known to all in
the city. Only two years later, (according to the most generally
received theory,) occurred the conflagration under Nero, and
the well known Christian persecution consequent on it. That

the Christians were at that time generally known in Rome is
not shown by this fact only, but by the express declaration of
the historian : " Nero subdidit reos et quæsitissimi pænis
affecit, quos, per flagitia invisos, vulgus Christianos appellabat."
(Tacitus, Annals, xv. 44.) How then is it possible that two
years earlier, Christianity could be so unknown in Rome as we
must assume it to have been according to the narrative in the
Acts of the Apostles, or how is it possible to suppose that the
Jews alone were ignorant of what everyone else in Rome was
acquainted with ? But, as far as regards the Jewish persecutions under the Emperor Claudius, on which Olshausen relies
for his statement, the importance so often attached to it is not
entirely warranted. That it included not only Jews, but
Christians also, is of course to be supposed, as at that time no
distinction could be made between Jews and Christians, and the
nearer the existing Christian Church in Rome was then to
the time of its origin, so much the greater would be the number also of its Jewish Christian members. There is no doubt
that by the " impulsor Chrestus," which according to Suetonius
in the Life of Claudius (chapter xxv.) was the cause of the
existing tumults on the part of the Jews, we must understand
nothing else than the Christianity which was then becoming
known in Rome, and which was received with acceptance by a
part of the Jews residing there, giving occasion to restlessness
and disputes, which existed even in the midst of Roman
Judaism. It would then be all the more natural, that the two
contending parties, the Jews and the Christians, would be
expelled from the city, and we see that Aquila and Priscilla,
who in consequence of this banishment met with the Apostle
Paul in Corinth, appeared to be by no means entirely unacquainted with the Christian faith. (Acts of the Apostles,
xviii. 2, &c.) But however we may decide on this, the prohibition of the Emperor Claudius can only have been of short
duration, and was attended with no important results. Such
prohibitions were never very strictly observed in Rome,

especially when a change in the government was expected soon after their issue. What Tacitus says of the mathematicians who were so often expelled not merely from Rome, but from Italy, that this " genus hominem in civitate nostra et retabitur semper et retinebitur,"* makes us all the more perceive the indulgence shown to the Jews; the mild treatment they received being also observable in the fact, that both Suetonius and the author of the Acts of the Apostles, agree in stating that they were only banished from the city of Rome, and not from Italy. How easy it must therefore have been for them to have returned from the near neighbourhood into the city itself, where they always had high patrons and protectors, and at that special time had such in Nero and Poppæa.† Some individuals, like Aquila and Priscilla, withdrew to a greater distance than the prohibition required, and went not only out of Rome but out of Italy, and although we find them at a later period still absent from Rome, we need not therefore conclude that this prohibition still maintained its full power and value. It may well be imagined that the more intimately Aquila and Priscilla became connected with the Apostle Paul, the less desirous

---

* History, i. 22. Under the reign of the Emperor Claudius, Tacitus speaks of a " de Mathematicis Italia pellendis factum Senatus Consultum," which is often identified with this prohibition against the Jews, as being " a trop et irritum."

† Compare on this the Programme of Professor C. Cless. Queritur de Coloniis Judæorum in Ægyptum terrasque cum Ægypto conjunctas post Mosem deductis. Part I. Stuttgart, 1832, page 32, where it is shown that many Jews lived as slaves and freedmen, and in high offices at the courts of princes. Ita in Cæsarum ædibus Acmen quandam, genere Judæam, Liriæ, servisse, Thallum, Samaritanum, Tiberii libertum fuisse scimus ; Poppæam, Neronis, qui et ipse Judæum, quendam mimum in deliciis habent uxorum Judæis sacris deditam, gentisque Judææ fautricem hujus mimi vel famulæ Judææ impulsu mentem hunc in modum flexisse, veri non est dissimili." According to Josephus, Antiq. of the Jews, xvii. 5, 7, xviii. 6, 4, xx. 8-11, where Poppæa is mentioned as a proselyte to Judaism by the expression θεοσεβής. Josephus relates in his life, chapter iii. that he had become acquainted with the Empress Poppæa through a Jewish μιμολόγος, who was in great favour with the Emperor Nero, and that through her, a Jewish priest who had been sent to Rome by the Procurator Felix, had obtained his release, and that she had even made him rich presents to enable him to return to his native land.

they were to return again to a Church in which without doubt an anti-Pauline tendency had early begun to develope itself. And finally how decidedly the undeniable existence of a Roman Church, not only at the time of the composition of the Epistle to the Romans, but (as we cannot avoid supposing,) for a series of preceding years, is shown by the fact that the residence of the Jews in the city of Rome at that time was no longer attended with any difficulty. It is therefore opposed to all historic probability, that in consequence of a past interdict of Claudius (which does not in any way justify us in speaking of a Jewish persecution under Claudius, as Olshausen maintains) and even in the time when Paul came to Rome, the number of Jews in Rome was only very small, and that the existing relations of the Christian Church in Rome, in consequence of this interdict, were in such opposition to the Judaism existing there, that Jews and Christians were in reality utterly unknown to each other in Rome. If the enigmatical phenomenon presented in the account in the Acts of the Apostles cannot be explained in this way, another way must be discovered. It is simply impossible that in Rome at that time such relations should have existed, and such a representation of the matter can only be explained by a special design on the part of the author. After our former investigations we can have no doubt with regard to this design. The author of the Acts of the Apostles represents the Apostle Paul as working with great success in the cause of Christianity, even during his Roman imprisonment (xxviii. 30, 31). He must have preached Christianity to the Gentiles in Rome as an Apostle to the Gentiles.

But it would seem necessary for him to be authorized for this work by a circumstance which would publicly exhibit in a striking manner the unbelief of the Jews who were opposed to the Gospel. Accordingly we find that the affair is represented in such a manner as to imply that the Jews in Rome now first acquired a knowledge of Christianity, and

resolved on their disbelief of it.   As we have here also a clear
proof that the author of the Acts of the Apostles, actuated by
a special interest, gives a wholly inconsistent account of the
real state of the matter, we must, keeping this interest in view,
use our judgment in deciding the analogous cases, in which the
Apostle observed the same course of action with regard to the
Jews; as these cases are according to our previous investigations highly improbable in themselves, and cannot be brought
into agreement with the strict limitations which the Apostle
lays down in his Epistle to the Galatians (chapter ii.) between
his ἀποστολὴ εἰς τὰ ἔθνη, and the ἀποστολὴ περιτομῆς.   But the
more earnestly the author of the Acts of the Apostles repeats
that the Gospel is to be preached to the Gentiles, wholly owing
to the Jews' own fault, and in consequence of their unbelief—
and the more evidently he subordinates this statement to his
special design—the less is it to be mistaken that he unites with
this statement an apologetic aim in respect to the Apostle Paul
as an Apostle to the Gentiles, and the more unavoidable is the
supposition that the author was induced to take this course by
regard to certain outward circumstances.   This is accordingly
the point in which the Acts of the Apostle coincides with the
Epistle to the Romans.   Both pre-suppose the same circumstances, and this indeed in that Church which had been in all
probability, according to the Acts of the Apostles, established
in Rome.   The Pauline author of the Acts of the Apostles, like
the Apostle himself in the Epistle to the Romans, states in the
same apologetic manner, that the Gospel is given to the
Gentiles owing to the fault of the Jews themselves, and in
consequence of their unbelief.   But in order to place this
fault in a clearer light, and completely to clear the Apostle
Paul from the reproof which had been made against him in
this respect, the author of the Acts of the Apostles represents
the case as though the Apostle had only so far respected
the Jewish national claim to priority that he transferred his
attention to the Gentiles when he considered himself justi-

fied in doing so by having been repulsed by the unbelief of the Jews. That which, according to the statement of the Acts of the Apostle, is of the last and highest importance, which the Jewish Christians would never consent to relinquish, that which could not fail to awaken, as soon as the question was raised, the greatest anxiety and conscientious scruples in the Apostle, is the primacy of his nation above all other nations —the national and theocratic prerogative, which he himself as a Christian would not allow to be endangered or abridged.

Before we investigate any further into how the Apostle treated this last stronghold of Judaism, we must first have a decided idea as to the question who the readers of this Epistle were ? After what has been said above, how can we doubt that they must principally have been Jewish Christians ? And yet there is a general assumption that the Roman Christians must have been Gentile Christians. Neander says, in his accustomed manner,* " It is very possible that the seed of the Gospel may have been brought much earlier to the Jews in Rome by the Jewish Christians, as we may conclude from the greeting at the conclusion of the Epistle that there were persons in Rome who belonged to the oldest Christians, but these certainly did not constitute the chief support of the Church, for the greatest part undoubtedly consisted of Christians descended from Gen- tiles, to whom the Gospel had to be preached by men of the Pauline school, independently of the Mosaic Law, to whom Paul, as the Apostle to the Gentiles, felt himself called on to write, and to whom, in consideration of his relation to them as such an Apostle, he could speak in a freer manner. Similar cir- cumstances to those which were for the greater part found in those churches where the Gentile Christian element preponde- rated, existed in this Church, although here a Jewish Christian one may also have existed, &c." In spite of all this, the exact opposite must be evidently true ; no historical proof of it is wanting, and it may be gathered from the Epistle to the Romans

---

* In the work already cited, page 384.

itself, and this not only from the whole tenor of the Epistle, but from individual indications contained in it.   If we accept, as I maintain we are justified in doing, that the section of the Roman Church to which the Epistle is chiefly directed was the predominant party in the Church, we must likewise assume Jewish Christians to have constituted the chief part of the Roman Church, and this is the more likely as the early origin of a Roman Church was manifested by the great number of Jews who were in Rome.   We cannot conclude with any certainty, from the last chapter of the Epistle to the Romans, that the Gospel in Rome was preached by men of the Pauline school; but if we conclude anything from this chapter, be it genuine or not, we find indications of a time in regard to the origin of the Roman Church in which a Pauline Christianity did not yet exist, as Andronicus and Junia, the ἐπίσημοι ἐν τοῖς ἀποστόλοις had been Christians before Paul himself had become one.   In fact, the idea to which Eichhorn gave currency, that disciples of the Apostle Paul had decided influence on the constitution and growth of the Roman Church, can only be founded on the general opinion that Gentile Christians alone could have constituted the chief party in a Christian Church in Rome, the centre of the Gentile world, and that the Apostle must have stood in a closer connection to the Romans before he would have written in so detailed and urgent a manner to them.   The Roman Christians would seem to have possessed this nearer relation as Gentile Christians only, but how could they have been converted to Christianity except by disciples of the Apostle ?   All this becomes worth nothing as soon as we relinquish all preconceived notions of the composition of the Epistle itself.   The Epistle to the Romans indeed leaves no doubt on the point, that at the period in question, not only Jewish but Gentile Christians also belonged to the Roman Church, but we do not know in what way they were converted, and we only see how in any case they stand in a subordinate relation to the principal subject and chief design of the Epistle.   From the very circumstance that the Apostle,

when he purposely turned to the Gentile Christians, addressed
himself to them in such a special manner as he did, (for
instance, in xi. 13-24,) shows that he had not so much care
for the Gentile as for the Jewish Christians. They are
brought forward at the conclusion of the chief argument as
a part of the whole, and appear therefore, (as is indicated also
by the special address, xi. 13, ὑμῖν γὰρ λέγω τοῖς ἔθνεσιν,) in a
subordinate relation to the whole, to which subject no such
special reference was needed.   Therefore, although the whole
concluding section, xi. 13-35, may be devoted to the Gentile
Christians, (as is indicated by the repeated ὑμεῖς, 28, 30, 31,
and confirmed by the right reading of the section, 25-29,) and
as the main idea, that in spite of the πώρωσις ἀπὸ μέρους, in
reference to Israel, and in spite of the πλήρωμα τῶν ἐθνῶν, the
οὕτω πᾶς Ἰσραὴλ σωθήσεται, refers not to the Jewish but to
the Gentile Christians, the address turns back after this section,
as after a digression, to the especial subject on which it was
before enlarging.*   That the Apostle commenced the composition of his Epistle with a view to Jewish Christian readers,
is besides indicated by many minor features, in which may be
recognized the stamp and general tone of the Epistle ; as for
instance in the beginning, which is very evidently influenced
by Old Testament ideas, (εὐαγγέλιον θεοῦ, ὃ προεπηγγείλατο διὰ
τῶν προφητῶν αὐτοῦ ἐν γραφαῖς ἁγίαις, περὶ τοῦ υἱοῦ αὐτοῦ τοῦ
γενομένου ἐκ σπέρματος Δαβίδ, i. 2, 3.) But what the Apostle
says in the introduction to his Epistle with regard to his mission of preaching the Gospel to the Gentiles, is not to be taken
with Neander, as meaning that the Apostle says he feels
himself called to write to the Romans as an Apostle to the
Gentiles.   It cannot be otherwise, (as has also been remarked
by the better commentators), than that by ἔθνη, verses 7 and 13,

---

* It is accordingly incorrect for Olshausen to maintain that the Gentile Christians alone were addressed, chap. ix.-xi. They are addressed only, xi. 12-35. How
such an interpreter of the Epistle to the Romans as Olshausen can maintain that
chapter ix.-xi, is certainly meant to apply to the Gentile Christians, I am unable
to perceive.

must be understood not only the Gentiles, but the nations generally. The Apostle explains that the reason which prompted him to write to the Romans, arose out of the obligation imposed on him by his apostolic office, of preaching the Gospel to all men without distinction of race or education. If he had intended to address the Gentile Christians especially, he would have contented himself with simply calling himself an Apostle to the Gentiles. On the contrary, he reminds the Jewish Christians of the universality of his mission, and states that from the wide circle of peoples to which that mission extended, the Roman Jewish Christians could not be excluded. In order to evade the deduction, that as an Apostle to the Gentiles, he stood in no relation to the Jewish Christians, he includes the Jews themselves as a distinct people in the general idea of the ἔθνη. He is also desirous of justifying himself to the Jewish Christians with regard to the Epistle which he is about to write.

If we now pass on to the main question which still remains unanswered, of the relation which the dogmatic portion of the Epistle bears to its tendency, as far as this has been explained, the problem must only be how to place it under the same anti-Judaistic point of view. As Judaism, in its claim to the primacy, which it considered as its natural theocratic prerogative, and as the most inalienable national privilege of the Jews over all other nations, brought forward in the most urgent manner all which could be said against Paulinism, so the Apostle Paul asserts the contrary in the most pointed way ; he goes to the deepest root of the matter, and the whole dogmatic treatment of the Epistle can be considered as nothing but the most radical and thorough-going refutation of Judaism and Jewish Christianity. How decidedly the principal anti-Judaistic tendency of the Epistle is shown in the first chapter, when the Apostle, after the statement of his chief subject, contrasts the δικαιοσύνη θεοῦ ἐκ πίστεως εἰς πίστιν, the righteousness of God, with the unrighteousness of man, and represents it as a notorious historical fact that not only was it steadfastly resolved to place Gentiles and Jews on a perfect equality ; and from the beginning, his argument evidently aims at bringing home to the Jews the consciousness of their own unrighteousness, as well as the unrighteousness of the Gentiles. He places the idolatry and sinful crimes of the Gentile world in the clearest light, and then suddenly turns to the Jews in order to say to them in the words contained (chapter ii. 1), that they who judged the Gentiles and rejected them as sinners, did the same things themselves as the Gentiles did ; if they did not actually commit the same sins and vices, still they did so virtually, inasmuch as the criminality of such modes of action consisted in the fact that those who in spite of the better knowledge which, as the necessary result of moral fitness, was not even denied to the Gentiles (1-19), committed those actions which all knew that no one could commit without rendering himself worthy of death. Considered in this manner, Gentiles and Jews stand on the same footing ; if any difference exists, it can only reside in the degree of consciousness with which those actions are committed which should not be committed, but even this difference results to the disadvantage of the Jews. The Gentiles are not wholly without law—they have the law of their own conscience ; but if the Jews in addition to this natural law had the advantage of another law, everything of which he boasts, relying on his law, speaks against him. The highest advantage of the law is that a man may know the Divine Will and can tell whether a thing is right or wrong ; the Jew is only all the more worthy of punishment the more clearly and completely he knows from the law what he ought to do, and yet in spite of it does exactly the contrary. Whilst therefore the true moral worth of man only consists in practice, in doing what he is conscious he ought to do, in this one thing the distinction between Jew and Gentile is cancelled, uncircumcision is as circumcision, and circumcision is as uncircumcision ; from which it follows " that he is not a Jew which is one outwardly," but " he is a Jew who

is one inwardly in the heart before God" (chapter ii. 1, 29).
The fresh instance also, which commences (chap. iii. 1) with
the question, "What advantage therefore hath the Jew?" as he
is thus obliged to yield up any advantage he had over the Gentile through his circumcision, the Apostle answers with fresh
humility, whilst now by the testimony of the Jewish law itself
he endeavours to bring the Jew to recognize his own liability to
punishment. He has in fact no advantage whatever, and there
still remains the accusation already brought forward and attested
by the Scripture itself, that Jew and Gentile are both under sin.
But we know that what is said by Scripture or by the law, is
said to those who are under the law. Therefore all the passages
of Scripture complaining of the sins of men refer especially to
the Jews; and it results from all this that no man can be justified before God on account of works of the law; the law can
so little produce righteousness, that rather through it do men
acquire a knowledge of sin (iii. 1-20). If a righteousness be
granted, it has nothing whatever to do with the law—it is
the righteousness of God through faith in Jesus Christ, to
whom man may become united by faith as by the free gift of
God. Faith alone corresponds to the universal conception of God.
If men could attain righteousness and salvation through the
works of the law as the Jews think, who hold circumcision to be
a saving work of the law, then the Jews alone would possess this
righteousness, and God would only be the God of the Jews,
but God is equally the God of the Gentiles as of the Jews. In
faith, therefore, all difference between circumcision and uncircumcision vanishes, and everything must be referred to faith
alone (iii. 20-31). But now if faith is opposed to works, and
together with works considered as the works of the law, the law
itself comes to nothing; the question arises, in what position the
law now stands? With this question the Apostle arrives at a point
from which he no longer argues so roughly and sharply against
Judaism, and where he assumes a purely negative attitude with
regard to it. He cannot avoid granting that the Jew has this ad-

vantage over the Gentile, that he can always appeal to the absolute importance of the law, which cannot be simply set aside;
and therefore the Apostle sets himself to explain the law in such
a manner, that whilst he recognizes and maintains its absolute
importance, he also shows, notwithstanding, how the law in
comparison with faith, has a merely subordinate, relative, and
negative significance. This is the chief point of view to which
the Apostle adheres in the address which follows. After having,
in chapter iv. indicated, with regard to Abraham and David, a
νόμος πίστεως (iii. 27) raised above a νόμος ἔργων, a righteousness obtained by faith as an objective means of salvation
founded on the law; and in pursuance of his chief idea, after
having brought forward, in v. 1-11, in one general view the
greatness of the blessings arising from justification by faith,
he assumes his highest standpoint in v. 12-21, namely, that of
its religious historical consideration, in order from this height
to examine and refute the absolute pretensions of Judaism, as
well as to lay open to the Judaizers a point of view from which
their Old Testament Scriptures might most easily be reconciled
with the new doctrines. The religious teachings of Judaism
contain, if they are rightly understood, all the essential points
of the Apostle's doctrines. We ought to look at the course
which the history of mankind took from Adam to Christ, with
special reference to the main idea which is designated in the
contents of chapter v. 12-21, and then only one scheme of
salvation is seen as possible for it, namely the δικαιοσύνη. It
is, so to speak, an absolutely necessary condition in the history
of the world and of revelation, that there is not only a question
of condemnation to death, but of justification to life, and in
the scheme of the world which is conditioned by this, the
whole history of mankind divides itself into two opposite
periods, each of which contains in itself its own peculiar distinctive principle. But with the same necessity we must maintain on this objective historical view, that the law and the whole
scheme of salvation depending upon it belongs to a subordinate

stage of religious developments, and that consequently it possesses only a relative importance, and can only hold a negative place in regard to what comes after it.   In the following section, where he begins a new train of thought (vi. 1), it is still the idea of the law which is pursued in the Apostle's address. The law can only be fulfilled by works—but the works which the law requires are a moral demand.   The Apostle had formerly shown that the claim made by the law was allowed through the works of the law.   Now this is no longer the case; the contrary state of things rather prevails.   Immorality, unrighteousness, sin, so that, as no man is justified through the works of the law, the unrighteousness of men can only be opposed to the righteousness of God, and the opponents of the absolute importance of Judaism supported by the law may draw from his doctrine of faith in opposition to works, the conclusion that he places the idea of the law in contradiction to the interests of morality.   In order to meet this reproof, the Apostle, in chapter vi., takes the exactly opposite standpoint, by maintaining that so little is this the case, that the scheme of salvation preached by him is rather the actual and radical annihilation of sin.   The union with Christ, in which the Christian is already so dead to sin that in reality it no longer exists for him, makes it actually and morally impossible for him to commit sin (vi. 8-23).   But, absolutely as the bonds which bind men to sin are loosed by the death of Christ, so absolutely is the union with the law also dissolved.   Just as little as a Christian, as such, is under the dominion of sin, is he also under the dominion of the law.   Sin and law stand in a perfect parallel to each other, and the law can not be more completely overthrown than it is here, when the same thing which is said of sin is applied also to the law.   If, hitherto, the Apostle had denied the efficacy of justification through the works of the law, and had said of the law that through it came the knowledge of sin (iii. 20)—that the law had multiplied sin in the period between Adam and Christ (v. 20), and that now, instead of the dominion of the law, the dominion of grace prevailed (vi. 15), so, the two ideas of sin and the law had, in their development, now entered into such close relation that they might actually be held as identical, and the Apostle, himself, feels obliged to ask the question (vii. 7), " What shall we say then ? is the law sin ?" Here the question about which he is at issue with the readers of his Epistle is pursued to its sharpest polemic point, but this is a point also, on attaining which he must explain more closely the nature of the law. He founds the identity which is implied by his words between the two ideas of the law and sin, in the fact that he considers the difference between what the law is for itself, and subjectively for mankind, lies in the whole psychological process, in which indeed Judaism and Christianity approach each other as nearly as possible—but the limits can never be passed which separate the Jew, as such, from Christianity, and which exclude him from its blessings as long as he remains a Jew.

If we refer to the Apostle's entire course of thought, as it lies before us in the first eight chapters of his Epistle, how can we imagine that the Apostle had any other readers except Jewish Christian ones in his mind, or that the chief purport of this section was any other than to indicate the opinions and scruples which still prevented his readers, as Jewish Christians, from giving complete adherence to the Pauline universalism ; and what else among these opinions and scruples was the greatest obstacle, which could with the greatest difficulty be set aside, than that which the Apostle makes the chief subject of the rest of his address, namely, that the Jews were no better than the Gentiles ; that in reality they possessed no advantage over them, and that even the law did not justify them in giving that absolute importance to Judaism which they were willing to ascribe to it ? How earnestly he must have entered into a question fraught with such weighty interest, not only for himself but for his readers, when in the same passage, where he closes the first great division of his Epistle with an expression of the most vivid joy, with the most enthusiastic description of the eternal blessed fellowship of the Christian with God and Christ, he adds, with words of the deepest sorrow and anxiety, the assurance of his most heart-felt sympathy in the destiny of his countrymen, in the great contrast it presented to the reality just described, and assures them of his sympathy, inspired by the thought that all this blessedness was lost to those for whom it was principally intended. For they are Israelites, all the blessings and riches of the religious fellowship of the Old Testament belong to them, the adoption and the glory, the covenants and the giving of the law, and the service of God and the promises; they have Abraham, Isaac, and Jacob as their fathers, and from them, " as concerning the flesh," came Christ, wherefore " God who is over all be blessed for ever." Now, we assume that the same thought to which the Apostle here gives the full expression of his sympathy, had been present to him from the beginning of his Epistle, had decided its whole intention and conception, and had been present to his mind throughout its accomplish-ment, we can then penetrate far enough into the motives which originated it as to be able to explain it historically. Both divisions of the Epistle are connected in the closest manner, so far that in each the most essential and most radical questions concerning Judaism are treated. That no man can attain righteousness by means of works of the law, that the Jews have in no degree whatever any advantage over the Gentiles in the righteousness that is by Faith, that on the side of the law there is only unrighteousness and sin—these subjects form the contents of the first eight chapters, and in the three following the same claims of the Jews and the Jewish Christians, which are set forth in the first part, are combated and refuted only with more decided reference to the grounds on which they are founded, and this is done with the greater energy, the more that the Apostle has now to treat of the circumstances actually existing at the time. If the Jewish exclusiveness had been as much as possible overcome, there would still have existed the

23 *

question whether ἐκπέπτωκεν ὁ λόγος τοῦ θεοῦ, ix. 6. The ancient promises of God to the nation could not have been so completely void as to leave the Jews no national advantage whatever over the Gentiles. This is the mildest, the most purely theocratic form of the Jewish exclusiveness, confiding in the fidelity and truth of God, but all the more decidedly was it necessary to weed out from it, although in this form, every root of inherent justification. Something there was required in which the Jew should have the advantage over the Gentile ; and what could this be but a righteousness supported on works ? But such an one does not exist, there is but one righteousness of God exclusive of all human actions. In this line of thought the Apostle writes what he intends to be the culminating point of his Epistle, in order to carry on his subject dogmatically, and to express at the conclusion with the most lively pity the conclusion to which he had been led, that under the new scheme of salvation appointed by God, those who possessed all these national advantages would not be saved. They would always possess them ; and although, indeed, the word of God could never be untrue, his promise never be unfulfilled, this would be in a manner totally independent of any human co-operation. With what justice could any man relying on the old national privileges, trouble himself about the rejection of the nation, to take exception at it, and to allow himself to be led into error by it ? God can do what he pleases through his own free absolute will, and the Jews have only themselves to blame if they are deprived of salvation, as, without reflecting that the life of the law has an end in Christ, they had rejected a scheme arranged by God. What accordingly is there to hinder us from finding a perfectly satisfactory connection between the outward apparent purport of the Epistle and its real inward meaning ? The main idea running through its entire extent is the absolute nothingness of all claims founded on Jewish exclusiveness. The aim of the Apostle is to confute the Jewish exclusiveness so thoroughly and radically that he fairly stands in advance of the consciousness of the time, and in the Epistle to the Romans we see this idea the more clearly and completely carried out the closer the connection is in which its two principal portions stand to each other.

The parenthetic part of the Epistle, beginning with chapter xii., is distinguished by the general moral precepts which are principally given in the twelfth chapter, by exhortations to obedience, to authority, and to mutual patience with regard to certain practices and observances. As far as regards the latter, the commentators, as is well known, are in great uncertainty with respect to the " weak," who call for especial mention from the Apostle in chapter xiv. That this section is to be understood as referring to the relation of the liberal Gentile Christians to the fettered and anxious Jewish Christians may be correctly assumed; but in order to arrive at a closer knowledge of the matter, we must come to a more precise historical understanding as to the Judaising character of the Roman Church. The Roman Jewish Christians, like most of the Jewish Christians of the ancient Churches, held more or less thoroughly Ebionitish principles.*

Only in the Ebionites do we meet with the same traits as we must assume to have characterized the Jewish Christians in Rome, according to chapter xiv. Those who are designated by the Apostle as weak, refrained from eating meat, and eat only herbs, (λάχανα, verse 2, as distinguished from κρέας, vegetables generally). So also they drank no wine (καλὸν τὸ μὴ φαγεῖν κρέα, μηδὲ πιεῖν οἶνον, xiv. 21). That the Ebionites on principle refused to eat meat we are told by Epiphanius,† and this indeed, as they themselves explain, because all meat is created by copulation. They also held the eating of meat to be polluting, and in this light it must also have been considered by the

---

* Epiphanius, Haer. 30. 18, makes Ebion appear as the nominal Founder of the Ebionites in Rome as well as in Asia, by his κήρυγμα.

† Haer. 30. 15. Καὶ κρεῶν, καὶ πάσης ἄλλης ἐδωδῆς τῆς ἀπὸ σαρκῶν πεποιημένης Ἐβίων καὶ Ἐβιωνῖται παντελῶς ἀπέχονται, διὰ τὸ ἐκ συνουσίας καὶ μίξεως σώματα εἶναι αὐτά.

Roman Jewish Christians, as the Apostle feels himself obliged to remind them, ὅτι οὐδέν κοινὸν δι' αὐτοῦ εἰ μὴ τῷ λογιζομένῳ τι κοινὸν εἶναι, ἐκείνῳ κοινόν (verse 14) and πάντα μὲν καθαρὰ ἀλλὰ κακὸν τῷ ἀνθρώπῳ τῷ διὰ προσκόμματος ἐσθίοντι (verse 20). If they held flesh as in itself impure, what other reason could they give for this impurity but that given by Epiphanius? According also to the pseudo-Clementine homilies, the unnatural eating of meat is of demoniacal origin, and derived from those giants who, in accordance with their bastard nature, took no pleasure in pure nourishment and only lusted after blood, Hom. viii. 15. Therefore the eating of meat is as polluting as the heathen worship of demons, with its sacrifices and sacrificial feasts, through participation in which a man becomes an ὁμοδίαιτος of demons. In the place of the custom of eating meat, rejected by the Ebionites, they introduced eating vegetables (λάχανα) only. Testimony as to this is not wanting. In the Homilies, the Apostle Peter, in the description of his manner of living which he gives to Clement, says (xii. 6): ἄρτῳ μόνῳ καὶ ἐλαίαις χρῶμαι καὶ σπανίως λαχάνοις. If the Apostle Peter, for the sake of the higher holiness, dared only seldom to eat λάχανα, all the more did it behove the Jewish Christians in general to use the same luxury in the same manner. According to certain passages in the writings of Clement of Alexandria,* the Apostle Matthew and James the Lord's brother lived on vegetables only. Not without some show of reason is such a manner of living ascribed to both these men. Both especially represent the characteristics of the oldest Jewish Christian Church, in which the strict Ebionite element was far more predominant than is generally supposed. Nothing is expressly stated with regard to abstinence from wine, but

---

* Clement of Alexandria, Pædag. ii. 1. Ματθαῖος, ὁ ἀπόστολος σπερμάτων, καὶ ἀκροδρύων καὶ λαχάνων, ἄνευ κρεῶν, ἐλάμβανε. Augustin Adv. Faustum, book xxii. 3. Jacobus, frater Domini seminibus et oleribus usus est non carne nec vino. The description also which Hegesippus (Eusebius, H. E. ii. 2, 3) gives of this James, has quite the stamp of Ebionite thought and manner of living, and it is especially said of him, οἶνον καὶ σίκερα οὐκ ἔπιεν, οὐδὲ ἔμψυχον ἔφαγε.

that the stricter Ebionites held the drinking of wine to be unlawful, is to be gathered without doubt from the fact that according to Epiphanius they celebrated their annual Eucharistic mysteries with unleavened bread and pure water; and the Roman Ebionites of the Homilies must also have had this custom, as Peter solemnized the Eucharist after the baptism with bread and salt only (Hom. xiv. 1). That the Roman Jewish Christians, to whom the Apostle is writing, regarded certain days under a religious aspect, we see from xiv. 16. We must remember the importance which the Sabbath, and new moon, and other days of this kind had among the Jews. But it must be expressly remarked of the Ebionites, that next to the rite of circumcision, they held the Sabbath festival as the most holy command given by the Jewish religion. There is therefore nothing more probable than that the Apostle had in his mind the custom which had so long prevailed in the Jewish Christian Church of keeping the Sabbath and the Passover according to the Jewish manner.

In the exhortation which the Apostle (chap. xiii. 1) gives to obedience to authority, interpreters do not fail, in order to explain the persistency and detail with which this is enforced and made into a duty, to call to mind the position of the Christians with regard to the power of the State, which from the beginning was mistrustful of the new religious community, and was influenced in the highest degree by its direct enemies the Jews and priests (Acts of the Apostles xvii. 7, xix. 26), and had taken every illegal act of its members as a pretext for oppressive measures. They also refer to the very conceivable fears of the pernicious influence of certain prejudices and errors entertained by the newly converted.

The ordinary Jew would have held the Jewish theocracy only for a legitimate government (Deuteronomy xvii. 15) and would have reckoned the Gentile kingdom on the contrary as founded and carried on under the influence of the devil (Luke iv. 6, Revelation ii., Ephesians iii. 12, John xii. 31); he would only obey on compulsion, and especially held the imposition of taxes as a robbery of the Temple at Jerusalem (Matthew xxii. 17). These fanatic ideas, to which the hope of a Messiah and the oppression of the magistrates gave great strength, had made the people, especially in Gentile countries, inclined to agitation and revolt, of which the capital had shown an example shortly before (Acts of the Apostles xviii. 2, and Suetonius, Vita Claud. 25.) All this indeed is not altogether groundless, but it has not any firm historical support. It may serve as a confirmation of the view we have here taken, that by it we gain an idea of the cause which prompted the Apostle to make such an exhortation, as well as a more decided point of view from which to consider its tendency. The chief subject of the exhortation which the Apostle gives, lies in the proposition that all authority, especially the governing power of the state, is of God. This assertion, so universally maintained, seems to pre-suppose as universal an antithesis—the opposite view, that the authoritative power not merely in certain isolated cases but wholly and generally, springs not from God, but from an ungodly source. The Ebionites, indeed, entertained this view, although, according to their dualistic idea of the world, they considered the whole present world with all its earthly powers in contradistinction to the future, as the kingdom of the devil.* Indeed,

---

* Δύο τινὰς συνιστῶσιν, says Epiphanius, Hær. 30, 16, ἐκ θεοῦ τεταγμένους, ἕνα μὲν τὸν Χριστὸν ἕνα δὲ τὸν διάβολον καὶ τὸν μὲν Χριστὸν λέγουσι τοῦ μέλλοντες αἰῶνος εἰληφέναι τὸν κλῆρον, τὸν δὲ διάβολον τοῦτον πεπιστεῦσθαι τὸν αἰῶνα ἐκ προσταγῆς δῆθεν τοῦ παντοκράτορος κατὰ αἴτησιν ἑκατέρων αὐτῶν. In harmony with this, the author of the Clementine Homilies says, xv. 7, The true Prophet teaches that God the Creator of all things has made two Beings, one good and one bad, and also two kingdoms. To the bad he gave the lordship of the present world, with the law that is necessary to punish the ill-doer, and he bestowed on the good the future eternal world. But God allows each man to choose freely which he will, either the present evil or the future good. Those who choose the present world ought to become rich, be content, and enjoy themselves as much as they can, for they have no part in the future world. But those who decide for the future world must consider nothing as belonging to them in this present world, belonging as it does to a strange Ruler; nothing, that is to say, but bread and water (according to xii. 6, olives and vegetables, also λαχάνα), and this means

we must take this form of Ebionism, which is presented to us in the writings of Epiphanius and the pseudo-Clementine Homilies, as the only and originally prevailing one among the Ebionites ; all that was harshest and most prejudicial in Ebionism belonged to it in its later aspect as opposed to the Catholic Church, and as regards the point in question the similarity between the later Ebionites and the Roman Jewish Christians does not hold so good. But all the less is it possible to deny, without ignoring the limitations which are involved in the nature of the case, what great harmony and close relations are presented between the view of the world taken by the Roman Jewish Christians and that held by the Ebionites. They saw in the world which surrounded them, the nearer they approached to the seat and centre of the power that ruled it, nothing but a principle at enmity with God, and striving against him, and therefore they submitted themselves to the ruling powers of the state, not under the idea that even in outward appearance anything good and divine, any decree ordained by God could be recognized in that most ungodly power, but they submitted with inward unwillingness and opposition, as though they were only restrained from rebellion against an adverse power of evil, by fear of material violence. To this we owe the expression of the Apostle's opinion, that there exists a moral necessity for submitting to authority, not merely for fear of punishment, inasmuch as refusing to submit would be a matter of absolute impossibility, but with the inward conviction of the right which submission had on its side : (ἀνάγκη ὑποτάσσεσθαι, οὐ μόνον διὰ τὴν ὀργὴν, ἀλλὰ καὶ διὰ τὴν συνείδησαν), that the cause of fear was not to be sought in authority itself, as such, as if in its principle it were a hard adverse power, but in the moral relations of the subjects which came under its jurisdiction : (οἱ γὰρ ἄρχοντες οὐκ εἰσὶ φόβος τῶν ἀγαθῶν ἔργων

of subsistence they must win by the sweat of their brow, because no man ought to take his own life. The children of the future world are therefore in this present one, in the forbidden kingdom of a monarch at enmity with them.

ἀλλὰ τῶν κακῶν· θέλεις δὲ, μὴ φοβεῖσθαι τὴν ἐξουσίαν ; τὸ ἀγαθὸν ποίει, 3, compare 4) that men are not to look upon authority as something evil in itself, objectionable, abhorrent, as a diabolic power simply adverse to God (οὐ γάρ ἐστιν ἐξουσία, εἰ μὴ ἀπὸ θεοῦ—θεοῦ γὰρ διάκονός ἐστι, σοὶ εἰς ἀγαθόν, verses 1-4). Only if we may suppose that in the view combated by the Apostle there existed so harsh a contrast, the antithesis, that in the principle governing the world and exercising its power in the existing civil authority, there was to be found nothing divine, but something wholly earthly and devilish—we can quite understand why the Apostle, leaving all the other questions, on which we should have imagined he would have enlarged in an address concerning the relations of subjects to the higher powers, should confine himself to one chief general point, to which no exception could be taken : οὐ—ἐστιν ἐξουσία εἰ μὴ ἀπὸ θεοῦ. This negative form of the main idea, shows how he kept in mind the maintenance of the antithesis that authority is not of divine but ungodly origin. If this position is in no case tenable, except on the hypothesis of an absolute dualism, what therefore can authority be εἰ μὴ ἀπὸ θεοῦ? This is the negative position, which has to be maintained against opponents. Authority is not of the Devil—the affirmative directly states : it is of God. Only in this connection can we understand the strict, absolute, universal sense in which the Apostle recognizes a divine appointment in the actual existing authority, even in the case of a Nero as ruler. This position is, therefore, really true, as the truth which lies at its foundation pre-supposes that the power ruling the visible world cannot be an evil, ungodly principle. According to the Ebionites indeed the Devil can only be commissioned to carry on the government of the Aeons, ἐκ προσταγῆς τοῦ παντοκράτορος—but it is also true, that in this direct government entrusted to the Devil, a great predominance is conceded to dualism, and how easily may the great idea of monotheism have thus become secondary to that of dualism, at least in the consciousness of ordinary

Christians. We can the less avoid the theory of the harmony between the Jewish Christian view of the world which is combated in the Epistle to the Romans, and the views of the Ebionites, as the author of the Clementine Homilies himself, from his dualistic point of view, gives a fresh reading of the advice contained in the Christian command, rather to suffer wrong than to do it. This reading consists in the idea that those who had chosen the future world might still enjoy many things in the present one, in which they are placed in connection with evil-doers, for instance, life and light, bread and water, and other things which really did not belong to them, whilst the children of the present world have no part in the future one, so that those who suffer unjustly are really those who act unjustly, and those who act unjustly are those who suffer unjustly (Hom. xv. 8). How could the Apostle, if the Ebionites thought thus, have felt himself obliged to caution the readers of his Epistle against the ἀντιτάττεσθαι τῇ ἐξουσίᾳ ? But this we cannot suppose to have been a prevailing view of life, and such a recommendation and reading of the command rather to suffer injustice than to do it, as we find it in these Homilies, can only justify us in the supposition that they have found a place in them because the author, writing in the Ebionite spirit, must have been as far from considering them superfluous, as does the Apostle in his exhortation given in the Epistle to the Romans.

There is nothing more natural than that a spirit of opposition so deeply grounded, so essential, should be always threatening to break out in actual reaction. Accordingly, everything here seems to speak of a dualistic view of life, closely related in its principles to a later form of Ebionism, and which is represented as being held by the Roman Jewish Christians, and this appears the less strange, as dualism in the civil life stands in a very natural connection with the view which recognizes in the natural life also, an impure, demoniacal, contradictory principle, inciting to enormous crimes, compare xiv. 14-20.

But, it is objected that if the Apostle had had such opponents as these in his mind, his argument would have been a completely different one. We must suppose, says Neander (in the work already cited, page 394, &c.,) that these persons had gone so far as to declare the eating of meat to be something plainly sinful, and this they would not have done, unless they had been in agreement with a decided dualistic theosophy. But Paul would not have treated such a view with such tolerance. It certainly cannot be imagined that Paul would only have treated such people as these as "weak;" so much forbearance towards them indicates, that he did not feel inclined to carry on a further opposition to the tone of thought which lay at the foundation of this standpoint. If we do not assume that a consciously expressed dualism, which he was bound to combat, lay at the foundation of these opinions, still he would not have taken so mild and indulgent an attitude towards an ascetic pride of this kind, which in any case stood in such harsh contradiction, as well to the nature of his doctrine of justification, as to the nature of Christian humility. This opinion is strengthened, when we see this tendency connected with a dualistic view of the world, referring all earthly authority to an evil principle. Notwithstanding I cannot concede any great weight to this objection. It is in itself a doubtful matter to decide how the Apostle would have argued against his opponents under certain circumstances. If once the supposition is sufficiently established on historical grounds, that the readers of his Epistle entertained certain and decided views and principles, we must also be convinced that the Apostle's argument would contain matter which would be the most to the point under the given circumstances. For, on the very uncertain data which are commonly presented to us in these cases, to enable us to see clearly into the various circumstances, and matters which have to be taken into consideration, who can so confidently weigh one thing against another as to be able to say with certainty, that in this, and in no other way must the Apostle

have expressed himself? The chief point is only, that what
the Apostle really did say suits the supposition and brings
forward an essential crisis in the matter under consideration.
How clearly this is the case with the question before us!
How decided are the antitheses which the Apostle places before
the narrow conceptions and perverted principles of his readers,
how strikingly is the almost self-evident critical point of the
affair brought under the influence of Christian consciousness!
But should it be said that if the Apostle had such opponents in
view, he ought to have kept a sharper eye on their peculiar principle of dualism, it would be necessary not only that the Apostle
should enter, as he does no where else in his Epistle, on a course
of speculative ideas, which lie outside the direct sphere of Christian faith, but it would also be presupposed that the theoretic
side of the dualistic view of the world entertained by the Roman
Christians ought to have been represented in a decided and
characteristic manner. But although at that time a certain
speculative view of the world may perhaps have existed in an
undeveloped state among them, they manifested only their practical side in their relation to certain relations of life. The Apostle
does not conceal that he does not hold as objectively correct the
views entertained by the Jewish Christians, which restrained
them from eating meat and drinking wine, and pointed out
vegetables alone as pure and lawful food; he expressly calls
these Christians "weak," and strictly forbids them to pass a condemnatory sentence on those who do not share their opinions
as to eating and drinking. (xiv. 1.) The stronger brethren
also he exhorts not to judge of, and treat their weaker brethren
in a depreciatory manner on acoount of their narrow-minded
views. After these exhortations to each party, having for their
especial aim to represent the affair objectively considered as
one indifferent to the Christian faith, in so far as no man has
any right to exalt himself into a judge and ruler over others, or
to interfere in a matter which does not concern him; and after
stating indeed that a man is not his own master, but belongs to
Christ, and all things of this kind are of importance only in the

absolute relation which each man knows how to give to them,
according to his conviction with regard to Christ, the Apostle
comes, in verse 13, &c., to the subjective side, and shows how
important it is that a man should give no cause ˉof offence to
his brother. Such a cause of offence could only be given by
those more liberally-minded brethren if, by the manner in which
they made no allowance for the narrowness and timidity of the
weaker ones, they placed an obstacle in their way, thereby
either exposing them to a condemnatory sentence, or making
them act against their conscience. For this reason the Apostle
exhorts the liberal-minded Gentile Christians, εἰ δὲ διὰ βρῶμα
ὁ ἀδελφός σου λυπεῖται—μὴ τῷ βρώματί σου ἐκεῖνον ἀπόλλυε
—μὴ ἕνεκεν βρώματος κατάλυε τὸ ἔργον τοῦ θεοῦ—καλὸν τὸ μὴ
φαγεῖν κρέα, μηδὲ πιεῖν οἶνον, &c., he also exhorts them at
the same time to eat no meat and drink no wine, and thus
to accommodate themselves to the scruples of the Jewish
Christians. But yet this exhortation is not to be understood as if he wished to lay on the Gentile Christians the
obligation to adopt the principles of the Jewish Christians with
regard to eating and drinking; what he intends to say, as far
as we can judge from the whole aim and connection of his
exhortation, is only this; he is desirous to prevent this
question of eating and drinking from becoming an obstacle
and cause of offence, but it by no means follows that the Gentile Christians, as long as they did not give any occasion for
excitement and anger to the Jewish Christians, should not go
on rejoicing in their own freedom. Although this is the
general mode in which the Apostle deals with such questions
as this he is all the more careful to do so in writing to the
Roman Church, as he is so desirous of doing away with everything which might be prejudicial to the unity of the Church, in
the mutual relations of the Jewish and Gentile Christians,
which, to attain that end, ought necessarily to be friendly ones.
The more solemn the truths which he had to present to the
Jewish Christians here, and even the more that he seemed to
give a preference to the Gentile Christians by thus combating

the claims and prejudices of the Jewish Christians—the more is he obliged to oppose the over self-appreciation of the Gentile Christians, and to remind them of the duties which they were to observe in their intercourse with the Jewish Christians. How energetically (xi. 18, μὴ ˙κατακαυχῶ τῶν κλάδων, &c.) he speaks of the arrogance which we may easily understand to have existed among the Gentiles, on account of the advantage which would seem to belong to them on account of their reception into the kingdom of God! We must judge also of the section, xiv. 13-23, from the same point of view.

There is besides an ancient authority in favour of the theory of the Judaistic character of the Roman Church, that of a commentator, whose works are added to those of Ambrose.* With the view of explaining the circumstances of the Roman Church from its establishment, ut rerum notitia habeatur plenior, principia earum requirere, the author of this Commentary remarks on the introduction to the Epistle to the Romans : Constat temporibus Apostolorum Judæos propterea; quod sub regno Romano agerent; Romæ habitasse, ex quibus hi, qui crediderant, tradiderunt Romanis, ut Christum profitentes legem servarent. Romani autem, audita fama virtutem Christi, faciles ad credendum fuerunt, utpote prudentes nec immerito prudentes, qui male inducti (so far as they were converted by Jewish Christians) statim correcti sunt (through the Epistle of the Apostle) et permanserunt in eo. Igitur ex Judæis credentes et improbe sentientes de Christo legem servandam, dicebant quasi non esset in Christo salus plena. Ideo negat illos spiritualem gratiam consecutos. Hi ergo ex Judæis ut datur intelligi,

---

* To the works of Ambrose (in the Benedict. Edition, Vol. iv. appendix. p. 33 f. there are added Commentaria in xiii. Epistolas Paulinas. Augustin, who cites a passage from this Commentary (contra duas Epist. Pelag. iv. 7), names as the author one Hilarius, who apparently was a deacon of the Roman Church in the time of the Roman Bishop Damasus in the middle of the 4th century. In any case the Commentary seems to be of very early date, and to have been written by an author acquainted with the circumstances of the Roman Church.

credentes Christo non accipiebant, Deum esse de Deo, putantes uni Deo adversam* quamobrem negat illos spiritualem Dei gratiam consecutos, ac per hoc confirmationem eis deesse. Hi (Jewish Christians of this kind), sunt, qui et Galatas subverterant, ut a traditione Apostolorum recederent, quibus ideo irascitur Apostolus, quia, docti bene, transducte fuerant, Romanis autem irasci non debuit, sed et laudare fidem illorum, quia nulla insignia virtutem videntes, nec aliquem Apostolorum, susceperant fidem Christi, ritu licet Judaico, in verbis potius quam in sensu, non enim expositum illis fuerat mysterium crucis Christi. Here also the author shows how completely he was aware of the most critical point of the distinction between Pauline and Jewish Christianity. The death of Christ possessed no essential importance for all Jewish Christians, as it is only mentioned once in the pseudo-Clementine Homilies, (Hom. iii. 19.) Propterea quibusdam advenientibus, qui recte crediderant, de edenda carne, et non edenda: (the author seems to refer not merely to the participation in the Gentile sacrificial feasts,) quæstiones fiebant, et utrumnam spes, quæ in Christi est sufficeret, aut et lex servanda esset. In the same reference, page 38, 39, to Romans i. 10 and 13, it is remarked: Carnalem illos sensum assecutos significat, quia sub nomine Christi non illa, quæ Christus docuerat, fuerant assecuti, sed ea, quæ fuerant a Judæis tradita. Si autem cupere citius venire, ut ab hac illos traditione abstraheret, et spirituale illis traderet donum. Hinc datur intelligi, superius non fidem illorum laudasse sed facilitatem et votum circa Christum: Christianos enim se profitentes, sub lege agebant simpliciter, sicut illis fuerat traditum. Propositum et votum secum ostendit quod quidum scire illos non ambigit per eos fratres, qui ab Hierusalem vel confinibus civitatibus causa suæ religionis ad urbem

---

* For a long period afterwards the Jewish representation of the person of Christ was the prevailing one in the Roman Church. The Unitarians, at whose head stood Artemon, relied for their doctrine on the ancient mode of teaching of the Roman Church, and the doctrine in the pseudo-Clementine Homilies, that Christ was God of God, was considered as in opposition to the Jewish Monotheism.

(this genuine Roman description of the city of Rome indicates with great certainty a Roman author of this Commentary), veniebant, sicut Aquila et Priscilla, votum ejus insinuantes Romanis. Cum enim sæpe vellet venire et prohiberetur, sic factum est, ut scriberet epistolam, ne diu in mala exercitatione detenti, non facile corrigerentur. Et fratres eos vocat, non solum, quia renati erant, sed et quia inter eos licet pauci qui recte sentirent.

The author, as is made clear by these last remarks, by no means holds the view which the more modern commentators suppose to have prevailed for a long period on this subject, namely, that the Apostle wrote to the Romans as to a Church on friendly terms with him. It ought rather to be considered that he wrote to them as to opponents, or as to those who now were to be brought for the first time to the true Gospel faith, and according to the contents of the Epistle itself, and the entire aspect of the circumstances of the Roman Church, this theory ought undoubtedly to be entertained.

The last two chapters of the Epistle deserve a special critical consideration. Manifold objections have been taken to them, and many things in them have been found strange. One of these is the Doxology, which occurs very abruptly not only at the end of chapter xvi, and after the concluding benediction, but which, according to ancient authority, was also placed at the end of chapter xiv: and the contents of chapter xvi. also, with regard to which, the remarks made by Origen cannot be left unnoticed, that the two last chapters are wanting in Marcion! *

Although this may be ascribed to the well-known arbitrary mutilation which, according to the assertion of the Fathers of the Church, Marcion allowed himself to make use of, with regard to the writings of the New Testament, yet the

---

* At the end of the Commentary on the Epistle to the Romans (Libr. x. 43) on the Doxology, xvi. 25-27, he says: Caput hoc, (the Doxology) Marcion a quo scripturæ evangelicæ atque apostolicæ interpolatæ sunt, de hac epistola penitus abstulit et non solum hoc, sed et ab eo loco, ubi scriptum est: Omne autem quod non est ex fide, peccatum est. (Romans xiv. 23), usque ad finem cuncta dissecuit.

24

supposition is in itself perfectly probable, that he may not have found these two chapters in the manuscripts of which he availed himself. But far more important than all the suspicions attached to isolated passages and urged with regard to them, is something else, which ought to be looked on from another standpoint, and in a more decided light than is generally done, namely, the contrast in which these two chapters stand to the whole character and contents of the Epistle. The section, xv. 1-13, contains nothing which the Apostle has not already said better than he does here in xii. 1, &c. To what purpose should he go back to exhortations already given, and that indeed in a tone which we do not perceive any where else in the whole Epistle; only on one theory can such a recurrence seem desirable, and that one in which everything is evidently referred to the Jewish Christians. How palpably the Messianic passage quoted, v. 3, is utilized in order to appeal to the whole Old Testament for a confirmation of the good doctrine which is given. How can we imagine that the Apostle, in an Epistle of such a nature, and after all that had passed on the subject, would make such a concession to the Jewish Christians as to call Jesus Christ a minister of the circumcision to confirm the promises of God made unto the Fathers.* The series of Old Testament passages commencing in verse 9, is also introduced for the purpose of pacifying the Jewish Christians as much as possible with regard to the admission of the Gentile Christians, which is here exclusively represented to the Jewish Christians as an act of grace, τὰ δὲ ἔθνη ὑπὲρ ἐλέους δοξάσαι τὸν θεὸν, verse 9. The

---

* Olshausen remarks on xv. 7, 8, the Apostle represents the relation of Christ to the Jews as a necessary one, in a peculiar manner; according to which God was obliged to send Christ to the Jews on account of his promises to the Fathers for his Truth's sake, but Christ was preached to the Gentiles out of mere pity and mercy. The whole of this representation must naturally be understood by κατ' ἄνθρωπον, for in chapter x. Paul reproves the Jews for thinking God owed them any grace. But is it then so natural to make the Apostle speak merely κατ' ἄνθρωπον, i.e. the exact opposite of what he had before said?

author may have had before him the passages ix. 24-29, but this similarity shows precisely the difference between the mode of argument in these passages. In chapter ix. 24, the Apostle is pursuing a masterly argument in connexion with the adoption of the Gentiles, and the justification of the consequent exclusion of a part of the Jews from the Old Testament prophecies; but here, in chapter xv. 9-12, there is a mere accumulation of Old Testament passages, according to which the Jewish Christians in their behaviour so little answered to the τὸ αὐτὸ φρονεῖν ἐν ἀλλήλοις κατὰ Χριστὸν Ἰησοῦν, and to the ὁμοθυμαδὸν ἐν ἑνὶ στόματι δοξάζειν τὸν θεὸν, καὶ πατέρα τοῦ κ. ἡ. I. Χρ., that they had again to be reminded that in the Old Testament itself the calling of the Gentiles to a common worship with the Jews had been proclaimed. Still more are we led to wonder in what follows, how the Apostle could think in this way to excuse himself for writing to the Romans. If indeed the Roman Christians, to whom the Epistle is addressed, were not merely so thoroughly well intentioned, but also so filled with all knowledge, and so fitted to admonish themselves, as the Apostle declares to be his conviction in verse 14, it would in fact be merely superfluous to have written such an Epistle. That πνευματικὸν χάρισμα also, i. 11, which the Apostle wished to impart to them in order to establish their belief, could not have been wanting to them, as spirituality is the very essence of such knowledge as he declares them to possess. It therefore could only be considered as a captatio benevolentiæ when he asserts this to his readers; and it must have been in the same frame of mind, that he called his Epistle in certain respects a great act of boldness, for which he had to excuse himself, and for which he did excuse himself, inasmuch as he had committed it as one who, on account of the grace of God which was given him, was enabled to put them in mind that he, as a minister of Jesus Christ to the Gentiles, was chosen to the priestly office as a preacher of the Gospel. He also refers to his mission to the Gentiles, and whilst (as he declares in

24 *

verse 18) he will not dare to write anything falsely of what Christ had wrought by him, of what in fact was not wrought by him but by others, his entire apology is aimed to meet the supposition that he had assumed to himself something to which he was not entitled in his preaching of the Gospel, whilst his principle had especially been not to "build upon another man's foundation," verse 20. But what caused him to endeavour to ward off the appearance of such an assumption is nothing else than the Epistle to the Roman Church itself, that τολμηρότερον ἔγραψα, to which he had been forced by the pressure of circumstances, and in the course of his missionary calling (23). When once this bold Epistle had been written, it seems to the author of chap. xv. that he can only remove the bad impression by representing the Apostle as declaring that he is aware he ought to keep within the limits of his missionary sphere, and that he had entered into these relations with the Roman Church in the efforts he made to keep within these limits. With this aim the Apostle (verse 19) mentions the sphere of his activity as extending from Jerusalem into Illyricum ; but how can we suppose that the Apostle himself dated the starting point of his apostolic course from Jerusalem, and then in order to establish this as certainly as possible, strangely enough included in the Jerusalem circuit, Arabia, Syria, and Cilicia, which countries, according to his own assurance (Gal. i. 22), he visited on his mission of preaching the Gospel ? Is not this too evidently a concession made to the Jewish Christians, according to whose views every preacher of the Gospel ought to start from Jerusalem only ? Commentators do not know what they should understand by this Illyricum— there is no trace whatever of any journey of Paul's in that rude, inhospitable land, which was then still inhabited by barbarians. One would rather suppose the Apostle to have mentioned, merely in an oratorical manner, the country at whose borders he had arrived in one of his Macedonian journeys, than that he adopted the political meaning which in common parlance the Romans gave to Illyricum, as the boundary between the East and West. By these two defined boundaries, Jerusalem and Illyricum, as well as by the expression πεπληρωκέναι τὸ εὐαγγέλιον Χριστοῦ (which can only be understood as stating that he had planted the Gospel in that whole district), the Apostle's task is represented as lying entirely in the East. This is referred to in what the Apostle says in continuation, that in " these parts," *i. e.* in the East, there was no more room to preach the Gospel, for all places were so filled with the Gospel preached by him, that he had nothing more to do. But we may well ask how the Apostle could say this ? and after all the attempts which have been made to explain it, no reasonable answer can be found. But is it not clear that the Apostle must only have represented his mission in the East, as so completely accomplished, in order from the threshold of his passage into the West, to make this step appear as one to which he was necessarily forced by the nature of the case, and thus obtain the best justification for writing to the Roman Christians ?

He stands now on the borders of the West, and can only in the West find a wider sphere of action ; but why does he here at the same time speak of being bound in honour only to preach the Gospel in those places where Christ was " not named ?" Why does he arrange to go to Rome, where for many years he had had a great desire to go, but yet only propose to accomplish this visit on his way to distant Spain ? Does it not seem as if there were here drawn a geographical line between two apostolic spheres of action, and that Rome and Italy with the countries near them were to be considered as an ecclesiastical province, in which the Apostle could only appear as a passing traveller, to avoid the suspicion of being officially in a strange territory ?

The author of chapter xv. represents Rome and Italy and the bordering countries as being under another apostolic authority whose sphere was extended far enough for the Apostle to be obliged to reach Spain in order to find a country in which he would be at liberty to act as an Apostle to the Gentiles, and was certain not to build on the foundation of others, nor to intrude into ground already appropriated. Although Gaul at that time was still an unconverted country, it was considered, as we find in the later traditions respecting its conversion, as a country so closely connected with, and belonging to the Roman Church, that the Apostle could merely pass through it on his journey. Only by a man so completely Pauline as the author of the Acts of the Apostles, could the Apostle be made to speak and act in such a manner as this—an author who has no scruple whatever in representing his Apostle as making all kinds of concessions to the Jewish Christians. In this way he is allowed to take his stand with the other Apostles, if not as one of equal pretensions, still as a preacher of the Gospel, or as a λειτουργὸς Ἰησοῦ Χριστοῦ εἰς τὰ ἔθνη, as he is called in verse 16, with an evident design to avoid calling him by the name of "Apostle," which name had not yet been granted to Paul by the Jewish Christians. All this, undoubtedly, was meant to serve as an apology for the τολμηρότερον ἔγραψα, but could it have entered into Paul's head to make any apology at all for his Epistle? If he really believed, according to the opinions ascribed to him (verse 20), that his field of work lay exclusively in the Gentile world, he would never have conceived the idea of writing an apostolic Epistle to the Romans. For what was it but an οἰκοδομεῖν εἰς ἀλλότριον θεμέλιον, for him to write an Epistle of such a nature as this Epistle to the Romans to a Jewish Christian Church not founded by him, and this indeed with the view of establishing it in Christianity by imparting to it such a πνευματικὸν χάρισμα, i. 11, or rather with the purpose of raising it from a state of dependence on Judaism to one of really evangelical Christianity? Whether this instruction was conveyed by word of mouth or by letter the essential principle was the same. In either case the Apostle would have acted in a manner which, judging by the principles enunciated by himself, could not

be brought into harmony with his apostolic mission. Is this probable ? and why does he express himself in this manner at the
conclusion of his Epistle, and not at the beginning ? Does not
the commencement of the Epistle come into complete antagonism with the end, when in the commencement the Apostle
does not express the least anxiety with regard to his justification in writing such an Epistle, but declares it to be his
duty to work without making any exception, and without regard to any distinction of nationality or cultivation, among
all peoples—the ἔθνη, to which idea he gives the widest meaning ? It is impossible that the Apostle should have fixed on
such an excuse for his Epistle. A further ground of doubt
with regard to the genuineness of these chapters, is the relation
in which they stand to the second Epistle to the Corinthians,
especially to the passage, x. 13-18. Here we have the original,
from which the unknown author has borrowed the material for
this supplement to the apostolic Epistle. Both extracts agree
so completely, both in contents and expression, that we can
only ask whether it is probable that the Apostle here makes
use of what he had at an earlier period said to the Corinthians, or whether another person has done so. As the subject
of the whole passage, 2 Cor. x. 13-18, is the καυχᾶσθαι, so the
Apostle in Romans xv. 17, speaks also of his καύχησις ἐν Χριστῷ
'Ιησοῦ, referring to τὰ πρὸς τὸν θεὸν, and as in 2 Cor. xii. 12,
he says, τὰ σημεῖα τοῦ ἀποστόλου κατειργάσθη ἐν σημείοις καὶ
τέρασι καὶ δυνάμεσι, so in Rom. xv. 18, he will not dare to say
anything respecting ὧν οὐ κατειργάσατο Χριστὸς δι' ἐμοῦ λόγῳ
καὶ ἔργῳ (compare 2 Cor. x. 11) ἐν δυνάμει σημείων καὶ τεράτων,
ἐν δυνάμει πνεύματος ἁγίου. The chief point of the parallel,
however, lies in Romans xv. 20, where, from the words of the
Apostle that he is φιλοτιμούμενος εὐαγγελίζεσθαι οὐχ ὅπου
ὠνομάσθη Χριστὸς ἵνα μὴ ἐπ' ἀλλότριον θεμέλιον οἰκοδομῶ, it is
very clearly shown that what he lays down as his rule, 2 Cor.
x. 16, εἰς τὰ ὑπερέκεινα ὑμῶν οὐκ ἐν ἀλλοτρίῳ κανόνι εἰς τὰ ἕτοιμα
καυχήσασθαι, or as he, in verse 15, says in the same sense, οὐ

καυχᾶσθαι ἐν ἀλλοτρίοις κόποις. In this last passage, the
Apostle speaks of his καυχᾶσθαι, founded on the objective
success of his labours, in opposition to the vain, empty, aimless,
subjective, arbitrary καυχᾶσθαι of his opponents, which is only
a καυχᾶσθαι ἐν ἀλλοτρίοις κόποις. They make the labours of
other men the subject of their own boasting—selfishly intrude
on his apostolic province, appropriate to themselves what he
had achieved in the preaching of the Gospel, and give themselves out to be the peculiar founders of the Corinthian Church,
just as if he had never been in Corinth at all.   In opposition
to this, he declares that it is not his way to boast of himself at
the expense of others, as where others had already laboured to
achieve work different from his, he always adhered to his rule to
remain within the limits of the sphere of action allotted to him
by God, and hopes through the increase of faith in the Corinthian Church to become so great in his own line that he may
even have an abundance, so that he may preach the Gospel even
beyond Corinth, without boasting "in another man's line made
ready to his hand."   The Apostle, in Romans xv. applies the
rule for his apostolic labours in such a manner that he declares
himself as only justified in going to Rome because he would
have to pass through it on his journey.   He even confesses,
that he shall go to Rome only as a passing visitor, in order that
he may have the company of the Romans on his further journey, and be brought on his way by them, as soon at least as
he had enjoyed their company as much as was possible under
the circumstances, verse 24 (—ἐὰν ὑμῶν πρῶτον ἀπὸ μέρους
ἐμπλησθῶ.)*   He would also only go to Rome in order that he
might continue his journey further—but whither then did he
intend to travel?   In order to go as far as possible from the
neighbourhood of Rome he intended to go to Spain.   This
journey of the Apostle into Spain, is in fact one of the most
improbable things that has ever been introduced into the his-

---

* "Non quantum vellem, sed quantum licebit," as Grotius strikingly puts the
sense of this passage.

tory of his life. No one else says anything about it, and if this passage is the only testimony in favour of its occurrence, nothing can be more doubtful than the supposition that the Apostle ever entertained the idea of such a journey. We must consider what motive he could have had for such an intention. Because the Apostle had so filled the East with his preaching, that he could not remain in it without being idle, and because if he went to Rome he would be in a place where he could not remain without building on another man's foundation, nothing remained but that he should go to Spain! How completely without motive all this is. Why then had he so great a desire to go to Rome, if, as he himself is obliged to confess, he has nothing at all to do there, but must appear as a stranger, and even more as perhaps as an unwelcome guest? As the author of chapter xv. does not give a very clear idea of this journey into Spain, we may explain his composition by the original passage in the Epistle to the Corinthians and thus get at the exact truth of the matter. The Apostle writes to the Corinthians, x. 15, 16, "I hope εἰς τὰ ὑπερέκεινα ὑμῶν εὐαγγελί-ζεσθαι." He speaks here also of his intention, to extend his missionary journey still further, and to preach the Gospel in the countries lying beyond Corinth and Achaia. If the word ὑπερέκεινα, which indicates something lying beyond, more exactly than the word ἐπέκεινα, and allows so wide a sphere of action, that it is quite as admissible for us to think of a country at a distance, as of a nearer one, we may very easily assume that the meaning of this ὑπερέκεινα may most properly be attached to the idea of Spain, and this in agreement with the interests of the apostolic authority, which extending already to Rome and Italy, would claim as wide a missionary sphere as possible. If we cannot avoid perceiving, from the dependence of the εἰς τὰ ὑπερέκεινα εὐαγγελίζεσθαι, on the πορεύεσθαι εἰς τὴν Σπανίαν, that the author of chapter xv, had the second Epistle to the Corinthians before him, and that he utilized in favour of the Judaizing tendency the principle enunciated by the Apostle him-

self, (from which standpoint this heterogeneous addition to the
Epistle to the Romans must be considered,) verses 25-27 contain a further proof of this dependence. The subject here
treated of is the journey of the Apostle to Jerusalem, for the
purpose of transmitting the contribution made in Macedonia
and Achaia, for the Christians of that city ; and this is spoken
of in the same manner as the Apostle speaks of it himself in
2 Cor. ; and the reason for this duty reminds us of the κοινωνία
which the Christians of those churches and of the one at Jerusalem concluded amongst themselves, 2 Cor. viii. 13, 14, ix.
12, &c.* How clearly is the Jewish Christian interest of the
author of chap. xv. expressed, when he recommends this contribution as only a labour of Christian love, and represents it
as a token of thankfulness from the Gentile Christians, which
they have to show, since they are allowed by the Jerusalem
Christians to participate in the πνευματικὰ, the good gifts of
Christianity. On this subject the Apostle says nothing in
those passages of his Epistle in which this idea, if he had ever
entertained it, must have been present to his mind, he does
not even attach this sense to the κοινωνία of which he speaks ;
there is not in any way the least hint, that he had ever thought
of the Church at Jerusalem as the Mother Church, as sustaining
such a relation to the Gentile Christian Churches, but only that
it introduced the Gospel to them. It would not accord with the
independence of which he makes so great a point with so much
emphasis in his preaching of the Gospel, if he were here to
represent the Christian blessings which through him had fallen

---

* The dependence on 1 and 2 Corinthians is especially obvious in Romans xv.
27, where ὀφειλέται αὐτῶν εἰσιν, εἰ γὰρ τοῖς πνευματικοῖς, &c., is only another
phase of the thought in 1 Cor. ix. 11 : εἰ ἡμεῖς ὑμῖν τὰ πνευματικὰ ἐσπείραμεν.
The author also depends on 2 Cor. ix. 6, for here also there is mention made of a
σπείρειν and θερίξειν. There is also obvious here an agreement in expression as
is generally the case with dependent passages of this kind. Compare διακονεῖν
τοῖς ἁγίους, Romans xv. 25, and διακονία εἰς τοὺς ἁγίους, 2 Cor. ix. 1, κοινωνία
εἰς τοὺς πτωχοὺς τῶν ἁγίων ἐν Ἱερ. Romans xv. 26, and κοινωνία τῆς διακονίας
τῆς εἰς τοὺς ἁγίους, 2 Cor. viii. 4. Also the expression εὐλογία, Romans xv. 29,
is a repetition, 2 Cor. ix. 5.

to the share of these Churches, as only having been conferred on them by the Church at Jerusalem. The matter could only have been represented in this manner, by an author of so different a stamp as the author of chapter xv., where with regard to the dangers which threatened the Apostle in Judea, he is spoken of in a manner which bears a strong analogy to the method employed by the author of the Acts of the Apostles, xx. 22.

Finally, these last chapters on which such doubt must be cast when we look at them with reference to the preceding part of the Epistle, bear the stamp of a later origin. The long series of persons whom the Apostle greets has quite the appearance of a catalogue of those who at that time were recognized as the notabilia of the most ancient Roman Church. As the relation of the Apostle Paul to the Roman Church became afterwards a subject of party strife, it would seem to be the interest of a follower of Paul to give a proof by such a document as this, that the Apostle already stood in very near and confidential connection with the best known members of the first Church, and that many among those persons had won special praise from the Apostle. This is particularly expressed. We may quote verse 4, οἵτινες ὑπὲρ τῆς ψυχῆς μοῦ τὸν ἑαυτῶν τράχηλον ὑπέθηκαν, and verse 6, ἥτις πολλὰ ἐκοπίασεν εἰς ἡμᾶς. In order to make the union of the Apostle with these most ancient Roman Christians more immediately apparent, mention is repeatedly made of the relations which the Apostle had among them ; verse 7, τοὺς συγγενεῖς μου ; verse 11, τὸν συγγενῆ μου. Also verse 13, τὴν μητέρα αὐτοῦ καὶ ἐμοῦ, the idea of relationship is at least brought forward as far as the expression goes. If we accept verse 21, where amongst those greeted the συγγενεῖς of the Apostle are named, we may justly ask in what other passage of his genuine Epistles does the Apostle speak so much of his relations ? Besides, how suspicious is the account and description of some of these persons ? Aquila and Priscilla, according to 1 Cor. xvi. 19, are in Ephesus, according to Romans xvi. 3, they are in Rome. It is possible that in the not very long interval between the composition of these two Epistles they may have gone again from Ephesus to Rome ; but this is only a mere possibility, of which there is no further proof. Besides this there are many suspicious things in this chapter, and the supposition is forced upon us that they are only named because they are of course obliged to be placed at the head of such a catalogue as this, in pursuance of the design entertained by the author of enumerating the most ancient Roman Christians who were in close connection with the Apostle.

It is justly remarked* that the words (1 Cor. xvi. 19) added to the mention of Aquila and Priscilla, σὺν τῇ κατ' οἶκον αὐτῶν ἐκκλησίᾳ, are precisely the same as those in Romans xvi. 5, καὶ τὴν κατ' οἶκον αὐτῶν ἐκκλησιάν. The question also presents itself, " How did Epanetus, the beloved of Paul, who is boasted of as the first-fruits of the Christians in Asia (verse 5) come to Rome ?" This is evidently taken from the conclusion of the first Epistle to the Corinthians, where (verse 15) it is said of Stephanas, ὅτι ἐστὶν ἀπαρχὴ τῆς 'Αχαΐας. This is now transferred to one of the Roman Christians, only instead of in Αχαΐας, it is placed in 'Ασίας, which reading some manuscripts give, in Romans xvi. 15, for the honour of this ἀπαρχὴ can only be applied to one person. But 'Απαρχὴ 'Ιταλίας, as we may imagine, cannot well be said, as this Epanetus as ἀπαρχὴ must have been converted by the Apostle as Stephanas was (1 Cor. xv. 15) ; and Andronicus and Junia were converted to Christianity even before the conversion of the Apostle himself (verse 7). But all the more, these two ancient Roman Christians must be placed at least as συγγενείς, in the nearest connection with the Apostle, as they are also made to have held friendly relations to the elder Apostles as ἐπίσημοι ἐν τοῖς ἀποστολοις. But how they could have been called his συναιχ-

---

* D. Schulz, Theol. Stud. und Kritik. page 609. Schulz urges more reasons against chap. xv. in his Review of Eichhorn's and de Wette's " Einleitung," and thinks that if it must be considered as written by Paul, it is more likely to be written by him to Ephesus than to Rome.

μάλωτοι, at a time when the Apostle was no longer remaining in a lengthy imprisonment, (for the foregoing φυλακαὶ, 2 Cor. vi. 5, xi. 23, could not have involved such a predicate) is inexplicable, but it becomes very clear if placed at a later period when greater value would be laid on such a predicate. That in such a connection as this there follows a section respecting the Judaising false teachers, is quite in harmony with our theory, as the writer, placing himself in the person of the Apostle, would consider an argument against such opponents as the chief criterion of an Epistle of Paul. This part of the Epistle contains nothing characteristic in its details, but is Pauline only in the most general way with regard to what it says of the false teachers. On the other hand, certain emphatic expressions, as verse 20, θεὸς συντρίψει τὸν σατανᾶν ὑπὸ τοὺς πόδας ὑμῶν, verse 18, δουλεύουσι τῇ ἑαυτῶν κοιλίᾳ, compare Phil. iii. 19, give indications of an ambiguous tone. To this category belongs the expression (ver. 4) ὑπὲρ τῆς ψυχῆς μου τὸν ἑαυτῶν τράγηλον ὑπέθηκαν.

If we add to this the abrupt way in which verses 17-20 are introduced between the greetings, verse 1-16, and 21-24, and how uncertain the position of the concluding doxology is, we certainly possess sufficient grounds for considering this chapter as not written by Paul. The criticism of the last chapters can only be concluded by saying that they must be attributed to a disciple of Paul, who, in the spirit of the author of the Acts of the Apostles, in the interest of peace and harmony, wished to replace the keen anti-Judaism of the Apostle by a milder and more accommodating influence in favour of the Judaizers.

END OF VOL I.

SECOND PART.

THE EPISTLES OF THE APOSTLE PAUL.

SECOND CLASS OF THE PAULINE EPISTLES.

THE EPISTLES TO THE EPHESIANS, COLOSSIANS, PHILIPPIANS, TO
PHILEMON, AND TO THE THESSALONIANS.

THE EPISTLES OF THE APOSTLE PAUL.

FOURTH CHAPTER.

THE EPISTLES TO THE EPHESIANS AND TO THE COLOSSIANS.

THE Pauline origin of the Epistle to the Ephesians has only recently been challenged; yet, with the exception of the Pastorals, there is none of the shorter Pauline Epistles the genuineness of which is more questionable. The bold and original method of criticism which Schleiermacher applied to the First Epistle to Timothy was adopted by De Wette in his treatment of the Epistle to the Ephesians; by the same process, namely, by demonstrating its dependence upon another work, he raised the gravest doubts as to its authentic apostolic origin. And the verdict of criticism on this Epistle,[1] which De Wette was the first to pronounce, is, that it is nothing but a rhetorical expansion of the Epistle to the Colossians. It is of no avail to insist upon the contrast between the flowing style and copious language of this Epistle, and the thoughtful conciseness of that to the Colossians; on the contrary, this very difference, when considered along with those other elements in our Epistle which certainly cannot belong to the apostle, brings us very easily to the conclusion that it was formed upon the model of the other. In the same way, as Schleiermacher showed, the First Epistle to Timothy resulted from a free use of materials borrowed from the other two pastoral

[1] De Wette's judgment was still wavering in the fourth edition of his Einleitung in das N. T. 1842 ; but in the Kurze Erklärung des Epheserbriefs, 1843, p. 79 (p. 89 in 2d Edition), we find him pronouncing distinctly for its spuriousness.

A

Epistles. This assertion of criticism has indeed given great offence, and a world of trouble has been expended in seeking to prove the Epistle genuine;[1] but the discovery once made was not one that could be proved either untrue or unimportant; and it only remains to be seen whether what happened in the case of the pastoral Epistles will happen here, that the doubts of criticism, once aroused by the proof of such a relation existing between the two writings, will not endanger only one of them, but draw both the Epistles so connected into the same condemnation.

The relation between the two Epistles is certainly striking enough,[2] and by the nearly unanimous judgment of critics and interpreters[3] it is the Epistle to the Ephesians, and not that to the Colossians, which must be held to be dependent on the other. How is it then, if this Epistle be genuine, that the apostle, who is not in general at any loss for ideas, writes to two different churches not far separate from each other, under the same circumstances, and, as is almost universally supposed, at the same time, two letters so very like each other? The resemblance which this Epistle bears to that to the Colossians in many of its arguments, ways of thinking, and expressions, is sought to be explained by

---

[1] This is done by Rückert in a very boisterous manner; Der Brief Pauli an die Eph., 1834, p. 303 *sq.* "Only a man such as Paul was can be the author of this Epistle, and if it was not he, point out to me the spirit in that age that was his peer. It is impossible that he can have passed over the world and left no trace behind. I ask then, who was he, and where? In the ranks of the imitators, the compilers, or the quacks, we dare not seek him; where then?"

Critical doubts then, it appears, may be simply disposed of even now-a-days with declamations like this. The author of a canonical Epistle, such writers imagine, must either have been an apostle, or one of the most despicable class of men, "the botchers, forgers, and wooden-headed compilers" (p. 299); or, if he were not a compiler, he must have been known to us by reputation, since he could not have gone through the world without leaving his mark on history. But is not this product of his genius itself a sufficient trace of his existence?

[2] Compare the tabulated comparison of the passages given by De Wette in his Einleitung, p. 259, and the Commentary on the Epistle, p. 79. (Edition of 1847, p. 89.)

[3] The only exception here is Mayerhof, Der Brief an die Colosser, etc. (The Epistle to the Colossians critically examined, with special reference to the three Pastoral Epistles, 1838.)

supposing that Paul had been writing that Epistle a short time before, and that the direction of thought induced by his controversy with the sects there combated was still prevailing in his mind ; hence, it is further said, it is clear that he must have written the Epistle to the Colossians the first of the two. This is the account of the matter given by Neander,[1] and to the same purpose Harless says :[2] " A writing directed by the apostle to a second body of Christians, just after he had discharged the mournful duty to which he saw himself compelled, of defending the infinite riches of the wisdom of God against the inroads of poor human wisdom, this Epistle naturally exhibits much greater play and movement in the treatment of its materials, while at the same time a multitude of similarities clearly demonstrate its kinship with that which he had just composed." In a word, then, the apostle wrote these two Epistles at the same time ; this is the solution of the difficulty with which we are presented. But what, we cannot help inquiring, could induce the apostle, after finishing the Epistle to the Colossians, to continue writing in the same attitude of thought, and to compose another letter, which was not particularly called for, in addition to the first ? Is it the apostle's habit to write such letters ? And, if the only way to account for the character of this Epistle be to assume that it was intended as a circular in which Paul, as the apostle of the Gentiles, addressed himself to all the Gentile Christians of those regions, just because they were Christians, and in which he condescended to no special circumstances, but dealt with the one great interest which was common to them all, the indisputable efficacy of the gospel among the heathen,[3]—what does this amount to, but a statement of the great peculiarity of our Epistle, that the stamp of individuality, the colour, form, and manner, which the genuine apostolic Epistles carry on their front, are wanting here ? Yet in fact, the assumption we have mentioned, not only does not explain the actual facts

---

[1] Planting and Training, i. 329.
[2] Comm. über den Br. Pauli an die Eph., 1834, Einleitung, S. 39.
[3] Neander, *ubi supra*.

of the case as they lie before our eyes ; it is but another attempt
to deny these facts. The peculiar phenomena presented to us in
the relation of these two Epistles are by no means adequately
described by speaking of mere points of resemblance, or even of
a multitude of points of resemblance. The whole contents of the
two Epistles are substantially the same, and what are called points
of resemblance are not merely chance repetitions of his former
words, such as the writer might employ unconsciously. On the
contrary, we find whole sentences repeated word for word, or with
such alterations as clearly betray that the original was present to
the writer's mind. And this is the case, whether we assume, on
the one hand, that the Epistle to the Colossians was written first,
and that its shorter and conciser contents were extended in that to
the Ephesians, or that the lengthier contents of the Epistle to the
Ephesians were drawn upon, and a sort of abstract of them produced
in the Epistle to the Colossians. In either case, what we have
before us is a reproduction of the one Epistle in the other, such as
cannot be explained by any fortuitous and unconscious coincidence
of thought, but only by a distinct intention on the part of the
writer of one of these Epistles to give a more or less full recast of
the other ; and even though interpreters and critics should succeed,
while defending the Epistles' genuineness in demonstrating that there
is a difference between the two letters as well as an agreement, it
will be found that whatever can be made good in this direction
will not tell in favour of the Epistle to the Ephesians, but of that
to the Colossians. It is only the latter which, in addition to the
general contents that are common to both, contains reference to
peculiar local and individual circumstances, such as the letters of
the apostle generally present, and so provides against total identity
with the other Epistle. Such being the case, it is not to be
wondered at that a recent critic has sought to solve the problem,
not by assuming the contemporaneousness of the two Epistles, but
in a totally different way. That the Epistles were written at the
same time, says Schneckenburger,[1] " would explain a general

---

[1] Beiträge zur Einleitung ins N. T., 1832, p. 141 *sq.*

correspondence of ideas, but not such a similarity as we have here in details, nor what I must almost call such a mechanical use of materials.   Nor is there any probable reason for Paul's sending two letters of so similar contents to the same district, and about the same time." Schneckenburger's opinion is, therefore, that the Epistle to the Ephesians (this Epistle is here put first, as that to the Colossians by the advocates of the other view) must have been before the apostle's eyes when he composed the Colossian Epistle. Why should it appear so improbable that when the occasion arose for writing to the Colossians, the apostle took up the earlier letter he had sent to the same region ?   There is no need to think of a scroll or draught of that letter, but it is easy to suppose, that having drawn out a sort of summary of Christian doctrine and morals for the use of his friends in Asia Minor, either he himself took a copy of it with a view to future use in the service of similar inquirers, or, if he did not do so, that his amanuenses copied it for their own improvement and instruction.   Then when he had to write to the Colossians, he may have taken up that earlier letter, and so certain similarities of arrangement and expression may have found their way quite naturally into the letter he was writing.   But the apostle would never have copied himself in this manner, nor does this hypothesis, any more than the other, escape from the objection that the agreement of the two Epistles is not the result of chance, but is certainly intentional.   And to whom can this intention be imputed with the greater likelihood ? Shall we impute it to the apostle ?   But we can conceive no reason why he should have appeared on this occasion as a re-writer of his own letters.   Shall we not rather impute it to another man, who, by the very fact of his conceiving the idea of personating the apostle, and writing letters in his name, showed that he had some special end to serve, and who thought, perhaps, the better to further his end by putting in circulation two editions of one letter ?

In addition to these considerations regarding the external form of the Epistle, we have further to consider that if it was actually addressed to the Ephesians, it cannot possibly have been written by Paul. They were a church in the midst of which he had lived for a considerable time, and with which he was intimately acquainted; and how could he write to them as to a church that was strange to him, and speak of their faith as a thing he had learned about through others? (Cf. i. 15.) The title and address which are found in the text (i. 1) are indeed doubtful; but even in the case that the Epistle was not an epistle to the Ephesians, even though the local address were wanting altogether, or ran thus, "To the Laodiceans," this indistinctness and the uncertainty of the destination (which even in the last case is not removed), would of themselves afford a presumption against the Pauline origin of the Epistle.

If now we turn to the contents of the Epistle, or rather of the two Epistles,—for their contents are so essentially the same that they cannot well be distinguished,—and seek for internal evidence of their Pauline character, we shall meet here also with much that is peculiar. First of all, it strikes us as strange that in both Epistles the eye of the writer is directed chiefly to the transcendental regions of the spirit-world; and there is an effort visible throughout to magnify Christ on the side of his higher dignity by predicates borrowed from this supersensuous domain. The nearest approach to the theology of Paul is in the passage, Eph. i. 20 *sq.*, where it is said of Christ, that God raised him from the dead, and that he set himself at his right hand in the heavenly places, ὑπεράνω πάσης ἀρχῆς καὶ ἐξουσίας καὶ δυνάμεως καὶ κυριότητος, καὶ παντὸς ὀνόματος ὀνομαζομένου οὐ μόνον ἐν τῷ αἰῶνι τούτῳ, ἀλλὰ καὶ ἐν τῷ μέλλοντι, καὶ πάντα ὑπέταξεν ὑπὸ τοὺς πόδας αὐτοῦ. This coincides with the apostle's conception of Christ's exaltation, who subjects everything to himself till the process reaches its highest stage, 1 Cor. xv. 24. But in which of the principal Epistles of Paul do we find those ἐπουράνια (cf. iii. 10), those regions of the supernatural world, classified as they are here, and in Colossians i. 16, 17,[1] according to the different spirits

---

[1] In Rom. viii. 38, only ἀρχαί and ἄγγελοι are spoken of, but nowhere do we find with Paul the θρόνοι and κυριότητες of this passage; and still less, what is

which, rising step by step, one above the other, severally inhabit them; and where do we find Christ placed, as he is here, at the head of the whole system of the spirit-world? The Christology of these two Epistles, however, does not confine itself to the contemplation of the dignity of Christ from beneath upwards, as shown in his exaltation; it also regards Christ as having been from the beginning the absolute principle of all existence. For it is asserted of him (Col. i. 15) that he is the likeness of the invisible God, the first-born of the whole creation, because in him all things were created, the visible and the invisible, whether they be thrones, or dominions, or principalities, or powers. Everything was created through him and to him (in him, that is, is the final purpose in which every created thing finds its realization), and he is before all, and all things subsist in him. To him, then, as the creative principle of everything existing, there is attributed absolute pre-existence. This is found explicitly only in the Epistle to the Colossians; but since that to the Ephesians presupposes the other, there can be no doubt that the Christology of both is in the main the same. It is true that we find certain hints of similar views in the homologoumena of the Apostle, but they are no more than hints, the meaning of which is open to question; while here, on the contrary, the absolute pre-mundane existence is the dominating idea, the pervading element within which the whole thought of these Epistles moves. Christ is the centre of the entire spirit-realm; his activity is represented as bearing chiefly on the invisible and supersensuous world, or at least as comprehending heavenly and earthly things, the visible and the invisible, at once and in the same degree. For this not only is there no analogy in Paul's writings, but we are here transported to a circle of ideas which belongs to a totally different historical era, viz., to the period of

evidently implied in these two passages above, such regular gradations of rank. It is true that in 1 Cor. xv. 24, Paul says of Christ that he καταργήσῃ πᾶσαν ἀρχὴν καὶ πᾶσαν ἐξουσίαν καὶ δύναμιν, but it is impossible to find here the different classes of an angelic hierarchy, and so this passage should not be used as a parallel.

Gnosticism. The properties which the Gnostics distributed in their myths among a number of æons, all of whom always resolve themselves again into the same central conception, are here united in the one Christ, in whom, as in the Gnostic Nous or Monogenes, the supreme and absolute God unfolds and reveals his secret essence, as the εἰκὼν τοῦ Θεοῦ τοῦ ἀοράτου, the πρωτότοκος πάσης κτίσεως, the highest principle of all life and being. In him, as on the one hand αὐτός ἐστι πρὸ πάντων, so on the other, ἐκτίσθη τὰ πάντα, καὶ τὰ πάντα ἐν αὐτῷ συνέστηκε, Col. i. 15 sq., for he is the Χριστός, who is τὰ πάντα καὶ ἐν πᾶσι, Col. iii. 11.[1]

The Gnostic systems rest upon the root idea that all spiritual

---

[1] According to the doctrine of the Valentinians, Christ sent out of the pleroma the Soter, ἐνδόντος αὐτῷ πᾶσαν τὴν δύναμιν τοῦ πατρὸς καὶ πᾶν ὑπ' ἐξουσίαν παραδόντος καὶ τῶν αἰώνων δὲ ὁμοίως, ὅπως ἐν αὐτῷ τὰ πάντα κτισθῇ τὰ ὁρατὰ καὶ τὰ ἀόρατα, θρόνοι, θεότητες, κυριότητες, Iren. Adv. Haer. i. 4, 5. Theodoret (Haer. Fabb. i. 7) mentions the same as the doctrine of the Valentinians, namely, that Christ sent the Redeemer Jesus, ὥστε ἐν αὐτῷ κτισθῆναι καὶ τὰ ὁρατὰ καὶ τὰ ἀόρατα, καὶ θρόνους, καὶ κυριότητας, καὶ θεότητας, ὡς αὐτοὶ λέγουσι. It is usually assumed that the Valentinians derived these representations and expressions from the Epistle to the Colossians; but how is it that this letter itself answered so closely to the forms of their thought and expression? We see from Iren. i. 3, 4, how they used other passages of these two Epistles for their own purposes, ὑπὸ Παύλου φανερῶς εἰρῆσθαι λέγουσι· καὶ αὐτός ἐστι τὰ πάντα (Col. iii. 11), καὶ πάλιν (Col. ii. 9) ἐν αὐτῷ κατοικεῖ πᾶν τὸ πλήρωμα τῆς θεότητος, καὶ τὸ ἀνακεφαλαιώσασθαι τὰ πάντα ἐν τῷ Χριστῷ διὰ τοῦ Θεοῦ (Eph. i. 10) ἑρμηνεύουσιν εἰρῆσθαι, καὶ εἴ τινα ἄλλα. It may very reasonably be supposed that the later Valentinians, whom Irenaeus is refuting, appealed to these passages in support of their doctrines, but that the agreement of these passages with their doctrines results from the fact that the circle in which those Epistles arose was permeated by similar Gnostic ideas. The first beginnings of Christian speculation coincided, as we know, with the beginnings of Gnosis, and thus Gnosis, when developing itself, and giving its peculiar impulse to Christian speculation, gave currency to many representations and expressions which, though springing from the soil of Gnosticism, and though containing Gnostic elements, yet were not offensive to the unprejudiced Christian consciousness. Even then, however, every speculation was not received equally as Christian; it is remarkable that the Epistle to the Colossians speaks of κυριότητες, but not of θεότητες, an idea at which the Valentinians took no offence. There can be no doubt that all these expressions, ἀρχαί, ἐξουσίαι, θρόνοι, κυριότητες, θεότητες, αἰῶνες, πλήρωμα, etc., belong to a circle where speculation about the spirit-world was carried on with peculiar zest; but where did this interest arise before Gnosticism began to take form? And with what other direction of thought is it more closely and more naturally connected than with the Gnostic?

life which has proceeded from the supreme God has to return to its original unity, and to be taken back again into the absolute principle, so that every discord which has arisen shall be resolved into harmony. Thus in these Epistles Christ's work is mainly that of restoring, bringing back, and making unity; the final purpose of it is, εἰς οἰκονομίαν τοῦ πληρώματος τῶν καιρῶν (*i.e.* according to the idea of a religious dispensation developing itself in the fulness of the times, that is, in definite epochs, in a series of momenta mutually conditioning each other), ἀνακεφαλαιώσασθαι τὰ πάντα ἐν τῷ Χριστῷ, Eph. i. 10, καὶ δι᾽ αὐτοῦ ἀποκαταλλάξαι τὰ πάντα εἰς αὐτόν, Col. i. 20. From this point of view both Epistles lay special weight on the consideration that Christ is, in respect of his death also, εἰρήνη ἡμῶν, ὁ ποιήσας τὰ ἀμφότερα ἕν, Eph. ii. 14, the εἰρηνοποιήσας, and that εἴτε τὰ ἐπὶ τῆς γῆς, εἴτε τὰ ἐν τοῖς οὐρανοῖς, Col. i. 20. It is in the light of this lofty and comprehensive conception that the work of Christ is here contemplated, *i.e.* as a mediation and atonement whose effects extend to the whole universe. And though it may be possible to harmonize this conception with the Pauline Christology and doctrine of atonement, yet it is certain that with Paul these ideas never assume the prominence which they have here. We have, therefore, good grounds for asserting that in these Epistles we are presented with a new and peculiar circle of ideas which is distinctly later than that of the Pauline Epistles. It is a transcendental region, into which Paul did look out now and then, but of which he had no definite views, and which he never introduced into his Epistles from a taste for metaphysical speculation.

As even the Christology of these letters bears unmistakably the impress of Gnosticism, we meet also with other Gnostic conceptions and modes of representation. Especially does that πλήρωμα, which holds so prominent a place in both Epistles, naturally suggest to us the Pleroma of the Gnostics. Indeed the two are so intimately connected, that the one can only be explained by the other. The Gnostic Pleroma is not the absolute itself; it is that in which the absolute displays itself as absolute, realizes the conception of itself, and fills itself with its own definite contents. According to the doctrine of the Valentinians, the Bythos, the original divine source, is not in and of itself the Pleroma, but only in so far as it is thought as the sum of the aeons by which it is filled. " These thirty aeons," says Irenaeus (i. 1. 3), " as the Valentinian doctrine of aeons represents them, are τὸ ἀόρατον καὶ πνευματικὸν κατ᾽ αὐτοὺς πλήρωμα, which is divided into an Ogdoas, a Dekas, and a Dodekas." The Logos, who is produced by the Nous or Monogenes, is called the ἀρχὴ καὶ μόρφωσις παντὸς τοῦ πληρώματος, that is, the being in whom the Pleroma first receives its form, in whom the conception of it is defined ; since the Logos, in connexion with Ζωὴ as his σύζυγος, is the πατὴρ πάντων τῶν μετ᾽ αὐτοῦ ἐσομένων, and contains in his own nature the whole Pleroma, as he is himself only the more definite and more realized form of the Nous or Monogenes. The supreme and absolute God is not therefore himself the Pleroma, but has it in himself as his contents.[1]

Now this is just the conception of the Pleroma which we find in both our Epistles ; the only difference is that there is no express mention here of a plurality of aeons as the complement of the pleroma, and that not the supreme God himself, but Christ, is the pleroma, since only in Christ does the self-existent God emerge from his abstract being, and unfold himself to the fulness of concrete life. For ἐν αὐτῷ, it is said, Col. i. 19, εὐδόκησε (ὁ Θεὸς), πᾶν τὸ πλήρωμα κατοικῆσαι. Col. ii. 9 : ἐν αὐτῷ κατοικεῖ πᾶν τὸ πλήρωμα τῆς θεότητος σωματικῶς, καί ἐστε ἐν αὐτῷ πεπληρωμένοι· ὅς ἐστιν ἡ κεφαλὴ πάσης ἀρχῆς καὶ ἐξουσίας. Eph. i. 22, 23 : αὐτὸν ἔδωκε κεφαλὴν ὑπὲρ πάντα τῇ ἐκκλησίᾳ, ἥτις ἐστι τὸ σῶμα αὐτοῦ, τὸ πλήρωμα τοῦ τὰ πάντα ἐν πᾶσι πληρουμένου. Eph. iii. 19 : Γνῶναι . . . τὴν ἀγάπην τοῦ Χριστοῦ, ἵνα πληρωθῆτε εἰς πᾶν τὸ πλήρωμα τοῦ Θεοῦ. Eph. iv. 13 : τὸ πλήρωμα τοῦ Χριστοῦ.

---

[1] Compare Iren. ii. 1 ; i. 2 : Deus—solus pater et continens omnia.—Quemadmodum enim poterit super hunc alia plenitudo aut initium aut potestas aut alius Deus esse, cum oporteat Deum, horum omnium pleroma, in immenso omnia circumtenere et circumteneri a nemine.

Here we observe a further remarkable agreement. According to the doctrine of the Valentinians the aeons, who together make up the Pleroma, are divided into male and female, and form the so-called syzygies, pairs bound together as if in marriage. The propator is united in syzygy with his ἔννοια (the thought of himself, his self-consciousness) ; in the same way, the Monogenes, or Nous, with Aletheia, the Logos with Zoē, the Anthropos with Ecclesia. From these the other aeons proceeded, also as syzygies. In the same way Christ forms, according to the Epistle to the Ephesians, a syzygy with the Church. Christ is indeed the head of the Church, but, in the same way, the man is the head of the woman, and husbands are exhorted to love their wives, just as Christ also loved the Church, and gave himself for her, that he might sanctify her to himself, and present her glorious to himself without spot or blemish, Eph. v. 23 *sq.* This is the great μυστήριον of which the writer of the Epistle speaks in reference to Christ and the Church (ver. 32), that she is his wife, as it were, united to him in marriage. In virtue of this relationship the conception of the pleroma is transferred to her also. As Christ is the πλήρωμα, so also is the Church ; that is to say, she is the πλήρωμα of Christ, since he himself is the πλήρωμα in the highest sense. This is the simple meaning of the words of which so many interpretations have been attempted : τὸ πλήρωμα τοῦ τὰ πάντα ἐν πᾶσι πληρωμένου. What is meant is simply that Christ is the pleroma in the highest and absolute sense, inasmuch as it is all things absolutely that he fills with himself as the absolute contents. The conception of the πλήρωμα suggests the relation of one thing to another, the relation of abstract and concrete being, of absolute unconditioned being, and its manifestation or realization, or the relation of form and contents. As Christ is the pleroma because the absolute essence of God manifests itself and enters upon concrete existence in him, because the conception of God is here filled with its definite contents, so when the Church is called the pleroma of Christ, she is conceived as possessing a more concrete and realized existence than Christ himself. But if the Church, as the pleroma, is the concrete real existence with

which Christ fills himself as his contents; on the other hand, and
in a higher sense, Christ, as the form of these contents, is himself
the contents with which everything that has existence, the self-
existent, fills itself. The expression πλήρωμα, then, implies
always a concrete and real existence,—the contents of another
existence with which it combines to form a unity of form and contents. Thus the expression πλήρωμα is to be taken neither as
simply active nor as simply passive. Both senses pass and
repass into each other, for that which fills—which makes full—
becomes itself that which is filled, is full, is informed with its
definite contents. As πληρούμενος τὰ πάντα ἐν πᾶσι, Christ is the
πλήρωμα which fills the πάντα ἐι πᾶσι with its definite contents,
and this pleroma itself again is the absolute all, replenished with
its absolute contents.

As with the conception of the πλήρωμα, so with that of the
σῶμα. The church is the σῶμα of Christ, Eph. i. 23, iv. 12. But
Christ himself is called σῶμα, the σῶμα of the Deity, inasmuch as
there dwells σωματικῶς in him πᾶν τὸ πλήρωμα τῆς θεότητος, all,
that is to say, that informs the idea of the Deity with the concrete
contents that belong to it, Col. ii. 9, an expression which can only
be explained by the line of thought which we have indicated. If
then he himself is the σῶμα of the Deity, the church can be his
σῶμα only in a more concrete sense, since he, as σῶμα of the
Deity, is the head of the church, and the principle, ἐξ οὗ πᾶν τὸ
σῶμα συναρμολογούμενον καὶ συμβιβαζόμενον διὰ πάσης ἀφῆς
τῆς ἐπιχορηγίας, κατ᾽ ἐνέργειαν ἐν μέτρῳ ἑνὸς ἑκάστου μέρους,
τὴν αὔξησιν τοῦ σώματος ποιεῖται εἰς οἰκοδομὴν ἑαυτοῦ ἐν ἀγάπῃ,
Eph. iv. 16. Here the church is described, in true Gnostic fashion,
as an organism fitted together by the concord of its members
inwardly, and living in the idea of its own unity. The relation
also in which the church stands towards Christ as his σῶμα
brings us back to the idea of syzygy; according to Eph. v. 28,
the γυναῖκες are the σώματα of their husbands, a representation
where we again encounter the Gnostic idea of the pleroma, since
here also the idea is present that the being of the husbands

receives its full contents only in that of the wives,—only there realizes its own conception.

The Gnostic representations afford, I think, the only satisfactory explanation of the obscure passage, iii. 9. The οἰκονομία μυστηρίου consists in this, that God has created all things, ἵνα γνωρισθῇ νῦν ταῖς ἀρχαῖς καὶ ταῖς ἐξουσίαις ἐν τοῖς ἐπουρανίοις διὰ τῆς ἐκκλησίας ἡ πολυποίκιλος σοφία τοῦ Θεοῦ κατὰ πρόθεσιν τῶν αἰώνων, ἣν ἐποίησεν ἐν Χριστῷ Ἰησοῦ τῷ Κυρίῳ ἡμῶν. The final cause of the creation is here alleged to be that the σοφία τοῦ Θεοῦ should be known by the heavenly powers, and that through the medium of the church; the final cause of the creation is thus realized by a movement going back into the pleroma, an ideal movement, however, which is placed in the knowing of the ἀρχαί and ἐξουσίαι, which occupy the same position here as the aeons of the Gnostics. According to the doctrine of the Valentinians, the final end of the creation takes place in the return of Sophia, along with the spiritually-minded who make up the church, back to the Pleroma. Now the author of our Epistle could not place Sophia in this position at the realizing of the final cause of creation, for he had not made Sophia, but Ecclesia, the σύζυγος of Christ. But Sophia could not be altogether omitted, and she is placed here ideally as the divine wisdom which realizes itself in the realization of the divine world-scheme; she is made known as such to the celestial powers who form the highest spirit-world, and that through the church, which, as the object of this knowledge, is the medium through which it is communicated. The church, however, can be the object of this knowledge only in her syzygy with Christ. The Gnostic doctrine represents Sophia returning into the Pleroma as a bride united with her bridegroom, the Redeemer; and thus the realization of the purpose of creation is placed here in the marriage of the church with Christ, inasmuch as it is in her that the wisdom of God is known by the heavenly powers.[1] In this accomplishment of the ends of creation in the

---

[1] ἵνα γνωρισθῇ can only be construed along with τίς ἡ οἰκ. τοῦ μυστ. : Grace is given to me to proclaim the gospel and to instruct others τίς ἡ οἰκ. τοῦ μυστ.,

γνωρίζειν of the ἀρχαὶ καὶ ἐξουσίαι, the πρόθεσις τῶν αἰώνων, the purpose of the aeons, or that which God has ideally proposed to himself in the aeons, returns into itself, having been accomplished and realized in Christ. The αἰῶνες here are like the Gnostic aeons (the αἰῶνες του αἰῶνος, Eph. iii. 21, the aeons of God as the primal Æon), the subjects of the Divine ideas of the world-plan which is developed and realized in the sequence of the aeons, ἐν τοῖς αἰῶσι τοῖς ἐπερχομένοις, Eph. ii. 7, and they constitute the being of God. All this, it is clear, can only be grasped and understood in the light of the Gnostic modes of thinking. The predicate, also, which Sophia here receives—πολυποίκιλος, this strange and singular compound, which has given so much trouble to the interpreters—cannot be rightly explained save from the same circle of ideas. Harless inclines ultimately to the view (which De Wette also in the main supports) that this πολυποίκιλος σοφία is so called on account of the difference of the present from earlier revelations, the revelations of God in nature and in the law. It is, that is to say, the wonderful wisdom, which adjusts the conflict between law and grace ; it is the thought, συνέκλεισε γὰρ ὁ Θεὸς τοὺς πάντας εἰς ἀπείθειαν, ἵνα τοὺς πάντας ἐλεήσῃ, which in another passage moves the apostle to exclaim, ὦ βάθος πλούτου καὶ σοφίας, etc., Rom. xi. 32 *sq.*; it is the *preparatio evangelica* of the Old Testament revelations, of which it is said at the beginning of the Epistle to the Hebrews, πολυτρόπως πάλαι, etc. The apostle, it is said, is not speaking here directly of that series of earlier revelations, for the wisdom he describes is that which is manifested through the church of the New Covenant, but he glances at all the various revelations of God, and calls the last and final one a revelation of the manifold wisdom of God. All this is perfectly sensible, still it does not preclude the question, why, if this was what the apostle had to say, he should have chosen such a peculiar expression as πολυποίκιλος, and should have spoken of a manifold (multiform) wisdom, when in reality it was the unity of it, as

namely, that this οἰκονομία τοῦ μυστηρίου finds its accomplishment in this ἵνα γνωρισθῇ, etc.

against the multiplicity of former revelations, that he wanted to express. I believe this πολυποίκιλος σοφία can only be explained thus : that the writer saw hovering before his mind that Gnostic σοφία of which this predicate is characteristic more than any other; for it was of the essence of that Sophia to pass through a series of the most varied forms and conditions. We even find Irenaeus using the same expression in speaking of the suffering condition in which for the most part she dwells.[1]

In this connexion we cannot set it down to chance that an idea occurs in one of these Epistles to which the apostle Paul never makes the slightest allusion. I refer to the passage, Eph. iv. 8. In spite of the reclamation of most modern interpreters, it appears to me that we cannot, with any regard to the natural meaning of the words, refer this passage to anything but the descent into hell. Harless urges that this would be the only passage where the descent into hell would appear as a characteristic of Christ's appearance, which it certainly is not. But to this I can allow no weight, nor do the other reasons to which Harless appeals in support of his rendering appear to me to be more forcible. It is said that the antithesis of earth and heaven is alone suited to the context ; but this is simply to take for granted that the two clauses of ver. 8 are to be referred to the same subjects, those, namely, whom Christ had won for himself upon the earth. It may be very true that in the psalm from which the words in verse 8 are taken, there is no trace of any reference to death or to a descent into hell ; but Harless asserts further, "only then could we prove that the Apostle found such a reference in the psalm, if he quoted the passage in a connexion in which the death or the descent of Christ was directly before him, but that here the very contrary is the case ; and what connexion can be shown between the gifts of grace which Christ gives to his own people, and his death or his *descensus ad inferos ?* If the Apostle seeks to demonstrate that the procedure of God triumphant who brings his captives with him without waiting till

---

[1] Adv. Haer. i. 4. ̓ 1, συμπεπλέχθαι τῷ πάθει, καὶ μόνην ἀπολειφθεῖσαν ἔξω παντὶ μέρει τοῦ πάθους ὑποπεσεῖν, πολυμεροῦς καὶ πολυποικίλου ὑπάρχοντος.

they render themselves to him, is also the procedure of the Son, who also places his people in the Church on earth in the place he fixes for them, what need is there here for any reference to the death or the descent of Christ?" With all this I disagree, just because the reasoning assumes that the passage can be understood in no other sense but one exclusive of the descent into hell. But what is more natural than to take αἰχμαλωτεύειν αἰχμαλωσίαν of those captives whom Christ, when he descended into Hades, brought up with him as his own captives, *i.e.* as those whom he had set free? And this was the original and common view of the purpose of the descent. It is very true that the preceding verse 7 prepares us for only the second clause of verse 8, but what hinders us from assuming that it was just the passage he was quoting from the Old Testament, which led the writer to the further thought expressed in the first clause, namely, the idea of the descent into hell, and that then he worked out this idea in verses 9, 10, and came back in verse 11 to the connexion of verse 7? And as for the question what the gifts of grace which Christ gives his people have to do with the descent into hell, the answer is not far to seek. It is given us in this very passsage in the words πληρώσῃ τὰ πάντα, and that so clearly as to exclude all doubt on the subject. It might be possible to take the κατώτερα μέρη τῆς γῆς as simply a circum-locution for γῆ, if that phrase stood alone, but it is altogether im-possible in a passage arranged as this one is, where the writer speaks of an ἀναβαίνειν and a καταβαίνειν, and where the one is called ἀναβαίνειν ὑπεράνω πάντων τῶν οὐρανῶν, that is, an ascend-ing to the highest height, as far as it is possible to ascend : it is impossible to take the καταβαίνειν εἰς τὰ κατώτερα μέρη τῆς γῆς, which forms the antithesis to ἀναβαίνειν ὑπεράνω πάντων τῶν οὐρανῶν, in any more limited sense than that which the nearest and most natural meaning of the words demands. By doing so we should take from the principal clause, ἵνα πληρώσῃ τὰ πάντα (all things without exception, as the article indicates) its unre-stricted meaning. What the author here seeks to express, is the activity of Christ which extends equally far upwards and downwards, which descends from the highest height to the lowest depth, and ascends again from the latter to the former, which embraces and replenishes the whole universe, so far as it is inhabited by intelligent beings, with its gracious and redeeming influence. It is the idea of the pleroma belonging to Christ in the highest sense, which is here dealt with on the side of its scope and extension. If Christ is the pleroma absolutely, then the activity, which according to this conception he exerts, cannot come short of comprehending everything in the widest possible circle, and of binding the highest and the lowest together.

If this be the sense of our passage, then not only does it contain the idea of Christ's descent into hell,—it exhibits to us very distinctly the genesis of that idea. Christ as the πλήρωμα is also the τὰ πάντα πληρώσας, and if he be the τὰ πάντα πληρώσας, thus he must also be the εἰς τὰ κατώτερα μέρη τῆς γῆς καταβάς. Now even if it were not possible to trace the idea of the descent of Christ into hell so distinctly as we do as one of the Gnostic doctrines, yet the Gnostic origin of this passage could not be doubtful, when we considered the inward connexion of these ideas, and the relation which, as we showed, exists between the Christology of these Epistles and the Christology of the Gnostics. Some Gnostic systems, notably the Valentinian, make the redeeming spirit return and close its earthly work before the catastrophe of death, and of course such a scheme as this can scarcely have contemplated a further action to deal with the under-world. But this was not universally the Gnostic conception; we know about Marcion at least, that in his system, Christ went down into the under-world after his death.[1]   And it is not probable

---

[1] "Super blasphemiam," says Irenaeus, i. 27. 3, "quae est in Deum, adjecit et hoc (Marcion), Cain et eos, qui similes sunt ei, et Sodomitas, et Aegyptios et similes eis et omnes omnino gentes, quae in omni permixtione malignitatis ambulaverunt, salvatas esse a Domino, cum descendisset ad inferos et accucurrissent et in suum assumpsisse regnum : Abel autem et Enoch et Noe et reliquos justos—non participasse salutem—non accucurrerunt Jesu neque crediderunt annuntiationi ejus, et propterea remansisse animas eorum apud inferos. Cf. Epiph. Haer. xlii. 4 : Χριστὸν (ἤλει Μαρκίων) ἄνωθεν ἀπὸ τοῦ ἀοράτου καὶ ἀκατονομάστου πατρὸς καταβεβηκέναι ἐπὶ σωτηρίᾳ τῶν ψυχῶν καὶ ἐπὶ ἐλέγχῳ τοῦ Θεοῦ

that Marcion, a man who borrowed so much from old Gnostic systems, and whose only peculiarity almost was to give a dualistic turn to what he borrowed, was the first to set this view in circulation. It fits so naturally into the whole Gnostic set of ideas, that we may well believe it to have existed before him. The greater the height was from which the Christ of the Gnostics came when descending from the all-encircling pleroma, the greater the number of heavens through which he had passed, the more natural was it to think of his descending also as far as it was possible to descend, not only down into the world, but even down into the underworld. And again, a thorough working out of the hostile relation in which Christ and the demiurge were conceived to stand to each other would itself suggest that Christ should visit the place where those souls lay whom the demiurge had caught and bound, and who had no hope of freedom in any other way.[1]

Besides all this, how many references do we find in these Epistles to Gnostic ideas and expressions! How often do they speak of a μυστήριον, a σοφία, a γνῶσις, etc.—cf. Eph. i. 8, 17; iii. 3, 9, 19; iv. 13; vi. 19; Col. i. 6, 9, 26; ii. 2; iii. 10, 16. With what peculiar meaning and emphasis is the word αἰών used, as for example Eph. iii. 21. The αἰῶνες might seem here to be nothing more than the γενεαὶ (as in Col. i. 26, αἰῶνες and γενεαὶ are coupled together), but the aeons and the γενεαὶ τοῦ αἰῶνος τῶν αἰώνων, in the same sense in which God himself, as the extratemporal unity of time, individualizes himself in the aeons, as the several stages of time, while unfolding itself. In the πρόθεσις τῶν αἰώνων also,

---

τῶν Ἰουδαίων καὶ νόμου καὶ προφητῶν καὶ τῶν τοιούτων, καὶ ἄχρι ᾅδου καταβεβη-κέναι τὸν κύριον, ἵνα σώσῃ τοὺς περὶ Καὶν, etc.

[1] Thus what Irenaeus says, v. 31. 2, about the Gnostic denial of the idea of the descent into hell, refers only to those Gnostics for whom the whole history of Christ seems to have had a merely symbolical meaning, *si Dominus legem mortu-orum servavit—commoratus usque in tertiam diem in inferioribus terrae, post deinde surgens in carne—adscendit ad patrem, quomodo non confundantur, qui dicunt inferos quidem esse hunc mundum, qui sit secundum nos, inferiorem autem hominem ipsorum, derelinquentem hoc corpus, in supercoelestem adscendere locum ?* Thus there were those who understood the *adscendere ad patrem* even with reference to Christ, only of the Spirit of man. This was, however, by no means the general view.

Eph. iii. 11, the conception of the aeons in their relation to time, corresponds with the Gnostic conception of them as spiritual beings who are the bearers of the thoughts of God. Still more striking is this in the expression αἰὼν τοῦ κόσμου τούτου, Eph. ii. 2. The interpreters think that the passage is sufficiently explained by giving the word the meaning "earthly life," "course of the world," "era of the world," and declare it to be quite a mistake to render αἰὼν in the Gnostic sense. Yet it can scarcely be denied that the expression is at least not very unlike the Gnostic conception, and why should not the subject αἰὼν τοῦ κόσμου τούτου be parallel to the other subjects, namely, the ἄρχων τῆς ἐξουσίας τοῦ ἀέρος and the πνεῦμα ἐνεργοῦν? The only Pauline expression with which this one can be compared is Θεὸς τοῦ αἰῶνος τούτου, 2 Cor. iv. 4, and that instead of Θεὸς we have here αἰών, and that the αἰὼν τοῦ κόσμου τούτου is mentioned by the side of an αἰὼν τῶν αἰώνων, can only be explained by the influence of Gnostic ideas. In the same passage, on inspecting it more closely, and comparing it with the kindred passage vi. 12, we detect still more Gnostic representations and expressions in which the eye of the author expatiates in the supernatural world of darkness, as at other times it does in the brighter regions of the spirit-realm. The κοσμοκράτορες τοῦ σκότους, Eph. vi. 12, cannot disown their Gnostic origin. The Valentinians gave the name of Kosmocrator to the devil. To the same origin with Kosmocrator are the δαιμόνια and ἄγγελοι to be referred. What he is in unity, these are in plurality.[1] Marcion gave the name of Kosmocrator to the demiurge, who is in his system the representative of the evil principle.[2] Now if the κοσμοκράτορες cannot be subordinated to any principle but the αἰὼν τοῦ κόσμου τούτου, then the αἰὼν is the κοσμοκράτωρ. As κοσμοκράτωρ, he is, according to Eph. ii. 2, the ἄρχων τῆς ἐξουσίας τοῦ ἀέρος and the πνεῦμα τὸ ἐνεργοῦν, etc., that is, the devil described in Gnostic phrases. For the peculiar expression, τὰ πνευματικὰ τῆς πονηρίας, Eph. vi. 12, there is no parallel to be found but in the language of the Gnostics.[3]

---

[1] Irenaeus, Adv. Haer. i. 5. 4.   [2] Irenaeus, i. 27. 2.

[3] Irenaeus says of the Valentinians (i. 5. 4): Ἐκ τῆς λύπης (of the Sophia) τὰ

That in connexion with such representations the contrast of light and darkness should be peculiarly dwelt upon (Eph. ii. 2, iv. 18, v. 8 ; Col. i. 18), may not be a very important circumstance ; yet the universal proposition, Eph. v. 13, πᾶν τὸ φανερούμενον φῶς ἐστι, is worthy of remark. This sentence affirms, according to the Gnostic theory of light, that light is the principle through which everything that is and has existence for consciousness, is mediated, All becoming takes place just by that which existed already in its essence becoming manifest to consciousness. The Valentinians used this proposition in this way in their explanation of the pro- logue to John's Gospel, when they said, When John called ζωὴ the φῶς ἀνθρώπων, he meant to include in the word ἀνθρώπων the ἄνθρωπος and the ἐκκλησία, ὅπως διὰ τοῦ ἑνὸς ὀνόματος δηλώσῃ τὴν τῆς συζυγίας κοινωνίαν, ἐκ γὰρ τοῦ λόγου καὶ τῆς ζωῆς ἄνθρωπος γίνεται καὶ ἐκκλησία· φῶς δὲ εἶπε τῶν ἀνθρώπων τὴν ζωὴν, διὰ τὸ πεφωτίσθαι αὐτοὺς ὑπ' αὐτῆς, ὃ δὴ ἐστι μεμορφῶσθαι καὶ πεφανερῶσθαι. Τουτο δὲ ὁ Παῦλος λέγει· πᾶν γὰρ τὸ φανε- ρούμενον φῶς ἐστι·[1] ἐπεὶ τοίνυν ἐφανέρωσε καὶ ἐγέννησε τόν τε ἄνθρωπον καὶ τὴν ἐκκλησίαν ἡ ζωή, φῶς εἰρῆσθαι αὐτῶν. Life is called the light of man and the church, because the origin of the syzygy of the man and the Church is nothing but its becoming visible. Everything that arises simply emerges to the light out of

πνευματικὰ τῆς πονηρίας διδάσκουσι γεγονέναι, ὅθεν καὶ διάβολον τὴν γένεσιν ἐσχηκέναι, ὃν καὶ κοσμοκράτορα καλοῦσι, καὶ τὰ δαιμόνια καὶ τοὺς ἀγγέλους καὶ πᾶσαν τὴν πνευματικὴν τῆς πονηρίας ὑπόστασιν. The different states of mind are here described, into which Sophia or Achamoth fell outside of the Pleroma. Each of these states of mind is, through the subjective becoming objective, the principle of a definite sphere of the material and spiritual world. Sorrow objectivated itself to the substance of the air (ἀέρα γεγονέναι κατὰ τῆς λύπης πῆξιν), but from the same λύπη arose also the πνευματικὰ τῆς πονηρίας, and especially the διάβολος or κοσμοκράτωρ, who has his seat ἐν τῷ καθ' ἡμᾶς κόσμῳ. So in our Epistle the αἰὼν τοῦ κόσμου τούτου, who presides over the κοσμοκράτορες τοῦ σκότους, is the ἄρχων τῆς ἐξουσίας τοῦ ἀέρος. The spiritually evil beings are the inhabitants of the atmosphere which envelopes the earth, and as such, the κοσμοκράτορες τοῦ σκότους. The conceptions air and darkness are the physical substratum of the spiritually evil.

[1] This is, moreover, one of the oldest pieces of evidence for the supposed Pauline origin of the Epistle to the Ephesians, and should not be omitted from the catalogue.

what it was essentially before. There is, therefore, and this expresses accurately the Gnostic view of the universe, no becoming or originating, but everything that becomes and originates simply begins to exist for consciousness, for everything that is, is absolutely. Nothing therefore acquires essential existence ; all becoming and originating is true only for the sphere of consciousness. The whole process of the world's becoming is just the process of the development of consciousness. If then such be the true sense of the supposed Pauline proposition, who does not perceive that it has come into this connexion out of a totally different set of ideas, and that the moral purport here given to it can only be properly understood if it be explained by the metaphysical meaning which underlies it?

The striking affinity of these two letters with Gnostic ideas and expressions has been for the most part disregarded by interpreters, but where this has not been the case, only two explanations seem to have been considered possible : (1.) That the Gnostics derived those views from the Pauline Epistles, or, (2.) That ideas like those of the Gnostics were already in circulation at the apostle's time, and that he set himself to combat and correct them. The latter alternative is thoroughly improbable; on the one hand there is no proof of the existence of Gnostic ideas at so early a period, and on the other, the Epistle to the Ephesians exhibits no trace of even an indirect polemic against the Gnostic doctrines. On the contrary, the apostle would have been playing into the hands of the Gnostics both in this and to some extent also in the Colossian Epistle. And the former alternative is just as unlikely or even more so. Tertullian has been appealed to in support of it.[1] But what can Tertullian prove for an opinion that has against it the whole constitution of the Gnostic systems, especially of the Valentinian system, the structure of which is far too original to be explained by what Tertullian says of it, that Valentine *materiam ad scripturas excogitavit.*[2]

---

[1] Compare Harless on Eph. i. 23, where he cites Tert. de praescr. Haer. c. 38.

[2] Non ad materiam scripturas (as Marcion), et tamen plus abstulit et plus adjecit, auferens proprietates singulorum quoque verborum et adjiciens dispositiones non comparentium rerum.

If, then, both alternatives are equally inadmissible, both those sides combine to make us think that the Epistle to the Ephesians especially is of post-apostolic origin, and dates from a time when the Gnostic ideas were just coming into circulation, and still wore the garb of innocent Christian speculations.

We are the more led to think of this period, that the same Epistle to which these remarks chiefly apply, namely that to the Ephesians, indicates an acquaintance with another phenomenon of the age of Gnosticism, viz., Montanism. We may remark here that the elements out of which Montanism arose were in existence long before the reputed founder of that sect, and were as far as may be from being heretical. And thus, though we should find in our Epistle the echoes of Montanism, we should not be compelled to place it at too late a date. The emphatic designation of the πνεῦμα as the distinctive principle of Christian consciousness and life might of itself appear to point out such a relation. Compare Eph. i. 3, 13, 17 ; ii. 18 ; iii. 5, 16 ; iv. 3, 30, 23 ; v. 18 ; vi. 17 ; and Col. i. 8, 9 ; iii. 16. With the Montanists, the conception of the πνεῦμα was identical with that of σοφία ;[1] it was to them the principle of Christian wisdom, of knowledge and insight, which constituted the peculiar distinction of the Christian, if at least he understood his position in the world. In this sense Tertullian speaks of the administratio paracleti quod intellectus reformatur quod ad meliora proficitur.[2] Through the agnitio paracleti which distinguishes them from psychical men, the Montanists are also instructiores per paracletum.[3]

Shall we seek here for an explanation of the fact that in both our Epistles, that to the Colossians also, the essence of Christian perfection is so often made to consist in σύνεσις, in σοφία, γνῶσις, etc. ? (Compare in addition to the passages last cited, Eph. v. 15 ; Col. ii. 23 ; iii. 16 ; iv. 5 ; i. 9.) The Montanists held the view

---

[1] In Epiphanius, Haer. xlix. 1, the Montanist prophetess Priscilla, or Quintilla, says that Christ had appeared to her in female form, καὶ ἐνέβαλεν ἐν ἐμοὶ τὴν σοφίαν καὶ ἀπεκάλυψέ μοι, etc. Cf. Eph. i. 17, πνεῦμα σοφίας καὶ ἀποκαλύψεως.

[2] De vel. Virg. c. 1.　　　　　　　　　　　　[3] Tert. ad. Prax. c. 1.

of a divine Revelation which unfolds itself in definite successive stages, and is completed in the period of the Spirit, and
in these stages the Christian perfection, which approves itself
through the σοφία, etc., was reckoned analogous to the ripeness
of manhood. So far, they held, had the Church advanced through
the manifestations and communications of the Paraclete within
her.[1]

The Epistle to the Ephesians takes up the same idea for the
principle of the development of the Christian Church, which, as
the body of Christ, has still to grow up to maturity, iv. 11 sq.
" He has given some as apostles, others as prophets, others as
evangelists ; others as pastors and teachers, that the saints might
be prepared for the work of ministration, for the building up of
the body of Christ, till we all come to the unity of faith, and of the
knowledge of the Son of God, to the perfect man, to the measure
of the age of the Church at which Christ is filled with her,[2]—that
we should be no more children." Here also the end of the corporate
life of the Christian Church is held to be reached by a progress
stage by stage, from the state of infancy to that of manly maturity.
But while Montanism held that end to be already attained
in the presence of the Paraclete, the author of our Epistle, seeking to think the thoughts of the apostle, represented it as yet
to be attained through the harmonious co-operation of all the
Church's members.

That the age to which our Epistles belong was one in which
there was a practical interest to take this idea as the principle
of the development of the Church, is rendered still more likely by
the fact that the Epistle to the Colossians also contains it, i. 28 ;

---

[1] Compare the fine passage Tert. de Vel. Virg. c. i.   Justitia primo fuit in rudi-
mentis, dehinc per legem et prophetas promovit in infantiam, dehinc per evan-
gelium efferbuit in juventutem, nunc per Paracletum componitur in maturitatem.

[2] It is incorrect to take τὸ πλήρωμα τοῦ Χριστοῦ in the sense of being filled
with Christ ; it is the fulness of Christ, or the contents with which Christ fills
himself, that is, the church.   The πλήρωμα Χρ. is thus equivalent to the σῶμα
τοῦ Χρ. in the preceding verse, and it cannot be said that the Montanist phrase
would be πλήρωμα τοῦ παρακλήτου.

καταγγέλλομεν (Χριστόν) διδάσκοντες πάντα ἄνθρωπον ἐν πάσῃ
σοφίᾳ, ἵνα παραστήσωμεν πάντα ἄνθρωπον τέλειον ἐν Χριστῷ.[1]
But the most striking references to the ideas and institutions of
the Montanists are contained in the passages, Eph. ii. 20; iii. 5;
iv. 11; where the apostles and prophets are named together, and
in each case the prophets after the apostles. Only a superficial
method of interpretation, a thing, however, which is not absolutely
unknown in the later commentaries, could hold this placing of the
prophets after the apostles to be merely accidental, and so understand the prophets here spoken of to be the prophets of the Old
Testament. Harless has with perfect justice repudiated this interpretation; but he goes on to say that the want of the article
before προφητῶν shows the apostle to have united the two sub-
stantives at ii. 20, and iii. 5, as forming together one conception,
that is, that he gives the apostles the additional designation of
prophets; and that this is done in reference to the description of the
state of the heathen Christians, ii. 12, who were there said to be
without promise and without hope, but who now possess the promise which the apostles, as the bearers of the promise of the new
covenant, have brought them. We cannot follow him in this; the
interpretation is far too artificial to be a real solution of the difficulty. The text iv. 11 shows distinctly that the apostles are
distinguished from the prophets. Harless remarks indeed that
the ἀποστολή involves the προφητεία, while the προφητεία does
not involve the ἀποστολή; and this is true; yet it is clear from
iv. 11 that there were prophets who were distinct from the
apostles, and the question must still be asked, Who are these
prophets, and how came the author of our Epistle to couple them

---

[1] Cf. the Kritischen Miscellen. zum Epheserbriefe; Theol. Jahrb. 1844, p. 381
(now in Schwegler's Nachap. Zeitalter, ii. 371.—*Editor*), where it is justly remarked that Paul cannot have had these ideas. He regarded the end of all time
and the second coming of Christ as imminent, and could not contrast his own
time as the period of νηπιότης to the age of manly maturity, as an age still distant, the goal of Christian history to be attained historically through an immanent
process of development. This is a later standpoint which, reflecting on the
past, conceived the idea of such a division of epochs.

with the apostles ? That it came about from a consideration of the contrast between the present and the former state of the Gentile Christians might possibly account for the passage ii. 20 ; but that the same expression should be found in two other passages and in wholly different connexions, evidently points to something peculiar in the circumstances of the age, or of the Church to which the Epistle is addressed.

The apostolic letters show no trace of an order of prophets who stand on the same level with the apostles. The passage which falls to be considered on the subject, 1 Cor. xii. 28, shows that Paul regarded prophecy as a χάρισμα among other χαρίσματα, and by no means as containing in itself all the gifts of grace, or the special criterion of the true Church. And this is the position of the author of our Epistle ; with him the apostles and the new prophets, the latter manifestly as successors and representatives of the apostles in the post-apostolic Church, are the depositaries of divine revelations, the θεμέλιον, the foundation of the Church.[1]

Not Paul, but Montanism, attributed to the prophets such a position and such importance. The Montanist Tertullian co-ordinates apostles and prophets in the same way, as equally organs of the Spirit ; what the apostles were formerly, the prophets are now.[2] And the author of our Epistle, identifying himself with Paul, and speaking of the whole time from the apostles to the date at which he was writing, says, iii. 5 : νῦν ἀπεκαλύφθη (τὸ μυστήριον) τοῖς ἁγίοις ἀποστόλοις αὐτοῦ καὶ

---

[1] Krit. Misc. 1844, p. 380.

[2] De Pudic. c. 21, where Tertullian is speaking of the power to forgive sins, which, he says, belongs only to God and to those to whom it is committed by God, viz., the apostles, as it had been to the prophets of the Old Testament. *Exhibe igitur et nunc mihi, apostolice,* so he addresses the Roman bishop, *prophetica exempla, et agnoscam divinitatem, et vindica tibi delictorum ejusmodi remittendorum potestatem.—Sed habet, inquis, potestatem ecclesia delicta donandi. Hoc ego magis et agnosco et dispono, qui ipsum Paracletum in prophetis novis habeo dicentem : potest ecclesia donare delictum.* If the Roman bishop appeal to Peter, Matth. xvi. 16, what right has he to apply to himself what is there said to Peter ? *Quid nunc et ad ecclesiam et quidem tuam, psychice ? Secundum enim Petri personam spiritualibus potestas illa conveniet, aut apostolo aut prophetae. Nam et ecclesia proprie et principaliter ipse est spiritus.*

προφήταις ἐν πνεύματι. The addition ἐν πνεύματι is certainly significant. Several interpreters wish to refer ἐν πνεύματι to προφήταις
exclusively, but this is justly condemned by Harless and others.
If it be asked what reason can be alleged that this predicate, which
the context shows to be a pregnant one, should be applied only
to the prophets, and not to the apostles also, we must go a
step further and ask, Why is it given to both? It was for the
sake of the prophets that it was inserted and applied to the
apostles also. The author lived at a time when the prophets
were recognised as new organs of the communication of the Spirit;
only this can account for his expressly calling the apostles and
prophets *spiritales*, as Tertullian calls them in the same sense.[1]
And if in the third passage, iv. 11, the ποιμένες refer to the
same ecclesiastical personages as are commonly termed ἐπίσκοποι,
then we see here just that depreciation of the bishops for which
the Montanists are censured by Hieronymus.[2]

It arose from the nature of the case that the materials for these
critical investigations were drawn chiefly from the Epistle to the
Ephesians. The Epistle to the Colossians, however, has not been
by any means lost sight of, and there is a further special task
which it presents to criticism. It is well known how many
theories have already been advanced about the so-called false
teachers of this Epistle, without, however, finding for them any
definite place in history, and least of all at the time of the apostle
himself. It is even doubtful whether they were Jews or Christians;
and this is certainly striking. If they were so considerable a
power that the apostle thought it necessary to write an Epistle
specially against them, we should expect that they had left some
clearer traces of their historical existence. And certainly we
should expect to find in the Epistle itself a more distinct indication
of what they were. Yet how hard is it to construct the peculiar
character of the sectaries in question from the various single
traits, mostly the merest hints, which are given us of them; and

[1] Loc. cit.
[2] Epist. 27: ita in tertium, i.e. paene ultimum locum episcopi devolvuntur.

how little does the polemic of the author, indirect as it is, rather than direct, show these heretics, supposed to have been so dangerous, to be the real subject-matter of the Epistle, and the central point from which the whole contents are to be explained. In seeking then to sift this matter to the bottom, it is not only permissible, but necessary, to drop the common hypothesis that these so-called false teachers were the historical occasion of our Epistle, and to set up the contrary view, that all that is said about them is said only by the way, to strengthen and enforce that which is in reality the principal theme.

And where is it more natural to find the chief theme of our Epistle than in that which is said about the higher dignity of Christ as the central point, not only of the Christian Church, but of the universe in general, and about the great mystery that has been made manifest in him? The author comes to this as soon as he has despatched the necessary introduction, and added to it, in the ordinary way, his expression of sympathy with the Christians to whom he is writing; he at once enforces this as the chief point to which the whole contents of his Epistle are to be referred. Now if Christ has this high and absolute importance, if he be considered in his divine supra-mundane nature, the substantial centre both of all spiritual and natural existence generally, and specially of the corporate life that is developed in the Christian Church, then it is of the first importance to hold steadfastly to this one foundation, and to suffer nothing to be brought by any one into competition with that communication of religious weal which is only possible through him, as if anything else could be the channel of such virtue. In this argument the author does certainly encounter some conflicting views which serve him for the further development of his main thesis; but these have not the special historical reference which is commonly attributed to them. They belong merely to certain phenomena here and there, which are a part of the general character of the time. We might think of gnosis in this connexion; we find it elsewhere, even as early as the Pastoral Epistles, a chief mark of Christian polemics. But

gnosis was, in the stage it had then reached, too nearly akin with
the tendency of our Epistles to be spoken of in such a spirit;
besides that gnosis also sought to place Christ as high as possible,
and to adequately express his absolute dignity. Ebionitism, on
the contrary, especially in the form in which it was most closely
connected with Judaism, and in which it afterwards became a
heresy, contained elements with which the higher conception of
the person of Christ could not fail to come in conflict, as it became
more and more intent upon excluding everything that might be
put on the same level with Christ as a channel of grace. The
polemical references of the Epistle to the Colossians are best
explained by referring them to Ebionitism, and if this be so, then
the special local occasion which is said to have led the writer of
this Epistle to his task disappears; for what is here condemned
as opposed to the Christian consciousness belongs to the whole
general character of Ebionitism, as it stood over against the freer
form of Pauline Christianity, not only at Colosse, but all over Asia
Minor. A polemical reference of this nature is manifestly present,
in what is said, ii. 11 *sq.*, against circumcision. The maintenance
of circumcision is characteristic of Ebionitism; we see this early
in the case of the antagonists of the apostle in the Epistle to the
Galatians, and it continues to be so with those Ebionites who were
too stiff to surrender their Judaism. Epiphanius expressly remarks
this of his Ebionites, as well as of Cerinthus and his followers.[1]

Then, as for the principles about eating and drinking, and the
observing of certain days and seasons, which gave occasion for the
warning, ver. 16, we know further from Epiphanius that the
Ebionites rejected altogether the use of animal food, considering
that it defiled the eater, a view which is clearly to be recognised
in those words of emphatic prohibition, μὴ ἅψῃ, μηδὲ γεύσῃ,
μηδὲ θίγῃς, ver. 21. They must also have held it unlawful to drink
wine, for they celebrated their mysteries, namely, the Eucharist,
with unleavened bread and unmixed water.[2] They were also

---

[1] Haer. xxx. 2, 16, 28; cf. xxviii. 5.
[2] Haer. xxx. 15, 16; cf. Clement. Hom. xiv. 1.

distinguished by their strict religious observance of certain days and seasons. Epiphanius mentions repeatedly the rite of circumcision and the celebration of the Sabbath as the ordinances of the Jewish religion which the Ebionites held most sacred.[1] The νουμηνίαι are to be understood not only of the new moons, but generally of the festivals, the date of which was determined by the moon, and the phrase may bear special reference to the Jewish or Ebionite celebration of the Passover, which was customary in Asia Minor. But most of all do the worshipping of angels and the transcendental speculations about the spirit-world that were bound up with that worship, as it is described, ii. 18, appear to be a characteristic trait of Ebionitism. Not only did the Ebionites attach great importance to the doctrine of angels and the religious worship of them, they closely connected Christ himself with the angels, and even considered him to be one of them.[2]

And it is just here that we see what was the point of the polemics of the Epistle to the Colossians. The Ebionites agreed in saying of Christ that he was created before all, exalted above the angels, the ruler of all created things. But then again they placed the angels in a co-ordinate relation to Christ, ascribed to them also a redeeming and mediating function, even invoked them directly in this capacity, and regarded Christ as only ἕνα τῶν ἀρχαγγέλων. The Epistle to the Colossians, on the contrary, insists strongly on the point that the dignity of Christ is not a question of degree, but consists in an absolute superiority over

[1] Haer. xxx. 2, 16, 17.

[2] According to Epiph. Haer. xxx. 2, the Ebionite doctrine about Christ (though, as Epiphanius remarks, they were not all together at one on the subject, or perhaps he was unable to harmonize the statements which he had before him) was in the main this: λέγουσιν ἄνωθεν μὲν ὄντα πρὸ πάντων δὲ κτισθέντα, πνεῦμα ὄντα καὶ ὑπὲρ ἀγγέλους ὄντα πάντων δὲ κυριεύοντα, καὶ Χριστὸν λέγεσθαι. Cf. c. 16 : οὐ φάσκουσι δὲ ἐκ Θεοῦ Πατρὸς αὐτὸν γεγεννῆσθαι, ἀλλὰ ἐκτίσθαι ὡς ἕνα τῶν ἀρχαγγέλων, μείζονα δὲ αὐτῶν ὄντα αὐτὸν δὲ κυριεύειν τῶν ἀγγέλων καὶ πάντων τῶν ὑπὸ τοῦ παντοκράτορος πεποιημένων. Tertullian also says (De carne Christi, c. 14), "*Ebionem constituisse Jesum plane prophetis gloriosiorem ut ita in illo angelus fuisse dicatur.*"

everything created. Christ is accordingly not merely πρὸ πάντων κτισθεὶς, but the πρωτότοκος πάσης κτίσεως; so far.from being himself created, that on the contrary all things are created in him. Hence it is strongly asserted that Christ is the κεφαλὴ both τοῦ σώματος, τῆς ἐκκλησίας, and πασῆς ἀρχῆς καὶ ἐξουσίας; and the chief proposition of the whole contention is, in contrast to that Ebionite οὐ κρατεῖν τὴν κεφαλήν, that in so pre-eminent a sense is Christ to be held as head, that whatever is not itself the head cannot be thought to stand to him in any relation but that of absolute dependence. What is said both against circumcision and against the στοιχεῖα τοῦ κόσμου, is to be regarded from the same point of view, namely, as opposition to everything that might detract from the absolute dignity of Christ. Now a doctrine which made man dependent in religion on his natural, physical being or material nature, which made religious welfare obtainable through the purifying and sanctifying power that was ascribed to the elements and substances of the world,[1] through the influence which the heavenly bodies were said to exercise on the sublunary world, through what was naturally clean as distinguished from what was held for unclean,—this doctrine placed the στοιχεῖα τοῦ κόσμου in the position which only Christ, as the Redeemer, ought to occupy. Just in this way do we find, ver. 8, that the στοιχεῖα τοῦ κόσμου and Christ are placed over against each other. This then is what our writer calls philosophy in the same sense in which the essence of philosophy is called worldly wisdom. It is the science which deals with the στοιχεῖα τοῦ κόσμου; it is only a κοσμικὴ παιδεία, as philosophy is termed in the Clementine Homilies (Hom. i. 10), in contrast with the doctrine of the true Prophet. It thus contains nothing to raise man above the world to God. It is a mere cosmology, not a theology, a distinction which seems to be before the writer's mind when he proceeds, after

---

[1] As was the case with the Ebionites, cf. Epiph. in loc. cit. They ascribed such virtue especially to water. According to the Clementine Homilies in the Contestatio pro eis, qui librum accipiunt, one is to invoke as μάρτυρας . . . οὐρανὸν, γῆν ὕδωρ, ἐν οἷς τὰ πάντα περιέχεται, πρὸς τούτοις δὲ ἅπασιν καὶ τὸν διὰ πάντων διήκοντα ἀέρα οὗ ἄνευ οὐκ ἀναπνέω.

the words, κατὰ τὰ στοιχεῖα καὶ οὐ κατὰ Χριστὸν, and adds that it is in Christ that the πλήρωμα· τῆς θεότητος dwells. It is this divine element which distinguishes Christianity from a philosophy which deals with nothing more than the στοιχεῖα τοῦ κόσμου. Such a doctrine is nothing but a philosophy; it may be called a κενὴ ἀπάτη, a mere παράδοσις τῶν ἀνθρώπων.

If, as can scarcely be denied, the polemical references of the Epistle to the Colossians are rightly accounted for by what we have brought forward, it must be admitted that the position occupied by our writer in this controversy is a totally different one from that of the apostle Paul in the Epistle to the Galatians. He was dealing there with the naked opposition in which Christianity was coming to stand towards Judaism, and with the question whether, in addition to faith in Christ, Jewish circumcision could have a place as a necessary condition of salvation. But here the stress of the antithesis is no longer, as formerly, in the sphere of soteriology (which was of course the first and chief contents of the Christian consciousness), it has advanced to the sphere of Christology, and the important point is now to bring what was thought to be the soteriological contents of Christianity to its absolute expression in the clearer and more definite conception which was coming to be formed of the person of Christ. The process of the development of the Christian consciousness consisted just in this, that instead of the immediate consciousness of the blessings of Christianity, there came a stage where these blessings were taken for granted, and here only such a conception of the person of Christ was admissible as would represent him with full capacity to produce all those effects, inwardly intense, and outwardly extensive, in which the work of redemption was held to consist. In this sense the absolute conception of the person of Christ is the theme of both Epistles, and if we find them (a point to which we must recur afterwards) insisting upon a unity in which all differences are done away, then Christ himself must be taken as the central point of that unity. Thus the dispute with Ebionitism was of importance only as the views of that body came into collision with the conception of the person of Christ which was thus being developed.

Thus the more special subjects which seemed to give this Epistle an advantage over that to the Ephesians, fail to dispel the suspicion of its post-apostolic origin. But apart from the historical phenomena by which both epistles are to be explained, there are numbers of smaller points about them which would lead us to conclude that the author stood at some distance from the apostolic age. If Paul were the author of these Epistles, how could he himself have given to the ἀπόστολοι the predicate ἅγιοι? iii. 5. De Wette at once remarked this, and justly considered it as weighing against the apostolic origin of the Ephesian letter. To this Harless answered "that the predicate ἅγιοι was positively required by the context. Why, he said, should the apostle, who calls all Christians ἅγιοι, carry his modesty so far as to scruple to call the apostles the same, even though he himself was one of them?[1] Does he call himself so κατ᾽ ἐξοχήν, or was it such a virtue in the apostles to be ἅγιοι, that they should not have ventured to mention it, however unobtrusively? Those whom he calls ἅγιοι are the apostles called by God, and so distinguished from other men." But the chief point is that this designation is not found in any other passage of an apostolical letter, but becomes a standing predicate of the apostles in a later age, which the greater the distance from them, looked up to them with the humbler reverence. The author of the Epistle, then, seems here to have made a slip, and to have betrayed himself involuntarily as a different man from the apostle, and as living in a later age. But on the other hand, we cannot fail to see how earnestly he tries to convince us of his identity with him. Thus he makes the apostle assure us again and again that he is Paul, the apostle of the Gentiles, the prisoner for the sake of the gospel. In Eph. iii. 1 the apostle says of him-

---

[1] As remarked in the Krit. Misc., p. 282, there is something remarkable in the frequent use of the predicate ἅγιοι as a convertible phrase with "believers" or "church." Compare with this the emphasis with which the Epistle to the Ephesians dwells on the sanctity of the Church, *e.g.* v. 27.

self: ἐγώ Παῦλος, ὁ δέσμιος τοῦ Χριστοῦ Ἰησοῦ ὑπὲρ ὑμῶν τῶν ἐθνῶν... τοῦ εὐαγγελίου, οὗ ἐγενόμην διάκονος κατὰ τὴν δωρεὰν τῆς χάριτος τοῦ Θεοῦ... ἐμοὶ τῷ ἐλαχιστοτέρῳ πάντων τῶν ἁγίων ἐδόθη ἡ χάρις αὕτη, ἐν τοῖς ἔθνεσιν εὐαγγελίσασθαι τὸν... πλοῦτον τοῦ Χριστοῦ· iv. 1, παρακαλῶ οὖν ὑμᾶς ἐγὼ ὁ δέσμιος ἐν Κυρίῳ· vi. 20, πρεσβεύω ἐν ἁλύσει. Col. i. 23, τοῦ εὐαγγελίου... οὗ ἐγενόμην ἐγὼ Παῦλος διάκονος· ver. 24, ἡ ἐκκλησία ἧς ἐγενόμην ἐγὼ διάκονος, κατὰ τὴν οἰκονομίαν τοῦ Θεοῦ, τὴν δοθεῖσάν μοι εἰς ὑμᾶς... ἐν τοῖς ἔθνεσιν. Is it the apostle's custom to speak thus of himself and his apostolate? How different are those passages which we naturally compare with the above, 1 Cor. xv. 9, 2 Cor. x. 1, Gal. v. 2. Is it not remarkable that the same thing should be insisted on again and again? How many words are used, how the expressions rise higher and higher! A notable instance of this exaggeration of expression is the peculiar form ἐλαχιστότερος, where the writer evidently had 1 Cor. xv. 9 (ἐγὼ ὁ ἐλάχιστος) before his mind. This simple and natural form, however, did not content him, nor did the phrase ἐλάχιστος τῶν ἀποστόλων, for which, with the same love of extremes, he substitutes ἐλαχιστότερος πάντων ἁγίων. And what a contrast to this ἐλαχιστότερος πάντων ἁγίων does it present, when the apostle not only reckons himself among the ἅγιοι, but even writes to the Church at Ephesus that they will be able to see from his Epistle how great insight he possesses into the mystery of Christ (iii. 4, 5).

Such digressions into personal matters, such exaggerations of the materials which are used,[1] such contradictions, in which the personation that is going on is clearly betrayed,—these are among the characteristic features of our two Epistles, as they are of the Pastorals. Here we have also to mention what De Wette justly remarks on the passage, Eph. ii. 20, that the apostle, who was actively engaged up to the end of his life, and who was conscious that his position was no other than that of a labourer for the kingdom of God, could hardly have

---

[1] Col. iii. 11 is also such a passage; it is evidently formed after the passage Gal. iii. 28, and exaggerates the differences there spoken of.

regarded himself (as we find in the passage named) as the foundation already laid, and still less in conjunction with other apostles
who laboured in a different spirit from his. Such a view would
be appropriate, as De Wette remarks, only to a disciple of the
apostle who saw before him the complete results of the apostolical labours, who was filled with reverence for them, at whose
time, moreover, the gift of prophetic inspiration had ceased to be
generally diffused throughout the Church, so that the prophets of
his age appeared to him in a higher light than that in which the
apostle Paul regarded them.

The same late date of composition is betrayed in the passage,
Eph. iv. 14, ἵνα μηκέτι ὦμεν ... κλυδωνιζόμενοι καὶ περιφερόμενοι
παντὶ ἀνέμῳ τῆς διδασκαλίας, ἐν τῇ κυβείᾳ τῶν ἀνθρώπων, etc.
This unstable swaying to and fro between different and constantly
changing doctrines, which is mentioned here as a state of things of
which there had already been experience, is quite out of place as
a picture of the apostolic age.

In conclusion, we may notice the salutations sent from Mark
and Luke, Col. iv. 10, 14. Mark and Luke are mentioned at the
close of the Second Epistle to Timothy, and as soon as doubt is
thrown upon the genuineness of that Epistle, we are led to believe
that there was some special reason for mentioning them. Their
Gospels were at that time highly valued as a basis for that
general unification of the Church which every one desired, and
thus there was a motive to call attention on every occasion to the
harmonious relation that existed between these two men, and
between them and the apostles. Thus the mention of their names
in the Epistle to the Colossians can scarcely be without some underlying motive. The mention of Mark is connected with a further
difficulty. According to the Second Epistle to Timothy (iv. 12),
which must have been the last of the apostle's letters, he was to be
called to Rome at that date, while, according to the Epistle to the
Colossians, with which that to Philemon agrees (ver. 24), he was
with the apostle at Rome already. And this is the more remarkable, that the journey of Tychicus to Ephesus, mentioned at the

same time, 2 Tim. iv. 12, can scarcely be a different one from that spoken of, Eph. vi. 21 ; Col. iv. 7. We must therefore imagine the apostle's assistants to have taken journey after journey from the east to the west, and from west to east again, if these different dates are not to stand side by side in the most glaring contradiction.

It has long been acknowledged that in expression and style these Epistles have a character of their own, and are distinguished from the Epistles of Paul ; especially is this true of the Ephesian letter. In its heavy long-drawn periods, laden with far-fetched and magniloquent expressions, we miss both the lively dialectical process and the wealth of thought for which the apostle is distinguished. In the Colossian letter this is less strikingly the case, yet in many passages it also gives us the impression of a composition without life or spontaneity, moving forward in repetitions and tautologies, and sentences grouped together with a merely outside connexion.

What, then, we have still to ask, is the true object of these Epistles, if they be not by Paul, and can only be understood in the light of the features of that later age from which they sprang ? The central idea around which everything else revolves in them is to be found in their Christology ; but it is impossible to assume that the object for which they were written was the purely theoretical one of setting forth those higher views of the person of Christ. The occasion out of which they arose must have been some practical need in the circumstances of the time ; and even the idea of the person of Christ is at once brought into a certain definite point of view. Christ, it is manifest, is taken here as the centre of the unity of all opposites. These opposites embrace the entire universe ; heaven and earth, the visible and the invisible, and everything that exists has in Christ the basis of its existence ; in him, therefore, all oppositions and distinctions disappear ; even up to the highest spirit-world there is nothing that has not its highest and absolute principle in him. This metaphysical height is sought, however, only in order to descend from it to the immediate present and its practical necessities; for here also there are opposites of which only Christ can be the reconciling and atoning unity. Here, accordingly, we find the stand-point from which the object and the contents of the Epistles can be satisfactorily comprehended. It is obvious that they point to the distinction of Gentile and Jew Christians; and thus they clearly belong to a time when these two parties were still, to some extent, opposed to each other, and when the removal of their mutual opposition was the only road to the unity of the Christian Church. How strongly the need of such unity, to be realized by the mutual approaches and the gradual fusion of the two still separated parties, was felt at the time when our Epistles were written, is clear on the face of them; first, in the earnest exhortations to unity, as especially Eph. iv. 1; in the repeated commendations of love as the bond of peace, Eph. iv. 25, v. 2; Col. ii. 2; iii. 14; and further, in all those passages where the Church is described with such emphasis as an organism sub-sisting in the idea of its own unity and the inward connexion of all its members with each other. This unity of the Church as an organic whole is the object towards which those Epistles labour with all their powers; they seek to make it clear that this oneness with the principle on which the Christian Church is based is necessarily contained in Christ as the head of the Church, and thus that the important point is to become fully alive to that which is already a fact, to recognise it practically, and carry it out. We find three momenta in which the conception of the person of Christ possesses itself its essential unity, and which supply the motives for this effort after unity which belongs to the idea of the Church. 1. The Epistle to the Colossians takes up the highest metaphysical stand-point: here Christ in his pre-mundane exist-ence as the image of the invisible God, is the principle of creation itself; if all things be created in him and through him, then all have in him their perfect unity and their highest teleological reference. As everything comes forth from him, so everything must return to him; and there is no opposition, no distinction, which is not done away in him, the principle of all unity, from the

beginning and absolutely : τὰ πάντα δι᾽ αὐτοῦ καὶ εἰς αὐτὸν
ἔκτισται, Col. i. 16. 2. The second momentum is Christ as the
κεφαλὴ τῆς ἐκκλησίας, as the Lord raised through his resurrection
and ascension, to be the head of the Church as his body. Here the
view goes upwards from beneath, as in the first instance it went downwards from above, so that both are but the two sides which cannot be disjoined, of one and the same unity realizing itself through
their difference. This second momentum is enforced with equal
emphasis in both Epistles : Col. i. 18, *sq.*, and Eph. i. 20, *sq.* Here
it is clearly set forth how in Christ, as the head of the Church,
all oppositions and differences in the Church, and indeed in the
world, must disappear, since he is pre-ordained, ἀνακεφαλαιώσασθαι
τὰ πάντα in himself as κεφαλή ; everything without distinction,
both things in heaven and things on earth (this could not be the
case were he not the absolute principle of all things existing, as he
is described, Col. i. 15). The very obvious inference is drawn
from this, how much it is the interest of the various parties in the
Church to overlook all differences that keep them from each other,
and in the consciousness of the unity of their common principle,
to come together themselves to actual unity. 3. To these two
momenta, standing as they do over against each other, comes the
third in which they are mediated. This is found in the death of
Christ. It is one of the peculiarities of those Epistles that they
regard the death of Christ in the light of an arrangement made by
God with the view of destroying the wall of partition between
Gentiles and Jews, and of reconciling both at once to God through
the peace that has thus been brought about. There is nothing
that both Epistles together insist upon more than this general
εἰρηνοποιεῖν, and ἀποκαταλάττειν, through Christ : Eph. ii. 14, *sq.* ;
Col. i. 20, *sq.* All distinction between Jews and Gentiles is abolished;
the absolute superiority which the Jew had over the Gentile is
taken from him ; for through the death of Christ the Mosaic law,
the handwriting that was against us of a law consisting in positive
commandments and ordinances of direct authority, is now destroyed.
Since, then, in Christianity all national differences and oppositions,

with everything else that divides men from each other in the
various relations of life, are abolished through the death of Christ,
there appears in it the new man who has now to lay off more and
more in practical reality the old man that still cleaves to him, Col.
iii. 9 ; Eph. ii. 10, 15 ; iv. 22. Connected with this, and starting
from a metaphysical idea of the person of Christ, the Epistle to the
Colossians represents the effects of his death in doing away with
all distinctions and oppositions, as affecting even the invisible
world.   In that sphere, also, Christ has reconciled all things
through the relation in which they stand to him, has made peace
through the blood of his cross, and brought back all things, both
in heaven and earth, to the unity that is in him.   So essential a
part is it therefore of the peculiar task of the Christian church to
strive after unity, and to realize the idea which she sees presented
to her in Christ, who is the highest and absolute principle of her
existence, as he alone can be the goal of all her efforts.

All this carries us to that period when, not without the ferment
and commotion of conflicting elements, the Christian church was
coming to realize herself and to achieve her unity.   With all the
authors of the immediately post-apostolic age whose writings
have come down to us, the prominent interest of the time appears
to have been the unity of the Church, the necessity of which they
recognised, and which they strove in various ways to usher in.
We have thus before us a state of affairs which lies beyond the
stand-point of the apostle Paul.   His task was to lay the foundations of the Gentile Christian churches ; but here we see the two
parties fully formed, and confronting each other, and the great
point is to bring them nearer to each other, and to bridge over the
gulf which still divides them.   Our Epistles find the point of
meeting where these differences may be reconciled chiefly in the
death of Christ.   In the same way the author of the Johannine
Gospel regards the unity which binds the different elements of
the Church into one body as an effect which nothing but the death
of Christ could have procured.[1]

[1] Cf. Abhandlg. über das joh. Ev. ; Theol. Jahrb. 1844, p. 621 (Unters. über
die Evang. 316).

To the apostle Paul himself this view is not familiar. It is true that the death of Christ is to him also the principle of a new creation, a new life, but with him this is only in essence, theoretically, generally, and in connexion with his doctrine of faith, inasmuch as to him who believes in Christ and his atoning death, old things are passed away, and all things are made new. But he never made a definite practical application of the death of Christ to the differences existing between the two parties out of whose union the Christian Church was to arise, such as is made here; still less did he ever ascribe to the death of Christ such an influence in the super-sensuous world as we find in our Epistles; that could be done only from the stand-point of their peculiar Christology.[1] Thus even here there is a very noticeable difference; on a closer view, however, we become aware that even the Pauline doctrines of justification by faith, and of the relation of Judaism and heathenism to each other and to Christianity, are modified in a way which can only be explained from the circumstances of the time in which these Epistles were produced, and the peaceful tendency which these circumstances impressed on them. The writer of the Epistle to the Ephesians cannot, as a true follower of Paul, degrade the Pauline doctrine of justification from the position which belongs to it; yet hardly has he mentioned faith, when he appears, although unconsciously, to be unable to refrain from going on to speak of works or love. This is most strikingly the case, ii. 8, where the sentence, τῇ γὰρ χάριτί ἐστε σεσωσμένοι διὰ τῆς πίστεως, καὶ τοῦτο οὐκ ἐξ ὑμῶν· Θεοῦ τὸ δῶρον· οὐκ ἐξ ἔργων, ἵνα μή τις καυχήσηται, indorses the Pauline doctrine with laboured and abundant emphasis; but with how little inward sequence does the next sentence follow it, a sentence adopted from the doctrine of James: αὐτοῦ γάρ ἐσμεν ποίημα, κτισθέντες ἐν

---

[1] Col. i. 20; Eph. iii. 9, *sq.* The Epistle to the Colossians represents the death of Christ as peculiarly a victory over the evil powers; Christ stripped them of their power, made a show of them openly, and triumphed over them, ii. 15. This is not found with the apostle in such immediate connexion with the death of Christ, but is a feature of later, particularly of Gnostic representations; Cf. Gesch. der Lehre von der Versöhnung, p. 27, *sq.*

Χριστῷ Ἰησοῦ ἐπὶ ἔργοις ἀγαθοῖς, οἷς προητοίμασεν ὁ Θεὸς, ἵνα ἐν αὐτοῖς περιπατήσωμεν. Works are thus to go by the side of faith, but instead of faith being alleged to be the foundation of them, they are placed by the side of faith as the final purpose of the creation of men. It is the same with love; the apostle Paul expresses by his phrase, πίστις δι' ἀγάπης ἐνεργουμένη, the inward unity of faith and love; in place of which the author of the Epistle to the Ephesians has only love by the side of faith, iii. 17, 18, and vi. 23, ἀγάπη μετὰ πίστεως. The Epistle to the Colossians prefers to take faith and works together as the moral praxis of the Christian life, i. 10; iii. 9, sq. By setting faith and love in this relation to each other, justice is to be done to both parties; and we see that in these Epistles, Gentile and Jew Christians are placed side by side, as equally privileged members of the Christian Church. Thus Judaism and heathenism equally occupy a negative position in relation to Christianity, Eph. ii. 11; Col. i. 20; yet as concessions may have been made to the Gentile Christians for the sake of unity, so out of regard for the Jewish Christians there are certain concessions made to Judaism of which the apostle Paul would not altogether have approved. It is said of the Gentiles, Eph. ii. 11, that they who were called uncircumcision by that which is called circumcision in the flesh, had been, during the whole period of heathenism, without Christ, aliens to the citizenship of Israel, unacquainted with the covenants of promise, without hope and without God in the world; but that now, they who before stood far off have come near in the blood of Christ. That is to say, the heathen have only received a share of what the Jews had before; and thus Christianity is not the absolute religion in which the negativeness of heathenism and that of Judaism come to an end together; on the contrary, the substantial contents of Christianity are just Judaism itself. Thus the universality of Christianity consists in this, that Judaism is extended to the heathen through the death of Christ. In it the hostility, the wall of division, and every thing positive that separated the two parties, has an end; both are reconciled to

God in one body and in one spirit, both have the same access to the Father. It is true that the heathen have thus, as Christians, everything that the Jews have; yet they are in the position of having been admitted, of having come near, of having received a share; for they, as the ἔθνη, are merely συγκληρόνομα καὶ σύσσωμα καὶ συμμέτοχα τῆς ἐπαγγελίας ἐν τῷ Χριστῷ. They are merely partakers of that to which the Jews have the first and indisputable claim. Now, if we consider how the Apostle expresses himself on this subject, especially in the Epistle to the Romans, we cannot admit this to be a genuine Pauline view. The deeper reason of the difference is, that the peculiar Pauline conception of faith is not familiar to these Epistles. They know nothing of faith as an inward process in the consciousness, the most essential part of which is a personal conviction and experience of the impossibility of justification through the law. Hence the object of this faith, the death of Christ, remains purely external to them. The death of Christ has indeed brought about the cancelling of the law as well as the forgiveness of sins; but the law, which is set aside in the death of Christ, appears to be here little more than the injunction of circumcision.[1]

It is in this way that the chief result of the death of Christ is the reconciliation of heathens and Jews: this reconciliation was a thing of course, as soon as the wall of partition, that is, circumcision, the difference between περιτομὴ and ἀκροβυστία, was taken away. Such is the Christian universalism of these Epistles; it is not based upon the profound idea of the Apostle's religious anthropology, but only upon the coalition of heathens and Jews, which is one of the outward effects of the death of Christ. It is the same external universalism which the pseudo-Clementine homilies make the object of Christ's death in addition to the

---

[1] The καθ' ἡμῶν χειρόγραφον τοῖς δόγμασιν, ὃ ἦν ὑπεναντίον ἡμῖν, Col. ii. 14 (cf. Eph. ii. 15, ὁ νόμος τῶν ἐντολῶν ἐν δόγμασιν), is quite adequately accounted for by referring it to the penalty connected with the injunction of circumcision, that every man not circumcised was to be regarded as liable to be put to death.

forgiveness of sins. The Christian identifies himself with a new
man, who, according to these Epistles, arises out of Christianity,
so that he, as Christian, is neither Jew nor Gentile (cf. Eph. ii. 15),
and, as Christian, has now to put off all the impurities of heathenism. Judaism thus loses, it is true, the absolute claim it made
through the law of circumcision; but for this loss the Epistle
to the Colossians seeks to provide a compensation; it is at some
pains to show that even in these altered circumstances there is a
circumcision, not ἐν σαρκὶ χειροποίητος, but ἀχειροποίητος, ἐν
τῇ ἀπεκδύσει τοῦ σώματος τῆς σαρκὸς, the περιτομὴ τοῦ Χριστοῦ,
which takes place in baptism, in which rite Christ makes alive
the νεκροὺς ὄντας ἐν τῇ ἀκροβυστίᾳ τῆς σαρκὸς, for in baptism
they renounce all sensual desires, and dedicate themselves to a
pure and holy life. This statement that Christian baptism was
to have the same meaning with Jewish circumcision, is one
we meet with elsewhere in post-Apostolic writings. The more
importance the author of the Epistle to the Colossians attaches to
the foundation thus gained for the union of Gentile and Jew
Christians, the more must he have been led to controvert the
principles of Ebionitism, a sect which repudiated universalism
if coupled with such conditions, and would hear of no renunciation of those elements which, as he shows, were irreconcilable
with the absolute Christian principle.

It is quite clear that the Epistle to the Ephesians is secondary
to that to the Colossians; but it may be doubted whether it was
written much later, and whether by another author. May not the
twin Epistles have gone forth into the world together? A comparison of the contents of both suggests that the materials have
been divided between them purposely with some such view. All
that is polemical, special, and individual, is given to the Colossian
letter: the Ephesian letter seems purposely to avoid all such topics,
while, on the other hand, it treats the general subject of the Colossian letter more at large. The close relation of the Epistles to each
other makes it somewhat striking that they seem to contain references to one another; the writer to the Colossians tells his readers

expressly, iv. 16, that they are to communicate their letter to the Laodiceans, and to get another letter from Laodicea communicated to themselves. The question is naturally suggested whether our Epistle to the Ephesians is this Laodicean epistle. Marcion asserts that the Epistle had the title, *To the Laodiceans;* but Marcion may have had no other authority for this statement than the passage, Col. iv. 16, itself. Yet though the letter was originally addressed *To the Ephesians*, and intended for them, i. 1, we may still suppose that the writer imagined the letter to have been taken by Tychicus to Ephesus, but to have been meant for other churches also ; and thus it might reach Colosse from Laodicea. This would explain why the words, iv. 16, are not τὴν εἰς Λαοδικείας, but τὴν ἐκ Λαοδικείας. If the address, Eph. i. 1, contained originally nothing more than τοῖς ἁγίοις καὶ πιστοῖς ἐν Ἰησ. Χρ., the addition τοῖς οὖσιν ἐν Ἐφέσῳ, might easily arise from 2 Tim. iv. 12, where Tychicus is spoken of, the same who is named, Eph. vi. 21, Col. iv. 7, as the messenger of the apostle and the bearer of the Epistle, Τύχικὸν δὲ ἀπέστειλα εἰς Ἔφεσον. Tychicus is thus, in any case, named as the bearer of both Epistles. Now it is curious to find it said, Eph. vi. 21, ἵνα δὲ εἰδῆτε καὶ ὑμεῖς τὰ κατʼ ἐμέ, τί πράσσω, πάντα ὑμῖν γνωρίσει ὁ Τυχικός, etc. This καὶ before ὑμεῖς can only be explained from Col. iv. 7. The author of the Epistle to the Ephesians writes as if he, that is, the apostle, had just before been writing to the Colossians the letter intended for them. This may indeed be the invention of the author of the Ephesian letter writing later than the other author. But the circumstance can be accounted for equally well by supposing that the authors of both Epistles are one and the same man. He will then have referred, Eph. vi. 21, to the Colossian epistle, as, in Col. iv. 16, to the Ephesian epistle. What makes this the more likely is, that it is hard to see why the readers of the Colossian epistle should be referred to another epistle about to reach them from Laodicea, if there were not such an Epistle in existence at the time. The same author will thus have purposely divided into two letters what he could have said in one ; and why ? Probably because he thought that what was said in the same way in two letters would produce the greater impression. The passage, Col. ii. 1, shows also how the author of this Epistle had two churches in his mind when he was writing, so that even this passage, taken in connexion with iv. 16, might make it seem not unlikely that as his subject was of equal importance to both churches, he felt himself induced to write two separate letters to them. Thus the more important the subject appeared to him with which both Epistles deal, the easier did it seem to imagine how the Apostle came to write these Epistles to two churches with which he was personally unacquainted (for this is especially remarked, Col. ii. 1, and the same thing is inferred, Eph. i. 15).[1] These explanations may have appeared necessary to the later author, but what reason could have induced the Apostle himself, judging even by the contents of our Epistles, to write to two churches with which he did not stand in any intimate relations? The Epistle to the Romans cannot be appealed to here as a case in point, unless a comparison were possible between the contents of the Epistle to the Romans and the contents of these two Epistles, which are so far inferior.

Whatever may be thought of the theory here advanced of the identical authorship of both Epistles, there can be no doubt of this, that the two are so much interwoven that they must stand or fall together in their claim to apostolic origin.

---

[1] If it be assumed that the Epistle to the Ephesians was addressed to Laodicea as a circular, we have still the difficulty that Col. ii. 1, iv. 16, mentions only Laodicea. Then it is to be considered that if Paul could not possibly write to the Ephesians in the words ascribed to him, i. 15, neither could an author, writing under his name, write in such terms, since the Apostle's relations with the Church at Ephesus were too well known to be passed over. Both Epistles appear to be written purposely to churches which were not personally known to the Apostle. Considering all this, and in addition to this, the close connexion which the Epistles bear to each other, one can scarcely avoid taking the Ephesian Epistle, in spite of its title and the οὖσιν ἐν ᾽Εφέσῳ, to be an Epistle to the Laodiceans.

FIFTH CHAPTER.

THE EPISTLE TO THE PHILIPPIANS.

THE critic who first ventured to cast doubt on the genuineness of the Epistle to the Ephesians, has lately asserted of the Epistle to the Philippians that its genuineness is above all question.[1]   It is true that no sufficient reasons have been alleged as yet for doubting its apostolic origin; yet I think there are such reasons, and I deem it necessary to state shortly, for the further consideration of criticism, what they are. I think there are three points to be considered.[2]

1. This Epistle, like the two we have just discussed, is occupied with Gnostic ideas and expressions, and that not in the way of controversy with Gnostics, but employing them, with the necessary modifications, for its own purposes.   The passage, ii. 6, one of great importance for dogmatics, and of as great difficulty, can

[1] *De Wette:* Einl. in's Neue Test. 4 Aufl. 1842, p. 268. [In his Fifth Edition, published in 1848, de Wette referred to the doubts expressed on the subject in this work and by *Schwegler*, Nachap. Zeit. ii. 133, *sq.*, but only very cursorily, characterizing them, without reason shown, as an "attack on frivolous grounds." *Lünemann* (Pauli ad Philipp. Epist., Göttingen, 1847) ; *Brückner* (Epist. ad Philipp. Paulo auctori vindicata) ; and *Ernesti* (über Philipp. ii. 6, *sq.* ; Theol. Stud. und Krit. 1848, 4 H., pp. 858-924) defended the authenticity of the Epistle against Baur at greater length.   He judged only the last of these arguments to possess any scientific value, but replied to them jointly in the Theol. Jahrb. viii. 1849, pp. 501-553 (in a section of the paper, " zur neutestamentlichen Kritik "). Ernesti returned to the subject in the Stud. und Kritiken, 1851, pp. 591-632, and was answered by Baur, Theol. Jahrb. xi. 1852, pp. 133-144, in the paper "uber Philipp. ii. 6 f." I shall refer to these two essays where they add anything to the discussion in the text, and shall reproduce the more important parts of them.]

[2] Cf. Theol. Jahrb. viii. 502. " What appears suspicious to me in the Philippian Epistle may be reduced to the following three heads :—1. The appearance of Gnostic ideas in the passage, ii. 6-9. 2. The want of anything distinctively Pauline. 3. The questionableness of some of the historical data."

scarcely be explained save on the supposition that the writer's mind
was filled with certain Gnostic ideas current at the time. What an
extraordinary conception is it that Christ, though he was in the
form of God, did not count it robbery, or, to give the words their
exact grammatical force, did not think that he must make it the
object of an *actus rapiendi*, to be equal with God. If he was God
already, how could he wish to become what he was already? But
if he was not equal with God, what an eccentric and perverted and
self-contradictory thought must it have been, to become equal with
God! Is it the inconceivableness of such a thought that is to be
expressed in the words οὐχ ἁρπαγμὸν ἡγήσατο? But how came
the Apostle to say of Christ a thing so inconceivable, even were it
merely to deny it? Though Christ did not proceed to such an act
of rapacity and arrogance, yet it seems it was possible to him, not
morally indeed, but abstractly. How is this to be explained?
The doctrines of the Gnostics show us how our author may have
come to entertain such a conception. It is a well-known Gnostic
representation, that in one of the aeons, the last of the series of
them, the Gnostic Sophia, there arose the passionate, eccentric, and
unnatural desire to penetrate forcibly into the essence of the All-
father, in order to connect herself directly with him the absolute,
and to become one with him. This desire is described as a προάλ-
λεσθαι, a darting forward, as a rash and passionate striving, as a
τολμὴ, a bold and violent attempt.[1] That aeon then sought
forcibly to seize and to appropriate what according to its nature
could never belong to it, and what it had no claim to. This whole
act, and what it aims at accomplishing, is a thing purely spiritual.
Sophia wished, as the Gnostics express it, κεκοινωνῆσθαι τῷ πατρὶ
τῷ τελείῳ, to associate herself with the father, the absolutely Perfect, and, καταλαβεῖν τὸ μέγεθος αὐτοῦ, to take up into herself
spiritually his greatness, his absolute essence. This amounts to
such an identity with God the Absolute, as is conveyed by the expression of our Epistle, τὸ εἶναι ἴσα Θεῷ, and only this consideration, that, according to the original Gnostic conception of it, the

---

[1] Iren. adv. Haer. i. 2. 2.

act was a purely spiritual one, makes it intelligible how our Epistle comes to speak of such a self-contradictory attempt as εἶναι ἴσα Θεῷ. On the one side, the identity with God is a thing still to be realized ; on the other, the reality of it is presupposed. The interpreters of the Epistle are thus driven to assert that the correct rendering of οὐχ ἁρπαγμὸν ἡγήσατο, is compatible only with such a view of εἶναι ἴσα Θεῷ, as makes it a thing which Christ did not yet possess ; for otherwise it could not be said that he did not wish to seize it for himself. But, they say, in order that the renunciation may be conceived as a voluntary one, we must ascribe to Christ the possibility which lies in the ἐν μορφῇ Θεοῦ ὑπάρχων. Christ then had the divine glory, *potentia*, in himself, and could have claimed it, could have made it appear in his life. But since it did not consist with the purpose of the plan of redemption that Christ should at once receive divine honour, it would have been a robbery, an act of presumption, if he had taken it to himself. But what, we must ask, was Christ, if, while ἐν μορφῇ Θεοῦ ὑπάρχων, he yet possessed the divine glory only *potentia*, if, though actually God, he yet was not God ? And what conceivable reason is there for saying that he voluntarily renounced a thing which, from the nature of the case, it was impossible that he should have ? This being and not being, this having and not having, is possible only in the spiritual sphere ; the distinction drawn is that between what is essentially and what is not only essentially, but also for consciousness. And the Gnostic aeons are the categories and conceptions in which the absolute becomes the object of the subjective consciousness : they are themselves the spiritual subjects in which the absolute subjectivates and individualizes itself ; or they are the subjective side, on which the absolute is not only the absolute in essence, but is also the absolute self-consciousness. Since, however, they are in plurality what the absolute is in unity, the descending series of aeons exhibits an ever-growing divergence between the consciousness of which the absolute is the object, and the absolute itself as the object of consciousness. The consciousness of these spiritual subjects, these aeons in which consciousness shows

itself as the subjective side over against the other objective side,
can, by its own nature, deal with nothing but the absolute, and yet
the further off they stand, the less can they with their consciousness embrace and comprehend it (καταλαβεῖν). Thus, then, the
aeon we spoke of directs itself to the absolute with the whole
energy of its spiritual force, seeks to grasp the absolute, to comprehend it, to become equal with it, to be one with it ; but in this it
undertakes a thing which is in itself impossible, by which it overleaps the boundaries of its own spiritual nature, and seeks, as it were,
to commit an unnatural robbery of the absolute. Thus, in the very
nature of the case, it cannot possibly succeed ;[1] and if it let itself
be borne along by this impulse, it will only become aware of the
negativity of its own being,—a thing which the Gnostics represented
by saying that the aeon fell down out of the πλήρωμα into the
κένωμα.[2] Thus one passage speaks also of a κενοῦν in connexion
with the ἁρπαγμὸς, and it is very clear from this that our author
is familiar with the same representations, that he proceeds upon
them, only with this difference, that what had a merely speculative
interest to the Gnostics, has with him a moral significance. With
the Gnostics the ἁρπαγμὸς is a thing that actually takes place, but
by its unnaturalness comes to an end without spreading further, and
has merely negative consequences ;[3] in this case, however, there is

---

[1] διὰ τὸ ἀδυνάτῳ ἐπιβαλεῖν πράγματι. Iren. loc. cit.

[2] Iren, i. 4. 1 : ἐν σκιαῖς καὶ κενώματος τόποις ἔξω φωτὸς ἐγένετο καὶ πληρώματος. 4. 2 : ἐν τῷ σκότει καὶ τῷ κενώματι. Compare Theodoret, Haer. Fab. i. 7,
ἔξω τοῦ πληρώματος, ἐν σκιᾷ τινι καὶ κενώματι διάγειν.

[3] This statement, however, requires to be qualified (as is observed, Theol.
Jahrb. viii. 507) : "That aeon which sought to grasp and comprehend the absolute essence of God, and fell from the πλήρωμα to the κένωμα, through attempting
the impossible, did yet at last arrive at the πλήρωμα. For the πλήρωμα does at
last, at the consummation of the world's history, receive all spiritual beings, and
in it they all become one with the absolute. This shows us what the unnatural
attempt spoken of here really signifies. It was unnatural, in that the aeon in
question desired to attain immediately and at once, what could not, according to
Gnostic conceptions, be attained save as a result of the whole process of the
development of the world. The attempt was suggested to the aeon by a subjective and unreasonable impulse. It was however, at the same time, the beginning
from which the development of the world proceeded, and was thus a necessary
momentum. If the genesis of the world be regarded as a falling away (and this

a moral self-determination, which stops short of such a ἁρπαγμὸς. It is not, in this case, that the action has failed, but that it has not taken place at all: there is a voluntary renunciation and self-abasement, and instead of the Gnostic γενέσθαι ἐν κενώματι we have a ἑαυτὸν κενοῦν. Thus the voluntary act of refraining from ἁρπαγμὸς, in our Epistle, is a modification of the speculative ἁρπαγμὸς of Gnosticism. When the question is made an ethical one, as it is here, there seems to be little need for saying that Christ did not seek to seize a thing before his moral probation, which could only be attained in the way of moral probation. What can be gained only through moral effort, that will no one gain, save as the fruit of his moral effort. This is so self-evident, that if it be said, as it is here, we have a right to conclude that the statement has reference to, and is occasioned by, some previous speculation. The statement could not otherwise have been made, at least in the form in which we find it.[1]

is the point of view here), then it is of course both subjectively arbitrary and objectively necessary." The ἁρπαγμὸς therefore denotes "that the aeon sought to assert at a leap, as it were, at once, through a violent act or a robbery, that identity with the absolute which could only be realized through the whole cosmic process;" that it "sought to seize by an act of will, violently and prematurely, what it could only gain by a certain definite process." Christ did the opposite of this: he did not seize the εἶναι ἶσα Θεῷ, the divine worship that should place him on an equality with God, violently, as a right belonging to him in virtue of his divine nature (the μορφὴ Θεοῦ), but earned it by voluntary self-abnegation (cf. Theol. Jahrb. xi. 134 sq., viii. 508 sq.). The author also admits distinctly (Theol. Jahrb. xi. 142) that ἁρπαγμὸς cannot be shown to be a Gnostic term; he thinks, however, that this is of no great importance if the idea denoted by the word is found in Gnostic systems.—Editor.

[1] The author insists again on this point in Theol. Jahrb. viii. 508 sq. "If," he says, "Christ was ἐν μορφῇ Θεοῦ ὑπάρχων, then his nature was from this very fact divine. Now if this ἐν μορφῇ Θεοῦ ὑπάρχειν was not equivalent to εἶναι ἶσα Θεῷ, this must mean that what he was essentially, as ἐν μ. Θ. ὑπάρχων, could only proceed to the εἶναι ἶσα Θεῷ (i.e. become the true and actual contents of his consciousness) by his vindicating his divine nature in the way of moral effort— by the proof of his obedience. But if the εἶναι ἶσα be thus a question of moral achievement, how could it be said of Christ that he ever dreamed of the possibility of attaining, without moral action, that which could not exist save as the fruit of moral action? It is clear that the author is referring here to certain other views. It could never have suggested itself to him to connect with Christ such an absurd and self-contradictory idea or intention, even though it were only to deny that he cherished it. The idea must have been suggested to him from without."

D

The other expressions used in this passage afford additional evidence of Gnostic modes of thought and expression having been before the author's mind. The contrast μορφὴ Θεοῦ and μορφὴ δούλου looks indeed sufficiently simple, yet the peculiar conception indicated by μορφὴ Θεοῦ can only be understood by a reference to the use of those terms by the Gnostic. The expressions μορφὴ, μορφοῦν, μόρφωσις, were very common with them. That which constitutes the peculiar character of one of the higher spiritual beings is the μορφὴ of that being; hence the Gnostics said of the fallen aeon, that when it passed out of the light and the pleroma, it was ἄμορφος καὶ ἀνείδεος, ὥσπερ ἔκτρωμα, and that διὰ τὸ μηδὲν κατειληφέναι because that was wanting to him which was necessary to make up his definite spiritual nature. Hence when Christ was sent out of the pleroma to help him, the first thing he did to him was τῇ ἰδίᾳ δυνάμει μορφῶσαι μόρφωσιν, τὴν κατ᾽ οὐσίαν μόνον, ἀλλ᾽ οὐ τὴν κατὰ γνῶσιν.[1] The aeon was to come to itself out of the state of utter negation in which it had been lying; it was to receive its own μορφὴ, and that in two stages. The first stage of the process of μορφοῦν was the μόρφωσις κατ᾽ οὐσίαν, referring to that which the aeon was in essence, in substance; then followed the μόρφωσις κατὰ γνῶσιν, by which he became in consciousness also what he was already in essence. This of itself shows us that the ἐν μορφῇ Θεοῦ ὑπάρχειν means the same thing, and is identical with εἶναι ἴσα Θεῷ.[2] But this can be distinctly proved to be according to the Gnostic use of terms.

Ernesti admits the force of this, but finds the suggestion in the Mosaic narrative of the Fall. Baur replies, op. cit. viii. 509 sqq., xi. 138 sqq., that this parallel is little to the point, and that our passage exhibits no trace of any reference to that narrative. He points out that the condition of our first parents before the Fall does not in the least correspond to the μορφὴ Θεοῦ here ascribed to Christ; that the robbery of the tree in Paradise which they committed is entirely unlike the ἁρπαγμὸς said to have been before the mind of Christ; and that the εἶναι ἴσα Θεῷ, which he did not obtain through a ἁρπαγμὸς, is quite a different thing from the ἔσεσθε ὡς θεοὶ, promised to our first parents by the serpent, and which they actually attained by eating the forbidden fruit. This latter was simply the knowledge of good and evil.—Editor.

[1] Cf. Iren. i. 4. 1 ; 5. 1.   Theod. Haer. Fab. i. 7.
[2] With the difference however (as the author explains, Th. Jahrb. viii. 507) of

The Gnostics said of the νοῦς or μονογενὴς that he was ὅμοιός τε καὶ ἴσος τῷ προβαλόντι, to the primal aeon, or the absolute ground of existence, as the μόνος χωρῶν τὸ μέγεθος τοῦ πατρός, since he only comprehends the absolute greatness of the Father, and in him the absolute unfolds itself to consciousness.[1]   On this account he is also called the sum of all the aeons of the Pleroma, the ἀρχὴ καὶ μόρφωσις παντὸς τοῦ πληρώματος. The number of the aeons is completed by Christ and the Holy Spirit. Christ taught the aeons that the essence of the Father is in itself quite incomprehensible, and that the knowledge of it is possible only through the μονογενὴς, and that the cause of the eternal existence of the aeons was that absolute, and for them quite incomprehensible, being of the Father; the cause of the existence of the Monogenes, however, through whom alone the Father is known, and of his μόρφωσις, was that which is comprehensible in the Father, ᾧ δὴ ἰσός ἐστι (ὁ μονογενὴς). Thus he is equal with him, identical with him, inasmuch as he comprehends the Father, and is subjectively what the Father is objectively.   This ἴσος εἶναι τῷ πατρὶ is accordingly his μόρφωσις or his μορφή, and since this μορφή is nothing but the being equal, the being one with the Father, he is himself in fact the μορφή of the Father, or ὑπάρχων ἐν μορφῇ Θεοῦ.   Through the Holy Spirit all the aeons were held to have become μορφῇ καὶ γνώμῃ ἴσοι, equal to each other, so that each was what the others were, and thereby as much ἴσος to the Father as the Nous or Monogenes is; and their μορφή consisted just in this, that they were thus ἴσοι.[2]   In a writer so obviously influenced by Gnostic ideas, it cannot surprise us to find a close approach to the Docetism of the

that which is essentially, and that which is not only essentially, but also for consciousness.

[1] Iren. i. 1. 1.

[2] To see how great the difficulties are with which this classical passage must be surrounded, so long as the solution is not sought in the way I have indicated, one has only to look at the exertions expended on it by USTERI (Entw. des paul. Lehrb. 4 A., pp. 309-315).   In his position these exertions are certainly not uncalled for.   The chief difficulty is, as he seems to be aware, to decide whether the expression ἐν μορφῇ Θεοῦ ὑπάρχων and ἴσα εἶναι Θεῷ, and their correlatives, are to be taken in an ethico-religious or in a physical and substantial sense.

Gnostics. This is undoubtedly the case in verse 7. If, as ἐν ὁμοιώματι ἀνθρώπων γενόμενος, Christ was only ὅμοιος to men, then he was no true and actual man, but only seemed to be so. The expression ὁμοίωμα can signify only similarity, analogy; it cannot denote identity or parity of essence (compare Rom. vi. 5). The passage Rom. viii. 3, where it is said of the Son that God sent him ἐν ὁμοιώματι σαρκὸς ἁμαρτίας, cannot be reckoned a parallel to this. The ὁμοίωμα there predicated of the Son is that likeness which as the Son he necessarily wears to the σὰρξ ἁμαρτίας. Here, however, the ὁμοίωμα is extended to human nature generally : and this is just the difference between the Docetic view and the orthodox. That this is the meaning of ὁμοίωμα in our passage is sufficiently clear from the phrase σχήματι εὑρεθεὶς ὡς ἄνθρωπος, which stands close beside it, and does not admit of any other interpretation. Though we should not press the ὡς and εὑρεθῆναι (ὡς indicates no more than an opinion, a view, a comparison, and εὑρεθῆναι is not equivalent to εἶναι; it refers merely to the outward appearance, to the qualities by which a subject presents itself to external observation), yet in σχῆμα we have as clearly as need be the notion of an *externus habitus*, of a thing changing, passing, and quickly disappearing (cf. 1 Cor. vii. 31).[1]

Purely Gnostic, again, is the author's view of the three regions, the heavenly, the earthly, and the subterranean, to all of which equally the power and rule of Christ extend. The καταχθόνιοι cannot but remind us of the Gnostic idea of the descent into hell. The peculiar manner, noticeable both in this Epistle and in the two which we last considered, in which Gnostic and Catholic conceptions are mingled and pass into each other ; the unsuspecting use the writers make of notions, bearing unmistakeably the stamp of Gnosticism, and which they modify only so far as the practical and religious objects they had to serve, made it necessary to do so— these things manifestly belong to a time when Gnosticism had not yet become the definite and striking phenomenon that it was afterwards, and when it was still in process of development out of

---

[1] Compare on this point Th. Jahrb. viii. 515 *sq.*, xi. 144.

the various elements then present. It was the era of the first awaking of Christian speculation, excited by the floating ideas of the time, from which speculation the Christian consciousness itself was to receive its peculiar dogmatic contents. At its outset Christian speculation found its leading and most powerful interest in the idea of the person of Christ; it was around this idea that the absolute contents of the Christian consciousness crystallized into their definite objective form. This growing occupation with the person of Christ comes out very strongly in doxological passages, such as Eph. i. 19 *sq.*; iii. 8 *sq.*; Col. i. 15 *sq.*, and, more than in any of these, in the passage we have been considering, which has quite the air of a doxology.

2. This affinity with Gnosis is the chief feature which the Epistle to the Philippians has in common with those to the Ephesians and Colossians. It differs from them chiefly in its prevailing subjectivity of tone. This is generally extolled as the peculiar beauty of this Epistle, and the sentiments and dispositions which it exhibits to us are certainly sweet and touching; yet this must not blind us to the fact that the Epistle is characterized very decidedly by monotonous repetition of what has already been said, by a want of any profound and masterly connexion of ideas, and by a certain poverty of thought, of which the writer himself seems to have been somewhat painfully aware, as he says in excuse, iii. 1, τὰ αὐτὰ γράφειν ὑμῖν, ἐμοὶ μὲν οὐκ ὀκνηρὸν, ὑμῖν δὲ ἀσφαλὲς. Connected with this there is another consideration which must count as an important element in judging of the Epistle, viz. that we find no motive nor occasion for it, no distinct indication of any purpose, or of any leading idea. There is certainly polemic against Jewish opponents, yet one can hardly avoid the impression that this is there simply because it seemed to belong to the standing character of Pauline Epistles. There is nothing fresh or natural in this polemic; the circumstances do not stand out with any palpable form. Could any description of the opponents of Christianity be more vague or general than this?—iii. 18 : πολλοὶ περιπατοῦσιν, οὓς πολλάκις ἔλεγον ὑμῖν, νῦν δὲ κλαίων λέγω, τοὺς ἐχθροὺς τοῦ

σταυροῦ τοῦ Χριστοῦ, ὧν τὸ τέλος ἀπώλεια, ὧν ὁ Θεὸς ἡ κοιλία, καὶ ἡ δόξα ἐν τῇ αἰσχύνῃ αὐτῶν, οἱ τὰ ἐπίγεια φρονοῦντες. The statements added by the interpreters in order to fill up the character of these Judaizing opponents and false teachers are borrowed from other Epistles; our Epistle itself affords no special features; it does not even appear where these opponents are to be looked for, whether at Rome or at Philippi. It is in vain that our author uses the strongest phrases to describe his antagonists; they fail to bring his polemic the colour which it wants. How harshly does his argument begin with the rude words, iii. 2, βλέπετε τοὺς κύνας; and how forced is the contrast that is attempted to be drawn between κατατομὴ and περιτομή, circumcision and concision! The Christians, that is, are the περιτομή; the Jews, the spurious circumcision, or the κατατομή. But how inaccurate is this; the difference between the true circumcision and the false is a qualitative one, but is here represented as quantitative by the exaggeration of περιτομὴ to κατατομή. Nor is this peculiar and unnatural contrast required by anything lying in the writer's way; it is evidently brought in in order to give the apostle an opportunity to predicate περιτομὴ of himself, that he may then go on to discourse of his own person. This, as we have already remarked, is always an important point to the writers of pseudo-apostolic letters, so conscious are they of their double personality.

Let us, however, examine the passage in which the apostle speaks of himself; it is manifestly nothing but an imitation of the passage in 2 Cor. xi. 13 sq. In the ἐργάται δόλιοι, verse 13, we have the κακοὺς ἐργάτας of our passage, and then the one passage follows the other in a number of details, even the introduction of the apostle's person through the idea of περιτομὴ finding its precedent in the original. In 2 Cor. xi. 18 sq. the apostle speaks of his καυχᾶσθαι in contrast to the καυχᾶσθαι of his Judaizing opponents, which he characterizes, verse 18, as a καυχᾶσθαι κατὰ τὴν σάρκα. To it he replies that if so great importance is to be attached to outward things of that sort, he himself can boast of the same distinctions as they possess, reluctant though he be to speak of them. Now the author of our Epistle refers this καυχᾶσθαι κατὰ τὴν σάρκα especially to the distinction of circumcision, and so puts these words into the apostle's mouth, verse 3, ἡμεῖς γάρ ἐσμεν ἡ περιτομή. Then, in order to ascribe to the apostle the true περιτομή, he takes the idea of circumcision first in a spiritual sense; οἱ πνεύματι Θεῷ λατρεύοντες, καὶ καυχώμενοι ἐν Χριστῷ Ἰησοῦ καὶ οὐκ ἐν σαρκὶ πεποιθότες. In the following words, however, καίπερ ἐγὼ ἔχων πεποίθησιν καὶ ἐν σαρκὶ, he returns to the idea of bodily circumcision. Here we recognise what the apostle says of himself, 2 Cor. xi. 18, κἀγὼ καυχήσομαι, i.e. ἐν σαρκὶ; and as in what follows there (cf. verse 23, ὑπὲρ ἐγὼ) he seeks to outbid his opponents with his καυχᾶσθαι, so here also we read: εἴ τις δοκεῖ ἄλλος πεποιθέναι ἐν σαρκὶ, ἐγὼ μᾶλλον. This πεποιθέναι ἐν σαρκὶ, which is merely another expression for the καυχᾶσθαι κατὰ τὴν σάρκα of 2 Cor. xi. 18, is then carried out into detail, verse 5, the περιτομὴ being placed at the head of the enumeration as the principal item. After the words περιτομῇ ὀκταήμερος, it is said ἐκ γένους Ἰσραὴλ, instead of Ἰσραηλῖταί εἰσι: κἀγώ, and Ἐβραῖος ἐξ Ἐβραίων, instead of Ἐβραῖοί εἰσι; κἀγώ, 2 Cor. xi. 22. This, however, is merely to give the apostle an occasion to speak more at large about himself, and to contrast his present Christian view of life with that πεποιθέναι ἐν σαρκὶ. Can it possibly be doubted that the author had before his eyes that passage of the Corinthian letter, and followed it as the apostle himself could never have done? The use of the expression κύνες can only be explained from the strong and vehement language in which the apostle denounces his opponents, 2 Cor. xi., and from the accustomed exaggeration of imitators. But how uncalled for and how forced does this speech of the apostle about himself appear when we compare it with the manner in which he deals with his opponents in the original passage. There we see at once what it is all about. How weak and lifeless is this imitation! What the apostle is made to say about his former life is just what nobody could fail to know. How petty is the mention of the circumcision

on the eighth day, how far from Pauline is the conception of a δικαιοσύνη ἐν νόμῳ, how dull and uninteresting is the whole episode!
There are other thoughts and expressions in this part of the Epistle
which remind us of the Corinthian Epistles ; cf. verse 10 with 2 Cor.
iv. 10 sq.; verses 11-14, with 1 Cor. ix. 24 sq.; verse 15, τέλειοι,
with 1 Cor. ii. 6 ; verse 17, συμμιμηταί μου γίνεσθε, with 1 Cor.
xi. 1, μιμηταί μου γίνεσθε; verse 19, with 2 Cor. xi. 15; verse 21
with 1 Cor. xv. 47 sq. This more or less obvious reappearance of
passages out of the older Epistles, together with the intentional
leading of the discourse to the apostle's own person, his earlier and
his present life, must certainly excite a prejudice against our Epistle.
Nor do we find any clear reason which could have led the apostle
to write this Epistle, and which might thus create an impression in
its favour. A special reason is indeed mentioned, iv. 10 sq., in the
shape of a present which the Philippians are said to have sent to
Rome for the apostle's support. This, however, is spoken of in connexion with former subsidies in such a way as to fail entirely to
satisfy us. Speaking of this last subsidy, iv. 15, the apostle reminds
his readers of the fact that from the commencement of his preaching
of the gospel, ever since his departure from Macedonia, he has
received such gifts from no church but that of Philippi, and that
during his stay at Thessalonica they sent him assistance more than
once. Now we must ask how this is to be reconciled with the
apostle's distinct assertion, 1 Cor. ix. 15, according to which he
stood in no such relation towards any church whatever : ἐγὼ οὐδενὶ
ἐχρησάμην τούτων, namely, ἐκ τοῦ εὐαγγελίου ζῆν. His μισθὸς
was ἵνα εὐαγγελιζόμενος ἀδάπανον θήσω τὸ εὐαγγέλιον τοῦ Χριστοῦ, εἰς τὸ μὴ καταχρήσασθαι τῇ ἐξουσίᾳ μου ἐν τῷ εὐαγγελίῳ.
Now the exactness of the truth of these words is certainly qualified
by the apostle's own confession, 2 Cor. xi. 9, that during his stay
at Corinth, brethren who came from Macedonia supplied his wants.
The statement of the first passage, however, is only qualified, not
entirely falsified, by the second ; and the case mentioned, 2 Cor.
xi. 9, can only have been an exception. But here, Phil. iv. 15, it
is made to appear as if there had been a system of subsidies all along,

as if the apostle had received regular contributions from the
Philippians, and had a sort of account of debtor and creditor with
them (λόγος δόσεως καὶ λήψεως). The explanation of this is, in
our opinion, that the author had the passage 2 Cor. xi. 9 before
him, and drew from it a conclusion which it does not warrant,
failing to allow due weight to the other passage. The λόγος
δόσεως καὶ λήψεως is evidently our author's equivalent for the
balance spoken of, 2 Cor. xi. 9, in the words προσαναπληροῦν τὸ
ὑστέρημα.

Another curious circumstance here claims our attention. The
interpreters of this Epistle agree with us in thinking that there is
a reference to 2 Cor. xi. 9 : they say that the words ὅτε ἐξῆλθον
ἀπὸ Μακεδονίας point to the subsidy received at Corinth, and that
then (verse 16) the apostle goes back to what he had received at
different times at Thessalonica in order to make his enumeration
complete. De Wette thinks that the καὶ requires this interpretation, and that the reason why the enumeration does not follow
the chronological order is that the subsidy received at Corinth was
the most considerable, and so suggested itself first to the apostle's
mind. But if it was so considerable, why is it not expressly mentioned ? The words ὅτε ἐξῆλθον ἀπὸ Μακεδονίας cannot be held
to refer specially to a subsidy received at Corinth ; the statement
made is a general one, that he received assistance from them from
the time of his leaving Macedonia. The apostle could not have
passed over the most important instance without mentioning it,
and it is evidently not he himself, but some other man who expresses
himself in this way. This other writer considered that the case
mentioned in 2 Cor. was so well known that he did not need to
refer to it specially ; he took it for granted, and went on to speak
of other acts of assistance, introducing them with the particle καὶ.
This καὶ cannot be explained in any other way. Now if these
subsidies were so frequent that the apostle was in a position to
count upon them as ordinary occurrences (at least in the case of
the Philippian church), it is hard to see how much is left of the
principle which he asserts in 1 Cor. ix. 15. There is evidence, more-

over, to show that the apostle cannot have received many such
subsidies at Thessalonica : for according to the Acts he did not reside there for any length of time. Thus hardly any other conclusion
is open to us than this, that the author exaggerated what he found
in 1 Cor. ix., about the ἀδελφοὶ ἐλθόντες ἀπὸ Μακεδονίας, and was
thus led to represent the apostle as having been assisted by regular
contributions from the Philippian church from the date when he left
Macedonia (ὅτε ἐξῆλθον ἀπὸ Μακεδονίας); or rather, as soon as he
left Philippi, since his residence in Thessalonica, a town which was
also in Macedonia, is counted along with the ὅτε ἐξῆλθον ἀπὸ
Μακεδονίας. Hence we notice that under the ἀδελφοὶ ἐλθόντες
ἀπὸ Μακεδονίας, this writer understood none but Christians from
Philippi. Thus what is told us, in chap. iv. 10, of a special occasion for the writing of the Epistle gives us no clear insight into
the apostle's circumstances at the time, and this of itself might
lead us to conclude that we have here no set of actual historical
circumstances, but only an imaginary situation. The more we consider the historical groundwork of the Epistle, the more probable
does this appear.

3. We have still to consider what is said in chap. i. 12, both
about the great progress of the Gospel in Rome, and of the deep
impression which the captivity of the apostle and his preaching
of the Gospel are said to have produced in the whole Praetorium
and throughout that city.[1] This statement stands quite alone and
unsupported ; it is not corroborated either by the Epistles which
profess to have been written from the apostle's captivity in Rome,
or from any other quarter. Yet the fact is not in itself incredible,
and no one would have thought of calling it in question had not
the author himself taken up into his Epistle another fact which
gives us so clear an insight into his plot, that it is impossible for
us to take his assertions as simple history. The attention which
the Gospel commanded in the whole Praetorium, and in Rome
generally, is supposed, as we see from iv. 22, to have had for one

---

[1] ἐν ὅλῳ τῷ πραιτωρίῳ καὶ τοῖς λοιποῖς πᾶσι : who are those λοιποὶ πάντες, but
the general Roman public ?

of its consequences that there were believers even in the imperial household. Ἀσπάζονται ὑμᾶς, the author says at the conclusion of his letter, πάντες οἱ ἅγιοι, μάλιστα δὲ οἱ ἐκ τῆς Καίσαρος οἰκίας. This is obviously meant to draw attention to the brilliant and noteworthy results of the apostle's preaching at Rome ; and there can be no doubt that in the λοιποὶ πάντες, i. 13, the author was thinking particularly of those ἐκ τῆς Καίσαρος οἰκίας. How is it then that this remarkable result of the apostle's activity at Rome during his imprisonment, a thing so important for the history of Christianity, meets us nowhere but in the Epistle to the Philippians ? The key to this question is found in the Clement who is mentioned, iv. 3 ; it is certainly a remarkable circumstance that this Clement, named nowhere else in the apostolic Epistles, is named here as sending greeting in a letter in which no other of the apostle's friends or assistants is mentioned as doing so. This marked mention of Clement cannot be held to be without significance. Since neither history nor tradition knows of any other Clement at that time, this must be the same who is placed elsewhere in the closest relations with the apostle Peter, and who is said to have been ordained by him as the first bishop of the Church at Rome. Now in the early legendary history it is reported of this same Clement that he was connected by blood with the imperial household. The Clementine Homilies, which derive their name from this Clement, represent him as the disciple, the companion, and the successor of the apostle Peter, and narrate his life in the form of a Christian romance, say of him that he was ἀνὴρ πρὸς γένους Τιβερίου Καίσαρος. Legend, then, was acquainted with a Clement who was a member of the imperial house, and who was converted by an apostle ; and the Clement of our Epistle is exactly the man in whose person Christianity is represented in the imperial house. One being thus given, our author meant us to infer that there were several believing members of the imperial house, and so made his apostle send greetings from the whole of them to the Church at Philippi. But how had Christianity gained access to the imperial house ? How could even the report

of it get there ?   There was another well-known circumstance at
hand to explain this, namely, the position which Paul had come to
occupy as a Roman prisoner in the Praetorium.   The Praetorium
was closely connected with the imperial household, and the apostle
had been committed, at his arrival in Rome, to the praefectus
praetorio, the στρατοπεδάρχης of Acts xxviii. 16, and guarded by
a soldier of the imperial guard.   Here, then, was a door through
which, as soon as it had gained belief in the Praetorium, Christianity might penetrate to the house of the emperor.   Thus one
circumstance fits into another in a perfectly natural way, and it is
easy to account for the emphatic mention of the προκοπὴ τοῦ
εὐαγγελίου and the φανεροὺς γενέσθαι ἐν Χριστῷ τοὺς δεσμοὺς ἐν
ὅλῳ τῷ πραιτωρίῳ καὶ τοῖς λοιποῖς πᾶσι at the beginning of the
Epistle.   The two facts given are, on the one side, the Roman
Clement, and on the other side the praefectus praetorio.   What
lies between the two—the interest of the whole Praetorium in Paul
and in Christianity, and the conversion of several members of the
imperial house—this seems scarcely more than the natural inference
by which these two facts are linked together.   Yet we must not
conclude that because this combination seems so natural, the facts
actually followed each other in this order ; what we know of the
Roman Clement will not allow us to do so.   He cannot, indeed,
be said to be altogether the creature of legend ; there is some fact
or other at the root of the legend ; but the facts, so far as we know
them, only serve to show that the apostle himself could not have
named the Roman Clement in this way.   It has long been remarked, and justly,[1] that the *fundus fabulae,* in the case of the
Roman Clement, is that Flavius Clemens who is known to us from
Suetonius,[2] Dio Cassius,[3] and Eusebius.[4]   The correspondence can
hardly be mistaken, and is remarkable as an example of the
process of formation of a Christian legend.   We can see to the
bottom of the process, and that in the case of so important a

---

[1] Even by Cotelier, Recogn. S. Clem. 7, 8.   Patr. Apost. vol. i. p. 554.
[2] Domit. c. 15.
[3] In the extract of Xiphilinus, lxvii. 14 (iii. 2, 23, in Appendix to Dio Cassius).
[4] H. E. iii. 18.

personage in Christian legend as the Roman Clement. It is reported of both, of the Clement of the Roman imperial history and of him of Christian legend, that they were related to the imperial family. Suetonius calls Flavius Clemens a *patruelis* of Domitian. We are warranted to hold him to have been a friend and adherent of Christianity, for the ἀθεότης for which he was sentenced to death by Domitian, and which is equivalent in the narrative of Dio Cassius to the ἤθη τῶν Ἰουδαίων, mentioned by him in the same connexion, is the common heathen designation of Christianity. The *contemtissima inertia* with which Suetonius charges him, agrees with this very well ; as a Christian he could not take any great interest in the politics of Rome, and this must have come out markedly during his consulate ; hence, as Suetonius reports his fate, Domitian *repente ex tenuissima suspicione tantum non in ipso ejus consulatu interemit.* Then, as the family of the Clement of the Homilies was forced to quit Rome by some dark fatality menacing them, and returned thither only after manifold vicissitudes, so the wife, at least, of Flavius Clemens, Flavia Domitilla, experienced a similar change of fortune. According to Dio Cassius, she was banished to the island Pandateria for the same reason for which her husband lost his life ; but she afterwards returned to Rome, since Domitian, as Tertullian says, when speaking of his mode of persecuting, *facile coeptum repressit, restitutis etiam, quos relegaverat.*[1] This is the historical basis of the legend of the Roman Clement ; there is no historical authority for any Clement but this one, and we have no warrant to assume an apostolic Clement different from him. The passage in the Epistle to the Philippians cannot count as evidence, if there be reason to doubt the apostolic origin of that Epistle.[2] The death

---

[1] Apolog. ch. 4.

[2] The Epistle extant under the name of Clement cannot be appealed to in evidence that there was actually an apostolic Clement different from the other. Whatever be the date assigned to that Epistle, the name prefixed to it can never prove that it was written by the Clement of Christian legend. We are not obliged to hold the Epistle of Barnabas to have been written by the Barnabas with whom we are acquainted, because it bears the name of Barnabas.

of Flavius Clemens is said to have been accompanied by certain
terrible phenomena (*continuis octo mensibus*, says Suetonius, *fulgura
facta nuntiataque sunt*), and to have been much spoken of on this
account; and this would make it the more intelligible how this
Clement, as one of the first Romans of good family to confess
Christianity, and to become a martyr to that faith, received so
prominent a place in Christian legendary history. In order to
make him a companion of the apostles and the successor of Peter
in the Roman Church, he was removed further back, and made a
relative of Tiberius instead of Domitian. Now if he became a
Christian only in the reign of Domitian, how could the apostle
Paul call him his συνεργὸς? This connexion with the apostle
Paul can only have been ascribed to him by one writing in the
post-apostolic age, when the Clement we have spoken of had
already been transformed into the well-known Clement of the
Roman legend. The mention of him in the Epistle to the Philippians is thus a criterion in judging of the genuineness of that
Epistle; and more than this, it throws a new light on the whole
composition of the Epistle. From this Clement and the interest,
of which he was held to be the evidence, which the οἰκία
τοῦ Καίσαρος took in the cause of the Gospel, the Epistle obtains
the προκοπὴ τοῦ εὐαγγελίου, i. 12, and this is the reason of that
fervent joy which is expressed all through the Epistle as the deep
and prevailing sentiment of the apostle's heart. Whatever the
author makes the apostle write about, no single subject is left
without a reference to his prevailing joyfulness, that χαίρω καὶ
συγχαίρω πᾶσιν ὑμῖν· τὸ δ᾽ αὐτὸ καὶ ὑμεῖς χαίρετε καὶ συγχαίρετέ
μοι, ii. 17, 18 (cf. iii. 1, χαίρετε ἐν Κυρίῳ: iv. 1, χαρὰ καὶ στέφανός
μου: v. 4, χαίρετε ἐν Κυρίῳ πάντοτε, πάλιν ἐρῶ χαίρετε: v. 10,
ἐχάρην δὲ ἐν Κυρίῳ μεγάλως) is found again and again as the
refrain of every passage. This predominant feeling outweighed
the pressure, the restraint, the clouded future in which there was
so little prospect of further action in the cause of the Gospel, and
all the cares of his position at the time. In this respect the Epistle
to the Philippians presents such a contrast with the second to

Timothy, that it has long been felt that these two writings must be placed at very different periods of the apostle's captivity at Rome. Nothing but this prevailing feeling of joy can explain to us how the author ventures to make his apostle express the hope of speedy deliverance from his imprisonment. And yet it appears very natural that an author living at a later period could not quite conceal how the well-known death of the apostle was present to his mind. Mixed with his feelings of joy, we find thoughts of an approaching death, and these two conditions of his spirit neutralize each other in sentences such as these : ὡς πάντοτε καὶ νῦν μεγαλυνθήσεται Χριστὸς ἐν τῷ σώματί μου, εἴτε διὰ ζωῆς, εἴτε διὰ θανάτου· ἐμοὶ γὰρ τὸ ζῆν Χριστὸς καὶ τὸ ἀποθανεῖν κέρδος. Εἰ δὲ τὸ ζῆν ἐν σαρκὶ, τοῦτό μοι καρπὸς ἔργου, καὶ τί αἱρήσομαι, οὐ γνωρίζω· συνέχομαι δὲ ἐκ τῶν δύο, τὴν ἐπιθυμίαν ἔχων εἰς τὸ ἀναλῦσαι, καὶ σὺν Χριστῷ εἶναι, πολλῷ γὰρ μᾶλλον κρεῖσσον, τὸ δὲ ἐπιμένειν ἐν σαρκὶ ἀναγκαιότερον δι᾽ ὑμᾶς, i. 20-24. Can it be questioned that a frame of mind alternating thus between life and death is far less appropriate to the apostle, if at least it be true that prospects so unexpectedly wide and splendid had been opening up before him for the success of the Gospel, than for an author who saw before him as a historical fact that end of the apostle which so little harmonized with all these expectations ? It cannot be without some special purpose that the author of our Epistle places the Roman Clement, the genuine disciple of Peter, as he is always accounted, at the side of the apostle Paul as his συνεργὸς. He also is to be a link of that harmonious relation in which the two apostles were more and more to be exhibited,[1] and

---

[1] Clement was a very suitable personage for this. He was a Gentile by birth, and had yet attached himself to Peter and to Jewish Christianity ; thus he was a natural mediator between the Judæo-Christian and the Gentile-Christian parties, and his great reputation could be serviceable in procuring acceptance for the Judaizing form of Christianity. He appears in this mediatorial capacity in the Shepherd of Hermas, L. i. vis. 2, where the Church appears to Hermas in the form of an old woman and commands him to write down the new revelations :— " scribes duos libellos et mittes manum Clementi—mittet autem Clemens in exteras civitates (Gentile-Christian churches) illi enim permissum est." With this agrees the description given in the *Epitome de gestis Petri*, c. 149 (cf. the Martyr. Clem.

how was it possible that a man of such importance for the Roman Church could have been unacquainted with the apostle Paul ? for was not the Praetorium the only quarter from which the imperial house was accessible to Christian teaching ?

In general, the object of this Epistle may be said to be to give a representation of the apostle's personality, through which he should appear as great and as illustrious as possible. To this end everything conspires that the writer has to say ; the great success of the apostle's preaching at Rome, the martyrdom, for it was nothing less, and it could never be sufficiently recognised, which he endured in his long incarceration, his affectionate and sympathetic feelings towards the Christian churches, and the constant direction of his spirit to Christ, in whom alone he lived. In conclusion, we may add that neither the ἐπίσκοποι and διάκονοι at the beginning of the Epistle, nor those persons named in the last chapter in such a peculiar and mysterious way, Euodia and Syntyche (in view of the exhortation to concord they might be thought to be rather two parties than two ladies), with the yet more peculiar σύζυγος γνήσιος, are in accordance with the apostle's manner in other Epistles.

ADDENDUM.[1]

No other Epistle contains so many passages, which from one

in Cotelier's Patr. Apost. i., p. 808) of the character of Clement, that he as " tertius post magnum Petrum in excelso romanae ecclesiae throno sedens, ipsumque virtutis certamen suscipiens, magistri vestigiis insistebat, apostolicamque doctrinam ipse quoque praeferebat et similibus moribus effulgebat, non Christianis dumtaxat placens, verum etiam Judaeis ac ipsis gentilibus et omnibus omnia factus ut et sic omnes lucrifaceret Christoque praesentaret ac verae religioni connecteret." As middleman between Jewish and heathen Christians, he was represented as the depositary of all the traditions held for apostolic, which were to be valid and obligatory for Jewish and heathen Christians equally. Cf. my Abh. über den Ursprung des Episcopats ; Tüb. Zeitschr. für Theol. 1838, 3 H. p. 126.

[1] The foregoing section (from p. 45) has received so considerable additions in the discussion Theol. Jahrb. viii., pp. 517-532, that I think it best to print this part of that discussion entire ; it would scarcely be possible to make extracts from it.

cause or another require to be explained, so many sentences wanting in clearness, loosely connected, and made up of nothing but repetitions and commonplaces.   After the introduction, in which Paul's style of introduction is closely imitated, take the first passage where there is a distinct thought expressed, i. 15.   Here we are at a loss to know who the τινὲς μὲν are, whether ἀδελφοὶ ἐν Κυρίῳ or others.   " Some preach Christ from envy and contentiousness, some from goodwill; some from love, because they know that I κεῖμαι for the defence of the Gospel."— What an expression, take it as we may !   " But others preach Christ from party-spirit, not with pure intentions, thinking to add affliction to my bonds."   What are we to conceive the difference between these two parties to have been ?   " What then ! notwithstanding, every way, whether from pretence or in truth, Christ is preached."   How could the apostle, who elsewhere judges his opponents with such severity, write this, and take pleasure even in those who preached Christ only προφάσει, without goodwill or honest intentions ?   If, as the interpreters remark, the doctrine which these people preached must have been anti-Pauline and Judaeo-Christian, since men of Pauline views would not have sought to counteract his influence, we know from other quarters what he thought of such opponents, and how he saw in them simply perverters of sound doctrine.   Why is he so indulgent here ?   Several explanations are attempted : that the church which these adversaries disturbed was not one which he himself had founded, and that in his situation at the time, he must have been impressed with the importance of the spread of the Gospel at Rome, even in the Judaeo-Christian form ; but all this is quite inconsistent with the apostle's character.   The passages cited could not have been written, save by an author who, considering that χαίρειν ought to be the key-note of the Epistle, made it so, and made the apostle look in that spirit beyond all disturbing and distressing influences, and who thought that the difference was quite capable of being harmonized.   Hence the χαίρω which recurs so often, and the intenser form χαρήσομαι.   And what is the cause

E

of his joy? The word τοῦτο which follows (ver. 19), fails to suggest any definite idea on the subject. And then the collocation of the δέησις of his readers and the ἐπιχορηγία τοῦ Πνεύματος Ἰησοῦ Χριστοῦ. Did the apostle ever call the intercession of his fellow-Christians, and the grace of God working in him in furtherance of his apostolic calling, an ἐπιχορηγία τοῦ Πνεύματος Ἰησοῦ Χριστοῦ, as he does here? Gal. iii. 5 speaks of an ἐπιχορηγεῖν τὸ πνεῦμα, and the author of our Epistle doubtless borrowed the expression from that passage; but then the apostle means by the ἐπιχ. τὸ Πν. the communication of the Spirit to Christians generally. And how could he, who said of himself as an apostle, δοκῶ κἀγὼ Πνεῦμα Θεοῦ ἔχειν (1 Cor. vii. 40), speak of an ἐπιχορηγία τ. Π. Ἰησοῦ Χριστοῦ only now reaching him? Whatever the τοῦτο (ver. 19) may mean, the apostle knows that it will fall out to his salvation, because he cherishes in general the hope that in nothing will he be put to shame, but ἐν πάσῃ παρρησίᾳ etc. What παρρησία means here is not apparent, but yet more curious is the expression μεγαλ. Χρ. ἐν τῷ σώματί μου. Of course it can only be taken in a qualitative sense, but in what other passage does the apostle use such an expression about Christ? Is it according to his ideas at all, to say that Christ is made great through him? or is it not rather Christ who glorifies himself through him and in him? As the writer's use of ἐπιχορ. τ. Πν. proceeded from a misinterpretation of Gal. iii. 5, so here his un-Pauline sentiment seems to have been suggested to him by the μεγαλυνθῆναι of 2 Cor. x. 15. What follows (ver. 20) εἴτε διὰ ζωῆς, etc., is a variation of the two passages, Rom. xiv. 7 and 2 Cor. v. 6. It was certainly quite in keeping with the situation in which the author of this Epistle conceived the apostle to be, to represent him as reflecting on his state, how he hovered between life and death; yet the whole passage, vv. 20-26, is nothing but a general meditation on life and death, and is not explained by anything special in the apostle's situation. The remaining verses of this chapter (27-30) contain an exhortation to a Christian walk, of so general a nature that it could have stood in any other epistle just as well. Yet traces of other passages are not wanting here.   It is usually said that ἥτις (ver. 28) refers grammatically to the following ἔνδειξις, but· factually to τὸ μὴ πτύρεσθαι.   But why should not ἥτις be referred to πίστις τοῦ εὐαγγελίου, so that καὶ μὴ πτύρ. . . . ἀντικ. should properly have stood after συναθλοῦντες?   Thus the πίστις τοῦ εὐαγγελίου is an ἔνδειξις ἀπωλείας to the one side, and σωτηρίας to the other, and that ἀπὸ Θεοῦ just as in the passage (2 Cor. ii. 15) where the apostle calls himself an εὐωδία Χριστοῦ τῷ Θεῷ ἐν τοῖς σωζομένοις καὶ ἐν τοῖς ἀπολλυμένοις, etc.   With regard to the καύχημα (ver. 26), compare 2 Cor. i. 14, 15.

It is principally the Second Epistle to the Corinthians of which we recognise the traces here.   The explanation of this is evident ; in no other Epistle do the apostle's personal relations to his readers appear so distinctly and directly as in that one, so that if the author was to make the apostle write a letter of so subjective a character as this one is, it was the Second Corinthian Epistle that he would naturally be led to follow.   I will not insist too strongly on the fact that he points his exhortation to unity τὸ αὐτὸ φρονεῖν (which is the chief purpose of the epistle, cf. ii. 1 *sq.*) by a reference to the person of Jesus, just as Paul enforces his exhortation to benevolence, 2 Cor. viii. 9.   But the passage ii. 19-30, it seems to me, must have been written under the influence of that chapter in the Corinthian Epistle.   And irrespectively of this there are several curious features in that section.   The apostle here expresses the hope that he will soon be able to send Timothy to the Philippians, that he also may be of good comfort by learning their state.   Why should he be longing so much for news, if Epaphroditus had brought him news from Philippi a short time before ?   And can we think that he would have parted with Timothy for this object ; the man of whom he says in this same passage, that he has no one on whose friendship and sympathy and straight-forwardness in the work of the Gospel he can so fully rely ?   It seems scarcely probable that he‧would have sent away a companion whose services he so much required in the position he was in, merely to take despatches to Philippi, which Epaphroditus, who was sent off at the same time, could have taken equally well, or to bring news from Philippi, a task which there was no reason why he of all men should undertake. How harshly does the apostle judge his fellow-labourers and friends, whom this matter leads him to refer to ! It is by no means enough to soften down the sentence by saying that Luke for one was no longer present at Rome at the time. Verse 21 is so general that we cannot help including Luke and Titus in the scope of it. Only a writer who projects the situations of his Epistle out of his own fancy could be led into such exaggerations. Now let us compare with this section the passage 2 Cor. viii. 17-24. As in our Epistle Timothy and Epaphroditus, so there Titus and another, are despatched on an errand of great importance, and here as there the messengers are recommended in the most honourable terms. In 2 Cor. viii. 23, the deputies are termed ἀπόστολοι ἐκκλησιῶν, and Phil. ii. 23 Epaphroditus is not called συνεργὸς as Titus is in that passage, but with regard to the Philippians their ἀπόστολος. The same word is used in both Epistles of the apostle's willingness in respect to this journey, with the difference that, at Phil. ii. 28, the σπουδαιότερος is the apostle who sends, and at 2 Cor. viii. 17 it is Titus, and ver. 22 the other ἀδελφὸς, the persons sent. Both passages conclude with a special exhortation to give the deputies a worthy reception. The expression, Phil. ii. 29, προσδέχεσθε οὖν αὐτὸν ἐν Κυρίῳ μετὰ πολλῆς χαρᾶς, καὶ τοὺς τοιούτους ἐντίμως ἔχετε, represents exactly the apostle's sentiment, 2 Cor. viii. 23, 24. It is, of course, obvious, that the two passages differ in many points ; the reasons alleged for the mission are different, for one thing. The author, that is to say, was not a mere copyist, only an imitator. But can it be regarded as a mere chance, that the two Epistles agree in the several common features we have noticed ? And do we not find here an explanation of the mission of Titus, which would otherwise appear so unaccounted for ? The writer of the Epistle wished to represent the apostle as giving the Philippians a peculiar proof of the love he bore them. He describes that as happening now, which had happened before in similar circum-

stances.   As Titus on that occasion, so here Timothy is sent with
another brother ; this other brother is very naturally Epaphroditus,
and the author gives them their recommendation in the highest
possible terms.

It may be urged that if analogies and resemblances like this are
to prove anything, the theory that is based upon them ought to be
shown to be capable of further demonstration.   But this is actually
the case here.   At iii. 1 we come to the passage, which, as I have
already shown (p. 54 *sq.*), is imitated from 2 Cor. xi. 13 *sq.*   The
two apologetes cannot of course allow that this is so ; they clearly
represent to us (Lünemann even by printing the texts side by
side) how different the terms of the two passages are ; and show,
with all due emphasis, how natural it is that the apostle should
speak more than once of such advantages, which there is no doubt
that he did possess, and how appropriately he does so here.   How
could I, they say, overlook, in speaking of the apostle's circumcision on the eighth day, that this was just the difference between
the born Jew and the Proselyte ; and a descent from the tribe of
Benjamin, the tribe which remained true to the house of David at
the division of the kingdom, was by no means a worthless distinction.   And if the passage 2 Cor. xi. 13 *sq.* be alleged to have been
made use of here, why not also Gal. i. 13 *sq.*, vi. 12, Rom. xi. 1 ?
Objections of this kind are not easy to answer, yet they cannot
destroy the impression which the passage makes on me, and I have
further to remark that this is not a mere question of words and
expressions which may be found here or there, but of the whole
character of the passage under consideration, and of a phenomenon
which is not isolated, but connected with many points equally
remarkable.   And a passage like iii. 1 *sq.* surely suggests pretty
clearly that if an Epistle such as this should not be reckoned
among the products of the apostle's own genius, he would be no
great loser.   What have the two apologetes done to justify this
passage against the charge that the spirit of the apostle is con-
spicuously absent from it ?   They cannot even clear the writer of the
Epistle of his own confession of constant repetition ; they go so far

as to say that the apostle wrote several other letters of this kind
to the Philippians; that the γράφειν (iii. 1) shows him to have been
in constant correspondence with them. (How this would agree
with ii. 19, we scarcely need to remark.) The τὰ αὐτὰ γράφειν
refers to nothing but the χαίρετε ἐν Κυρίῳ, that is, to the contents
of the Epistle generally, for the key-note and the leading thought of
it are expressed in this constantly recurring χαίρετε. De Wette
thinks it decisive against the reference to χαίρετε, that ἀσφαλές
could only refer to some danger such as is spoken of in the sequel,
and in the case of another writer this consideration would have
some weight. In our Epistle, however, there are so many awkward
and illogical connexions that it is not so pertinent. The objection
from the 'dogs' (iii. 2) is not removed by mentioning passages in
Homer where this predicate is given even to goddesses (Lünemann, p. 27). The apostle calls his opponents 'ministers of Satan'
(2 Cor. xi. 15), but there we know the reason for his doing so. Here,
however, we can discern no object, no train of thought leading up
to this climax. The only thread of connexion here is the
author's reminiscence of 2 Cor. xi. 12. Here, as there, the apostle
speaks of himself in contrast to his opponents. What he says of
himself there may be expressed in the general statement that he
desires to know of nothing but what he is in his relation to Christ,
and that he will let his grace be sufficient for him. His imitator
here makes him express the same idea in the words that he counts
all things but loss, damage to his true welfare, because of the surpassing excellence of the knowledge of Jesus Christ his Lord, for
whose sake he had suffered loss of everything that he had counted
or might yet count precious. What follows ver. 9 looks like an
attempt to give as general as possible an abstract of the teaching
of the Pauline Epistles; as if the apostle were to make a confession
of his faith, since he is speaking of personal subjects already, he is
made to expound and define with all due accuracy the chief proposition of the Pauline system, the doctrine of justification by
faith. Where else does the apostle speak of the righteousness that
is by faith with this purely subjective and personal reference to

himself? where else does he make the resurrection, the sufferings, the death of Christ, the subject of an abstract theoretical contemplation, as here, that he may know τὴν δύναμιν τῆς ἀναστάσεως, etc.? How differently does he speak of all this, 2 Cor. iv. 14 *sq.* v. 14-21, xiii. 3, 4, Gal. ii. 19, *sq.* etc. What is the import of the δύναμις τῆς ἀναστάσεως αὐτοῦ, ver. 10? How loosely are all these ideas connected with each other! When the apostle comes in other passages to speak of these, the great elements of his religious consciousness, he develops them in the fullest and most pregnant connexion with each other, and places them in such lights that we look at once into the whole profundity, and the whole inner necessity of the divine economy of salvation. And when he speaks of his own experience, he gives us a very different, and a much more life-like picture of his inner life.

Then the dubious εἴπως καταντήσω εἰς τὴν ἐξανάστασιν τῶν νεκρῶν, which is annexed to what precedes, and carries on the discourse to a discussion of this doubt. The apostle has been made to recapitulate his whole life, beginning at his circumcision, and now he goes on to the very end, to the resurrection from the dead. But how could the apostle be in any doubt as to his own attaining to the resurrection from the dead? Do not all the dead arise? He means, it is asserted, the blessed resurrection of which the apostle speaks, 1 Cor. xv. 52, but there certainly in a connexion which precludes the reader from thinking of any other. But even if this be what is meant, we must ask how the apostle could speak of the resurrection in a tone of doubt and uncertainty, as he does here. Take all these statements in connexion with each other; the apostle wishes to win Christ, and to be found in him with the righteousness that is by faith, in order to know the secret of the δύναμις τῆς ἀναστάσεως αὐτοῦ, and the κοινωνία τῶν παθημάτων αὐτοῦ, while he is made conformable to his death (this death, analogous to that of Jesus, can only be understood of the death of martyrdom). In these ideas ranged outwardly beside each other, it is hard to see what is the connexion between the practical συμμορφοῦσθαι τῷ θανάτῳ αὐτοῦ and the theoretical γνῶναι, and still harder to understand how he, being συμμορφούμενος τῷ θανάτῳ αὐτοῦ, can ask further as if in doubt εἴπως καταντήσω εἰς τὴν ἐξανάστασιν τῶν νεκρῶν. How differently, and with a consciousness how well assured, does the apostle speak elsewhere of his communion with the life and death of Christ! Compare Rom. viii. 11 : εἰ δὲ τὸ Πνεῦμα τοῦ ἐγείραντος Ἰησοῦν ἐκ νεκρῶν οἰκεῖ ἐν ὑμῖν, ὁ ἐγείρας τὸν Χριστὸν ἐκ νεκρῶν ζωοποιήσει καὶ τὰ θνητὰ σώματα ὑμῶν, διὰ τὸ ἐνοικοῦν αὐτοῦ πνεῦμα ἐν ὑμῖν. 2 Cor. iv. 11 : ἀεὶ γὰρ ἡμεῖς οἱ ζῶντες, εἰς θάνατον παραδιδόμεθα διὰ Ἰησοῦν, ἵνα καὶ ἡ ζωὴ τοῦ Ἰησοῦ φανερωθῇ ἐν τῇ θνητῇ σαρκὶ ἡμῶν. . . . εἰδότες ὅτι ὁ ἐγείρας τὸν Κύριον Ἰησοῦν, καὶ ἡμᾶς διὰ Ἰησοῦ Χριστοῦ ἐγερεῖ, καὶ παραστήσει σὺν ὑμῖν. How can he who regards himself as one συμμορφούμενος τῷ θανάτῳ αὐτοῦ, be in doubt even for a moment, that he has in himself, along with death, the living principle that shall awake him out of death? Εἰ γὰρ σύμφυτοι γεγόναμεν τῷ ὁμοιώματι τοῦ θανάτου αὐτοῦ, ἀλλὰ καὶ τῆς ἀναστάσεως ἐσόμεθα, Rom. vi. 5. Is it conceivable that views like these, wrought as they were into his inmost consciousness, should ever have left him? that at that particular time he could not speak with any such certainty of his union with the life and death of Jesus, or of the good and happy conscience he had so often spoken of before in looking forward to the supreme decision? If there be anything that our apostle cannot possibly have written, it is that dubious εἴπως καταντήσω εἰς τὴν ἐξανάστασιν τῶν νεκρῶν, where his whole fellowship with Christ is put in question. And where in the apostle's writings does the resurrection appear, as it does here, as the last event man has to look for, removed from all connexion with the momenta by which it is conditioned, and relegated, it appears, to the most distant future? To the apostle's mind the Parousia was so near, that for his own case his expectation was rather to be changed than to rise again. Can we, then, resist the conviction that the apostle himself would not have spoken thus, and that this dubious εἴπως can only have proceeded from him in the representation of another,—a writer who, not being the apostle himself, could not make him speak with that confidence and assurance, which a man can only have for his own person. The double consciousness which such a writer can never get quit of has for its natural result, that in matters of which he is not positively certain he makes the man under whose name he writes express himself waveringly and undecidedly, as if either the one thing or the other might be true. Then also, in the words τί αἱρήσομαι, οὐ γνωρίζω (i. 22), the writer imports into the apostle's consciousness his own uncertainty as to which course the latter would have chosen ; there can be no doubt that the apostle himself would have known quite well which of the two to choose. The same wavering uncertainty and want of definite views runs on in the following verses, 11-14, where the author makes the apostle review his own moral and religious condition in self-contemplations which have, as little as the foregoing, any resemblance to Paul's own ways of thinking. When the apostle says that he has not yet apprehended, but that he is already apprehended by Christ, we have here again, as i. 22, two propositions which mutually limit each other in such a way that it is hard to see what is meant at all. It is clear that if the apostle be laid hold on by Christ, he must lay hold of him also, but he says that he has not yet laid hold ; what does this mean ? of what has he not yet laid hold ? and how does the justification by faith, spoken of in verse 9, agree with this not having yet laid hold ? Has not he who has laid hold of Christ in faith (and we see this assurance of faith expressed everywhere in the apostle's writings), received in his faith everything on which it is necessary to lay hold in order to be certain of his union with Christ, and of his salvation ? Is there such a faith with Paul, as is not also an assurance of faith ? It seems indeed a very plausible explanation to say that the apostle could not yet have been assured of his moral perfection ; but let it be considered whether moral perfection, such as would be spoken of here, be a thing which the Pauline ideas recognise at all ? Faith, with all that faith comprehends, cannot be conditioned by moral perfection ; else this moral perfection would simply bring us back again to the old justification by works.

This is of a piece with the whole character of the Epistle; it is written altogether in a very soft subdued tone; differences are neutralized, not stated in their extremer forms. It appeared to the author that in an Epistle to the Philippians the apostle might be expected to speak much of himself; that in speaking to so dear a church, he would disclose his inmost heart in confidences and confessions. So he concluded that he could not make him speak too humbly, and meekly, and depreciatingly of himself. And in fact the apostle does speak of himself here in such a style that his true self is not recognisable at all. Humility is certainly a strong trait of his character, but where, even when speaking of himself most humbly, did he ever employ such an expression as this—οὐχ ὅτι ἤδη ἔλαβον? Deep as his humility is, it is lost in the preponderating sense of the unspeakable grace of God, which is mighty in him, even in his weakness, through which alone he is what he is; through which, however, he is already what he is to be. If he himself had been speaking here, there could not have failed to be some reference to this grace of God. In a passage where he looks to what still lies before him, and describes his striving towards that goal with the same metaphor which the author of our Epistle is using here, verse 14, he says to his readers: οὕτω τρέχετε, ἵνα καταλάβητε, but of himself he says: ἐγὼ τοίνυν οὕτω τρέχω, ὡς οὐκ ἀδήλως, οὕτω πυκτεύω, ὡς οὐκ ἀέρα δέρων, 1 Cor. ix. 24 sq. He knows nothing here of any οὐχ ὅτι ἔλαβον, διώκω δὲ, εἰ καὶ καταλάβω. It is simply the writer of the Epistle whose views are not sufficiently clear to distinguish the ideas of perfection in the ethical and the physical sense. The author has not yet quite reached the goal of his earthly career; martyrdom is not yet achieved but only impending, and so the writer thinks it necessary to throw doubt in this manner on the question of his having apprehended. I need not here comment further on the want of any clear and natural sequence of thoughts or language in the following verses; and the laborious efforts of interpreters to bring something definite out of these wavering statements, and especially out of the vague description of the apostle's opponents: cf. p. 54.

Another point which is by no means settled, is the occasion which may have led the apostle to write such an Epistle to the church at Philippi. The present of money said at the close of the Epistle to have been brought to the apostle by Epaphroditus, is generally held to be a sufficient explanation. If the Epistle vindicated its Pauline character in other respects, there could be no objection to this ; the apostle will then have written an epistle, the first object of which was to express his gratitude towards a church that had given him so flattering a proof of their continued attachment. Yet even this point does not stand out with any distinctness, nor have my doubts been removed by the utterances of the latest advocates of the Epistle. They insist that it is a misunderstanding on my part to take the words of the apostle, 1 Cor. ix. 12 *sq.* (that it is his principle to preach the gospel without recompence), as true generally ; instead of referring them especially only to the case of the Corinthian church. I will not discuss whether the words of the apostle in that passage, especially in the verses 15-18, admit of such a limitation. The question is merely whether what is said, Phil. iv. 15, of the subsidies received by the apostle from the Philippians, naturally suggests that in this particular also the author derived his information from the second Corinthian Epistle, and used what he found there for his own purpose. There is no trace in the authentic letters of the apostle of his having stood in such a special relation to the church at Philippi as is implied in Phil. iv. 15. The name of that church is not once mentioned ; he speaks only of the churches of Macedonia, and we might even conclude from 2 Cor. xi. 8, where he speaks of ἄλλαι ἐκκλησίαι, as distinct from the Corinthian church, from which he had received assistance in money during his residence in Achaia, that other churches also stood in this relation towards him. According to Phil. iv. 15, however, this relation subsisted only in the case of the Philippian church. It is said expressly : οὐδεμία μοι ἐκκλησία ἐκοινώνησεν εἰς λόγον δόσεως καὶ λήψεως, εἰ μὴ ὑμεῖς μόνοι. Thus it is very natural to suppose, and this agrees very well with the other considerations which make the origin of the Epistle doubtful,

that the author, having, as the Epistle shows, a special interest in
the church at Philippi, attributes the help which the apostle says
came to him from Macedonia, to that church specially and indi-
vidually. He thought very naturally that the Philippians would
not leave the apostle without aid during his imprisonment, and he
made use of this circumstance as the occasion of his Epistle to the
Philippians. It may indeed be argued that since, as we know
from 2 Cor., the apostle did receive aid from the Christians of
Macedonia, it is very probable that the Philippians actually did
what is reported of them, iv. 15. Since, however, the Pauline
origin of the Epistle is questionable on other and more general
grounds, the contrary supposition is equally probable; it simply exhibits in this one particular that derivative character of the Epistle
which has already been demonstrated on other grounds. In a
genuine Pauline Epistle we should expect that, besides what is
directly spiritual, there will be some new information not derivable
from other sources, about the position of affairs at the time, the
occasion of the writing, and the various matters of interest which
a piece of the original reality could not fail to bring with it. Here,
however, we have poverty of thought, want of any historical basis,
unconnectedness; we have nothing specific or concrete, nothing to
give us the impression of originality, nothing but a dull and
colourless reflection. As for the want of connexion, it is indeed
possible by making out a general view and index of the contents,
to bring to light a certain succession of sections, and thus to make
the transition from one to the other somewhat easier to the reader.
In this business Mr. Brückner shows a considerable amount of
dexterity (*op. cit.* p. 38 *sq.*). De Wette, again, calls the Epistle a
graceful contexture of two main themes, the affairs of the Philippians
and those of the apostle, and makes it apparent in a table that these
two themes come forward alternately. Yet at a passage, iii. 1,
where the connexion is difficult to trace, he is forced to take refuge
in putting a dash between the two chapters, a way of connecting
which is certainly not after the apostle's manner. The Epistle
consists of a multitude of independent sentences; the larger sections

are placed after each other with a merely external connexion;
χαίρετε forms the close of one and the beginning of another (ii. 18,
iii. 1), and there is a total want of any idea to bind the whole
together.   If it be alleged, in explanation of this, that this Epistle
is more properly a private letter than any of the others, it must be
said that 2 Cor. is such a letter quite as much.   Yet how different
is it in this particular !

As for my theory regarding the person of Clemens and the
historical statements connected with it, I have little to add.
Lünemann and Brückner bring all their acuteness to bear against
my view, and seek to prove that the Clement mentioned, iv. 3,
must be a Philippian.   Lünemann exalts the merit of his refutation
by the construction of the words of that verse which he gratuitously
imputes to me.   The critics might have said much more simply, as
Ritschl does in his review of my 'Paulus,' in the *Halle Allge-
meine Lit. Zeitung,* 1847, p. 1008 : "This Clement is, unless I be
greatly deceived, a member of the church at Philippi, and has
nothing to do with that Clemens Romanus so famous afterwards in
legend." What more is wanted to prove the authenticity of the
Epistle, if Messrs. Lünemann and Brückner agree in this opinion !
It is certainly quite in keeping with the vagueness of our Epistle
that nothing in it can be fixed to its own definite locality, so that
it is impossible to know where the persons spoken of belong to,
where the opponents who are impugned are to be sought for,
whether at Rome or at Philippi.   And the apostle himself speaks
in one passage of his bonds and his anticipations of death, and,
immediately after of setting out for Philippi (ii. 24).   Yet the chief
point is, and these critics seem to have overlooked it altogether, that
Clement is expressly called a συνεργὸς of the apostle, and thus is
reckoned one of those who worked with him and beside him, and
that for some time, in the proclamation of the gospel.   Although
nothing whatever is known from the apostle's own writings about
such a fellow-labourer, yet in itself it might quite well be the case
that besides the Roman Clement, who appears in other quarters as
an adherent of Peter, there was another apostolical man of this

name. But let it be considered what stage has been already reached in the criticism of our Epistle, before we come to speak of this Clement named at iv. 3. Here is an author who exhibits so little independence in other particulars, who has nothing to say that is new or peculiar to himself, whose sources of information can be pointed out in a number of instances. And from what other quarter should his Clement come than from that tradition to which the Clement already known to us belongs? With this the rest is explained at once. About the enigmatical σύζυγος of the apostle I have nothing to say any more than others. Schwegler thought of the apostle Peter, and this is at least as reasonable as the suggestion of Wieseler (Chronologie der Apostelgeschichte, p. 458), who takes this yoke-fellow to be Christ, "who helps every one to bear his burden," or that of Rückert, who recognises in him the brother-german of the apostle, said to be spoken of in the ἀδελφὸς, 2 Cor. viii. 18, 22.

An author writing in the name of the apostle was of course obliged to write a Pauline style, yet the language of the Epistle betrays the imitator in many particulars. There is a considerable number of words and expressions which are peculiar to this Epistle (cf. Zeller, Studien zur neutest.Theol., Theol. Jahrb., 1843, p. 507 *sq.*) I have also been struck with the repeated use of the particle πλὴν, which the author is fond of using as a particle of transition, to join together, externally, sentences, which have no very close connexion inwardly. In this short Epistle πλὴν is used in this way three times, i. 18, iii. 16, iv. 14. In the unquestioned Epistles of the apostle, the particle is found only once, 1 Cor. xi. 11. The particle ἄρα, on the other hand, which the apostle uses so frequently, is not once found here. Then the emphasis which the author seeks to gain by the repetition of the same word: i. 9, μᾶλλον καὶ μᾶλλον; ver. 18, χαίρω, ἀλλὰ καὶ χαρήσομαι; ver. 25, μένω καὶ συμπαραμενῶ; ii. 17, χαίρω καὶ συγχαίρω; ver. 18, χαίρετε καὶ συγχαίρετε; ver. 27, λύπην ἐπὶ λύπην; iii. 2, βλέπετε τοὺς κύνας, βλέπετε τοὺς κακοὺς ἐργάτας, βλέπετε τὴν κατατομήν; iv. 2, Εὐωδίαν παρακαλῶ καὶ Συντύχην παρακαλῶ; ver. 17, οὐχ ὅτι ἐπιζητῶ τὸ δόμα, ἀλλ' ἐπιζητῶ τὸν καρπόν. The same word used twice in the same verse (iii. 4, 8). Synonymous or similar expressions are used in conjunction : i. 20, ἀποκαραδοκία καὶ ἐλπίς ; ii. 1, σπλάγχνα καὶ οἰκτιρμοί ; ver. 2, ἵνα τὸ αὐτὸ φρονῆτε . . . τὸ ἓν φρονοῦντες ; ver. 16, οὐκ εἰς κενὸν ἔδραμον, οὐδὲ εἰς κενὸν ἐκοπίασα ; ver. 17, θυσίᾳ καὶ λειτουργίᾳ τῆς πίστεως ; ver. 25, Epaphroditus is called not only ἀδελφὸς καὶ συνεργὸς, but also, with the exaggeration characteristic of such writers, συστρατιώτης ; and on all this follows ὑμῶν δὲ ἀπόστολος, καὶ λειτουργὸς τῆς χρείας μου. In contrast to this the apostle calls Timothy, 2 Cor. viii. 23, simply his κοινωνὸς, and in reference to the Corinthians his συνεργὸς ; iii. 9, δικαιοσύνη ἡ διὰ πίστεως Χριστοῦ, ἡ ἐκ Θεοῦ δικαιοσύνη ἐπὶ τῇ πίστει ; iv. 7, τὰς καρδίας ὑμῶν καὶ τὰ νοήματα ὑμῶν ; ver. 12, ἐν παντὶ καὶ ἐν πᾶσι ; ver. 18, ὀσμὴ εὐωδίας, θυσία δεκτὴ εὐάρεστος τῷ Θεῷ. This phraseology is not specially Pauline ; the writer who used it was clearly one who sought to make up for what was wanting in his thought by the exuberance of his expression. Then again, there are expressions which though of rare occurrence with Paul are yet so specifically Pauline, that the use of them at once informs us of the quarter from which they were drawn,—Thus i. 8, μάρτυς γάρ μου ἐστὶν ὁ Θεὸς, ὡς, etc., cf. Rom. i. 9 ; Phil. i. 10, δοκιμάζειν τὰ διαφέροντα, as Rom. ii. 18. The apostle calls himself, 1 Cor. ix. 23, a συγκοινωνὸς of the gospel, and our author makes him say to the Philippians (i. 7), that they are συγκοινωνοί τῆς χάριτος ; Phil. i. 19, ἐπιχορηγία τοῦ πνεύματος, as Gal. iii. 5 ; Phil. i. 26, καύχημα ὑμῶν, as 2 Cor. i. 14 ; Phil. i. 22, ζῆν ἐν σαρκί, as Gal. ii. 20 ; Phil. ii. 16, εἰς κενὸν ἔδραμον, as Gal. ii. 2 ; Phil. ii. 30, τὸ ἔργον Χριστοῦ, as 1 Cor. xvi. 10 ; Phil. ii. 30, ἀναπληροῦν τὸ ὑστέρημα, as 2 Cor. ix. 12 ; Phil. iii. 3, καυχᾶσθαι ἐν Χριστῷ, 1 Cor. i. 31, 2 Cor. x. 17, etc. We are also reminded of the Apocalypse xiii. 8, by the expression used in Phil. iv. 3, ὧν τὰ ὀνόματα ἐν βιβλῷ ζωῆς.

SIXTH CHAPTER.

THE Epistle to Philemon takes its place beside the three Epistles to the Ephesians, Colossians, and Philippians, as bearing, like them, to have been written during the apostle's captivity at Rome.   It is connected most intimately with the Epistle to the Colossians, Philemon having been, according to the general assumption, a member of the Church at Colosse.   In this Epistle, indeed, there is no distinct indication of the fact, except that the persons from whom greetings are sent are the same as in the Epistle to the Colossians, with the exception of Jesus Justus, Col. iv. 11.   And there is no doubt that at Col. iv. 9, this same Onesimus, whom the author of the Epistle represents as sent to the Colossians along with Tychicus, is called one of themselves.   In the case of this Epistle more than any other, if criticism should inquire for evidence in favour of its apostolic name, it seems liable to the reproach of hypercriticism, of exaggerated suspicion, and restless doubt, from the attacks of which nothing is safe.   What has criticism to do with this short, attractive, graceful and friendly letter, inspired as it is by the noblest Christian feeling, and which has never yet been touched by the breath of suspicion ?   Yet criticism cannot possibly take an apostolic origin for granted here, and forbear from inquiries.   If indeed the other Epistles, which profess, as this one does, to have been written in the apostle's captivity, had been above all doubt, then the claim of this one to the same origin might have passed unchallenged.   But the case is quite different when this Epistle is regarded in the light of the critical doubts which those others have certainly appeared to us to warrant.   If so much can be urged

against the Pauline origin of these three Epistles, and still more of
the Pastoral ones, and if it be so extremely doubtful whether we
have any apostolical Epistles from the period of the imprisonment
at all, what claim has this small Epistle, a mere letter of friendship, and dealing with a purely private affair, to be considered an
exception to that judgment? Whatever weight may attach to this
inference from analogy, yet on the other hand the demand is
certainly fair, that we should look at the Epistle in itself, and
show, if not the probability, at least the possibility of its having a
non-apostolic parentage. The difference between Pauline and non-
Pauline Epistles cannot surely be so small that this one, if not
Pauline, should bear no mark whatever of its different origin. Now
what can be proved in this direction? We need not insist upon the
nature of the language used; on the fact that in this short Epistle
there is a considerable number of expressions which never occur in
the apostle's own writings at all, or only in the disputed writings; as
συστρατιώτης, ver. 2, in the metaphorical sense that later writers are
so fond of;[1] ἀνῆκον, ἐπιτάσσειν, ver. 8; πρεσβύτης, ver. 9 (the reference to his age is certainly peculiar); ἄχρηστος and εὔχρηστος, ver. 11;
ἀπέχω in the sense of "have back," ver. 15; ἀποτίω, προσοφείλω,
ver. 19; ὀνίνασθαι, ver. 20; ξενία, ver. 22 (the expression σπλάγχνα is
also striking, not as being un-Pauline, but as occurring three times
over, ver. 7, 12, 20). It is the contents of the Epistle that chiefly
arrest our attention: these contents are certainly peculiar, and
distinguish the Epistle from all others. Here there are no mere
commonplaces, no repetitions of things known long before, no indefinite doctrine; on the contrary, it deals with an actual occurrence
belonging to a certain definite set of circumstances. We must ask,
however, whether this subject, which is the occasion of the writing,
is not itself so very singular as to arouse our suspicions? A slave
has run away from his master because of some delinquency; a theft,
it is commonly assumed. His master is a Christian at Colosse in
Phrygia, and an intimate friend of the apostle Paul; the slave
comes to Rome, is brought in contact with the apostle in his im-

[1] Cf. Pastoralbriefe, p. 99.

F

prisonment, is converted by him to Christianity, and thereupon sent back to his master at Colosse as a Christian slave. This is a very remarkable concurrence of chances, such as rarely indeed takes place ; and the letter given to the converted slave by the apostle to carry to his master regards the occurrence from the Christian point of view, and makes it the subject of Christian reflection. The slave converted to Christianity is represented as a child born to the apostle in his old age and in his captivity, and therefore loved by him with all the greater tenderness. As a converted slave he has been changed out of an ἄχρηστος, one from whom his master derived no profit, but rather the reverse, into an εὔχρηστος for both, for his master and the apostle. Here there is a play, not only on the slave's name, Onesimus (from ὄνημι, ὀνίνημι, to be of use, serviceable), but on the Christian name itself, for the heathens often said Χρηστὸς instead of Χριστὸς, a thing which the Christians did not take at all amiss.[1]

The leading idea is this—that when the slave returned to his master he had become a Christian : this idea is expressed with all due clearness, and everything that the Epistle contains besides is just the development and illustration of what Christianity was held to imply. The beautiful idea is here taken as a part of Christianity, that those whom it connects stand to each other in a real community of essence, so that the one sees in the other his own self, knows himself to be completely one with him, and is thus included in a union which is to last for ever. The converted slave is no longer the slave of his master ; he is more than a slave, he is his brother beloved, all whose misdeeds and debts are now forgiven. The apostle who has converted the slave is not only the spiritual father of the man who through him is now regenerate ; the master of the slave receives in him not merely the convert, but

---

[1] Cf. Justin, Apol. i. c. 4 : Ἐκ τοῦ κατηγορουμένου ἡμῶν ὀνόματος χρηστότατοι ὑπάρχομεν. Χριστιανοὶ γὰρ εἶναι κατηγορούμεθα, τὸ δὲ χρηστὸν μισεῖσθαι οὐ δίκαιον. In the same way Athenagoras says of the heathens, Leg. cap. 2 : εἰς τὸ ὄνομα ὡς εἰς ἀδίκημα ἐνυβρίζουσιν, οὐδὲν δὲ τὸ ὄνομα ἀφ᾽ ἑαυτοῦ καὶ δι᾽ αὐτοῦ οὐ πονηρὸν οὔτε χρηστὸν νομίζεται. Tertull. Apol. 3 : Cum perperam Chrestianus pronuntiatur a vobis (nam nec nominis certa est notitia penes vos), de suavitate vel benignitate compositum est.

also the apostle who converted him. Σὺ δὲ αὐτὸν, τοῦτ᾽ ἔστι τὰ ἐμὰ σπλάγχνα, προσλαβοῦ, ver. 12. Εἰ οὖν ἐμὲ ἔχεις κοινωνὸν, προσλαβοῦ αὐτὸν ὡς ἐμέ, ver. 17. As the converted slave, being a Christian slave, is to the apostle in place of his Christian master, so through the same bond of identity, he unites the apostle who converted him with his Christian master, who must needs behold in him the converted, his converter also. Thus Christianity does away with all differences which separate men from one another ; as a new principle of life it creates a new set of relations, where one lives in the other ; the consciousness is a common consciousness in which all are one. The apostle becomes surety for the converted slave to his master, and answerable for his debt ; but then the Christian master himself is the apostle's debtor, ver. 19. What one is the other is also, because all are one in the same unity. The play on the word Onesimus in ver. 20 is doubtless meant to convey the same idea ; the apostle says, in a certain way, " as thy Christian slave has only now become an Onesimus worthy of his name, so shouldst thou, his Christian master, be my Onesimus ; let me rejoice in thee (ἐγώ σου ὀναίμην ἐν Κυρίῳ), give me the full enjoyment of thy love, let my inmost consciousness as a Christian consciousness repose on thine."

Among those sweet utterances of an author deeply imbued with the Christian spirit, there is another thought especially deserving of remark. The apostle writes to the master of the slave, ver. 15, that perhaps the slave who deserted him, but who has now become a Christian, departed from him for a season, in order that he might receive him back for ever. He receives him back for ever if he receives him as a Christian. This aspect of Christianity is dwelt upon in the pseudo-Clementine homilies : Christianity is the permanent reconciliation of those who were formerly separated by one cause or another, but who by a special arrangement of affairs brought about by Divine Providence for that very purpose, are again brought together ; through their conversion to Christianity they know each other again, the one sees in the other his own flesh and blood, himself.[1] The point of the

---

[1] Die Christliche Gnosis, p. 372 sq.

historical narratives in the homilies is to be found in these scenes
of recognition and reconciliation ; and if, on this account, they have
been called, and justly so, a Christian romance, why should not
our Epistle be the embryo of a similar Christian fiction? The
historical materials which it contains are not worked out, yet it
evidently contains materials for a more extended treatment. The
author of the Epistle, however, does not dwell on his story for its
own inherent interest ; he rather pre-supposes the story as a vehicle
for the idea which it is his object to set forth. The moral of the
story is, that what one loses in the world, one recovers in Christianity, and that for ever ; that the world and Christianity are
related to each other as separation and reunion, as time and
eternity. This idea is expressed with all proper clearness in the
words, ver. 15 : τάχα γὰρ διὰ τοῦτο ἐχωρίσθη πρὸς ὥραν, ἵνα
αἰώνιον αὐτὸν ἀπέχῃς. The occurrence spoken of is thus to be
considered teleologically ; but the teleological view of history is the
mother of historical fiction, and if once the idea be regarded as the
substance of what has taken place, it is no great step to regard
what has happened as having happened only in representation,
and that it might serve as the outward form of the idea. Thus it
cannot be called either an impossible or an improbable construction
of this Epistle, if we regard it as a Christian romance serving to
convey a genuine Christian idea.

If this Epistle be interpreted in the way in which it must be,
as soon as we regard it, not merely in itself, but in its historical
and critical connexion with the other Epistles which stand nearest
to it, then the peculiar excellence for which it is extolled becomes
much more questionable. The excellence is, that it contains
nothing of importance either in relation to doctrine or to Church
history, but is invaluable as a document, bringing before us the
apostle's cheerful and amiable personality, and as a practical
commentary on Col. iv. 6. But if the Epistle be actually written
by Paul, is it not remarkable that the occurrence, which in that
case actually happened, is simply used to illustrate a certain
idea, and that the enforcement of this idea is the real aim and
subject of the Epistle?

SEVENTH CHAPTER.

THE second of these Epistles has already been attacked by criticism; but the first has as yet excited no suspicions. The reason of this is probably to be found in the nature of its contents, in which there is nothing at all striking or peculiar. In the whole collection of the Pauline Epistles there is none so deficient in the character and substance of its materials as 1st Thessalonians. With the exception of the view advanced in iv. 13-18, no dogmatic idea whatever is brought into prominence, as is certainly the case in the Epistles to the Ephesians, Colossians, and Philippians, and even in the short Epistle to Philemon. The whole Epistle is made up of general instructions, exhortations, wishes, such as appear in the other Epistles merely as adjuncts to the principal contents; what is accessory in the other cases is here the preponderating and essential element. This might appear at first sight to favour the opinion that the Epistle is genuine—there is so little for criticism to lay hold of. The very insignificance of the contents, however, the want of any special aim and of any intelligible occasion or purpose is itself a criterion adverse to a Pauline origin; but not merely do these negative considerations demand explanation: a closer view of the Epistle betrays such dependence and such want of originality as is not to be found in any of the genuine Pauline writings. The chief part of the Epistle is nothing but a lengthy version of the history of the conversion of the Thessalonians as we know it from the Acts. It contains nothing that the Thessalonians would not know already, and the author may have taken his account of the transaction either from the Acts or from some other source. To begin with i. 4 *sq.*, εἰδότες, ἀδελφοὶ ... τὴν ἐκλογὴν ὑμῶν, etc.; this merely states how the apostle preached the gospel to the Thessalonians, and they received it; ch. ii. 1, αὐτοὶ γὰρ οἴδατε, ἀδελφοὶ, τὴν εἴσοδον ἡμῶν τὴν πρὸς ὑμᾶς ... προπαθόντες καὶ ὑβρισθέντες, καθὼς οἴδατε, ἐν Φιλίπποις, etc., points more distinctly to the circumstances of the apostle's coming to Thessalonica, and the way in which he worked there. In the same way iii. 11 *sq.*, εὐδοκήσαμεν καταλειφθῆναι ἐν Ἀθήναις μόνοι, καὶ ἐπέμψαμεν Τιμόθεον, etc., refers to what happened only a short time before, and what the Thessalonians were quite well aware of. As the writer admits by the perpetually recurring εἰδότες (i. 4), αὐτοὶ γὰρ οἴδατε (ii. 1), καθὼς οἴδατε (ii. 2), μνημονεύετε γὰρ (ii. 9), καθάπερ οἴδατε (ii. 11), αὐτοὶ γὰρ οἴδατε (iii. 3), καθὼς καὶ ἐγένετο καὶ οἴδατε (iii. 4), οἴδατε γὰρ (iv. 2), only such things are spoken of as the readers knew well already; the history which is recapitulated is not an old one, but, on the contrary, quite fresh and new. In addition to all this, we find in the narrative reminiscences more or less distinct, of other Pauline Epistles, particularly of those to the Corinthians. The passage (i. 5) τὸ εὐαγγέλιον ἡμῶν οὐκ ἐγενήθη εἰς ὑμᾶς ἐν λόγῳ μόνον, ἀλλὰ καὶ ἐν δυνάμει, is manifestly an imitation of 1 Cor. ii. 4;—i. 6, μιμηταὶ ἡμῶν ἐγενήθητε καὶ τοῦ Κυρίου, of 1 Cor. xi. 1;—i. 8, ἐν παντὶ τόπῳ ἡ πίστις ὑμῶν ... ἐξελήλυθεν, reminds us of Rom. i. 8, ἡ πίστις ὑμῶν καταγγέλλεται ἐν ὅλῳ τῷ κόσμῳ. The passage ii. 4 *sq.* is a brief recapitulation of the principles enunciated in the Corinthian Epistles : cf. 1 Cor. ii. 4; iv. 3 *sq.*; ix. 15 *sq.*, and particularly 2 Cor. ii. 17; v. 11. The following expressions especially remind us of the second Corinthian letter, πλεονεξία (ii. 5), cf. 2 Cor. vii. 2; with δυνάμενοι ἐν βάρει εἶναι (ii. 6), μὴ ἐπιβαρῆσαι (ii. 9), cf. 2 Cor. xi. 9 ; ii. 7 also reminds us of 1 Cor. iii. 2. Thus the Corinthian Epistles are easily recognizable both in the thoughts and the expressions of the two first chapters. Of the passages referring to the story of the conversion of the Thessalonians, ii. 14-16 is particularly noticeable.

The writer makes the apostle say here that the Thessalonians had become imitators of the Christian Churches in Judæa, since they had suffered the same things from their own countrymen as the Jewish Churches from the Jews, who killed the Lord Jesus and the prophets, and persecuted him, the apostle, and pleased not God, and were contrary to all men, forbidding him to preach the gospel to the heathen, that they might be saved, to fill up their sins always; wherefore at last wrath is come upon them. This passage has a thoroughly un-Pauline stamp. It agrees certainly with the Acts, where it is stated that the Jews in Thessalonica stirred up the heathen against the apostle's converts, and against himself;[1] yet the comparison is certainly far-fetched between these troubles raised by the Jews and Gentiles conjointly and the persecutions of the Christians in Judæa. Nor do we ever find the apostle elsewhere holding up the Judæo-Christians as a pattern to the Gentile Christians. It is, moreover, quite out of place for him to speak of those persecutions in Judæa; for he himself was the person principally concerned in the only persecution to which our passage can refer. Then do we find in any other passage that the apostle couples together, as he does here, his own sufferings for the sake of the Gospel with those which the Jews inflicted upon Jesus and the prophets? (in what a very different sense does he speak of his νέκρωσις Ἰησοῦ? 2 Cor. iv. 10). Is this polemic against the Jews at all natural to him; a polemic so external and so vague that the enmity of the Jews to the Gospel is characterized solely in the terms of that well-known charge with which the Gentiles assailed them, the *odium generis humani?* It is this which is alleged against them, ver. 15, when it is said that they are not merely Θεῷ μὴ ἀρέσκοντες, but also πᾶσιν

---

[1] We may take this opportunity of observing the unhistorical elements of the story, Acts xvii. 6. The Jews are said to have stirred up the heathen with the words: οἱ τὴν οἰκουμένην ἀναστατώσαντες οὗτοι καὶ ἐνθάδε πάρεισι. This ἀναστατῶσαι is thus said to have taken place at the time when Paul came first into these districts; how long afterwards was it that Christianity appeared to the Romans so politically dangerous as implied in the words used here: ἀπέναντι τῶν δογμάτων Καίσαρος πράττουσι?

ἀνθρώποις ἐναντίοι, ver. 15. It is evident on the face of this passage that the story in the Acts is the only source of its information; the expressions ἐκδιώκειν, κωλύειν, correspond accurately with the course of events described in Acts xvii. 5 sq. The expression τοῖς ἔθνεσι λαλῆσαι ἵνα σωθῶσι clearly suggests to us the author's familiarity with the Acts. This expression is quite after the manner of that work (xiv. 1 ; xvi. 6, 32 ; xviii. 9), but one which the apostle Paul himself never uses of his own preaching.[1] And when it is said that after the Jews have continually filled up the measure of their sins, ἔφθασε δὲ ἐπ' αὐτοὺς ἡ ὀργὴ εἰς τέλος, what does this suggest to us more naturally than the punishment that came upon them in the destruction of Jerusalem ?

It is generally supposed that the apostle wrote the First Epistle to the Thessalonians during his first residence at Corinth, soon after Silas and Timothy had arrived from Macedonia (Acts xviii. 5). Our Epistle agrees perfectly with the Acts in making Timothy, who had left Thessalonica along with Paul, but remained at Berœa while Paul went on to Athens, rejoin him at Corinth, (iii. 6). It represents Timothy, however (iii. 1), as having already been with Paul at Athens, and sent back thence to Thessalonica. The news which Timothy then brought the apostle (iii. 6) was obtained on this second journey. All this happened shortly after the apostle's first visit to Thessalonica, and so the Epistle must have been written a few months after that visit. If this be so, it is certainly strange how he could write to the Thessalonians at such length about things which must have been fresh in their memory ; it is strange also that he should give such a description of the state of the Church as, it is obvious, can only refer to a Church that had been some time in existence. How can it be said of Christians belonging to a Church only lately founded, that they were patterns to all the believers in Macedonia and Achaia, that the fame of their reception of the word of the Lord has not only gone abroad in Macedonia and Achaia, but

---

[1] λαλεῖν, 1 Cor. ii. 13, iii. 1, cannot be compared to the above expression; the meaning of λαλεῖν in these passages is simply " speak ; " it is not equivalent to λαλεῖν τὸν λόγον.

that their faith ἐν παντὶ τόπῳ ἐξελήλυθεν, that people of every place were speaking of them, how they were converted, and turned from their idols to God, i. 7 *sq.*? How can the apostle say after so short an absence that, as he greatly desired to see them face to face he had been not only once, but twice on the point of coming to them? (ii. 17, iii. 10.) Here we have an echo of the Corinthian letters, where there is frequent mention of such repeated journeys and designs of travel. How can the brotherly love of the Thessalonians, which they exhibited to all the brethren in all Macedonia, be spoken of as a virtue already so widely proved? (iv. 9.) Were admonitions to a quiet and industrious life, such as are given in iv. 11, 12, necessary even at that early period? It is usual to pass very lightly over all these things, and perhaps to place the date of the Epistle somewhat later. Another critic, on the contrary, brings all his acuteness into play to find out new possibilities, and defend the old view as being after all the most probable. Such palliatives, however, fail to remove the infirmity; it lies deeper, and can only be covered over for a moment by the treatment.

As for the section, iv. 14-18, and the view it contains of the resurrection of the dead, and the relation of the departed and the living to the second coming of Christ, this seems to agree very well with 1 Cor. xv. 52; but it goes far beyond what is taught there, and gives such a concrete representation of those transcendent matters as we never find in the apostle. Yet, if only the apostolic character of the Epistle stood firmer upon other grounds, the countenance it obtains from the passage named would save it from condemnation as unapostolic. Since, however, this is not the case, and since not only does the exhortation on the subject of the second coming occupy a prominent place (iv. 13-18; v. 1-11), but the letter is pervaded throughout by the expectation of that event (i. 10; ii. 19; iii. 13; iv. 6; v. 23), it would appear that the First Epistle arose out of the same interest in the second coming which is more decidedly expressed in the Second. With regard to this leading thought, both Epistles are intimately connected with each other. The main purpose of the First must therefore be to give a comforting view of the second coming, such as the Christians of that age required.

This is the chief theme of the Second Epistle, and here the question arises, whether such absorption in the visions of the second coming of Christ as we find in the first, and much more markedly in the second, of these Epistles, can be considered as properly belonging to our apostle. The essential part of the Second Epistle is the section ii. 1 *sqq.*, and what we have here is the Christian representation of Antichrist in its essential features, as it rose out of its sources in Judaism, especially from the prophecies of the book of Daniel. Now it cannot be considered unlikely *a priori* that the apostle Paul shared the views of his Jewish countrymen at the time ; his undisputed Epistles afford us abundant evidence how much his thought and imagination were still imbued with Jewish elements. On the other hand, however, we must remember that here is a man who resolutely broke through the limits of the national consciousness, and rose to a point of view essentially different from the Jewish, to whom, therefore, we must beware of ascribing more sympathy with Jewish ways of thinking than there is good evidence for. We must not overlook the fact that in this matter of the second coming of Christ, as much as in anything else, the strongest repulsion must have been discovered between the Pauline view of Christianity and the Judæo-Christian view. If, according to the apostle Paul, the Christian consciousness was taken up almost exclusively with the subjective relation of the individual man, feeling his need of salvation, to Christ and all the different elements of that relation, then the Christian's attention must simply have been turned away from a circle of ideas, where the essence of Christianity was made to consist only in the outward realization of the Messianic kingdom, conceived according to the form of the Old Testament theocracy. If the Pauline character of the section now under review is to be judged by any definite canon, that canon must be its measure of agreement with the genuine letters of the apostle. The question is thus narrowed to the relation which the two passages dealing with the *parousia* in the Thessalonian Epistles, bear to those passages which alone fall to be considered here, 1 Cor. xv. 23-28, and 51, 52. Here the apostle is occupied with the same class of ideas, and we shall see in what sense he accepted them, and how far he was disposed to give himself up to them. But what a difference is here! In 2 Thess. at least this is the all-engrossing question, it is specially discussed; in 1 Cor. it is only touched by the way as a very subordinate question, and that in a connexion where the apostle is taking a broad sweep over the chief epochs of the development and final consummation of the kingdom of God, and cannot avoid touching on the point. And with what measured reserve does he say the little that he thinks it necessary to say; how carefully does he seem to avoid what does not belong to the matter in hand, or what seems to have a less immediate practical interest, such as the question how it is to be with those who are living at the time of the *parousia.* The last trumpet is the signal of the resurrection, which takes place at once when it has sounded; the curious view of an ἀπάντησις ἐν νεφέλαις is not even hinted at; and when the subjection of hostile powers is spoken of as preparing the way for this final catastrophe, the last enemy who is overcome is not Antichrist, but death. The views expressed in 1 Cor. are entirely free from the specific Jewish stamp of the later period, the two representations of the last time are related to each other as the Messianic prophecy of Ps. cx. quoted in 1 Cor. xv. 25 *sq.*, and that of the prophet Daniel, ch. vii. and xi. It is therefore scarcely probable that an author who expresses his views of the last things with such caution and reserve, as in 1 Cor. xv., should, in a writing of earlier date, have entered into the question so fully and given evidence of a belief entirely preoccupied with Rabbinical opinions.[1] We may

---

[1] It is said that Acts xvii. 7 shows the apostle's preaching at Thessalonica to have been mainly apocalyptical, to have hinged, that is to say, upon the expectation of the coming of Christ as king of the kingdom of God, so that the Jews took occasion to raise a charge against his adherents, as if they were about to desert from the emperor to another king, Jesus. This interpretation of the passage is entirely arbitrary; cf. De Wette, Thess. Brief, p. 92.

go further, and assert that the view expressed in 2 Thess. ii. is in direct opposition to the apostle's own expectation, 1 Cor. xv.; for he writes, 1 Cor. xv. 52, on the assumption that he himself is to witness the *parousia,* and to be changed, along with those living at the time. Here there is a simple and confident faith in the immediate approach of Christ's coming. In 2 Thess. ii., however, we find a theory introduced to explain why the *parousia* cannot take place so soon; thus it had evidently been expected for some time when this was written. Now it was impossible to give up faith in the reality of the event, and so it was said that it had been delayed by some obstructive agency in the way. This obstruction, this κατέχον, the agency through which the final catastrophe was still delayed, was believed to be the Roman Empire, as the fourth monarchy of the prophecy of Daniel, which had to fulfil its definite period before the kingdom succeeding it, the kingdom of Christ, could appear. At the time when the Second Epistle was composed, the increasing sin and godlessness of the world were believed to be the signs of the impending catastrophe; the elements of evil were now consolidating themselves into the definite form and personality of Antichrist; yet the actual advent of the catastrophe was still relegated to the dim and distant future. The principal exhortation that our Epistle contains is therefore to the effect that Christians should not be disquieted by any delusive assertion of the approach of the *parousia,* nor surrender their calm and rational frame of mind; since it was impossible for Christ to appear before Antichrist came, and Antichrist could not come as long as that continued which had to precede the beginning of the last era. How far does this take us, not only beyond the apostle's point of view, but beyond the period in which he lived!

The view expressed in the First Epistle on the subject of the *parousia* is similar on the whole to the apostle's own view, 1 Cor. xv. 51; inasmuch as the principal element in it is the exhortation regarding the living and the departed. And here our Epistle simply repeats what the apostle himself had said. The Second Epistle differs from the apostle's views on the subject, and goes therefore beyond the First. Yet this relation of the two Epistles to each other can scarcely warrant us to attribute the Second Epistle entirely to the writer's intention to correct the representation of the nearness of the *parousia* in the First Epistle by his own doctrine of Antichrist which removed that event further off. It is perfectly conceivable that one and the same writer, if he lived so much in the thought of the *parousia* as the two Epistles testify, should have looked at this mysterious subject in different circumstances and from different points of view, and so expressed himself regarding it in different ways. However this may be, the Epistles are alike in this, that they are greatly wanting in original matter, and that this deficiency discredits their apostolic authorship. The First Epistle merely repeats what was well known before. The dependence of the second on the first shows that the writer looked about him for some precedent which might warrant him in investing his doctrine of the *parousia*, which was the main thing he had to bring forward, with the form of a Pauline Epistle. The whole of the first chapter has reference, as has justly been observed, to the First Epistle. The commencement exactly resembles the commencement of 1 Thess. ; what is said about θλίψις for the sake of the gospel has several parallels in 1 Thess. ii. and iii.[1] At ver. 6 the author goes on to the main idea of the *parousia*, as it had already been expressed in 1 Thess. ; only that his view of Antichrist and of the judgment to follow his subjection is even here before his mind, as an addition to and modification of that earlier view. Ver. 11 *sq.* is similar to 1 Thess. i. 3, iii. 12 *sq.*, v. 23 *sq.* As little can ii. 13-17 deny its similarity to 1 Thess. i. 4 *sq.*, iii. 11 *sq.* The form of address ἀδελφοὶ ἠγαπημένοι ὑπὸ Κυρίου, which occurs nowhere in Paul's own writings, is found here, and is evidently derived from 1 Thess. i. 4. Chapter iii. contains a number of sentences borrowed and extended

---

[1] De Wette (K. Erkl. p. 129) insists upon the present αἷς ἀνέχεσθε against Kern (whose Abh. über 2 Thess., Tüb. Zeitschr. f. Theol. 1839, 2 H. S. 20 *sq.* may be compared). This present, however, merely serves to show us how the author transferred what had been said in 1 Thess. to his own time.

from 1 Thess. Compare 2 Thess. iii. 1-2 with 1 Thess. v. 25 ; 2 Thess. iii. 5 with 1 Thess. v. 24, iii. 11-13 ; 2 Thess. iii. 6-12 with 1 Thess. ii. 6-12 ; iv. 11 *sq.*, v. 14 ; 2 Thess. iii. 16 with 1 Thess. v. 23. The writer's want of originality is also apparent in the phrase μὴ ἐκκακήσητε καλοποιοῦντες, which is evidently borrowed from Gal. vi. 9 ; and only seeks variety by changing τὸ καλὸν ποιεῖν into καλοποιεῖν. Phrases like εὐχαριστεῖν ὀφείλομεν are not, indeed, absolutely un-Pauline, yet circumlocutions such as this, instead of the simple Pauline εὐχαριστεῖν and with the further addition καθὼς ἄξιόν ἐστιν ; conscious exaggerations, as ὑπεραυξάνει ἡ πίστις ὑμῶν καὶ πλεονάζει ἡ ἀγάπη ἑνὸς ἑκάστου πάντων ὑμῶν (compare with this 1 Thess. iii. 10-12) ; strange and far-fetched expressions, as ἐπιστεύθη τὸ μαρτύριον ἡμῶν ἐφ' ὑμᾶς (i. 10) ; δέχεσθαι τὴν ἀγάπην τῆς ἀληθείας (ii. 10) ; with vague and confused relations of object to subject, as ἀξιοῦν τῆς κλήσεως, πληροῦν πᾶσαν εὐδοκίαν ἀγαθωσύνης (i. 11), are certainly not calculated to give evidence for a genuine Pauline origin. And lastly, the καὶ before διὰ τοῦτο (ii. 11), and αἱρεῖσθαι (ii. 13) instead of ἐκλέγεσθαι, for the idea of election, are distinctly un-Pauline.

The conclusion, iii. 17, 18, affords strong evidence against this Epistle. In order to understand it properly, we have first of all to dispose of the incorrect assertion that the greeting is contained in ver. 17 itself, and not in the benediction which follows in ver. 18. De Wette argues against this latter view, that in 1 Cor. xvi. 21, Col. iv. 18, the benediction does not immediately follow the words, ὁ ἀσπασμὸς τῇ ἐμῇ χειρί ; that, on the contrary, in the former passage, these words are succeeded by something quite opposite to the spirit of blessing, namely, by malediction. But this does not prove anything ; the Pauline benediction is not wanting in either of these Epistles. All Pauline Epistles have the same benediction at the close, though with some verbal differences ; and so the ἀσπασμὸς in this case is evidently meant to stand at the close of the Epistle after the Pauline manner, in the words ἡ χάρις τοῦ Κυρ. etc. Where is the greeting, if not in these words ? for ὁ ἀσπασμὸς, etc., is not itself the greeting, but only announces it. Now, the statement made here that the apostle added this greeting and benediction to his Epistle with his own hand, is not in itself peculiar ; the same statement is made, 1 Cor. xvi. 21, Col. iv. 18. But if we compare the conclusion of our Epistle with that of 1 Cor., we notice a very remarkable difference. Why does the apostle add the greeting to 1 Cor. with his own hand ? clearly in order to give his readers one more living proof of his affection towards them. But in our Epistle the author has made it very apparent what a different intention the assertion is meant to serve. He says, ὅ ἐστι σημεῖον ἐν πάσῃ ἐπιστολῇ· οὕτω γράφω. The words, then, stand here, not to enhance the affection of the greeting, but as a sign whereby the Epistle is to authenticate itself as Pauline, as a critical mark, to distinguish the genuine from the spurious. Not only is this quite un-Pauline in comparison with 1 Cor. ; it is an unmistakeable proof that our Epistle was written at a time when spurious apostolic writings were known to be in circulation, and there was cause for inquiry into the genuineness of each production. Against this inquiry no one could have a stronger motive to take precautions than one actually engaged in giving a pretended Pauline letter to the world. How far is the apostle himself from any such idea of spurious Epistles ; in how different a spirit did he write his autograph greeting, and how could it ever have occurred to him to set up in an Epistle, which, according to the general view, is one of the very first of the series, a criterion applicable to each one ; there being, on this hypothesis, several of them already in circulation ? Are we to suppose that, at the time when the apostle had written hardly any Epistles at all, pretended Pauline ones had already made their appearance, which called for caution in discriminating, such as is given here, ii. 2 ; or could he foresee so distinctly, even so early as this, that he would have a large correspondence afterwards ? And more, how could he reasonably regard such a criterion of the genuineness of his Epistles to be of the slightest value ? For as soon as the mark became known, it would be used with all due care to foist in any Epistle that needed it. The idea of taking the Pauline form of salutation in this sense can only have occurred to a later writer, who had a series of Pauline Epistles already before him, and who, being about to augment their number with a new one, not only provided his own with this badge of Pauline origin, but thought it necessary to draw attention to the fact. The repeated mention of Epistles, 1 Thess. v. 27, 2 Thess. ii. 2, 15 ; iii. 17, seems to ascribe an importance to the writing of Epistles, which it is impossible it should have had for the apostle, at least at the time from which these Epistles are professedly dated, but which it very naturally possessed in the eyes of a writer for whom the apostle himself existed nowhere but in his Epistles. How clearly does the exhortation given, 1 Thess. v. 27, with all due emphasis, reproduce the views of a time which regarded the apostle's letters no longer as the natural channels of spiritual intercourse, but as sacred objects to which the proper reverence was to be shown by forming as minute as possible an acquaintance with their contents, especially through public reading of them. In this way the custom arose of reading those Epistles, and others deemed important, before the congregation. But how could the apostle himself have thought it necessary formally to adjure the Church to which his Epistles were addressed, not to leave them unread ? That could be done only by an author who was not writing in the living pressure of the circumstances of which he treated, but transporting himself while writing into an imagined situation, and who wished to vindicate for his own pretended apostolic Epistles the consideration with which the original apostolic Epistles had become invested by the growth of custom.

The accustomed apologetic method will doubtless bring up one objection and another to the arguments I have here advanced. Yet if they be fairly weighed in their whole connexion, they can scarcely produce any other impression than this : that both the Epistles are entirely destitute of marks of original Pauline authorship. Their character is best explained on the hypothesis that they are letters formed on the Pauline model, in order to impress upon the Christian consciousness an idea for which the passage

1 Cor. xv. 51 seemed to afford good grounds for claiming the apostle's authority,—the idea of the *parousia*, with the definitions and modifications which the time seemed to require.[1]

[1] The above discussion has been printed, without alteration, from the first edition. If the author had reached this point in his revision of the work, he would have remodelled this chapter, and, for one thing, have incorporated in it the substance of his treatise "die beiden Briefe an die Thessalonicher, u.s.w." (Th. Jahrb. xiv. 1855, p. 141). I, of course, have not felt myself warranted to introduce this change, but as that treatise not only contains valuable investigations, especially with regard to the second Epistle, but also advances a different view from the above of the relation of the two Epistles to each other, I have printed it in the Appendix to this volume.

G

THIRD CLASS OF PAULINE EPISTLES.

EIGHTH CHAPTER.

EVEN at the present stage of the criticism of the Pauline Epistles, the Pastoral ones stand distinctly marked off from the class we have been considering, as a set of deutero-Pauline writings, doubts of whose authenticity are generally recognised as reasonable. The suspicion which Schleiermacher first conceived with respect to the First Epistle to Timothy has since then struck deep roots in the soil from which the three Epistles sprang; so that we need no longer fear any very decided reclamation when we appeal to those three Epistles in proof of the fact that there are forged Pauline letters in our canon. The more carefully and impartially these writings are examined, critically and exegetically, the less will it be possible to doubt their late origin. One critic and interpreter, the competency of whose judgment cannot be denied, has already declared, as the result of repeated examinations and of exegetical treatment in which no point was left untouched, that the verdict that they are spurious is the only possible one for him, and, he believes, for any one who does not close his eyes.[1] As this simply confirms the conclusions which I reached some time ago, and published in a work devoted to the subject, dealing especially with

---

[1] De Wette : Kurze Erkl. der Briefe an Titus, Tim., und die Hebr. 1844, Vorr. S. vi. Credner (das N. T. nach Zweck, Ursprung, Inhalt für denkende Leser der Bibel, 1841-43) has also, Th. ii. S. 96 *sq.*, renounced his previous eclectic opinion, and declared unconditionally his belief that the three Epistles are spurious.

these Epistles,[1] and as I still adhere to the view developed in that work, I need not now do more than indicate the point at which that view strikes in upon our present discussion. I will, therefore, content myself here with briefly mentioning the chief considerations on which the judgment of criticism respecting these Epistles rests, so far as it is already established.

To one seeking to form a correct judgment of the nature of the Pastoral Epistles, a main question for investigation must be found in the heretics who are mentioned here as playing a considerable part in the world. In the work I have mentioned, I was the first to assert, and to give evidence for the assertion, that in these heretics we recognise throughout the familiar features of Gnosticism ; and nothing of importance has since been urged against this view. It is no arbitrary theory, but the nature of the case, that shuts us up to this one conclusion, that these heretics can belong to no other school. What the latest defender of the genuineness of the Pastoral Epistles[2] urges against this conclusion, is nothing more than this : that "at the period from which the Pastoral Epistles spring, the higher spirits are not yet developed and arranged into systems, that they appear as mere loose formless existences, and that, though they contain the elements or bases for more developed growths, yet what they want is just that form which, as members of the Gnostic systems, they possess." But how unnatural is the assumption that if the author of the Pastoral Epistles wished to controvert the Gnostics, he would himself have described their systems ; and how unfair and absurd is the demand made on those who seek to prove that those Gnostic-looking representations actually belong to Gnosis! If the true state of affairs is really to be acknowledged, two things must first of all be allowed : first, that there may have been Gnostic systems in existence at the time, which may possibly be referred to here, even though the writer of the Epistles does not set

---

[1] Die sogenannten Pastoralbriefe des Apostels Paulus, 1835.

[2] Matthies, Erklärung der Pastoralbriefe mit besonderer Beziehung auf Authentie und Ort und Zeit der Abfassung derselben, 1840, S. 165. Compare my review of this work in the Jahrb. für wissensch. Kritik, 1841, Jan. Nr. 12 f.

forth the heresies which he is combating in their systematic form,
but only characterizes them in general terms; and then, that the
task of historical criticism is to make combinations on the grounds
of probability, and thus to arrive at the actual state of the case.
If these two things be allowed, then we have simply to determine
whether the features of the doctrine controverted in these Epistles
warrant us, from what we can understand of them, to assume that
it is no other doctrine than the Gnosis known to us in history.
That this conclusion is warranted, De Wette now allows;[1] he only
does not take the further step with me, that the Gnostics attacked
here are the Marcionites in particular. And yet in the face of
such clear indications of the Marcionite doctrine, as we have 1 Tim.
vi. 20, this conclusion ought not to offer any great difficulty; if the
apostolic origin of the Epistles is fairly given up, then half-a-century
backwards or forwards in the date of their origin cannot so much
matter, at least where, as is here the case, no further reasons can
be adduced against a later date. This late origin of the Pastoral
Epistles has a further point in its favour, which is not noticed in
my work on those Epistles, but of which I spoke later in another
place.[2]

The passage quoted by Eusebius, Eccl. Hist. iii. 32, from the
historical work of Hegesippus, is an important one for the criticism
of the Pastoral Epistles, especially of 1 Tim. Hegesippus says
here distinctly, in speaking of the origin of the heresies and of their
entrance into the Church, till then pure and immaculate, that only
when the choir of the apostles became extinct did the ψευδώνυμος
γνῶσις boldly lift up its head. Now how could Hegesippus have
said this, if the apostle Paul, as author of the pastoral Epistles,
had mentioned this ψευδώνυμος γνῶσις by the same name as a
phenomenon existing at his time? We might suppose that
Hegesippus happened not to know of 1 Tim. as a Pauline Epistle;
yet the fact that there had been at that earlier period a Gnosis

---

[1] *Op. cit.* p. 119 *sq.*, cf. p. 117.

[2] In the essay on the origin of the episcopate, which may be consulted on this
whole subject, Tub. Zeitschr. für Theol. 1838, 3 H. S. 27 f.

falsely so called, could not possibly have escaped him. This piece of evidence speaks with all possible distinctness against the apostolic authorship of our Epistles, and the passage from which it is taken is the more remarkable, that in other points also it betrays an affinity with our Epistles which cannot be altogether the result of chance. Not only is the peculiar phrase ψευδώνυμος γνῶσις found there as well as here, but the phrase ἑτεροδιδασκαλεῖν (with which Schleiermacher was so much struck, and which seemed to him to imply the existence at that time of the word ἑτεροδιδάσκα-λος, a word which, he thought, did not occur)[1] finds its parallel in the term ἑτεροδιδάσκαλοι which Hegesippus (*in loc. cit.*) applies to those heretics. Again, Hegesippus speaks of a ὑγιὴς κανὼν τοῦ σωτηρίου κηρύγματος, and in the same way the phrase ὑγιαίνουσα διδασκαλία is used of sound doctrine, 1 Tim. i. 10, and elsewhere. There are only two possible explanations of this : that Hegesippus had our Epistle before him, or the writer of our Epistle the work of Hegesippus. But Hegesippus can scarcely, considering his Ebionite views, have drawn from an Epistle supposed to be by Paul ; and thus we are shut up to the latter alternative which is in itself the more probable of the two. Thus the origin of 1 Timothy at least belongs to the period of the Marcionite Gnosis. Hegesippus[2] enumerates Marcionites, Carpocratians, Valentinians, Basilidians, Saturninians, as sects who, with Simon Magus at their head, and springing from the seven Jewish heresies (it agrees very well with this that the heretics of the Pastoral Epistles are characterized in part as judaizers), as ψευδόχριστοι, ψευδοπροφῆται, ψευδαπό-στολοι, ἐμέρισαν τὴν ἔνωσιν τῆς ἐκκλησίας φθοριμαίοις λόγοις, or as it is expressed before, ἀκοαῖς ματαίαις. This agrees with the ἐξ-ετράπησαν εἰς ματαιολογίαν of 1 Tim. i. 6. How then can it be thought so improbable that the Marcionite is one of the Gnostic doctrines attacked in these Epistles ?

A second point in the criticism of the Pastoral Epistles, and one of no less importance than that just spoken of, is the reference

---

[1] Sendschreiben über den sogenannten ersten Brief des Paulus an Timoth., p. 29.   [2] Eusebius, Eccl. Hist., iv. 22.

they contain to the government and the external institutions of the church. This second point is intimately connected with the first. The Gnostics, as the first heretics properly so called, gave the first occasion for the episcopal constitution of the church. Now, if there were heretics of the same stamp in the age of the apostle Paul, then it was quite natural and proper that the importance of a well-defined constitution for the Christian church should have been urged at that earlier period. If, however, it appear unlikely that there were such heretics at that time, then this also must appear unlikely ; then these ecclesiastical arrangements will be devoid of any historical occasion or connexion. And if the mention of such things in a Pauline Epistle be in itself a curious and suspicious circumstance, then the argument it furnishes against the authenticity of the Pastoral Epistles is all the stronger. In any case it must appear very remarkable that only in these Epistles do we find the apostle Paul insisting with such serious emphasis on ecclesiastical institutions. In those Epistles which supply us with the surest standard of his principles, he never betrays the slightest interest in such things, not even when they might be thought to lie directly in his way, as in his dealings with a church like that of Corinth. And this want of interest in such things is not merely accidental ; it is founded deep in the whole spirit and character of Pauline Christianity, so that we may not without substantial reasons make him the author and supporter of institutions which were not long in showing how closely they were akin to the hierarchical spirit of Judaism. This feature in the pastoral Epistles is so peculiar, that those who defend their genuineness have felt themselves compelled to seek for special motives, which may have led the apostle to impart such pastoral instruction in this instance. It must have been, it is alleged, very necessary and very beneficial for these churches, that the greatest attention should be bestowed on organization ; and it was very fitting that this should be done in private letters, such as these, addressed to men who were functionaries in the church and associates of the apostle. But it is not proved that in this case there was any

such special need ; and this explanation is bound up with
hypotheses which stand themselves in need of proof. The consideration that, as private letters, these Epistles afforded peculiar
opportunities for imparting such instruction can weigh for nothing,
if we reflect that the form of the writing would not determine the
object, but, on the contrary, the object the form.[1]

A further point in the criticism of the pastoral Epistles is that it
is impossible to find a suitable place for the composition of them
in the apostle's history as we know it. The latest attempt, that
made by Matthies, furnishes an additional proof of this assertion.
The Epistle to Titus is said to have been written during the

---

[1] One of the most decisive proofs of later origin is the ecclesiastical institution
of widows, spoken of 1 Tim. v. 3. This passage is still misunderstood. The
explanation given by Matthies is quite beside the mark. De Wette (Preface, p.
vi.) thinks he has cleared up the whole difficulty. But the passage can never
appear in a clear light so long as the expression χηρά is not taken in the sense
which I have shown to be the ecclesiastical one (cf. especially Ignat. Ep. ad
Smyrn., c. 13). If the χῆραι, vv. 11 and 14, be actually bereaved persons, then
we are met by the great difficulty that the apostle gives two directly contradictory precepts about them. According to vv. 11 and 14, the younger widows
should marry again ; and, according to ver. 9, a second marriage is to exclude them,
should they become widows again, from the viduatus of the Church. De Wette
says the distinction was a rare one, to which many did not aspire, and that the
author set up the regulation, ver. 9, only out of respect for the custom of the
church then subsisting ; but this is very superficial. How can it be thought that
a writer who gives such precepts would deal so loosely with second marriage, a
thing so repugnant to the sentiment of the time ? Not to insist upon the simple
and unqualified γαμεῖν, ver. 14, the passage does not apply even to the younger
widows, who alone would be spoken of here. If the χῆραι, vv. 11, 14, be widows
proper, then these younger widows, as distinguished from the older, ver. 9, must
include all under the age of sixty. But how can such persons be meant in the
general directions? vv. 11, 14. The whole passage applies, it is evident, only to
younger females ; and the sense becomes still clearer if we do not, as is generally
done, take νεωτέρας χήρας together, but take νεωτέρας as subject, and χήρας as
predicate, and παραιτοῦ as a negative of καταλεγέσθω. The words then bear the
plain and natural meaning : Do not admit young persons of the female sex into
the catalogue of the χῆραι, for they are at an age when they cannot be trusted ;
for if they feel the sexual impulse, which is incompatible with faithfulness to
Christ, they will marry. And if it thus appears that the passage can be satisfactorily explained only out of the ecclesiastical vocabulary of the second century,
this is the clearest possible proof that the Epistle cannot belong to the apostolic
age, when the church had no special order of the kind.

apostle's three months' residence in Greece before his return to Jerusalem, Acts xx. 2. There was also, it is said, plenty of time during this period for a journey to Crete. He made this journey with Titus for his companion, laid the foundation of the church there, then left Titus behind to take charge of further arrangements for the cause of the Gospel, and then wrote this letter to him,[1]—wrote to him in fact, what he could have said just before by word of mouth, and that much better. The result of this author's investigation regarding 1 Tim. is that shortly before Paul began his return journey from Achaia to Jerusalem, he sent Timothy before him to Ephesus with verbal messages (the passage 1 Tim. i. 3 is interpreted thus, though its natural meaning is entirely different, in order to harmonize it with Acts xx. 4); that he thought of going there himself, but did not know positively if he would do so, and that, a good opportunity presenting itself, he wrote this Epistle to Timothy from some place in Achaia or Macedonia, in order to give him some instructions that might be of use to him in the meantime.[2] But this account of the matter is full of contradictions. In the Acts Timothy accompanies the apostle on the journey through Macedonia to Troas, and presumably to Ephesus also; and 1 Tim. makes Timothy remain at Ephesus, when the apostle, after spending nearly three years in that city, leaves it for Macedonia; the apostle then writes this Epistle to him immediately after his departure, with a view to a complete ecclesiastical organization, and this while intending shortly to return there. What a mass of improbability is this! How plainly do we see that the apostle's departure and Timothy's remaining are arranged in this way simply to find an occasion for the Epistle! In a word, the Epistle is, as De Wette also judges, historically incomprehensible. And these Epistles are all alike in this. At whatever point a new attempt is made to rescue them, the proofs which are set up at once break down. In the great sea of possibilities, it may perchance be possible to find a calm spot for the Epistle to Titus and the second to Timothy

[1] Matthies, Comm., p. 194.   [2] *Op. cit.*, p. 486.

(though in the case of the latter, the second Roman captivity is incapable of proof, and quite improbable, and is thus a sufficiently decisive piece of evidence); but their entire similarity to, and their intimate connexion with the first to Timothy—this is, and will be, the chief betrayer of the false fraternity—involves them all alike in the same condemnation.

In addition to all this, a close inspection reveals to us much that is peculiar and un-Pauline in their language, and in many of their conceptions and views.[1] In this particular also the three Epistles are so much alike that none of them can be separated from the others, and from this circumstance the identity of their authorship may be confidently inferred.

---

[1] Compare on this subject De Wette's Kurze Erklärung, p. 118 *sq.*

NINTH CHAPTER.

FROM the foregoing investigation I think every unprejudiced student will be led almost irresistibly to conclude that each of the shorter Pauline Epistles, regarded separately, presents more or less formidable critical difficulties, and that there are some of them which it is scarcely possible to regard as authentic. If we take a general view of all these Epistles together, the verdict to be passed on them, as compared with the Epistles universally acknowledged authentic, can scarcely be in their favour. The comparison reveals at once how far they stand below the originality, the wealth of thought, and the whole spiritual substance and value of those other Epistles. They are characterized by a certain meagreness of contents, by colourlessness of treatment, by absence of motive and connexion, by monotony, by repetition, by dependence, partly on each other, and partly on the Epistles of the first class, which are often referred to in a style evidently not that of a writer at first hand. It is not the object of any of those Epistles, as of the principal ones of Paul, to develop fully some one peculiarly and essentially Pauline idea ; even the higher Christological idea which distinguishes the Epistles to the Ephesians, Colossians, and Philippians, has no intimate relation with the Pauline system ; on the contrary, it is foreign to that system. The general character of these Epistles is, we may say, a certain smoothing of the specific Pauline doctrine with a dominant practical tendency. This may be recognised in the frequent recommendation of good works, and in the instructions and admonitions regarding the Christian behaviour, the ἀξίως περιπατεῖν τῆς κλήσεως, περιπατεῖν ἐν ἔργοις ἀγαθοῖς (Eph. ii. 10 ; iv. 1). It is clear that the point of view from which these letters are written is not that of one seeking to make good, and to develop a general principle which has still to vindicate itself, and on which the Christian consciousness and life are to be formed; but rather that of one applying the contents of Christian doctrine to practical life with its various circumstances. Very striking and significant is the difference between these later Epistles and the older ones, in all that belongs to the peculiar plan and composition of a Pauline Epistle. The authentic Pauline Epistles have a true organic development; they proceed from one root idea which penetrates the whole contents of the Epistle from the very beginning, and binds all the different parts of it to an inner unity, through the deeper relations in which it holds them, even though they appear at first sight to be only outwardly connected. They are founded in one creative thought, which determines not merely the contents of the Epistle, but its whole form and structure. Hence they exhibit a genuine dialectic movement, in which the thought possesses sufficient inherent force to originate all the stages of its development, and to advance from stage to stage in accordance with their inner connexion with each other. Especially does this merit distinguish the greater Epistles of the apostle, that to the Romans, and the first to the Corinthians. It would be a great mistake to think, of these Epistles, that the order in which they deal with the various matters contained in them, and pass from one subject to another, is merely fortuitous. The only way to grasp the whole contents of such an Epistle is to place one's-self within that one idea, from which, as the centre, each single part is assigned its place in the connexion of the whole; and this immanent movement of thought may be traced in each important section of those Epistles. Remark, for example, how methodically the apostle goes to work with the instruction he has to give about speaking with tongues (1 Cor. xii. 14); how he discusses the matter in all its various aspects; how what is said about love (chap. xiii.) is an essential element in helping his argument forward; and how he makes the thought with which he is chiefly concerned pass through the necessary stages of its

evolution in their order.   In the shorter Epistle to the Galatians
we find the same ; the rapid movement which brings the apostle
at once to speak of himself and his own personal concerns does
not come merely from the passionate warmth with which he
speaks ; it is the immediate grasp of the subject of his Epistle at
that point at which it presents itself to him in all its lines of influence at once.   He who has recognised this depth of conception
from which each genuine Epistle of Paul proceeded, this metho-
dical development and dialectical process, as the characteristic
distinction of these Epistles, will be prepared to admit how little
of all this there is to be found in the smaller Epistles.   Here the
authors move forward not without visible effort ; they draw out
one and the same thought with laboured expansion and manifold
repetition ; the contents of their Epistles consist more of piece
added to piece externally, than of any one subject developing
naturally under their hands.   If these Epistles were genuine
productions of the apostle, why should they thus belie their
Pauline origin ; how is it that none of them bears the features of
that origin with any distinctness ?   Even the Epistle to the
Colossians, which might in many respects be best qualified to put
forth such a claim, can make no pretence to equality with the
older Epistles in these particulars.

Such is the position of these Epistles in respect of their inward
character ; and in respect of the outward historical circumstances
by which their origin is to be explained, the difference is equally
striking.   The older Epistles rest, with regard to their occasion
and drift, on the whole historical connexion of circumstances to
which they belong, in such a way that everything fits in perfectly ;
their roots are native to the soil of the time in which they arose,
and we cannot have the least doubt as to their historical position
and reference.   How little this is the case with the later Epistles
has already been shown ; how uncertain and indefinite they are in
nearly all their historical bearings, and by what feeble threads
they are connected with the chief features of the apostle's life.
The most of these Epistles presume to have been written during

the Roman captivity, but we nowhere find any pressing reason why they should have been written during that period (and if the apostle had been so fertile in correspondence, he might have written such letters as well during his two years' imprisonment at Cesarea, as has been surmised not without reason, and yet quite incorrectly), or any clear account of his personal condition at the time. If the apostle was to be made the author of other letters after the true ones, the Roman captivity certainly presented itself as a very suitable situation for that purpose. During the considerable period over which it seems to have extended, it might well be thought that he had ample leisure to write letters. Then when this situation had been used to a considerable extent, the letters ascribed to him were dated also from an earlier period, as we see in the case of the two Epistles to Timothy ; the first of these, which is manifestly of later composition, dates, not like the second, from the imprisonment, but before it ; and the two Thessalonian letters are probably later than Ephesians, Colossians, and Philippians.

The nature of the case may explain why we have not spoken hitherto of the external testimony to these Epistles, and why we merely touch upon it now. Testimonies to these Epistles, such at least as are deserving of any confidence, do not exist. In this respect also they are inferior to the older Epistles, which have at least the early testimony of the Roman Clemens. Evidences to the existence and the apostolic origin of these Epistles date only from the time of Irenæus, Tertullian, and Clemens of Alexandria, that is, from a period in which it is quite conceivable that post-apostolic Epistles, even though produced far on in the second century, could have come to count as genuine works of the apostle.

What gives these Epistles their claim to the name of the apostle is simply the circumstance that they profess to be Pauline, and make the apostle speak as their author. But if even one of them be unable to make good its apostolic name, and with regard to 1 Tim. this can scarcely be denied, then we see at once how little that circumstance can prove of itself ; it must then be admitted that what has happened in one case may have happened

·equally in several others. The great and prominent spirits of the ancient world count this among the proofs of their greatness and importance, and of the power with which they dominated the whole consciousness of their time, that whatever was thought in their spirit was, as a matter of course, invested, when published, with their name. The continued working of their overshadowing personality manifests itself in this, that even after their death they are made to speak and write as they spoke and wrote in their lifetime. Thus there are pseudo-Pauline letters, just as there are not only Platonic but pseudo-Platonic dialogues, and the form in which a new body of philosophical or religious thought was expounded seemed so much a part of the thought itself, that in order to reach the original stand-point of the thinker, it was held necessary to employ his forms of thinking. A Paulinist who wished to write in the sense of Paul had to employ the Pauline epistolary form, as a Platonist held that he must not make use of his master's dialogue-form without thinking himself into the spirit and personality of Plato as he wrote. From the unity of the form and contents of such modes of composition, it was thought that they could not be severed from the names of their originators; their imitators felt bound to write in their names. Viewed in this light, a Pauline Epistle is, equally with a Platonic dialogue, a classical form of representation, to the original type of which one sought, therefore, to be faithful as far as possible. Both these forms, indeed, arose in the same way, out of a definite circle of peculiar circumstances, in which a new form of consciousness had prepared for itself its outward shape by its own creative power. It is therefore a true observation which has frequently been made, that the forging of such Epistles must not be judged according to the modern standard of literary honesty, but according to the spirit of antiquity, which attached no such definite value as we do to literary property, and regarded the thing much more than the person.[1] There is therefore no reason to think here of deception

[1] De Wette, Kurze Erkl. der Briefe an Titus, u.s.w., S. 122 f. Cf. Schleiermacher, Der chr. Gl. ii. 372 f.

or wilful forgery ; yet even if it be asserted that the matter is not intelligible except on this hypothesis, that cannot be maintained as an argument against its possibility and likelihood.

The Epistles which thus carry us beyond the age of the apostle, and, as their contents for the most part clearly show, to a later set of circumstances, come under the same category with the legends of the apostle's last fortunes. They belong, not to the biography of the apostle himself, but to the history of the party which used his name, and to their party circumstances. How Paulinism was developed, what modifications it admitted, with what antagonisms it had to contend, what influence it exerted in moulding the features of the time, from the varied elements of which the unity of the Christian church was to emerge, this is what we find in these Epistles. It may be ground for regret that we cannot see in them genuine products of the apostle's genius, or sources for history of the same importance as attaches to his undisputed Epistles (and yet in no case could they be placed on a level with these ; their intrinsic value and the nature of their contents remain just the same, whether they be apostolic or not). But in the other scale we have to place this immense advantage, that these letters, as soon as they are critically examined, make it possible for us to obtain a somewhat clearer view of the circumstances of a period which is of such importance for the history of the development of early Christianity. If it be considered how meagre the materials are for the history of that period, and how valuable every new source that is opened up must be, what inducement can we have to maintain the apostolic character of letters, whose apostolic origin is surrounded by doubts which the ablest advocacy can never entirely overcome ; and the attempt to dispel which presents to us, at the best, not the natural truth of history, but a confused web of artificial combinations ? It is out of place to speak of any real loss in a case where that is simply given back to historical truth which rightfully belonged to it from the beginning.

THIRD PART.

THE DOCTRINAL SYSTEM OF THE APOSTLE.

INTRODUCTION.

THE sphere of our representation grows always more contracted as we approach the spiritual centre of the apostle's historical appearance and personality. It has been our task up to this point to detect the spurious elements both in the history of his life and work and in those Epistles which have reached us under his name. By this process we have sought to get at the true historical basis of his personality, and to confine it within those limits which he himself indicates to us in the true productions of his genius, and in the principles of action expressed in them. Having laid this foundation, our task is now to separate the essential and universal from the less essential, the fortuitous, and that which has reference only to the special circumstances of his time. The substance and contents of Paul's Epistles consist in nothing but his peculiar system of doctrine ; and our task with regard to this is not only to impute to him nothing that is not really his, but also to seek to comprehend that which is essentially his, at the point from which it took its organic connexion and developed into a definite whole.

The following discussion of the Pauline system differs in three points from the treatment which the subject has commonly received :—

I. It follows, of course, from our critical investigations, that our representation of the apostle's doctrine can be founded on the contents of those Epistles only which are to be regarded as indisputably his. Whether the objections raised against the genuineness of the smaller Epistles be or be not well founded, at any rate till they are completely and manifestly refuted (and there is no great reason for expecting this), it is impossible to be certain that the use of these Epistles will not introduce features into our view of the doctrine which will give it a physiognomy more or less different from what it had at first. A representation of the apostle's doctrine, which abstains completely from using these Epistles as materials, will, at the same time, yield a palpable proof how small their importance is in this respect, in comparison with the others, and how little their rejection will create any gap in the apostle's teaching. As his proper teaching is sharply defined and clearly recognised, we shall see distinctly how un-Pauline the doctrine and statements of these Epistles are, throughout nearly their whole extent. Attention has already been drawn to this in the proper place in our critical discussions, and it is not necessary to compare further the two doctrines, or to insist on their divergences.

II. The following representation seeks to avoid an error which has been made in the reconstruction of the Pauline system, by not clearly distinguishing, nor, in consequence, placing in their proper relation to each other, the two sides which ought to be distinguished. A comparison of the views of Usteri,[1] Neander,[2] and Dähne,[3] will show at once how far they differ from each other in the position they give to the different doctrines, and in the construction of the whole. Usteri divides his treatment of the subject into two parts of unequal extent, the first dealing with the ante-Christian, and the second with the Christian period. The ante-Christian period embraces both Judaism and heathenism, both being comprehended in the conception of sin. The general ruin of the human race points backwards to that beginning from which the dominion of sin and death arose ; how this came about, how sin came to extend its power, the relation of sin and death to the law, the inadequacy of the law for justification and salvation, the end of the law, and the longing for redemption which was the result of the ante-Christian period,—all these points are considered here. In the second part, which deals with the provision for redemption made by God through Christ, the first section deals with the

[1] Entwicklung des paulinischen Lehrbegriffs in seinem Verhältniss zur biblischen Dogmatik des N. T.   4th Edition 1832.

[2] Planting and Training, etc., i. pp. 416-531.

[3] Entwicklung des paulinischen Lehrbegriffs, 1835.

realization of redemption in the individual, while the second treats of Christians as a body,—the church of Christ. In passing to the second part, Usteri himself remarks, that the distinction here drawn between the life of the individual and the life of the body is a relative one, which cannot be carried out strictly, because the one always passes over into the other ; he thus admits that his view and arrangement of the subject are unsatisfactory. The distinction is a just one, and the reason why it cannot be carried out is, that it is made in the wrong place. If a distinction is to be maintained between the life of the individual and the life of the body, the former must not be subordinated to the latter as if it issued in it at one definite point; the two should be set over against each other as independent momenta. Again, the contrast between the ante-Christian and the Christian period may have been clear enough to the apostle's mind, yet it was only something secondary ; he had to start, in fact, from the individual life in order to obtain such a view of corporate life, of historical development, as should explain to him theoretically, looking at it historically, that which was the immediate result of his own most intimate experience. Thus what Usteri places first is not the first in fact, but presupposes something else.

Equally mistaken again is the procedure of Neander and Dähne. Starting from the idea of νόμος and δικαιοσύνη, and from the great proposition of the Pauline doctrine of justification that man requires for his salvation and justification by God out of grace, they subordinate the corporate to the individual life, and introduce, before the Pauline doctrine of justification, which moves entirely within the sphere of the individual life, has been developed in its connexion, propositions which belong to the sphere of the corporate life. Usteri's division is simply applied subjectively by Dähne, when he divides his subject into two sections : first, man needs for his salvation a justification before God through grace (and the guilt of Gentiles and Jews is spoken of in this connexion, there being no further review of the historical connexion of Heathenism and Judaism with Christianity) ; second, justification before God

through grace is offered to man in Christianity. I can discern
no principle of division in the arrangement of Neander, which is
as follows : First, the ideas of δικαιοσύνη and νόμος, the central
point of the doctrine ; Second, the central point of the Pauline
anthropology, human nature in opposition to the law ; sin, origin
of sin and death, suppression by sin of the natural revelation of God,
the state of disunion ; Third, preparations for redemption, Judaism
and Heathenism ; Fourth, the work of redemption ; Fifth, the appropriation of salvation by faith, etc. How can the development
of the ideas δικαιοσύνη and νόμος be separated from the apostle's
doctrine of justification, and how one-sided is it to make Judaism
and Heathenism follow the doctrine of sin as being a preparation
for redemption, when Judaism and Heathenism are just the domain
where the principle of sin and death has its supremacy ; and their
relation to Christianity can only be defined by the opposition in
which sin and grace, death and life, law and faith, stand to each
other ? For the same reason that they do not distinguish with sufficient accuracy the subjective and the objective sides, the representations of Neander and Dähne are deficient in this point also,
that the religious historical position of Christianity in relation to
Judaism and Heathenism is not specially considered. It is not possible to maintain order, connexion, and unity in our view of the whole,
and to give the respective doctrines their proper place, except in
this way : that the apostle's doctrine of justification with all that
belongs to it be recognised as constituting his representation of
the subjective consciousness, and kept separate from his view of
the objective relation in which Christianity stands to Judaism and
Heathenism in the religious development of mankind. The more
this objective side is kept distinct from the other, the more clearly
do we see what importance it also had for the apostle.

III. It is important to give more exact definitions, both grammatical and logical, of the various conceptions on which the
Pauline system is based, and to place them more precisely in the
order of their arrangement than has been done in former treatments
of this subject.

NOTE.

In the following review of the Pauline doctrine, the author first discusses (Chap. I.) " *The principle of the Christian consciousness*," as it is determined by Paul. He finds the peculiar feature of the principle to be its absoluteness; namely, that the Christian has the Spirit in himself, and cannot therefore consider his salvation to be depending on anything outward; that he is conscious of his immediate union with God, of the identity of his spirit with the Spirit of God, of his own freedom and infinity. How the Christian arrives at this consciousness is explained by the apostle through his doctrine of justification; and this doctrine is discussed here (Chap. II.) in its negative, and (Chap. III.) in its positive aspect.

Chap. II. develops the proposition that man does not become righteous through the works of the law, and that the reason of the incapacity is to be found in the σάρξ.

Chap. III. shows that according to the apostle's teaching faith is the only way to justification; but it is this only in virtue of its contents, as faith in the atoning death of Christ. Thus the author inquires here what significance the apostle discovered in the death of Jesus. He then goes into an examination of the idea of justification, the question being, How far man can become a δίκαιος through faith in the death of Christ? He proceeds to discuss the nature of that faith through which he acquires the righteousness, a main element of it being shown to be a real and living fellowship with Christ.

Christianity having thus been considered as a subjective principle of life, the author turns (cf. p. 118) to the objective relation in which it stands towards Judaism and Heathenism.

In Chap. IV. he speaks of " Christ as the foundation, and the principle of the Christian society," or what amounts to the same thing, the church as the σῶμα Χριστοῦ, and takes up in this connexion the Christian charisms, and Baptism and the Lord's Supper.

In Chap. V. he deals with the relation of Christianity to Judaism and Heathenism. This relation is, broadly speaking, that of opposition. Sinfulness is the character of the ante-Christian time, and accordingly Paul's doctrine of the origin and reign of sin has been kept for discussion at this point. Then his view of the law, his estimate of the Jewish religion, are taken up ; and lastly, his views on heathenism.

In its relation to the preceding and subordinate forms of religion Christianity asserts itself as the absolute religion, and thus appears " as a new principle of the world's historical development." It is regarded from this point of view in Chap. VI., where we have a description of the Pauline doctrine of the first and the second Adam, and of the periods of the world inaugurated by each, which naturally introduces the Pauline eschatology.

Hope has reference to this future, faith to the past ; and in its reference to the present, the Christian consciousness is love. Chap. VII. deals with " faith, love and hope, as the three momenta of the Christian consciousness."

Chap. VIII. adds to the foregoing, in the form of an appendix, a " special discussion of certain dogmatic questions not involved in the main system," the successive sections of which deal with the following points :—1. The nature of religion ; 2. The doctrine of God ; 3. The doctrine of Christ ; 4. The doctrine of angels and demons ; 5. The doctrine of the Divine predestination ; 6. The heavenly habitation of 2 Cor. v. 1.

Chap. IX. is entitled, " On certain features of the apostle's character," and is an attempt to gather up the various traces of his character which are to be found in his writings, that we may thus form acquaintance with its most prominent features, though the data at our command do not carry us further.

The author's later discussion of the subject in his *Vorlesungen über Neutestamentliche Theologie* (128-207) deviates considerably from this one not only in many points of detail, which I shall notice in their place, but in the arrangement of the whole. The central point of the apostle's religious consciousness and of his doctrine is found in that work in the fact of his opposition on principle to the law, in the proposition, namely, that that which

Judaism is not able to effect is now effected by Christianity. This proposition, as is here remarked, was a natural and immediate corollary from the view the apostle had come to entertain of Jesus as a sacrifice. In demonstrating this proposition the apostle arrives at his peculiar doctrine of justification. Judaism and heathenism are comprehended in the common conception of religion; the task of both, which is indeed the ultimate object of all religion, is to bring man into union with God,—into that harmonious relation towards God with which God will be satisfied. Now, à priori, there appear to be two ways in which this may be accomplished; the way of the fulfilling of the law, and the way of faith. The distinctive peculiarity of Judaism is that it adopts the first of these two ways; Christianity, on the other hand, adopts the second. The apostle's contention is, then, that man obtains δικαιοσύνη not through works of the law, but through faith. The negative part of this assertion, the οὐ δικαιοῦται ἐξ ἔργων νόμου is treated first (p. 134 sqq.), and is provided with three proofs drawn from Paul's different arguments : the purely empirical, Rom. i. 18-iii. 20; the religio-historical, provided by the contrast of the first and the second Adam, Rom. v. 12 sq.; and the anthropological, consisting mainly of the apostle's doctrine of the σάρξ and the νόμος in their relation to sin (pp. 141-153). The positive part of Paul's central doctrine, the assertion of justification by faith, is then taken up (pp. 153 sqq.) and looked at from the different points of view : (1.) of actual facts ; (2.) of anthropology; (3.) of religious history. Under the first of these heads the author speaks of the significance of the death of Jesus regarded as an atonement ; under the second, of the real influence of that death as overcoming the σάρξ; and, under the third, of the Pauline view of the law as an essentially imperfect and transitory dispensation, meant only to prepare for the coming of the true religion. In pp. 174-182, he defines the notion of justifying faith, and the relation of faith and works ; p. 182 sqq., he discusses the relation of faith to the freedom of man and the predestination of God ; then p. 186, he comes to speak of Christ as the object of faith ; p. 195, he enters on an

estimate of the importance Paul attributed to the death of Christ
for the development of mankind, especially to his resurrection as
the prototype of ours; p. 198, he takes up the doctrine of the
influence the glorified Christ exerts upon the Church, of the
church as the body of Christ, and of the sacraments; 202 *sq.*,
eschatology; and concludes, p. 205 f., with the apostle's definition
of the idea of God.—*Editor's Note.*

FIRST CHAPTER.

In order to apprehend the principle of the Christian consciousness in all its depth and peculiarity, as it existed in the view of the apostle, it is necessary for us to refer as far as possible to what was characteristic in the fact of his conversion. In proportion as this change, not less decisive than rapid and immediate, not merely from Judaism to Christianity, and from one form of religious consciousness to another, but also from one direction of life into the very opposite direction, was characteristic of the man, it reveals to us the power and significance which Christianity had for him. That the same man, who just before was persecuting Christianity with the most violent hatred, should come all at once to believe in him whose followers he had been seeking to destroy, and that in this faith he should become a totally different man ;—what is this but a victory which Christianity owed to nothing but to the might of its own inherent truth ? Of all those who have been converted to faith in Christ, there is no one in whose case the Christian principle broke so absolutely and so immediately through everything opposed to it, and asserted so triumphantly its own absolute superiority, as in that of the apostle Paul. First of all, then, the Christian principle has this peculiarity with him, that it declares itself in its absolute power and importance, and asserts itself in its absoluteness, by overcoming all that conflicts with its supremacy. In the fresh consciousness of a stand-point, in the still recent attainment of which all his strength and energy had been engaged, the apostle stands upon the absoluteness of his Christian position, and Christianity is thus to him the absolute power of the spiritual life forcing its way through and overcoming the most formidable obstacles. The spiritual process he passed through in the act of his conversion is simply the key to the Christian principle as unfolded in his person. The absoluteness of the Christian principle consists, however, simply in this : that it is essentially identical with the person of Christ. The entire absolute importance of Christianity resides, in the apostle's view, in the person of Christ ; hence it was in that person that the Christian principle came to his consciousness as that which it essentially is. This is what he asserts when he says of his conversion (Gal. i. 15, 16) that it pleased God, who separated him from his mother's womb, and chose him for this particular destiny, and called him by his grace, to reveal his Son in him, that is, to disclose the person of Jesus (against whom he had hitherto acted such a hostile part, as not only not to recognise him as Messiah, but to behold in him merely a false Messiah, quite repugnant to the true idea of the Messiah), in his consciousness, through an inward act of the consciousness, as that which he really was, the Son of God. The expression " Son of God" denotes the essential change which took place at his conversion in his view of the Messiah, and we must examine what this change was in order to appreciate its importance. It has already been remarked that up to that time the difference between the believing and the unbelieving Jew consisted mainly in this, that the former regarded Jesus of Nazareth as the Messiah already actually come, as the same who was to appear as Messiah, according to the promises and prophecies of the Old Testament, and that notwithstanding that his whole appearance, and particularly the manner of his death, presented so great a contrast to all that the common imagination expected the Messiah to be and to do. The belief in the resurrection of Jesus did away with that contradiction, and thus the most essential element in the apostle's conviction of the Messianic dignity of Jesus was, that he believed in him as the risen One (1 Cor. xv. 8). But the peculiar inward process through which the belief in Jesus, as the Messiah, had arisen in him, made his conception of the Son of God, which he now recognised Jesus as being, one of far wider meaning than that of the other disciples. For these latter the belief in the resurrection, which removed the offence of the death of Christ, meant simply that there was a prospect of a second appearance of the risen One, and that then all that had remained unaccomplished at the first coming would be realized (Acts iii. 19 *sq.*). For the apostle Paul, on the contrary, the death of the Messiah was in itself simply inconceivable, except by such a revolution in his Messianic consciousness as could not but produce the greatest effect in his whole view of Christianity. Everything that was national and Jewish in the Messianic idea (and this had been modified in the consciousness of the other apostles only by their changing the form of it and referring it to the second coming of Jesus) was at once removed from the consciousness of our apostle by the one fact of the death of Jesus. With this death everything that the Messiah might have been as a Jewish Messiah disappeared ; through his death, Jesus, as the Messiah, had died to Judaism, had been removed beyond his national connexion with it, and placed in a freer, more universal, and purely spiritual sphere, where the absolute importance which Judaism had claimed till then was at once obliterated. It is of this complete reversal of his Messianic consciousness, brought about by contemplation of the death of Jesus, that the apostle speaks in a passage which is important in this connexion, and which finds an appropriate place here in the sense in which it was formerly explained, 2 Cor. v. 16. He says here, that since he began to live for Christ who died for him as for all, and who rose again, he knows no Christ κατὰ σάρκα any longer. This is equivalent to saying that from the moment when the full meaning of the death of Jesus burst upon him, he had renounced all the limitations of his Jewish stand-point, and of the Jewish Messianic ideas. The Jewish Messiah was to him a Messiah after the flesh ; as a Messiah who had not passed through death, he was not free from the carnality which only death, as the destruction of the flesh, can put away. The apostle therefore saw in the death of Christ the purification of the Messianic idea from all the sensuous elements which cleaved to it in Judaism, and its elevation to the truly spiritual consciousness where Christ comes to be recognised as (that which he was to the apostle) the absolute principle of the spiritual life. The absolute importance which the person of Christ has for the apostle is the absoluteness of the Christian principle itself; the apostle feels that in his conception of the person of Christ he stands on a platform where he is infinitely above Judaism, where he has passed far beyond all that is merely relative, limited, and finite in the Jewish religion, and has risen to the absolute religion.

A further definition of the absoluteness of the principle of the Christian consciousness, as it is presented in the person of Christ himself, is this : that in this principle the apostle is conscious of the essential difference of the spirit from the flesh, of freedom from everything by which man is only outwardly affected, of the reconciliation of man with God, and of man's union with God. It is the same absolute character of the Christian consciousness which finds its expression in all these different relations. The term "spirit" is used by the apostle to denote the Christian consciousness. He asks the Galatians, who were wavering in their Christian faith (iii. 2), whether they had received the spirit by the works of the law, or by the faith that had been born in them of the preaching they had heard ; and if it were not the height of folly, having begun with the spirit to end with the flesh,—to relapse from Christianity the spiritual to Judaism the fleshly and material. The apostle refers the Galatians here to an immediate and undeniable fact of their Christian consciousness ; this is that which declares itself most immediately in the Christian, which indeed constitutes his Christian consciousness itself, that he has within him the spirit, an essentially spiritual principle, which forbids him to regard anything merely outward, sensuous, material, as in any way a condition of his salvation ; that he is conscious of his immediate communion and union with God. It is as a purely spiritual principle that the Christian consciousness, inasmuch as it proceeds upon a faith which rests on certainty of the divine grace, is the consciousness of the sonship of God ; for all who are impelled by the spirit of God are also sons of God; they do not receive a spirit of bondage, which could only work fear, but a spirit of adoption in which they cry, Abba, Father; the spirit itself witnesses with our spirit that we are children of God (Rom. viii. 14-16), *i.e.*, since the πνεῦμα ἡμῶν (ver. 16) is the same πνεῦμα which, according to Gal. iii. 2, is itself one we have received, the spirit of God, as it is found expressed in our Christian consciousness, is at the same time so identical with the objective spirit[1] of God (the spirit as the objective principle of the Christian consciousness), that this sonship of God rests on the testimony of both, and thus is no mere subjective assertion of our subjective Christian consciousness, but has, in the absolute self-existent spirit of God himself, its objective reality and absolute certainty. This συμμαρτυρεῖν of the αὐτὸ τὸ πνεῦμα with the πνεῦμα ἡμῶν, this identity of the spirit as it appears in us with the spirit as it is in God, is thus the highest expression for the absolute truth of that which the Christian consciousness asserts as its own immediate contents.[2]

The spirit, as principle of the Christian consciousness, is thus traced back to the objective spirit of God, and identified with it. The apostle takes up the same absolute stand-point in the passage

[1] Geist an sich.

[2] Gal. iv. 6 is exactly parallel to Rom. viii. 14; in the former passage we read, Because (ὅτι must be taken in this sense) ye are sons, God has sent out the spirit of his Son into your hearts; thus the sending of the spirit pre-supposes the υἱὸς εἶναι. This is to be explained simply by the relation of faith to the spirit, which is the principle of Christian consciousness. One becomes υἱὸς Θεοῦ at once through faith, but this is a merely abstract relation, and the concrete contents which it must have in the living reality of consciousness come only through the spirit, which is nothing else but the very principle of the Christian conscious-ness. The apostle purposely writes: ἐξαπέστειλεν ὁ Θεὸς τὸ πνεῦμα τοῦ υἱοῦ αὐτοῦ, ver. 6, to correspond to ἐξαπέστειλεν ὁ Θεὸς τὸν υἱὸν αὐτοῦ, ver. 4. What the first ἐξαποστέλλειν is objectively as an objective historical fact, the second is subjectively; the sending of the Son becomes an inward experience, experimen-tally a fact of consciousness, only through the spirit, in which alone does objec-tive Christianity become subjective. This subjective stage is indicated by the apostle by the addition εἰς τὰς καρδίας ὑμῶν; and as this is merely the subjective experience corresponding to the fact expressed in that objective ἐξαποστέλλειν, he calls the πνεῦμα here very appropriately the πνεῦμα of the Son. The Christian consciousness, of which the spirit is the principle, is communicated by Christ himself, is Christ himself becoming inward.

1 Cor. ii. 9 *sq.*, where he expresses the infinity of the contents of
his Christian consciousness in the words, " what no eye hath seen,
no ear hath heard, what has entered into no heart of man, that has
God prepared for those who love him.   (The υἱοὶ Θεοῦ, Rom. viii.
14 ; Gal. iv. 6.)   But God hath revealed it to us by his spirit ;
for the spirit searcheth all things, even the deep things of God.
As what is human is known only to the spirit of a man that is in
him, so only the spirit of God knows what is divine.   But we have
not received the spirit of the world, but the spirit from God, that
we might know that which is given us by God."   The Christian
consciousness is thus an essentially spiritual one ; what speaks in
it is the spirit, as the principle of it ; for the divine, which is the
contents of the Christian consciousness, must be what only the
spirit can know.   For it is the spirit that searches all things, and
all searching and knowing as such, the more therefore in proportion
as its contents are the absolute, the divine, can only take place by
means of the spirit.   And this spirit which knows the divine is
the spirit from God, not merely the spirit which God has communicated, but as the spirit of the Christian consciousness, identical with the spirit of God himself, with that spirit, which just
as the human spirit is the principle of the human self-consciousness, is in God the principle of the divine self-consciousness.
Thus in the unity of this spirit, the knowledge a man has of the
contents of his Christian consciousness is the knowledge of God
Himself.   In his Christian consciousness as an essentially spiritual
one, the Christian knows himself to be identical with the spirit of
God ; for only the spirit, the spirit of God, the absolute spirit,
can know the divine contents of the Christian consciousness.   On
this high and absolute stand-point does the Christian stand in the
contents of his Christian consciousness which God has revealed to
him.   It is a truly spiritual consciousness, a relation of spirit to
spirit, where the absolute spirit of God, in becoming the principle
of the Christian consciousness, opens itself up to the consciousness
of man.

Being in this sense spiritual, the Christian consciousness is also absolutely free, absolved from all limits of finality, and unfolded to the full clearness of absolute self-consciousness. Now the Lord, says the apostle (2 Cor. iii. 17), the Lord as the contents and the principle of the Christian consciousness, is the spirit : but where the spirit of the Lord is, or the Lord as spirit, as principle of an essentially spiritual consciousness and life, there is liberty,—the liberty of self-consciousness. The apostle develops this idea in the passage we have named, in a connexion which asks for careful consideration. At the end of chapter ii. he was speaking joyously of the victorious issue of his apostolic activity, which the influence of his teaching seemed to render certain ; but in order to exclude everything subjective, as if he should praise himself, or ascribe too much to himself, he turns (chapter iii.) to the self-consciousness of the Corinthians themselves, which must attest the fruits of his activity, and where everything could be read as if in an Epistle. Here there is not merely something subjective, but something real and actual. Here there is a result which cannot be denied ; yet even with regard to this work that he has wrought, the apostle is unwilling to dwell upon himself as the author of it. It is not he, who, as author, by his merely subjective activity, has brought this to pass ; it is his work only in so far as he is a διάκονος καινῆς διαθήκης. The personal is to be sunk entirely in the official, and here the apostle takes occasion, as against his Judaizing opponents, to discuss the nature of the καινὴ διαθήκη, and to show from it that the double dealing, reservation, and insincerity with which they charge him, are quite incompatible with the nature and principle of this διαθήκη, so that they cannot be the character of its διάκονος. As the principle of this διαθήκη is an absolute one, so the consciousness of a διάκονος of it cannot harbour any elements of disturbance or of restraint, or any limitation such as would destroy its absoluteness. The apostle shows that Christianity as the καινὴ διαθήκη is the absolute religion in contrast to the old, by the antithesis, verse 6, in which he develops the difference between the old religion and the new. The new religion is not letter, such as the old διαθήκη which was written upon tables of stone, but spirit,

I

and so does not kill as the letter does, but makes alive. The apostle then argues from the glory on the face of Moses, as a symbol of the glory which even the old διαθήκη possessed, how greatly the glory of this διακονία τοῦ πνεύματος outshines all others. The Old Testament has indeed its own glory ; but if the two differ from each other, as letter does from spirit, and condemnation from justification, in the same proportion does the glory of the one differ from the glory of the other. Thus, so far as the glory of the old διαθήκη had a real existence, it was not permanent, verse 10, on account of the glory of the new διαθήκη which outshone it, for how could this be other than a far-exceeding glory (εἰ γὰρ, verse 11) ? If that which was finite and vanishing had its own glory, the glory of the abiding must be vastly greater. Since, then, he goes on, I have such hope that the glory of the new διαθήκη is one which abides for the future, and will disclose itself more and more, I act quite freely and openly,[1] and not like Moses, who put a veil on his face, to the effect that the Israelites did not see the end of that which came to an end according to its finite nature. As Moses, the apostle means, covered his shining countenance with a veil, the Israelites were unable to perceive how long the glory lasted which rested on his face, and which lasted only a certain time in each instance. This is the first reference of τὸ τέλος τοῦ καταργουμένου ; but in this expression the apostle points further to the finiteness of the old dispensation, of which the periodical splendour of the face of Moses was a symbol. The Israelites could not see the δόξα τοῦ προσώπου αὐτοῦ, the καταργουμένη, and so could not know whether or not it still continued ; and in the same way the Israelites are not now aware that a διαθήκη, which was designed from the beginning to last only a certain time, has come to an end simply because the καινὴ διαθήκη has appeared. What is characteristic of Mosaism is the opposite of that παῤῥησία spoken of, verse 12. This

---

[1] παῤῥησία is here properly the freedom of self-consciousness, such as is possible only from the Christian stand-point. As the principle of the Christian self-consciousness is the complete liberty of the spirit, nothing can remain before it concealed or confined, and thus all reserve and double-dealing is necessarily foreign to the Christian. It is clear that the apostle opposes this παῤῥησία to his opponents' charges, as being the principle of his own conduct.

opposite is not, however, as the interpreters have incorrectly understood the passage, a *tecte* or even *fraudulenter agere* on Moses' part,
as if he had arranged intentionally to deceive the Israelites and to
keep from them the true state of the case. Nor is it, as De Wette
thinks, that he covered up the truth with symbols; we must look
on the matter from the stand-point of the Israelites in their position towards Moses, and then we shall see that the point is, that the
finiteness of the old διαθήκη was not recognised. That they had
no idea of this finiteness,—this was the barrier in their consciousness, which, as long as it was unremoved, prevented them from
being anything more than Jews. The step from Judaism to Christianity could only be made by recognising that Judaism was merely
a finite form. That the Jews did not recognise this, and that on
this account their minds were sealed against Christianity, such was
the κάλυμμα, the covering, the concealing veil which, as the apostle
says still more plainly, verse 14, lay upon their consciousness as
upon the face of Moses. They do not see the end; their thoughts
are become obtuse, for to this very day the same covering remains
at the reading of the Old Testament, which, as long as it is not removed, prevents them from coming to perceive that the old διαθήκη
is at an end in Christ. Yes, to this very day a veil lies upon their
hearts when Moses is read (and here, still more distinctly than in
the foregoing, it is intimated in the words ἐπὶ τῇ ἀναγνώσει, that
this κάλυμμα is only subjective, and is to be accounted for, not by
that which is read, by the writings of the Old Testament, by Moses
himself, but only by the subjective condition of those who read and
hear these writings); but when they turn to the Lord, the veil will
be taken away; and as soon as this takes place, everything that
is needed will follow. The conversion to the Lord is the taking
away of the veil, but the Lord whom one has after the veil is
taken away is the spirit, and where the spirit of the Lord is, there
is liberty. And hence he who stands on this platform and is a
διάκονος of this διαθήκη cannot but have that perfect freedom and
unclouded self-consciousness which sets him far above all that was
limited, concealed, and finite, in the stand-point of the old διαθήκη.

And this, the apostle says, is true not only of me, the apostle, as the διάκονος of this διαθήκη :—it is true generally of us all. We have all of us in Christ the principle of spiritual freedom, of a consciousness released from all finite limits, from all dim and obstructing media. What Christ is to us objectively, as the object of our consciousness, as the δόξα which we see before us as in a glass, he is to become to us subjectively ; that which is now objective is to become identical with ourselves by our being changed into the same image from glory to glory. This cannot but be the case, since the transformation proceeds from the Lord, whose whole essence is spirit.

The essence and principle of Christianity is thus defined here as simply spirit, and in what sense it is such is very clearly apparent from all those contrasts between the old διαθήκη and the new. It is spirit, because in the consciousness of the man who stands upon this platform there is no barrier, no veil, nothing disturbing or obstructing, nothing finite or transitory ; it is a consciousness clear and free within, and one with itself. Or the Lord is the spirit, for the principle of Christianity and of the Christian consciousness is, in one word, an absolute principle, in which everything else, as being merely relative and finite, naturally comes to an end. He who is at this stand-point is conscious of his freedom and of his own infinity ; he knows himself as the subject of all things, all things have their final reference to him, to his own self, which can never become a mere object for others ; everything is for him, for he is above all. "All is yours," says the apostle (1 Cor. iii. 21), in order to awaken in the Corinthians a Christian self-regard which should make it impossible for them to surrender themselves to others, who would make them the mere puppets of their own sectarian egoism, "all is yours : whether Paul, or Apollos, or Cephas, or the world, or life, or death, or things present, or things to come ; all is yours ; and you are Christ's ; and Christ is God's." You then are the absolute subject, but only in that identity with Christ and God which is to the Christian the principle of his consciousness and of his life. At this point of absolute self-consciousness, the whole view of the world which the Christian has is a different one from that of other men, because he can look at things only from the point of view of the absolute idea, the consciousness of which has been engendered in him by Christianity. The apostle shows this in 1 Cor. i. 19, and iii. 18. "If any man," he says in the latter passage, "thinks himself wise in this world, let him become a fool, that he may be wise. For the wisdom of this world is folly before God." From the stand-point of the Christian consciousness, wisdom and folly change places. What is wisdom is in fact folly; what is folly is in fact wisdom. So great is the difference and the contrast in which the divine in Christianity stands to all that is human. They are related to each other as finite and infinite, as relative and absolute. At the stand-point of one contemplating the absolute, everything that is not the absolute itself, everything finite, whatever importance it may seem to have when regarded by itself, can appear no otherwise but in its finiteness and nothingness; while, on the contrary, to him who lives only in the finite, and has never learned to direct himself towards the absolute, the absolute does not exist at all; it is a sphere entirely closed to his consciousness; it is a thing altogether transcendent and incomprehensible; he can hold it for nothing but foolishness. This is the difference between the psychical and the pneumatical man; the psychical man does not receive into himself the spiritual, the divine, that which is the contents of the spiritual Christian consciousness, for to him it is foolishness; it transcends his consciousness, he cannot comprehend it, because it must be spiritually comprehended. The spiritual man, on the other hand, possesses the adequate form of comprehension for everything, but he himself is beyond the adequate comprehension of every one who is not himself spiritual (1 Cor. ii. 14, 15). This is the absolute superiority of the stand-point of the Christian consciousness. He who occupies the absolute standpoint possesses in it the absolute standard for everything that is merely relative; but he who holds to the relative, the finite, will always remain in an inadequate relation to the absolute. In all this we have the explanation which the apostle himself has given us of the principle of his Christian consciousness.

SECOND CHAPTER.

THE DOCTRINE OF JUSTIFICATION.—(1.) IN ITS NEGATIVE ASPECT :
ὁ ἄνθρωπος οὐ δικαιοῦται ἐξ ἔργων νόμου.

THE Christian consciousness is, in its principle, as we have shown, an essentially spiritual one ; the spirit which speaks in it is the spirit of God himself. Being a spiritual consciousness in this sense, it is further the consciousness of the sonship of God, of communion and union with God, of reconciliation with Him. Since, however, this reconciliation with God is, as the Christian idea of it implies, a thing that has had a beginning, the first question to be asked in order to a more definite understanding of the contents of the Christian consciousness is, how this reconciliation has been brought about. The answer to this question is found in the chief proposition of the Pauline doctrine,—that man is justified, not by works of the law, but by faith. In this antithesis of the δικαιοσύνη ἐξ ἔργων νόμου, and the δικαιοσύνη ἐκ πίστεως, the apostle's doctrine moves through its essential momenta. In the conception δικαιοσύνη, it has its roots in the soil of the Jewish religion, to which that conception belongs ; but in the peculiar Christian conception of faith, it departs from that religion, and takes up an attitude of decided opposition to it. These two conceptions are what we have first of all to consider in seeking to develop the Pauline doctrine.

In the idea of δικαιοσύνη, Judaism and Christianity have their point of meeting, a fact which of itself may show that the meaning of the term must be wider than the Jewish use of it, viz., righteousness as the statutory perfection of the citizen in the theocratic state, or, morality in its merely legal aspect. In the apostle Paul's language δικαιοσύνη is a conception applicable to both Judaism and Christianity, and must thus have a higher and more general meaning ; righteousness is not here a term of a particular religion, but of a universal one.   By the expression δικαιοσύνη, the apostle denotes that adequate relation towards God, to bring man into which is the highest task of religion.   Religion is to make man blessed, to give him that ζῆν, that ζωή, which is so closely related to δικαιοσύνη.   Man can become blessed only by having in himself that which is the condition of blessedness, and the conception of δικαιοσύνη is in general just this moral conformation which is the condition of his blessedness, and therefore puts him in his right relation towards God.   The expression denotes, broadly, the adequateness of the relation subsisting between God and man ; and since this adequateness can be realized only on the side of man, by man's having in himself what answers to the idea of God, the word δικαιοσύνη comes to have an almost entirely subjective meaning ; it signifies that condition of man which answers to the will of God, or his justification.   Since however, this subjective element on man's side has a real meaning only in so far as it answers to something objective, the word δικαιοσύνη is used further in a more definite sense to express this objective relation. Δικαιοσύνη is called δικαιοσύνη Θεοῦ (Rom. i. 17, iii. 21, 22, x. 3, 2 Cor. v. 21).   The genitive Θεοῦ does not signify the originator, so that the δικαιοσύνη Θεοῦ would be the δικαιοσύνη which God gives ;. if so, it would only refer to the δικαιοσύνη ἐκ πίστεως ; it could not refer to δικαιοσύνη generally (as in the passage Phil. iii. 9, to which the interpreters who take Θεοῦ in this sense appeal, it is yet only δικαιοσύνη ἐκ πίστεως which is δικαιοσύνη ἐκ Θεοῦ), the Θεοῦ can only be taken objectively ; the δικαιοσύνη Θεοῦ is that δικαιοσύνη which is occupied with God, which can take its direction only towards God, and can be determined only by the idea of God, by that which God essentially is, and sets up as the absolute standard.   In so far it may be said that the δικαιοσύνη Θεοῦ is the righteousness which avails before God (compare with this, δικαιοῦσθαι ἐνώπιον Θεοῦ, Rom. iii. 20 ; δικαιοῦσθαι παρὰ Θεῷ,

Gal. iii. 11; δίκαιον εἶναι παρὰ τῷ Θεῷ, Rom. ii. 13) or the *integritas quæ Deo satisfacit*, since what is to avail before God, and to be acknowledged by him as adequate, can be nothing but what is founded in his own being, and has its absolute basis in him the absolute.[1] This δικαιοσύνη Θεοῦ, then, is, generally speaking, the adequate relation founded in God's own nature, in which, as the idea of religion requires, man has to stand towards God. There are two forms in which this conception may be realized. It will be either δικαιοσύνη ἐξ ἔργων νόμου or δικαιοσύνη ἐκ πίστεως. Of the former, however, the apostle asserts that though it is theoretically a possible form of the relation, yet it never exists in fact; that man οὐ δικαιοῦται ἐξ ἔργων νόμου, that it is not possible in

---

[1] Usteri (Entwicklung des Paulin. Lehrb., 4 Ausg. 89) explains δικαιοσύνη Θεοῦ incorrectly. He says:—" The righteousness which man seeks to achieve for himself is called ἰδία (ἐμή) δικαιοσύνη, Rom. x. 3, Phil. iii. 9. The other righteousness is that which God imputes to men, which is given to men in the way which God has instituted, by his free gift. This righteousness is οὐ κατὰ τὰ ἔργα ἡμῶν, but δωρεὰν χάριτι, κατὰ τὸν αὐτοῦ ἔλεον, and is therefore called δικαιοσύνη ἐκ Θεοῦ, Phil. iii. 9, or simply δικαιοσύνη Θεοῦ, Rom. x. 3. The δικαιοσύνη Θεοῦ being thus the righteousness (of men) which emanates from God, is also a manifestation of the divine nature (in men). And so the expression is used as indicating simply a divine attribute, to signify that God's essence is both righteousness in itself, and the source of righteousness."

The conception δικαιοσύνη Θεοῦ will not be properly understood unless we regard it as the general, which may appear in the form either of δικαιοσύνη ἐξ ἔργων νόμου, which is theoretically a possible form of the relation, or of δικαιοσύνη ἐκ πίστεως. The δικαιοσύνη is the general which is implied in these two particular forms of δικαιοσύνη, and in which these forms satisfy their own conception. But, not to insist on this, the δικαιοσύνη Θεοῦ cannot possibly be taken as an attribute of God. God manifests his righteousness in it, it is true, but that implies that man has that which places him in an adequate relation towards God. It is this relation which is called δικαιοσύνη Θεοῦ. Now the δικαιοσύνη ἐκ πίστεως is an act of grace and not of righteousness (justice), and righteousness is not the attribute that would be spoken of in the connexion. The author speaks somewhat differently, Neutest. Theol. 134. The genitive Θεοῦ might be taken as the genitive of the object: "the δικαιοσύνη which is founded on the nature of God, or which avails before God;" but the correct interpretation is to take it as the genitive of the subject, "the righteousness proceeding from God as its cause, or produced by God, *i.e.* the way in which God brings men into an adequate relation to himself, the way opened up by God for this purpose, or indeed, the new theory of justification which God has proclaimed." He therefore asserts that δικαιοσύνη Θεοῦ is not a general term, including both Judaism and Christianity, and to be divided into the two forms, the δικαιοσύνη ἐξ ἔργων and that ἐκ πίστεως.—*Editor*.

this way to obtain justification, salvation, life, and all that makes up man's highest welfare. This is the apostle's distinct and perpetually recurring assertion. We have now to examine more closely what this assertion implies and means.

Δικαιοσύνη ἐξ ἔργων νόμου is the Jewish form of the δικαιοσύνη Θεοῦ, and is mediated by the law. The law is given to man simply that he should observe it and work it out in practice ; and thus, the law being given and known, the way in which man can set himself in that adequate relation to God which answers to the idea of religion consists in that practical disposition which issues in active obedience, in keeping the commandments of the law. The law, the works of which are the ἔργα νόμου, is the law of Moses, and thus it is only in the domain of the Jewish religion as the religion of the law that the δικαιοσύνη ἐξ ἔργων νόμου can be expected or attained. The moral law generally and the Mosaic law were not distinguished from each other in the apostle's view, since the Mosaic law in which God had declared his moral requirements, was the most perfect expression of the moral law with which he was acquainted. Yet the heathen were not simply ἄνομοι to him. What the law aims at in general is the ἐργάζεσθαι τὸ ἀγαθόν, Rom. ii. 10. The law is first of all to bring home to man's consciousness the good which he is to realize practically. Now it cannot be denied that it is possible for the heathen also to do right, and therefore they must be supposed to have at least something analogous to the law. When the Gentiles, the apostle says, ii. 14, do by nature, without positive revelation, what the law commands, they are, without having any law, a law to themselves, whereby they practically prove that the essence of the law (this must be the sense of τὸ ἔργον τοῦ νόμου; that which the law is abstractly, according to its fundamental contents, apart from the particular form in which it is expressed, as in the Old Testament ; the ἔργα νόμου in their unity) is written in their hearts, while their conscience bears witness at the same time with the thoughts which of themselves accuse and excuse each other. There is thus, as a standard of moral conduct, a natural law independent of all positive revelation, manifesting itself in conscience, to the truth of which the conscience bears witness. Hence if it had been possible at all to obtain the δικαιοσύνη Θεοῦ through the ἔργα νόμου, this road was not quite closed against the heathen. In their case also it was possible to obtain by the ἐργάζεσθια τὸ ἀγαθὸν that blessedness in which religion recognises the aim of man in his relations Godward. But the δικαιοῦσθαι ἐξ ἔργων νόμου is not possible at all ; there is no δικαιοσύνη ἐξ ἔργων νόμου, even where the law is declared with perfect clearness and impressiveness. On this negative proposition, first of all, the apostle's doctrine of justification is based, and we have only to inquire in what way he arrives at it. What is the reason that no true δικαιοσύνη Θεοῦ can be attained by any ἔργα τοῦ νόμου whatever ; is the reason of this to be found in the law itself ? We might almost be led to think so when we find the apostle saying, Gal. iii. 21, εἰ ἐδόθη νόμος ὁ δυνάμενος ζωοποιῆσαι, ὄντως ἂν ἐκ νόμου ἦν ἡ δικαιοσύνη. If, that is to say, such a law were given in the Mosaic law as could itself give life or save, then righteousness would actually come by the law ; then it would be possible to be justified in the way of law, through works of law. But this is by no means the case ; on the way of the law no righteousness is to be obtained (cf. iii. 10). Thus it is directly asserted here that the law οὐ δύναται ζωοποιῆσαι ; but how can this be if it be promulgated by God, and given to men on purpose to ζωοποιῆσαι? Do we not read, Gal. iii. 12, Ὁ ποιήσας αὐτὰ ζήσεται ἐν αὐτοῖς? Nor can the apostle find the reason of this οὐ δύνασθαι ζωοποιεῖν in the nature of the law itself, for he recognises fully that the nature of the law is in itself spiritual and good. Οἴδαμεν γὰρ ὅτι ὁ νόμος πνευματικός ἐστιν, Rom. vii. 14 (cf. ver. 12 : ὥστε ὁ μὲν νόμος ἅγιος, καὶ ἡ ἐντολὴ ἁγία καὶ δικαία καὶ ἀγαθή). In any case, then, it was not the defectiveness or imperfection of the law that produced the want, but on the contrary, the perfection of it, its spirituality, that it stands too far from him, and too high above him for man to be able to fulfil it. This may be regarded as a defect in the law, but, in order to decide how far the law itself is to blame, we must pass from the side of the law to the side of man, and inquire into the nature of man in its relation to the law. This relation has already been suggested by the expression used of the law, Rom. vii. 14, that it is πνευματικός. If man's nature were as spiritual as the law is spiritual, both would agree together, so that any contradiction between them would be out of the question. The spiritual purpose of the law would find itself naturally and completely fulfilled in the spiritual nature of man. But this harmony cannot take place, since man is not only spiritual, but carnal. In the flesh lies the reason why the νόμος is not δυνάμενος ζωοποιῆσαι, as for its own part it might be. The apostle speaks, Rom. viii. 3, of the ἀδύνατον τοῦ νόμου ἐν ᾧ ἠσθένει διὰ τῆς σαρκός. The law's inability, as things are, to effect what for its own part it might have effected, is due to this,—that the flesh crippled its power, that the strength of the law was broken against the opposition which the flesh presented; and so it appeared in this case only in its weakness and inability. As man then is not only spirit, but, on one side of his nature at least, is flesh also, and as the law, which is spiritual in its nature, cannot effect what for its part it might have effected, what takes place in man when the law comes to him with its demands is just that opposition by which his whole nature is brought into conflict with itself, in which the flesh lusts against the spirit, and the spirit against the flesh; and as soon as the flesh obtains the mastery, all those works appear which the apostle calls τὰ ἔργα τῆς σαρκὸς, Gal. v. 19 *sq.* The σάρξ is in one word the seat and organ of ἁμαρτία, and the wages of sin is death, Rom. vi. 23. Where sin is, death is also, as, even in the first man, death came into the world along with sin, Rom. v. 12. How then can the law make alive, when man, following the impulses of his nature, and entangled in sin, which is the natural operation of the flesh, falls at once and entirely under the power of death ? The law cannot but condemn what is opposite to the law in man, and so is worthy of condemnation. It must pronounce the verdict of death upon sin. Regarded in this light, the law is simply the γράμμα which kills, and its office is the διακονία τῆς κατακρίσεως, τοῦ θανάτου, 2 Cor. iii. 6 *sq.* If, however, we are to understand aright this opposition which the law, originally and naturally life-giving, finds in the flesh of man, we must not take up too narrow an idea of what is meant by the flesh. Man is flesh, not only on one side of his nature ; regarded according to his natural constitution he is flesh altogether. The spirit, which is the opposite of the flesh, has been imparted to man only through the grace that was given in Christ. Originally, then, he can have been nothing else but flesh. The flesh is therefore not merely the body with its bodily impulses, it is the sensuous principle which dominates the whole man in soul and body. Out of this arises sin in all the various aspects it assumes in human life, so that sin does not consist merely in the indulgence of bodily lusts and desires.[1] In himself, as he is by nature, man is only σαρκικὸς or ψυχικὸς (hence κατὰ σάρκα περιπατεῖν is, with our apostle, identical with κατὰ ἄνθρωπον περιπατεῖν), he becomes πνευματικὸς when, through faith in the grace of God in Christ, he has received the spirit into himself as the principle of his Christian consciousness and life, cf. 1 Cor. ii. 14 ; iii. 1 *sq.* Thus it is very natural that while man has no ἔργα νόμου to point to, but in place of these only ἔργα σαρκὸς, there can be no δικαιοῦσθαι ἐξ ἔργων νόμου. If the law be, as the apostle says, a νόμος πνευματικὸς, then the whole relation of the law to man must bring to light that state of contradiction between spirit and flesh in which the law is nothing but the condemnation of ἁμαρτία as the operation of the σὰρξ, and can hold no other relation towards man but that of negation and hostility. But the δικαιοῦσθαι ἐξ ἔργων νόμου, as the apostle speaks of it, must be held to imply that ἔργα νόμου exist as well as ἔργα σαρκὸς. And thus, though man be essentially flesh, yet there must be in him a spiritual principle which is at least analogous to the divine πνεῦμα, and makes it possible for him not only κατὰ

---

[1] In the Neutest. Theol. (and compare my observations, Theol. Jahrb. i. 83 *sq.*, xiii. 301) it is asserted distinctly that according to the fundamental ideas of the Pauline anthropology the σὰρξ is the material body, which, however, is not conceived as inanimate, but as a being with life and peculiar impulses and powers inherent in it ; that thus the ψυχή proceeds from it, and also the νοῦς or human πνεῦμα, to be carefully distinguished from the divine πνεῦμα.

σάρκα περιπατεῖν, but to raise himself above the sphere of the σὰρξ and of the ἄνθρωπος σαρκικὸς or ψυχικὸς. This must indeed be the case; for if man had nothing spiritual in him by nature, he would not have even that natural receptivity which is necessary for the entrance of the spiritual element, to be communicated by God's grace. If then there be ἔργα νόμου, which are essentially different from the ἔργα τῆς σαρκὸς, how can it be maintained at the same time that there is no such thing as δικαιοσύνη ἐξ ἔργων νόμου? Though they be not perfectly adequate to the law, yet they must be of such a nature as to stand in no positive opposition to it, as the ἔργα σαρκὸς do, but only in a position more or less inadequate. How then can it be said so nakedly that they have no justifying power, and stand in a merely negative relation to the δικαιοσύνη Θεοῦ? Yet this is the apostle's assertion, and the reason for this assertion is, that the ἔργα νόμου cannot do away with the might of the ἁμαρτία which reigns in man's σὰρξ. Thus, in this case also, the law can only condemn that which is sin; but the peculiarity of the apostle's doctrine here is, that not only does the law pass the condemning verdict on the sin actually existing in contradiction to itself, but that it also brings sin to its full reality in man. The reason of the οὐ δικαιοῦσθαι ἐξ ἔργων νόμου is thus in the law itself after all. The negative part of the apostle's doctrine of justification comes to a point in the proposition which sounds so paradoxical: ἡ δύναμις τῆς ἁμαρτίας ὁ νόμος, 1 Cor. xv. 56. What gives sin its power, its significance, and its reality— what makes it become that which it is, what makes it sin, is the law. How can this be?

The answer to the question lies in the undeniable truth, that sin is what it is essentially and simply through man's consciousness of it; where there is no consciousness of sin, there is no sin. Now the consciousness of sin comes by the law; for it is just the law that says to man what he is to do or not to do, and thus the law is to man the standard of his whole moral behaviour, to conform to it or not. This is what the apostle insists upon so emphatically in Rom. vii. At ver. 5, he says, " As long as we were living the life which is dominated by the flesh, the passions which lead to sins were active in our members, being stirred up by the law, in order to bear fruit for death." Then at verse 7 he asks, "What do I say then? is the law sin? certainly not, but I would not have known sin except through the law, and I would have known nothing of lust if the law had not said, Thou shalt not covet. But sin, taking occasion therefrom, worked in me through the commandment the whole of lust, for without the law sin is dead. I lived once without the law, but when the commandment came, sin revived, and I fell into the power of death, and the commandment which was given for life, was found by me to be a thing leading to death. For sin, having thus taken its occasion, misled me through the commandment, and by it slew me. The law indeed is holy, and the commandment is holy, just, and good. Did that which is good then become death to me? No, but sin; that it might appear how sin through that which is good works death to me, that sin through the commandment might appear as sinful as possible." Vers. 7-13.

Thus sin is dead or slumbers in the consciousness as long as the absence of consciousness of any law or prohibition precludes transgression; so soon, however, as one knows what one may do or not do, sin begins at once to stir; it awakes, as it were, out of its slumber, one becomes aware of the possibility of doing what he should not do. With the knowledge of what is forbidden comes also the desire to do it; and if sin has once been committed, the consciousness cannot be wanting that through it one has fallen into the power of death, which the law makes the consequence of sin. In proportion, therefore, as the consciousness of sin is awakened through the law (διὰ γὰρ νόμου ἐπίγνωσις ἁμαρτίας, Rom. iii. 20), sin itself reaches its reality, because sin exists essentially just in the consciousness that one has of it. Thus without the law there is no sin, and yet the law is not the cause of sin. The more the law brings home to a man the consciousness of sin, the less is a justification through the law, a δικαιοῦσθαι ἐξ ἔργων νόμου, possible. He feels only his antagonism to the law, or if he has ἔργα νόμου to show, he feels only the inadequate relation in which they still stand to the law; if the law can justify through ἔργα νόμου, it can only justify him whose ἔργα νόμου are completely adequate to the law, and extend to all its commandments. But what does the moral consciousness say here, when it is brought to confront the law? All who seek to obtain justification in the way of ἔργα νόμου are under the curse, for it is written, "Cursed is every one who does not keep all that is written in the book of the law to do it," to carry it out in his acts. As long as the law stands, therefore, no one can be justified before God, Gal. iii. 10. This is the testimony which every man's moral consciousness bears to him, and it is confirmed by universal experience among heathens and Jews, as the apostle shows in the first chapters of the Epistle to the Romans. But not only does the law awaken the consciousness of sin by saying to every man what sin is, and how much in what he does and leaves undone is simply sin, so that at no point in his life does he stand in a perfectly adequate relation to the law, so that he never is what he ought to be; the law also computes what is or is not possible, and makes men aware of the impossibility of fulfilling it. The more it quickens the perceptions with regard to sin, the more does it weaken the consciousness of any power in the will, so that in respect to sin, knowledge and will stand to each other in an exactly inverse ratio. The apostle speaks of this in the same section of Romans, vii. 14; he describes the antagonism of the carnal man and the spiritual law; as carnal, man stands under the power of sin, is as it were sold under sin. "For what I do, I do not consciously, with the full consciousness of my freedom, for not what I will do I, but what I hate, that I do. But if I do that which I would not, then I consent to the law that is good. But now it is not I who do it, but sin that dwells in me. For I know that in me, that is, in my flesh, there dwells nothing good : for to will is present with me; but how to perform that which is good I find not. For not the good that I will do I; but the evil that I will not, that do I." Thus there reside in man two antagonistic laws. " I find the law that when I would do good, evil is present with me.

I delight in the law of God after the inward man : but I see
another law, which in my members opposes the law of my spirit,
and brings me into captivity to the law that is in my members.
O wretched man that I am ! who shall deliver me from the body
of this death ?" (from the body which is the actual seat of sin,
because it is in it that the consequences of sin are accomplished,
namely, death.)

If the passage, vii. 7 *sqq.*, be regarded in its whole connexion with
what precedes and follows it, we can have no scruple in rejecting
as quite erroneous the opinion of those who would understand the
condition depicted by the apostle, vii. 14 *sq.*, to be the condition of
the regenerate. The contrast of the condition under the law and
that under grace could not be expressed more forcibly than is done
by the apostle, vii. 24, 25, and viii. 1. The apostle is here
describing how the law in its bearing on the moral volitions and
acts of man determines his self-consciousness. The highest state of
mind man can reach, as long as he merely stands over against the
law, is to recognise the good which the law prescribes, and to will
to do it. But that he should never get past mere willing, that the
possibility implied in willing never becomes a reality, that instead
of the good he willed to do, he should do the evil which the law
forbids, and which he himself does not will ; this is the imperfection and defect inherent in the condition under the law, and which
cannot be explained but by assuming the presence of a power
opposing man's will in its recognition and desire of what is good.
This power can only be in the flesh, which, as it directs itself only
to the sensuous, is the principle of sin, and which enables the
sin that dwells in man, and manifests itself through the flesh as
its organ, to become a special power, determining the man's whole
actions. The apostle calls this power a law, inasmuch as that may
be called a law which underlies a constant tendency as its
determining principle. There is thus a νόμος ἐν τοῖς μέλεσι, which,
as the sensual impulses accomplish the results to which they
exclusively tend, becomes a νόμος ἁμαρτίας ; and there is a νόμος
τοῦ νόος, a tendency determined by the rational principle, which is

opposed to the sensual. Thus, even in the state under the law, before man has received into himself by faith the divine πνεῦμα, there is, beside the σάρξ, a higher and better principle which is spiritual in its nature. The apostle calls it reason, νοῦς, to mark it as distinguished from the πνεῦμα, which is the result of a communication from without, and as belonging to man's own nature. It is the inward man (ὁ ἔσω ἄνθρωπος, ver. 22) in opposition to the outward or carnal man; it is the higher spiritual self-consciousness which is determined by reason, as opposed to the sensual consciousness, the determining principle of which is the σάρξ.[1] This νοῦς becomes the νόμος τοῦ νόος which answers in so far to the νόμος τοῦ Θεοῦ, as it is a spiritual principle, and, by its nature as such, cannot but recognise the law, which is also spiritual, feel itself one with that law, and make it the principle of its thought and will. But as this thought and will never grows to anything more than thought and will, does not realize itself in practice, the more man becomes conscious of his union with the law, the more does he grow conscious of his opposition to it. Taking the law up into his consciousness, and being thus aware of that Shall which his union with the law brings home to him, he finds that this is only to discover how far he stands below that Shall, and how little it is possible to him to fill up the gap within him between the Shall and the Am. The whole being of the man is divided between two hostile powers which strive against each other; and the one is so greatly stronger than the other, that it might seem that this latter is only saved from extinction in order that the man, so divided and drawn to and fro in contrary directions, should feel the whole torture of the opposition and struggle with which he is fighting against himself. This is the difference between the νοῦς and the πνεῦμα; the spiritual principle of the νοῦς can never be the invader and conqueror of the σάρξ; what it is, it is only

---

[1] This shows distinctly, as the author goes on to say, Neutest. Theol. i. 48, that the Pauline doctrine of sin is different from the Augustinian doctrine. In the Theol. Jahrb. xiii. 29. 5 *sqq.*, I have entered more fully into the relation of the Pauline doctrine of sin and grace to the Augustinian and the early Protestant doctrine.—*Editor.*

K

potentially, and can never come to be actually.[1] This is the condition in which man finds himself as long as he is under the law, it is a state of distraction, disunion, conflict; an unhappy consciousness, in which one longs for the redemption which can deliver from its torture. In this longing the man can do nothing but cry out, "O wretched man that I am! who will deliver me from the body of this death ; as for me, as I am in myself, I serve the law of God, but with the flesh the law of sin." Reason is the better principle in him, but the flesh is the predominant and ruling principle. Man cannot emerge from this state of division and distraction so long as he is under the law, and the law itself is there, just to create in him the full consciousness of the division. But as soon as he becomes conscious of the enormity of the division, and begins to long for deliverance from it, he has in reality got past it, and the lower negative standpoint is now looked back upon and judged by a standard which only the superior standpoint has given. It is seen namely, and that from above, how the position under the law is that of a mere naked Shall, which can never be fused into union with the human consciousness in its entirety. We have therefore a right to say that no one ever felt so truly this disunion of man with himself—this division which prevails at the standpoint of the law—as the apostle, who, when he felt it, had already overcome it. In this respect the interpreters are right, who hold that the so-called *gratia praeveniens* has to be presupposed to Rom. vii. 15. Only in presentiment of the state of grace can one feel rightly what is wanting in the

---

[1] This is the difference between Rom. vii. 18 *sq.* and Gal. v. 17 *sq.* In the ἐπιθυμεῖν of the σάρξ κατὰ τοῦ πνεύματος and of the πνεῦμα κατὰ τῆς σαρκός, the πνεῦμα gains the victory just because it is the πνεῦμα. In the words, verse 17, ἵνα μὴ ἃ ἂν θέλητε, etc., the apostle does not mean that the struggle is so undecided that no ποιεῖν ensues at all, but only that this ποιεῖν cannot take place save through the subjection of an opposing power. These two tendencies, impulses, principles, are at strife with each other, as if they only aimed to effect that you shall not do just what you wish to do. But if in this contest of the two principles, in which the victory is yet undecided, you give yourselves to be determined by the πνεῦμα, and the πνεῦμα thus obtains the preponderance, then you will not only not fulfil that which the flesh desires,—you will also cease to stand under the law, you will have Christian freedom.

state of law.¹   A δικαιοῦσθαι ἐξ ἔργων νόμου, or an ἰδία δικαιοσύνη, obtained through the fulfilling of the law (with regard to
which only a ζητεῖν, διώκειν, is possible, which must not grow to
an opinion of actual legal righteousness, Rom. x. 3, ix. 30) has thus
no existence, not only because the ἔργα νόμου which man has to
point to are never fully adequate to the law, but still more because
he can never feel the possibility of fulfilling the law,—can never
know himself one with the law in the totality of his self-consciousness.   Διότι ἐξ ἔργων νόμου οὐ δικαιωθήσεται πᾶσα σάρξ, Gal. ii.
16 ; Rom. iii. 20.   If this union, this δικαιοσύνη τοῦ Θεοῦ, is ever
to be reached, that can only be in a word, in this way :   that the
νοῦς (which is the highest element in this stand-point, and in which
nevertheless we only see its negativity) is changed into the
πνεῦμα.   How this is brought about is the other side of the Pauline
doctrine of justification.

---

¹ We are here supplied with a simple answer to the question how far the
apostle is speaking in the first person at Rom. vii. 7 *sqq.*   He is speaking generally, and what he says applies not only to himself, but to all who are in the same
case.   At the same time, only he himself is properly the subject, and he has to
use the first person in speaking of himself, because no one had gone through the
same experience before him.

THIRD CHAPTER.

THE DOCTRINE OF JUSTIFICATION.—(2.) IN ITS POSITIVE ASPECT :
ὁ ἄνθρωπος δικαιοῦται ἐκ πίστεως.

It is not in the way of the works of the law, it is only in the way of faith, that the true δικαιοσύνη is to be realized. Faith is the indispensable and all-important element and condition of justification, as the apostle very clearly intimates in the passage Rom. i. 16, where he states the main proposition of the whole subsequent discussion in the words, " I am not ashamed of the gospel : for it is a power of God to salvation for every one that believes ; both Jew and Gentile. For righteousness, the adequate moral relation to God, is manifested in it as one which goes from faith to faith, as it is written : The just shall live by faith." The apostle thus regards faith as all-important ; he cannot speak of righteousness, even at the very threshold of his Epistle, without at once declaring faith to be its essential element. The peculiar expression which he uses here is to be explained by the supreme importance which faith possessed to him. He says of the δικαιοσύνη Θεοῦ that it ἀποκαλύπτεται ἐκ πίστεως εἰς πίστιν, i.e. it is manifested in the gospel as a righteousness which begins with faith and ends with faith, of which faith is the beginning, middle, and end ; the essential and pervading element of which is simply faith : cf. Rom. iii. 22, δικαιοσύνη Θεοῦ διὰ πίστεως Ἰησοῦ Χριστοῦ, εἰς πάντας καὶ ἐπὶ πάντας τοὺς πιστεύοντας.[1] Thus everything depends on faith ; now what is faith ? It comes externally from

---

[1] In this passage also the two prepositions only serve to add strength to the one conception. The addition of εἰς πίστιν to ἐκ πίστεως is best illustrated by the passage 2 Cor. ii. 16 : ὀσμὴ θανάτου εἰς θάνατον, ὀσμὴ ζωῆς εἰς ζωήν.

hearing the preaching of the gospel (ἀκοὴ πίστεως, Gal. iii. 2, 5, Rom. x. 17), and thus it is primarily a recognition of the truth of the contents of the gospel, πίστις τοῦ εὐαγγελίου. Now as Christ is the essential contents of the gospel, this πίστις becomes πίστις Ἰησοῦ Χριστοῦ, Gal. ii. 16, *i.e.* the faith of which Christ is the object, or πίστις ἐν Χριστῷ Ἰησοῦ, Gal. iii. 26, the faith which has in Christ the principle on which it rests. This πίστις is further defined as πίστις ἐν τῷ αἵματι αὐτοῦ, Rom. iii. 25, since what faith apprehends in Christ as its proper object is the atoning death of Jesus. And here the apostle defines the contents of faith yet further, as πιστεύειν ἐπὶ τὸν ἐγείραντα Ἰησοῦν, τὸν Κύριον ἡμῶν, ἐκ νεκρῶν, ὃς παρεδόθη διὰ τὰ παραπτώματα ἡμῶν, καὶ ἠγέρθη διὰ τὴν δικαίωσιν ἡμῶν, Rom. iv. 24, 25. Thus the object of faith is narrowed stage by stage, and in proportion as this is done the faith grows more intense and inward. From theoretical assent it becomes a practical trust in which the man's deepest interests find expression. This trust becomes in turn a certainty of conviction, in which what has once been taken up into the subjective consciousness, even though a mere representation or expectation has all the force of an immediate objective reality. Now this faith, awakened first by an external agency, but then proceeding to discover and to rest upon its own inward resources, has for its object the death of Jesus. How has the death of Jesus come to occupy this position, and how does the δικαιοσύνη Θεοῦ result from the direction of faith to this its object?

At the standpoint of the law, the δικαιοσύνη Θεοῦ was sought to be attained through the works of the law; thus what the ἔργα νόμου sought to effect, but, being an ἰδία δικαιοσύνη, could not, is now to be effected through faith as a δικαιοσύνη τοῦ Θεοῦ. Faith then must have what works had not. But faith does not of itself possess this mediating power; all that it is, it is only in virtue of the object to which it is directed. There must, therefore, be something in the death of Jesus which qualifies faith to effect what the law with its works could not. This relation of the death of Jesus to the law is most explicitly stated by the apostle in the passage, Gal. iii. 13, "Christ has bought us free from the curse of the law, in that he became a curse for us; for it is written in the Scriptures, 'Cursed is every one that hangs on a tree.'" There is thus a curse in the death of Christ on the cross; this curse cannot have been incurred by Christ himself,—it must have been laid upon him. It is the curse of the law, for the result at which one arrives on the way of the δικαιοῦσθαι ἐξ ἔργων νόμου is just this, that ὅσοι ἐξ ἔργων νόμου εἰσὶν, ὑπὸ κατάραν εἰσί, Gal. iii. 10, since man has not those ἔργα νόμου which he ought to have, and, instead of the righteousness of the law, has only sin, which the law can do nothing but condemn. It is this curse, then, which Christ has taken on himself, for he suffered the penalty which the law demanded for the sins of men, viz., death. By this men are bought free from the curse of the law; the demand which the law made upon them for penalty has been met, hence the law has now ceased to have any valid claim against them; in respect of the law they are free. That principle which the law sets up as its *ultimatum*, that only ὁ ποιήσας αὐτὰ ζήσεται ἐν αὐτοῖς, and that thus every one who does not exactly observe all that the law prescribes, τοῦ ποιῆσαι αὐτὰ, has fallen under the curse of the law—this principle has ceased to apply to them. Man is thus free from the curse of the law—the κατάρα τοῦ νόμου, the curse, the penalty, which the law denounced, or the curse of which the law was the cause, the objective ground of which resided in the law. This deliverance is given to men, only in so far as Christ has died for their sake; but if he died for their sake, then this mutual relation between him and them must come home to their consciousness, must be recognised by them. They must, in order to appropriate to themselves what he has done for them, feel that they are one with him. Faith is this relation; only in faith in him, and in the death which he died for them upon the cross, are they free from the curse of the law. Faith is this union of man with Christ, by means of which the deliverance from the law which the death of Christ has effected, becomes his own deliverance from it. Here, however, something would seem to be wanting in the logic of this theory. For though man be bought free from the curse of the law, all that is effected thereby is that that demand is cancelled which the law made on them in respect of sins already committed. But does it follow from this that the law itself is done away? The law remains what it is, it continues to be binding, the obligation to keep it can never cease, and every failure in the observance of it involves the same demand for penalty, the same curse; and so man remains under the curse of the law. How then can the apostle say that the law in itself is done away? This implies that the constant repetition of the law's demands is met by the death of Christ being constantly set over against them, and constantly producing the same effect in respect of them. Thus if the death of Christ be really a deliverance for men, then its doing away with the law must be a doing away with it for ever, or as such. And that is so : what the law could not effect because of the constant failure to observe it, and indeed cannot possibly effect, that the death of Christ accomplishes by doing away with the law ; it accomplishes it without the law, but only in so far as it is the object of faith. How it is the object of faith can only be explained at a later stage in our discussion. The question before us now is in what way it is the abolition of the curse which lies upon man because of the law. The chief passage in which the apostle expresses his views on this point is Rom. iii. 21-26, " Now is made manifest without the law the righteousness which avails before God, as it is attested by the law and the prophets, *i.e.* that which is to be regarded as the condition of the adequate relation of man to God. This adequate relation is mediated by faith in Christ Jesus, so that all in general are merely such as believe, for there is no difference; all have sinned, and have nothing to glory of before God. They are justified freely through his grace through the redemption in Christ Jesus, whom God has set up as a propitiatory sacrifice through faith in his blood, for a proof of his righteousness, because he had passed over the sins that had been done before, in the long-suffering of God, for a proof, that is, of his righteousness at the present time, that he might be just, and might justify him who is willing to be justified by faith." Here we have to distinguish two momenta which the apostle, in regarding the death of Jesus as an object of faith, keeps separate from, and opposes to each other. On the one hand, the redemption which is effected through the death of Jesus is an act of the free grace of God; sinners as they are, men can only be justified through the grace of God; but, on the other hand, there has been manifested in the death of Christ the righteousness of God, which cannot suffer sin to go unpunished. Redemption, which has been effected through the death of Jesus, is an act of grace, but with this qualification, that that death is a bloody sacrifice presented for the propitiation of God. In this sense the apostle calls the death of Jesus a ἱλαστήριον, an atoning sacrifice, and that in order to prove God's righteousness, which cannot but cause the guilt to be followed by the punishment of sin. This righteousness of God had therefore to be satisfied, and this was done by the penalty of sin being actually borne. De Wette justly remarks that this passage leads up to the Anselmic doctrine of justification; but as for the view held by our apostle there is no reason here to travel beyond the idea of ἔνδειξις, which does not imply that God requires such a sacrifice for the expiation of sins on his own account, in order to satisfy the claims of his own righteousness, but only that this was done for men to demonstrate his righteousness to them. Yet this distinction is seen ultimately to be unreal, for what God does can never be for the mere external purpose of an ἔνδειξις,—it must have its objective ground in God's own nature. Since it was inconsistent with the idea of the righteousness of God to leave sins unpunished that had been already committed, it was necessary that Christ should die for the punishment of the sins of men. Yet this is not to say that the obstacle to the forgiveness of men's sins which was to be removed by Christ's death was actually and essentially in God's nature, in his penal judgment, or his wrath against men. It was not that God himself is to be appeased; and though the apostle speaks of a reconciliation, a καταλλαγή, a καταλλάτεσθαι, the reconciliation that he speaks of is not such a one as should have brought about a change of disposition towards man in God himself. We have received the reconciliation, says the apostle, Rom. v. 10, 11 ; though ἐχθροὶ ὄντες, we have been reconciled to God through the death of his Son. This ἐχθροὶ ὄντες must be understood rather of men's enmity against God than of God's enmity against men,—of that ἔχθρα εἰς Θεὸν which has its seat in the φρόνημα τῆς σαρκὸς, Rom. viii. 7. Of course the death of Christ must have some reference to the righteousness of God, and what it was in this aspect may be said to have been the removal of the wrath of God, Rom. v. 9, and in so far a reconciliation of God with men ; but here, however, we must remember that it is God Himself who is the reconciler, who brings about the reconciliation of men with himself through Christ, Θεὸς ἐν Χριστῷ κόσμον καταλλάσσων ἑαυτῷ, 2 Cor. v. 19. This implies the gracious disposition of God towards men as the condition without which the whole transaction would not have taken place, and on which alone it was possible for them to enter on a new relation towards him. Thus it rests entirely with men to cease from their enmity against God, and to allow that disposition with which God has always regarded them, and which he has actually proved through the death of Christ, to pass over into their minds ; or since God by His gracious and conciliatory disposition has reconciled the world to Himself in Christ, to let themselves be actually reconciled to Him. The καταλλαγὴ is nothing but the manifestation of the grace of God for men's acceptance. By their acceptance of it they enter upon a relation towards him where there is εἰρήνη πρὸς τὸν Θεὸν, and all enmity between the two parties has disappeared. Here we may already discern the relation which those two elements bear to each other, which are distinguished in the passage Rom. iii. 21-26, as the opposite aspects of the death of Christ, viz., righteousness and grace. The death of Jesus is to be regarded in the light of the Divine justice as having to do with a matter of guilt and penalty, yet this is merely the outside of the affair ; the merely judicial aspect pertaining to the sphere of law where that justice which is

based upon the law which God himself has given dare not be
violated. The inward motive, however, of the provision made by
God in the death of Jesus, that element in it in which God's
essential nature is most distinctly revealed, is the grace of God
(ἡ αὐτοῦ χάρις, Rom. iii. 24). This factor predominates so greatly
over the other, that even the strong claim which God's justice puts
forth in the death of Jesus may be regarded as simply a result of
his grace. The ἔνδειξις of his δικαιοσύνη in the death of Jesus
could never have taken place had he not, before he showed himself the just one, already been the gracious one, who gave the
greatest proof of his graciousness in this, that so far as the penalty
of sin had to be enforced in order to give his justice what it
claimed, he desired it to be enforced not in men themselves, but in
another for them. This leads us from the idea of satisfaction to
the intimately related idea of substitution. The satisfaction which
has met the divine justice in the death of Jesus could not have
taken place without the grace of God; and so intimately is the
idea of grace which gives rise to this whole process related to that
of substitution, that the one preposition ὑπέρ stands for both ideas,
denoting both that which is done for men and that which is done
in the place of men. On the one hand, what is done for men, in
their interest, is done merely to make them partakers of the
benefit of the grace of God. And it is truly remarked that the
preposition ὑπέρ does not of itself imply the idea of substitution,
and that that other meaning, in which the death of Jesus is
represented as having been for men, in their interest, is predominant. On the other hand, however, it is also certain that the idea
of substitution cannot be dissevered from that one; the preposition ὑπέρ, which is so much used in this connexion, contains both
these ideas constantly passing over into each other, and present in
each other. In the passage Rom. v. 6, it is said "Christ died when
we were yet weak" (without value or importance, without any of
those qualities which can determine another to do something for
one; it is thus that ἀσθενεῖς must be understood in distinction
from δίκαιος and ἀγαθός, and in opposition to δικαιωθέντες, ver. 9,

since, in their character as δικαιωθέντες they have in themselves
something that gives them importance in God's sight) ; hardly does
one die for a just man, for a good man (such a one as is more than
δίκαιος, who has won the love of others through his amiable
qualities) one might dare to die more readily than for another, but
God proves his love to us in this, that when we were still sinners,
Christ died for us.   Here and in many similar passages the
ἀποθανεῖν ὑπέρ is merely a dying in the interests of others ; but
in the passages Rom. iv. 25, παρεδόθη διὰ τὰ παραπτώματα ἡμῶν ;
Gal. i. 4, τοῦ δόντος ἑαυτὸν περὶ τῶν ἁμαρτιῶν ἡμῶν ; Rom. viii. 3,
περὶ ἁμαρτίας κατέκρινε τὴν ἁμαρτίαν ἐν τῇ σαρκὶ ; 1 Cor. xv. 3,
Χριστὸς ἀπέθανεν ὑπὲρ τῶν ἁμαρτιῶν ἡμῶν ; 2 Cor. v. 15, εἷς ὑπὲρ
πάντων ἀπέθανεν, ἄρα οἱ πάντες ἀπέθανον, καὶ ὑπὲρ πάντων
ἀπέθανεν, ἵνα οἱ ζῶντες μηκέτι ἑαυτοῖς ζῶσιν, ἀλλὰ τῷ ὑπὲρ αὐτῶν
ἀποθανόντι καὶ ἐγερθέντι, the idea of substitution cannot certainly
be rejected as out of place.   If Christ died because of sin (διὰ,
περὶ, ὑπὲρ), that is, from a cause which lay in the sins of men,
inasmuch as death is the necessary penalty of sin, then he bore in
his death that penalty which men had incurred through the guilt
of their sin, and so should have borne themselves.   He died then
not merely for them, but also in their place, as the one instead of
the many, who, just because he died for them and took their place,
did not actually die themselves, but are regarded as having died in
him their substitute.   This comes out most clearly in the passage
2 Cor. v. 14, where, from the proposition εἷς ὑπὲρ πάντων ἀπέθανεν,
the apostle at once draws the conclusion, ἄρα οἱ πάντες ἀπέθανον.
This is not the spiritual death of which the apostle speaks, Rom.
vi. 2, nor a mere ought-to-die ; it is simply said that what is true
of one is true of all, just because (as the article shows) these
are the πάντες, those, namely, whose place the one has taken.
Only if he died instead of them, and for them, have they also died.
Only the one has actually died, but they are all contained in him
ideally ; if not really, yet essentially ; and for his sake who died in
their place and for them, they may all be regarded as dead themselves.   The idea of substitution implies two things, first, that

the one who is to take the place of many others, and to be counted for them, is the same as they are; and secondly, that he possesses something which they have not; that, namely, the lack of which makes it necessary that he should represent them. If Christ has died for the sins of men, then he must have been without sin himself, in order that his death, which could not be a sacrifice on his own account, might avail as the penalty of the sins of others. Thus it is merely the development of the idea of substitution found at 2 Cor. v. 14, where the apostle says, ver. 21, that God made him who knew of no sin, who did not know from his own self-consciousness what sin was, to be sin for us, that is, to be an object of sin, and therewith one in whom sin is to be punished. But in order that he might thus represent the sins of men in himself, it was necessary for him to be a man like the men whose place he was to take; only in one point which was common to them all, he could not be like them, namely, in sin. Thus though he had a σὰρξ, yet since the σὰρξ of all men is a σὰρξ ἁμαρτίας, his σὰρξ could only be a ὁμοίωμα σαρκὸς ἁμαρτίας, Rom. viii. 3. Thus he was not quite as they were, but only similar to them; with all his identity with them, he had this essential difference from them, that his σὰρξ was not, like the σὰρξ of all other men, the seat of sin. This being a difference between him and them, the difference was done away and changed into perfect unity; through his becoming what they were, ἁμαρτία, they became free from ἁμαρτία, from the penalty of sin. This was the negative condition of the δικαιοσύνη Θεοῦ. God made him ἁμαρτία that we might become δικαιοσύνη Θεοῦ ἐν αὐτῷ, that which it is necessary for us to be in order to stand in that relation to God which is adequate to the idea of God. Thus by one man's satisfying justice on behalf of all men, a justification was attained which sets men free from death, and makes them partakers of life. Through the obedience of one many were made righteous, 2 Cor. v. 21, Rom. v. 18, 19.[1]

---

[1] The author discusses at page 164, and more at length in his Neutest. Theol. 166, *sqq.* (cf. also my observations, Theol. Jahrb. 1. 87, *sq.*) another effect of

This δικαιοσύνη γίνεσθαι or δίκαιοι καθίστασθαι, which is equivalent to δικαιοῦσθαι, brings us back again to the conception of faith. Since faith is the subjective condition on which alone men can enter into the relation these words denote, the result of the foregoing is to confirm the proposition ὅτι οὐ δικαιοῦται ἄνθρωπος ἐξ ἔργων νόμου, ἐὰν μὴ διὰ πίστεως Ἰησοῦ Χριστοῦ, Gal. ii. 16. Faith is subjectively what grace is objectively (the object of faith is indeed just the grace of God which has appeared in Christ), and thus grace is the objective principle of the Pauline doctrine of justification. Everything here depends on grace, as being the outcome of the divine love, which is the primary cause of the work of redemption in God's own nature, Rom. iii. 24, v. 8. We are δικαιούμενοι δωρεὰν τῇ αὐτοῦ χάριτι, and the antithesis between δικαιοῦσθαι ἐκ πίστεως and the δικαιοσύνη νόμου consists just in this, that the former is done freely through grace alone. For if there be a righteousness of the law which it is possible to attain through works of the law, then Christ has died in vain, Gal ii. 21, because the grace which his death has purchased would then be completely superfluous. There would then be no need of it, because the δικαιοσύνη διὰ νόμου proceeds on the directly opposite principle, that as the apostle says, Rom. iv. 4, τῷ ἐργαζομένῳ ὁ μισθὸς οὐ λογίζεται κατὰ χάριν, ἀλλὰ κατὰ ὀφείλημα. That which comes about κατὰ ὀφείλημα, from indebtedness, is the opposite of what comes about κατὰ χάριν or δωρεάν; the former is what a man has a right to claim, since it is nothing but an effect, arising from, and implicitly contained in, a cause which is present in ourselves. Here effect follows cause of necessity and without external intervention. He who has the ἔργα νόμου receives the δικαιοσύνη κατὰ νόμον by the same law by which the workman receives wages proportioned to his labour. With the δικαιοῦσθαι ἐκ πίστεως, however, the case is entirely different; the one is related to the other as λογίζεσθαι and οὐ λογίζεσθαι. In the case of the ἐργάζεσθαι and the consequent δικαιοῦσθαι ἐξ ἔργων νόμου, there can

the death of Christ, viz., that in his body, the σάρξ, and with it the sin which resides in the σάρξ, is destroyed in its principle.

be no question of any λογίζεσθαι; but there is this in the case of δικαιοῦσθαι ἐκ πίστεως. Faith itself λογίζεται εἰς δικαιοσύνην, namely, τῷ μὴ ἐργαζομένῳ, who does not hold to ἔργα, πιστεύοντι δὲ ἐπὶ τὸν δικαιοῦντα τὸν ἀσεβῆ, Rom. iv. 5. The one δικαιοῦσθαι is thus related to the other as the mere representation and supposition of a thing to the truth of the thing itself. Thus starting from the δικαιοῦσθαι ἐξ ἔργων, faith would require, first of all, to overcome the contradiction that the godless, the unjust, is held for just; that he, who in himself is unjust, is yet just. This is the proper contents of faith, through which δικαιοῦσθαι becomes a δικαιοῦσθαι ἐκ πίστεως. He who is to be justified by faith must first of all believe that this is so, and since the objective truth of justification consists in this, that what the justified person is to his own consciousness, he is also in the consciousness of God, in the judgment of God concerning him, in which the justifying act takes place, it must be a fact in the consciousness of God that he who in himself is unjust, is yet just. The Pauline doctrine of justification appears here in its greatest hardness. It supposes as actually existing what does not actually exist; its δικαιοῦσθαι is not an actual *being just*, but a mere *being held* or *being declared* just, and faith, as the principle of this δικαιοῦσθαι, is thus the imagination arrived at in looking to Christ, that what really is not, yet is.

If this be so, then the δικαιοῦσθαι ἐκ πίστεως certainly affords no occasion whatever for a καύχημα such as there might be in the case of δικαιοῦσθαι ἐξ ἔργων, Rom. iv. 2 ; indeed man has nothing in himself at all that could set him in the adequate relation to God which is required in order to δικαιοῦσθαι; for how is it possible that faith as a mere opinion that a thing is as it should be, although it is in fact the very opposite, could have any influence whatever to procure such a relation ? We are here at the extreme point where faith in this merely putative sense, as a thing devoid of contents, seems destitute of all reality, and where at the same time it becomes clearly apparent, that if faith is to be the principle of δικαιοῦσθαι, it must contain in itself those definite contents without which it can have no reality. Whence then is faith to

draw these contents ? When the apostle says, Rom. iv. 5, that to
the πιστεύων ἐπὶ τὸν δικαιοῦντα τὸν ἀσεβῆ λογίζεται ἡ πίστις
αὐτοῦ εἰς δικαιοσύνην, he regards the faith which is imputed for
righteousness as itself the δικαιοσύνη, as itself the subjective condition of δικαιοῦσθαι. Faith is δικαιοσύνη, or the moral quality
which, when it is present, enables man to come into that adequate
relation towards God which the idea of δικαιοῦσθαι represents.
The moral element of faith can only consist in this, that the
believer (not as Rückert observes on Rom. iv. 5, though he is not
righteous yet, yet has the wish to become so, a consideration which
is out of place here, but) believes the δικαιῶν τὸν ἀσεβῆ in this
very point, that the ἀσεβὴς is no longer an ἀσεβὴς, but a δίκαιος.
But how can he believe this without being at the same time
conscious of the foundation on which this faith rests ? The
foundation on which this faith rests can only be Christ. While
the believer makes Christ the contents of his faith, the
πίστις which was reckoned for δικαιοσύνη, or the δικαιοσύνη
which consists in nothing but πίστις, the δικαιοσύνη which
faith does not realize but only takes for granted, and which is
therefore only an imagined δικαιοσύνη, is turned into a real one.
For it is impossible to believe in Christ without knowing one's-
self one with him, and in this conscious unity with him, being
aware of that which is the proper object of faith in Christ, as an
immanent determination of one's own consciousness.

Faith is therefore counted for righteousness to those who believe
in him who raised up Jesus our Lord from the dead ; and in the
faith in God as the raiser up of Jesus, there is implicitly contained faith in Jesus himself, as the one who was delivered for
our sins, and raised again for our justification, Rom. iv. 24, 25.
While believing in him we know at the same time that we are one
with him and we become in him the δικαιοσύνη Θεοῦ, 2 Cor. v. 21, the
δικαιοσύνη which he is made to us of God, 1 Cor. i. 30. His
death is the cause why we, being now free from all the guilt of
sin, can be the same as he is, without sin, and being in this sense
righteous, are able to stand in the same adequate relation towards

God, in which he stands towards him. It follows, however, from his death, that our faith in him brings us not merely this negative righteousness, consisting in freedom from the guilt of sin ; he is also a δικαίωμα εἰς πάντας ἀνθρώπους εἰς δικαίωσιν ζωῆς (Rom. v. 18). As he shows himself righteous in his death, so his death is for all men the ground of a justification which leads to life. For as in the disobedience of the one man, the many who have their unity in him became sinners, so through the obedience of the one man, the many who have their unity in him are made righteous. In his obedience, in which he himself appeared as δίκαιος, they themselves become δίκαιοι in virtue of their faith in him ; such, namely, as have in themselves the subjective condition of the adequate relation between man and God. In that negative aspect the liberation of men from the guilt and penalty of sin has removed everything that might have proved to men the cause of wrong relations towards God. There is, as the apostle says, Rom. viii. 1, nothing subject to condemnation in those who are in Christ Jesus ; all who stand in communion with Christ, who have become one with him in faith, are, as justified persons, no longer subject to the divine sentence of condemnation. But not only have they in themselves this negative righteousness ; they are positively, through a principle that has become immanent in them, placed in an adequate relation towards God. What renders the δικαιοσύνη διὰ νόμου impossible, is that the law, though in itself spiritual, could not take up its place in man as spiritual, and thus become a unity with him. Now, however, what man takes up into himself through faith in Christ, as the mediating agency of his justification, is the νόμος τοῦ πνεύματος τῆς ζωῆς ἐν Χριστῷ ᾿Ιησοῦ. The law of the spirit (that is, the spirit as the principle which determines the whole direction of the man, the principle of the Christian consciousness as the vital principle of those who believe in Christ, and find in him alone the principle of their spiritual life) has made me free, the apostle says in the same passage, from the law of sin and death, from the power they have as a dominating principle. For what was impossible through the law because it was too weak through the flesh, God has done by sending his Son in the likeness of the flesh of sin, and on account of sin, condemning sin in the flesh, that that which, according to the law, is accounted righteous, as the act which is highest, and which corresponds to the idea of righteousness or morality, might be realized in us, inasmuch as we walk not according to the flesh, but according to the spirit. For those who are after the flesh think only fleshly things, but they who are after the spirit think spiritual things. The νόμος τοῦ πνεύματος, as the apostle here designates the principle of the Christian consciousness, distinguishing it both from the νόμος Θεοῦ which one serves only with the practically impotent νοῦς, and from the νόμος ἁμαρτίας, which comes out through the σάρξ, is the highest expression for the Pauline conception of justification, the δικαιοῦσθαι ἐκ πίστεως in its opposition to the δικαιοῦσθαι ἐξ ἔργων νόμου. There must be πίστις before there can be πνεῦμα, yet πίστις is only the form of which πνεῦμα is the contents ; it is only in the πνεῦμα that πίστις becomes the living reality of the Christian consciousness, informed with its positive contents. It is in the πνεῦμα, therefore, that the whole process of justification, as the apostle traces its development through its different stages, is at last completed. The true Christian δικαιοῦσθαι is no longer a δικαιοῦσθαι ἐκ πίστεως in the sense in which πίστις λογίζεται εἰς δικαιοσύνην to the πιστεύων ἐπὶ τὸν δικαιοῦντα τὸν ἀσεβῆ, in which case the relation of the person justified to God rests on a merely imaginary δικαιοσύνη, since, though essentially an ἀσεβής, he is regarded by the δικαιῶν as a δίκαιος, and pronounced to be δίκαιος. On the contrary, it is a true and real δικαιοῦσθαι, because in the νόμος τοῦ πνεύματος, in the πνεῦμα as the principle which determines his whole consciousness and life, he is truly and actually placed in the relation to God which is adequate to the idea of God. The relation which, in the case of faith imputed for righteousness, was a merely outward one, has now by means of the πνεῦμα, in which God communicates his spirit to man, and in which he dwells in man as the spirit of Christ, become a truly inward one, Rom. viii. 9. It is now a

L

relation of spirit to spirit, in which the spirit, as the principle
of the subjective consciousness, is drawn into union with the
spirit of God, as the spirit of Christ which is its objective basis.
The δικαίωμα τοῦ νόμου, the moral contents of the law as the
moral self-determination of man, is fulfilled and realized in this,
that the justified persons walk, not according to the flesh, but
according to the spirit. This walking according to the spirit is not
indeed that ἐμμένειν ἐν πᾶσι τοῖς γεγραμμένοις ἐν τῷ βιβλίῳ τοῦ
νόμου, τοῦ ποιῆσαι αὐτά, Gal. iii. 10 ; for that remains even in this
case a demand which can never be satisfied ; but in place of this
merely quantitative fulfilment of the law, there has come the
qualitative fulfilment ; the spirit is the principle of the fulfilment
of the law or of moral conduct, and the spirit, the totality of disposition, contains in itself also the totality of the law, the δικαίωμα
τοῦ νόμου. The δικαίωμα τοῦ νόμου which is thus satisfied is the
δικαιοσύνη Θεοῦ realized in man, and this δικαιοσύνη is also ζωή,
for the νόμος τοῦ πνεύματος is the νόμος τοῦ πνεύματος τῆς ζωῆς
ἐν Χριστῷ Ἰησοῦ, and the spirit of God who dwells in us as the
spirit of Christ is as the πνεῦμα, ζωὴ διὰ δικαιοσύνην. Where
δικαιοσύνη is, there is also ζωή, because the principle of the one as
well as of the other is the divine spirit which has come to reside
in man as the principle of his Christian consciousness and life.
Thus, though the body still carries in itself, that is, in the σάρξ, the
principle of sin, and is consequently subject to the power of death,
yet in the spirit the man has in himself the principle of life ; the
spirit which dwells in him, the spirit of him who raised up Jesus
from the dead, and will penetrate what of him is mortal more and
more with the power of life, Rom. viii. 10, 11. Thus that δίκαιος
ἐκ πίστεως ζήσεται, in which the apostle concentrates his whole
doctrine of justification, has now become a truth and a reality.
All that he says in the same connexion, Rom. viii. 12-17, of the
spirit of the sonship of God, which makes itself heard in the
Christian consciousness, is simply the definition of that highest
stage, in which the whole process of justification comes to its
completion and passes into the living reality of the immanent
Christian consciousness.

Thus the spirit is the element in which God and man are related to each other as spirit to spirit, and where they are one with each other in the unity of the spirit. But this union of man with God, in which the essence of justification consists, is only possible on the condition of faith. The spirit is indeed the true and living medium of the union of man with God; yet it must not be forgotten that since we only receive the spirit on the ground of faith, the essential element of justification is nothing but faith, and that the bond of union, in which justification consists, is formed by faith only, being here the union of the man with Christ. Faith of itself transfers the man from his former condition into a totally different one—into a new circle of tasks and duties. We see this in the Epistle to the Romans. The apostle describes the life of justification in its highest stage, viii. 1-17, but before this he has deduced from the conception of δικαιοῦσθαι ἐκ πίστεως, and of the divine grace which is given in faith, Rom. v., the manner in which the union of man with Christ which faith has formed is to realize itself in practice, Rom. vi. What faith in Christ lays hold of first of all is the grace of God reconciling men to himself in the death of his Son, and not imputing their trespasses to them, Rom. v. 10, 2 Cor. v. 19. But where grace is, there the law is no longer; throughout the whole domain of grace there is an end to every claim the law could make. If we be under grace, says the apostle, Rom. vi. 14, 15, we are no more under law; law and grace are mutually exclusive of each other, Gal. ii. 21. Now if this be the relation between law and grace, if grace have so much the predominance over the law as to abolish the law altogether by grace, and render null and void all claims which it could make on account of the guilt of sin, then it appears that sin is not such a serious affair, and why should a man not sin if he be certain that grace is stronger than the law and sin? The apostle takes up this question, Rom. vi. 1, and shows, first, that his doctrine of justification is not open to the charge of allowing licence to sin; and then, that the justification which he teaches kills and extirpates sin from its very roots. The law is indeed abolished by grace, but grace has faith as its essential condition, and faith places a man in such a state of union with Christ, that what is true of Christ must also be true of him who has faith in him. In the fellowship with Christ's life and death which faith procures, sin is put an end to in two ways : first, the death of the σὰρξ is also the death of sin; and, second, in the new life to which he who has died with Christ must rise in virtue of his union with him, sin can find no place. All who are baptized into Jesus Christ, says the apostle, Rom. vi. 3, are baptized into his death ; they are, therefore, buried with him through baptism into death, that as Christ has been raised up from the dead through the glory of the Father, so they also should walk in a new life. For if they be grown together with him in the likeness of his death, they will be one with him in his resurrection. The first of these two points, the being dead with Christ, is then further defined, verse 6 ; for we know that our old man is crucified with Christ, that the body of sin should be destroyed, so that we should no more serve sin, for he that is dead is absolved from sin. In order to apprehend correctly this latter proposition which embodies the general truth, on which the apostle's argument proceeds, we have to remember how he regards the σὰρξ as the principle and the seat of sin. It is through his σὰρξ, his physical nature, that man is subject to sin and death. This dominion of sin and death can last only so long as the σὰρξ is vitally active and capable of asserting itself. As soon as it is dead, man is free from its dominion over him, and absolved from the claim which it makes on him ; if in the death of the σὰρξ he himself has died to the σὰρξ, then he has discharged his debt to it ; not only is he free from it, but he has, as it were, formally and judicially cleared off scores with it, so that he stands over against it as a δίκαιος, a justified person. The apostle expresses this relation by the phrase, δεδικαίωται ἀπὸ τῆς ἁμαρτίας. The σὰρξ, however, is dead, or the man in the σὰρξ has died to it, because he has died with Christ ; for Christ is crucified for this purpose, that the body of sin might be destroyed, Rom. vi. 6. Inasmuch as he died, he died unto sin; in reference to sin, Rom. vi. 10, since he condemned sin in the flesh. Through the surrender of his body to crucifixion he took from sin the power which it possessed in the sinful body.

Now from this the apostle draws the immediate inference that he who believes in Christ cannot, being dead, live in respect to sin, or in the service of sin, ver. 11. "Thus do you also regard yourselves, that you are dead for sin; let not sin therefore reign in your mortal body (the physical mortality of which ought to symbolize to you that other mortality, that it is already νεκρὸν τῇ ἁμαρτίᾳ), so that you should obey the lusts thereof. Nor do you yield your members as instruments of unrighteousness unto sin, for sin will not or cannot have power to rule over you, because you stand no longer under the law, but under grace." He, then, who is dead to sin, is also dead to the law, Rom. vii. 4, for this simple reason, that the law can reign only so long as sin reigns; for only under the rule of the law does sin develop its whole power, Rom. vii. 5. Thus the law itself seemed to call forth sin just in order that, in the guilt and punishment of sin it might appear in its whole power over man (hence there was at last nothing for it but to die to the law through the law, since it stood self-condemned in its insufficiency for man's salvation, Gal. ii. 19). A further reason why he who is dead to sin is dead to the law also is, that he who has died to sin can have died to it only in one way, viz., that Christ in his crucified body has destroyed the body of sin. As being dead with Christ, he now belongs, in virtue of this unity, to Christ alone, and thus through the death of Christ, all who have died with him are freed from the bond which binds mankind to the law. The apostle shows this, Rom. vii. 1 *sq.*, through the analogy of a wife who is bound to her husband only so long as he lives. As death is in this instance the termination of a legal obligation, so in the case of the law; the law's binding power ceases so soon as he who stands under the law is dead; thus, as soon as a man has died to sin through that unity with Christ which faith procures him, he is no longer subject to the law,—the old relation has ceased, and in the death of Christ, a new one has been formed. You have, says the apostle, Rom. vii. 4, become dead to the law through the body of Christ, that you should belong to another, to Christ, who has risen from the dead; and that in this fellowship you should no longer, as when under the dominion of the law, the flesh, and sin, bear fruit to death, but should bear fruit to God, Rom. vii. 4-6. Thus the second of the momenta above mentioned, life with and for Christ, is conditioned by the first, the being dead with Christ. The bond which binds a man to the law is loosed because he has died to sin, and has been absolved from the law; the new bond now takes the place of the old one, the bond of union with Christ, whose life is also his life; and he who lives in and with Christ lives to God. "If we be dead with Christ, we believe that we shall also live with him; for we know that Christ, being raised from the dead, dies no more. In that he has died, he died to sin for ever; in that he lives, he lives to God. So we also must regard ourselves as those who are dead to sin, and live to God in Christ Jesus," Rom. vi. 8-11. Christ himself lives in us as the higher principle which directs our whole being and life, in which everything in us that is merely finite, and belongs only to our self, or private *ego*, is done away, that we should live no longer to ourselves, but only to him. I am crucified with Christ, says the apostle, Gal. ii. 20; he who is crucified with Christ, who knows himself one with the crucified Christ, has also the life of Christ in himself. In this unity of life with Christ, then, do I live, but I live only in such a way that that which lives is not this *ego* of mine; I for myself do not live at all, but Christ lives in me because I am one with him, and in this unity with him, he only can be the principle of the life that is lived. It is true that my fleshly life itself has not on this account entirely ceased, so that I should no more live in the flesh at all; but I live, so far as I live in the flesh, in faith in the Son of God, who has loved me, and given himself for me; my life in the flesh is entirely a life of faith, and its being a life in faith causes it to be both these things at once, a life in the flesh, and a life of Christ in me; faith, as the bond of union with Christ, makes it possible for these two to exist together. What gives faith the power to unite the believer with Christ, or that in Christ which attracts faith, and unites us to him in faith, is the love through which he died for us and in our stead; for the love of Christ to us constrains us as a power coming upon us;

while we consider that he, as one, died for all, and that thus they are all dead; and he died for all, that they, in so far as they live, should no longer live to themselves, but to him who died for them, and is risen again, 2 Cor. v. 14. All that is particular, individual, self-concerned is done away in him, and, in the thought of his self-sacrificing and devoted love, disappears before the universality of a spiritual principle. This love of Christ proceeds itself from the love of God, who caused him to die for us, and it works love in us when it is received by us through faith; faith passes over into love as the πίστις δι' ἀγάπης ἐνεργουμένη, Gal. v. 6. Faith contains from the first the element of love, as its practical principle. What faith is in itself as faith must become practical, and this takes place through love; love is practical faith. Love in its connexion with faith is thus an important feature of the Pauline doctrine, for in it the law which was done away in the death of Christ is taken up again, only with a higher meaning. Love is indeed the whole sum of the law; in it the law becomes the law of Christ himself, Gal. v. 14, vi. 2 (cf. ἔννομος Χριστοῦ, 1 Cor. ix. 21). Though the law is abolished through the death of Christ, it is not abolished altogether; only that in it is taken away which was merely external, which was merely positive. Set free from its outward form, the legal becomes the moral,—the law is received back into the self-consciousness of the spirit, and the law of Christ is the moral consciousness in its essential oneness with the Christian consciousness. Thus what on the one side is freedom, is on the other side subordination. The Christian is called to freedom as being free from the law, but it is not a freedom in which the flesh, his sensual nature with its sensual impulses, may have its play with less constraint; his freedom is δουλεύειν ἀλλήλοις δι' ἀγάπης, Gal. v. 13. The ideas of freedom and unfreedom (servitude, constraint) pass here into each other. So long as a man is a servant of sin he is free from righteousness (ἐλεύθερος τῇ δικαιοσύνῃ, i.e. free over against righteousness, so that he is not bound by it, will not be determined by it, Rom. vi. 20); but when he is freed from sin, he is a bondsman to righteousness, and has now to make his members, which were formerly members of lawlessness, servants of righteousness to holiness of life, Rom. vi. 16 *sq.* This also is a condition of bondage, and bears a certain analogy with the condition of the man under the law and sin, so that it also may be regarded as a δουλεύειν and δουλωθῆναι ; but where faith is, that is, the faith that works by love, there is also the spirit, and they who will be led by the spirit do not stand under the law, because they walk in the spirit, nor do they fulfil the lusts of the flesh ; as those who belong to Christ, they have crucified the flesh with its affections and lusts, Gal. v. 16, 18, 24. Thus the spirit, the principle of the Christian consciousness, which is the highest stage of justification, is also the principle in which the adequate relation in which justification places man towards God, is practically realized. The spirit presupposes faith as the subjective form in which man takes up the spirit into himself. Through the spirit, that which he is as a justified person in his relation to God, in his consciousness of sonship of God, is practically operative. It brings in a life which, in its relation to God, approves itself a holy one, and such that man is a temple of God through the spirit dwelling in him, 1 Cor. iii. 16. In its reference to men, this life approves itself as one which brings forth out of itself the fruits of faith, which consist in love. In both these references, it is a life in which we live not to ourselves, but to Christ who lives in us.[1]

[1] The same subject is dealt with by the author, Neutest. Theol. 174 *sq.* He there enters more specially into the question how Paul's demand for good works consists with his propositions as to the impossibility of justification by works of the law. To this he answers, p. 180 *sq.* (in agreement with my views, Theol. Jahrb. xiii. 303 *sqq.*), that the reason why Paul never thinks of any inconsistency here is,—that his doctrine of justification refers entirely to the relation of Christianity to Judaism ; that to be a Christian and to be justified are one and the same thing to him (so that the question could never arise in his mind whether the good works which have their origin in Christian faith contribute anything to justification). At the same time, he remarks that the antithesis of faith and works is only one of abstract thought and of general principle ; that in reality the two are not thus independent of each other, so that the one might be present and the other entirely absent ; and that thus the opposition of justification by faith and justification by works is reconciled and brought to rest in the simple moral truth of such passages as Rom. ii. 6, 1 Cor. iii. 13 *sq.*, ix. 17, 2 Cor. v. 10, ix. 6, Gal. vi. 7 *sq.*—*Editor's Note.*

FOURTH CHAPTER.

CHRIST AS THE PRINCIPLE OF THE CHRISTIAN COMMUNITY
WHICH HE FOUNDED.

THE doctrine of justification by faith was entirely within the sphere of the individual consciousness. It is only the relation of the individual to Christ that is there in question. Faith in Christ is first of all a personal thing; the most prominent fact of the believer's consciousness is what Christ is for him, in this definite relation to him. But he cannot be conscious of this relation in which Christ stands to him without being aware, at the same time, that what is true of him is true of all the others for whom Christ died, as he died for him, since he, as the one, died for all, 2 Cor. v. 14. The Christian consciousness which is awakened and inspired by faith in Christ is necessarily also the consciousness of a communion of believers, whose unity consists simply in this, that Christ is the principle of their fellowship. In order to denote the organic unity with each other of those who stand within this communion, the apostle compares them with the organism of the human body, Rom. xii. 4. "As we have many members in one body, but all the members have not the same office; so we, being many, are one body in Christ, and as for each individual regarded separately, we are related to each other as members." The apostle reminds his readers of this, in order to exhort them to unity and unanimity. As the body has different members, so in the Christian community there are different gifts of grace, according to the grace that is given to every man. There is prophecy according to the proportion of faith, there is ministry, doctrine, exhortation, etc. All these gifts then ought to work together for the common good of those who are combined in the one fellowship, Christ being looked up to by all as the principle of this communion, it being always remembered that we ἓν σῶμά ἐσμεν ἐν Χριστῷ. But not only are we one body in Christ, as the apostle says, that is, as Christians, in so far as we are one with Christ in faith; we ourselves also are, as he says, 1 Cor. xii. 27, σῶμα Χριστοῦ καὶ μέλη ἐκ μέρους. This is generally taken as if the apostle called the Christian community, the ἐκκλησία, of whose different offices and gifts he is speaking in the passage, itself the body of Christ. But it must not be overlooked that the phrase is only σῶμα Χρ., not τὸ σῶμα Χρ. Now σῶμα Χρ. (gen. obj.) is only a body which has the objective reason of its existence in Christ; it is only in view of its relation to Christ that it is called a body, that is, it is a body (as the apostle expresses it in the first passage) inasmuch as we ἓν σῶμά ἐσμεν ἐν Χριστῷ. This designation of the Christian fellowship as *a* σῶμα Χρ., not *the* σῶμα Χρ., seems intended to bring out the merely figurative intent of the term ; and the apostle explains his meaning more fully, verse 12 : " As the body is one (a unity equal to itself) and has many members, but all the members of the body, though they be many, are one body, so it is with Christ." Here it might appear very natural to understand ὁ Χριστὸς as standing simply for the Christian church ; yet the apostle's meaning in this case also is probably that as there is a natural body, so also there is, in a figurative spiritual sense, a body, the whole significance of which—the proper conception of the essence of which—is in Christ; a σῶμα Χριστοῦ. And as every natural body is both one and complex, and consists of many members which are different from each other, and yet bound together to the unity of a whole, so also with the Christian community as a spiritual body. The principle of unity of this spiritual body is originally Christ, but Christ operates here through the spirit. Thus in the spirit all who became Christians are one body, however they may differ in their natural extraction and in other particulars. For we are all, says the apostle, verse 13, baptized in one spirit to one body (so that as baptized persons we form one and the same society), and have been all made to drink of One Spirit.[1]   Since, then (we must supply this thought after verse 13), all who have been baptized form in this way one body in the fellowship of the same spirit, this unity cannot be formed by any one man for himself, but only by all together ; or, this unity can only be brought about by the difference of the many from each other, and must be such a unity as will allow each man to have his rights and free development (in the transition from ver. 13 to 14 the apostle brings the idea πάντες into prominence, that all are to be taken together, that it is to be kept in view that in their unity they are also a plurality of subjects existing beside each other).   For the natural body also does not consist of one member, but of many ; and thus no single member must assume such importance for its own individuality, as to seek to exist only for itself and not as a member of the body.   Thus no member can tear itself from its connexion with the body and with all the other members, as if to be only for itself, and itself to compose the whole body ; for the organism is that of a human body, a unity in plurality, and a plurality in unity, and can only subsist in all together.   In this sense, then, does the apostle regard the Christian fellowship as one body ; it is a totality, the constituent members of which form a unity by their reference to Christ ; and it is an organic unity in which no one excludes the other, but every one receives the complement of all the others to make up the unity of the whole.   The conception of this fellowship includes those two momenta, that of unity and that of variety ; and the principle which enables these two to exist together is the spirit. The spirit resolves the variety into unity, and introduces variety into the unity, and reconciles unity to itself through variety. The Christian community is a thing that is only becoming, and that it may be realized, it is necessary that every difference which

---

[1] There can be no doubt that the only admissible reading is καὶ πάντες ἐν πνεῦμα ἐποτίσθημεν, and if this be so, then ἐποτίσθ. can only refer to baptism. Our reception into the Christian church by baptism at the first planting of our Christian life was effected through the same spirit, and through the same spirit was that principle communicated to us in baptism, which is to serve for the continual nourishment and furtherance of our Christian life.

originates elsewhere, every natural difference by which men are divided in their national, their political, or any other relations, should be done away. This is brought about, as the apostle says, by all being baptized in one spirit to one body. But the spirit which makes all differences disappear in unity makes them disappear only that they may proceed again out of itself; and that having taken them up into itself, and purified and spiritualized them in its own essence, it may send them forth as forms of its own nature. The very idea of its nature impels it to destroy itself, to disintegrate and divide itself into its elements, to cause the conception of its essence to separate into its essential momenta; for here there is not only a unity, but in the unity also a diversity, without which there is no living organic unity, no vital development. This is what the apostle says very significantly in the words : διαιρέσεις χαρισμάτων εἰσὶ, τὸ δὲ αὐτὸ πνεῦμα, 1 Cor. xii. 4. The one spirit individualizes itself in the various charisms which make one man to differ from another. As Christianity itself is χάρις, and the spirit is the principle through which what Christianity is essentially, objectively, becomes a living reality in the subjective apprehension of the individual, so the charisms are the various operations and appearances which Christianity assumes, according to the nature of the different individualities in which it finds expression. Thus, while the spirit individualizes itself in the several charisms, it can do so only in accordance with the different individualities in which these charisms are deposited, and which become Christian personalities only through the agency of the spirit. The natural, then, is given to Christianity; it has only to penetrate and inspire it with its own spirit. The charisms are originally nothing but the gifts and qualities which each man brings with him to Christianity ; and these gifts and qualities are exalted into charisms because the Christian consciousness and life are found on them, and reared on the materials which they bring, and moulded by the operation of the spirit into their different individual forms. What the διαιρέσεις χαρισμάτων are in relation to the spirit as their principle, the διαιρέσεις διακουἱῶν are in relation to the Lord, since they have no object save to be used, through the services which every one can yield with his charisms, for the welfare of the fellowship of the Lord, and to be means towards the realizing of the common good. Thus the διακονίαι are only another phase of the χαρίσματα, and are related to them simply as the outward to the inward. The διαιρέσεις ἐνεργημάτων are essentially the same, only regarded from another point of view. Here these same operations are referred to the causality of God, which works all in all, as the first cause. They are also phenomena in which (as was the case with some of them) a peculiar divine influence is manifest. The spirit manifests itself in each of them after its individual character for the general good.

The special charisms which the apostle mentions as wrought by the same spirit are the λόγος σοφίας, the gift of delivering a lecture or discourse of special instructiveness in point of form and contents ; the λόγος γνώσεως, a discourse in which the deeper spiritual sense of Scripture is unfolded, chiefly by means of allegorical interpretation,[1] πίστις, the faith in divine providence, which exhibits its special strength in extraordinary circumstances and emergencies. Then the χαρίσματα ἰαμάτων, the gift of uttering a prayer full of faith in cases of severe illness, and that with such peculiar power and intensity as to elevate and soothe both the sick persons and others who are present. In this prayer the sick persons were commended to the divine succour, and their recovery was promised, if according to God's will, with more or less assurance ; and thus the ἰάματα to which this charism referred were not a consequence which followed in every case, but rather what was aimed at—what was made the object of faithful prayer. Then the ἐνεργήματα δυνάμεων, the gift of coming forward and working in special cases with remarkable energy, in the interests, and for the cause of Christianity, of exercising extraordinary vigour of spirit and power of action ; to work δυνάμεις, wonders, in this wide sense : the προφητεία, the διακρίσεις πνευμάτων, the gift of distinguishing whether those who declared

---

[1] Γνῶσις sometimes stands specially for allegory. Cf. die Chr. Gnosis, p. 85 *sq.*

themselves prophets really were so, whether the Spirit of God really spoke through them, the γένη γλωσσῶν, and the ἑρμηνεία γλωσσῶν.[1] All this is worked by one and the same spirit, who divides and distributes himself to each man specially as he will. All these charisms are free gifts and operations of the divine spirit, which manifests itself in them in its divers forms, and as it were disintegrates itself into the momenta of its own conception. All of them are simply the manifestation of that spiritual life which proceeds from the spirit as the principle of the Christian communion, to display and diffuse itself in that communion as the whole fulness and manifoldness of its σῶμα Χριστοῦ. And as it is the same divine spirit which produces all these operations, so it is the same which, as the spirit identical with itself, operates through all the periods of the Christian Church, in the same fundamental types of the Christian life. These types are, indeed, subject to modification, with the diversities of different ages and individuals, yet they are always present in the deep tendencies which are perpetually recurring and exhibiting the same variations and contrasts. The whole history of the development of the Christian Church is only the unfolding of the divine spirit, and shows how it more and more individualizes itself and distributes itself into all its variations. As it can become manifest only because there are διαιρέσεις χαρισμάτων, as it διαιρεῖ itself in them, so the variety which this fact implies must work itself out in an ever-widening circumference. The greater the fulness of the spiritual life which it includes within itself as the principle of the Christian body, the greater must be, not only the manifoldness, but also the divergency of the forms in which the idea of the Christian Church moves towards its realization. In this way everything which the one spirit that works in the Church contains within itself must be brought forth and made to appear. Only this must be observed, that however great the variation and the contrast of the forms may be in which the

[1] Cf. with reference to these latter charisms the essay mentioned, vol. i. p. 15.

Christian life is developed, the bond is nevertheless not severed which connects them with each other, and with the spirit, and makes them one ; the spirit goes forth out of itself, only to return into itself, and to take back into itself the phenomena in which it has become external and objective to itself. It is this other side (essentially connected with that first one) on which the spiritual process in which the Christian life is developed comes back to itself again in the unity of its own inward motion, and becomes the process of the spirit mediating itself with itself, that the apostle has in view, when he insists again and again upon the point, that the principle of all those various charisms is that same spirit, identical with itself ; when he insists so strongly that the one purpose of them all is to serve as means to further the common purpose of the Christian fellowship ; and when in this connexion he speaks of love as the element in which all diversity and contrast, all particular and subjective interests must subside, and be subordinate to the unity of the idea. Thus what he says of the nature of love (1 Cor. xiii.) has an intimate connexion with his doctrine of the charisms and of the Christian community. In that love which inspires all her members, the church ought to realize the idea of her own unity ; in that love she should seek to return from all her differences to her unity. To this unity from which she comes forth, and to which she returns again when she is perfected, she is to be built up on the foundation which is laid once for all, which is no other than Jesus Christ. Everything that contributes to the furtherance of the Christian life is termed very fittingly, in the Pauline language, a building up ; in this building up, the common work is to be advanced towards its end by every one doing his part in his own sphere, under the continual operation of the Holy Spirit. Thus the Christian Church is, as a whole, what each individual ought to be for himself, a temple of God, in which the Spirit of God dwells ; as the temple of God is holy, so Christians should be holy, for they are a temple of God (1 Cor. iii. 16 *sq.*) The notion *holiness* comprehends here everything that the Christian communion has to be in its most general character, as the kingdom of God founded by Christ, and working out its accomplishment in Christ. The spirit which dwells and governs in the Christian communion, both in the whole and in every individual, is named the Holy Spirit—this is his specific predicate; and the object of his activity can be nothing else than the holiness of the Christian Church, to be realized in the progressive sanctification of all her members. Christ himself is eminently the ἅγιος, who has himself the πνεῦμα ἁγιωσύνης; and Christians are not merely κλητοί, persons called to the Messianic blessedness through the free grace of God in Christ, κλητοὶ Ἰησοῦ Χριστοῦ, but also ἅγιοι; as κλητοί, they are also ἅγιοι, κλητοὶ ἅγιοι, or ἡγιασμένοι ἐν Χριστῷ Ἰησοῦ (1 Cor. i. 2), *i.e.* those who have in Christ the principle of their being made holy, who are themselves holy persons in their union with him, the Holy One. The fundamental and ever-recurring thought of the apostle is, that only in union with Christ can the Christian be what he is and ought to be as a Christian, that in him alone has he the essential principle of his being and his living, or is he himself a Christ, a Christian, as the German language expresses so significantly in the Christian name.[1] The name χριστιανοί, used only by the adversaries of Christianity, expresses nothing but the external side of this relation; the expression ἐπικαλούμενοι τὸ ὄνομα τοῦ Κυρίου ἡμῶν Ἰησοῦ Χριστοῦ (1 Cor. i. 2), turns from the outward to the inward side of the relation; but the ὄντες ἐν Χριστῷ, 1 Cor. i. 30; 2 Cor. v. 17, expresses its most intimate principle. In the ὄντες ἐν Χριστῷ, Christ is the immanent, substantial principle of their being and life; in them, as a σῶμα Χριστοῦ, he is himself to be beheld in his identity with them; what is true of them is true of him. Whatever interferes with or destroys the unity of the Christian communion; whatever, instead of drawing its members closer together in the unity of the spirit, divides them, or rends them asunder, is not merely a severance of the bond which connects the individual with Christ—it is a division and dismemberment of Christ himself (μεμέρισται ὁ

---

[1] The German word for Christian is *der Christ*, the Christ.

Χριστὸς ; 1 Cor. i. 13).   As the εἶναι ἐν Χριστῷ is, in its original
conception, true of the individual as well as of the whole, it is a
merely figurative way of stating the relation of the church to
Christ, to compare it with the marriage-bond. The apostle says
of himself (as founder of the Corinthian Church) (2 Cor. xi. 2) that
he had espoused her to one man, in order to present her as a chaste
virgin to Christ. The church is therefore united as a bride with
Christ her bridegroom. The comparison, however, is merely
figurative, and used for the purpose of exhortation. It is devoid
of the dogmatic intention with which the idea is accompanied in
Eph. v. 23 *sq.*[1]

Entrance to the Christian Church, admission to it in order to
incorporation in it as a σῶμα Χριστοῦ, takes place by means of
baptism, for all who are baptized into Christ put on Christ, Gal.
iii. 27. They are baptized into Christ, because baptism is in His
name, and thus accompanied with believing acknowledgment of
all that that name implies. One cannot, therefore, be baptized into
Christ without believing in him, and becoming one with him,
so far as faith makes the believer one with him. This relation
to Christ which is brought about by baptism is called putting
on Christ, an expression which represents the relation, not as an
outward, but as an essentially inward one. He who puts on a
garment goes altogether inside it, and identifies himself with it,
and since all who are baptized into Christ become one with him in
the very same way, there is an end in this identity of everything

---

[1] A comparison of the Epistle to the Ephesians shows distinctly throughout,
how, at the standpoint which it occupies, the ideality of the Pauline conception
of the Christian church has passed over into the material conception of the
Catholic church. What is with Paul quite ideally σῶμα Χριστοῦ is here quite
definitely τὸ σῶμα τοῦ Χριστοῦ, Eph. iv. 12 ; there is one Lord, one faith, one
baptism, iv. 4. A unity of faith in this objective sense, as the faith of the church,
is not known to our apostle ; he merely says, πάντες εἶς ἐστε ἐν Χριστῷ Ἰησοῦ,
Gal. iii. 28. Nor is Christ called κεφαλὴ in the earlier Epistles, because the conception of the σῶμα has not yet reached, as a whole, this concrete and material
development. The whole machinery of the organism of the church may be clearly
recognised in the expressions of the Epistle to the Ephesians, iv. 12, 16. Cf.
Misc. zum Eph. Brief, Theol. Jahrb. 1844, p. 385 (Schwegler, Nachap. Zeit. ii.
381 *sq.*).

in the outward circumstances of life that divides or distinguishes them from each other. In this new relation which is entered externally by baptism, internally by faith, there is neither Jew nor Gentile, neither bond nor free, neither male nor female, all are one in Christ Jesus. In this unity with Christ they are all one among one another, every man is simply a Christian, as all the others are, Gal. iii. 28, cf. 1 Cor. xii. 13. In order to be one with Christ, it is also necessary to partake in everything that is inseparable from his person. He who is one with him lives in him and with him; but in order to live with Christ, one must also have died with him as he himself died. Therefore baptism, as baptism into Christ, is itself a baptism into his death, and in its form as an immersion, baptism represented this fellowship in Christ's death as symbolically a fellowship in his burial. It was very graphically represented in the rite, how one had to descend with Christ into death, and the grave, and the under-world, in order to rise with him again to a new life, Rom. vi. 3 *sq.* Being a baptism into the death of Jesus, it is, of course, a baptism for the forgiveness of sins, or, figuratively speaking, a washing away of sins. But this negative includes in itself all that is positive. When the apostle says of Christians, 1 Cor. vi. 11, that they are washed, that they are sanctified, that they are justified, in the name of the Lord Jesus, and in the Spirit of God, this is nothing but a general description of the Christian character as imparted to the Christian even in his baptism. The operative principle by which one is incorporated at baptism into the Christian fellowship is the spirit; the spirit communicates itself in the rite as the principle of Christian consciousness, 1 Cor. xii. 13.

Along with baptism, the apostle speaks of the Lord's Supper (not perhaps at 1 Cor. xii. 13, where, according to the correct reading and interpretation, there is nothing said of the Lord's Supper; yet) at 1 Cor. x. 1, where he says of the Israelites, that "they were all baptized unto Moses in the cloud and in the sea; and all ate the same spiritual food; and all drank the same spiritual drink." This is all said with typical reference to baptism and the Lord's Supper, as the two essential elements of the religious life of the Christian community. The apostle here goes back to the analogies which the Jewish religion presents to Christian baptism and the Christian supper, in order to get a foundation for his argument about participating in the Gentile sacrificial feasts ; he impresses the thought upon his readers, that the higher the stage one has reached in the religious life, the more need is there for caution lest one fall : that all the privileges and blessings by which a religion is distinguished can give no security against the penalties which God inflicts on those who violate the religious communion that is sacred to him, or who fall away from the one true religion to heathenism and idolatry. Baptism and the Lord's Supper are thus equally essential elements of the Christian communion, and both equally contain in themselves that which constitutes its peculiar character and superiority. If it be through baptism that a man is incorporated in the Christian fellowship, the Lord's Supper, on the other hand, must be a means for the furtherance of the religious life in this fellowship, and as baptism not only unites all who are baptized into one body, but makes them a body of Christ, translates them, as it were, into the communion of one and the same vital organism with Christ, so, in the Lord's Supper, the reference to Christ must be the same, and of equal scope. The apostle regards it from this point of view when he asks, 1 Cor. x. 16, if the cup of blessing which we bless be not a fellowship with the blood of Christ ? and the bread which we break a fellowship with the body of Christ ? Since it is one loaf, the many are one body, for they all partake in the one bread. It can scarcely be thought accidental that in this connexion, where he is speaking of the body of Christ, he calls the Christian fellowship a body, and that because in it many are bound together into a unity. The leading thought on which the apostle is here insisting is, that by partaking of the cup and the bread, many are brought into one and the same common relation to Christ, and partake of Christ in the same way. And here the idea was probably before his mind, that the reason why Christ called the bread with which he instituted the Lord's Supper his body, was that this action makes the Christian fellowship a σῶμα Χριστοῦ, since many take part in that same relation to him which his death has brought about. What the apostle, however, considered the chief object of the institution of the Lord's Supper was, as he explains in the second passage which the same Epistle contains on the subject, xi. 23 *sq.*, that it was to be an action for the con-. tinuous remembering of Jesus, and especially of his death, in which he gave himself for men, and brought them into a new relation towards God. The cup is the new covenant, or contains a representation of the new covenant as founded on the blood of Christ,—on the death of Christ on the cross. As often, then, as one eats of the bread and drinks of the cup, one is to show forth the death of the Lord till he come ; what the partakers have before them, as the body and the blood of Christ, is to take the place of Christ himself, and to be to them instead of his own personal presence. The peculiar action of the rite is to be one connecting the past, in which he was personally present, with the future, in which he is to come again in person, and that by the most graphic and living commemoration. And this commemoration, having to serve such a purpose, could fasten only on that crisis in the life of Christ, in which he was on the point of completing, by the sacrifice of himself, that which was the essential basis of the new religion he was founding. Thus the peculiar idea of the Lord's Supper is, that in the elements the partakers have him, as it were, before them, as one who died for them ; and in the elements become conscious of his bloody death on the cross, and thus regard them as the symbols of his body and blood. And so there can be no greater offence in reference to the Lord's Supper than to partake of the bread and wine without being distinctly conscious that they are the body and blood of Christ. By doing this, the partaker becomes guilty of a sin against the body and blood of Christ, because, not keeping in his mind the great difference that obtains between this eating and drinking, which are so full of meaning, and every other, he fails thereby to realize the object for which the

Lord's Supper was instituted—the ever-recurring proclamation of the death of Christ, and the continuous representation of his personal presence. Taking all this together, we see that the chief significance of the Lord's Supper consists, with the apostle, in the historical commemoration of Christ as the founder of Christianity. As he himself received what referred to it in the way of historical tradition, 1 Cor. xi. 23, so the Lord's Supper is itself to be a chief means of keeping alive the historical memory of Christ as the founder of Christianity. As a historical religion, Christianity depends on, and is bound up in, the person of its founder, and to keep up the historical connexion with him, constantly and livingly, is thus an essential condition of the continued existence of the Christian communion. The more nearly and the more immediately, then, the Lord's Supper connects the members of the Christian fellowship with Christ, the more does it become itself the actual centre of that fellowship, and that which constitutes its characteristic difference from all other religious fellowships. The central point of a religion must be just where its professors become most immediately conscious of that which is the essential contents of every religion,—atonement with God. According to the apostle's own comparison of Christianity with Judaism and heathenism in this respect, 1 Cor. x. 18, this central point is, in the Jewish religion, the sacrificial altar of the one temple ; in the heathen religion, the sacrificial *cultus* generally ; in the Christian religion, the Lord's Supper. The Lord's Supper is the showing forth of the death of Jesus, and thus of the atonement effected through him. One can appropriate this atonement only by historically remembering the fact of the death of Jesus on the cross. Thus the Lord's Supper, as the central point of the Christian religion, cannot be dissociated from this historical commemoration, and he who fails to hold the feast in living consciousness of what it means must thereby be removed more or less from the centre of the Christian religion. It is only in the living reference to Christ and to his atoning death, as brought home to the consciousness in the Lord's Supper, that the Christian community becomes a σῶμα Χριστοῦ.

FIFTH CHAPTER.

THE RELATION OF CHRISTIANITY TO JUDAISM AND HEATHENISM.

THE deep inward foundation on which the apostle's doctrine of justification rests is the moral consciousness of man : it is in the moral consciousness of man, as he is while yet standing under the law, that the law works out the proof of its own inability to save him. In this sphere law and faith stand over against each other in the relation of division and atonement. Now this contrast, which is found deepest and most intense in the individual human consciousness, presents itself also as a great historical contrast in the relation of Judaism and Christianity. It was through a breach with Judaism that the apostle's Christian consciousness first took shape, and thus it came about that he regarded Christianity in the main as the opposite of Judaism. His deep conviction that Christianity was a new διαθήκη, and that it contained a totally new principle of the religious life, rendered it inevitable that he should define the relation of the two διαθῆκαι to each other as a relation of contrast. In describing this contrast, he exhibits profound and comprehensive ideas of the historical development of religion.

The apostle sums up the chief result of the ante-Christian history of religion in the proposition, Rom. iii. 9, that Jews and Gentiles are both equally under sin, i.e. that it cannot be said of any one in the Jewish or heathen world that he was a truly justified person, because no one is without sin, and without faith there can be no forgiveness of sins. The apostle's discussion in the three first chapters of the Epistle to the Romans amounts to an empirical proof of the proposition with which his doctrine of justification had already furnished him, that no man can be righteous without faith.

If there be no righteousness without faith, the whole pre-Christian period must attest the fact by its predominant and continual sinfulness. While, however, the apostle takes sinfulness to be the general character of the whole pre-Christian period, he refers it at the same time to a general principle. In that period sin reigns alone; there was as yet no opposing principle to break the power of sin. Sin itself is the ruling principle of that period, and the ante-Christian and the Christian time, or Adam and Christ, are related to each other as sin and grace, as death and life, or as law and faith. The apostle deals with this great contrast in the passage Rom. v. 12 *sqq.* After contrasting the want of δικαιοῦσθαι ἐξ ἔργων νόμου in the ante-Christian time with the δικαιοῦσθαι ἐκ πίστεως as the new principle of religious life which has appeared in Christ, he rises to the general standpoint we have indicated, from which the ante-Christian and the Christian time are regarded in their essential difference. The universality of the reign of sin and death is proved by the simple fact that both had their beginning in the very first man; from him they have been diffused to all men. Therefore—the apostle draws this conclusion from the preceding— it is the same with Christ as with Adam; the one is, equally with the other, the beginning and the principle of a great world-historical period. It is here, as it is there, where through one man sin entered into the world, and death by sin, and so death passed upon all men, for a distinct proof that all have sinned. This rendering of the words ἐφ' ᾧ πάντες ἥμαρτον, which are the key to the whole passage, is at variance with the explanations of that phrase which have hitherto been current, but I think it is the only admissible one. Grammatically ἐφ' ᾧ cannot be taken in any other sense than "because," which is undoubtedly very common; nor, if the statement ἐφ' ᾧ π. ἥμ. be taken only in its connexion with the foregoing, is there any objection to this rendering. Do not the apostle's words yield a perfectly adequate sense, if we interpret them thus; when once through Adam sin and death, thus intimately connected with each other, acquired the force of a dominating principle, death passed upon all men, because they have all sinned?

Even if the apostle do regard sin and death as a general principle
which rules irrespectively of the individual, that does not by any
means preclude the supposition that the connexion between sin
and death, which was first established through Adam, is brought
home to each individual by means of his own sin. In order that
it might not appear as if the sin of the individual were the only true
cause of his death, it was sought, instead of translating ἐφ' ᾧ simply
"because," to give it the meaning, "the fact being that," "under the
additional circumstance that," "in such a way as that." In this
way death would not be deduced from the sin of each individual,
but this sin of the individual would be merely mentioned as a circumstance which takes place in connexion with that death which
reigns already because of Adam's sin. But what end can it have
to give the sentence ἐφ' ᾧ π. ἥμ. a merely subordinate importance,
and how ambiguously must the apostle have expressed himself if
all he did to deny that the sin of the individual was the cause of
his death, was merely to use a particle which, in addition to its first
indisputable meaning, "because," perhaps possessed that other
meaning; for even though ἐφ' ᾧ = ἐπὶ τούτῳ, ὅτι, as well as ἐπὶ
τούτῳ ὥστε, yet "under condition that," "and under the circumstances that," are not entirely the same. The question that has to be
answered for a proper rendering of ver. 12 can be no other than
this; why in the second part of the verse the apostle places death
first, and sin after it; why he does not say, after the analogy of
what precedes, "and so all men have sinned, and death has passed
upon all." But it is no answer to this question merely to take from
ἐφ' ᾧ the meaning of causality, and make the death as far as possible
independent of the ἐφ' ᾧ π. ἥμ.; what we have chiefly to attend to
is the connexion with what follows, since the apostle goes on with
γὰρ, ver. 13. And this is the great mistake in the way the passage
has been treated hitherto: no regard has been paid to the connexion
of ver. 12 with ver. 13, at least no satisfactory explanation of that
connexion has been given. To make the connexion clear, we have
to take the passage in this way: that, as in ver. 13, the apostle infers
the presence of sin from the fact of the dominion of death, so also,

in ver. 12, he infers the universality of ἥμαρτον from the universality of death, or regards the latter as a proof of the former. Through one man sin entered into the world, and through sin death, and so death passed upon all men, which shows that, which involves the presupposition that, all have sinned. For until the law sin was in the world; not even this period was without sin; but sin is not imputed where there is no law, and it might therefore be said that there was no sin during this period; but the presence of sin in this period is clearly demonstrated by the death which reigned from Adam to Moses. The men of this period must have sinned also, though their sins were not altogether like those of Adam, who sinned against a positive injunction. The apostle's idea here is that sin as well as death is universal, and that they are inseparably linked to each other. The universality of sin, however, is not so immediately and clearly apparent as the universality of death, and so it is inferred that sin is universal from the fact that death is universal, there being no death apart from sin, which is its cause. The whole argument, therefore, shows distinctly that though he sees in sin and death the operation of a principle reigning in humanity since Adam, he yet conceives the death of man to be brought about only by the imputation to each individual of his own actual sin. The passage thus proves the very opposite of what has generally been drawn from it as a *locus classicus* for the doctrine of original sin. The only question is whether ἐφ' ᾧ can be taken in the sense here alleged, and of this there can hardly be a doubt. The ordinary meaning "because," is simply stated more distinctly in the phrase "proceeding on the fact that," "it being presupposed that." The difference is simply that what "because" expresses objectively, is by that other rendering logically defined for the subjective consciousness. For the purpose of a logical demonstration, cause and effect, the thing implied and that which proceeds upon it, are held apart. ʽΟ θάνατος διῆλθεν, ἐφ' ᾧ π. ἥμ. means accordingly: Death came to all under the presupposition that all sinned, *i.e.* the coming of death is a thing which involves, which cannot be explained except on the supposition that, all sinned; the one always implies the other. If there

be a time in which it might be expected that there was no sin, it
is the time from Adam to Moses, and yet, as certainly as death
reigned during this period, so certainly it was not without sin.
That this logical explanation of cause and effect is the proper sense
of ἐφ' ᾧ, may be shown from the other two passages of the New
Testament in which the phrase occurs ; 2 Cor. v. 4; Phil. iii. 12. In
these passages, also, the meaning I have indicated affords a much
better sense than the ordinary "because." In the first of these passages the apostle says ; as being in the body we groan under the burden; now if he goes on, *because* we do not wish to be unclothed, but
to be clothed upon, this yields no clear sense. Here also we must
take ἐφ' ᾧ as marking the purpose of the argument. In the body
we sigh under a burden ; yet this does not imply that we desire to
be unclothed, but only that we desire to be clothed upon; what is to
be inferred is not the wish to ἐκδυς., but the wish to ἐπενδ. The second
passage is commonly taken thus : but I follow after, if I may also
apprehend that for which I also have been apprehended. This, however, is neither accurate nor clear. The proper rendering of ἐφ' ᾧ
must be this : which presupposes that, etc.; I follow after, if I may
also apprehend it, which, of course, is only possible on the presupposition that I have been apprehended by Christ. A comparison of
these three passages shows at once that ἐφ' ᾧ is inseparable, and is
to be taken as a conjunction. Thus that other interpretation, which
certainly adheres more closely to the ordinary meaning of the preposition ἐπὶ, but makes ᾧ refer to θάνατος or to the sentence εἰς
πάντας διῆλθεν, cannot be defended. Death is said to be the established consequence of sin, under the presupposition of which all
individuals sinned, or the pre-ordained result to accomplish which
they sinned. This, however, would require not ἐφ' ᾧ, but εἰς ὅν.

It is thus explained in what sense Adam is a type of the future
or second Adam. These two, Adam and Christ, stand over against
each other as the dominion of sin and death, and the reign of
grace, in which the dominion of sin and death is done away. What
the apostle remarks, ver. 15, of the difference between the two,
is less essential and serves only to increase the contrast. It is

not, he says, with the gift of grace as with the trespass. For if by the trespass of one many died, much more (the more there were who died) has the grace of God and the gift in grace of the One Man, Jesus Christ, proved effectual in many. And it is not as it happened there through one that sinned, with the gift of grace. The judgment came from one man, as a judgment of condemnation; but the gift of grace from many trespasses, as a judgment of justification. If through the transgression of the one death reigned through the one, much more shall they who receive the abundance of the grace and the gift of righteousness reign in life through the one Jesus Christ. (The contrast is thus not merely the quantitative one of ἐξ ἑνὸς and ἐκ πολλῶν, ver. 16, but also a qualitative one, inasmuch as the reign of life through grace is infinitely better than the reign of death through sin, ver. 17.) As, then, through one transgression it came to a judgment of condemnation for all men, so through one judgment of justification it came to justification for all men. For as through the disobedience of the one man the many were made sinners (those who are bound up in him, under the principle he represents), so through the obedience of the one the many shall be made righteous. The relations denoted in these antitheses are, in fact, more outward than real; but they serve to bring into prominence the leading thought of the passage, that Adam and Christ are each the representative of a world-historical principle. The whole period before Christ was the period of the reign of sin and death. Though each individual dies on account of his own sin, and each man's sins are reckoned to him as transgressions, just as Adam's sins to Adam, yet there was a principle developed and realized in the first sin from the power of which principle no man could afterwards be free. This principle is identified with the person of Adam, and thus Adam has a determining influence over all his posterity, since the principle reached actuality in him, and operates from him downwards. The question of Adam's own relation to the principle which in him became as it were a living personal power, whether the appearance of the principle is to be regarded as the consequence of an act performed by him while yet in the state of freedom, or whether this act itself is to be accounted for by the operation of the principle, this question lies outside of the apostle's sphere of vision. So far as the development of his views allows us to judge, there can have been no question in his mind on either of these two points : that the principle does not operate without, but only in and through freewill, and that it is a power independent of, and standing above, freewill. We cannot here discuss how the relation to each other of the two principles represented by Adam and Christ is worked out further in detail. It is time that we should turn to Judaism and the relation it bears to Christianity.

The ante-Christian period was the period of the reign of sin ; and in this description Judaism is included : in Judaism also sin reigned. Now Judaism is distinguished from heathenism by its law ; Judaism and the law are so identical to the apostle, that where the Mosaic law is not in force, he sees nothing more than something analogous to the law. How then is the reign of sin in Judaism related to the law ? does the law restrict it or confirm it ? It might appear hardly necessary to raise the question ; that it needs no further answer than what the apostle says, Gal. iii. 19, that the law was given because of transgressions, *i.e.* as a barrier against them. But the apostle makes two seemingly contradictory assertions : that the law conflicts with the reign of sin ; and that the law has confirmed that reign. He says very clearly, Rom. v. 20, that the law entered the reign of sin just on purpose to increase the transgression ; to let sin, as it were, manifest all that it is and can effect, and work out its reign to the utmost. It can scarcely be wondered at that a seeming paradox like this has frequently proved a stumbling-block to the apostle's readers. If the law were given for a certain definite purpose, surely that purpose must have been the prevention, limitation, and subjection of sin, and not its increase or furtherance. And yet from the apostle's standpoint the difficulty is very easily solved. The explanation given by Rückert and others cannot indeed be deemed satisfactory : that the apostle does not recognise any such thing as chance, that with him everything that happens is willed and ordained by God, and especially everything bearing on the great plan of redemption, so that when he considered that the law had brought about not less sin but more, and that by this means mankind grew riper and more prepared for the acceptance of salvation, that grace might find at last her great opportunity, he could come to no other conclusion than that this result—the increase of sin through the law which lay before him as a matter of observation—had been willed by God. But God can never have willed the increase of sin through the law ; if the law paved the way for grace through the increase of sin, then God willed sin or the law only for the sake of grace, and the question is not removed how, even on this hypothesis that the way to grace is to be through sin, the increase of sin could be brought about by the law ? If this be an essential characteristic of the law, then God could not will the law without willing this as a condition attached to it. But how is it that the law, which is essentially and necessarily the negative of sin, was a positive means for the furtherance of sin ?

Here we have simply to remember what the apostle's conception of sin was, that it is what it is only through the consciousness a man has of it. The law has increased, intensified, and confirmed sin, inasmuch as it was through the law, because the law was there, that sin came into consciousness, and in consciousness sprang into vital existence and reality. Διὰ γὰρ νόμου, says the apostle, Rom. iii. 20, ἐπίγνωσις ἁμαρτίας, and ἁμαρτία οὐκ ἐλλογεῖται μὴ ὄντος νόμου. Here it might be said that the qualitative side of sin cannot be all that the apostle has in view ; that he would have expressed himself differently if all he meant to say was that actions which are not sinful in themselves receive the character of sinfulness only through the law, since one becomes conscious of their disagreement with the law when they are held up to it ; that he would have spoken not merely of παράπτωμα (Rom. v. 20), but of ἐπίγνωσις ἁμαρτίας. But a correct analysis of the apostle's proposition διὰ νόμου ἐπίγνωσις will show us that this qualitative relation of the law to sin is not essentially different from the quantitative relation, the πλεονάζειν τὸ παράπτωμα ; that the one is the subjective and the other is the objective expression for the same quality and operation of the law. Of course the law is not the immediate cause of sin ; it does not itself produce those actions which are to be regarded as sin ; it only brings out their disagreement with the law, and shows them to be sinful. Now, the more the law becomes the universal and exclusive standard for judging of men's actions, the more deeply it sinks into their consciousness, the more does sin increase in quantity ; sin is heaped on sin, because in the light of the law there is so much that must be judged to be sin. In this way the law appears to serve no other purpose but to multiply men's transgressions and fill up the measure of their sins. What it produces, however, to this end, is not sin itself, but the consciousness of sin, and thus if we confine ourselves to the objective side of the matter, we may say that the law was added to sin for the purpose of increasing it, or to cause the process of sin to complete itself in its whole quantitative extent, by the πλεονάζειν τὸ παράπτωμα ; and this process is completed just in this way, that what is already sin in essence becomes sin to the consciousness. The law is given therefore for the realization of sin, only in so far as sin is not sin without the consciousness of it. Here we see in what way it is true that the law is for sin as well as against it. It is for sin, because sin runs its course through the law, and not without it ; because without the law there is no sin, or without the consciousness of sin there is no sin. It is against sin because the consciousness of sin is in another aspect the necessary condition on which alone sin can be removed. Only where there is a vivid apprehension of what sin is, is there a possibility that it will be removed ; the stronger the consciousness of sin is, the more is the power of sin broken even in this very fact. Where, the apostle says, Rom. v. 20, sin has reached its utmost measure, there grace predominates all the more ; that, as sin has reigned in death (in the element of death), so grace might reign through righteousness to eternal life. The apostle's view thus sees in the law only a *stadium* in the reign of sin, of which he is speaking in the section Rom. v. 12-21. The law must come in order that the reign of sin may have full swing. Sin and death are the reigning powers of this period ; but this is not to be taken objectively : it is only in the subjective sense in which the apostle says, 1 Cor. xv. 56, that ὁ νόμος is the δύναμις τῆς ἁμαρτίας.

This is enough to show us that Judaism in the form of the law does not stand in such a merely negative relation to Christianity as the apostle's words seem at first sight to imply. Judaism, as law, is opposed to the grace of Christianity, and thus admits of no other religious position than that which the apostle describes as arising out of the impossibility of any δικαιοῦσθαι ἐξ ἔργων νόμου. But Judaism is further the subjective mediation of this opposition ; for the knowledge of sin is only possible through the law. And this brings Judaism incomparably nearer Christianity than heathenism ; indeed, the way from heathenism to Christianity lies, properly speaking, through Judaism, since that knowledge of sin, which is the indispensable and only preparation for the reception of grace, can only come from the law. But the relation of Judaism, or the Old Testament dispensation, to Christianity is more than this : not only is it in virtue of the law a preparatory mediating and necessary stage : the Old Testament and the New are related to each other as promise and fulfilment ; the Old Testament contains ideally what is realized in Christianity. The most essential, the central point in Christianity, justification by faith, as opposed to justification by the works of the law, is prefigured in the Old Testament. The faith of Abraham is essentially the same thing as the justifying faith of the Christian. Judaism, or the Old Testament, is not, therefore, to be regarded in the narrower sense in which it is equally with heathenism a particular form of religion, and stands in a negative relation to Christianity. It is something more than this ; it rests on a foundation from which it looks beyond everything particular, and contains the same universality that is characteristic of Christianity. This is what the apostle means when he calls justification by faith a law, a νόμος πίστεως. Here, from what is specific in the law, he abstracts this as its essence, as the proper conception of it, that it is more than anything else a religious norm for the determination of the relation subsisting between God and man. Thus the law, as the law of works, is only the particular of that universal which is present even in this instance, and which is differentiated to one or other of two modes, the νόμος ἔργων or the νόμος πίστεως. And as the particular cannot be thought here without the general, which it presupposes, so, as the apostle says in the same connexion, the God of Judaism is not only the God of the Jews, but also of the Gentiles; he is God absolutely, and as such, as the one Absolute, he must set up one universal norm of justification, and both for circumcision and uncircumcision this can be nothing else than justification by faith. How can it then be said that the law is made void through faith, when justification by faith simply realizes that which the law contains already as its universal, as the conception breaking through the particular form? With this the apostle passes on to his discussion of the faith of Abraham, Rom. iv, 1 *sqq.*[1]; and shows that in Abraham's faith in the Divine promise there was that very imputation of faith as righteousness which belongs to the Christian idea of justification. Abraham's faith was imputed unto him, and that while he was yet uncircumcised; circumcision was by no means the reason of this imputation, but only a consequence of it. He received circumcision merely as a sign of that justification by faith which he had received while yet uncircumcised; so that he might be a father of all them that believe, though they be not circumcised, and a father of the circumcision to them who are not of the circumcision only, but who also walk in the steps of that faith of our father Abraham, which he had being yet uncircumcised, *i.e.* to those who, although circumcised, yet do not find the essence and the ground of justification in circumcision, but in faith, and so do not seek to

---

[1] I take the passage, Rom. iv. 1, thus: If then the law itself consists essentially of faith, and everything depends on faith, what shall we say that Abraham, our father, gained by circumcision (κατὰ σάρκα can only refer to circumcision, even though the expression is a general one)? He gained nothing by it, as little as by other works of this kind which belong to the same category with circumcision.

be justified by the law, but only by faith. The apostle now goes on to show how little the law (that is, in its particular and specific sense) has to do with the promise which was given to Abraham in consequence of his faith. The promise given to Abraham or his posterity was the possession of the world. This possession, however, was to be theirs not through the law, but through the righteousness of faith. Indeed, from the nature of the case it could not be otherwise ; for if they had been to receive it in the way of the law, through the keeping of the law, then faith would have been void and the promise made of none effect. For the law works wrath, *i.e.* the opposite of that disposition from which the promise comes—law and sin being correlative ideas, so that where there is no law there is no transgression, but where there is law there is also sin and punishment, and the punitive displeasure of God. Since, then, the law had nothing to do with this matter, they were to receive the possession not in the way of the law, but in the way of faith, that they might receive it in accordance with grace, in order that the promise might be valid for all posterity, not only for the posterity from the law, but also for those from the faith of Abraham, who is the father of us all (as it is written : I have made thee the father of many nations) before God, in whom he believed, as in him who makes the dead to live and calls into existence the things that are not. Thus faith showed itself even in Abraham to be the principle through which alone man can arrive at a saving relation towards God. As Abraham believed God, and his faith was reckoned to him for righteousness, so do Christians now believe, and as believers they are the children of Abraham, for it was in respect that God justifies the nations by faith, that the Scripture promised Abraham that all nations should be blessed in him, Gal. iii. 6. So far then is the Christian justification by faith, as opposed to the law, from being an encroachment on the religion of the Old Testament, that on the contrary it merely carries out what the Old Testament itself declares with regard to the law ; it fulfils a prophecy which was given before the law, and the superiority of which to the law cannot possibly be questioned. The apostle

N

shows, Gal. iii. 15, that this is the true position of the law, that the place it occupied in the organism of the Old Testament religion was only a subordinate one, and that it stands as far below Christianity as below the promise given to Abraham, which simply prefigured that which was to arrive at full maturity in Christianity. To his argument in this passage he prefixes the following principle as a truth universally recognised :—"A man's testament, when it is legally executed and ratified, no one sets aside nor adds to it, nor alters anything in it by subsequent modification. If then even a man's testament, when properly confirmed, is beyond the power of any one to set aside, or modify, still less can this take place in the case of a divine testament." This major, containing the universal, is now followed in the apostle's argument by the particularizing minor. "Now in the promise made to Abraham in respect of his σπέρμα there is a distinct divine disposition ; it is defined in such a way that it can only point to Christ, can only be realized in him. Thus (this is the conclusion) the disposition made by God, or the promise given by him to Abraham, can by nothing be set aside or made invalid ; it must be fulfilled in Christ to whom it refers." Owing to the intervention of the explanation about the σπέρμα the apostle intimates his conclusion somewhat loosely, with the phrase, verse 17, τοῦτο δὲ λέγω, by this I mean, etc. If the divine disposition cannot be made void at all, then it cannot be made void by the law. The discussion turns on the law ; what is to be proved is that the law cannot interfere with the continued validity of the διαθήκη in question. A disposition having reference to Christ and already confirmed by God cannot possibly be invalidated by the law which was not given till 430 years afterwards, so that the promise should become of none effect. For the promise would be made of none effect : for though the law also promises a blessing, so that those who keep the law may expect an inheritance (the κληρονομία, blessedness, as the reward and fruit of the fulfilment of the law : as even in the Pentateuch the possession and continuous inheritance of the land of Canaan is coupled with the condition of keeping the law), yet this κληρονομία or inheritance is

in form a totally different one. If the κληρονομία comes from the
law, it is conditioned by the keeping of the law, and can only be
realized in proportion as the law is actually kept; now as the law
is always kept so very imperfectly, the κληρονομία ἐκ νόμου is as
good as none at all ; while, on the other hand, if salvation be the
result simply of the promise, then it is entirely free, bound to no
limit or condition : it is an affair of grace alone. And this was the
manner of the salvation which God promised to Abraham : δι᾽
ἐπαγγελίας κεχάρισται, verse 18. And if this be so, if everything
depends on that διαθήκη, and on it alone, on the promise given to
Abraham, and if the law is to be left out of consideration altogether
by virtue of this promise, then what is to be said of the law,—what
importance attaches to it ? The apostle had to meet this question
here : he could not rest satisfied with the merely negative relation
of the law to the promise ; it was necessary for him to say something positive about it, if his utterances were not to lead to the
conclusion that the law had been without purpose or significance.
But the answer he returns to the question allows the law only a
very subordinate function. The significance ascribed to the law
is only intermediate, secondary, provisional : it was added, he says,
τῶν παραβάσεων χάριν. It was given after the promise had been
given already, and was to have effect only during the interval
between the promise and its fulfilment in Christ. The promise is
and remains the most important, the substantial foundation of the
whole relation in question ; the scope of the law is entirely subordinate ; it was added, so to speak, only *per accidens*, τῶν παραβάσεων χάριν. The whole tenor of the passage shows that the
view these words were meant to express was, that the law was
given to set bounds to transgressions, to hold men in check in
regard to transgressions, lest they should go too far in them. All
that the apostle says, be it observed, is that the law was given
τῶν παραβ. χάριν, *i.e.* because there were transgressions ; the article
points, as Rückert justly observes, to transgressions which had
already been committed. The passages, Rom. iv. 15, and vii. 8,
seem to assert that before the νόμος there is no παράβασις, but we

have to distinguish two meanings of παράβασις, a wider and a restricted meaning. The παράβασις cannot, of course, precede the νόμος as the transgression of a positive law ; this is the sense of Rom. iv. 15 ; but inasmuch as the way man had to choose according to the will of God was always in some sense prescribed, there were always transgressions and deviations. Ἀμαρτία is indeed χωρὶς νόμου νεκρὰ, but that does not mean that without the law there was no sin at all, but only that sin does not properly awake nor disclose itself in its full extent until it finds in the positive law the object in comparison with which it thus appears ; the more is commanded, the more is sinned.

But scarcely has the apostle conceded to the law that it is a useful barrier against transgressions, when he at once adds two qualifications which serve no other end than to point out the subordinate position of the law as distinguished from the promise. First, that it was given by angels (in accordance with the later and peculiarly Alexandrine view, which did not allow even the giving of the law to be thought of as an immediate act of God, who is exalted absolutely above the material world) : second, that it was given through a mediator, Moses. The passage, verse 20, in which the apostle defines the office of the mediator, is one of the most vexed passages in the New Testament : yet it only requires to be looked at from the point of view which the context naturally suggests, in order to receive a very clear and simple meaning. The distinction drawn above, between the ἐπαγγελία and the νόμος, was that the former was given directly by God, and the latter through the mediation of angels (and here this can only be said in depreciation of the law, though it is true that angels are made elsewhere to exalt the glory of the legislation, Acts vii. 53). The phrase ἐν χειρὶ μεσίτου must thus denote something by which the law is made subordinate to the promise. And as διαταγεὶς δι' ἀγγέλων does not touch the inward difference between the νόμος and the ἐπαγγελία, but dwells on a merely external feature, so the definition contained in verse 20 is to be taken in the same way, as merely external. The question is, it is true, the idea of the mediator, but what is dwelt upon first in defining this idea, is not the essence of the matter, viz., that the mediation he effects presupposes a conflict, that he has to mediate between two divided and discordant parties. The first thing to notice about a mediator is this merely external and local feature, that he stands in the middle between two parties standing over against each other ; that he occupies the middle position, and so mediates the one with the other. It is thus that the idea of *mediator* is understood in the rabbinical passages which the interpreters have adduced, in order to explain μεσίτης. The function Moses has to discharge as *mediator* is simply to take what is delivered to him, given into his hands, by one of the parties, and to hand it over to the other. *Data est lex manu mediatoris*, it is said in one of these rabbinical passages, and in the same way ἐν χειρὶ, verse 19, directs attention to the hand which bears and delivers the document of the law ; it is thus that the mediator's peculiar function is characterized. The sense of this passage, which has been twisted to so many purposes, is therefore this :—That the mediator belongs not to one party, but to both parties ; the mediator as such cannot be conceived of otherwise than as standing between the two parties : he is not himself therefore one of the parties, he stands in the middle between them in order to be the middle person between the one party and the other. But God is one, *i.e.*, God is not such a mediator : he is only one of the two parties, he stands only on one side, and not between the two parties, who stand over against each other on the one side and on the other ; he is thus one party for himself, as the other of the two parties, with which God is dealing in a διαθήκη, such as the ἐπαγγελία to Abraham, is one party for himself. Thus interpreted the passage bears a very simple and natural meaning ; it at once becomes clear why the apostle says the first time ἑνὸς οὐκ ἔστιν and the other time εἷς ἐστιν, and that without any further definition, since indeed none is required. It is hard to see what objection can be raised to this interpretation. Thus ὁ δὲ Θεὸς εἷς ἐστιν does not refer in the least to the absolute, eternal and unchanging unity of God ; this is entirely apart from the discussion ; God is one simply as standing for himself, as one of the two contracting parties in this party-relation. And as for the law, what is said about it is the merely external statement that the νόμος has a quite subordinate importance, just as the position of the μεσίτης, as one who is not εἷς, or rather (what can be said of none but him) who ἑνὸς οὐκ ἔστιν, is a merely subordinate position. The ἐπαγγελία as a διαθήκη in which God εἷς ἐστιν, and in which no μεσίτης is concerned, stands higher than the νόμος, which cannot be thought of without the μεσίτης and is essentially conditioned by him. The law belongs to the same sphere as the μεσίτης, to whom it is bound, and whose position is determined for him by the conception of what he is. One is not therefore warranted to place the νόμος on the same line with the ἐπαγγελία, to compare it with or exalt it above the promise. All these other ideas about the relation of the ἐπαγγελία and the νόμος which interpreters have fancied they discovered in our passage, have simply been imported into it ; however correct they may be in themselves, they do not belong to this passage. The apostle has indicated his meaning with sufficient clearness, and we need not travel beyond it.

Up to this point the apostle has spoken of the νόμος in such a way as if it were of no importance whatever, in comparison with the ἐπαγγελία. He admitted indeed, in verse 19, that it τῶν παραβάσεων χάριν προσετέθη, yet no sooner was this said than he placed it far below the ἐπαγγελία, saying that it was διαταγεὶς δι' ἀγγέλων ἐν χειρὶ μεσίτου ; and when he added ὁ μεσίτης ἑνὸς οὐκ ἔστιν, ὁ δὲ Θεὸς εἷς ἐστιν, he represented the relation of the νόμος to the ἐπαγγελία as one of actual opposition. Thus he comes very pertinently to put the question : Is the law, then, so far below the promise, that we should think there is an actual opposition and conflict between the two, that they are mutually exclusive of each other, and that thus in comparison with the promise the law is to be held not only unnecessary and useless, but an element of disunion and conflict ? To this he answers : That is by no means the case. I am far from wishing to set up so disparaging a view of the law, and one which so little recognises its significance. I do not depreciate the law to such an extent as to consider it of no further importance to me. Yet, on the other hand, I cannot, as the Jewish Christians do, value it so highly as to make δικαιοσύνη ἐξ ἔργων νόμου my highest principle. I must declare against this view. For if the Mosaic law contained such a law as could make alive or save, then righteousness would actually come from the law, then it would be possible to be justified in the way of the law, by the works of the law. But this is far from being the case : in the way of the law there is no righteousness to be attained ; the scripture itself asserts the contrary and declares the result of the operation of the law to be the very opposite. The scripture declares (συγκλείειν in the declaratory sense, as Rom. xi. 32) that all is held under the might of sin, stands under the principle of sin, so as to be more or less affected by it. It declares this in passages such as those quoted, Rom. iii. 10 *sq.* And this has come to pass in order that through the knowledge (the apostle here expresses objectively and teleologically a process which cannot be conceived, but as subjectively mediated) that one cannot be saved in this way, the promise in the way of faith in Jesus Christ might be given to them that believe. And it is just this consideration, that that which, according to the scripture, is the result of the operation of the law, the manifest universality of sin, serves simply to prepare the way for the promise being fulfilled through faith, it is just this that leads us to the true view of the law, that it is to be regarded in itself, in its whole essence, as a mediating and preparatory stage. The chief stages in the apostle's view of the world's religious history are the ἐπαγγελία, the νόμος, and πίστις (πίστις, though in itself subjective, is here taken objectively, the apostle regarding the subject entirely from the objective point of view as a divinely ordained historical process). Now before faith came, faith that is, as a new stage of the objective process of development, we were kept under the law as if shut into a prison with a view to the faith which should afterwards be revealed. Thus the law was our schoolmaster till Christ, that we might be justified by faith. Here the apostle is merely drawing a conclusion which results of itself from the foregoing; and the idea of the παιδαγωγὸς contains nothing that was not present in the foregoing; he simply reverts to the principal idea prefixed to this section in verse 19, that the law τῶν παραβάσεων χάριν προσετέθη. He now takes up this idea again as it has been defined and substantiated in the intervening verses. The paedagogic nature of the law must thus, from the context, refer to its holding back from transgressions, setting a limit to them. In the same way the law is likened, verse 23, to a prison where a man is detained and watched. It is only in this negative sense that the law is to be regarded as a παιδαγωγὸς, nor must what follows lead us to ascribe to it the function of an educator, as if it had been meant to lead to Christ by awaking the inward longing for redemption : the words εἰς Χριστὸν simply express that the law retained this interim and provisional importance, until, in the course of this development, the time came at which Christ could appear.[1] And in this negative sense the word points to another class of men, so named among the ancients, the slaves namely, who accompanied boys not so much for education or training, as merely to watch over them. It is such a tutor and guide that the law is said to be. It was God's intention, and the scope of this whole scheme of religious history that only when Christ had come, should justification by faith begin, a thing which was impossible under the law. This paedagogic state was only for the interval, only a preparation, and so it came to an end at once, and of itself, as soon as a new stage of the religious consciousness and life had come with the appearance of πίστις. Thus we

[1] Neander says, *op. cit.* i. 435 : " Since the law put an outward check on the sinful propensity, which was constantly giving fresh proofs of its refractoriness, as by this means the consciousness of the power of the evil principle became more vivid, and hence the sense of need both of the forgiveness of sin and freedom from its bondage was awakened, the law became a παιδαγωγὸς εἰς Χριστόν." Here two stages are taken together which neither belong to each other essentially, nor are thus connected by the apostle, at least in this Epistle. As a rein, a check, the law awakens in the first instance merely the consciousness of hinderance, of opposition, in which the man seeks to be freed, not from sin, but only from the law. [There are some modifications of the above view of the παιδαγωγὸς and the μεσίτης in my N. Theol. 166 *f.—Editor.*]

stand no longer under the νόμος παιδαγωγὸς ; for us the law has lost its meaning and its use. Here the questions naturally arise whether πίστις has made an end altogether of the παραβάσεις, for the sake of which the law was given ? why, if the νόμος be so far inferior to faith, the latter had not appeared before ? and whether those, who as being under the law had nothing but the δικαιοῦσθαι ἐξ ἔργων νόμου, had not been justified nor saved at all ? The apostle does not enter into those questions in this passage, he only takes a broad view of the process as it moves through the three stages, ἐπαγγελία, νόμος, πίστις. Πίστις is just the ἐπαγγελία fulfilled and realized ; the actual appearance of that which was implicitly contained in the ἐπαγγελία. Thus the chief difficulty is presented by the νόμος, which stands between these two, how it comes to be there at all. The apostle almost seems to say that it should not properly have been there at all : the relation of the νόμος to the other two momenta is at any rate taken as purely external : the νόμος has no inward connexion with the other ; it is there merely τῶν παραβά-σεων χάριν, that there may not be a total want of government and order in the interval until πίστις arrives, and that there may be something to serve as a thread, though in a merely external way, for the religious development. As long as man stands under the law's discipline and severity, he is in a condition of bondage ; law and faith are related to each other as servitude and freedom, or as the slave to the son and heir of the house. The apostle finds this relation also prefigured in Abraham, in his two sons, Ishmael and Isaac. Ishmael the son of the bondwoman, the slave by birth, stands for the law, because the law places man in a position of bondage before God. Isaac, the son of the free woman Sarah, born, moreover, after a special divine promise, is the type of Christians as τέκνα τῆς ἐπαγγελίας. The one is a son only in the literal outward sense, the other not in a literal, but in a higher spiritual sense. The mothers of these two sons represent the two διαθῆκαι, or forms of religion, Hagar the Jerusalem that now is, Sarah the upper, heavenly Jerusalem. This upper Jerusalem, the free, is our mother : for we Christians are Christians simply in virtue of our Christian consciousness which assures us of our freedom from the law. Having this freedom, we belong to a διαθήκη essentially different from the Mosaic, Gal. iv. 22 *sq.*

When we consider the position which the apostle assigns to the law, and the terms he uses to describe its distinctive character, we see that the law is here degraded from its absolute value, and reduced to the rank of a subordinate stage. Thus we can easily understand how Gnostics of the most pronounced Antinomianism appealed to our apostle's authority. The law is given only for discipline and punishment, it is to act as a barrier, as a dam against men's constantly increasing transgressions, that they may not exceed all bounds. And the law has not proved adequate even for this negative task of prevention; the scripture and the law itself attest that under the law sin acquired an unlimited sway. The law then is there only to appear in its impotence as against the might of sin, which it has failed to subdue. The apostle has not further explained what in his view was the reason why the law was thus, as it appeared, so uselessly interposed between the promise and faith, as if to hold the two as far as possible asunder, and cause an interval to intervene before the promise was fulfilled in faith. But we are able to infer the thought which was present to his mind on this point, from his comparison of the law to a παιδαγωγὸς, a functionary who has only children to deal with. Then he calls the man who stands under the law an infant (minor) in a state of dependence, in which he differs nothing from a bondsman, and is under tutors and governors, and who cannot emerge from that state of pupilage and become the master of his inheritance until a certain fixed period. Gal. iv. 1 *sq.* In the same connexion it is said expressly that only when the time had come to its fulfilment, when this period had expired, did God send his Son. Considering this statement, and in conjunction with it the term στοιχεῖα τοῦ κόσμου which is applied to Judaism, Gal. iv. 3, we see that the apostle stands here at the standpoint of a great and wide historical view, in which he distinguishes two periods of the history of the world and of religion. The former of these, the ante-Messianic, as commonly distinguished in the Jewish view of history from the Messianic, he regards as in general the period of the *tirocinium* of the world or of the world's history, in which, as it must be at the beginning of everything that is to have a great history, all was yet rude and wild. This character, which the world as a whole possessed at that period, belonged also to the law : its *raison d'être* as a νόμος παιδαγωγὸς was to take the Jews under its hard discipline, and hold them there till the beginning of a new period of cosmic and religious history. This new period was that of spiritual freedom, in which the unfree servile condition had reached its term, and humanity, hitherto a pupil and in need of a tutor, had grown into a free and independent man. Short as the apostle's words are, they are so chosen as to exclude every thought of chance or caprice entering into this process. The apostle places himself within the process, one which had indeed been predetermined in God's decree, but which was nevertheless conditioned by the successive stages of a historical development, and in which no other cause than this was possible, since, as he indicates, humanity as a whole, no less than the individual man, is appointed to pass through certain periods of life. From this point of view the apostle recognised in the law simply a pedagogue appointed for the period of youth, and whose office was little more than to curb the wild outbreaks of sin. But the law proved unequal to this office, and simply demonstrated by its powerlessness the universality of the reign of sin. Thus in one aspect the apostle recognised in the law a mere παιδαγωγὸς, but, on the other hand, he looked at it in the light of a divine plan of education ; could he then rest satisfied with this merely external view of the law? We see from the Epistle to the Romans that he did not confine himself to this view of it ; and the harsher view of the law which we find in the Epistle to the Galatians is clear evidence that that work belongs to an earlier stage of the apostle's activity. To apprehend the deeper meaning of the law, it was necessary to regard it not as a mere instrument of correction thrust in externally between the ἐπαγγελία and πίστις, but as itself an essential and influential factor in the religious development under review. And this could only be through the assertion of a more inward relation between the law and sin. The object of the law was not now to be sought in the transgressions which stood over against it externally and existed independently of it and before it ; and its relation to which was one of mere repression and prevention : the trans-gressions must be referred to their principle, ἁμαρτία, and this latter could not be understood in its essence except in the light of the law. If the essence of sin be not what it is objectively, but what is subjective about it, the consciousness one has of it, then sin can only be realized through the law ; but as it is realized only in the element of consciousness, the law, in proportion as it brings it to reality, brings about also the inward possibility of its removal. Sin, being thus developed by the intervention of the law, comes to a head in the division of the man with himself which it brings about. Here the man realizes the whole power of sin ; but in this state of mind he is already inwardly loosed from it and turned towards the operation of grace. Thus the law is not merely an outward stage of the history of religion : it is an inward momentum in the de-velopment of the religious consciousness : it is the consciousness of sin turning in upon itself, and it fulfils its mission in the re-ligious development simply by appearing as the consciousness of sin to mediate between sin and grace. This is the apostle's stand-point in the Epistle to the Romans, where it is said of the law not merely that it τῶν παραβάσεων χάριν προσετέθη, but that it is δύναμις τῆς ἁμαρτίας, and that because διὰ νόμου ἐπίγνωσις τῆς ἁμαρτίας.

We come now to heathenism and its relation to Judaism and Christianity. It might be thought that the principle stated by the apostle, Rom. v. 13, that where there is no law sin is not imputed, furnished us with his moral estimate of heathenism. But, on the one hand, the universality of death attests the universality of the reign of sin among the heathens also ; and, on the other hand, if they were judged incapable of having sin imputed to them, this would not elevate them in the scale of moral and religious life, it

would, on the contrary, degrade them in that scale ; for unconsciousness of sin must necessarily be followed at some time or other by
consciousness of it. But the principle appealed to is not applicable
to heathenism ; though the heathens did not possess the Mosaic
Law, and were to that extent ἄνομοι (Rom. ii. 12, 1 Cor. ix. 21),
yet they were not absolutely without law. The place of a positive
law is supplied in their case by the natural moral consciousness,
which of itself informs them what they ought to do, and what to
leave undone, Rom. ii. 14 *sq.* Thus the same reign of sin is found
to prevail in heathenism as in Judaism, and even more strikingly
than there ; for the natural law could not be so effective a barrier
against transgressions as the positive law, and the reign of sin declares
itself in exhibitions of the grossest sensuality, which reduce heathenism morally far below the level of Judaism. But the characteristic
difference between Judaism and heathenism is not to be looked for
on this moral side, where both alike fall to be included under the
idea of sin. The essential conception of heathenism is that it is
a declension from the true idea of God, a denial and perversion of
the original consciousness of God. There is an original and universal revelation of God to humanity in which the heathens shared,
which comes from nature and history as well as from conscience,
and which was sufficient to make them acquainted with the nature
of God, so far as it can be the object of human apprehension. It
is therefore entirely their own fault that they did not preserve
and complete the knowledge which God himself had thus given
them of his true nature. This is a moral delinquency to be charged
to their own free-will, the source of which is to be looked for
mainly in their ingratitude, Rom. i. 21. But when once through
their own free-will they had turned away from the true God, their
thought and imagination could not but turn from the truly existent to the non-existent, the vain, the empty shadow. Their consciousness being no longer enlightened by the true idea of God, fell
into an obscurity which not only debarred them from seeing the
true, but caused them to set the false in the place of the true.
Wanting the true knowledge of God they wanted also the absolute

principle of truth; they could place the standard of truth nowhere
but in themselves, and so they came to regard their own thoughts
and imaginations as the highest wisdom. Φάσκοντες εἶναι σοφοὶ
ἐμωράνθησαν, says the apostle, Rom. i. 22, obviously with reference
to the Hellenic philosophy or culture. He saw in this philosophy
a knowledge that was nothing more than subjective, devoid of all
objective truth, sprung from the turbid source of human egoism.
For, of course, heathenism could not be simply the negation of the
true idea of God; it necessarily set up something else to take the
name and honour of the absolute, in place of the true Absolute
whom it denied. Though the absolute contents of the idea of God
had vanished from consciousness, yet there remained behind the
formal postulate that there must be something absolute. Hence
heathenism is not merely a turning away from the true Absolute,
but the perversion of it to its opposite ; it is the falsehood that that
which is essentially finite and transitory is the absolute itself.
This is the character of the heathen idol-worship, in which the
δόξα which properly belongs to the absolute God alone is transferred to finite beings, and the latter are substituted, as a spurious
likeness, for the former. Heathenism, as the apostle apprehends
it, is the theoretical confusion of the finite with the absolute, the
identification of the true, the real, which is the nature of none but
God himself, with the untrue, the unreal, the lie,—the placing of
the creature on the level of the Creator. As the radical error of
heathenism is an unnatural transposition of the true natural order
of the universe, so its practical outcome in the moral life of man
could be nothing but a perversion of the natural relations.
Heathenism and Judaism both fall under the common term
ἁμαρτία ; the difference between them is the difference between
sin and vice : vice differing from sin in this, that it is not merely
the transgression of a specific injunction, which may have reference
to a merely outward act, but an inward immorality, a degradation,
disgrace, the pollution of the man's nature. This is what the
apostle means in the words, Rom. i. 24, παρέδωκεν αὐτοὺς ὁ Θεὸς ...
εἰς ἀκαθαρσίαν (verse 26 : εἰς πάθη ἀτιμίας) τοῦ ἀτιμάζεσθαι τὰ

σώματα αὐτῶν ἐν ἑαυτοῖς. In enumerating the heathen vices, the apostle gives precedence to those, as most characteristic of heathenism, in which the unnatural perversion of the order of nature appears most clearly, verses 26, 27. He deduces this practical perversion from that theoretical perversion of the consciousness which all heathenism exhibited, verse 28. And as they did not like to retain God in their knowledge, God gave them over to a reprobate mind, so that they did what is not convenient. The moral self-debasement into which they sank was the natural, and in so far divinely ordained, consequence of the inadequate relation which their religious consciousness sustained to the idea of God. This view of heathenism followed of necessity from the idea with which the apostle started, and which is the corner-stone of his whole thinking on the subject, that it is an apostasy from the true idea of God, which arises out of a moral aversion of the will from him.

Striking and profound as the apostle's description and explanation of heathenism are, yet to trace it altogether to moral perversity is only half the truth. There is another and an equally essential consideration to be added, namely, that this moral deflection could never have gone so far if the consciousness of God had been clearer and deeper to begin with. When all the elements are considered which go to make up the conception of the heathen religion, this must not be forgotten, that the consciousness of God originally present in it was not so deep and clear as elsewhere, that it laboured from the beginning under this radical defect, and stood in a position from which it had yet to develop itself, by working itself clear of the natural element with which it was entangled. At Rom. i. 19 *sq.*, where he is concerned with a moral estimate of heathenism, the apostle devotes himself chiefly to the first of these two sides ; but the other was not necessarily excluded, since he distinguishes different stages and periods of the religious development of mankind. We saw from Gal. iii. 19 *sq.*, iv. 1 *sq.*, that he regarded Judaism from this point of view, and so we might expect that he would look at heathenism in the same way. Accordingly we find that in that section of the Galatian Epistle he expressly

comprehends heathenism and Judaism in one term which places
them both at the same subordinate stage in the development of
religion.   There can be no doubt that this is the force of the expression used, Gal. iv. 3, 9, τὰ στοιχεῖα τοῦ κόσμου.   The στοιχεῖα
τοῦ κόσμου are not the elements as the ultimate principles of the
world in a physical sense, but the elements as beginnings of instruction, appropriate for those who are still νήπιοι, still in the age of childhood.   The στοιχεῖα must certainly include the law : and as the
νήπιοι for whom the στοιχεῖα are designed have already been placed
(iv. 1) in the category of bondsmen, the apostle is here characterizing the relation to the στοιχεῖα as a relation of bondage.   Yet
the point of view from which the law is regarded in the expression
στοιχεῖα is different from that where it is called a παιδαγωγὸς.
There is at any rate something more than mere discipline and punishment ; here the law is not merely for this negative purpose, but
also for the positive end of instruction.   The νήπιος is to be instructed, as befits his age, in the first elements.   As for the words
τοῦ κόσμου, the writer is treating of the periods of religious development, and κόσμος can only signify cosmic or religious history.   The
primary elements in which the νήπιος is instructed are the elements
and beginnings of the world itself at the very beginning of its history, when it was in a state still rude and imperfect, and the forms
it had assumed were hard and severe.   It is true that the law is
the first and most important of these στοιχεῖα τοῦ κόσμου ; but
that is only in so far as it is regarded generally under the aspect
of a religious development which still bears the features of a rude
beginning.   Thus it is probable that the apostle meant to include
in the στοιχεῖα τοῦ κόσμου both Judaism and heathenism.   In verse
9, however, there can be no doubt that this is so.   Here he is addressing Gentile Christians whom Jews were seeking to influence
in the direction of Judaism.   He calls their leaning towards
Judaism a return to those στοιχεῖα, weak and beggarly elements,
as he terms them, because there is nothing in them from which a
strong spiritual life could be evolved.   Where God is not yet
known as a spirit, where religion is occupied with nothing but

the material, sensual, carnal (for this is the idea of the στοιχεῖα), there all is dead and empty, there is no true vital principle, the religion is void of spiritual contents. These two religions are at the most elementary stage of religion ; they are occupied with the material, not with the spiritual ; they place the essence of religion in things which belong entirely to the region of the physical life. The στοιχεῖα are thus the first beginnings, the elements of religion, and the word conveys further the impression that this elementary religion is occupied with nothing higher than the elements, principles, and substances of the outward physical life. Judaism contained many of those purely natural elements : it also was bound to the natural, the material, as to days, months, fixed times ; thus it also was a nature-religion, based upon those physical στοιχεῖα, the natural being invested as such with religious significance. The στοιχεῖα, then, the elements of religion[1] of which the apostle speaks

---

[1] The meaning generally given to στοιχεῖα, elements of religion, or beginnings of religious knowledge, is asserted by Neander to be inadmissible, because Paul would then be indicating by it a common conception, applicable to a certain extent to heathenism and Judaism equally (Pl. and Tr. i. 465). "But how," he says, "could this agree with the views of Paul, who regarded Judaism as indeed a subordinate and preparatory stage of religion, but yet as one founded on a divine revelation ; who saw in heathenism, on the other hand, that is, in idolatry, of which he is speaking here, not a subordinate stage of religion, but a thing entirely foreign to the nature of religion, a suppression, brought about by sin, of the original knowledge of God ?" He proposes, instead, the following interpretation : the entanglement of religion in sensuous forms, that is, her state of servitude under the elements of the world, is what is common to Judaism and heathenism. But we must ask if this be not as much as the other a common conception, applicable to a certain extent to Judaism and heathenism equally ? What difference is there logically between the one interpretation and the other ? And what difficulty is there in supposing that Paul placed heathenism on one side on the same level with Judaism, and on another side beneath it ? [In his Neutest. Theol., 171, Baur adheres only to one side of the above interpretation of στοιχεῖα τοῦ κόσμου (on the meaning of the term in the Epistle to the Colossians, vide p. 30). He says there that the στοιχεῖα τοῦ κόσμου are physical elements and substances as the basis of the heathen nature-religion, that is, the constellations : that in many things, in its symbols and ceremonies, its feasts, and its sumptuary laws, and in many other ordinances, such as circumcision, Judaism had the same physical character ; that the radical ideas of both, the principle of the religious consciousness in both, were so much bound up in the natural, the material, the sensuous, as to place man before God in no higher relation than that of bondage :

O

here, are the physical elements, which were reckoned objects of reverence in both religions, the Jewish and the heathen, and served in a slavish and unspiritual way.

Though this be so, yet heathenism stands far below Judaism : for the latter consists not only in the στοιχεῖα, but also in the law, and in the promises which stand above the law. Heathenism has indeed a law in itself, yet it is essentially different from the law ; and in the same way it is a religion, and yet no religion, because the conception of religion is only realized in the form of revelation. Thus Judaism, negative as its relation to Christianity is, is yet on the same line with Christianity in this,—that it is a διαθήκη, a special institution of God, through which he has entered on a definite relation towards man. There is an old and there is a new διαθήκη, 2 Cor. iii. 6, 14, and the two διαθῆκαι are so closely and so essentially connected, that the new could not have come into existence without the old. It is true that circumcision has no religious significance for the Christian ; yet the way from heathenism to Christianity does, in a certain aspect, lie through Judaism ; it is impossible to understand the new διαθήκη without being acquainted with the old. This explains to us why when the apostle speaks of the Old Testament in his Epistles he makes no distinction between the Judæo-Christian and the Gentile-Christian sections of his readers ; and how, even when addressing Gentile Christians, he does not scruple to call the members of the old dispensation their fathers, 1 Cor. x. 1, thus indicating how in his view the two dispensations formed one connected whole. This is the essential advantage which Judaism has over heathenism, περιτομή over ἀκροβυστία. Though there is no distinction between Jews and Gentiles in their relation to Christianity, though in this respect the two are precisely equal, yet as soon as a comparison is instituted between the two, the Ἰουδαῖος is preferred to the Ἕλλην, Rom. i. 16. The Jew stands at a higher stage of religious consciousness,

so that in neither religion was God known as a spirit. In this he follows Schneckenburger : was sind die στοιχ. τ. κ. Theol. Jahrb. vii. 1848, p. 445 sq.— Editor.]

or, as the apostle defines the superiority of the περιτομὴ to the ἀκροβυστία, Rom. iii. 2, ἐπιστεύθησαν τὰ λόγια τοῦ Θεοῦ τῇ περιτομῇ. This, it is evident, does not refer to circumcision as such, but to Judaism as the religion of the circumcised. There is committed to Judaism something that heathenism does not possess. There is a peculiar treasure deposited in Judaism for preservation. God has declared himself in it in a special manner ; or, in a word, the religion it contains is the religion of revelation. Being the religion of revelation it is also the religion of the promise, in which that is contained in idea, which is realized in Christianity. It is to the Israelites that the sonship belongs, and the visible presence of God, the covenants, and the giving of the law, and the service of God, and the promises ; to whom belong the fathers, of whom Christ came according to the flesh ; wherefore God who is exalted above all is to be blessed for ever, Rom. ix. 4, 5. This also is part of that relation of identity in which Judaism stands to Christianity, that in it everything that is distinctive and valuable in Christianity is already contained typically, symbolically, allegorically. The baptism of the Israelites unto Moses is a type of Christian baptism. The food and drink with which they were supplied in the wilderness is a type of the Christian supper, 1 Cor. x. 1 *sq.* ; the slain paschal lamb is a type of Christ killed at the feast of Passover, 1 Cor. v. 7. Thus Judaism is related to Christianity as the type to the antitype.

SIXTH CHAPTER.

CHRISTIANITY AS A NEW PRINCIPLE IN THE WORLD'S
HISTORICAL DEVELOPMENT.

THE relation of Christianity to heathenism and Judaism is, as we have seen, defined as that between the absolute religion and the preparatory and subordinate forms of religion. We have here the progress from servitude to freedom, from nonage to majority, from the age of childhood to the age of maturity, from the flesh to the spirit. The state left behind is one in which the divine spirit is so little apprehended, that those dwelling in it are without any higher guiding principle : this is heathenism, 1 Cor. xii. 2, 3 : or it is the torturing conflict between the law and sin, beyond which Judaism can never pass. The state now reached is a truly spiritual consciousness charged with its own proper contents and at one with itself. It is only in Christianity that man can feel himself lifted up into the region of the spirit and of the spiritual life : it is only here that his relation to God is that of spirit to spirit. Christianity is essentially the religion of the spirit, and where the spirit is there is liberty and light, the clear and unshadowed identity of the spirit with itself. Now what Christianity thus is as the absolute religion it is only through Christ. And the explanation can only be found in Christ, how the transition is effected from the first period, including heathenism and Judaism, to the second. This of itself, of course, should warn us not to think of a transition lying in the nature of the case and proceeding naturally out of it. In the apostle's view Christ's entrance into the world and into the life of humanity is a thing entirely supernatural. Christianity comes into existence by God's sending his Son. Yet this does not prevent the apostle from regarding the appearance of Christ and of Christianity in the light of a process developing itself in history and advancing through various stages. In all those contrasts in the light of which Christianity is regarded, as that between servitude and freedom, nonage and majority, sin and grace, death and life, the first and the second Adam, we trace the idea of an immanent process of development, proceeding by the conflict of mutually reacting momenta. Supernatural though the appearance of Christianity is, it is not entirely incomprehensible. It is to be comprehended, in part philosophically, from the essential inward connexion of one momentum with another, and in part historically, from the historical conditions in which it appeared. As for the first, Christianity is the natural outcome of the process in which sin grows by the operation of the law into the consciousness of sin ; for this is the necessary condition for the approach of grace. The latter is most clearly stated by the apostle in the passage Gal. iv. 4. When the fulness of the time was come, God sent his Son, as one γενόμενον ἐκ γυναικὸς, γενόμενον ὑπὸ νόμον, ἵνα τοὺς ὑπὸ νόμον ἐξαγοράσῃ, ἵνα τὴν υἱοθεσίαν ἀπολάβωμεν. That is to say, that God placed the man Jesus when he destined him to be the Messiah, or the Son of God, in that historical crisis where the fulness of the time was to ensue and the one period was to pass over into the other. On this account he was to be essentially man, and to enter into the world just as any other man, as one γενόμενος ἐκ γυναικὸς. This expression for being born as man does not directly exclude a supernatural generation, but in the connexion it certainly seems very unlikely that such an idea was entertained. He who is born of a woman is simply a man coming into existence in the ordinary and natural way. He is γενόμενος ἐκ γυναικὸς, and he is γενόμενος ὑπὸ νόμον ; he bears the impress and character of the στοιχεῖα τοῦ κόσμου. The apostle's idea seems to be that since the transition from one period to another was to be made in his person, it was necessary that he should represent the first period in his own person. As he entered at his birth into the conditions of humanity, he stood also under the law : the law made the same claim on him that it makes on all other men. Indeed he became the curse of the law, but not on his own account,—it was that by dying on account of the curse and discharging the claims of the law, he might bring in freedom from the law and make men children of God, υἱοὶ Θεοῦ. He himself is in a special sense the υἱὸς Θεοῦ : for in him humanity rises to the consciousness of unity with God, in him there is for humanity the principle of its new existence, where it is not servile, but free, not under guardianship, but of full age. Thus as it belongs to human nature that the man passes from the restrictions of infancy and youth to the independence of maturity, from the unfree to the free, from the servant to the son, so Christ entered into humanity as a Son at the time appointed for that event, that is, when humanity had arrived at its maturity. In this view Christianity is not merely a thing that has been imported into humanity from without ; whatever conception be formed of Christ's person, Christianity is a stage of the religious development of the world which has proceeded from a principle that is internal and immanent in humanity. Christianity is reached by the progress of the spirit to the freedom of its own self-consciousness, and humanity cannot arrive at this period till it has traversed that of unfreedom and servitude. Christ as the principle of this period of human development is the second Adam over against the first. This antithesis as much as the others suggests that Christianity is one of the stages of an immanent process of development. This antithesis contains the main ideas with which we are concerned in this chapter.

In the period of the first Adam sin and death are the ruling powers. Death is the wages of sin : that is, so certainly as a man sins, so certainly does he also die. The universal reign of death is what chiefly distinguishes the first period from the second. But do not men die in the second period just as much as in the first ? And if death comes because of sin and is the punishment which sin deserves and draws after it, then how can the apostle say, as he does, Rom. iii. 25, that God has left unpunished the sins committed before Christ ? If men died during that period, then their death paid the penalty their sins had incurred and they required no other means of expiation. And if the death of Christ be a means of expiation set up by God, available to all men for the forgiveness of their sins, if sin has ceased to have such a hold on men that nothing but their death can discharge the penalty of it, and the power of death which reigned throughout the first period is thus broken in the second, then those who have received into themselves the grace bestowed in Christ and therein the justification by which life is imparted, should not die in this latter period. But if they do die in this period as much as in the former, then what is the difference between the two ? Or are we to understand the long-suffering which God manifested in the first period to have consisted in this : that he did not suffer the human race to die out altogether, and that the dead were always succeeded by the living ? But this is the case in the second period as well, and we fail to see in what sense it is true that the one period is distinguished from the other by death being the dominating principle of the one and life of the other. The solution of this difficulty lies in an accurate apprehension of what the apostle means by the words ζωή and θάνατος. He uses these words in a double sense, as including both the physical and the ethical, and neither of these two spheres is thought of without an implicit reference to the one and original element in which both have their common root. Death and life stand over against each other as the first and the second Adam. In the first Adam men die, in the second they rise to life, those namely who believe in him. From this qualification of the statement, that only those rise who believe in him, we see how the physical notion of life and the ethical are interwoven. If it be said that men die in the first Adam, the death here spoken of is first of all physical death ; they die because sin runs its course in them and is followed by death, the wages of sin. But this is merely the physical death to which man is liable at any rate in virtue of his bodily constitution, and which is not necessarily the extinction of his whole existence. Why should so great importance be attached to death in this sense ? This arises from the Jewish view of the nature and office of the body as an essential element of the human personality. Without the body man is in this view without any material basis for his existence ; if death asserts its power over his body, then the power of death reigns over him in his entirety ; all the privations bound up in the idea of death are now realized in him ; there is no longer any life for him, nor any salvation, nor any connexion with the kingdom of God.   And if death is not to be the total severance of this connexion, if he is to look for a life worth having after death, then he must be assured of this point first of all, that death has no power entirely to destroy his physical life.   Hence the great importance which the resurrection of Jesus possesses for the Christian consciousness.   It is the positive and actual evidence of a power of life by which death is overcome.   Physical death is abolished by physical life : in the resurrection of Jesus a new principle of life has entered into humanity.

But physical death is not merely the natural end of life : it also results as the wages of sin under God's decree of condemnation. Thus the life imparted to humanity through the resurrection of Jesus must be something more than physical life.   Over against the κατάκριμα of death there stands, as the apostle says in a pregnant expression, Rom. v. 18, the δικαίωσις ζωῆς.   That is to say, the life given to humanity in the resurrection of Jesus is co-extensive with the change which transfers a man from the state of sin into the state of justification ; it comes in that change, and so is more than physical life, though it includes that also—it is life in the fullest and truest sense.   But the chief evidence that there is such a life, in which death is conquered and abolished, is the great fact of the resurrection of Jesus.   The apostle regards the resurrection as the principal doctrine of the Christian faith.   He writes to the Corinthians, 1 Cor. xv. 3, that among the chief points of the doctrine which had been delivered to him, and which he had communicated to them, were these : that Christ died for our sins according to the Scriptures, and was buried, and that he rose again on the third day.   Now that Jesus rose again after his death is an outward historical fact, from which Christianity derives its objective historical character.   In virtue of this fact it is the λόγος τοῦ σταυροῦ, a doctrine founded on a distinct historical basis, and thereby essentially different from such truth as is evolved from pure reason, 1 Cor. i. 18.   It is therefore all-important that that fact should be properly authenticated ; and the apostle brings forward evidence on the subject, appealing to the appearances of Jesus both to the older apostles and to himself.   One great function of the apostles in their preaching of the Gospel is to be witnesses of the resurrection of Jesus, 1 Cor. xv. 15.   But the resurrection is something more than this single historical fact : it also involves a general truth.   For if it were in itself impossible that the dead should rise, then Christ could not have risen.   Christ's resurrection therefore has made it clear and certain to us that resurrection from the dead is possible, that there is such a resurrection.   This knowledge is due to Christianity ; nor is its connexion with Christianity a merely outward or accidental one ; Christianity as a whole is based upon the fact that a resurrection from the dead is possible, and that it has actually come to pass in Christ.   If Christ be not risen, the apostle says, verse 17, then the faith that Christians have is vain and delusive : then there is no forgiveness of sins, and the guilt of sin is not removed from us ; hence the Christians who have fallen asleep are lost.   Death reigns over them with the same dominion which it exercised from Adam to Christ : then there are no more miserable men than Christians are,—they have much to suffer for their faith, and their hope in Christ is limited to this world, there is no hope in him beyond.   If the death of the body be not done away, if death as the end of this life be not succeeded by another life, then there is no power of life to overcome the mortality of man.   Inspiriting and blessed as the Christian faith is even for the present, with its assurance of mercy, of justification, and of atonement with God, yet it is always liable to be disturbed and darkened by the thought of the death which is coming to the body ; and there is no way out of this darkness and perplexity unless the Christian can become assured that out of the death of the body he will rise again to a new life.   Even the spiritual life, which is the contents of the Christian consciousness, would be no true life at all, if it were not at the same time a physical life. Without the resurrection of the body the personality cannot continue, and the spiritual life of Christianity must embrace this, and bring the Christian the assurance that he will continue to exist with the same personality as at present. Christianity is therefore meaningless, and its absolute idea is untrue except in the light of this fact—that there is a resurrection of the dead. It is not only that Christ rose from the dead —he could not have risen if resurrection were in itself impossible,— but that what happened in his case is also to happen to all others.

Thus in Christ and through his resurrection a new principle has been introduced into humanity ; that principle has to be developed in humanity. This is what the apostle means when he says that Christ was raised up from the dead as the ἀπαρχὴ τῶν κεκοιμη- μένων. As death reigns over the period beginning with Adam, so the new principle of life which appeared in Christ rules over the second period. The two periods and principles agree in this, that, Adam and Christ are both human, since Christ is a man as much as Adam ; the one principle as well as the other is immanent in humanity. Christ as much as Adam belongs essentially to humanity, is subject to all its conditions and part of its history, and hence it is, that the principle which he brought in becomes incorporate with and a living power in humanity. As then in Adam all die, so in Christ shall all be made alive, verse 22. They are made alive in him because of their common nature with him, because he, who has in himself the principle of life, is a man like them. Now how are we to account for this sweeping statement, " All shall be made alive "? On the one side, only those who are in Christ are made alive ; on the other side, the life is spoken of as co-extensive with the death in Adam. The reason of this is that the physical and the ethical idea of life are not held apart from each other. The life that comes from Christ is the life of the resurrection, and therefore a physical life ; but, on the other hand, only those can obtain it who have the spiritual life that is awakened by faith in Christ. The life which comes from Christ, then, is a thing which is mediated by the spiritual life of faith, and must be life in the highest sense, the blessed life. The being made alive would thus seem to mean nothing more or less than salvation. But it is asserted of all universally, and this plainly implies the apostle's belief that the principle which has come to actuality in Christ is of sufficient energy and power to quicken all men for the resurrection to the blessed life. His whole argument on the subject leads to this conclusion. Adam and Christ are related to each other as death and life, as dying and rising again. The same human nature which perishes in the one rises again in the other. In contrasting Adam and Christ with each other as the physical and the spiritual principle, the apostle goes on to show that the one cannot exist without the other, that the two things, death and resurrection, are essential momenta in one and the same process of development. For so it is written, he says, verse 45, " The first man Adam·was made a living soul, the last Adam was made a quickening spirit. Howbeit that was not first which is spiritual, but that which is psychical ; and afterward that which is spiritual. The first man was of the earth, earthy ; the second man is the Lord from heaven. As the earthy was, so are they that are earthy ; and as the heavenly was, so are they that are heavenly. And as we have borne the image of the earthy, we shall also bear the image of the heavenly. For flesh and blood cannot inherit the kingdom of God ; nor can the corruptible inherit incorruption." There is thus not only a material earthly life, but also a spiritual, heavenly life ; not only a physical, but also a pneumatical Adam. Some think that as the apostle is discussing the resurrection he must be speaking merely of the bodily constitution of the first man, with a view to showing that there are different kinds of bodies, higher and lower, physical and pneumatical, and that man rises from the lower to the higher. The human race, the apostle is thought to argue, is first endowed with an earthly body after the type of the first man, and only at a later period does it attain to a higher, more than earthly nature, after the type of the Redeemer, *i.e.* of his glorified body. The present human body, then, is to be changed and glorified. But this is not what the apostle is saying. It is not only the bodily structure that he is thinking of when he calls the first Adam a living soul, and the second a quickening spirit,—the one psychical and earthy, the other spiritual and heavenly. He is thinking of the whole personality of the two. This is quite clear when we remember how he does not regard the resurrection as being merely the restoration of the body, but as that state of higher greater life of which the glorified body is to be the seat.[1] The resurrection does not consist, in his view, in a change of the human body taking place instantaneously at a certain crisis through a supernatural operation of God. This was the unspiritual Jewish view. But to the apostle the resurrection is a form, a stage, of life, to which the whole system of organic life, natural and human, bears witness. He adduces the following arguments to show the possibility of the resurrection. 1. That nature presents us with phenomena precisely analogous to it, changes in which new life springs from death and corruption in the same individual. The most appropriate symbol of the resurrection is the seed-corn which dies and yet lives again, verses 36-38. 2. Nature presents to us a great multiplicity and diversity of bodies or existences, some less perfect, and some much more perfect. Hence we conclude that man also may have not only a mortal but an immortal nature, verses 39-43. 3. The two elements that make up man's nature being the ψυχὴ and the πνεῦμα (ψυχὴ here as the sensuous part, and including the σὰρξ, the ψυχικὸς being equivalent to the σαρκικὸς), and the two opposite sides of human nature which are combined to a unity in him, being represented by Adam and Christ, the first and the second, the earthly and the heavenly man, the relation of the

---

[1] When the apostle says, 1 Cor. xv. 44, σπείρεται σῶμα ψυχικόν, ἐγείρεται σῶμα πνευματικόν· ἔστι σῶμα ψυχικόν, καὶ ἔστι σῶμα πνευματικόν, this refers to the whole personality and substance of the man in the two distinct periods. It is not to be overlooked that σῶμα is to the apostle a different thing from σὰρξ, and a much higher thing. He knows of no resurrection of the σὰρξ ; the σὰρξ is no part of the man's personality after the resurrection. Those who resurge exist only in a σῶμα πνευματικόν ; σῶμα is thus to the apostle the concrete form in which the substance of any being's existence is contained.

present life to the future cannot be conceived to be anything else than an advance from the psychical life to the pneumatical. If in his present state man stands at the stage of the psychical life, what is more natural than that this subordinate stage should be succeeded by a higher, should develop into the stage of the pneumatical life? (verse 44.)

Now the contrast drawn by the apostle between Adam and Christ is not merely that they are the antagonist principles of life and death, and that in the one men die, and in the other rise again. They are also the representatives, the one as ψυχή, the other as πνεῦμα, of the two great historical periods in which the life of humanity runs its course. The collective life of mankind is treated here after the analogy of the individual life. As with the individual the psychical element predominates in the earlier period of life, the spiritual principle being quite undeveloped as yet, though of course not wholly wanting; and as this psychical period is succeeded by another in which the spiritual principle asserts itself more and more, till in the man's full and mature age when he has reached the freedom of the spiritual self-consciousness, it gains complete ascendency,—so is it with humanity. The two periods are determined by their respective principles, Adam and Christ. In the first period it is only the psychical, sensual, carnal, side of human nature, that side which suffers the dominion of sin, that comes to the surface. In the second the spiritual is the predominating principle, the whole thoughts, desires, and actions of men are determined by it. If human history be thus divided into two periods represented by and depending on Adam and Christ respectively, then we reach two important conclusions on the nature of these two periods. 1. The apostle does not seek to deduce the sin of Adam and of his posterity from any other source than their own free-will; yet, at the same time, he could not altogether escape from the idea that the reign of sin during the first period was simply the natural predominance of the sensuous side of human nature at the time. The relation of the two elements of human nature to each other dictated a certain course which the development of humanity could not but follow: no other course was possible. An earthly sensual man, as Adam was, he lacked the strength required to master the sensual impulses of his nature and to resist the tendency to sin which was inherent in his constitution. Abstractly his free-will may have been competent for such an effort, yet his will was insufficiently informed by motives, many of which could only be supplied by the reason and the spiritual sensitiveness to be reached at a later stage. This predominance of sense, this impotence of the moral will, this tendency to sin, were a part of human nature from the beginning, and the apostle does not suggest in the remotest way that this was a result of the sin of the first man. Indeed he cannot have thought so; for if Adam was to stand in such a contrast with Christ, he must have been essentially ψυχικὸς and ἐκ γῆς χοϊκὸς. 2. As Adam represents this side of human nature, and is its principle and the common root of all those in whom it is predominant, so we behold in Christ the principle of the other, spiritual side of human nature. This contrast of the two principles, however, shows us that it is something more than the resurrection and the state to follow it in the future, and the abolition it involves of the death inherited from Adam, that Christ is regarded as procuring. What is obtained through him is the higher spiritual consciousness of man, awakened by Christ and invested with permanent authority and power. Christ is the principle of this consciousness, and the reason why the apostle speaks of it as a resurrection still in the future, is that the victory ·of the new principle over the old, of life over death, is most vividly represented in that form. The power of the new principle, moreover, can be best recognised and appreciated when viewed in its effects in the future world and in bringing about the final consummation. These future results throw a strong light back on the beginnings of Christianity, and show the immense importance of the epoch in the development of humanity which Christ brought about. The principle which has been brought to light in Christ is thus of infinite extension: and it is also infinite intensively as realized by the individual. It is the infinite Christian consciousness, as a truly spiritual consciousness. The apostle expressly calls the principle with which Christ stands over against Adam, pneumatical, and that though he is speaking of the resurrection. But the ideas of physical and spiritual life are so closely interwoven here, that the Christian principle could not be the principle of the resurrection, save in virtue of what it is in itself. The Christian principle includes and proceeds upon faith in Christ, on the assurance of reconciliation and unity with God, on the fellowship of the spirit, whose communications are the beginning and the condition of the whole new relation ; and it lifts the Christian up so high in the religious life, that all things give place to the idea of the absolute with which he is inspired : he knows that neither death nor life, neither things present nor things to come, can separate him from the love of God in Christ Jesus. In this absolute consciousness he already possesses that life which is superior to everything worldly, fleeting, and finite ; and all that remains is that this life should manifest itself outwardly and extensively in the resurrection of the body.

In order to understand how the physical and the spiritual elements are both comprehended and united in this life of which Christ is the principle, we have only to remember that the apostle represents the development of this life as the continued negation of the opposite principle of death. It is in the victory it achieves over death that its power and energy are manifested. To the Christian consciousness death is already abolished ; it remains that it should be abolished in outward fact. The resurrection is not merely a life given to men by Christ at a certain definite point of time : it is a life which men receive now, and which carries with it the triumph of life over death. Each stage in the development of this principle is thus a stage in the victory over death. Every man rises again in his own order, the apostle says, verse 23. There are therefore several distinct stages of the process. The first negation of death is the resurrection of Christ himself, for he is risen from the dead as the firstfruits of them that slept : the principle is identical with his person, and he was necessarily the first in whom it proved its power to conquer death. The second negation of death is the resurrection of those who belong to Christ, at his coming. At the Parousia of Christ, those who are dead rise again, those who are still living at the time are changed. Though they have not yet died and fallen under death's dominion, yet the principle of death is in them, and they would necessarily succumb to it sooner or later. In them also, therefore, death has to be overcome, the mortal in them has to be transmuted into immortality, else they cannot share that life which begins with the resurrection for those who rise. Flesh and blood cannot inherit the kingdom of God, nor can the corruptible, this material and sensuous life which is composed of earthly elements, inherit incorruption. On this account the apostle designates as a mystery what was an unavoidable feature of his view of the future life as a post-resurrection life. It was a mystery in so far as it was not clearly realized—that all would not have died at the time of Christ's coming, but that all would undergo a transformation (since the resurrection is also a transformation); in a moment, in the twinkling of an eye, at the last trump, as soon as it sounds, the dead will be raised incorruptible, and the living will be changed. For according to the order ordained by God, in which the whole process moves, from which the victory of the principle of life over the principle of death is to result, it cannot but be the case that this corruptible shall put on incorruption, and this mortal, immortality, 1 Cor. xv. 50-53. After the resurrection of the dead, and the transformation of the living, comes the end, the end of the whole present history ; then, that is to say, when Christ delivers up the kingdom to God and the Father, when he shall have destroyed every rule and every authority and power, for he must reign till he has put all his enemies under his feet. The last enemy that shall be destroyed is death, for he has put all things under his feet. But when it is said that all things are put under him, it is manifest that this means all things except him who put all things under him. And when all things are subdued under him, then shall he himself, the Son, subject himself also to him that put all things under him, that God may be all in all : vv. 24-28. It is very evident that the apostle here regards the whole history of the world and men as the scene of the conflict of two principles, one of which has sway at first, but is then attacked and conquered and entirely destroyed by the other. The first of these principles is death ; the history of the world begins with this one, and comes to a close when death, and with death the entire dualism of which the course of history is the development, has entirely disappeared from it. In order to break the might of the principle of death, Christ appeared at the time appointed him as the Son of God the Father. God caused him, as it were, to issue from himself, enters in him into the process of history, and subjects himself in him to the limitations of the world in its subjection to the principle of death ; that in the finite the principle of infinity may be born and appear, and the world of death be changed into the world of life. The power of the death-principle is broken by the resurrection of Jesus, yet the life-principle cannot assert its full supremacy as long as the world's history still goes on in time. Thus the common division of history into the ante-Messianic and the Messianic period is replaced in the apostle's mind by the higher view that we are now in the αἰὼν οὖτος, and that the αἰὼν μέλλων is to follow it. Now is the world of opposition and of struggle : Christ bears rule in the name of God, but only that he may subdue all hostile powers in which the principle of death continues to assert itself. The world to come is the higher world where the battle between life and death has been fought out, and the victory is complete ; where every jar is stilled. Here the eternal and absolute God, who stands above all, takes back into himself, out of the historical process in which the world he had created stood over against him, all that is his, and embraces it all in the eternal unity of his own undivided essence. If the conflict of the two principles, life and death, be now concluded, and transformed to unity, then Christ, who is identical with the principle of life, cannot be any longer outside of God,—he must be in God. The opposition through which God sought to bring about the unity of

P

the world with himself has now come to an end, and there is no longer any need of mediation or of a mediator. Corruption has put on incorruption, the mortal has put on immortality, and the words of Scripture are fulfilled: death is swallowed up in victory; death is robbed of its sting. The apostle adds, The sting of death is sin,.and the strength of sin is the law; but the victory is given through the Lord Jesus Christ. In these words he recapitulates the momenta through which the transition from the one principle to the other takes place inwardly as well as outwardly. The mediation consists, in a word, in this : that the life in which death is overcome and abolished is the δικαίωσις ζωῆς (Rom. v. 18).

Here we might ask if God's being all-in-all is held to imply the final cessation of evil by the conversion of the wicked and of the devil. The question might be answered in different ways, but is of slight importance. It makes little difference in the main, whether the evil powers continue to exist in a state of entire exhaustion and impotence, or whether they be at last attracted by the irresistible power of good. Whatever be thought on the question, it must be perfectly clear that if death is to be robbed of his last sting, then there can be no eternal punishment.

Among the changes to take place in this development of the world's history there are two which we may mention specially. They are connected with the great final catastrophe, one in the physical, the other in the moral world. The first is the transfiguration of external nature spoken of by the apostle, Rom. viii. 19 *sq.* Nature is to be set free from the vanity and finiteness to which she has been made subject, and to be raised to the state of liberty which is the glory of the sons of God. Thus external nature also is one day to wear the likeness of that unshadowed Christian consciousness which is at one with itself and God, and is absolved from every limitation. The other occurrence which the apostle expects from the future is the conversion of the Jews. The blindness of a part of the Jews, he says, Rom. xi. 25, will last only till the fulness of the Gentiles be come in to the Christian body. Then all Israel will be saved. If this is to happen only after the conversion of all the Gentiles, then it must be at the end, just before the Parousia, and the general resurrection. And the apostle expected that he himself would live to see the Parousia! What mighty events did he compress into the immediate future! But he has not given his reasons for these two expectations, nor did he make definite doctrines of them.

SEVENTH CHAPTER.

FAITH, LOVE, AND HOPE, AS THE THREE MOMENTA OF CHRISTIAN
CONSCIOUSNESS.

THE process of the world's history is thus divided into two great
periods, with Adam at the head of the first and Christ at the head
of the second. The first comes to an end in the present world;
the second has its beginning here, but stretches into the infinite
beyond of the world to come. The Christian consciousness is
similarly divided between the two elements of the past and of
the future. It goes back in Adam to the past, and follows the
whole process of the history that lies between Adam and Christ;
and in Christ it directs its view to the most distant future, reaches
out to the consummation of all things, and finds its rest in the
result that lies behind that consummation, in God who has then
become all in all. As directed to the past, the Christian consciousness is Christian faith; as directed to the future, it is
Christian hope. Christian faith must of necessity be directed to
the past. It is indeed the living present consciousness of Christ's
dwelling in us through his spirit; yet the proper object of faith
is something that has happened, that is past, and in this instance
it is the death of Christ upon the cross. All the different
momenta of Christian faith are centred in the cross. And it is
impossible to understand these momenta except by tracing them
backwards, and going up through the series, sin, death, law, to
Adam, with whom the series originated. Christian faith is essentially historical; what is immediate in it has yet been mediated
by past events, and has its roots in the past. Faith, therefore,
goes back to the past. It does not, however, take its stand at any

one point of the past, it is under the necessity of going back to the beginning; from the beginning it is led forward again from stage to stage, from the past to the present, from the present to the future. Thus faith stands in the present as an element of consciousness, but lives in the past. This attitude of the mind towards the past comes out very distinctly in the view that everything in the past has reference to us, and happened principally for our sake. In the history of the Old Testament, in the fortunes and vicissitudes of the ancient people, the apostle finds a multitude of types of the various aspects of Christianity. He says, 1 Cor. x. 6, after mentioning a number of occurrences from the Old Testament, ταῦτα τύποι ἡμῖν ἐγενήθησαν, that we should not lust after evil things, nor be idolaters, etc. All this happened to them as a type, and had reference to the future. The past thus contains a picture of the future, and does not find the object which it serves save in that future. Hence it is written for our admonition, εἰς οὓς τὰ τέλη τῶν αἰώνων κατήντησεν, on whom the end of the world's history is advancing, on whom the last eventful time is just about to break, in which that history shall reach its end and consummation. The whole interest of the world's history is concentrated in the τέλη τῶν αἰώνων; here every event is solemn and important; to this period all past events have been converging; this period all past events have been prefiguring. Thus the past is consulted for an explanation of the present. But not only so : the present itself points us forward; it also is to reach a fulfilment in the future. The chief interest of the Christian consciousness is in the future, and thus faith, including as it does all the momenta of the Christian consciousness, yet admitting of different aspects and expressions, comes to be hope or longing. In thinking of the future, the faith which justifies assumes the character of hope. In the spirit, the apostle says, Gal. v. 5, that is, in our Christian consciousness, we look through faith for righteousness or justification as the object of our hope (ἐλπὶς δικαιοσύνης as 2 Cor. i. 22, ἀρραβὼν τοῦ πνεύματος, the πνεῦμα as ἀρραβὼν), we expect that that δικαιοσύνη, which is the object of our hope, will be realized.

Though justification belongs to the present as being πνεύματι and ἐκ πίστεως, yet as ἐλπὶς δικαιοσύνης it is placed in the future. The divine act of justification is only accomplished in the blessedness of the future ; this is a part of δικαιοῦσθαι, thus faith may come to be more occupied with the future than with the present, and then it will be hope. The Christian's whole thought, and desire, and effort is occupied with the future ; he is drawn to it by all the ties by which he is bound to Christ. He knows—for the apostle's words, 2 Cor. iv. 14, may be understood of Christians as Christians—" that he who raised up the Lord Jesus from the dead will raise up us also by Jesus. For this cause we do not weary, but though our outward man perish, yet our inward man is renewed day by day. For our transitory light afflictions procure for us a transcendently exalted and eternal glory, while we look not at the things that are seen, but at the things that are not seen, for the visible is temporal, but the invisible is eternal." The visible present is a vanishing momentum of the future which is as yet invisible ; if the two be held side by side it cannot but appear that the sufferings of the present time are of no account whatever in comparison with the glory which the future will make manifest in us. The Christian cannot but long for this glory, the thought of which engrosses him ; his whole mind and soul are possessed with longing, and he even imputes his own mood to outward physical nature and thinks that it sympathizes with his yearning. " For expectant nature waits for the manifestation of the sons of God, for the catastrophe at which they shall appear in their glory as the sons and heirs of God. For nature was made subject to vanity, not willingly, but for the sake of him who subjected her ; the hope being reserved to her, that she also should be freed from the bondage of corruption to the freedom which is the glory of the sons of God. For we know that all nature groans with us, and is in travail from of old till now : and not only she, but we also, who have the firstfruits of the spirit, we also groan within ourselves, waiting for the adoption, the redemption of our body. For we have been saved for hope (our salvation is only the object of hope) : but a hope which is visible is no hope : for what a man sees he can no longer be hoping for. But if we hope for what we see not, then we wait for it with patience," Rom. viii. 18-25. Thus everything is summed up in hope : the deepest feeling of the Christian's heart is yearning,—the patient waiting for what is yet to come. Even the spirit, which the Christian has already received, and in which the blessings of the gospel are already consciously his, even the spirit is only an ἀπαρχὴ, only the sacred initiation, only the pledge of something higher which has yet to come, of this namely : that the mortal shall be swallowed up of life, 2 Cor. v. 5. This being so, the apostle proceeds :—" I have always good courage, and look beyond the present to the future. I know that so long as I am in the body I am absent from the Lord, for we walk in faith not by sight,. but I have good courage and wish rather to go forth out of the body and to be at home with the Lord," vv. 6-8. By force of yearning after the Lord and reaching forth towards him beyond the present to the future, the present and the future come to appear to the apostle to lie quite close together. Everything seemed to be pressing on to the close, all existing relations and arrangements were uncertain, and on the brink of being dissolved, 1 Cor. vii. 29. The future world was already beginning to appear, he believed that he himself was to live to see the appearance of the Lord when he should come again and close the world's history by his arrival, 1 Cor xv. 52.

Thus the Christian lives only in the future ; the present has no interest except as pointing to the future ; so little does it weigh in itself, that if the present has been filled with a hope in Christ which is not to have its fulfilment in the future, then Christians are of all men most miserable ; that if there be no resurrection of the dead, then those are right who say : Let us eat and drink, for to-morrow we die, 1 Cor. xv. 19, 32. The consciousness of the Christian has nothing in itself to hold on to, if it do not go out beyond the present. The consciousness of atonement and unity with God is indeed such a blessed thing that there is no greater happiness for a man than to be by his holy life a temple of the indwelling God ; and yet here it is as if it were not so, as if all this blessedness and holiness of soul were nothing in itself, and were of value only in the light of the future. There could be no stronger expression of the Christian's dependence on the world to come.

And is it then the case that the Christian has nothing in himself now, and irrespective of what the future is to bring, that can lift him up absolutely above the limitations of his existence ? Is the infiniteness of the Christian consciousness a thing yet to be attained, and not already present ? To this we answer, that where faith is as yet nothing more than hope, and the spirit works only as the ἀπαρχὴ, there love comes in as a new element. The apostle describes the nature of love in the classical passage, 1 Cor. xiii. ; without it, he says, the most distinguished spiritual gifts are nothing worth, since it is love alone that teaches how to use them well, so that they are really serviceable. Of the highest practical virtues it is the same, the utmost devotion and self-sacrifice are worthless if they do not proceed from love. He goes on to describe love and invest it with every possible distinction as the moral quality by means of which man becomes free from every selfish feeling, lives not for himself, but only for others, and has no ends but such as are lofty and universal. Thus it is love which gives the Christian consciousness and life its absolute value. Even faith is nothing without love, though love again is simply faith actively operative. In comparison with faith and hope, then, the apostle distinctly calls love the greatest, since she is what she is immediately and absolutely, and therefore always remains what she is. She is greater than hope, for when the fulfilment comes hope ceases to exist ; and she is greater than faith, for faith does not reach its object immediately, but mediately, it is not a περιπατεῖν διὰ εἴδους. Our present knowledge is obscure and dim, not a seeing face to face. This knowing in part has to give place to perfect knowledge, this mediate and reflected knowledge to the immediate and direct. Even faith as a form of knowledge will cease to be when it rises into sight. Thus love is the greatest of the three momenta of the Christian consciousness; it remains what it is, it has absolute value even in the present. Now if love have absolute value in herself, if it be possible for the Christian even now to be filled with a love which leaves everything that is particular, egoistic, and limited, behind, and is her own reward instead of having to expect her reward in the future world,—if this be so, then is it not quite untrue to say that if there be no resurrection of the dead there is nothing better to be done than to eat and drink, since this life makes an end of all, and it is all the same whether a man lives so or so? If love be in herself of absolute value, then she is so without the resurrection, and all the more the more she is without any ulterior interest to inspire her. But the reason of her having this absolute value is that the principle of the Christian consciousness from which she also springs, faith with all that makes up its living contents, has absolute value in itself. Faith, love, and hope, are the three momenta of the Christian consciousness, the three essential forms in which it finds expression; but while to faith and hope that infinity of the subject which Christianity promises is reserved for the transcendent hereafter, and is unattained here, love possesses that infinity here and now as her own immanent virtue. *Πίστις δι' ἀγάπης ἐνεργουμένη* is *πίστις* in possession of those absolute contents, which to *πίστις* as expressed in *ἐλπίς* were still unattained and only to be expected from the future world. Love, therefore, or faith in the form of love, is a greater thing than hope. What faith is theoretically love realizes, a consciousness that is free within itself, and absolved from all limits and barriers. Thus the three momenta in which the apostle while at the highest stage of his contemplation sums up the whole contents of his Christian consciousness coincide with that principle, as we sought to apprehend and to develop it at the outset of our discussion.

EIGHTH CHAPTER.

SPECIAL DISCUSSION OF CERTAIN SUBORDINATE DOGMATIC QUESTIONS.

In the preceding chapters we have been considering the Pauline doctrine as a connected and organic system, in which one idea rose logically out of the other, till the whole stood before us. We have still to consider some questions which may serve to throw light on individual points of the apostle's system, though they do not materially affect its main positions. The question of greatest importance under this head is, how the apostle conceived of the higher nature of Christ. His doctrine of Christ is not indeed a key to his system; that system can be quite well examined and described even before this question is discussed; yet we must of course devote some attention to it, and we may dispose of several other points at the same time.

1. The conception or the essence of religion.

If it be asked what is the apostle's conception of religion, or what he held to be the essential element of religion, we must, of course, answer—Faith. This is man's part in religion; what is to put man in a right relation towards God is faith and what springs out of faith. The chief proposition of the apostle's doctrine of justification, ὁ ἄνθρωπος ἐκ πίστεως ζήσεται, contains his definition of religion. Religion is essentially faith. Faith is taken here not in its contracted, but in its widest sense; it is faith in that which God must have in himself in order to make man blessed, confidence in his omnipotence. With regard to faith in Jesus, faith, that is, in its more specific sense, when the apostle means to exhibit that element in it which belongs to religion generally, he uses the expression πιστεύειν ἐπὶ τὸν ἐγείραντα Ἰησοῦν τὸν Κύριον ἡμῶν ἐκ νεκρῶν (Rom. iv. 24).

And the distinguishing feature of Abraham's faith is that he be-lieved in God as the ζωοποιῶν τοὺς νεκροὺς καὶ καλῶν τὰ μὴ ὄντα ὡς ὄντα (ver. 17). This faith, that God can bring about what seems impossible, contains, on the one hand, an expression of absolute dependence on God, and, on the other, an attitude of mind, in which the standard of possibility is not taken from what actually is, which surmounts the present reality, and takes account not only of the visible, but also of the invisible. Faith here means, to abstract from self and from one's own subjectivity, and to cast one's-self on the objective by which the subject is determined. It is the trustful surrender of the whole man to God. The ground of this confidence is not only God's omnipotence, but also his love ; but first of all it must be his omnipotence, because if God is to be the object of con-fidence, he must, first of all, have the power to do what love sug-gests. The most essential element of religion is thus, that man feel his dependence on God, and place an unlimited trust in him.

The apostle, however, counts not only faith and confidence to be of the essence of religion, but also a certain amount and kind of action. He says, Rom. ii. 13, that not the hearers but the doers of the law are just before God; the difference between circumcision and uncircumcision is given up, but is replaced by that between the observance and the non-observance of the law. For circum-cision profits if one keeps the law, but if one be a transgressor of the law then circumcision is made uncircumcision. If then uncir-cumcision observes what the law pronounces to be right and good, then uncircumcision is counted for circumcision. And the uncir-cumcision that is by nature, if it fulfil the law, judges him who with the letter and with circumcision is a transgressor of the law. For it does not matter what one is outwardly, but only what one is inwardly in regard to the spirit with which he keeps the law (Rom. ii. 25). Compare 1 Cor. vii. 19: Circumcision is nothing and un-circumcision is nothing; the main point is the τήρησις ἐντολῶν Θεοῦ. This view of the essence of religion rests on the idea that justification by works of the law is abstractly a possible road to attain that salvation which is religion's ultimate end. If we omit, what the apostle teaches further, that this road does not actually lead to that end, then the essence of religion must be the doing, the observance, of the commandments of God. But works and faith are related to each other in respect of the essence of religion as δικαιοῦσθαι ἐξ ἔργων νόμου to δικαιοῦσθαι ἐκ πίστεως; works, as distinguished from and separate from faith cannot but be imperfect, and can only be the essence of religion in one of its lower stages. At a higher stage that essence is faith.

There are, however, some indications that the apostle regarded knowledge as the highest region in which religion moves, and placed knowing above both doing and believing.

He draws a contrast between dim and obscured seeing in a mirror, and seeing face to face; between his piecemeal knowledge now, and that which was to come, the knowing perfectly as he was known (1 Cor. xiii. 12). These last words may be understood either generally, thus : I shall be both the subject and the object of the knowledge of the future world, where all is clear and transparent; or they may be taken of the knowledge of God: my knowledge of God will be as immediate and absolute as God's knowledge of me. In any case the highest stage and form of religion is to the apostle that in which it is an immediate relation of spirit to spirit; if man's knowledge of God be as absolute as God's knowledge of man, then it is nothing but a knowledge identical with itself, the identity of subject and object in pure knowledge. Of the same knowledge the apostle says, 1 Cor. viii. 3, If any man love God, the same is known of him. The context of the passage is not satisfied by the interpretation *Deo probatur.* The apostle is speaking, verse 2, of the γνῶσις which φυσιοῖ, of the γνῶσις which is disjoined from love; and says that this is not the right knowledge, that there can be no right γνῶσις without the καθὼς δεῖ γνῶναι, which nothing but love can supply. Then he takes up the converse, verse 3, referring γνῶσις to ἀγάπη, and here he cannot mean anything but this,—that in the true ἀγάπη the true γνῶσις is also contained. In such a man the conception of γνῶσις is realized through his being known by God in loving God. This passive, being known, implies the active, knowing: as the object of the absolute divine knowledge he is also the subject of it, in so far as it is in him, as he, the object of it, has it in himself. Thus he is not only the object, but also the depositary, the subject of this divine knowledge of him. Thus religion is also knowledge—the highest absolute knowledge on man's part, as on God's part. God is known by man in the same absolute way as man by God; in this same absolute knowledge God and man are one.

2. The doctrine of God.[1]

What is most remarkable in the apostle's doctrine of God is how he seeks to remove from the idea of God everything particular, limited and finite, and to retain nothing but the pure idea of the absolute. The final result of the whole world-process is that God may be all in all, and this point of view is consistently adhered to throughout. Whatever subject he happens to be considering, its reference to God is always an essential part of it; and the more he labours to grasp the subject in all its various aspects, and exhibit the whole system of its parts and connexions, the more does the whole train of thought seem to carry him at last by a natural attraction to the absolute idea of God, to find there his conclusion and resting-place. As everything proceeds from God, so everything is to be referred to him. The one God is the Father, ἐξ οὗ τὰ πάντα καὶ ἡμεῖς εἰς αὐτὸν (1 Cor. viii. 6), or in the more comprehensive expression of Rom. xi. 36, ἐξ αὐτοῦ καὶ δι᾽ αὐτοῦ καὶ εἰς αὐτὸν τὰ πάντα, all things proceed from him, all things come to actuality through him, all things have in him their final purpose. As God in this absolute sense, he is further the Father of Jesus Christ, by whom the whole work of redemption was ordained: τὰ πάντα ἐκ τοῦ Θεοῦ, τοῦ καταλλάξαντος ἡμᾶς ἑαυτῷ διὰ 'Ιησοῦ Χριστοῦ (2 Cor. v. 18). This constant reference to the one and universally efficient causality of God, and the consequent feelings of gratitude and wonder at God's greatness and goodness, causes the apostle to break out in direct doxology, as in Rom. ix. 5, 2 Cor. i. 3, xi. 31. This view of the absoluteness of the idea of God is the root of the

[1] Cf. Neutest. Theol. 205 *sq.*

apostle's universalism; he declares repeatedly that God is as much
the God of the Gentiles as of the Jews, and that in this matter there
is no respect of persons with God (Rom. ii. 11, iii. 29, x. 12). Christianity indeed is simply the negation of all particularism to the end
that the pure and absolute idea of God may be realized in humanity.
The barriers which divide Jews from Gentiles are removed in the
justification that is by faith, because faith is the freest way of justification, and the only way that answers to the absolute idea of God
(Rom. iii. 30). But God has proved himself from the very beginning to be the God of the Gentiles; he did not leave them without
a witness; he could not do so, for it belongs to the idea of God
that he should manifest himself. *Τὸ γνωστὸν τοῦ Θεοῦ φανερόν
ἐστι ἐν αὐτοῖς,* the apostle says (Rom. i. 19),—for God has manifested it to them, for the invisible things of him are spiritually beheld since the foundation of the world, both his eternal power and
his divinity. This sentence implies, on the one hand, that it belongs to the essence of God to reveal himself, and, on the other,
that his absolute nature cannot be revealed by any revelation.
Invisible as it essentially is, it became visible so far as the invisible
can become visible, through the creation of the world and all that
God has been doing since then, through all God's works in nature.
But then this is brought about only through the instrumentality
of thought: *τὰ ἀόρατα ... νοούμενα καθορᾶται*: it is only through
thought that it comes to presentation. This knowledge of God
through the works of nature is not immediate but mediate; nature
may be made the subject of thought and contemplation, and, from
the operations that are visible there, we may infer an invisible
cause. The apostle thus indicates that the conclusion from effect
to cause is the natural way to the knowledge of God. That which
is known of God in this way is his power, and in general the
divinity of his nature. Whether *θειότης* be understood specially
of the goodness of God as a further element in his nature, and
different from his power, or, more accurately, of the sum of his
divine attributes in general, in any case the apostle places the
power of God before all his other attributes. It is the property by

which God calls the non-existent to exist (τὰ μὴ ὄντα ὡς ὄντα καλεῖ, Rom. iv. 17). By his omnipotence God created the world; and Christianity, as a spiritual creation, is also to be referred to his omnipotence. The same God at whose command light shone out of darkness has also, as the apostle says (2 Cor. iv. 6) (here he is speaking of himself personally, but what he says is true of all Christians), shined into our hearts, to give us a clear knowledge of the glory of God as it appears on the face of Jesus Christ. Christianity is a creation of light, as the first appearance of the world was; as creator of the world God called the non-existent into existence, and that important event on which Christianity depends, the resurrection of Jesus, is a similar act of his omnipotence (the Apostle places the ζωοποιεῖν τοὺς νεκροὺς in the same category with the καλεῖν τὰ μὴ ὄντα ὡς ὄντα, Rom. iv. 17). Thus while the general conception which the Christian consciousness entertains of God is that he is the Father of Jesus Christ, this conception is further defined in this way: that God is he who raised up Jesus from the dead (Rom. iv. 24, 25, 2 Cor. iv. 14). The reason for the omnipotence of God occupying so large a place in the Christian consciousness of him is, that it is essential to be assured that he δυνατός ἐστι καὶ ποιῆσαι what he has promised (Rom. iv. 21). Next to his omnipotence, however, is his love: for his love is the first and highest cause to which the whole work of redemption which he ordained and set in motion, is to be referred (Rom. v. 8, viii. 38, 2 Cor. xiii. 13). But his love cannot have its way without satisfaction being done to his justice: for his justice is the attribute through which that relation between God and man which is adequate to the idea of God must be accomplished. Thus Christianity and the scheme of salvation which it declares is itself a revelation of God's justice (Rom. i. 17). When his justice has been satisfied then his love appears in the forgiveness of sins as grace, and, where grace prevails, the wrath of God, his retributive justice, has no longer any part to play.

3. The doctrine of Christ.

Our consideration of the Pauline doctrine has not as yet carried us beyond the idea of the κύριος, the risen and glorified Lord. All that that doctrine involves in regard to the person of Christ is that Christianity could not have inaugurated the new epoch, which dates from the resurrection of Christ, and reaches its full accomplishment at the end of the world, if Christ did not possess in the higher dignity to which he has ascended the principle of that new life which is to prevail when death has been subdued. But the higher dignity which Christ attained after his resurrection suggests to us very naturally that we should direct our view backwards and inquire, what is Christ? What was he before he entered on his human existence? He was sent as the Son of God : he entered as the Son of God, at the time which God had fore-ordained, into the history of humanity and of the world (Rom. viii. 3, Gal. iv. 4). This, however, indicates nothing more than his exalted office as Messiah. These expressions do not inform us whether he was the son of God before he was sent, or became the son of God by being sent. We have therefore to look for something more than this υἱὸς Θεοῦ, and to inquire how much is implied in his pre-existence. This question has been frequently discussed of late,[1] yet the apostle's position on this subject has never yet been accurately determined. It is clear on the one side that a pre-existence such as that of the Johannine Logos-doctrine cannot be traced in our apostle's writings ; yet on the other side, it is equally clear that we cannot believe him to have regarded Christ's personality as originating only in his human existence. We have to define what the view is that is situated between these two extremes.

By this time there should surely be little doubt among interpreters that Christ is not called God at Rom. ix. 5. When we consider how absolute the idea of God is to the apostle, how ·powerfully the absoluteness of God had taken possession of his mind, and how distinctly and consistently he represents the rela-

---

[1] Cf. my Geschichte von der Lehre der Dreieinigkeit u.s.w., 1 Thl. p. 81. Zeller, Ueber einige Fragen in Betreff der neutestamentlichen Theologie, Theol. Jahrb. 1842, p. 51 *sq.* Köstlin, der Lehrb. des Evangeliums und der Briefe Joh. und die verwandten neutest. Lehrb. 1843, p. 290 *sq.* Theol. Jahrb. 1845, p. 89 *sq.*

tion of Christ to God as one of subordination, we cannot possibly believe that in this one passage he meant to describe Christ as the absolute God exalted above all. The Pauline mode of thought on such subjects recognises the limits of the monotheism of Judaism, and such an expression would be simply inconsistent with that monotheism. Nor is there any reason why these doxological phrases should be taken in a different sense from the other doxologies which occur in the apostle's writings. Why should they not be a doxology referring to God ? For this is what the context requires. It is said that the preceding τὸ κατὰ σάρκα leads us to expect some higher predicate to be ascribed to Christ. But that is not the case : the apostle's intention here is not, as Rom. i. 3, to expound his conception of Christ in all its elements, and to indicate that in him which is more than the σάρξ. If this were his intention, it is certainly carried out in a very different way from what we find in Rom. i. 3,—indeed in a very peculiar and inexplicable way. What he is saying here is simply that one of the great advantages by which the Israelites are distinguished, is that Christ appeared among them, and as a descendant of their fathers, that Christ, in fact, belongs first of all to them. He feared, however, to allow too much to the particularism of the Jews, and so he had to modify what he had said of Christ's descent by adding that this applied only to the natural extraction of the Messiah ; that it was only κατὰ σάρκα. And this did not require to be balanced by another opposite predicate any more than the γενόμενος ἐκ γυναικὸς of Gal. iv. 4. Here then we have a passage in which the apostle sums up all the benefits and advantages conferred on the Israelites by God : and the climax of all these is said to be that the Messiah appeared among them, and as the descendant of their fathers ; and what is more natural than that, when he arrived at that climax, he should give utterance to his feelings of thanks and adoration ? In doing so he uses the words εἰς τοὺς αἰῶνας, as if to indicate that proofs like these of the divine favour, which the Israelites had enjoyed, could never be obliterated, nor cease at any future time to be a ground of gratitude and praise. De Wette thinks it unnatural that God should be spoken of as the Being who is all in all, as if purposely to overshadow Christ : yet it cannot be alleged that there is no sufficient reason for thus subordinating Christ to God, and for this doxology in which God is praised. The passage, if properly understood, proves exactly the opposite of what is commonly deduced from it ; it proves, namely, how little it consisted with the apostle's ideas to place Christ on an equality with God, and to give him the name of God.

The passage 1 Cor. viii. 6 affords much more plausible grounds for the assertion that the apostle ascribed divine pre-existence to Christ. That this is the force of the words δι' οὗ τὰ πάντα καὶ ἡμεῖς δι' αὐτοῦ, is argued on the following grounds :—1. That it is implied in the analogy of these words with the preceding ἐξ οὗ τὰ πάντα, and that the expression used of God, Rom. xi. 36, is precisely identical.   2. That it is implied in the collocation of πάντα and ἡμεῖς, the latter being understood most naturally of the whole body of Christians, and the former of the totality of things existing. 3. That the context requires it. The reason given here why Christians need not scruple to eat meat offered to idols is the same as that given x. 25 sq., viz., that the meat which is dedicated to idols belongs in fact to the God of the Christians.   This is what is meant by the words ἐξ οὗ τ. π.   Now what is said here of Christ must be meant to have the same force as what was said before of God, and the conclusion is : You are at liberty to eat what the heathens have presented to their masters, for this also belongs to your master, Christ, since it, with all existing things, was made by him.[1]   In spite of all this, I still fail to see that this is the correct interpretation of the passage.   As for the last of the three points, the words do not bear the meaning that is put into them; there is no such immediate reference to the flesh offered to idols.   What the apostle means is just this, that the εἴδωλα as such have no reality, for though there be many so-called gods, higher and lower (θεοὶ and κύριοι), yet they are no true existences.   Christians only have the one God, the Father, from whom all things are, and to whom the

---

[1] Zeller, op. cit. p. 57.

Christian has to refer all things; and the one Lord Jesus Christ, through whom all things are, and through whom Christians also are. Thus if the formal distinction drawn in heathenism between θεοὶ and κύριοι be a correct one, yet only in Christianity are there a θεὸς and a κύριος who answer to the distinction. In this passage also we have to observe that Christ is not himself called God; he is placed beside the one God as κύριος, as a subordinate being, corresponding to those beings of lower rank whom the heathens worshipped in addition to the beings they called gods, and who stood in a more familiar relation to men than the gods did. What does this show with regard to the pre-existence of Christ? If the distinction between the θεὸς and κύριος be a clear and well-defined distinction, then it is very improbable that the apostle ascribed to Christ as κύριος the highest prerogative of deity, the creation of the world. If everything were created by him, then, of course, he would be not only κύριος but Θεὸς. The Logos is Θεὸς, just because all things were made by him. The only conclusion open to us in interpreting this passage is therefore that between the creation (ἐξ αὐτοῦ τὰ πάντα) and the consummation (ἡμεῖς εἰς αὐτὸν), the apostle interpolates what is attributed to Christ, in the words καὶ εἰς . . . δι᾽ αὐτοῦ, that is, the government and preservation of inanimate beings. Τὰ πάντα will then be all that is continually coming to pass throughout the course of time; all things that come to pass in whatever way come to pass through Christ; and we also are what we are through him.[1]

This rendering of the πάντα attributed to Christ is certainly quite consistent with his character as κύριος; yet if we reflect upon the sense in which the apostle uses the particle διὰ of Christ in other passages, we shall see that this rendering of πάντα ascribes too much to him. 2 Cor. v. 17, 18, he says that at the standpoint of the Christian consciousness all things are become new, τὰ δὲ πάντα ἐκ τοῦ Θεοῦ τοῦ καταλλάξαντος ἡμᾶς ἑαυτῷ διὰ Ἰησοῦ Χριστοῦ. Here also all things are of God, because God is always the ultimate causality from which all things proceed. But these

[1] Köstlin, *op. cit.* p. 309.

words are obviously inclusive of the τὰ πάντα διὰ 'Ιησοῦ Χριστοῦ. All that Christ has done for the redemption and salvation of men is regarded by the apostle as done by God through Christ (διὰ—Rom. i. 5, iii. 24, 25, v. 2, 9, 10, 11, 18, etc.) This πάντα διὰ 'Ιησοῦ Χριστοῦ is a part of the τὰ πάντα ἐκ τοῦ Θεοῦ. Thus we see that the words 1 Cor. viii. 6, ἐξ οὗ τὰ πάντα καὶ ἡμεῖς δι' αὐτοῦ, refer not only to the creation of the world, but also to the work of redemption in all its parts. Now is it not obvious that the words immediately following these, δι' οὗ τὰ πάντα καὶ ἡμεῖς δι' αὐτοῦ, do not cover more than the τὰ πάντα of 2 Cor. v. 18, and signify all things referring to the redemption and atonement wrought by God διὰ 'Ιησοῦ Χριστοῦ.

Another of the principal *loci* from which it is sought to show that the pre-existence of Christ occurs in Paul's writings is 1 Cor. x. 4. There may be a question, it is said, as to the exact sense in which Christ is called the spiritual rock which followed the Israelites in the wilderness; yet there can be no question, that he is represented as living, and in some way active at that time. I do not see that even this is necessarily implied in the passage. Christ is called a πέτρα πνευματικὴ in that sense only in which it is said of the Israelites that they τὸ αὐτὸ βρῶμα πνευματικὸν ἔφαγον and τὸ αὐτὸ πόμα πνευματικὸν ἔπιον. Now the reason why the manna is called a spiritual food, and the water which sprang up in the wilderness a spiritual drink, is simply that they are invested with a symbolical reference to the Lord's Supper. Here as elsewhere that is called pneumatical which appears to be the higher spiritual sense of Scripture in the light of allegorical interpretation. And when the apostle calls Christ the πνευματικὴ πέτρα, that simply means that he gave an allegorical meaning to the rock which followed the Israelites, and discovered in it a type of Christ. We should at any rate require more evidence before we could allow that this passage contains an assertion of Christ's pre-existence, and of his actual working in his pre-existent state.

Nor is this pre-existence to be extracted from the passage 2 Cor. viii. 9. Accurately interpreted that passage simply affirms that Christ was poor (not became poor), although he was rich : *i.e.* that he lived in poverty and low estate, though as the redeemer he was rich enough to make us rich with the grace of the redemption which he brought us.[1] It is true that spiritual riches are not a direct contradiction to outward poverty; but the point is just that we ought to have the same self-sacrificing spirit as Christ had, who was poor and lowly, though exalted so far above us in the riches of his grace.

Thus none of these passages is enough to prove that the apostle ascribed pre-existence to Christ, a divine glory antecedent to his human existence. None of the predicates which he applies to Christ refers to a previous existence : he calls him simply κύριος, never Θεὸς. Indeed it cannot be allowed that he could possibly have regarded him as God. He calls him a man, not meaning thereby that there was a human side of his nature; he calls him man in a way which precludes us from thinking of a higher divine nature essentially belonging to him. Over against the one man through whom sin and death entered into the world, he is the εἷς ἄνθρωπος Ἰησοῦς Χριστὸς, in whom the grace of God has been extended to many, Rom. v. 15. As by a man came death, so by a man came the resurrection of the dead, 1 Cor. xv. 21. As Adam was the first man and earthy, so he is the second man, the Lord from heaven, verse 47. What does the apostle mean by such statements as these, but that Christ was essentially man, man like Adam, only man in a higher sense? All that is left for us to ask is what that higher conception is which is to be connected with the person of Christ over and above that of human nature. The apostle calls the higher principle of the person of Christ the spiritual, the heavenly, in him, and that not in the sense that a divine principle different from human nature had been added to that human nature from without; the higher principle is the purer form of human nature itself. As the pneumatical man, as the Lord from heaven, Christ is, in a word, the archetypal man; and this archetypal man does not exist merely in idea, he exhibits in a real form what man

---

[1] Köstlin, p. 310.

is according to the principles of his nature. Adam is the earthly, psychical man, who has fallen under the power of sin and death, but Christ is the spiritual heavenly man, the man in whom the lower side of human nature has completely given place to the higher, the sinless man. That Christ was without sin (μὴ γνοὺς ἁμαρτίαν, 2 Cor. v. 21) is an essential part of his character as distinguished from that of Adam. As sin began to manifest its power in Adam, so the principle of death also made its appearance in his person; Christ, on the other hand, as he is free from sin, is also free from death : not only was he not subject to the principle of death, he had within himself the opposite principle of life, the life-giving spirit. Thus though Christ had a physical nature like all other men, he yet differed from them in this respect, that his σὰρξ was not affected by the principle of sin and death, and was only a ὁμοίωμα σαρκὸς ἁμαρτίας, Rom. viii. 3. This expression refers simply to the sinlessness of his human nature. As being free from sin, he ought not to have died ; yet he was subject to the necessity of death, not on his own account, but in virtue of his office, in which he took upon himself the sins of men. But how could he die ? Though descended κατὰ σάρκα from the fathers of his nation and from Adam, yet he had in himself no element of death ; the principle of his nature was the opposite of that of Adam's, was the life-giving spirit. The explanation of this is, that though flesh, sin, and death are inter-dependent, and proceed the one out of the other, yet the σὰρξ cannot be conceived but as essentially mortal. If the σὰρξ did not carry in itself the element of liability to death, it could not be considered that the death of Christ as one dying only in the ὁμοίωμα σαρκὸς ἁμαρτίας was a true and actual death. Yet though he died truly and actually, he died only in the flesh ; the life-giving spirit in him, the spiritual principle which constituted his true essence, could not be affected by death. How is it then that the apostle regards it as an act of God's omnipotence that Christ was not subdued by the death that had reigned since Adam, but rose again from the dead ? Was this not a necessary consequence of his immortal, spiritual, and heavenly nature? It cannot be asserted that his resurrection was only the resurrection of his body; for the resurrection is, in the apostle's view, the entrance into humanity of that principle of life which Christ procured for it, and by which the reign of death was broken. If Christ had not risen, this would not import merely that his body had not been revived, while the spiritual principle that was identical with his person still continued. It is only through his resurrection that he has become the πνεῦμα ζωοποιοῦν in which πάντες ζωοποιηθήσονται. How then can that be regarded as an operation of the divine omnipotence, and one extending only to Christ's body, which is simply the manifestation of his higher spiritual nature in its superiority to the mortality of the body? Here we see the apostle involved in the inconsistency which attaches unavoidably to every attempt to hold at the same time to a theory carried out logically to its ultimate consequences, and to the miracles of supernaturalism. The whole of Christianity depends in his estimation on the miracle of Christ's resurrection; yet, at the same time, we see him deducing his view of what Christianity is essentially, as the communication of a new life-principle, or as the stage at which man becomes conscious of the infiniteness of his nature, from purely historical and logical considerations. While holding its supernatural origin, he yet demonstrates how it springs naturally from the opposition of the psychical and the pneumatical, of the earthly and the heavenly, or of Adam and Christ, that is of man on the lower, and on the higher side of his nature, as these opposites form the successive momenta of a process which is developed in accordance with an immanent principle.

Christ is thus essentially man, the archetypal man in whom the higher principle of human nature appears. Did he begin to exist as such only when he was born as a human individual in the person of Jesus of Nazareth? The first is not the pneumatical, as the apostle says, 1 Cor. xv. 46, but the psychical, and the pneumatical follows it; at the same time, however, both of these are momenta of, and are included in, a unity. That the pneumatical comes after the psychical is true, of course, only of the development in time. The pneumatical is not accounted for by indicating its origin in time. And if Christ represents in himself this higher principle of human nature, then this conception of what he is refers us back, beyond his merely individual existence, to the general out of which the individual proceeds. Thus we are not unprepared to find our apostle familiar with the idea of Christ's pre-existence. Besides the passages we have already discussed, Rom. i. 4 has been interpreted in this way, and it has been thought that the πνεῦμα ἁγιωσύνης there spoken of is itself the element in which the higher pre-existent personality of Christ consists.[1] Before this can be admitted, however, we must ask how these two things consist with one another : firstly, that Christ is, as the apostle declares, essentially man ; and secondly, that his personality is distinctively spirit : so that the spirit existed in him, antecedently to his human existence, in the form of a human personality. We are shut up to regard this as his conception when we remember how he calls Christ the spiritual, heavenly man, the Lord from heaven, 1 Cor. xv. 47, the Lord of glory, 1 Cor. ii. 8, the spirit, 2 Cor. iii. 17, and that not only in respect of his having been exalted and glorified through his resurrection, but without qualification, in respect of his whole being. Christ is, as the apostle says, 2 Cor. iii. 17, τὸ πνεῦμα, the spirit itself ; the substance of his being is spirit. Now the apostle appears to have conceived the essence of spirit to be an immaterial light-substance ; in unfolding his conception of the spirit which the Lord is, he says that we all, who behold with unveiled face the glory of the Lord, are changed into the same image, from one glory to another, as could not fail to be the case, since the Lord is the spirit. The essence of the spirit, and consequently the essence of Christ, is thus clearness, brilliancy, δόξα ; it finds its analogy in the brilliant light of which the apostle speaks as shining from the face of Moses. In this spiritual brilliance of Christ the eternal luminous essence of God himself is reflected. The apostle speaks, 2 Cor. iv. 6, of God, the creator of light, shining into our hearts

---

[1] Zeller, on the πνεῦμα ἁγιωσύνης, Rom. i. 4. Theol. Jahrb. i. 486 *sq.*

πρὸς φωτισμὸν τῆς γνώσεως τῆς δόξης τοῦ Θεοῦ ἐν προσώπῳ Ἰησοῦ Χριστοῦ, to make clear the knowledge of the glorious light reflected from the face of Christ as it was once reflected from the face of Moses. Christ is himself the image of God, and as the glory of God is reflected in him, so it is reflected again from him in the gospel (εὐαγγέλιον τῆς δόξης τοῦ Χριστοῦ), the knowledge of which produces a bright light in the man who receives it, 2 Cor. iv. 4. Thus we see distinctly that Christ is related as he is to God just because he is essentially spirit; it belongs to the spiritual light-nature of God to reflect itself in something outward, and thus, as Christ is τὸ πνεῦμα he is also κύριος τῆς δόξης, essentially spirit and light. And he is this not only in consequence of his exaltation, but essentially and originally. His exaltation brought about the full realization of what he was already, what had not been visible when he was crucified by the ἄρχοντες τοῦ κόσμου. But though thus the κύριος τῆς δόξης, he is also essentially man,—the pneumatical, heavenly man. The apostle thus appears to have conceived of Christ's pre-existent personality as the spiritual luminous figure of the archetypal man. And here a further question is suggested : what are the relations between this ideal first man and the historical first man, Adam ? On one side they are far asunder ; on another side they bear a relation to each other, which is analogous to the relation between God and Christ. The passage 1 Cor. xi. 3 may give us some insight into the apostle's peculiar ways of thinking here. It is said there that the head of the man is Christ, that the head of the woman is the man, that the head of Christ is God. The man is the εἰκὼν καὶ δόξα Θεοῦ, the woman is the δόξα, the luminous reflex, of the man. From this point of view it seems that the first man can be nothing but the reflex and the likeness of the archetypal man, of Christ. There is however this mighty difference between the two, that the one is merely earthly and psychical, while the other is heavenly and spiritual. The apostle does not indicate further how this contrast arose ; we may be certain, however, that he did not conceive that Adam existed first in a state of perfection, and came to be what he was afterwards ; he says of him, speaking of his essential nature, that he was merely a ψυχὴ ζῶσα, 1 Cor. xv. 45. The apostle considers it according to the universal order of nature that the psychical should be developed first in humanity, and then the spiritual ; and if this was the case, then of course what Christ was ideally, as the archetypal man, could not be realized in humanity till after the period of the earthly, psychical man. Not till then did God cause the archetypal man, the κύριος δόξης, to enter into humanity as his Son, his own Son, Gal. iv. 4, Rom. viii. 3, 32. He entered into humanity as one ἐν ὁμοιώματι σαρκὸς ἁμαρτίας, γενόμενος ἐκ γυναικὸς,—predicates which agree very well with the conception of the person of Christ which we have arrived at above. It has been said, and with great justice, that the stress here laid upon the circumstances that the Son of God had a human body and was born of a woman, clearly shows the writer to have regarded his personality as not inseparable from a human body, as in the case of other men ; while it certainly shows at the same time that he considered Christ to have existed in such a body before his appearance in the world.[1] The apostle's view can scarcely have been any other than this, that Christ existed already subjectively for himself, and was invested with a ὁμοίωμα σαρκὸς ἁμαρτίας, at the time when he appeared as a man, and in order that he might so appear. The view would thus be the same as that expressed in the second Epistle of Clemens Romanus to the Corinthians, chap. viii., with the simple words, ὁ κύριος ὢν μὲν τὸ πρῶτον πνεῦμα, ἐγένετο σάρξ. This view is strictly consistent with the monotheism of Judaism, and differs radically from the Johannine view. The pre-existing subject is not the λόγος, Θεὸς, but the πνεῦμα, Christ, who, as the κύριος δόξης, is the πνεῦμα, 2 Cor. iii. 17. Now though Christ appeared only in a ὁμοίωμα σαρκὸς ἁμαρτιάς, yet his appearance in the σάρξ makes him really and perfectly a man. There is nothing to suggest a supernatural origin ; on the contrary, the apostle seems to exclude such an idea when he says that God sent his Son as one γενόμενον ἐκ

[1] Theol. Jahrb. 1842, p. 58.

γυναικὸς, Gal. iv. 4, or as one γενόμενον ἐκ σπέρματος Δαβὶδ κατὰ σάρκα, Rom. i. 3. How the apostle reconciled the sinlessness of Christ with his natural human generation we have no means of deciding. It is certainly unnecessary to assert that the two cannot possibly occur in one person ; this is an inference from the doctrine of original sin, a doctrine of a later age and with which Paul was unacquainted. With the apostle it is only through actual sin that the σάρξ becomes the seat of the ἁμαρτία.

Thus it is through his human birth that Christ enters into humanity as the Son of God. Over against the γενέσθαι ἐκ σπέρματος Δαβὶδ κατὰ σάρκα, however, the apostle places the ὁρισθῆναι ὑπὸ Θεοῦ ἐν δυνάμει κατὰ πνεῦμα ἁγιωσύνης ἐξ ἀναστάσεως νεκρῶν. What this πνεῦμα ἁγιωσύνης denotes is a further and somewhat obscure point in the Pauline Christology. As being πνεῦμα, it must, as we have already remarked, be that element in which the higher pre-existent personality of Christ consists. The peculiar expression, πνεῦμα ἁγιωσύνης, with which the πνεῦμα is further defined, can only be explained by an accurate examination of the passage Rom. i. 3, 4, where it is used. The apostle is seeking to express the fulness of his faith in the Messianic dignity of Christ at the outset of his Epistle by summing up all the momenta that enter into that conception. Christ is the Messiah in virtue of his being the son of David: to the Judæo-Christians at Rome, this was the first and principal criterion. But to the apostle a much more important criterion of his Messiahship is his resurrection from the dead. What Christ is physically as the son of David, he is spiritually through his resurrection ; this is the spiritual credentials of his Messianic dignity, for this first of all supplied an actual proof that the spirit which alone could make him the Messiah was actually resident in him. And this is the proper meaning of the πνεῦμα ἁγιωσύνης. Christians are ἅγιος, because Christ himself is *par excellence* the ἅγιος ; and he is the ἅγιος because he has in himself absolutely the πνεῦμα, the πνεῦμα ἅγιον. The spirit is the principle in virtue of which Christ is the Messiah, it is the immanent principle of his Messianic office ; and the apostle calls this spirit, which is essential to the Messiah, the πνεῦμα ἁγιωσύνης. As being born of the seed of David he was the Messiah, the Son of God, according to the flesh ; but he has been attested to be the Son of God in a powerful manner (the apostle says ἐν δυνάμει, either to mark the resurrection as an act of the divine omnipotence, or to indicate that this alone was the true and real attestation of Christ's Messiahship), by the resurrection of the dead which took place in him in accordance with the Messianic spirit indwelling in him. The πνεῦμα ἁγιωσύνης is thus simply the Messianic spirit, and would not by itself be any proof of pre-existence. We have not, however, to regard it by itself, but in its connexion with the other momenta we have been discussing. The πνεῦμα ἁγιωσύνης presupposes the πνεῦμα, in which Christ's personality is broadly said to consist.

We have thus three momenta in which the personality of Christ is defined : 1. Christ is essentially and substantially spirit, ὁ κύριος τὸ πνεῦμα ἐστὶν, 2 Cor. iii. 17, *i.e.* spirit absolutely, as God himself is essentially spirit. This spiritual nature of Christ necessarily implies the idea of pre-existence. 2. In Christ's appearance in humanity, πνεῦμα, the essential element of his personality, assumes the form of the Messianic spirit ; it is the πνεῦμα ἁγιωσύνης. 3. The resurrection proves Christ to be the Son of God in the highest sense ; at this point the πνεῦμα ἁγιωσύνης asserts itself in its full power and significance as the πνεῦμα ζωοποιοῦν, 1 Cor. xv. 45. What the πνεῦμα ἁγιωσύνης is for Christ's own person, the πνεῦμα ζωοποιοῦν is for humanity ; it is the life-principle that works in humanity, makes an end of sin and death, and raises the mortal σὰρξ to the glorious image of the heavenly man. All that he is as τὸ πνεῦμα, as the κύριος τῆς δόξης, the κύριος ἐξ οὐρανοῦ, the εἰκὼν τοῦ Θεοῦ, the πνευματικὸς ἐπουράνιος ἄνθρωπος, as the archetypal man in whom the image of God resides and is displayed, all this is introduced into humanity by his coming in the ὁμοίωμα σαρκὸς ἁμαρτίας, to kill and to destroy the σὰρξ. And all this that he is, is accomplished and realized in humanity when the whole of humanity is formed after his image. For those who become the children of God through the spirit of God or the spirit of Christ, them God προώρισε συμμόρφους τῆς εἰκόνος τοῦ υἱοῦ αὐτοῦ, εἰς τὸ εἶναι αὐτὸν πρωτότοκον ἐν πολλοῖς ἀδελφοῖς, Rom. viii. 29. It is an essential thought of the Pauline Christology that Christ is the image of God. This image of God, which he wears in his spiritual light-nature, prefigures the unity of God and man. Christ is essentially man ; but as the archetypal, spiritual, heavenly man, he is also the God-man, or the Son of God, the ἴδιος υἱὸς Θεοῦ. But the apostle never calls him simply God. This characteristic of the Pauline Christology shows us how strictly Jewish its conceptions are. The apostle has nowhere ignored the barrier which separates the Son of God from God, on the contrary, he holds fast to the position that Christ is essentially and substantially man. He is at the same time τὸ πνεῦμα, the spiritual man untainted by sin. Thus he is the ideal and archetypal man, and in this sense the κύριος τῆς δόξης.[1]

4. The doctrine of angels and demons.

In the Epistles of which we take account in this inquiry, the apostle speaks very little of angels, and where he does speak of them it is not with any dogmatic intention, but only by way of illustration, and proverbially : Rom. viii. 38, 1 Cor. vi. 3, iv. 9, xiii. 1 ; Gal. i. 8, iv. 14 sq. We notice especially that he does not even mention the relation of the angels to Christ, as is the case in the Epistle to the Hebrews, where the higher dignity of Christ is defined by his relation to the angels. This lay outside of the apostle's sphere of vision ; Christ, though he be the κύριος τῆς δόξης, is yet with him too essentially a man to be thought of in such relations. The apostle's ideas about the angels are altogether vague ; to him they are certain superior snperhuman beings standing between God and the world of human life. He even assumes, in accordance with the later and especially Alexandrine tradition, that the law was given through the angels ; but this merely proved to him that the Mosaic legislation was of a subordinate character.

---

[1] The Vorlesungen über neutest. Theologie, pp. 186-195, agree in the main with the above discussion.

It would hardly be worth while to make special mention of the
apostle's angelology were it not for one passage in his Epistles, from
which it might appear that he laid greater stress upon this doctrine
than his other expressions on the subject would lead us to expect.
I mean the passage 1 Cor. xi. 10. Here the apostle is admonish-
ing the Corinthian women not to let themselves be seen with
uncovered head, and for this he gives a reason : For this cause
ought the woman to have a sign of the power (not of the power
which she has, but of the power which her husband has over her ;
this is unquestionably the meaning of ἐξουσία) upon her head,
because of the angels. Women are thus to wear a veil because of
the angels ; but why, what is the connexion between the one thing
and the other ? Different explanations have been advanced, but
they are all alike unsatisfactory. An attentive consideration of
the contents and connexion of the passage can lead us to but one
conclusion : that as the words διὰ τοὺς ἀγγέλους cannot possibly
have arisen out of anything in the apostle's own religious consciousness, they cannot be considered to be part of the original text.
Observe how unconnected these words are here, and how they
destroy the sense. The apostle's main proposition is this : the
woman must wear a veil as a sign of her subjection to the man,
for she is, as the apostle explains, ἐξ ἀνδρὸς and διὰ τὸν ἄνδρα.
Therefore ὀφείλει ἡ γυνὴ ἐξουσίαν ἔχειν. It is clear that διὰ
τοῦτο refers to what goes before ; so far the argument is clear.
But how is it interrupted and confused if διὰ τοὺς ἀγγελοὺς be
added, as if a parallel to διὰ τοῦτο ? The reason given before was
quite sufficient; there is no place for this new and foreign reason,
a thing to which not the slightest reference is made either in what
precedes or in what follows. Our apostle is not such a writer as
could destroy the logic of his argument with such an awkward
interpolation. The sense most probably to be attributed to these
detached and isolated words suggests to us that they were originally
a gloss on the text. An early Christian, such a one as was much
occupied with Jewish representations, might imagine, what the
apostle Paul himself could never imagine, that the veiling of

women was advisable as a precaution against what had once happened to the angels before, Gen. vi. 1. Or he may have thought that the custom of women's wearing veils had been instituted as a memento of that occurrence, and for a standing admonition. The words διὰ τοὺς ἀγγέλους were added as a gloss to indicate this view, and were then taken up into the text without regard to their effect on the sense. The view we have indicated was actually current during the early centuries ; we find it actually applied to impress upon women that their head-dress should be such as to give no occasion for unchaste desires. This appears most clearly from a passage in the Testament of the twelve patriarchs, in the Testament of Rubens, chap v. : προστάσσετε ταῖς γυναιξὶν ὑμῶν καὶ ταῖς θυγατράσιν, ἵνα μὴ κοσμῶνται τὰς κεφαλὰς καὶ τὰς ὄψεις αὐτῶν· οὕτω γὰρ ἔθελξαν τοὺς ἐγρηγόρους (the angels as guardian spirits) πρὸ τοῦ κατακλυσμοῦ.[1] A Christian who was acquainted with these views would very naturally be led to think of them in connexion with this passage. To dispense with the veil he would think was to hold out one of the most dangerous of all temptations. Both of these considerations, then, the isolated position of the words, and the probability of their having originated in a gloss, make us hesitate to ascribe such a view to the apostle. He may have held a view like this, but never as a thing of such importance.

With regard to demons, the point we have to consider is how the apostle conceived them to be related to the heathen deities. The question arises in two passages : 1 Cor. viii. 4-6, and x. 19-21.

[1] Cf. Tertullian, De Velandis Virg., c. 7 : Si propter angelos scilicet quos legimus a Deo et coelo excidisse ob concupiscentiam feminarum, quis praesumere potest, tales angelos maculata jam corpora et humanae libidinis reliquia desiderasse, ut non ad virgines potius exarserint quarum flos etiam humanam libidinem excusat. Debet ergo adumbrari facies tam periculosa, quae etiam ad coelum scandala jaculata est, ut cum Deo adsistens, cui rea est angelorum exterminatorum, caeteris quoque angelis erubescat, et malam illam aliquando libertatem capitis sui comprimat, jam nec hominum oculis offerendam. C. 17 : Nobis dominus etiam revelationibus velaminis spatia metatus est. Nam cuidam sorori nostri angelus in somnis cervices, quasi applauderet verberans, elegantes, inquit cervices, et merito nudae. Bonum est usque ad lumbos a capite veleris, ne et tibi ista cervicum libertas non prosit.

The first passage has greatly perplexed the interpreters. Rückert thinks it most likely that the apostle does not admit with regard to the idols of the heathen that they are truly gods, but does admit that there are many other beings of higher than human nature, and that these possess a certain power over men and over the inanimate world, in virtue of which power they may be called κύριοι, and even θεοὶ, though destitute of any proper title to be worshipped by men as θεοὶ. The apostle, Rückert thinks, actually assumed the existence of such beings as angels and demons. But he does not speak of angels and demons; he speaks of θεοὶ and κύριοι. And he denies that they have any objective existence—as the argument and the idea of the passage distinctly prove. His immediate object is to represent the eating of meat offered to idols as a thing entirely indifferent. There are no idols, he says; an εἴδωλον is a thing that has no reality in the world. Such gods as those of the heathens do not exist at all; there is only one God. For though there be so-called gods in heaven and on earth, as people talk of gods in the plural and believe in them, as in this sense there are many gods and many lords, yet for us, to our religious consciousness as Christians, there is only one God and only one Lord. There can be nothing clearer than that the apostle makes the existence of the heathen gods a matter of mere λέγεσθαι ; allows their existence only in so far as they are represented and spoken of after the manner of polytheism as gods really existing. They are θεοὶ and κύριοι not really, but only to the imagination. We have to remark, however, on the other hand, that the reality and objective existence of the heathen gods is denied only in so far as it is claimed for them that they are θεοὶ and κύριοι, gods properly so called. This does not exclude the supposition that these beings who have no real existence as gods do yet exist actually and objectively not as gods but as demons. This is the apostle's position in the second passage. Here he takes up the other side of the question. His former assertion that an εἴδωλον is nothing, and that therefore neither is an εἰδωλόθυτον any true εἰδωλόθυτον (for nothing can be offered to an idol which has no existence), is not recalled but modified and supplemented by a further statement. This is, that what the heathens offer they offer to demons and not to God, and that one cannot therefore partake in the heathen sacrificial feasts without coming into communion with demons. For it is from the nature of the case impossible—it is a contradiction—to drink the cup of the Lord and at the same time the cup of demons ; to partake of the Lord's table and at the same time of the table of demons ; to practise religious rites which connect us with beings of entirely opposite natures. Thus the apostle appears to have held the view which afterwards became so general, that heathenism was the empire of demons, and essentially demoniacal. With the apostle, however, the view has two sides : on the one side heathenism is demoniacal, on the other it does not deal with realities at all, it is a mere matter of imagination.[1] But the one element of heathenism cannot be separated from the other. The apostle regards the relation of heathenism to Christianity as one of absolute contradiction, not only in the subjective sense that one who has

[1] What Neander says (Planting and Training, i. 243 and 511) on the two passages under discussion is in part indefinite, and in part manifestly erroneous. In the passage viii. 5 he thinks the apostle is merely contrasting two different subjective standpoints, and that there is nothing said of the relations these bear to the objective. What is spoken of here, however, is not two subjective standpoints, but the subjective nature of polytheism, whose gods are merely imagined gods, and the objective nature of Christian monotheism. On the passage x. 20 Neander says, " verse 20 is to be interpreted in the light of the preceding verse. If we admitted that Paul described the heathen deities as evil spirits, then we should need to suppose that he wished to guard against that misunderstanding to which the previous comparison might have given rise, that he really acknowledged their divinities to be divine. But this is inconceivable. On the other hand, his words might be understood in such a way as if he considered these divinities to be real beings (though evil spirits), and hence ascribed objective importance to what was offered to them. To correct this mistake he says now, that he is speaking only of what the heathens believed subjectively from their own standpoint, which was the opposite of the Christian, that those beings to whom they sacrificed were δαιμόνια in the Hellenic sense of the term." How misty, how mistaken ! What business have the δαιμόνια in the Hellenic sense here ? The apostle means demons in the ordinary Jewish sense, and he says clearly enough that he holds them to be the beings to whom the heathens sacrifice. The matter becomes intelligible at once when we admit the light of the apostle's simple distinction. He denied the existence of the heathen gods as gods or idols (εἴδωλον is a supposititious god) : he had room, however, for the assumption that they were evil spirits.

R

become a Christian cannot be a heathen at the same time, but
objectively. The two are related to each other as the false
religion and the true. For what fellowship has righteousness with
unrighteousness, or light with darkness, and what concord has
Christ with Belial, etc. ? 2 Cor. vi. 14.

5. The doctrine of the divine predestination.

With the apostle everything runs up into the absolute idea of
God ; this is his favourite point of view for every subject he may
be considering. And thus he deduces the salvation of man, from
its first beginning to its final accomplishment, from a decree passed
by God on the case of each individual. We know, he says, Rom.
viii. 28, that all things work together for good to them that love
God, to those who are called in accordance with a decree which
he has passed. For those whom he foreknew (fixed in his consciousness as objects of knowledge), them he also predestinated
to be conformed to the image of his Son, that he might be the
first-born among many brethren ; and those whom he predestinated, them he also called ; and whom he called, them he also
justified ; and whom he justified, them he also glorified. Here the
apostle makes it as clear as possible, that in the first beginning,
which he places in the divine decree, the whole series of the subsequent stages was contained, which proceed by necessary sequence
one out of the other. The first stage, the being foreknown, implies
the last, the being glorified into the image of Christ, as its natural
and necessary consequence. So soon as the divine decree has been
arrived at, the process, the objective realization of the idea, moves
forward by logical necessity. The subjective element in the
realization is not, however, excluded, for as it was said before, it is
only those who love God who can be the objects of his decree. In
the ninth chapter of the Epistle to the Romans, on the other hand,
we seem to find the idea of an absolute predestination. Here,
however, everything depends, as we have already indicated, on a
proper apprehension of the position which this chapter and the
doctrine it contains occupy in regard to the whole system. The
apostle is dealing with the different aspects in which the relation

of Israel to the kingdom of God, or the benefits of Christianity, is to be regarded. He goes back to the absolute will of God, and argues that no one can derive from his outward position any right to make definite claims on God, since in such things as depend on the absolute will of God there can be no such thing as injustice towards one party or another. This standpoint, where we are referred to the absolute will of God, is of course liable to be compared with another where the man complaining of injustice at God's hands is reminded of his own sins voluntarily committed. The apostle, however, makes no attempt to reconcile these two positions. Neither here nor anywhere else does he feel called upon to deal with speculative extremes. And in whatever way the question between freedom and predestination be adjusted in speculation, the two positions, that of absolute dependence and that of moral self-determination are both involved and rooted in the immediate Christian self-consciousness. Thus all that is hard, repellent, and one-sided in the argument of Rom. ix., is to be regarded merely as the extreme logical consequence of one of two positions. It is true, we must admit, but then there is the truth of the opposite position, which the apostle himself takes up afterwards, to be placed over against it. In making the practical application of his main pro-position, verse 30, as he had developed it, verses 6-29, the apostle turns from the objective view of the matter to the subjective. The will of God being an absolute will, it is necessary to recognise it as such, and to remember our absolute dependence upon God. As the absolute will of God is not determined by anything human, so men's guilt is great if they refuse to recognise this dependence. With regard to the promises of God, the question is not whether a man belongs externally to the people of God, but whether he is himself elect of God, verses 6-9. It is of God's free choice to prefer one and to reject another, verses 10-13. Nor is this arbitrary choice to be regarded as an injustice on God's part, for man has no right to reclaim against him, the Lord of his fate, verses 14-21. And man is the less entitled to dispute God's absolute right of disposal when he considers that in those who are devoted to

destruction, God's longsuffering and retributive justice and omnipotence are manifested, and in the others the fulness of his grace,
since he has called us as vessels of mercy from among both Jews
and Gentiles, verses 22-29. The conclusion that is reached through
all these considerations is that it does not depend on a man's willing and running; that the heathen obtained what they were not
seeking, and the Jews did not obtain what they were seeking,
namely, righteousness. And the reason of this was that righteousness is not to be obtained by seeking it through the law and the
works of the law, but by faith alone. Thus the Jews brought their
fate upon themselves; they did not obtain righteousness because
they attached value to their own righteousness and did not submit
themselves to the way of the divine appointment, through which
righteousness may be obtained. For with Christ the life that is
under the law has an end, and righteousness may now be obtained
through faith by all, both Jews and Gentiles. Salvation is only
to be had through faith. Though Moses teaches a righteousness
that is to be achieved in the way of the law, yet it cannot be
obtained, nor the salvation that proceeds from it, save by doing all
that the law contains. But the righteousness that comes from
faith is so near every man that he need not go far to seek it, either
to heaven, as if Christ had to be brought down from above, or
to the depths, as if he had to be brought up from the dead. It is
offered freely and at once, and has only to be laid hold of. There
can be no excuse for the want of a faith like this.

It is obvious that as in chapter ix. the apostle seems to argue for
absolute predestination, so in chapter x. he takes up the opposite
position. Here the cause of the rejection of Israel is found not in
the will of God, but in their own wilful unbelief. This is no solution of the problem of predestination; the one position is simply
set over against the other. In chapter xi., however, the apostle
approaches the same question in a different way. From the subjective side he recurs again to the objective. Israel is undoubtedly
the chosen people of God, the subject of his promises. And what
God has promised must be fulfilled. God cannot have rejected

the people whom he foreknew (προέγνω, xi. 2, in the same sense as viii. 29). What then of the unbelief of the people ? how can God's decree be accomplished in spite of their unbelief ? To bring out this point the apostle enters on a teleological view of the world, from which it appears that everything must be subjected sooner or later to the absolute idea of God. The decree of the election of Israel is accomplished in the following momenta :—1. God has not cast away his people, since a part at least of them is accepted in virtue of his gracious choice, though the rest are hardened, xi. 1-10. 2. This hardening is certainly in contradiction with God's decree, yet it is not without its uses ; it is not meant to lead to the final exclusion of the Jews, but only to provide an opportunity for the conversion of the Gentiles. 3. The hardening is only for a time, and will issue at last in the general conversion of Israel. This last point is reached by way of deduction from the other two. If the fall of them be the riches of the world, and the diminishing of them the riches of the Gentiles, how much more will their general entrance into the Messianic kingdom and blessedness bring about a great era of salvation? For if the casting away of them be the reconciling of the world (of the Gentiles with God), what can the receiving of them be but the quickening of the dead, the last great catastrophe which we look for at the resurrection of the dead at the end of the world ? If then the hardening of Israel be so full of blessing even for the heathen, it cannot but have blessed consequences for Israel also. The final and universal conversion of the Jews may also be inferred from the beginning which has already been made. For if the first fruit be holy, the lump is also holy, and if the root be holy, so are the branches. The hardening of a part of the Jews, then, can only last till all the heathens have entered in, and then all Israel will be saved. The apostle grounds this hope and confidence on the original election of Israel attested by the divine promises. For if in regard to the gospel they be hated of God for the sake of the Gentiles (inasmuch as the Gentiles believe—as it is God's will that the Gentiles should obtain salvation—through the unbelief of the Jews), yet as regards the election they are beloved of God for the fathers' sake. For God cannot revoke his gifts and calling. As the Gentiles were once disobedient to God, but have now, through the disobedience of the Jews, become the objects of God's mercy, so have the Jews in their turn become disobedient, that in consequence of the mercy shown to the Gentiles they also might obtain mercy. For God has concluded them all in unbelief, that he might have mercy upon all. And here the apostle sees the depth of the riches of the wisdom and the knowledge of God; the unsearchableness of his judgments; the mystery and hiddenness of his ways; the absolute dependence of all on God, since from Him all things proceed, through Him all things come to pass, and to Him all things tend.

The apostle's main idea is the universality of the grace of God; no man can be excluded from it, it must extend at last to all, both Jews and Gentiles, in order to achieve the end it has in view. Grace being absolute, and it being impossible that what God has promised should remain unfulfilled, the apostle infers that the ends of grace must be realized universally. This universalism of grace, however, contains a decidedly particularist element. Grace may be universal in its operation, yet the peculiar object of the divine decree of the bestowal of grace and salvation (the πρόθεσις κατ᾽ ἐκλογὴν Rom. ix. 11, the ἐκλογὴ xi. 28, ἐκλογὴ χάριτος, xi. 5) are the Jews as descendants of the patriarchs to whom God gave his promises. God's decree is therefore particular, inasmuch as it applies only to the Jews and not to the Gentiles. And it is also an absolute decree, for the election of the Jews precludes the possibility of their being cast away; it cannot be thought that the promise God has given to the Jews can remain unfulfilled. Now, how does it agree with this particularism and this absoluteness that the Gentiles have been brought into the kingdom of God, and that by far the greater part of the Jews is excluded from it? It is inconceivable except in this way, that each of these two events, the reception of the Gentiles and the exclusion of the Jews, is considered as itself constituting a momentum in the realization of the divine decree. The apostle does so regard the reception of the Gentiles when he asserts that the Gentiles have been received only for the Jews' sake. The Jews have stumbled, he says, xi. 11, not to fall for ever; but rather through their fall salvation has come to the Gentiles, to provoke the Jews to emulation. Through their unbelief the Jews have been broken off as branches from the olive tree, and the Gentiles stand by faith as branches on the tree, verse 20. But blindness happened to a part of Israel, till the fulness of the Gentiles should have come in to the kingdom of God, verse 25. For the fact that the Jews did not receive the Gospel the apostle has no explanation but this : that what was wanting on the side of the Jews for the accomplishment of the divine decree was to take place on the other side, that of the Gentiles. The Jews did not submit themselves to the divine ordinance of justification by faith; and so, as justification could only be by faith, it had to be received by the Gentiles. Thus the unbelief of the Jews has provided, as it were, an opportunity for the Gentiles to obtain a part of that salvation, to which they had no claim in virtue of any election. They take part in it because in justification by faith God has opened up a way in which it is possible for them also to obtain it. But the position which they occupy in thus partaking of the gospel is in reality merely that of substitutes for the Jews. They receive the gospel in virtue of that election of which the Jews were the objects originally; they, the branches of a wild olive tree, are grafted into the good olive tree. Here the particularism of the election appears in a very strong light. Particularism is to lead to universalism at last, but the idea of the particular decree is not departed from. Now if the divine mercy has been extended to the Gentiles in this way, it is impossible that the Jews, on the basis of whose election the Gentiles have obtained mercy, should continue to be excluded from that mercy themselves, verse 31. Their blindness cannot shut out mercy from them for ever; their election cannot remain for ever unfulfilled. And though they be at present in a state of blindness, unbelief, and disobedience, that merely shows that their unbelief is a stage upon the road to the divine mercy.

For it is God's intention to carry out his decree of grace through disobedience and not otherwise. He has concluded all in disobedience, in order to have mercy upon all, says the apostle. Thus he does not hesitate to ascribe this disobedience not merely to a permission, but to an ordinance, of God; he regards the disobedience as a momentum through which the mercy is mediated, and which disappears in mercy as the end and consummation which it subserves and ushers in.

What grace is in the absolute conception of it must of necessity be realized, and as grace would not be absolute if it were not universal, it requires the universal mercy of God for its realization. Now how is this absoluteness and universality of grace, this objective character of grace, to be reconciled with freedom on the part of man? The apostle's whole doctrine of faith shows how important the subjective element is to him, and even in the discussion of chapter xi. everything turns on faith and unbelief, obedience and disobedience. But what importance can be ascribed to the subjective element of faith, if it be the case that grace is so absolute that it necessarily overcomes sooner or later every possible opposition, and gathers in all things to the embrace of universal mercy? All that we can say on this point is that the apostle does not by any means slur over the subjective side in favour of the objective; that he lets the two stand side by side without showing how they harmonize. On the one hand, all that grace must be in order to be absolute is to be developed and to become actual; and on the other hand, there is to be no compromise of the self-determination of the subject, the free and voluntary exercise of faith. How these two can be reconciled the apostle has nowhere shown. He is indeed thoroughly familiar with all the processes of subjective consciousness, and has the faculty of illuminating its inmost recesses; yet his interest is engrossed still more in the objective development which is determined by the absolute idea of God. Heathenism, Judaism, and Christianity, are to him great historical opposites, general forms of religious development; he regards not the individuals, but the masses, and in the light of his well-assured Christian consciousness all the questions and riddles of the world find their solution in this one conception : that all things are to be subordinated at last to the absolute idea of Christianity, to be penetrated by it and received up into its unity. He takes a broad majestic sweep through the whole course of historical development, and traces it from stage to stage ; but his Christian consciousness hurries him forward so fast towards the final issue that he passes over many considerations which must be essential momenta of the process, and which had a claim to be considered. Grace is glorified at last, issuing forth as universal mercy, but who are the objects of this mercy? The apostle says indeed that God has mercy upon all as he has concluded all in unbelief; but who are the πάντες on whom he takes mercy? are they the same individuals as were shut up to unbelief? are those who ἐν Χριστῷ ζωοποιηθήσονται the same individuals who died in Adam?—for the necessary condition of ζωοποιεῖσθαι is εἶναι ἐν Χριστῷ. The resurrection, the last world-catastrophe, is to be the general *théodicée*, but only for those who as Christians have been changed or have risen from the dead. Sin and grace, reprobation and mercy, are demonstrated on their objective side, but not on the subjective. The two should have been interwoven, but the one is merely placed after the other. There is a gap here in the apostle's system, which none of the materials in our hands enable us to supply.

6. The heavenly habitation, 2 Cor. v. 1 *sq.*

The view contained in this passage is noticed here merely because the apostle's meaning in it has frequently been misunderstood, and a belief attributed to him which he was far from holding.

For us, the apostle says, iv. 16-18, who look not to the things that are seen, but to the things which are not seen (for the things that are seen are temporal, but the things which are not seen are eternal), there is an infinitely exalted glory. We shall take part in it, the death of the body is the porch to it. For we know that if this earthly house of our body were dissolved, we have a building of God, a house not

made with hands, eternal in the heavens.   For as long as we are in
this body we groan, yearning to be clothed upon with our heavenly
habitation.   What follows, εἴγε καὶ ἐνδυσάμενοι, etc. (read thus :
not ἐκδυσ.), can only be taken as an explanation of ἐπενδύσασθαι.   We
shall not be without the covering of a body, for of course as soon
as we are clothed upon in the way we expect we shall not be
naked, not without a body to cover us.   This is merely a repetition of ἐπενδύσασθαι, and is to say that in this ἐνδύσασθαι that
which was most repugnant to the feeling acquired by the Christians
from Judaism does not take place, namely, γυμνοὶ εὑρεθῆναι.   And
it is added that our longing in the present body is not to be understood to mean that we have any desire to be naked and without a
body altogether.   Being in the body we do indeed groan under the
burden, but it is not to be concluded from this that we desire to
be unclothed ; we wish to be clothed upon, that mortality might be
swallowed up of life.   The apostle's utterances here amount to
neither more nor less than the idea of the resurrection expressed
in 1 Cor. xv. 53.   In this passage it appears as a wish arising out
of the pressure of the present body, and which the apostle takes
care shall not be misunderstood.   If man is not to be naked and
without a body in the future, if he is to have another body consisting of better materials, then the future body must in one way
or another be identical with the present one, must be built up on
the same basis, and the change that is to take place must consist in being clothed upon.   Thus the substance of the man's
personality remains, even in its bodily features ; what of it is
earthly falls off from him, and it is thus transfigured and becomes
heavenly.   The man has even now an inward occult supersensuous
ground-work for a bodily existence different from the present one,
and that which he is essentially even in the present life emerges
at his death into reality.   This then is what is meant by the
οἰκοδομὴ ἐκ Θεοῦ, the οἰκία ἀχειροποίητος, the οἰκητήριον ἐξ
οὐρανοῦ.   These phrases have been wrongly thought to indicate a
heavenly body which true Christians were to receive immediately
after death, and which was to be united at the resurrection with

that which rose out of the physical body.   It is said that the connexion of verse 2 with verse 1 requires that the οἰκητήριον should be the same as the οἰκοδομὴ, that each of these is opposed to the ἐπίγειος οἰκία, and must therefore signify a body, and that therefore verses 1 and 2 must both refer to a body which true Christians are to have at once at their death.   Now, it is said, such a body can be no other than a heavenly body, quite different from the one we have, but to be united with it at the time of the resurrection. This curious imagination is quite inconsistent with the argument of our passage.   The apostle is seeking to lift up his readers to the surpassing glory of the world to come, and he would not have served his object by speaking of an intermediate body.   It is certainly true that this new body is represented as coming immediately after death.   But this difficulty, as it is held to be, is not removed by supposing that the apostle hoped to receive the new body without the painful process of the soul's departure from her old tenement.   It is said that what he desired was a painless change of his mortal body into an immortal, that to represent this change he passed from his former analogy of a house to the more convenient one of a garment, as if the new garment were put on over the old one, and the old one only then put off, or destroyed without pain, by the overpowering energy of the new one.   This, however, is a mere expedient of interpretation, and is sufficiently disposed of by the fact that the apostle is not speaking only of himself, but of Christians generally.   And supposing that the apostle overleaps here the middle stage between death and the resurrection, why should that be thought remarkable ?   Of course if the resurrection be conceived in the Jewish form, as the issue of a body from the grave, then there is a reason to inquire about a middle state.   But the apostle does not entertain any such conception.   In this passage he is not speaking of the resurrection at all, and what he says at 1 Cor. xv. 52 is that the dead will be raised ἄφθαρτοι.   Now if they are raised ἄφθαρτοι, what part of the resurrection-body can come up out of the grave, for the grave contains nothing but the corruptible ?   In the apostle's view the resurrection-body does not come out of the grave, but is a building of God, a house not made by men's hands, an eternal, heavenly habitation, following the earthly in accordance with the divine order which appoints the mortal and corruptible to be changed into the immortal and incorruptible. And if these two sides of the existence of man be of such a nature that they are intimately and immediately connected with each other, then neither can they be separated and held apart from each other in time. The Christian consciousness forbids us to think of a middle state as a stage of existence by itself; for that consciousness is so well assured (the ἔχομεν, verse 1, indicates this) that to it the mortal includes the immortal, and the incorruptible is present even in the corruptible. The corruptible is under the necessity of putting on the incorruptible, the mortal of being swallowed up of life. The apostle therefore adds, verse 5, we may with perfect confidence look forward to this state in which our earthly body will be transfigured into the heavenly, and our mortal nature into the immortal, and penetrated with the principle of life; for it is God who is to bring us to that state; the whole constitution which he, its creator, has given to our nature points to it, and the spirit that is given to us, which we have within us as the earnest of our destination in the future, vouches for it. The imaginations of Judaism were not without their part in the apostle's Christian faith; yet, as we see, his rational consciousness was able to assert itself against them.

NINTH CHAPTER.

ON CERTAIN FEATURES OF THE APOSTLE'S CHARACTER.

WE do not aim at a complete description of the apostle's character. Many data are wanting, without which it is not possible to make him stand before us as he was. What we propose is merely to take up a few noteworthy traits which appear prominently in his writings. And it is quite proper that this should follow at once on our discussion of the doctrine, for the apostle's doctrine is the immediate reflection of his spiritual individuality.

That the apostle was converted from Judaism to Christianity, that he was transformed suddenly and decidedly from a bitter persecutor of Christ's followers to a faithful and devoted disciple of Christ, this great fact gives us a deeper insight into his spiritual organization than anything else we know of him. This was a step from one of two extreme opposites to the other, so that we see here a spirit involved in a great struggle, in the throes of a travail which cannot be accomplished save with labour and conflict and high spiritual energy. And if the two alternatives, than which he saw no other, and each of which displayed itself to him in all its significance and gravity, were great and very contrary alternatives, then this reveals to us one great feature of his character, that he could never stop half-way, but followed up the one line as much as the other to its last conclusions. Thus, if he was to persecute Christianity, it was a war of extermination that he waged against it, Gal. i. 13. Here we have a very determined nature, for which the consequences of the idea it has formed have all the power of necessity, which throws itself into everything that it takes up

with its whole energy, which is what it is entirely and absolutely.
As a Christian, Paul would know nothing but Christ, and lived and
moved entirely in him; just so he had formerly been with his
whole soul a Jew, and the most zealous of all champions for the
religion received by tradition from the fathers. Προέκοπτον, he
says, Gal. i. 14, in describing his former ἀναστροφὴ ἐν τῷ Ἰου-
δαισμῷ, ὑπὲρ πολλοὺς συνηλικιώτας ἐν τῷ γένει μου περισσοτέρως
ζηλωτὴς ὑπάρχων τῶν πατρικῶν μου παραδόσεων. But the more
consistently and energetically a tendency is worked out which is
essentially one-sided and narrow, the more certain is it to suffer
shipwreck on its own narrowness; it crumbles down by its own
inward action, is overcome by the awaking consciousness of its own
finitude, and thus necessarily undergoes a revulsion to the directly
contrary tendency.   It seems to be the thing itself which runs
this course, and the subject in whom this takes place appears to
be determined by something objective and external to himself,
although the process is in reality his own spiritual act.   And the
vividness of the man's consciousness of this objective power
determining him is a standard by which we may measure the
depth of his nature as it withdraws into itself and works for itself
through the universal process of spiritual life.   It is this manifestly
objective character that shows the apostle's act to have been a
really great and wonderful event.   It was an act such as only
those natures are capable of whose movement is in the highest
regions of the spiritual life.   For we can detect no trace of any
subjective interest or motive having influenced or helped this
change; it was the immediate, purely objective impression of the
spiritual power that had come over him, which changed Paul into
that spiritual personality who appears before us as the apostle of
Jesus Christ.   It is of this characteristic of his spiritual nature, as
manifested at the most important epoch of his life, that the apostle
is thinking, when he calls himself with respect to his conversion to
Christianity an ἔκτρωμα, 1 Cor. xv. 8.   This phrase suggests not a
late birth, but a miscarriage; yet what he means is not that his
unworthiness and unfitness for the apostolate were so great that he

had as little right to be an apostle as the fruit of a miscarriage to continue in the world. What he means by the expression is, that his birth into the world as a Christian was after a violent fashion, that it was as it were a miscarriage. Grotius very truly remarks : hoc ideo dicit, quia non longa institutione ad christianismum perductus fuit, quo esset velut naturalis partio, sed vi subita, quomodo immaturi partus ejici solent. This applies, however, not merely to the fact of his becoming a Christian, but to the whole of the sweeping revulsion that was brought about in his consciousness by the objective power of events and tendencies, without his being aware that he was doing anything to help or hinder it. What took place in him seemed to belie his nature : the absolute truth of Christianity was brought home to him and forced upon him against his will by Christ's appearing to him. He could do no other ; little as he willed it for himself, he was constrained to yield the whole of thought and will to the obedience of Christ.[1]

He who has fought through such an inward conflict and in a personal spiritual process overcome the opposition which he there encountered, will, when the spiritual principle has worked its way through all and asserted itself in its own absolute superiority, know that he is himself the power that stands above the conflict. The principle which takes possession of his consciousness is now the immanent principle of his own self-consciousness ; he knows

---

[1] It is said, and very truly, that the apostle's conversion discloses to us the inmost depths of his spiritual nature, and that the ultimate subjective basis of that nature is to be explained and comprehended in the light of this one characteristic fact. If this be so, the problem of the apostle's character may be viewed in the light of the question, why he not only became a Christian like others who were converted from Judaism to Christianity, but believed himself to be called to be an apostle. This followed, it may be said, from the call addressed to him by Christ ; but what appeared to him objectively as the call of Christ was, subjectively considered, the inward impulse of his own spiritual nature. For it was the peculiarity of that nature that in every case it went straight to the results of its principles, and to the absolute. His spiritual nature thus carried him past a form of Christianity which was nothing but another form of Judaism ; he was the first to declare the Christian principle in its integrity, in a way in which none of the older apostles had declared it, and so could scarcely avoid considering himself to be a new apostle.

himself free from everything by which he was formerly constrained; he is conscious of his own independence and autonomy. The position which the apostle took up as the logical and necessary consequence of his conversion, involved of course that all those shackles of religious authority which he had recognised up to that time at once fell away. But it involved more: namely, that within Christianity the apostle recognised no other principle as having authority for him but his own immediate self-consciousness, rooted as it was in faith in Christ. One main feature of the apostle's individuality is this lively and powerful consciousness of freedom. He was quite alive to all that the principle of Christian freedom implied both for himself and for all Christians. It was in him, next to Christ, that this principle received its proper concrete contents; it was in him that it first became subjective and individual. This consciousness of freedom is frequently, and variously, and energetically expressed in the apostle's letters. It is expressed most directly and openly in 1 Cor. ix. 1, where he says: Am I not free? am I not an apostle? have I not seen Jesus Christ our Lord? have I not you to point to as my work in the Lord? These were the evidences which sustained his assured consciousness of freedom, independence, self-dependence as a Christian and an apostle. He calls himself free in the sense in which he spoke of Christian freedom in the eighth chapter (ἐξουσία, viii. 9), free, that is, as having an essential right to act in accordance with his own best convictions, without being bound by considerations regarding others, or being in the least degree subject to any superior authority.[1]

[1] The feeling of freedom is expressed most energetically where it meets with opposition. The opposition which the apostle had to encounter was the appeal made against him and in disparagement of him to the authority of the older apostles. Against them, then, he asserted his freedom in the fulness of its own native energy, and as not requiring any outward sanction, 1 Cor. ix. 4. They are to him only the δοκοῦντες. Their apparent dignity is no law to him; for wherever the truth of the gospel is concerned, there can be no respect of persons. If it be the apostles themselves that he calls οἱ ὑπερλίαν ἀπόστολοι, and not merely the Judaizing teachers of the Corinthian Church who appealed to their authority, then this is a very distinct assertion that there can be no external

The true freedom, however, is not without limitation ; it realizes the conception of freedom by the limit which it sets itself and then again makes to disappear : and that which is the greatest freedom from narrowing and enslaving forms is, on the other hand, the highest capacity for entering subjectively into forms the most diverse. This mark and evidence of true freedom was not wanting with the apostle. Though free from everything, free from all dependence on man, says the apostle, 1 Cor. ix. 19, " I have yet made myself the servant of all, that in this way I might gain the more. To the Jews I have become a Jew, that I might gain the Jews ; to those who are under the law as one under the law, that I might gain them that are under the law ; to them that are without law, as one without law (not that I was without law in reference to God, but obeying the law of Christ), that I might gain them that are without law. To the weak I became weak, that I might gain the weak : I am made all things to all men, that I might by all means save some." Only he can become all things to all men who is so free and master of himself as to be able to put on every form of self-restraint. And what makes this self-restraint possible to him is that he is subject to an infinite power, his freedom being simply the outward form in which this subjection appears. The utmost freedom of self-consciousness is thus, when looked at from another side, the utmost subjection ; he is free, but his liberty consists in his consciousness being altogether determined by Christ, it is only in his union with Christ as an ἔννομος Χριστοῦ that he knows himself free, and this his freedom consists in his subjection. It is with a view to this same freedom which consists in dependence on Christ that the apostle says, 1 Cor. vii. 23, " Ye are dearly bought ; be not ye the servants of men, do not be drawn into any spiritual dependence on men." In every event of life the

authority for him, by which he should consider himself bound. Λογίζομαι γὰρ μηδὲν ὑστερηκέναι τῶν ὑπερλίαν ἀποστόλων, 2 Cor. xi. 5, cf. xii. 11 οὐδὲν γὰρ ὑστέρησα τῶν ὑπερλίαν ἀποστόλων, εἰ καὶ οὐδέν εἰμι (though I be nothing in myself apart from the grace of God supporting me). And the reason of this is the assurance he had gained through the knowledge of the truth, εἰ δὲ ἰδιώτης τῷ λόγῳ, ἀλλ᾽ οὐ τῇ γνώσει.

Christian has this inward spiritual freedom, without it his consciousness would not be a Christian consciousness at all. He is
free inwardly though outwardly he be a slave. For in Christ
freedom and bondage pass into each other, and neither of the
two exists without the other. He who is called in the Lord
being a slave, is yet free in relation to the Lord : and he who is
called being free, is Christ's servant, 1 Cor. vii. 22. As there is
no contradiction in a man's being dependent on Christ and yet
free, nor in his being free and yet at the same time dependent,
so bondage externally does not in the least preclude inward
freedom. This inward freedom and independence of everything
outward comes only to the man who has found in Christ the absolute principle of his spiritual life. The more he feels his dependence on Christ, the more independent is he of everything but
Christ.

For a Jew who had been bound to the law from his childhood
and felt the law's authority and control in every part and province
of his life, to cut himself adrift from the law at once and altogether ;
to cast off its dictation, and with it to renounce all the natural and
national ties which bound Jew and Jew together,—this must have
been a step the gravity and far-reaching importance of which we
can scarcely measure. This step our apostle took in his conversion ; and in taking it he entered into a position of utter solitude ;
he was not attracted, though he became a Christian, to the older
apostles ; he was not drawn into fellowship with them, but remained alone. The boldness of this step may give us an idea of his
spiritual energy. Now the shaking off of authority and the advance to autonomy is not admirable in itself : the moral and
spiritual value of such a step consists in this, that it is not a capricious and arbitrary act, nor one brought about by merely outward
circumstances, but a step taken from a full conviction that truth
requires it. The autonomy which becomes the ruling principle
must, in a word, be the autonomy of reason. And we must keep
this in mind in considering the apostle's conversion ; for it was a
change from Judaism to Christianity, and Christianity, the absolute

religion, is also absolute reason. The apostle did, indeed, recognise in his conversion to Christianity a supernatural event, a miracle, a thing incomprehensible even to himself. Yet we see him labouring with all the power of his spirit to engraft this event which he had experienced, on his reason, to take it up into his thinking consciousness, thus to make it, what it could not otherwise be, his own spiritual act. In this fact more than anything else we have an explanation of the peculiar organization of his spiritual individuality ; for it is this spiritual process that is worked out in the whole development of his doctrine, and in the discussions, personal and otherwise, which form the main contents of his Epistles. To speak of nothing else, let it be considered how he deals with the idea of the law, how he analyses it in its various elements, and seeks thus to resolve it into itself, in order to justify to the thinking consciousness that degradation of the law from its absolute authority, that depreciation of it to the position of a merely subordinate stage, which was necessary from the standpoint of Christianity. The development of the apostle's doctrine of justification with all the ideas which belong to it,—what is it but an analysis of the Christian consciousness according to the inward connexion of its momenta as they act and react upon each other, the nature of justification being thus explained from the inner necessity of the case ? Here also we find the reason why the apostle's main developments of doctrine always grow in his hands into theories of religious history ; since the course of history cannot be understood save by regarding one stage as contained by implication in the preceding stage, and regarding the whole in the light of the immanent idea which is the principle of the whole movement. The different determining periods of history, the contrasts into which it is divided, the contrast of sin with grace, of the law which requires works with faith which justifies without works, of death with life, of the first psychical with the second pneumatical Adam, these are simply so many momenta of the conception as it works forward by its own inward power. The great distinguishing characteristic which appears everywhere in the apostle's writings is the innate impulse, springing from the

very roots of his nature, towards rational speculative contemplation.[1]

[1] It is a deep conviction of the apostle, and comes repeatedly and in various
ways to the surface in his writings, that Christianity is the truly rational, and
that in matters of religion nothing can stand that cannot justify itself to rational
contemplation. When he speaks, Rom. xii. 1, of a λογικὴ λατρεία, in which a man
is to present himself a living sacrifice to God, he means a service which does not
consist, like that of Judaism, merely in outward rites, but is spiritual in its nature
and founded in the spirit itself, so that in everything it contains the worshipper
must have the rational end and purpose of his act before his mind. And thus he
adds an exhortation not to hold exclusively to that which is in accordance with
the ruling tendency of the world and the time, but to be transformed in the
renewing of the spirit, (τοῦ νόος), *i.e.* to go back into one's self in thought, to consider and to prove in one's self what is the will of God, what is the good, and
acceptable, and perfect. And here, I think, we find the explanation of that distinction which the apostle sometimes draws between that which he is in his γνώμη,
and that which he is in pursuance of an ἐπιταγή of the Lord. It is not probable
that this ἐπιταγή refers to an utterance of Jesus which he had received through
tradition. A comparison of the various instructions which he gives on difficult
questions of social duty will show us what the nature of the distinction is.
Where he is conscious of a rational objective ground lying in the nature of the
case, his instruction at once and of itself assumes in his consciousness the form of
an immediate command of Christ. He speaks of a mere γνώμη in cases where
he could not deny the subjective nature of his view. Cf. 1 Cor. vii. 6, 10, 12, 25,
40. As the objective truth could only declare itself in the form of the subjective
consciousness, it is very natural that with the apostle the one constantly passes
over into the other. Thus he says, verse 25, that he has no ἐπιταγή of the Lord
in reference to virgins, but gives a γνώμη, ὡς ἠλεημένος ὑπὸ Κυρίου πιστὸς εἶναι,
i.e. an opinion deserving of all consideration, as given quite in accordance with his
apostolical consciousness. In the same way, verse 40, after the words κατὰ τὴν
ἐμὴν γνώμην, he adds, δοκῶ δὲ κἀγὼ πνεῦμα Θεοῦ ἔχειν. As his call was a fact
of his consciousness, the self-assurance of his consciousness was his highest principle of knowledge. His self-assurance, however, is not called forth by himself,
but rests on grounds of reason. The authority which he claims for himself as an
apostle must not be said to be founded on the external fact of the appearance of
Christ which he asserted he had had ; it was founded rather upon two inner
momenta : 1. The truth of his gospel, a thing to him irrefragably true, Gal. i. 8 ;
2 Cor. xi. 4, and resting ultimately in the absolute satisfaction of man's need of
salvation which it brought, in all that goes to make up faith in the Pauline sense.
2. The reality of the success of his work. He appeals to this as his strongest
argument against his opponents. Those whom he had converted could not but
bear witness that it was through him that they had become Christians, 1 Cor.
ix. 1-3 ; 2 Cor. iii. 2, 3. But how could they have become Christians through him
if he was not an apostle, and how could he have worked with such success as an
apostle, 2 Cor, x. 13-18, if it were not God's will that he should so work, and
how could this be God's will if it were not in accordance with the highest truth

If the first great characteristic of his personality be that he was as it were the receptive soil in which the principle of Christian consciousness should first take form and appear as a concrete consciousness, the second must be found in this, that that consciousness was expressed by him mainly in the way of thought. The apostle is conscious of the power of his thought; he declares to his opponents, 2 Cor. x. 2 *sq.*, how he intends to meet those who take him to be but a weak and ordinary man. For though, he says, I walk in the flesh, yet I do not war in a weak human way ; for the weapons with which I fight are not humanly weak, but divinely strong to the pulling down of strongholds. I cast down arguments, and every work that is erected against the knowledge of God, and bring every thought into captivity to the obedience of Christ. Far from being, as has been thought, the apostle's protest against the exercise of reason in things pertaining to faith, these words are an expression of the absolute confidence he reposed in his dialectical powers, that on the ground of reason he could never be defeated. The more we penetrate into the process of thought in the apostle's writings, the more minutely we analyse his mode of argument, the method of his development and representation, the more shall we be convinced that his is a thoroughly dialectical nature.[1] Here we may remind the reader of what was said, in our

and reason ? What he says, Gal. ii. 8, in the pregnant words that God ἐνήργησε ἐμοὶ εἰς τὰ ἔθνη is an argument from effect to cause, an argument which would have no force were it not understood that nothing can really take up a position in the world but what is more or less true and rational. The success of his preaching to the heathen is in his eyes a proof that his gospel is true. This was the best credentials of his apostolic calling. It says a great deal for the apostle's sober good sense that he never appeals to the appearance of Christ to him as a purely outward fact, such as the Acts represent it. There was a good deal of the ecstatical in him, as the ὀπτασίαι and ἀποκαλύψεις Κυρίου, 2 Cor. xii. 1, show us (the ecstasy described, verse 2, cannot, however, be identified with the act of his conversion ; the fourteen years, 2 Cor. xii. 2, cannot coincide with the fourteen years of Gal. ii. 1) ; but this element was so thoroughly subordinate to his clear and rational self-consciousness that it could never make him a visionary.

[1] It belongs to the essence of the dialectical method, that it proceeds by negation, and in order to deny, accentuates the opposite, the contrast, and thus has naturally an element of irony. In the apostle's dialectic irony is not wanting ; cf. 1 Cor. iv. 8 ; 2 Cor. xi. 18, 19 ; and Rückert's observations on the first of these

examination of the great Epistles, of their arrangement and the conception of thought from which it proceeds. We see everywhere in them the effort to place the subject treated of in the most general point of view it will admit of, to proceed from the general to the particular, and consider the main thought in all its aspects successively. What we have here is the true dialectical procedure ; namely that the thought is made to move through all its stages, and to arrive at the totality of its momenta, at which point its concrete determination coincides with and meets its abstract truth. Could the utter contemptibility of the sectarian squabbles at Corinth have been put more clearly than in the apostle's words : Is Christ divided ? Was Paul crucified for you ? Were you baptized in the name of Paul ? (1 Cor. i. 13.) Here a rapid turn of thought brings the question so entirely under the standpoint of an absolute contemplation, that we have nothing but an absolute Yes confronting an absolute No.[1] But the dialectical mediation follows at once. The apostle sees the source of the sectarianism of Corinth in the love of the Corinthians for worldly wisdom ; he therefore considers Christianity itself as wisdom. Wisdom is divided in his eyes into the wisdom of the world and the wisdom of God ; these are the two stages through which it moves ; through its negation in worldly wisdom it comes to affirm itself in the divine. At the opening of the Epistle to the Romans, in the same way, the apostle takes up the absolute standpoint of the δικαιοσύνη Θεοῦ, the two momenta of which are the δικαιοσύνη ἐξ ἔργων and the δικαιοσύνη ἐκ πίστεως. Here also the development consists in the conception passing

passages. The latter passage is a striking instance of his dialectic, as it fortifies itself with irony, and smites, overthrows, and crushes the opponent.

[1] Another notable instance of this is to be found in the passage 1 Cor. xi. 3. The question of women having their heads uncovered is at once put in this way : the head of the man is Christ, the head of the woman is the man : the head of Christ is God. The question whether the custom be a Christian one or no is placed under its absolute point of view : all that is asked is whether the custom be or be not consistent with the absolute dependence of Christ. Thus a question referring solely and simply to a case in practical life is identified with the very highest question, the relation to Christ. This rapid soaring up from the particular, the empirical, to the absolute, to the idea, to God, Christ, is a genuine Pauline trait.

through the stage of denial in order to affirm itself. The δικαιοσύνη Θεοῦ passes through the negation of δικαιοσύνη ἐξ ἔργων, and
becomes in δικαιοσύνη ἐκ πίστεως the true self-mediated δικαιοσύνη
Θεοῦ. It belongs to the dialectical method to take the object
which is to be explicated dialectically, in its various stages, both
negative and affirmative ; since it is only in the consciousness of
its mediation that the conception completes its dialectical movement.   And our view that dialectical thought was the apostle's
natural element is greatly confirmed by the fact that he never
forgets the practical side of his discussion in the theoretical.
What must be affirmed theoretically must often be denied practically ; for love, the principle of practical conduct, is also an element,
and has to be considered if the object is to be apprehended in the
totality of its momenta. That Christian love was a conspicuous
element in the apostle's character all that we know of his life and
work leads us to believe.   Here however we are more immediately
concerned with such traits as are provided in his writings, and
with the stamp of his essential spiritual character that is impressed
upon them ; and the place he has assigned to the element of love
even in his dialectical thinking is noticed only as a proof how free he
was in the whole attitude of his spirit from all onesidedness. Faith
was nothing to him in itself, if it did not work through love ; he could
not rest satisfied with a merely abstract theoretical view of anything;
his spirit urged him from the theoretical to the practical, from the
abstract to the concrete, from the essential thought to the realities
of life.   The end which he thus kept in view was of course the communion of Christian life inspired with the principle of love.   This is
well illustrated by those two sections of the First Epistle to the Corinthians in which the apostle expresses his views on the subjects of
eating the flesh of idolatrous sacrifices, and of speaking with tongues.
The eating of the heathen sacrifices seems to have been in itself a
thing of complete indifference to him ; yet he regards it as very important that the fact that the practice was objectionable to many
Christians should be recognised, and care taken not to wound them.
This consideration must be taken into account in order to a proper

settlement of the question ; and as soon as the question is regarded from this point of view it ceases to be indifferent to religion ; it acquires an importance which it might not of itself possess.   In the latter of the two sections we named, a place is even more distinctly and emphatically assigned to love, or the consideration due to others, to the common good, as a very important element in arriving at a decision.   In this case we see very clearly how it is just in this practical side of the matter that the dialectical solution of the whole problem is sought and obtained.   It is very obvious throughout that the apostle cares very little for the speaking with tongues.   He does not however regard it as unchristian, he recognises it as one of the various forms in which the spirit which dwells in Christians finds expression.   So he goes on to give it its definite position in the number of the Christian charisms, and to insist that each charism has an equal right to be considered, as making up along with the rest the unity of the whole.   Thus though the λαλεῖν γλώσσαις be in itself a charism, yet its true, real value depends on its practical operation, on its being through love a means to the furtherance of the common Christian life.   From this point of view the apostle pronounces a judgment on the λαλεῖν γλώσσαις which amounts to this : that from its small practical utility it ought to be as far as possible restricted.   Thus we see how in every case it is the apostle's object to exhaust the subject he has in hand in all its logical bearings, and to bring his discussion to a stage where the confronting momenta are mediated dialectically in the unity of the conception.   The apostle's whole representation, religious as it is, is filled to overflowing with the forms and elements of thought ; it is not only, what is commonly recognised as the great merit of the apostle's writings, that thought follows hard on thought : more than this, thoughts succeed each other as determinations and momenta of some one conception that is greater than all of them ; the thought unfolds itself, brings forth its own contents out of its own depths, and determines itself by taking up its own momenta.   Hence the peculiar stamp of the apostle's language : it is distinguished on the one hand for precision and compression; on the other hand it is marked by a harshness and roughness which suggest that the thought is far too weighty for the language, and can scarcely find fit forms for the superabundant matter it would fain express.[1] Yet in one way the form actually used is not uncongenial to the contents; the language is Hellenistic Greek, an easy and flexible instrument, and well fitted for such a peculiar writer.

The traits we have dwelt on thus far give us as their result a mind naturally and perfectly adapted to take up into itself and to develop the free, universal, and absolute principle of Christianity. This, however, is only one side of his individuality; there is another which we must not disregard. It is a thing of course that even so eminent a mind as Paul's is subject to a certain limitation. It is nothing but what we had to expect that besides all the splendid gifts that distinguished him we should find also a certain onesidedness, a con-

[1] The apostle indicates, 2 Cor. xi. 6, that he is not unconscious of this. He says he is εἰ καὶ ἰδιώτης τῷ λόγῳ, ἀλλ' οὐ τῇ γνώσει, a phrase which can refer to nothing but the struggle which it cost his thought to find expression. As for his language and style it has long been remarked, and very justly, that it bears a great resemblance to that of Thucydides. (We may mention the well-known work of Bauer, Philologia Thucydideo-Paullina, 1773, which, however, is merely a "notatio figurarum dictionis Paullinae cum Thucydidea comparatae," and deals chiefly with the outward expression.) As speech is the expression of inward thought, this similarity of modes of expression must be referred to a deeper similarity, namely of the mental idiosyncrasy of the two men. Such passages as 1 Cor. iv. 12, 13; vii. 29-31; ix. 20, 21; 2 Cor. vi. 9, 10 have the true ring of Thucydides, not only in expression, but in the style of thought. The genuine dialectical spirit appears in both in the love of antithesis and contrast, rising not unfrequently to paradox. Antithesis serves the dialectically thinking mind simply as a means to obtain a direct grasp of the conception in the whole of its bearings; it confronts the one with the other, negatives the one through the other, that the conception may thus determine itself through negation and affirmation. The analogy may be traced still further. Thucydides' critical method of dealing with history necessarily involved a breach with the great national consciousness which lived and had its being in the happy child-like Homeric-mythical theory of the world, proceeding to exhibit the conflict of Ionism and Dorism as a conflict within the larger whole, the nation. In the same way the apostle Paul could not take up the position of Christian universalism, in which the opposition of heathenism was done away, without renouncing the absolute importance of Judaism. With both these men the ties of national particularism give way before the generalizing tendency of their thought, and cosmopolitanism takes the place of nationalism.

sciousness in some way *borné*, a national particularism, which go to
make up this definite individual character which we have before us.
In our development of the Pauline doctrine the reader will remember how we came here and there on points in which it could not be
denied that the thoughts and views of Judaism were still discernible,
circumscribing his sphere of vision, directing his attention too exclusively to the future, and causing him to overleap momenta, which,
from a freer and more universal standpoint, could not have been
left unnoticed.   Then his expectation of the parousia—here we
see how his mind was influenced by the not very enlightened
national expectations that were current at the time, insomuch that
he expresses a firm belief that Christ's second coming would take
place in a short time, and that he with his contemporaries would
not need to pass through death and the resurrection, but would be
changed without dying.   We have already shown that this view is
not to be pressed to the apostle's disadvantage to such an extent as
some writers have done : and it is of importance in this regard not
to attribute to him anything that cannot be shown from Epistles
undoubtedly genuine to have been an element of his faith and
thought.   Yet this characteristic fact remains, that a view so manifestly peculiar and limited to the age in which it arose, and soon
to be left behind as events and thoughts moved forward, had such
influence as we see it had on the apostle's consciousness.   In this
case his view is narrowed by an idea peculiar to the nation and
the time ; but his whole position with reference to the Old Testament is another such restriction.   It was in opposition to the Old
Testament that he became aware of the perfect freedom of his Christian position, and everything that formed in his eyes an element of
Christian freedom was at the same time a liberation from the yoke
of the law, and from the imperfection and limitation of the Old
Testament dispensation.   Yet, on the other hand, how much do we
see him bound to the Old Testament, tied to the very letter of it ?
He rests his demonstrations of the most important positions of his
doctrine on inferences from passages of the Old Testament, and that
not merely out of regard for those to whom the Old Testament was

the supreme authority, in order to make it easier for them to believe in the Christian doctrine, but because the Old Testament is to him the source of all objective truth, the ultimate authority on which the certainty of the Christian faith must rest. When he reminds his readers of the cardinal facts of Christianity, that Christ died for our sins, that he was buried and rose again on the third day, he does not omit to add that this happened according to the Scriptures, 1 Cor. xv. 3, 4. The more he wants to establish the truth of any doctrine and preclude all doubt of it, the more does he labour to prove it from passages of the Old Testament. Even that most important truth of all, in which the whole doctrine of salvation consists, that the true righteousness which avails before God is not to be attained by works of the law, but only by faith, even this doctrine is made to rest directly on the fact that even in the Old Testament Abraham believed God, and that this faith was imputed to him for righteousness, Rom. iv. 1 *sq.* If, the apostle argues, Gal. iii. 7, one can only be saved as a descendant of Abraham, then those are the sons of Abraham who are saved through faith ; and as the promise was given to Abraham, that in him all nations should be blessed, this promise is now fulfilled in the fact that God justifies the heathen through faith. The promise was given to Abraham because the Scripture foresaw this event at the time when it was written. Christian faith is thus related to the Old Testament as the fulfilment to the promise : the former could not have taken place without the latter. And yet, as the apostle assures us in other passages, nothing can be more immediately certain than that which the Christian consciousness declares as its essential contents, or that which the divine spirit that is given to the Christian testifies to him.

The more the apostle enters into details in the inferences he draws from the Old Testament, the more striking does this dependence of the Christian consciousness on it appear. It is an authority lying outside of consciousness, and the deference paid to it arises simply from a personal subjective limitation. The most striking instances of this are to be found in two passages of the Epistle to the Galatians, in which, as is now acknowledged universally, the apostle deals with

the Old Testament passages from which he is reasoning in a quite
arbitrary way, and gives them a sense which they never could have
borne.   With regard to the passage, Gen. xxii. 18, which he takes
up, Gal. iii. 16, he simply adopts the interpretation which was
usually given it by the Jews at the time.   The seed of Abraham,
in which all the nations of the earth are to be blessed, he does
not take to be the posterity of Abraham generally, though this is
obviously the meaning of the expression, but one person, an
individual, Christ.   He deals with the passages Gen. xvi. 15, xxi.
2 even more capriciously.   His whole proof is nothing but a play
of allegory, and has no force whatever to prove anything.   The
whole argument is erected on the distinction shown to have existed
between Isaac and Ishmael, the two sons of Abraham, that the
former was the son of a slave, while the other was born not only
not a slave, but in consequence of a special divine promise.   In virtue of this difference they are made to represent the two διαθῆκαι.
Ishmael, the slave by birth, stands for the law, because the law
places men in a position of bondage before God.   The apostle
failed, however, to consider how little the subsequent history of
the two sons of Abraham fits in with the allegorical interpretation
he gives it.   Ishmael is made to represent the law, but the Mosaic
legislation never touched the sons of Ishmael.   It was they
who were free from the law, while those for whom the law was
given were none but the posterity of Isaac, the type here of the
διαθήκη of freedom ; and the promise connected with the person
of Isaac, in regard to which he was to be a type of Christians as
τέκνα τῆς ἐπαγγελίας, was only fulfilled by means of circumcision
and the Mosaic law, and the whole theocratic dispensation connected with the law.   Not only have the apostle's allegorical
demonstrations out of the Old Testament no objective basis in the
Old Testament itself,—they actually conflict with it.

There could be nothing more absurd than the efforts made by
interpreters to show the apostle's argumentation to be objectively
true.   *Flatt*, for example, remarks on this passage : " The apostle
received special divine instruction with a view to his expositions

of doctrine, and in that instruction the idea was communicated to him that Sarah and Hagar were types in the way he states. Thus he had a right to say that this history meant something else, had an inner meaning, that with regard to God's intention it was to be considered as a type, even though the author who wrote the history never thought of such a thing. The proposition,—This history has an inner meaning, is not, however, the same as the proposition, —When God caused the history in question to be narrated, he intended that it should be a prophecy in the form of a symbol: although we have a right to assume that in guiding the Old Testament writers God did not neglect to provide that the history should contain a certain amount of instruction for the future." What does all this mean? What a narrow petty theology is this! And what end does it serve? The apostle's subjective and capricious imagination, the mere play of his fancy, is to have its objective ground in the very spirit of God! And is the contradiction of historical truth which we find here removed by referring it back from the apostle to God himself? Luther had a healthier sense of truth, and judged: "The allegory of Sarah and Hagar will not hold water, for it is at variance with historical reason." This is the only true way of looking on the apostle's argument here; and thus the passage affords us a very curious proof of the position, both free and not free, which he occupied with regard to the Old Testament. In his view of the law that it places man altogether in the position of a bondman before God, a position of which the Christian consciousness knows nothing, he shows the greatest freedom of spirit, a self-assurance that has completely cast away all bonds of external authority. Here, on the other hand, we see him still confined to the old way of thinking about the Old Testament as if there were no other. For there cannot be a doubt that his allegory appeared to him to be the true sense of the Old Testament history, as an objective truth vouched for by the Old Testament. The Old Testament law is to be of force no longer, it has no power to constrain the religious consciousness; and yet the Old Testament stands before his mind with the undiminished weight of its divine authority. A thing that is objectively certain to him, being the immediate utterance of his self-consciousness, must yet, after all, be recommended and proved to him out of the Old Testament. The Old Testament itself is made to furnish proof that the law, its most essential part, has no longer any authority. The apostle makes out his case by means of allegory ; allegory is to him, as to his contemporaries, the equivocal expedient by which, while making use of the Old Testament, he yet cuts himself off from it, and places himself above it. Allegory holds to the Old Testament as its necessary object, and rests all its proofs upon it ; yet it only plays with the Old Testament, since the allegorist has already placed himself above it, though not fully conscious that he has done so. Yet, freely as he uses the Old Testament in his allegorical interpretations of it, allegory is itself the strongest proof of his subjection to it ; for otherwise he never could endure the unnatural restraint that allegory imposes on him. It might be urged that the two examples we have mentioned of arbitrary allegorical interpretation occur in the Epistle to the Galatians, undoubtedly the oldest that the apostle wrote, and in which his view of the law is not so fully developed as in the later Epistles. We must, however, remind the reader of 1 Cor. x. 1 *sq.*, a passage which shows us as distinctly as the others how fully the apostle shared with his contemporaries the allegorical ideas current in his time.

These limitations of the apostle's individuality on its intellectual side are little more than the widest and most general limitations, those of time and country. It cannot be required of any man that he should not wear the character of his time. Yet the more a man is conscious of the boundaries he lives in, the freer will be his attitude towards them, and the more will he be inclined to remember the limits to which every human individuality is subject, and to show to others the fullest consideration. How the apostle's spiritual freedom appeared in his regard and indulgence for weaker fellow-Christians, we have already shown. Yet we must add that in his dealings with others the apostle did not invariably maintain this standpoint. He cannot be said ·to have always looked at others from without, and to have been independent of his own subjective feelings. However convinced he was of the reality of his apostolical calling and of the absolute truth of his doctrine, still that cannot excuse his excesses in judging of his adversaries, and failing to distinguish involuntary from voluntary errors. Rückert remarks very justly on 2 Cor. ii. 17, that "Paul was apt to judge his opponents very harshly, and to impute motives for their conduct, which, in all probability, were not the true ones; since what he attributed to an unholy disposition might in many cases be the natural, and, considering the circumstances, must almost have been the necessary, outcome of honest prejudice (cf. Gal. i. 7, ii. 4, vi. 12). This harshness was part of his character as it was in the case of our own Reformer." He applies the same observation to the passage 2 Cor. xi. 12. What Rückert calls a harshness of character arises from inability to abstract from one's own subjective feelings, and transport one's-self into those of another. The apostle could not conceive the truth otherwise than as it appeared to him; and with regard to the different belief of another man he could not imagine that it had even a subjective foundation; what was asserted in their opinion being all the while nothing but that Judaism which was native to both them and him. With this influence which his idiosyncrasy exerted over his judgment of his opponents, we come down to the lower sphere of the peculiar bias and direction which he derived from character and temperament. We have already observed how this purely human side of the apostle appears chiefly in the Second Epistle to the Corinthians. The passage 1 Cor v. may also be compared. It can scarcely be denied that his character was marked by a certain excitableness or violence, which sometimes made him act precipitately, and rendered him liable to fitful and sudden changes of emotion. (This is particularly noticeable in 2 Cor. and in the Epistle to the Galatians.) We should obtain a deeper insight into the apostle's individuality, its psychical, and probably also its physical organization, if it were possible to form any clear ideas of the nature of the ὀπτασίαι and ἀποκαλύψεις, and the peculiar circumstances accompanying them, of which he speaks, 2 Cor. xii. But he gives us here only vague and distant hints on the subject, and it is impossible to fix any definite meaning on them, or to form any clear view of the subject from them.

But without this, what we have gathered while seeking for traits of his character is abundant confirmation of what he says of himself, 2 Cor. iv. 7, that he had a divine treasure in an earthen vessel.

APPENDICES.

APPENDIX I.

ON THE LITERATURE OF THE LEGEND OF PETER.

[See Part I. Chapter IX.]

THE first attack made on this legend proceeded chiefly from a general distrust of all such facts as were employed to provide a historical basis for the claims and encroachments of Rome. Such were the motives of those who either rejected the legend entirely or expressed grave doubts about it; first in the middle ages, when the assailants were parties in opposition, such as the Waldenses, or the declared enemies of the papacy, such as Marsilius of Padua, Michael of Casena and others; and then at the time of the Reformation and after it, when the assailants were Protestant historians, such as Matthias Flacius,[1] Claudius Salmasius,[2] and others.

[1] In his work published in the year 1554: Historia certaminum inter Romanos Episcopos et sextam Carthaginiensem synodum Africanasque ecclesias, de primatu seu potestate Papae, bona fide ex authenticis monumentis collata. Cf. p. 267, "Non constat plane, Petrum fuisse Romae. Nam quod Papistae scribunt, Petrum Romae 25 annos docuisse, cum usque ad 18 Ierosolymis docuerit, item in Ponto, ut aliqui tradunt, 5 annis fuerit, et Antiochiae 7, ad hoc etiam cum Babylone scripserit suam epistolam, propalam falsum est; inde enim efficeretur, ut longe ultra Neronis mortem vixisset, a quo tamen interfectus dicitur. Demonstratio item certa est, Petrum Romae non fuisse, quod Paulus Romam et Roma scribens, ac tam multos mediocres Christianos salutans et nominans, nusquam tamen vel unico verbo Petri tanti viri mentionem faciat." Flacius laid great stress on Gal. ii., p. 124: "Denique ego omnibus omnium mortalium historiis de Petro illam ad Galatas secundo a Paulo scriptam praefero. Ibi enim ille primum affirmat diserte Petro esse concreditum apostolatum seu episcopatum inter Judaeos, sibi vero inter gentes seu super gentiles. Deinde narrat, Petrum usque ad concilium Hierosolymitanum (quod circa 18 annos post ascensionem Christi, et septimo commenticii papatus Petri celebratum est) potissimum Judaeis praedicasse et de postero tempore sanctissimum datarum dexterarum foedus secum iniisse: quod

[2] Librorum de primatu Papae. P. 1 cum apparatu. Lugd. Bat. 1645.

By far the greater number of the Protestant divines, however, and especially those of the Reformed Church, who were much occupied with this field of historical research, considered the subject to be one calling for impartial treatment, and providing an opportunity to show their opponents how ready they were to respect the witness of history, when properly ascertained and resting upon fact.[1]

The first scholar who undertook a thorough historical investigation of the subject, and declared as the result of his researches that the common view was entirely destitute of historical reality, was Friedrich Spanheim. His Dissertatio de ficta profectione

ipse quidem velit praedicare Judaeis, Paulus vero debeat concionari gentibus. Ubi habes brevissime et verissime comprehensam historiam Petri, quae indicat, ei et a Christo potissimum super et inter Judaeos apostolatum, episcopatum seu papatum concreditum mandatumque esse : et eum tum ante Hierosolymitanam synodum, tum postea potissimum Judaeos docuisse, eoque potissimum ibi sedisse vel stetisse, ubi plurimi Judaei fuerunt, id est in Syria et aliis orientalibus partibus. Nam Romae non ita multi fuerunt : quandoquidem et nondum fuerant sic dissipati, sicut postea in eversione Hierosolymae, et Claudius eos Roma penitus expulerat." The Magdeburg Centuries do not express any distinct doubt of the supposed fact.

[1] Compare the whole series of the Protestant divines who held this position on the subject. F. Spanheim enumerates them in the treatise to be named below, p. 336 : Quinimo in Protestantium castris ἐπέχοντες non pauci, atque etiam largientes haud gravate plurimi, imo plerique, tantis auctoritatibus moti. Chamiero certe *non facile vellicandus videtur tantus consensus Patrum* sed neque Davidi Blondello, id perpetuo largienti, Romanam ecclesiam a Petro et Paulo fundatam atque instructam fuisse. Nec inficiati eam Petri inter Romanos praesentiam Th. Beza Annot. ad i. Petri v., Fr. Junius, Scaliger, Casaubonus, Petr. Molinaeus, Petitus, Usserius, Seldenus, Pearsonus, Fellius, Dodwellus, G. Cave, Bedelius ipse, et quotquot Ignatianis epistolis speciatim illi, quae est ad Romanos, patrocinantur, in qua Ignatius circa medium ad Romanorum coetum : οὐχ ὡς Πέτρος καὶ Παῦλος διατάσσομαι ὑμῖν. Quin Patricius Junius Notis ad Clementem, quod Petrus Romae vitam finierit martyrio dicit *potius* esse, quam ut in dubium vocetur. Similiter Hammondus vel his duobus testibus rem extra dubium poni, Caji scilicet et Dionysii Corinthiorum fide. Samuel Basnage at once followed Spanheim with a defence of the opposite view, in his Exercitat. histor. crit. de rebus sacris vel ecclesiast. Ultraj. 1692, p. 548. He declared : Me quod attinet, hic tantum antiquitatis auctoritas apud me valet, ut adventum Petrinum ad urbem orbis dominam in dubium adducere mihi sit religio, ita etenim, quae firmis cingunt historiam praesidiis, fama constans, testium vetustas atque fides incorrupta, pondus suffragiorum atque numerus, sub signis hujus narrationis militant ut historiae omni sit abroganda fides, si hac in re nutet.

Petri apostoli in urbem Romam, deque non unius traditionis origine, appeared in 1679.[1] Spanheim brings forward first the negative grounds, which make the occurrence appear so improbable *a priori*: Luke's silence on the subject in the Acts, where there was every reason to speak of it; the silence of Paul himself both in his Epistle to the Romans, and in the Epistles of the Roman captivity; the agreement arrived at by the two apostles, Gal. ii. 9, that the one should consider the ἔθνη as his province, and the other the περιτομὴ, after which it was not likely that Peter should have left his work in countries so distant from Rome, and taken part in the foundation of a church which consisted almost entirely of Gentile Christians. Spanheim then takes up one by one the oldest and most important authorities for the fact, and impeaches their credibility chiefly by the general argument, supported of course by special proofs in each case, that writers who accepted with avidity so many and so manifestly fabulous traditions, are unworthy of credence in the case of this tradition. He finds the roots of the tradition partly in a mystical interpretation of the name Babylon in the First Epistle of Peter, v. 13, partly in the myth of the journey of Simon Magus to Rome, Peter having followed him to that city; and partly in the ambition of the Church of Rome which could be satisfied with nothing less than this: ut Paulo in Romanae ecclesiae institutione, sed et in consummatione martyrii socius quoque Petrus adderetur, primus omnium apostolorum, πρῶτος in evangelio, πρωτόκλητος, προήγορος, ἀρχηγὸς, qui primum lapidem in aedificanda ecclesia posuisset, obsignaturus quoque fidem in ecclesiarum omnium prima (p. 383). Thorough as Spanheim's investigation was, and pertinent as his arguments on many points undoubtedly are, his treatise failed to do much to shake the old tradition. The church historians who followed him continued to think that the authorities were too strong to be impugned; they went further, and asserted (as, for example, Schrökh)[2] that it would be difficult to find another event in the history of the early

---

1 Opp. t. ii. (Lugd. Bat. 1703), pp. 331-388.
2 Kirchengeschichte, vol. ii., 2d ed., p. 185.

church that was established so firmly and beyond all question as
this one was by the unanimous testimony of the first Christian
teachers. Of the later church historians and critics, Eichhorn[1]
was the only one who ventured to assert the opposite, and this he
did with all his wonted boldness. He said that the apostle Peter's
residence at Rome, in company with Mark the Evangelist, was in
all probability a fable. The foundation of Peter's reported residence at Rome was, that his first Epistle was dated from Babylon,
(1 Peter v. 13); the early church interpreted this name figuratively, and said it stood for Rome; and this was the foundation on
which everything was built, Peter's labours for the Roman church,
his primacy and his martyrdom in that city, and all that has been
fabled of him in the old and in the new Christian world. It might
be asked with all confidence where any other piece of evidence
was to be found? And was this absurd evidence to be respected
by historical criticism? This startling attack was the chief means
of inducing another Catholic theologian to undertake a new investigation of the subject, looking at it in an unprejudiced way, which
is thoroughly deserving of respect. The results at which he arrived
were these : that it is quite unquestionable on historical grounds
that the apostle Peter came to Rome, that he taught and governed
the Roman church, and suffered death at last on account of his
faith ; but that his residence at Rome cannot have extended to
twenty nor to twenty-five years, but only at the outside to a few
months over one year.[2] While the Catholic party thus admitted
the necessity of setting bounds to the old tradition, and reducing
it to a minimum, Protestant historians and critics displayed a wish
to clear the controversy of polemical and party spirit, and met the
Catholics with a confession that some of their former writers had
gone too far. Neander and Gieseler were at one on this point.
The former[3] declared it to be simply hypercriticism, to throw doubt

---

[1] Einl. in's N. T., vol. i. p. 554. Cf. vol. iii. p. 603 *sq.*
[2] In the Essay on the apostle Peter's residence at Rome, being also a contribution to the chronology of the early Church, in the Theolog. Quarterly, published by
Drey, Herbst und Hirscher, Tüb. 1820, 4 H., p. 567 *sq.*
[3] Church History, vol. i. p. 296 (Bohn's Edition).

on the tradition that Peter had been at Rome, attested as it was by the consent of all the early authorities. This tradition was obviously to be referred to a period in which no one thought of exalting the church of Rome by the primacy of Peter. It was nothing but party and polemical spirit, Gieseler declared,[1] that led some Protestants to deny the reality of the event. Bertholdt,[2] Cölln,[3] Mynster,[4] and others, expressed themselves in the same way. Mynster for one thought that "what seduced the Protestant writers to throw doubt on a fact, attested as this was by the unwavering voice of all Christian antiquity, could have been nothing but polemical rancour, and that the writing in which these doubts had been collected, clearly betrayed by its title : Of the fictitious journey of Peter to Rome " (the essay of Spanheim), its true end and motive.

My essay, which appeared in 1831, has led the two church historians, Neander and Gieseler, to at least modify their former view. They are unwilling to give up the supposed facts at the root of the legend, yet they cannot deny the weakness of the evidence. Neander allows the possibility of the legend having arisen out of the circumstances of the Roman church which I referred to,[5] but hesitates to agree in my result, considering that the argument which we mentioned must still be allowed some weight. Gieseler's chief point of late is,[6] that if the legend proceeded from the Judaizing Christians in Rome, and was meant to give Peter the pre-ponderance over Paul, it is difficult to understand how it was not at once and strenuously contradicted by the Pauline party at Rome, and how the Pauline Cajus could be one of the chief author-

---

[1] Lehrb. d. Kirchengesch., vol. i. 2d Ed. 1827, p. 189.
[2] Hist. Krit. Einl. in das A. und N. T., Part V. p. 2690.
[3] Encyclop. of Ersch and Gruber, Part XVIII. p. 42.
[4] In the paper on the first residence of the apostle Peter at Rome in the Kleine Theol. Schriften, 1825, p. 143 *sq.* An arbitrary habit of wresting the statements of authorities from the context in which they occur, and allowing them just so much weight as suits the hypothesis to be established, is a prominent feature in Mynster's essay.
[5] Planting and Training, i. 379.
[6] Lehrb. d. Kirchengesch., 4th Ed. 1844, p. 103.

ities in favour of it. This requires no further notice after what we have already said.[1] Mayerhoff[2] gives his decided adhesion to my view and to the arguments on which it is based, while Olshausen[3] as decidedly opposes it. Of those who have given the weight of their authority for or against the legend without having thoroughly investigated the question, I name here Schleiermacher[4] and De Wette,[5] who both take the negative side. In the Catholic church, Windischmann[6] and Ellendorf[7] may be mentioned as having lately expressed their views on a question of such importance for their Church. The former seems to be excited by Protestant contradiction, and does battle for the truth of the old tradition with all the fervour of Ultramontane partisanship. But as for the conflict of authorities he has nothing better to allege than that Peter resided in Rome more than once, first between 42 and 51, and then between 64 and 68. The latter of these two writers brings his historical critical investigation to this result : " Peter may have been at Rome ; it is possible that he was there about the year 65 or 66. But it is nothing more than possible, and the opposite is equally likely, or even more likely. Nor can we take it ill of Protestants, if they follow the proofs offered by Holy Scripture, and by the earliest fathers, Clement and Justin, and hold Peter's residence at Rome, with all that is connected with it, to be a story drawn from the Apocrypha. Peter's residence at Rome can never be proved."

[1] Cf. vol. i. p. 252.

[2] Hist. Krit. Einl. in die Petrin. Schriften, 1835, p. 73 *sq.*

[3] Cf. vol. i. p. 247 *sq.*, where Olshausen's objections are met. On the assertions of Credner and Bleek, who are also defenders of the legend, compare my Abh. über den Ursprung des Episcopats, Tüb. Zeitschr. für Theol., 1838, H. 3, p. 45 *sq.*

[4] Vorlesungen über die Kirchengesch. (Sämmtliche Werke, zur Theol. Part II.), p. 69 : " I am one of those who disbelieve the entire story of Peter's residence at Rome."

[5] Einl. in das N. T., p. 314 : " The alleged fact is essentially improbable. The legend seems to owe its existence to an effort made on the part of the Judæo-Christians of the influential church at Rome, to prove Peter to have had a share in the foundation of that church."

[6] Vindiciae Petrinae, Regensburg, 1836.

[7] Ist Petrus in Rom und Bischof der römischen Kirche gewesen ? Darmstadt, 1841.

APPENDIX II.

COMPARISON OF THE PAULINE DOCTRINE OF JUSTIFICATION
WITH THAT OF JAMES.

[Supplement to Part III. Chapter III.]

THE main doctrinal position of the Epistle of James : ἐξ ἔργων δικαιοῦται ἄνθρωπος, καὶ οὐκ ἐκ πίστεως μόνον, ii. 24, is the direct opposite of the Pauline doctrine as it is stated, Rom. iii. 28, in the proposition, δικαιοῦται πίστει ἄνθρωπος, χωρὶς ἔργων νόμου. It cannot be denied that between these two doctrines there exists an essential difference, a direct contradiction. It may be urged that James says no more than οὐκ ἐκ πίστεως μόνον, that he thus refers δικαιοῦσθαι not exclusively to ἔργα, but partly at least to πίστις also. But the Pauline proposition, on the other hand, distinctly excludes ἔργα and refers δικαιοῦσθαι to that very faith of which James says that without ἔργα it is nothing, forms no element of the religious life at all. Those works, then, which Paul altogether repudiates are with James the ground of δικαιοῦσθαι; and that faith which with James has no religious value whatever apart from ἔργα, is with Paul the principle of δικαιοῦσθαι.

That the difference between Paul and James may not appear to be one of principle, it is generally assumed that they do not use the terms in question in the same sense : this is asserted either of δικαιοῦσθαι or of πίστις and ἔργα, and this difference in the use of terms is said to be quite consistent with agreement in thought on the main point at issue. One simple way of saving the harmony of the two apostles was to take the word δικαιοῦσθαι not in its Pauline sense of actual justification, but only of the manifestation of that which must flow from justification. Thus Calvin remarks on James ii. 24 : Certe Jacobus hic docere non

voluit ubi quiescere debeat salutis fiducia, in quo uno insistit
Paulus.   Ergo notanda est haec amphilogia, justificandi verbum
Paulo esse gratuitam justitiae imputationem apud Dei tribunal,
Jacobo autem esse demonstrationem justitiae ab effectis, idque
apud homines.   If the main difference is placed in the word δικαιοῦσθαι, then it is not necessary to take πίστις and ἔργα in different senses in the two writers.   The prevailing view is, however,
that the difference of the two is not to be sought merely in the
word δικαιοῦσθαι, but rather in the meaning they attached to the
words πίστις and ἔργα.   It is said that πίστις means with Paul
that faith in God which is founded upon Christ, and with James,
merely religious knowledge as such ; and that ἔργα are with Paul
the works of the Mosaic law, and with James, moral and religious
actions.[1]   Neander adheres to this method of reconciling the two
apostles, if, indeed, his wavering utterances on the subject yield
any distinct view at all.   He says, first, that Paul always regards
πίστις alone as that through which a man becomes and continues
to be a justified person before God, and from which all other
elements of good are spontaneously, and by an inner necessity,
evolved : and that Paul would never have said that faith and
works must co-operate in order to justification.   On the other
side, however, the material difference disappears.   For in this
apostle's thought, works are the expression of faith, and of the
δικαιοῦσθαι which faith procures, and are thus a necessary element
of the Christian life, faith having to approve itself through the
whole of life and conduct ; and so the apostle comes to say that
each man will receive his due according to the deeds done in the
body, whether good or evil, 2 Cor. v. 10.   Thus the Jacobean
type of doctrine is represented in Paul.[2]   If we are to regard these
remarks as actually shedding light on the subject, the chief
point in them must be this, that the ἔργα of James are different

---

[1] Cf. *e.g.* Pott in his Commentar zu Jak. ii. : Alium alio sensu vocabula πίστεως et ἔργων accepisse manifestum est—ita ut in tanta argumenti diversitate
neuter neutri repugnare potuerit.
[2] Planting and Training, ii. 23 (Bohn).

from those of Paul, that he means such works as proceed from faith, and are the fruits of faith. But Paul does not distinguish two kinds of ἔργα; he says quite broadly that it is impossible to δικαιοῦσθαι by them. This must apply to those that proceed from faith as well as to others; for if they proceed from faith, then faith is there already, and with faith justification: so that they cannot have been the means of justification.

Kern was thus perfectly justified in asserting that the difference between Paul and James is one of principle, and cannot be got rid of. James, he says, could never have made δικαιοῦσθαι depend on ἔργα, had not his notion of justifying faith been limited to faith as it manifests itself in action. Kern brings the difference to a point in the following propositions: with Paul, faith, because it is the faith which justifies, is the source of good works, of morally good conduct; with James, faith, because it is the source of good works and proves in them its own vitality, is the faith that justifies. With Paul justification is conditioned by faith, or justification and faith are both present together in the man who is justified by faith, and in faith works proceed from justification. With James justification is conditioned by moral conduct; here we must not even use the expression " by faith and by the works which it brings forth;" for this would separate faith and conduct from each other, which from the Jacobean standpoint is an inadmissible distinction; justification proceeds from works, in which faith proves itself a living faith. With Paul faith is regarded in the light of its origin and essence as the attitude of soul in which man is occupied entirely with his relation to God in Christ, and refers himself entirely to God, sinking all reference to himself or to his neighbour. Faith, being such, was of course for Paul the only possible channel of justification. In one aspect he could connect justification with love; for the beginning of love is present in that movement of the heart towards God which springs from confidence in his grace and seeks to appropriate it. But even in this case what the apostle has in view is simply and exclusively man's relation to God. Love is not considered as the man's principle of action, in his private or social relations ; it is spoken of merely because from the very nature of the moral life faith contains the germ of it. James, on the other hand, cannot conceive of faith but as issuing in that activity in which man brings forth what is in him both in reference to his neighbour, and to himself. To James, faith is nothing short of a principle of action, which man has acquired in order to act throughout the whole circle of his moral relations in a way that is in harmony with the will of God. Only when faith has thus proved itself sincere, and has reached its fulfilment, does man receive justification before God. According to this theory, then, active faith passes into consciousness of justification. With Paul, on the contrary, faith passes over from the consciousness of justification into that activity in which it proves itself a living faith by the influence it exerts in the man's private and social relations.[1]

This definition of the relation the two positions bear to each other is in the main accurate. Yet too large a concession is made to the unity of the two doctrines, when it is said that the πίστις of James is a principle,—a principle of action. We must go a step further in estimating the extent of the divergence, and assert that with James faith is not a principle of moral action at all. With Paul, faith evolves love out of itself, and shows itself active through love, and so faith is the principle of the practical ; it is the immediate unity of the theoretical and the practical ; there is no part of life that remains unaffected by it ; when it lays hold of a man it asserts its influence over every province of his spiritual nature. With James, faith has no practical element whatever ; it is never pointed out, as with Paul, that faith is the principle of ἔργα, of moral conduct. The faith of James is nothing higher than the faith of which Paul says, 1 Cor. xiii. 1 *sq.*, that the man who has it, and nothing more, is like a sounding brass and a tinkling cymbal. It was not to this faith that Paul ascribed the power to justify ; he says of it οὐδὲν ὠφελοῦμαι. To this vain and empty faith Paul opposes the faith which justifies, as the only

---

[1] Der Brief Jakobi, Tüb. 1838, p. 43 *sq.*

true one, but the former is the only faith with which James seems
to be acquainted. He says of faith indeed, that it συνεργεῖ τοῖς
ἔργοις, ii. 22, so that πίστις seems to be an active principle which
cooperates to justification; and he says that man is not justified
by faith alone (οὐκ ἐκ πίστεως μόνον, ii. 24); and justification by
works is called the fulfilment of faith, ἐκ τῶν ἔργων τελειοῦται ἡ
πίστις, ii. 22. Notwithstanding all this, however, he does not
seem to recognise any inner connexion between πίστις and ἔργα.
Had he done so, then πίστις must have appeared as the operating
principle of ἔργα, and πίστις would then be the main consideration; the ἔργα would be merely the form in which the inner πίστις
becomes external. But how can James have conceived πίστις as
standing in this relation to ἔργα, when he applies expressions to
it which deny that it has in itself any life and activity, qualities
which, had it been a principle, it must of necessity have had?
That cannot have the rank or importance of a principle, which, as
is said of faith in unmistakable terms, is dead for all further purposes, is devoid of strength or life, and must be likened to a body
that is without spirit, without any principle of animation (ii.
20-26). And how could James have attributed δικαιοῦσθαι simply
to ἔργα, if ἔργα were themselves to be referred to πίστις as their
principle, so that their power to justify was derived from πίστις?
It is evident that ἔργα and they alone are regarded as real and
substantial; they are not merely a form in which a substance
derived from something else that is greater is deposited; they are
what they are immediately, of themselves and in virtue of their own
nature, not merely the Outward of a different Inward, such as faith
would be. It is true that James places πίστις by the side of ἔργα
and even makes πίστις the presupposition of ἔργα, but what does this
amount to? It amounts merely to this: that faith is present as well
as works, but no more is asserted than that it is present. The συν-
εργεῖν of which he speaks signifies nothing more than this: that
πίστις, mere theoretical knowledge, is a concomitant element of
the religious consciousness, of which, however, works are the substantial form. The view implied rather than stated here is one

according to which the theoretical and the practical, knowledge on the one hand, and on the other the action which is in perfect harmony with will, do indeed stand side by side, but are quite unmediated with each other. Each exists for itself, and forms a sphere for itself beyond which it does not pass, and being thus unconnected with each other, they actually fall asunder. The unity is not reached in which the two sides are embraced and harmonized. It is by no means the case here, as with the Pauline conception of faith, that the theoretical and the practical are felt to form a unity, the latter being contained implicitly in the former, and being related to it as the outer to the inner. And if this interpenetration of the theoretical and the practical be wanting, and with it that unity of the spirit which the two ought to combine to form, if the two elements stand side by side without being mediated with each other, then, of course, the practical must appear to be the immediate and the independent, and the centre of gravity of the religious consciousness must fall on the side of the practical. This is plainly stated in the proposition that religion consists essentially in willing and in action, or that no δικαίωσις is possible, save what comes through ἔργα. Only ἔργα are reckoned to be real and objective, since they are what exists in the state of actuality. Now this amounts to saying that only what exists outwardly, empirically, to the senses, is true and actual. This outward existence, however, necessarily presupposes other existence in a different form, that is, in essence ; and even the Jacobean view recognises that ἔργα come after and presuppose πίστις. But the characteristic feature of the position is that what is in essence is held to be the unreal, the empty, the shadow, which, existing as it does in essence is held unimportant, and scarcely worth considering. Thus with James the relation of πίστις to ἔργα is this, that πίστις has scarcely any real existence in itself at all, that it is only in ἔργα that it begins to exist truly and actually. The Pauline doctrine of justification takes us to the very opposite pole ; here everything actual has reality only in virtue of that which it is in essence. Πίστις is what ἔργα pro-

ceed from and presuppose ; and the value of ἔργα consists entirely
in πίστις ; this is the substantial element in them, this is the
main point in question, and ἔργα are, as it were, a mere *accidens*
of πίστις. Not that which exists externally, but that which is essentially, is true and real; and only that which can be conceived as being
in essence can truly exist, as with Paul ἔργα are true, actual ἔργα
only inasmuch as they are operations of πίστις. Regarded from the
one standpoint ἔργα have their absolute value in themselves; they are
for themselves the absolute, and the fact must be overlooked that
as material phenomena they are and must be finite and imperfect.
Regarded from the other standpoint, the ἔργα appear as the particular, and bear a negative and inadequate relation to their own
essential conception. This negative character of the particular
must be constantly corrected by a reference to the unity of the
whole, namely to faith, the moral disposition which is the totality
of the particular actions. The contrast of the Jacobean and the
Pauline doctrine is thus not merely that of the Judaeo-Christian
and the opposite school of Christian thought : it is the contrast of
the empirical and the speculative. Paul rises in his doctrine of
faith from the empirical consciousness to the spiritual ; starting
from the position that works as the particular can only be finite,
inadequate, and negative, and that the consciousness of the absolute, if there be such a thing, cannot reside in works themselves
but must be something beyond and above them, he rises to that
which is essential, and which works presuppose. This is faith ;
it is as a unity, as a totality, what works can only represent in a
finite, inadequate and negative way. Looking at the doctrine of
James from this point of view, we cannot but consider it a retro-
gression from that of Paul. When James puts δικαιοῦσθαι ἐξ
ἔργων in place of the Pauline δικαιοῦσθαι ἐκ πίστεως, he ascribes
to works that absolute value which faith has with Paul. The
reason why Paul denied δικαιοῦσθαι to ἔργα was that there was
nothing absolute about them, and that they could only stand in
an inadequate relation to δικαιοῦσθαι. Now what does James do
but vindicate for works that absolute character which, according to

Paul, they cannot possibly have ? They could not have this absolute character except in virtue of their unity with faith, and
thus the absoluteness of works would not belong to works but to
faith. This absoluteness of faith, however, is just what James
denies. He must therefore place the absoluteness which works
must have in their reference to δικαιοῦσθαι in the works themselves, regardless of the proof that has been given that works cannot as such have any absolute value. What is this but going
back to a position which Paul had already overcome ? The absolute standpoint of Christian consciousness which Paul took up
in his doctrine of faith is degraded again to that of Judaeo-Christianity, at which a value is ascribed to works, which from their
very nature they cannot possibly have. The spiritual consciousness of faith is made to retreat before the empirical consciousness
of works.

But though the account here given of the relations the two doctrines bear to each other be accepted as satisfactory, the further
question will remain, whether the Epistle of James is to be regarded
as an intentional denial of the Pauline doctrine. This question is
so important for the history of Paulinism that we feel bound to
devote some attention to it. Schneckenburger[1] and Neander[2] have,
as is well known, maintained that this is not the case. Neander
asserts that the proposition of James, which most scholars
seem constrained to regard as a denial of the Pauline doctrine
of justification, belongs to quite a different province of religious
life from that doctrine, and is aimed at a tendency of the Jewish
mind, at the dead faith of Jewish religiosity. " It is mere imagination," Neander says, " to suppose that James alludes to the expressions and the illustrations of Paul. And is this allusion, if such
it be, so very striking ? Let it be remembered that the Pauline
phraseology arose out of Judaism, from the Judaeo-Hellenic use of
terms,—it was by no means made up of new expressions, but often
simply appropriated the old Jewish terms, employed them in new

[1] Annot. ad Epist. Jac. 1832, p. 126 sq., Beiträge zur Einl. in's N. T., p. 196 sq.
[2] Planting and Training, i. 357 sq.

combinations, applied them to new contrasts, and animated them
with a new spirit. Thus neither the term δικαιοῦσθαι in reference
to God, nor the term πίστις, was entirely new; both of these ideas
had long been familiar to the Jews. And the example of Abraham
as a hero of faith must have been obvious to every Jew," etc. All
this is very well known, and no one denies it; but what does it
prove with regard to the position to be assigned to the Epistle in
the history of the primitive Church? With regard to this, the
only question we have to ask is, whether the onesided and perverted
religious position which James denotes with the formula δικαιοῦσθαι ἐκ πίστεως can be regarded as a phenomenon which stands
in any natural connexion with Judaism. And this question must
undoubtedly be answered in the negative. Abstract notional faith,
such as the term δικαιοῦσθαι ἐκ πίστεως may denote when used
in a bad sense, was never one of the leading errors of the Jewish
religion. It is true that faith is an important feature of the Jewish
religion, faith, that is, in the One true God, or the γινώσκειν Θεὸν,
by which Judaism is distinguished from heathenism, This faith,
however, is an essentially practical thing; it is essential to it that
the knowledge of God should always be accompanied by the worship
of God through all the religious actions which are prescribed in the
law. Judaism is no mere speculative monotheism : it is the religion
of the one · true God who has revealed himself in the law; and as
the law demands, according to the very conception of its nature, to
be observed and kept, so action in conformity with the law is the
very essence and the distinctive characteristic of the Jewish religion. Thus except where confusion arose from the invasion of
foreign elements, the main errors of the Jewish religion were not
errors of theory, but of practice ; the form of religious life was
determined by the law in its various aspects and demands. Now
it is certainly possible that the main error of a legal religion such
as Judaism may consist in the mere knowledge of the law being
regarded as the most important point. But the law being in its
very essence a thing to be practised, knowledge thus divorced from
action cannot be considered a peculiar development of the legal

U

religion, but must be considered as simply irreligion. The dead knowledge of the law and the empty learning of the Scribes which Neander cites is not a form of religion, but an utter want of the true religious life. Now, even though δικαιοῦσθαι ἐκ πίστεως were a mere onesided development of Judaism, there must yet be something in it that might possibly become the principle of a definite direction of religious life. But no man could ever propound it as a principle to be seriously accepted and acted on, that mere knowledge is all that is wanted in order to satisfy the law. Where mere knowledge is made to take the place of action, it is not that a theory to this effect has been advanced or accepted; it is merely that there is a deficiency of practical conduct. In no case, however, could this mere knowledge, knowledge for its own sake and regardless of action, be rationally called πιστεύειν; knowledge and faith are not the same, and it would be hard to see what was meant by faith in such a connexion. The chief aberration of the religious life of Judaism is not to be sought on the side of the theoretical; but it is distinctly to be found on the side of the practical. The danger to which a religion that insists on legal obedience is most exposed is that action may be dissociated from disposition, that an action which is merely external and consists in the external performance of works may come to claim for itself a real religious value. In this regard there is no more notorious phenomenon in the whole history of religion than the legal formalism, the work-holiness, the *opus operatum* of the Jewish religion. Neander seeks, very naturally, to introduce the notion of the *opus operatum* as an element in this discussion. He finds the *opus operatum*, however, in such a faith in the one Jehovah and the Messiah as leaves the disposition unaffected; a notion entirely untenable, and, indeed, self-contradictory. An *opus operatum*, where such exists, cannot be an inward thing such as faith : it must be something outward, some work or performance. If then the δικαιοῦσθαι ἐκ πίστεως, which James condemns, be a product of Judaism, it would more aptly be called δικαιοῦσθαι ἐξ ἔργων. But there can be no doubt that the δικαιοῦσθαι ἐκ πίστεως which Paul condemns is an error chargeable to the Jewish cast of religion. Thus we should have the curious fact that the Jewish religion is charged with two opposite errors, δικαιοῦσθαι ἐκ πίστεως and δικαιοῦσθαι ἐξ ἔργων, by two writers who, on the hypothesis, are at one on the nature of the Christian δικαιοῦσθαι. This is somewhat difficult to grasp ; and it is equally difficult to see how, after James had denied δικαιοῦσθαι ἐκ πίστεως, Paul on the other hand came to deny δικαιοῦσθαι ἐξ ἔργων. To suppose that the denial of δικαιοῦσθαι ἐκ πίστεως preceded that of δικαιοῦσθαι ἐξ ἔργων is manifestly a perversion of the natural and logical order of affairs. The element of the Jewish religion, which must have excited the most lively repugnance in the fully formed Christian consciousness, as it appeared for the first time in Paul, was undoubtedly its empty confidence in outward works. From this it was necessary to appeal to the inner disposition,—to faith. Then, when the inward, or faith, had come to be regarded as the most important point, the suspicion might very naturally arise, that too much importance was ascribed to this part, and that action and practice were in danger of being neglected. And it is obvious how naturally this suspicion would arise in the form of a reaction against the Pauline doctrine of justification by faith in the minds of men whose whole history and habits of thought disposed them to place the essence of religion in the practical, or in works, that is to say, in the Judaeo-Christians who could scarcely be said to have left Judaism behind them. It is only in this way that Paul's denial of δικαιοῦσθαι ἐξ ἔργων, and James's denial of δικαιοῦσθαι ἐκ πίστεως can appear in that natural relation to each other, which they must have held in the course of the advance from Judaism to Christianity. Christian polemic on the subject of δικαιοῦσθαι can have found the object of its attacks nowhere but in Judaism, as Neander cannot but allow. Now if the first object of attack in this controversy were δικαιοῦσθαι ἐκ πίστεως, then (not to mention that Neander's rendering of it as an element of Judaism is utterly capricious and unwarranted) we should have this curious and unnatural state of affairs before us : that James calls the Jewish δικαιοῦσθαι a δικαιοῦσθαι ἐκ πίστεως, while Paul uses this expression of the Christian way of justification ; and that James calls the Christian δικαιοῦσθαι a δικαιοῦσθαι ἐξ ἔργων, the expression by which Paul denotes the Jewish. In this way the Jewish δικαιοῦσθαι would be the Christian, and the Christian the Jewish ; the two writers would be writing of the same thing, but in each of the two expressions that had to be employed on the subject, each writer would mean the opposite of what the other writer meant. The two expressions would thus exchange meanings, without a word of explanation being added, and although one of the two writers must have had the other before him. So unnatural a theory of the relation between James and Paul could only have been invented to serve some purpose. The reason why it was denied that the Epistle of James contained any reference to the Pauline doctrine of justification was that this was the evidence that had been used to prove its later origin or its spuriousness. Thus in this case also personal considerations were placed above considerations of fact and substance. One would have supposed that there was a sufficient contrast between the author of this Epistle, a writer so much at home in the Greek language and in Greek modes of thought, and a genuine Palestinian Judaeo-Christian like James, as we know him especially from the description of Hegesippus ; and that this would have been enough, had there been no other evidence, to preclude the idea that the latter could have been the writer.[1]

[1] As the Epistle undoubtedly presupposes the development of the Pauline doctrine, its date cannot be placed very early. The Pauline doctrine must have become generally known, and its opposition to Judaeo-Christianity perceived, before this Epistle was written. But it is not only the doctrine of the apostle Paul that we see to have been in existence at the time ; we find allusions to his Epistles, which leave little room for doubt that the author was acquainted with them. Compare i. 2 with Rom. v. 3 *sq.* ; i. 18 with Rom. viii. 23 ; i. 21 with Rom. xiii. 12 ; i. 22 with Rom. ii. 13 ; ii. 21 with Gal. iii. 6, Rom. iv. 3 ; iv. 1 with Rom. vii. 23 ; iv. 4 with Rom. viii. 7 ; iv. 12 with Rom. ii. 1, xiv. 4. As for the use made of the example of Abraham, this, as De Wette remarks, Theol. Stud. u. Krit. 1830, p. 349, cannot be held to prove that James was referring to Paul's Epistles to the Galatians and Romans. Paul and his followers may have used the argument frequently in their oral discourses. Yet in view of such a

The doctrine of this Epistle, then, must be considered as intended to correct that of Paul. But we should not do justice to the Epistle nor understand its doctrinal position if we judged that this correction of the Pauline doctrine was the chief end for which it was written. What is devoted to this subject is manifestly only a part of the contents of the Epistle, which are in general eminently practical, and consist chiefly of admonitions and instructions. The main characteristic of the Epistle is its practical tendency, and this can only be understood from the Judaeo-Christian standpoint from which it is written. What we have here is no longer the original harsh and rigid opposition of Judaism to Christianity, as we meet it in the Epistles of our apostle; the opposition has softened down, the harsher demands of the law are now departed from. There is nothing here to remind us of the Judaeo-Christianity of James, a man whom we know from Gal. ii.

series of analogous passages it becomes more probable that there was such a reference. A curious circumstance is the appeal made both in this Epistle and in that to the Hebrews to the example of Rahab ; James ii. 25, Heb. xi. 31. De Wette observes very truly :—"It is very improbable that the idea of quoting Rahab as an instance of faith occurred to any other mind than that of the writer to the Hebrews ; it is not faith that she is celebrated for in the Old Testament, and her character is not above suspicion. The peculiar train of thought, however, which that writer was pursuing led him to exalt her as a heroine of faith. It is therefore extremely probable that James made use of this Epistle, and this very obvious fact could scarcely be denied on the evidence that properly belongs to the subject. The reason for refusing to accept it must be drawn from some foreign motive, or must consist in mere prejudice. Let each man lay his hand upon his heart, and ask himself whether, if the deductions to be made from this fact were such as suited him, he could continue to deny it." Neander's reply to this consists in the question whether the allusions are so obvious after all. It is always possible to put such questions, but they do not conceal the underlying subjective interest and motive, which Neander indeed almost acknowledges, to make the Epistle of James earlier than Paul. Every unprejudiced person must see that an Epistle which contains references to that to the Hebrews must be post-Pauline. Compare De Wette's Einl. in d. N. T., p. 310, where the true verdict on the subject is given :—" The signs of later composition which the Epistle itself contains are abundantly sufficient to prove that it was not written by James the brother of the Lord, but by a later author who assumed his name. The fiction of which he availed himself, and of which moreover the unepistolary form of address is an additional feature, was one not uncommon in antiquity. This view is not new to the church, and it is only narrowness and timidity that will be startled at it now-a-days."

to have been impregnated with all the obstinacy of traditionary
Judaism, and to have been the uncompromising upholder of every
Jewish institution, even of circumcision. Christianity is indeed
regarded as a νόμος, but it is a νόμος which has cast off the
yoke of ceremonial Judaism ; all that the expression is meant to
convey is the idea of religion as moral action, as practical conduct.
It can never cease to be considered an essential element of religion
that it is a practical thing and must go forth in moral and religious
action or works : and this, the main substance of the religion of
the Old Testament, is asserted to belong to Christianity as well.
This suggests to us that though Christianity was at first identical
with Judaism in the eyes of the Judaeo-Christians, it had by the
time when this Epistle was written passed through a certain process of development, and had thus reached a stage much later in
time than that of Gal. ii. And when the writer calls the law the
νόμος τέλειος τῆς ἐλευθερίας, we see plainly enough the influence
that Pauline Christianity had been exerting in this quarter. The
Judaeo-Christian writer of the Epistle has come to entertain the
idea of freedom, an idea which can have signified nothing but the
liberation of the consciousness from everything which appeared
from the Christian point of view to be the yoke of Jewish bondage : and it was the apostle Paul who first introduced this idea
into Christian thought. This standpoint, belonging as it did to the
more educated Christian consciousness, was one which James was
far from having made his own, for we must not form our estimate
of his position from the Paulinizing account of him given in the
Acts. Nor can any one who has conceived even a tolerably rational
view of the history possibly consent to regard that Judaeo-Christianity which had passed through the Pauline process of development, and the original Judaeo-Christianity which rejected the
root-principle of Paulinism, as belonging to the same group or
epoch, or to disregard the wide gulf that lies between the two. It
is urged by Neander that the readers of the Epistle were none but
Judaeo-Christians and as such neither inclined nor able to attach
themselves to Paul or to assimilate the Pauline system. This may

be so ; yet they are not by any means unaffected by the Pauline
view of the law : the great concession is an accomplished fact, that
Judaism is to dispense with several of its most important institutions for the sake of the alliance with Christianity.　The main
point is now to maintain Judaism on its spiritual side, as
the religion of practical conduct or moral action.　Regarded in this
way the Epistle of James presents to us that form of Christianity
in which it was based upon Judaism indeed, but Judaism spiritualized and released from its positive forms, and was conceived as
mainly a practical religiousness.　Pauline Christianity devotes its
energies to the discovery of, and engrossment in, what is deepest in
the Christian consciousness ; it is aware of a certain tendency to
speculation ; it seeks to become a comprehensive theory, and to
grasp the contents of Christianity in the light of its absolute idea,
as represented in the person of Christ.　It is not content with a
simple declaration of the forgiveness of sins as a Christian truth, it
seeks to explain how the fact is possible, and by what ways and
means it is brought home to the consciousness.　It recognises and
asserts that the true essence of Christianity is found only in the
history and the person of Christ ; but it does not rest in this as a
fact declared ; it seeks to apprehend the person of Christ in its
highest, its absolute significance.　The standpoint of the Epistle of
James is an entirely different one.　Here the peculiar Pauline
ideas of the death of Christ and its atoning virtue, of the Holy
Spirit as the principle of Christian consciousness, and the subjective
appropriation of salvation, and of the person of Christ, are left out
of sight, not merely because they do not happen to come in the
writer's way (being however presupposed, as it is said), but because
they lie entirely outside of his sphere of vision.　The higher
dignity of Christ is but barely hinted at in the expression $X\rho\iota\sigma\tau\grave{o}s$
$\tau\hat{\eta}s$ $\delta\acute{o}\xi\eta s$, ii. 1.　This is the only passage in the Epistle where
Christ is named, so different is it in this respect from those of
Paul.　$N\acute{o}\mu os$ and $\kappa\acute{v}\rho\iota os$ are no more than mentioned, and the
latter in so indefinite a way that $\kappa\acute{v}\rho\iota os$ may be understood of God
as well as of Christ.　We see here what an Old Testament and

deistical thing, so to speak, Christianity would have become, if this had been the only channel of its development. There is no living impulse here to develop organically the specific Christian element as it is contained in the idea of the person of Christ: what is specifically Christian fades away into general religion, of which the practical is the substantial element. Christianity is indeed the word of truth (i. 18); not however as the eternal Logos, in the absolute idea of whom the Christology of Paul finds its satisfaction, but as the principle of a new moral creation and regeneration, through which it is to operate practically in moral conduct and action. As then Pauline Christianity, following up its theoretical tendency and going back to the inner principle of Christian consciousness, reaches a point where it seems directly to conflict with this mainly practical interest, it is inevitable that these two tendencies, the Pauline and the Jacobean, starting as they do from opposite poles, should at this point come into collision. This point is reached in the doctrine of justification by faith, as Paul propounds it; the opposition lurking in the two tendencies from the beginning appears in all its force in the conflicting statements : δικαιοῦται ἄνθρωπος ἐξ ἔργων, and δικαιοῦται ἐκ πίστεως.

Let it not be supposed, however, that this correction of the Pauline doctrine of justification was the writer's sole object in composing his Epistle. Had this been the case, the subject must have occupied a much more prominent position in the Epistle, and been distinctly marked as its principal topic. It is clearly its connexion with the rest of what he has to say that leads the writer to take up this point. It is not hard to discern that the task the writer proposed to himself was to give a systematic view of Christian life as it appeared from the peculiar standpoint which he occupied with his particular form of Judaeo-Christianity ; to show what form and aspect Christian life with all its parts assumed in the light of such views as he held. Now as this standpoint was a thoroughly practical one, for the character of the Jewish religion, with which Christianity is so intimately blended here, made this a thing of course, it is natural that the Epistle should be occupied mainly with the principal elements of practical moral life, as it displays itself in Christian actions and endurance.   The Christian is to be exhibited here—in the character he wears from this point of view, as an ἀνὴρ τέλειος; and the perfection of Christian life—which can be nothing but an ἔργον τέλειον.   The whole contents of the Epistle may be very simply and naturally arranged in the light of this idea.   But we do not enter further into these details, our object in making these remarks being simply to show the relation borne by the doctrine of the Epistle to that of Paul, and to restore the Epistle to its place in the history of the early development of Christianity, from which it has been removed by unfounded and arbitrary assumptions.

APPENDIX III.

THE TWO EPISTLES TO THE THESSALONIANS : THEIR GENUINENESS AND THEIR BEARING ON THE DOCTRINE OF THE PAROUSIA OF CHRIST.

[Supplement to Part II. Chapter VII.[1]]

DR. LIPSIUS has lately returned to the discussion of the First Epistle to the Thessalonians, and has referred to my criticism of it.[2] He is of opinion that it is possible to accept my account of the peculiar characteristics of the Epistle without being shut up to my conclusion with regard to its genuineness. All that is needed for this end, he thinks, is a correcter view of the object of the Epistle. "The marks of a controversy against Judaism, of which the Epistle contains a considerable number, have never yet been placed in the right light. The apostolical dignity of Paul has been impugned or threatened, and his object in celebrating as he does the praises of the Thessalonians is to draw attention to the success of his labours among them as the best evidence of his apostolical calling. The passage ii. 3 betrays a distinct personal interest of this nature. He had been charged, and this attack can only have come from the Jews, with πλάνη, ἀκαθαρσία, δόλος, and doubts had been raised as to the purity of his motives. The Epistle carries us back to the time when Paul had just founded the churches of Macedonia. His repeated appeals to the Thessalonians as to the effectiveness of his preaching and the divine origin of his doctrine, his eagerness to defend himself against the imputation of impure motives, the description of his unselfish con-

---

[1] From the Theol. Jahrbücher xiv. 1855, p. 141 *sqq.* Cf. above, p. 97.
[2] In the Studien und Kritiken 1854, p. 905 *sqq.* : Ueber Zweck und Veranlassung des ersten Thessalonicher briefs.

duct, by which he rebuts the charge, and the statement to which he recurs again and again, that he does not aim at the applause of men, all this reminds us of the closely analogous situation of the Corinthian Epistles, especially the second. But the chief interest of the First Thessalonian Epistle is derived from the fact that the opposition to the apostle is not yet so pronounced and definite as we find it in those to the Corinthians. The opposition party has not yet taken shape, but the elements of it are already discernible, and the apostle sees the storm brewing. In these circumstances he had to take measures as far as possible to fortify his own position against the libellous attacks of his enemies, and to secure the church he had founded from inward disorder and dismemberment."

The chief point that criticism has to consider in the case of the first of these Epistles is undoubtedly the striking resemblance which, as I have already shown, it bears in a number of passages to the Epistles to the Corinthians. Dr. Lipsius does not deny the fact of this resemblance; but he differs from me in holding this Epistle to be the original, while I hold it to be the copy. We have thus to inquire whether we can reasonably consider the circumstances spoken of in this Epistle to be the beginnings and elements of the similar, only more fully developed set of circumstances which we find in the church of Corinth, or whether there is anything to show that they have been adopted for literary purposes, such as a later author writing under the assumed name of the apostle might think himself justified in promoting in this way. I am decidedly of opinion that the latter is the case. Repeated investigations of the subject have confirmed my conviction that the passages in question in the Thessalonian Epistles give us nothing that is primary or fresh or self-evidencing; that they are the copy of an original, that the features of the original have lost much of their clearness in being reproduced for another circle of readers, and that only by going back to the original is it possible to infuse life and reality into these fainter outlines. I shall seek to prove this in detail.

The Epistle begins, after the Pauline greeting and benediction, with almost the same words as 1 Cor. i. 4: εὐχαριστοῦμεν τῷ Θεῷ πάντοτε περὶ πάντων ὑμῶν, and with a thanksgiving, as in the Corinthian Epistle, for all the blessings conveyed to the Thessalonians through the gospel that had been preached to and received by them. The contrast drawn, i. 5, between λόγος and δύναμις shows the author to be moving in the same circle of ideas as the apostle in the first chapters of First Corinthians, though he merely extracts the general drift of ideas which there appear in much greater detail. The words : ὅτι τὸ εὐαγγέλιον ἡμῶν οὐκ ἐγενήθη εἰς ὑμᾶς ἐν λόγῳ μόνον ἀλλὰ καὶ ἐν δυνάμει amounts precisely to what the apostle says in a connexion which gives the statements far greater force and meaning, 1 Cor. ii. 4 : καὶ ὁ λόγος μοῦ καὶ τὸ κήρυγμά μου οὐκ ἐν πειθοῖς σοφίας λόγοις ἀλλ' ἐν ἀποδείξει πνεύματος καὶ δυνάμεως, etc., and iv. 20, οὐ γὰρ ἐν λόγῳ ἡ βασιλεία τοῦ Θεοῦ, ἀλλ' ἐν δυνάμει. At 1 Cor. xi. 1 the apostle sums up his exhortations in the sentence : μιμηταί μου γίνεσθε καθὼς ἐγὼ Χριστοῦ; but, 1 Thess. i. 6, this imitation is spoken of and praised as a thing the Thessalonians had already practised. They are extolled for the pattern they had given and which had already attracted attention far and wide, 1 Thess. i. 7 sq. : ἀφ' ὑμῶν γὰρ ἐξήχηται ὁ λόγος τοῦ κυρίου οὐ μόνον ἐν τῇ Μακεδονίᾳ καὶ Ἀχαίᾳ, ἀλλα καὶ ἐν παντὶ τόπῳ ἡ πίστις ἡ πρὸς τὸν Θεὸν ἐξελήλυθεν, just as the apostle says in praise of the Roman Christians, Rom. i. 8 : ὅτι ἡ πίστις ὑμῶν καταγγέλλεται ἐν παντὶ τῷ κόσμῳ. But what reminds us more than anything else of the peculiar tone of the Corinthian Epistles is the reference, introduced with such earnestness, to the manner of the apostle's first appearance among the Thessalonians, and to the evidence their own consciousness must furnish of the success of his labours. Compare 1 Cor. ii. 1, κἀγὼ ἐλθὼν πρὸς ὑμᾶς, ἀδελφοί, ἦλθον οὐ, etc., verse 3, καὶ ἐγὼ—ἐγενόμην πρὸς ὑμᾶς: iii. 1, καὶ ἐγὼ, ἀδελφοὶ, οὐκ ἠδυνήθην λαλῆσαι ὑμῖν, etc. This appears even more markedly in the Second Epistle, especially i. 12, ἡ γὰρ καύχησις ἡμῶν αὕτη ἐστὶ, τὸ μαρτύριον τῆς συνειδήσεως ἡμῶν, etc., iii. 2, *sq.* etc. The passages analogous to these in 1 Thess. are i. 9 : αὐτοὶ γὰρ περὶ ἡμῶν ἀπαγγέλλουσιν, ὁποίαν εἴσοδον ἔσχομεν πρὸς ὑμᾶς ; ii. 1, αὐτοὶ γὰρ οἴδατε, ἀδελφοὶ, τὴν εἴσοδον ἡμῶν τὴν πρὸς ὑμᾶς ὅτι οὐ κενὴ γέγονεν ; verse 5, καθὼς οἴδατε, verse 9, μνημονεύετε γάρ ; verse 10, ὑμεῖς μάρτυρες ; verse 11, καθάπερ οἴδατε, etc. As in the Corinthian Epistles, so here, the meaning and aim of all the passages of this kind is to be found in the apostle's defence of himself against the imputations of his opponents. In the Epistle to the Corinthians other more general topics are made to lead up to this apology in one way and another ; it is intimately interwoven with the other contents of the Epistles, rather indirectly than directly. In the Epistle to the Thessalonians we have an abstraction from the concrete historical circumstances of the former case, and the apologetic aim comes to the front and is dwelt upon for its own sake. The imputations against which the apostle is made to defend himself are in part extremely general and vague, and partly of such a nature that the falsehood of the accusation is quite obvious and scarcely needs to be demonstrated. What is purposely kept to the end in the Epistles to the Corinthians is here taken up at the very outset. In 1 Thess. ii. 3-6, we find an echo of the last two chapters of the Second Epistle to the Corinthians, where the apostle vindicates his personal honour against his Judaizing opponents, and asserts himself to be no teacher of false doctrine, no deceiver, no flatterer, and that his conduct has not been selfish or ambitious or overbearing. As we read 2 Cor. xii. 16 *sq.* of δόλῳ λαβεῖν, πλεονεκτεῖν, ἐπιβαρεῖν, so also here. The peculiar expression ἐν βάρει εἶναι especially points unmistakably to 2 Cor. xii. 16 : ἐγὼ οὐ κατεβάρησα ὑμᾶς, and xi. 9, ἐν παντὶ ἀβαρῆ ὑμῖν ἐμαυτὸν ἐτήρησα, and can only be explained from these passages. When the apostle says, We have not sought honour from men, neither from others, nor from you, δυνάμενοι ἐν βάρει εἶναι, ὡς Χριστοῦ ἀπόστολοι, this can only mean, as it is generally interpreted, that he did not do this although he might quite well have assumed authority and asserted his position as an apostle of Christ.¹ But why is this conveyed with the expression ἐν βάρει εἶναι, which occurs nowhere else in the New Testament in this sense? The expression clearly ought to convey in accordance with its proper sense, the sense which it bears in both the passages of 2 Cor., the idea of burdensomeness to others, by means of oppressive demands on them, especially such as are dictated by covetousness and love of money. How is it then that πλεονεξία is conjoined with it in this passage, 1 Thess. ii. 5, where the former expression is used in quite a different sense, and where the two expressions do not supplement nor explain each other as in 2 Corinthians. It is evident from what follows that ἐν βάρει εἶναι at once suggested to the author the ἐπιβαρεῖν of the Corinthian Epistle, verse 9 ; he makes the apostle ask his readers to think of his labour and trouble, how working night and day, that he might not be burdensome to any of them, he preached to them the gospel of God. And here again we detect an arbitrary misinterpretation of a thing, which, as it occurs in the Corinthian Epistle, is quite natural and intelligible. The apostle himself speaks of a κόπος and μόχθος (the only other passage where these two occur in this conjunction is the parallel 2 Thess. iii. 8), but not in the special sense of a manual ἐργάζεσθαι : and in regard to the οὐκ ἐπιβαρεῖν, what he there asserts that he did out of consideration for the peculiar circumstances of the Corinthian church is in the Epistle to the Thessalonians represented as his universal practice. The section 1 Thess. ii. 1 *sq.* presents other points of analogy with the Corinthian Epistles (cf. verse 2, ἐπαρρησιασάμεθα with 2 Cor. iii. 12, πολλῇ παρρησίᾳ χρώμεθα, and the affectionate expressions with which the apostle speaks of the church as a child which he had nursed and cherished, 1 Thess. ii. 7, 11, with 2 Cor. xii. 14, 15). Dr. Lipsius can neither ignore nor account for these

¹ The interpretation of Lipsius is quite unnatural and grammatically impossible. As apostles of Christ we have no need of honour from men ; on the contrary we are able to be in burden and trouble, *i.e.* to endure persecutions and afflictions of all kinds with an even mind. Δυνάμενοι here, as δυνάμενος Gal. iii. 21, is the pure abstract *can ;* what one might do but does not actually do.

analogies. In the Corinthian Epistles there is never any doubt who the antagonists are against whom the apostle is defending himself; his whole argument is aimed at the Judaizing party who counteracted his influence in the Corinthian church. But who are the opponents with whom he is confronted in the First Epistle to the Thessalonians? Dr. Lipsius infers from ii. 14-16 that they were Jews who had made a personal attack on the apostle on account of the gospel he preached, because he had taken up the position of apostle to the Gentiles. " Thus it was an opposition which sprang from the same grounds as the Judaizing opposition in other quarters. The only difference is that the opponents dealt with here appear to stand for the most part outside of Christianity; the antagonism to the apostle had not yet reached the dangerous stage to which it rose in Corinth about a year later, when an anti-Pauline party made its appearance in the bosom of the Christian church itself. It was still possible to point to the churches of Palestine as examples of patient endurance of Judaistic persecution. This could never have been the case if emissaries had already arrived from Judaea for the purpose of stirring up the Christians of Macedonia against the apostle. What Paul feared was the formation at Thessalonica of an opposition, a Judaistically-minded Christ-party; since the attacks which proceeded here from the unbelieving Jews had been aimed at him in Galatia by the Judaeo-Christian party," etc. All this is entirely destitute of foundation; it is entirely imaginary. The churches of Palestine were the head-quarters of Christian Judaism, and how can they ever have been exposed to Judaistic persecution? And it is a mere unwarranted assumption, when Jews and Judaizers are classed together in this way as if what is true of the one were true of the other also. Both were, of course, hostile to the apostle; but is it conceivable that Jews expressed their antipathy to him with no graver charge than that of πλεονεξία, etc. They either rejected the gospel altogether as a σκάνδαλον, or they hated the apostle for being an apostate and an enemy of the law. It is, on the other hand, a very curious circumstance that while the opponents whom the apostle combats in his Epistles are Judaizers, and Judaizers only, the smaller Epistles which assumed his name are occupied with a controversy with the Jews, a controversy, however, the very vagueness and generality of which show it to be the product of reflection. Where shall we find a passage in the Epistles to the Galatians, Corinthians, or Romans, where the apostle reproaches the Jews, as he is made to do here, 1 Thess. ii. 15, with having killed Jesus and the prophets, and persecuted himself, with not pleasing God, and being contrary to all men? The adversaries with whom he comes in contact in his Epistles are of a different kind; but at a time when Paulinism had no longer any conflict with Judaeo-Christianity, and was interested rather in finding means of accommodation with it, the apostle was made to write not against the Judaizers, but against the Jews. He could not be conceived without a contest of some kind on his hands, and the Jews could be made to receive all that he had to hurl against the enemies of the gospel. And this explains the reference to the churches of Judaea as a pattern for Gentile Christians, 1 Thess. ii. 14. For this also we shall in vain seek a parallel in the admittedly genuine Epistles.

An analogy becomes always more undeniable the further it can be traced through a number of detached particulars. And this holds good in this instance. The next section, ii. 17-20 and iii. 1 *sq.*, bears very clearly the impress of the Corinthian Epistles, especially the second of them. It is curious how the apostle is said, ii. 17, not merely to have wished more than once, but to have actually formed the intention once and again, an intention which only Satan had hindered, of returning to Thessalonica. How could this be the case so immediately after his departure from that city, and when Timothy, whom he had left there on that occasion, had just rejoined him? How could he possibly have come to propose such a journey in the earlier stage of his residence at Corinth, and amid the stress of the anxieties and labours with which he was occupied and engrossed in founding a new church? When we consider, however, how much there is in this Epistle that is evidently drawn from the Epistle to the Corinthians, we are naturally led to think in this case also of the journeys and projects of travel which are so frequently referred to in those Epistles. The author adopted this as part of the plan of the Epistle he was writing, without noticing the improbability of it; he meant it to be simply an additional proof of the tender love and attachment which he makes his apostle express with so many phrases and ideas borrowed from the Corinthian Epistles. I have drawn attention to this already, but the argument may be greatly strengthened from what is said afterwards, iii. 1, about the sending of Timothy. The situation of the apostle which is described here is closely similar to that with which we are acquainted from 2 Cor. ii. 12, vii. 5 *sq.* According to those passages the apostle is in great anxiety and unrest on account of the state of the Corinthian church; he looks with restless solicitude for the news he is to receive from it, and in proportion to his anxiety is his delight when Titus comes and sets his doubts at rest with the assurances he brings of that church's continued attachment to him. We find all this repeated in 1 Thess. iii. 1 *sq.* The apostle cannot bear (verse 1, μηκέτι στέγοντες, cf. 2 Cor. ii. 13, οὐκ ἔσχηκα ἄνεσιν τῷ πνεύματί μου, vii. 5, οὐδεμίαν ἔσχηκεν ἄνεσιν ἡ σάρξ ἡμῶν) his anxiety for the Thessalonians any longer; he must have information about them; he fears they may have been shaken by their afflictions. He therefore despatches Timothy to them; and when Timothy returns he is rejoiced and comforted with the tidings of their steadfastness in the faith and their undiminished love to him, just as in the other case by the coming of Titus (2 Cor. vii. 6, παρεκάλεσεν ἡμᾶς ὁ Θεὸς ἐν τῇ παρουσίᾳ Τίτου— ἀναγγέλλων ἡμῖν τὴν ὑμῶν ἐπιπόθησιν—ὥστε με μᾶλλον χαρῆναι, 1 Thess. iii. 6 : ἄρτι δὲ ἐλθόντος Τιμοθέου πρὸς ἡμᾶς ἀφ' ὑμῶν— καὶ εὐαγγελισαμένου ἡμῖν—καὶ ὅτι ἔχετε μνείαν ἡμῶν—ἐπιπο- θοῦντες ἡμᾶς ἰδεῖν—διὰ τοῦτο παρεκλήθημεν, ἀδελφοί, ἐφ' ὑμῖν—

---

[1] Compare also 1 Thess. ii. 19, τίς γὰρ στέφανος καυχήσεως, ἢ οὐχὶ καὶ ὑμεῖς, καὶ ἡ χαρά ; iii. 7, ἐπὶ πάσῃ τῇ θλίψει καὶ ἀνάγκῃ ἡμῶν, with 2 Cor. vii. 4, πολλή μοι καύχησις ὑπὲρ ὑμῶν, ὑπερπερισσεύομαι τῇ χαρᾷ ἐπὶ πάσῃ τῇ θλίψει ἡμῶν.

X

322   LIFE AND WORK OF PAUL.   [APP. III.

ἐπὶ πάσῃ τῇ χαρᾷ, ἦ χαίρομεν, etc.) The disagreement of our
Epistle with the Acts in respect of Timothy is undoubtedly due to
the wish to give a copy of the scene of the Corinthian Epistle. In
the Acts, xvii. 14, Silas and Timothy stayed at Berea when Paul
went from there to Athens, and rejoined him afterwards at Corinth.
According to our Epistle, iii. 1, Timothy is with the apostle at
Athens; it is from Athens that the apostle sends this ἀδελφὸς καὶ
συνεργὸς (this latter predicate is given to Titus, 2 Cor. viii. 23) to
Thessalonica, probably for no other reason than that in 2 Cor.
the apostle is still on his journey, and his unrest and impatience
on the journey give so eloquent and vivid a proof of his vehement
desire for them. It is, of course, quite possible that these circumstances may have occurred more than once in the apostle's life;
but when we find so many things repeated under the same circumstances, and the same occurrence narrated with the same words,
we have a right to ask if the one account is not imitated from the
other.

The hortatory part of the Epistle, which begins in chap. iv., does
not contain such striking analogies; yet even here there are parallel sentences, the expressions of which are very similar to those
of the corresponding sentences in the older Epistles. Compare 1
Thess. iv. 3, ἀπέχεσθε ὑμᾶς ἀπὸ τῆς πορνείας, with 1 Cor. vi. 18,
φεύγετε τὴν πορνείαν. The exhortation 1 Thess. iv. 4 : εἰδέναι
ἕκαστον ὑμῶν etc., is quite analogous to that given by the apostle,
1 Cor. vii. 2 sq. in regard to the conduct of married people. The
exhortation 1 Thess. iv. 6, μὴ ὑπερβαίνειν καὶ πλεονεκτεῖν ἐν τῷ
πράγματι τὸν ἀδελφὸν αὐτοῦ answers to the apostle's rebuke, 1 Cor.
vi. 8, ὑμεῖς ἀδικεῖτε καὶ ἀποστερεῖτε καὶ ταῦτα ἀδελφούς, which
refers to πρᾶγμα ἔχειν πρὸς τὸν ἕτερον of verse 1. The sentences
1 Thess. v. 19 sq : τὸ πνεῦμα μὴ σβέννυτε, προφητείας μὴ ἐξουθε-
νεῖτε, πάντα δὲ δοκιμάζετε, τὸ καλὸν κατέχετε, are somewhat
different in sound, but in scope and spirit they are just the same
as the general concluding exhortation, 1 Cor. xiv. 39, 40, ζηλοῦτε
τὸ προφητεύειν, καὶ τὸ λαλεῖν γλώσσαις μὴ κωλύετε, πάντα δὲ
εὐσχημόνως καὶ κατὰ τάξιν γινέσθω.

Dr. Lipsius's attempt to defend the genuineness of the First Thessalonian Epistle would not of itself have induced me to return to the question regarding these two writings, had it not been that I thought myself in a position to give a further contribution to the settlement of it. The two Epistles are intimately related to each other by similarity of contents, certain passages proving that one of them must have been known to the writer of the other (cf. 1 Thess. ii. 9, and 2 Thess. iii. 8); and whatever verdict criticism may pass on one of them, will naturally determine our view of the other. The two simplest cases are that both are genuine or that both are spurious; there is another possible case, that the one is genuine and the other spurious, but this case can only be proved by such a careful comparison of the two as will show the spuriousness of the one to result from the genuineness of the other, or the genuineness of one from the spuriousness of the other. What has to be done first of all, however, is to find a point from which to determine the historical situation to which the Epistles belong. It is easy to deal in suppositions and probabilities, greater or less, with regard to such a monument of the primitive church; but what are they worth if there be no one fixed point for the hypothesis and combination to rest upon with some little solidity? The second of these Epistles is of greater value in the eyes of criticism than the first, its doctrine of Antichrist and of the Parousia being more definite and giving a better clew to the historical situation. Thus what we have first of all to examine is the eschatology of the chief passage of this Epistle. It has hitherto been considered, and I myself formerly held this view, that what we have in 2 Thess. ii. 1 *sq.* is the Christian view of Antichrist as it had arisen from a Jewish basis, chiefly in accordance with the prophecies of the book of Daniel; described in the chief features which it had assumed up to that time. This however gave too much room to suppose that the apostle Paul shared in the Jewish views of his contemporaries on the subject; and whatever trouble we may take to show his eschatology to be different from that of this Epistle, we shall always be met by the assertion that the one as well as the other lies inside the Jewish circle of ideas on the subject. We must therefore ask more definitely whether in 2 Thess. ii. we do actually find ourselves entirely within the sphere of Jewish eschatology, such as the apostle also may have adopted; or whether we do not find a view of Antichrist which can only have arisen on Christian soil, and which presupposes events and experiences that belong to a later age than that of the apostles.

There can be no doubt, when we consider it, that the key to the chief passage of the Epistle, and therefore to the aim and character of the whole writing, is to be found in the Apocalypse. The Apocalypse is the earliest writing in which we find the concrete representation of a personal Antichrist; here the absolute enemy of Christianity is identified with the person of the Emperor Nero, and the picture of Antichrist is composed accordingly of features which are clearly enough borrowed from Nero's history and character. The same belief appears in the description of our Epistle. Antichrist is a definite person, an individual appearing in history at a certain fixed date; he is the man of sin, the son of perdition, the adversary who exalts himself above all that is called God, and is an object of worship, to such an extent that he places himself in the temple of God and asserts of himself that he is God. This description of Antichrist derives several of its expressions from the prophet Daniel (compare especially xi. 36), but it also coincides with the description of the Apocalypse. The Apocalypse does not make Antichrist declare that he is God, but the actions of the false prophet who stands beside the beast all serve to represent the beast or Antichrist, as an object of worship, such as is due to the supreme God alone. Cf. Apoc. xiii. 12, 14, 15, xix. 20. And ἐπιδεικνύναι ἑαυτὸν, ὅτι ἐστὶ Θεὸς does not refer, if accurately rendered, to what Antichrist says of himself in words, but rather to what he represents himself to be by his acts, in his whole Antichristian behaviour. The difference thus comes to be that what the Apocalypse sets before our eyes in a succession of scenes by means of narrative and description, the author of our Epistle compresses into a general notion, and expresses concisely by means of accurate definition. There is nothing to prevent us from taking the Antichrist of our Epistle to be the same individual who is described more at large in the Apocalypse. The expressions ἀνομία and ἄνομος on the one side, and ναὸς τοῦ Θεοῦ on the other, may serve as an indication that we have to seek this individual in the circle of the heathen world. In what follows we recognise the views and images of the Apocalypse even more clearly.[1] Antichrist is the representative and organ of Satan, derives all power from him, and operates through false signs and wonders, through works of deceit, by which he plunges into destruction those who fall away from the truth and believe in him. Compare with παρουσία κατ᾽ ἐνέργειαν τοῦ σατανᾶ ἐν πάσῃ δυνάμει, Rev. xiii. 2, ἔδωκεν αὐτῷ (the beast or Antichrist) ὁ δράκων τὴν δύναμιν αὐτοῦ καὶ τὸν θρόνον αὐτοῦ καὶ ἐξουσίαν μεγάλην : with σημεῖα καὶ τέρατα ψεύδους, what the Revelation says of the false prophet, xiii. 13 sq., that he ποιεῖ σημεῖα μεγάλα, etc., cf. xix. 20 : ὁ ποιήσας τὰ σημεῖα ἐνώπιον αὐτοῦ ; with the ἐνέργεια πλάνης, through which men believe a lie, Rev. xiii. 14, πλανᾷ τοὺς κατοικοῦντας ἐπὶ τῆς γῆς, and xix. 20, ἐν οἷς ἐπλάνησε τοὺς λαβόντας τὸ χάραγμα τοῦ θηρίου, etc. The subjection of Antichrist is given differently in the Apocalypse, where the two organs of Satan, the beast and the false prophet, are at once hurled into the place of torment of the lower powers. The author of the Epistle represents Antichrist, whom he expressly describes as a man, as destroyed by the Lord through the breath of his mouth. This πνεῦμα τοῦ στόματος, however, is equivalent to the ῥομφαία ὀξεῖα which proceeds in the Revelation xix. 15, 21, ἐκ τοῦ στόματος αὐτοῦ, and by which all the remnant are killed. In all these particulars the Epistle to the Thessalonians and the Apocalypse are substantially agreed ; and there are some other points in the Epistle which appear inexplicable until the Apocalypse explains them. The most difficult problem in the

---

[1] *Kern* took it for granted in his discussion on 2 Thess. ii. 1-12, in the Tübingen Zeitschrift für Theologie 1839, H. 2, p. 200 sq., that the apocalyptical description of 2 Thess. is of a piece with the prophecy of the Revelation xiii. 3 sq., xvii. 10 sq., in which Nero returns in the character of Antichrist.

Epistle has hitherto been to find an interpretation for the κατέχον and the μυστήριον τῆς ἀνομίας which is already working. De Wette, for example, thinks that the mystery of iniquity should not be understood of any individual, but of the still uncollected and unformed mass of iniquity which was to assume form and personality in Antichrist, and of which the writer may have seen some manifestations in the opposition of fanatical Jews. But the expression ἀνομία prevents us from thinking of Jews : the reproach contained in the word was one for the Jews to bring against the apostle, not one to which they themselves were liable. The sense and substance of the passage are clear enough : that the beginnings and elements are already present of that which will make its appearance in full concrete reality in the person of Antichrist. But why is the word μυστήριον used to express this idea, and wherein does this μυστήριον consist, as Antichrist had not appeared at all, and what had appeared, the premonitory symptoms of his approach, was no secret, but manifest and visible ? The only probable meaning seems to be this : that Antichrist was present in essence in the still scattered and isolated manifestations of ἀνομία. This presence of Antichrist in essence is, however, too abstract a notion ; the statement is vague and shadowy; the power of evil that is working in the world is not fixed to any definite point, the person of Antichrist is not yet present at all, and his personal appearance is conceived merely as the concentration of all the various manifestations of the power of evil into a unity. Surely the writer must have meant something more than this. The difficulty is at once solved if we take the idea of Antichrist in this Epistle to be that of the Apocalypse. If it be the emperor Nero, then Antichrist is present as a person before he is fully revealed in the character of Antichrist. We have to think of the period in describing which the Apocalypse says of the beast, xvii. 8, ὅτι ἦν, καὶ οὐκ ἔστι, καὶ παρέσται. Nero, as emperor, has retired from the scene and is reported to be dead ; but he is still alive, and will come again as Antichrist. In this interval he is secretly and mysteriously active, and preparing to appear in the

full energy of Antichrist, as soon as his hour is come (εἰς τὸ ἀποκαλυφθῆναι αὐτὸν ἐν τῷ ἑαυτοῦ καιρῷ, verse 6). This then is the
meaning of the words : τὸ γὰρ μυστήριον ἤδη ἐνεργεῖται τῆς ἀνομίας.
Antichrist is already come, but not openly, and is preparing in
his retirement for the period when he is to appear. The word
μυστήριον answers this interpretation perfectly. It is used in the
same peculiar sense as in the Revelation xvii. 5, cf. verse 7. Here
it is said of the woman that she has a name written on her fore-
head as μυστήριον, namely Βαβυλὼν ἡ μεγάλη ; the meaning of
which is that the name Babylon is given to her only in a figurative sense, that the reader is to think of something else that is
merely hinted or suggested in this name ; that is, that the name
stands in reality for the city of Rome. In the same way the expression μυστήριον ἀνομίας, 2 Thess. ii. 7, is intended to indicate
that ἀνομία or the worker of it, the ἄνομος, stand for something
else not stated, which is to give the notion of Antichrist an actual
body and contents. What the word μυστήριον conveys is the
notion of a vague hint which has to be filled up and supplemented
by being referred to something actually existing in history. If
this be, as we think it is, an adequate solution of the μυστήριον
τῆς ἀνομίας, then the κατέχον, or as the writer says more definitely
ὁ κατέχων, no longer presents any difficulty. What can it refer to
but the intermediate government, which the Apocalypse agrees
with our Epistle in placing between the disappearance and the
return of Nero : the Roman emperor who occupied the throne
when the Epistle was written, not Galba (even the Apocalypse
makes him the sixth, followed by a seventh), but one of the
following emperors.[1] The further definition depends on other
considerations which we have still to notice.

---

[1] The Apocalypse makes the sixth emperor to be followed by a seventh, who is
to be immediately succeeded by the reappearing Nero. This limitation to the
number seven is owing to the writer's view that the seven hills of Rome symbolize
the number of her rulers ; xvii. 9 αἱ ἑπτὰ κεφαλαὶ ἑπτὰ ὄρη εἰσίν, ὅπου ἡ γυνὴ
κάθηται ἐπ αὐτῶν, κἀὶ βασιλεῖς ἑπτά εἰσιν. Thus there can only be seven Roman
emperors in all, and the seventh, the immediate predecessor of Antichrist, is the
κατέχων; *i.e.* the last before him. The notion of the κατέχων can only have arisen

We must now inquire into the purpose and occasion of the Epistle. The writer's mind is engrossed and preoccupied with the Parousia of Christ, the judgment that is then to overtake the unbelieving world, and the glory which the faithful may anticipate as the reward and compensation of their sufferings. He thinks it necessary, however, to warn his readers against the assertion that the day of the Lord is already come. They are not to be shaken out of their composure, nor to give way to terror, not even—there can be no doubt that this is the meaning—though some one make the announcement with prophetical inspiration, or appeal in support of it to a pretended declaration or letter of the apostle himself. They are to let no man deceive them by any means, nor delude them into thinking that the day of the Parousia is coming now. This must evidently refer to some movement that had arisen among the Christians. The exhortation εἰς τὸ μὴ ταχέως σαλευθῆναι appears to indicate that something had been done already betraying a want of self-control and a readiness to be excited and led away. Let us seek for the traces of something of this kind in the history of the time. The Parousia is closely connected with Antichrist, and Antichrist with Nero, and thus we are naturally led to think of some of the pseudo-Neronian disturbances. Indeed it is surprising that none of the interpreters have sought the occasion of the Epistle in this quarter. A passage in Tacitus, which is often quoted for other purposes, approaches our Epistle even in its expressions and might well have been employed in this way. " Sub idem tempus," Tacitus says, Hist. ii. 8, of the period after the murder of Galba,

---

from the view of the Apocalypse. The apocalyptical elements of the Epistle have not been properly attended to. In the first chapter as well as in the second, we meet with the ideas and the spirit of the Apocalypse. The sufferings of the Christians are regarded throughout from the point of view of retributive justice. The result of these sufferings is to be, for the righteous, that they will be glorified and judged worthy of the kingdom of God ; while the ungodly will be punished to avenge them. Compare 2 Thess. i. 5, and Rev. vi. 6 sq., vii. 14, xi. 18.

The appearing of the Lord when he comes with his mighty angels is described in the same way as in Rev. xix. 11 sq. Compare the ἐν πυρὶ φλογὸς 2 Thess. i. 8, with the φλὸξ πυρὸς of his eyes, Rev. xix. 12 ; and the ἄγγελοι δυνάμεως αὐτοῦ, 2 Thess. i. 7, with the στρατεύματα τὰ ἐν τῷ οὐρανῷ, Rev. xix. 14.

when Otho and Vitellius, and even Vespasian were taking up arms for their several interests, " Achaia atque Asia falso exterritae, velut Nero adventaret ; vario super exitu ejus rumore, eoque pluribus vivere eum fingentibus credentibusque. Inde late terror, multi ad celebritatem nominis erecti, rerum novarum cupidine et odio praesentium. Gliscentem in dies famam fors discussit."[1] Achaia, or Greece and Macedonia, and Asia Minor, were the chief seat of this disturbance, and Thessalonica was in these provinces. Even at that early date there were many Christians in these districts ; and as the reappearance of Nero meant to them simply the coming of Antichrist, the terror occasioned by the report would affect them more powerfully than their neighbours, and may have caused them to behave in such a way as to aggravate the general alarm and confusion.[2] There can be no doubt that prophets arose who applied the signs of the times in their own manner, and perhaps appealed to the Johannine Apocalypse, which was already well known. Pauline Christians did not fail for their part to point to the utterances of Paul, verbal or epistolary, in which he was held to have foretold the catastrophe. At the time when our Epistle was written, the excitement was spoken of as ταχέως σαλευθῆναι ἀπὸ τοῦ νόος, and set down to some unscrupulous person who had imposed on the general credulity ; the ludibrium falsi Neronis must thus have disappeared again, and the Epistle must have been written after the alarm was over. As we read of gliscens in dies fama, the commotion may have continued for some time, but its collapse was so sudden and complete (fors discussit) that there

[1] We know of three pseudo-Neros. The first is that spoken of above ; a second is mentioned by Zonaras (p. 578 c. cf. Reimarus on Dio Cassius, c. 64, 9). He appeared in A.U.C. 832 under Titus, gained a considerable following in Asia Minor and the regions of the Euphrates, and sought refuge at last with the Parthian king. The third is he, of whom Tacitus says, Hist. i. 2, that through him, mota prope Parthorum arma. According to Suetonius, vita Ner., c. 57, this was twenty years after Nero's death. The situation of our Epistle shuts us up to the first of these *falsi Nerones.*

[2] If the terror was so great and general as Tacitus describes, we are obliged to attribute it to the Christians more than others, for this among other reasons, that many of the Gentiles desired the return of Nero, and must have hailed the report of it. Cf. Theologische Jahrbücher, 1852, p. 332 *sq.*

could be no doubt of the utter groundlessness of the whole story, and it would naturally be spoken of as a thing of the past, just as we find in our Epistle. Yet we must not go too far beyond the date of the Neronian catastrophe ; in spite of the experience gained from the appearance of the false Nero, our writer does not by any means relinquish the belief that Nero is to reappear ; he knows that the μυστήριον τῆς ἀνομίας ἤδη ἐνεργεῖται, and that it is nothing but the existence of the κατέχων, the Emperor presently in possession of the throne, that causes his appearance to be delayed.[1]

It was important, therefore, to learn from the error that had been committed, and to deduce from it the principle on which the expectations of the future are to be formed. The newly made experience is vividly present to the writer's mind, and he derives from it the new criteria on which his new theory of the Parousia is based. The Parousia cannot take place until Antichrist has come, and Antichrist cannot come till after the falling away, and neither the falling away nor Antichrist can come until the κατέχων is taken out of the way. When, therefore, the ruling emperor has fallen, the catastrophe of the Parousia will begin. Now Galba had fallen already, so had also Otho and Vitellius, and notwithstanding this, the Nero of report had turned out to be a fictitious one. The several criteria here mentioned must therefore follow hard one on the other. With the fall of the present emperor comes Antichrist, with him must come the ἀποστασία, and this can be nothing but what the Apocalypse describes, xiii. 4, 8, 12, the idolatrous προσ-

---

[1] As the reigns of Otho and Vitellius were extremely short, the κατέχων is probably Vespasian, and the Epistle will then have been composed in the early years of his reign. It might be inferred from the καθίσαι εἰς τὸν ναὸν τοῦ Θεοῦ, 2 Thess. ii. 4, that the date is prior to the destruction of Jerusalem. Our only reason for doubting this is, that the Epistle shows the Apocalypse to have been already well known. The expression might be taken as a figurative one, formed after the prophet Daniel ; or ναὸς Θεοῦ may be equivalent to τόπος τοῦ ναοῦ. Even though the temple was not standing, the place where it had stood was considered equally sacred, as we see from the setting up of the idol under Hadrian. Cf. the krit. unters. über die kan. ev., p. 606 sq. The feeling of sanctity attached not so much to the temple as to the site on which the temple stood, as the temple itself is called ἅγιος τόπος ; Acts vi. 13 sq., xxi. 28.

κυνεῖν, namely, which is rendered to Antichrist at his appearance, when the whole unbelieving world hails him and espouses his cause. But this criterion is not enough ; it is not easy to be certain whether the following that a reputed Nero gets is sufficient in number and of such a character as to be a sure token of Antichrist. Antichrist must therefore reveal and declare himself to be what he is, the ἄνθρωπος τῆς ἁμαρτίας, the υἱὸς ἀπωλείας, the ἀντικείμενος καὶ ὑπεραιρόμενος ἐπὶ πάντα λεγόμενον Θεὸν ἢ σέβασμα, ὥστε αὐτὸν εἰς τὸν ναὸν τοῦ Θεοῦ καθίσαι, ἀποδεικνύντα ἑαυτὸν ὅτι ἐστὶ Θεός. The main point, in a word, is the ἀποκαλυφθῆναι αὐτὸν ἐν τῷ ἑαυτοῦ καιρῷ. Now what does all this amount to ? It is precisely the instruction and the warning that would be suggested by the experience just gained in the matter of the false Nero. That Christians were not to let themselves be imposed upon by any such ludibrium, nor led to think that the Parousia of Christ was to take place immediately ; that this belief would not be warranted until Antichrist had revealed himself so unmistakably with all his proper tokens, as to leave no doubt whatever of his actual presence. This is all intended, it is clear, to prevent the recurrence in the future of such commotions, as we see from the historical data that the affair of the false Nero had excited. The Christian is to consider it his duty to exercise caution and presence of mind, and to avoid all precipitation. With regard to the Parousia, he is to regulate his behaviour and his views strictly in accordance with the tangible evidence of facts.

The exhortations given in a later part of the Epistle are very appropriate to the historical situation we have traced. The belief in the Parousia could easily operate in a very demoralizing way. What was the use of caring for the future, or making orderly arrangements, if the Parousia might come at any moment and be the end of all ? This state of feeling could be more mischievous still. There were men to whom this state of things gave a welcome opportunity to indulge in their natural love of disorder. There were such men among the Christians : faith, *i.e.* the right Christian faith, was not a thing possessed by all, as is said, iii. 2 ; there

were not wanting ἄτοποι καὶ πονηροὶ ἄνθρωποι, who became a
burden upon other people. The main part of the writer's exhortations
is thus directed very naturally against disorderly life, against idleness and refusal to labour. The last was the chief evil; it arose
from the view that all things were on the verge of dissolution. It
was thought unnecessary to continue to work, men lounged about
in idleness, and thought no shame to live at the expense of others,
since those who had means would no longer be able, when the Parousia came, to make any use of them. It is those people who are
spoken of in iii. 11 : ἀκούομεν γάρ τινας περιπατοῦντας ἐν ὑμῖν
ἀτάκτως, μηδὲν ἐργαζομένους, ἀλλὰ περιεργαζομένους. Hence the
earnest admonition, not to go idle, but to work (μετὰ ἡσυχίας
ἐργάζεσθαι, iii. 12), and the insistence upon the principle, that he
who will not work, should get nothing to eat, iii. 10 ; which, however, is not to prejudice the exercise of the Christian duty of
beneficence towards those who are in want, iii. 13. In this connexion, where the writer is recommending work for the purpose of
self-support, and that Christians should beware of being burdensome to others, nothing could be happier than his appeal to the
apostle's own example, and to the principles enunciated by him in
his own Epistles. Αὐτοὶ γὰρ οἴδατε, πῶς δεῖ μιμεῖσθαι ἡμᾶς, etc.,
verse 7 *sq.* The writer is obviously thinking of the passage 1 Cor.
ix. 4 *sq.* ; he very appropriately generalizes what the apostle says,
1 Cor. ix. 12, that he did for a special purpose, and imputes to him a
wider motive : ἵνα ἑαυτοὺς τόπον δῶμεν ὑμῖν εἰς τὸ μιμεῖσθαι ἡμᾶς,
v. 9. In the sentences, μὴ συναναμίγνυσθε, ἵνα ἐντραπῇ—ὁ κύριος
τῆς εἰρήνης, iii. 14, 16, we find further points of resemblance to the
Corinthian Epistles. Cf. 1 Cor. v. 9, 11 ; 2 Cor. xiii. 2.

If this interpretation of the occasion and scope of the Epistle be
accepted, it certainly cannot be charged with any want of colour or
point, or historical character. The situation from which it is written
is such that we fully appreciate the necessity that existed for issuing
such a piece of Christian exhortation, and the desirability of investing it with the name of that apostle whom the Churches of those
regions for whom it was mainly intended revered as their founder.

One very obvious result of the foregoing investigation, however, is that the apostle Paul cannot possibly have written this Epistle himself. He could know nothing of an Antichrist appearing in the person of the Emperor Nero ; nor of a κατέχων, by whom the portentous catastrophe was in the meantime delayed, nor of the circumstances which called so urgently for exhortations like those to be addressed to the members of his Churches. Whom could the apostle possibly have meant with the κατέχων? It is said to be more than probable—De Wette shares this view—that he meant the Roman empire or the Roman emperor. There can be no doubt, it is said, that he had the book of Daniel before his mind, that the four monarchies of that book represented to him the whole course of the world's history down to the appearance of the Messianic kingdom, and that he unquestionably held the fourth to be the Roman empire, as did Josephus and the early fathers, so that this empire which still existed was the only obstacle in the way of the last catastrophe. He had before his eyes the condition of the world as it then was, and his vision carried him no further. He expected the speedy termination of the Roman empire, and after that the appearance of Antichrist, and finally, but still in his own lifetime, the second coming of Christ. All this, however, fails to explain how he formed this peculiar conception of a κατέχων. The Roman empire was the last ; and Antichrist might come sooner or later during its existence. Now if the Roman empire, or the Roman emperor, was held to be the κατέχων, it must surely have had some characteristic features showing it to be so, and contained some definite symptoms of the impending catastrophe. But if, as is generally assumed, the Epistle was written in the year 53 A.D., what reason was there to deem the then reigning emperor Claudius to be the κατέχων, the power which alone stood in the way of the appearance of Antichrist ? Or if the Epistle be placed at the very beginning of the reign of Nero, we know of nothing at that period that could lead any one to suppose that that Emperor would be the last. All that we find in this period is the general belief that the end of the world was near, but so long as this expectation derived no special strength or colour from anything personal to the then reigning emperor, it is hard to see why he should be called the κατέχων. Nor is it easy to explain why, if the apostle thought it necessary at that time to give such a careful and circumstantial opinion on the Parousia, he never returned to the subject in any of his subsequent Epistles. In the later Epistles he entirely ignores, on this hypothesis, the vivid expectation of Antichrist which he had awakened, when he represented him as already working in secret, and about to appear in the immediate future. Was it not somewhat strange that having presented these ideas with such emphasis to the Christian consciousness, he should all at once drop the subject ; that he should have nothing to say of the many prophecies he had uttered and which had remained unfulfilled, and pass at once to the announcement of the instant approach of the Parousia of Christ (1 Cor. xv. 51) ? To explain all this, we are reminded of the narrow limits of time, which the apostle spoke of in his prophecy, and are even told that as the events which he expected from the immediate future did not take place, it was unreasonable to expect the fulfilment of the prophecy from a future more remote. It is better, we are told, to acknowledge that Paul made a mistake, that his characteristic impetuosity made him imagine that he knew things which it is not given to man to know, not even to an apostle though filled beyond all other men with the spirit of Christ. If this be all that can be said, the Epistle stands before us a riddle utterly unsolved. Would it not be far simpler to refer it to the time to which all its characteristic features obviously point, and to accept the conclusion that the apostle himself was not the writer ? But, it may be objected, how could another writer make the apostle say these things if he could not possibly have said them himself ? how could a later writer make him speak of Nero as Antichrist, when this theory could have had no evidence nor reason at the time when the Epistle was represented as having been written ? The answer to this question is found in the precautions taken by the writer himself to meet it, if it should arise. In such a point we see very distinctly how the character of such an Epistle is insensibly determined by the double personality of the writer. The writer is the apostle and yet at the same time another person; the form of the Epistle is from the pretended, the contents from the real, author, and these two have to be made to harmonize in some way. There are several things in the Epistle which give us a tolerably clear glimpse of an age lying beyond the apostle's time; and yet these are so managed as not to make its apostolic authorship too palpably impossible or improbable. The special concrete individual elements of the later history are as far as possible generalized, as we see in the conception of Antichrist. It is not till we take Nero to be the actual subject of the predicates with which Antichrist is characterized, that the picture appears before us as that of a real person; and yet it cannot be said that any of the traits of the picture is so specifically Neronian as to show the writer to have forgotten the part he was playing. He does not mention a κατέχων without speaking first of τὸ κατέχον, the abstract instead of the concrete, a phrase which suggests nothing more than some hindrance or other in the circumstances of the times. Again, we see the writer trying to engraft his own interests on the personal history of the apostle, and to keep up the fictitious personality, by asserting again and again that the apostle had told his readers by word of mouth, when he was present with him, what he was now writing, cf. ii. 5; iii. 10. Thus should there be anything in the Epistle that is not quite clear, they are to imagine what he said orally as the commentary to it, and to remember that the original readers had been already acquainted with the apostle's meaning. The pretended apostle, as author of the Epistle, is thus made to assure himself again and again of his identity with the true apostle; which simply shows that the writer felt this to be the weak point in his literary undertaking. In the same way the frequent allusions to passages of the authentic Epistles are meant to confirm us in the belief that we are altogether within the familiar circle of the Pauline ideas. But the more pains such a production takes to prove itself a Pauline Epistle (as notably in the conclusion, iii. 17, 18), the more reason does there appear for holding its asserted origin to be doubtful.

We must now look back from the second Epistle to the first. If we have made up our minds about the second it will be less difficult to arrive at a definite opinion with regard to the first. As we saw that the genuineness of the first is doubtful, and as that of the second has even stronger evidence against it, we have now to inquire what, in this view of their origin, is the relation which they bear to each other.

The First Epistle deals in its exhortations with a wider range of subjects, and is at more pains than the second to explain by considerations personal to the apostle how the different topics it contains came to be taken up. Yet the question of the Parousia is evidently the foremost in the writer's mind, he thinks the time calls urgently for instruction and explanation on the subject. This point is kept prominently in view from the very beginning : even in the introduction, i. 3, the writer speaks of the ὑπομονὴ τῆς ἐλπίδος τοῦ Κυρίου ἡμῶν 'Ιησοῦ Χριστοῦ ἔμπροσθεν τοῦ Θεοῦ καὶ πατρὸς ἡμῶν, i.e. the hope of his return. He calls Jesus, i. 10, τὸν ῥυόμενον ἡμᾶς ἀπὸ τῆς ὀργῆς τῆς ἐρχομένης, and God, ii. 12, the καλῶν ἡμᾶς εἰς τὴν ἑαυτοῦ βασίλειαν καὶ δόξαν. He speaks repeatedly of the Parousia as the ultimate event which the efforts of Christians are to keep in view, ii. 19 : τίς γὰρ ἡμῶν ἐλπὶς — ἔμπροσθεν τοῦ Κυρίου ἡμῶν 'Ιησοῦ Χριστοῦ—ἐν τῷ αὐτοῦ παρουσίᾳ : iii. 13, εἰς τὸ στηρίξαι ὑμῶν τὰς καρδίας—ἐν τῇ παρουσίᾳ τοῦ Κυρίου ἡμῶν 'Ιησοῦ μετὰ πάντων τῶν ἁγίων αὐτοῦ. When he comes to speak of this subject specially, iv. 13, he makes the transition with the same formula with which the apostle generally introduces the more important passages of his Epistles : οὐ θέλομεν δὲ ὑμᾶς ἀγνοεῖν. On comparing the sections in the two Epistles which deal with the Parousia, we are struck by the fact, that though there is said to be a very short interval of time between the two, the first contains no trace of what the second treats as a matter of the first importance. The first seeks to reassure its readers concerning those who have fallen asleep, and to instruct them when the Parousia is to be expected; but there is not a word of Antichrist nor of the circumstances which are to herald his appearance. The interpreters have nothing to say on this point that bears the least semblance of probability. De Wette, for example, says that the strongly apocalyptical tendency of the apostle's preaching produced an extraordinary sensation at Thessalonica. The First Epistle did nothing to allay the excitement, but on the contrary insisted on the duty of being constantly on the watch for the immediate advent of Christ. The apostle felt it necessary afterwards to do something to cool down the fervour of the expectations the Thessalonians had formed. But this cannot surely have been necessary, for the picture of Antichrist that is drawn with such care must have been a fresh source of agitation. But why does Antichrist come on the scene at this point? According to 2 Thess. ii. 5, the apostle had spoken of Antichrist during his residence at Thessalonica, but even supposing the Second Epistle to be genuine, we cannot help asking why the First Epistle does not contain the least allusion to the subject. If the Second Epistle is to be fixed to the definite historical position we have indicated, it becomes impossible to frame any rational theory of the relation borne to it by the first, except on the assumption that the first was written after the second, and at a considerable interval after it. The expectation of Antichrist had died away of itself, since Antichrist had failed to appear at the time when everything in the Roman empire seemed to be ready for him. It was impossible to give up expecting the Parousia of Christ himself; but the longer it tarried, the more did doubts and questions arise on the subject, and these it was necessary to satisfy. This is what the First Epistle sets itself to do, and both the difficulty which it discusses, and the considerations it brings forward to meet them, belong to a later period. According to iv. 13, anxiety was felt on behalf of those Christians who had fallen asleep having waited in vain for the Parousia of Christ, and died before it came, lest, when it did arrive, they should be worse off than those who were living at the time. This might be (iv. 15) either by their

Y

not rising again till later, or perhaps even by their continuing permanently in the comfortless condition of the under-world, which they had already endured since their death, so that there would be no difference between them and the heathens (verse 13). In view of these anxieties the writer appeals to the resurrection of Christ as the warrant for believing in a resurrection of the dead, and goes on to assure his readers that the resurrection of those Christians who had died would be the first thing to take place when the Lord should descend from heaven, after which those who were alive should be united to those who had risen, and be for ever with the Lord. It is very difficult to harmonize this description of the Parousia with the series of events connected with the coming of Antichrist, as the Second Epistle, following the Revelation, details them. But not to insist on this, we are forced to ask when Christians began to regard the case of those who had fallen asleep as a matter of such anxiety. If the Epistle be genuine and was written to the young church at Thessalonica only a few months after it was founded, how many κεκοιμημένοι could there be—members of the church who had died after their conversion to Christianity? The question of the prospects of their fellow-Christians who had died would naturally rise into prominence with the church when there came to be a considerable number who had died without seeing what all hoped that they would live to see, when a whole generation perhaps had departed from the midst of the Christian community. At a time when the Parousia and the end of the world were thought to be so close at hand, the idea that the Christian community consisted of the dead as well as of the living could only arise gradually, and could hardly become familiar till the continual replacement of the dead by the living had come to show that a new order of things was now prevailing.

The apostle had indicated a belief that he himself would live to see the Parousia, and an author writing after his death would still make him express that belief, iv. 15, 17. Though the apostle had been mistaken, yet what he had said was true of those who did live to see the Parousia. But it marks a wide departure from the faith of the first Christians,—that they would be alive at the Parousia,—when instead of that expectation we find it urged that it did not make the least difference whether one became partaker of the blessings of that event in the ranks of the dead or of the living. The question whether the Parousia was to happen sooner or later was no longer one of paramount importance. The important thing was to cultivate that attitude of mind which the writer of the Epistle recommends to his readers, v. 1. The dogmatic significance of the question of the Parousia is here reduced to the practical exhortation that since the date of it was utterly uncertain it was necessary to be prepared for it every moment. This obviously implies, that a considerable time had passed since the Parousia began to be expected. χρόνοι and καιροὶ are spoken of, times and periods that have already passed without its coming, times and periods which may still have to pass before it comes, that is to say, simply the broad course of time, of which the ἡμέρα Κυρίου constitutes the closing scene. The only warning issued is against those who are seduced into too great security because the Parousia is so long delayed, and who forget that the day of the Lord comes suddenly and unexpectedly as a thief in the night, verse 2. Christians must thus be exhorted simply to be watchful and sober ; an exhortation which shows that the Christian consciousness had now rejected the ecstatic and eccentric elements that entered into the primitive belief of the Parousia. If the Parousia be contemplated with composure, that means that it is beyond the immediate sphere of vision ; and the further off it is conceived to be, the more room is there left for the circle of Christian life and duty. This sphere is filled up as much as possible by our author with moral instructions and exhortations to περιπατεῖν ἀξίως τοῦ Θεοῦ, ii. 12 ; cf. iv. 1, 2. In this department as well as in the other he has the Second Epistle before him, and borrows precepts which are much more natural and appropriate there than here ; though they had not ceased to be necessary at the later period. Such are νουθετεῖν τοὺς ἀτάκτους verse 14, φιλοτιμεῖσθαι ἡσυχάζειν, πράσσειν τὰ ἴδια, καὶ ἐργάζεσθαι ταῖς χερσὶν, iv. 11, and ii. 9 ; cf. 2 Thess.

iii. 7-12. The writer takes special care to let the reason and occasion of his moral precepts appear. For this purpose he avails himself largely of the apostolical framework of his Epistle. The apostle strives to stimulate his readers to be forward in the business of their Christian calling, partly by praising them for their good qualities, and partly by assuring them of his own love and attachment to them.

As for the passages which have commonly been held to show the dependence of the Second Epistle on the First, it is not difficult to convert them into proofs of the opposite relation. (In some cases they are obviously extensions and exaggerations of the parallels in the Second Epistle, as, *e.g.* iv. 15-17 is simply an explanation of the ἐπισυναγωγή, 2 Thess. ii. 1, and 1 Thess. v. 27, ὁρκίζω ὑμᾶς τὸν Κύριον, etc., is an assertion of the importance of the Epistle similar to that, 2 Thess. iii. 14, εἰ δέ τις οὐχ ὑπακούει, etc., only stronger.) And there seems to be no further consideration of any weight to be brought against the view we have sought to establish of the origin of the two Epistles, and their relation to each other. The First Epistle must accordingly have been written after the Second, and if we accept the most natural interpretation of the passage 1 Thess. ii. 16, we have the Epistle referring to the destruction of Jerusalem as an accomplished fact.[1]

---

[1] If the Epistle be considered to be by Paul, we must say on this point that he regards a thing, of which he merely foresaw the accomplishment, as already to all intents accomplished. The grammar admits of this, but is it natural to speak of an event, such as the destruction of Jerusalem, before it came about, as if it had taken place already? The ordinary interpretation thus provides a new proof, that the author of an Epistle like this could not indeed forbear to speak of the time in which he himself was living, but took care to choose expressions which should not be out of place as coming from the mouth of the author whose name he was assuming.

INDEX.

z